Paths to Civilization:
Readings in the Intellectual Heritage of the Western World

Volume I
Revised Printing

James L. Marra
Stephen C. Zelnick
Mark T. Mattson

KENDALL/HUNT PUBLISHING COMPANY
4050 Westmark Drive   Dubuque, Iowa 52002

Copyright © 1998, 1999 by Kendall/Hunt Publishing Company

Revised Printing

ISBN 0-7872-6312-5

All rights reserved. No part of this publication may be reproduced, stored in a retrieval system, or transmitted, in any form or by any means, electronic, mechanical, photocopying, recording, or otherwise, without the prior written permission of the copyright owner.

Printed in the United States of America
10   9   8   7   6   5   4   3   2

Contents

Classical Greek Foundations

Sappho
    "A Wedding Toast" 3
    "Lament for a Maidenhead" 4
    "Come to Us, Aphrodite" 4
    "Prayer to My Lady of Paphos" 5
    "He Is More Than a Hero" 6
    "Consoling a Friend" 6
    "The Departed Lover" 7
    Family of Gods/Royal House of Thebes 8

Pericles
    Funeral Oration from Thucydides, *History of the Peloponnesian War* 9
    The Athenian Empire—Map 12

Abraham Lincoln
    Gettysburg Address 14

Sophocles
    Oedipus 15
    ***Oedipus the King* 17**
        Study Guide for Sophocles' *Oedipus the King* 51
        Thucydides and the Plague in Athens 55
        Athens after the Oration: Realism vs. Idealism 56
        On Aristotle's *Poetics* 57
        The Hero—Chart 60
        Antigone 61
    ***Antigone* 63**
        Study Guide for Sophocles' *Antigone* 91

Plato
    A Brief Biography of Plato 95
    Outline for Plato's *Republic* 96
    ***The Republic* 98**
        Six Major Themes in Plato's *Republic* 123
        Introduction to *The Apology* 125
    ***The Last Days of Socrates: The Apology* 126**
        Introduction to Greek Foundations Timeline 141

Religious Foundations

- Introduction to the Bible   145
- *Hebrew Bible*   152
- **Genesis**   **154**
  - *Exodus*   181
- **Exodus**   **183**
- **Job**   **209**
- **Psalms**   **227**
- **Isaiah**   **231**
  - Introduction to the *Gospel of Matthew*   243
- **Gospel of Matthew**   **246**
  - A Seminar on the *Gospel of Matthew*   279
- **Gospel of John**   **281**
- **1 Corinthians**   **285**
  - *Qur'an*   286
  - Introduction to the *Qur'an*   288
- **The Story of the Qur'an**   **291**
- **The Qur'an**   **300**
  - Basic Features of Islam   328
  - English Words That Come from Islam   328
  - Spread of Islam—Map   329
  - Religious Foundations Timeline   330
  - Introduction to *Sundiata*   331
- **Sundiata: An Epic of Old Mali**   **334**
- **Creation Stories from around the World**   **374**

The Humanist Revival

Galileo
- Notes on Galileo   383
- Introduction to *The Starry Messenger*   385
- **The Starry Messenger**   **394**
- Galileo and Ancient Science   411

Machiavelli
- *The Prince*—Notes on Connections   413
- **The Prince**   **415**
- Notes on Machiavelli's *The Prince*   448

William Shakespeare
- Who Was William Shakespeare?   451
- Some Background on Shakespeare's Theater   453
- **The Tragedy of Othello, Moor of Venice**   **455**
- Notes on *Othello*   515
- Humanist Foundations Timeline   517

List of Contributors

G. Bernhard-Jackson is a member of the Department of English at Temple University. She is the senior Shakespeare scholar in that department and has taught for many years in the Intellectual Heritage Program at Temple University.

J. Scott Lee is an associate at the American Academy for Liberal Education in Washington, D.C. He is also National Director and co-founder of the Associate for Core Texts and Courses and a former Visiting Professor in the Department of English and the Intellectual Heritage Program at Temple University.

Michael Levin is a member of the Department of History at the University of Akron. He is a former Visiting Professor in the Intellectual Heritage Program at Temple University.

James Marra is a member of the Department of Journalism at Temple University. He is a former Associate Director of the Intellectual Heritage Program at Temple University and originated the Intellectual Heritage publication projects.

Mark Mattson directs the Cartography Laboratory of the Geography and Urban Studies Program at Temple University.

Robin Mitchell-Boyask is a member of the Department of Classics at Temple University and frequently teaches Intellectual Heritage.

Elie Noujain is a Visiting Professor in the Department of Philosophy at Temple University and frequently teaches Intellectual Heritage.

Grant Ward is a Visiting Professor in the Intellectual Heritage Program, a specialist in Biblical textual criticism, and an ordained minister.

Stephen Zelnick is a former Director of the Intellectual Heritage Program at Temple University, Executive Director and co-founder of the Association for Core Texts and Courses, and a member of the Department of English.

Introduction

Paths to Civilization is an ambitious attempt to represent the dynamism, variety, and power of the traditions of thinking that mark the Western world. These days we know more about more different things, and because of the speed and reach of technology, we encounter others of different backgrounds and traditions. Under these circumstances, it is particularly important that we who live in the Western world understand the ideas and the stories that have shaped us and our institutions.

The approach of *Paths to Civilization* reveals how very dynamic the traditions of the West are. As we move from one text to the next, we discover ongoing innovation, a constant bickering among writers, even among writers of the same culture.

We begin with the Greeks, for example, and soon learn that although we can use the term "Greeks," it encompasses very many different views. Pericles praises the daring of the Athenians who have created their glorious city by themselves and with no assistance from the gods; Sophocles, his contemporary and fellow Athenian disputes this view, arguing instead that only when the city blends the justice of the gods into its laws can things go well; Plato, another citizen of Athens, disputes both of the others, being an opponent to Periclean democracy and raising troubling questions about Sophoclean piety.

So there we are: three Athenians of the fifth century B.C.E., each an important figure in the development of Western thinking, and disagreeing fundamentally with one another. This is an excellent way to see how much the tradition we belong to, rather than being a self-confirming chorus of agreement, is instead an unfolding debate about basic principles.

This theme of innovation is also emphatic when we move from one cultural setting to another. The Greeks are polytheists. Sappho, for example, has her own god, the goddess Aphrodite, to whom the poet is devoted. For her, erotic love is the pathway to the divine, a religious devotion. For Odysseus, the goddess Athena sums up who he is and for him, what is important in life. Athena is the goddess of strategic wisdom, appearing as she does in warlike dress and carrying her spear. She expresses the amazing resourcefulness of Odysseus, his cleverness and cunning.

In a polytheistic setting, there are many ways for humans to approach the divine, and there is an honored place for many different kinds of people and the special soul of each of them. This variety of difference is appealing and provides an interesting advantage for democracy. However, as Plato begins to show, there are also decided disadvantages in such diversity. Plato's questionings about the inconsistencies of the gods—how is one to know what is right when the gods themselves offer so many different versions of excellence, and also so much confusion and misbehavior?—prepares the way for monotheism.

The Hebrew Bible accomplishes many things, but the central task is to dispel the many gods and put in their place the one true God whose excellence is assured. The way to know this God is not through an exercise of reason, as with Plato, but through a forceful and authoritative revelation. Jehovah blesses us not only through His power to create life and the richness of nature but by making Himself known to us and teaching us the laws of life.

However, the Hebrew Bible is far from a simple story or untroubled teaching. The negotiation between God and humans is unfailingly complicated in the Hebrew Bible. Human beings refuse to listen, or hear only what they wish to hear. They forget; they "lawyer" with God's words. In addition, God Himself seems willing to test and to learn about this odd creature who is so full of trouble. *Job* tells us a story of this sort.

Isaiah presents us with a major prophet, one who rails against his own people for having misappropriated or corrupted God's teachings. Prophets are plentiful in the *Hebrew Bible*, and they do what no other Scripture does—record the failure of God's chosen to achieve the excellence God set out for them. There is no comparable account of the failure of Christians or Muslims in their scriptures. Even within the *Hebrew Bible* there is endless criticism and a constant revising of the understanding of God's purposes and of the meaning of human history. Again, far from presenting an uncomplicated account, the *Hebrew Bible* is cross-hatched with conflict and contentiousness.

The New Testament offers a criticism of the law presented in the *Hebrew Bible* and offers a new emphasis on the meaning of life for human kind. Not only are the old laws "fulfilled" by the teachings of Jesus, but the entire perspective shifts from a revelation to the Jews exclusively to a revelation for all people. This universalism is something new, as is the promise of life everlasting for those who are saved.

Much in Christianity follows from the traditions of teachings of the Jews, and much else is appropriated from the Greeks, as *1 Corinthians* 13 shows. Nevertheless, Christianity offers another instance of bold innovation, and one that has formed the Western world decisively.

If we take the lesson of Intellectual Heritage firmly, we will also see that within the *Gospel of Matthew* itself there is a significant tension. In the "Sermon on the Mount," the reasons for obeying God's law are founded on the love of God purely. In the latter third of the same gospel, we hear a great deal about the punishments of hell and the glory of heaven. These are advanced as the source for obedience, and that represents a dramatic shift in emphasis.

The *Qur'an* represents yet another revelation from the same God, this time delivered to the Arab people but intended for all humanity. The *Qur'an*, though tolerant of Christianity and Judaism in places is also highly critical. The *Qur'an* presents a thorough-going account of God's law, like that of the *Hebrew Bible*; it is also, however, a universal religion, like Christianity. The Last Judgment is even more forcefully proposed than in the *New Testament*; and the proscription for a pious life is even more specific and all-embracing.

The *Sundiata*, an epic from West Africa, comes from a tradition not well known to the West, one that has had little influence on the Western world (though that would seem to be changing). It represents a perspective that helps us understand what is different in the Western outlook. *Genesis*, for example, insists that humankind is separate and apart from the rest of God's creation, the so-called "crown of creation" whose obligation is to "have dominion" over all the rest. In the *Sundiata* the animal world and the human interpenetrate; humans have totemic identities, the animals of the forest are our "dumb brothers in the bush," a view that modern science endorses. The *Sundiata* also argues for the superiority of oral culture over written, a view the West has abandoned, and perhaps with great loss to our culture and to ourselves. The *Sundiata* helps us think about our central traditions and, perhaps, what we have lost by being shaped so decisively by them.

The Renaissance tosses out much of what has come before. Galileo describes nature not through metaphor but through close physical observation and mathematical calculation. The ancients, lacking the appropriate instruments, could observe very little about the heavens. They turned instead to deduction following the pathway, often, of fanciful metaphor. The result, a beautiful physico-moral construction, comes crashing down when Galileo trains his "spy-glass" to the heavens. Disrupted, too, is the pleasing notion that the earth sits at the center of the universe. This displacement is the first of several relocations that have taught Western humanity a lesson is eccentricity and proportion and, in some odd sense, humility in the face of an unaccountable universe.

Machiavelli instigates the same sort of revolution in the social sciences. While Plato constructed "imaginary republics" to explore his notion of perfection, Machiavelli looks at what is, and draws from history and contemporary observation his lesson for wielding power and for constructing a successful polity based upon the severe moral and intellectual limitations of humanity.

Shakespeare concludes the first part of our itinerary in *Paths to Civilization,* and in *Othello* provides a Christian Humanism that draws together both the wisdom of the ancients and the close observation of the Renaissance. The play offers a critique of Machiavelli's power politics, perhaps an unfair one.

But Shakespeare's play represents for us another instance of what has become an obvious theme in our studies of the Western tradition. It is, after all, a tradition of restless criticism, innovation, and bold reconstitution. In every case, we encounter revolution, and indeed, the fate of many of these notable authors was unpleasant—Socrates drinks his hemlock; Jesus rouses the benighted who live in the shadows and moral confusion and pays dearly for it; Machiavelli is reviled, and Galileo imprisoned. Far from being a comfortable affirmation of shared values, the intellectual tradition of the West is an adventure that invites us all to see what is out ahead of us from the perspective of what has come before.

Classical Greek Foundations

Greece of the classical period (5th Century B.C.E.) was one of several powerful Mediterranean cultures of the ancient world. Egyptian culture was much older and continued to be politically powerful for a much longer period. The Persians, too, maintained a larger empire and for a longer time; and we have some records of remarkable accomplishments in science and mathematics attained by the Sumerians.

Why, then, do we single out the Greeks for special attention?

The answer is simple and straight-forward. The Greeks, and especially the city-state of Athens, left behind an astounding record of themselves—historians' accounts and administrative records, but, more importantly, plays, poems, and philosophical dialogues of great beauty and sophistication. It is told that a group of Athenian soldiers were captured by a bitter enemy and were to be put to death. However, when their captors discovered that these Athenians could recite passages from Aeschylus and Sophocles, their lives were spared so that their enemies could enjoy this beauty of language and thought. Even after the Greek city-states had lost their political and economic vitality, Greek scholars and teachers continued to make Hellenic culture essential to the Romans, the later ages of Egyptians, and to the emerging Christian world.

In *Paths to Civilization*, we do not study the Homeric epics, which were so influential, indeed almost sacred to the ancient Greeks. We do, however, read several poems by Sappho, an account of a speech by Pericles (which appears in The Peloponnesian Wars, written by Thucydides), and plays by either Aeschyles (*The Oresteian Trilogy*) or by Sophocles (*Oedipus, the King* and *Antigone*), and dialogues by Plato (*The Republic* and *The Apology*).

Western cultures are deeply indebted to these works of the Golden Age of Greece. The debates over various types of political constitutions (aristocracy, democracy, monarchy, etc.) were carried out energetically and recorded in the speech of Pericles and the works of Plato, among others. The ideas in these works have long had a powerful influence on Western thinkers—Lincoln, for example, is reported to have consulted the speech of Pericles in writing his Gettysburg Address in 1863.

Furthermore, the dialogues of Plato—in which his teacher Socrates is most often the main character—provided a powerful model for Western philosophical and religious traditions (one writer has concluded that all of Western philosophy is merely footnotes to Plato). Such important social formations as the Catholic Church owe a debt to Platonic thinking, especially in *The Republic*.

Greek literature has also had a profound effect upon later developments in Western literature. Sappho wrote lyric poetry of subtle simplicity about desire and love. Although centuries later Church authorities all but obliterated her works from the historical record, we still have enough to retain some sense of the charm and deep humanity of this splendid artist.

Many of the plays of Aeschylus and Sophocles (perhaps a quarter of the plays written by Sophocles) were preserved intact over the ages. Their philosophical richness and complexity is matched by the careful craftsmanship of their dramatic design. These Athenian playwrights established the criteria for dramatic construction that influence plays even today. For example, *Antigone* invites us to think about the relation of human and Divine laws and the meaning of civil disobedience. In the darkest moments of Nazi control in France, the playwright Jean Anouilh brought *Antigone* to the stage to rally the forces of opposition to inhuman tyranny. The tight construction of *Oedipus, the King* has taught generations of dramatists how to arouse an audience's involvement with the events on the stage and how, with a few deft strokes, to make a character believable and an object of our deepest concern.

The cultural roots of Western Civilization are deep in the events and productions of the ancient Greeks. Along with the Judeo-Christian heritage, the classical Greeks provide the foundation on which so much that is familiar to us is constructed.

Poems from Sappho (7th-6th Century B.C.E.)

A Wedding Toast

We drink your health

Lucky bridegroom!
Now the wedding you
asked for is over

and your wife is the girl you
asked for;
she's a bride who is

charming to look at,
with eyes as soft as
honey, and a face

that Love has lighted
with his own beauty.
Aphrodite has surely

outdone herself in
doing honor to you!

From *Sappho: A New Translation* by Mary Barnard. Copyright © 1958 The Regents of the University of California; © renewed 1986 Mary Barnard. Reprinted by permission of the University of California Press.

Lament for a Maidenhead

1st
Voice

Like a quince-apple
ripening on a top
branch in a tree top
not once noticed by
harvesters or if
noticed, not reached

2nd
Voice

Like a hyacinth in
the mountains, trampled
by shepherds until
only a purple stain
remains on the ground

Come to Us, Aphrodite

You* know the place: then

Leave Crete and come to us
waiting where the grove is
pleasantest, by precincts

sacred to you: incense
smokes on the altar, cold
streams murmur through the
apple branches, a young
rose thicket shades the ground
and quivering leaves pour

down deep sleep: in meadows
where horses have grown sleek
among spring flowers, dill

scents the air. Queen! Cyprian!
Fill our gold cups with love
stirred into clear nectar

---

* Aphrodite, Goddess of love

Prayer to My Lady of Paphos[*]

Dapple-throned Aphrodite,
eternal daughter of God,
snare-knitter! Don't, I beg you,

cow my heart with grief! Come,
as once when you heard my far-
off cry and, listening, stepped

from your father's house to your chariot
to yoke the pair[**] whose
beautiful thick-feathered wings

oaring down mid-air from heaven
carried you to light swiftly on
dark earth; then, blissful one,

smiling your immortal smile
you asked, What ailed me now,
made me call you again? What

was it that my distracted
heart most wanted? "Whom has
Persuasion to bring round now

to your love? Who, Sappho, is
unfair to you? For let her
run, she will soon run after;
if she won't accept gifts, she
will one day give them: if she
won't love you—she soon will

love, although unwillingly . . ."
If ever—come now! Relieve
this intolerable pain!

What my heart most hopes will
happen, make happen; you yourself join forces on my side!

---

[*] Aphrodite, born of sea foam, was washed ashore at Paphos
[**] The sparrows that drew Aphrodite's chariot

He Is More Than a Hero

He is a god in my eyes—
the man who is allowed
to sit beside you—he

who listens intimately
to the sweet murmur of
your voice, the enticing

laughter that makes my own
heart beat fast. If I meet
you suddenly, I can't

speak—my tongue is broken;
a thin flame runs under
my skin; seeing nothing
hearing only my own ears
drumming, I drip with sweat;
trembling shakes my body

I turn paler than
dry grass. At such times
death isn't far from me

Consoling a Friend

Yes, Atthis*, you may be sure
    Even in Sardis
Anactoria will think often of us

of the life we shared here, when
you seemed the Goddess incarnate
to her and your singing pleased
    her best

Now among Lydian women she in
her turn stands first as the
red-fingered moon rising at
    sunset takes

precedence over stars around
    her;
her light spreads equally
on the salt sea and fields thick
    with bloom

---

* Atthis and Anactoria were two girls in Sappho's circle.

Delicious dew pours down to
freshen roses, delicate thyme
and blossoming sweet clover; she

wanders aimlessly, thinking of
gentle Atthis, her heart hanging
heavy with longing in her little
    breast

She shouts aloud, Come, we know
    it:
Thousand-eared night repeats
    that cry
across the sea shining between
    us

The Departed Lover

I have not had one word from her
Frankly I wish I were dead.
When she left, she wept

a great deal; she said to
me, "This parting must be
endured, Sappho, I go
    unwillingly."

I said, "Go, and be happy
but remember (you know
well) whom you leave shackled by
    love

"If you forget me, think
of our gifts to Aphrodite
and all the loveliness that we
    shared

"all the violet tiaras,
braided rosebuds, dill and
crocus twining around your young
    neck

"Myrrh poured on your head
and on soft mats girls with
all that they most wished for
    beside them

"While no voices chanted
choruses without ours,
no woodlot bloomed in spring
    without song . . ."

Family of the Gods

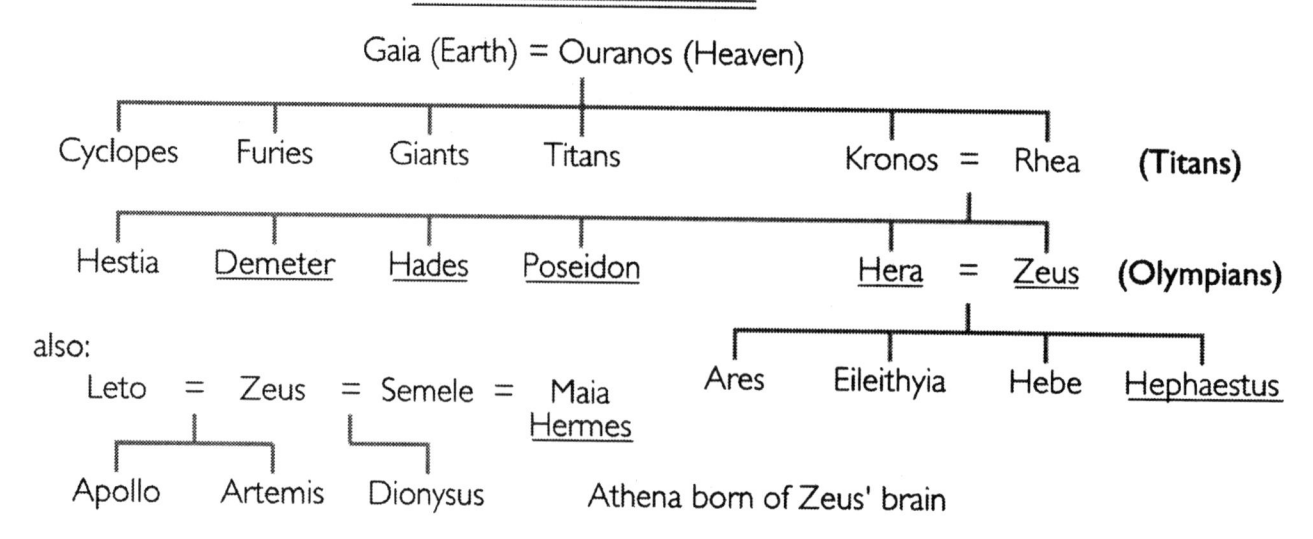

```
                Gaia (Earth) = Ouranos (Heaven)
    ┌─────────┬─────────┬─────────┬──────────────────┐
  Cyclopes  Furies   Giants    Titans           Kronos = Rhea    (Titans)
                                                    │
    ┌─────────┬─────────┬─────────┬──────────────────┐
  Hestia  Demeter   Hades    Poseidon            Hera = Zeus    (Olympians)
                                                    │
also:                                   ┌────────┬────────┬────────┐
   Leto = Zeus = Semele = Maia        Ares  Eileithyia  Hebe  Hephaestus
    │         │          Hermes
    │         │
  Apollo  Artemis   Dionysus      Athena born of Zeus' brain
```

Royal House of Thebes

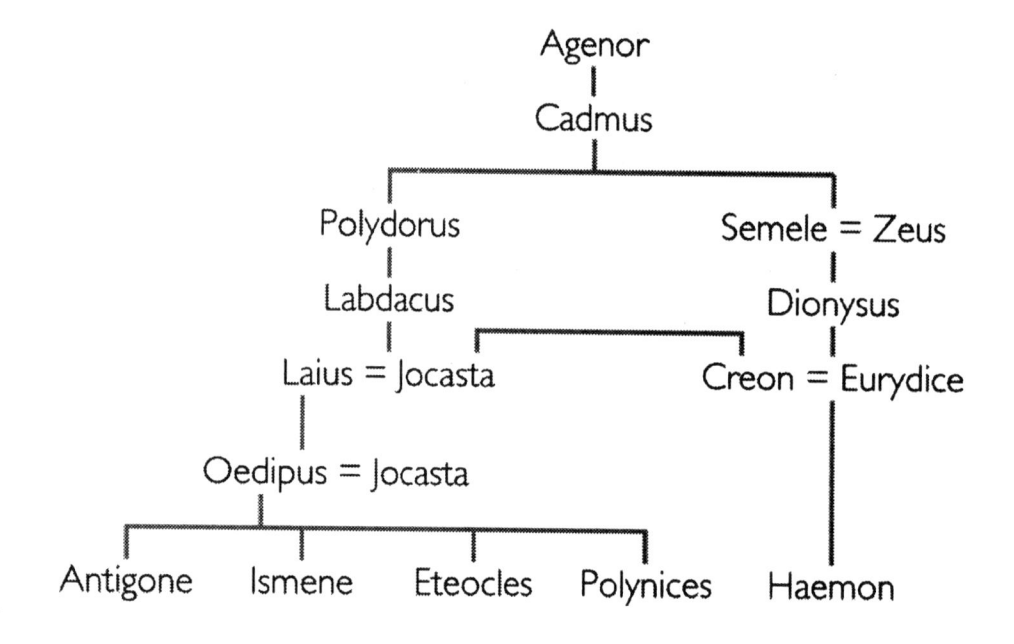

```
                Agenor
                  │
                Cadmus
         ┌────────────────────┐
      Polydorus          Semele = Zeus
         │                    │
      Labdacus            Dionysus
         │                    │
      Laius = Jocasta     Creon = Eurydice
              │                 │
         Oedipus = Jocasta
    ┌────────┬────────┬────────┐        │
 Antigone  Ismene  Eteocles  Polynices  Haemon
```

Pericles' Funeral Oration

Thucydides

from Thucydides, *History of the Peloponnesian War*

Thucydides' Introduction

That winter the Athenians gave a funeral at public cost for those who had first fallen in this war. It was a custom of their ancestors and was performed as follows. Three days before the ceremony, the bones of the dead are laid out in a tent which has been erected; and their friends bring to their relatives such offerings as they please. In the funeral procession cypress coffins are borne in wagons, one for each tribe. One empty bier, decked for the missing, celebrates those whose bodies could not be recovered. Any citizen or stranger who pleases, joins in the procession: and the female relatives are there to wail at the burial. The dead are laid in the public sepulchre, maintained for those who fall in war, in the most beautiful suburb of the city—with the exception of those slain at Marathon, who for their singular and extraordinary valor were interred where they fell. After the bodies have been laid in the earth, a wise and eminent man chosen by the state pronounces over them an appropriate panegyric; after which all retire. Such is the manner of burying; and throughout the war, whenever the occasion arose, the established custom was observed. Meanwhile, these were the first that had fallen and Pericles, son of Xanthippus, was chosen to pronounce their eulogium. When the proper time arrived, he advanced from the sepulchre to an elevated platform in order to be heard by as many of the crowd as possible, and spoke as follows:

The Speech of Pericles

"Most of my predecessors in this role have commended the man who made this speech part of the law, telling us that it is well that it should be delivered at the burial of those who fall in battle. For myself, I should have thought that in respect of men who have been good in action it would have sufficed to manifest our honor for them in action, as you now see we have done in providing for this public funeral; and I should have thought that the virtues of the many should not be jeopardized by being entrusted to one man, who might speak badly or well. It is hard to speak properly upon a subject where it is difficult to establish even the appearance of truth. On the one hand, the hearer who is familiar with every fact of the story may think that some point has not been fully set forth; on the other, a person lacking experience may be led by envy to suspect exaggeration if he hears anything above his own nature. For men can endure to hear others praised only so long as they can persuade themselves of their own ability to equal the actions recounted: beyond this point, envy and disbelief begin. However, since our ancestors have established this custom, it becomes my duty to obey the law and to try to satisfy your several wishes and opinions as best I may.

"It is both just and fitting that our ancestors should be honored first on an occasion like the present. They dwelt in this nation from generation to generation, and handed it down free to the present time by their valor. And if our more remote ancestors deserve praise, much more do our own fathers, who added to their inheritance the empire we now possess, and spared no pains to leave those acquisitions to us. Lastly, most of

---

Translated by R. Crowley. *Thucydides, Peloponnesian War*. The Modern Library, with modifications by E. Noujain and S. Zelnick.

our dominions have been increased by those of us here, who are still more or less in the vigor of life; Athens has been furnished by us with everything she needs for war or for peace. The actions in war which gave us our several possessions, or the ready valor with which either we or our fathers stemmed the tide of Hellenic or foreign aggression, is a theme too familiar to my hearers for me to expand on, and therefore I shall pass them over. But the road by which we reached our position, the form of government under which our greatness grew, the habits out of which it sprang; these are matters I may try to deal with before I proceed to my panegyric upon these men; since I think this is a proper subject upon the present occasion, and one to which the whole assemblage, whether citizens or foreigners, may listen with advantage.

"Our constitution does not seek to copy the laws of our neighbors; we are an example to others, not imitators of them. The name of this constitution is 'democracy,' because it pertains to the greater number, not to the few. In settling private disputes everyone is equal in accordance with the laws, while in public life, advancement depends on reputation and ability; for what counts is merit, not taking turns. Nor is poverty an obstacle: if a man is capable of conferring some benefit on the city, he is not hindered by the obscurity of his condition. As far as public life is concerned, we live as free men. In our daily habits, far from jealously spying upon one another, we are not angry with our neighbor for doing what he likes, or even for bad manners when they do no harm. But this ease in our private relations does not make us lawless as citizens. We obey the magistrates and the laws, particularly those laws which protect those who are wronged, whether such laws are actually on the statute book or belong to that code which, although unwritten, yet cannot be broken without disgrace.

"Further, we provide many ways to refresh the mind from the burdens of business. We hold contests and offer sacrifices all the year round, and the elegance of our private establishments forms a daily source of pleasure and helps to drive away sorrow. The magnitude of our city draws the produce of the world into our harbor, so that to the Athenian the fruits of other countries are as familiar a luxury as those of his own.

"In our military policy also we differ from our enemy. We throw open our city to the world, and never exclude foreigners from any opportunity of learning or observing, even though enemy eyes may occasionally benefit from our generosity, since we trust not so much in our preparations and our ruses as in our innate spirit for action. In education, where our rivals from their very cradles seek after manliness by a painful discipline, at Athens we live exactly as we please, and yet are just as ready to face every legitimate danger. In proof of this, notice that the Spartans do not invade our country alone, but must bring with them all their allies. We Athenians, however, advance unsupported into the territory of a neighbor, usually vanquishing with ease men who are defending their own property. Our united force has never yet been encountered by any enemy, because we deploy both our naval and land forces upon a hundred different services. When our enemies engage with some fraction of our strength, they magnify a minor success into a victory over all of us, and a defeat into a reverse suffered at the hands of our entire people. Yet, although we are prepared to face danger, our lives are easy, and we do not make a practice of toil, preferring to rely on courageous habits rather than the compulsions of the law. Thus we have the advantage of not suffering in preparation for future pain. Although we have to face hardship, we have proved ourselves equal to those who are committed to constant endurance.

"We are lovers of beautiful things with simplicity, and we cultivate philosophy without being soft. Wealth is to us an opportunity for action rather than for boastful words; and we place the real disgrace of poverty not in owning to the fact but in refusing to struggle against it. Our public men have, besides politics, their private affairs to attend to, and our ordinary citizens, though occupied with everyday pursuits, are able judges of public matters: of all our neighbors, we alone consider the man who refuses to take part in city affairs as useless, and not as someone who refrains from meddling. And rather than look upon discussion as a stumbling-block in the way of action, we think it an indispensable preliminary to any wise action at all. Again, in our enterprises we present the remarkable combination of daring and deliberation, each carried to its highest point, and both united in the same person; while with other nations decision is often the fruit of ignorance, hesitation of thoughtlessness. But the palm of courage will surely be awarded to those who best know the difference between hardship and pleasure and yet are never tempted to shrink from danger. In generosity we are equally singular, acquiring our friends by giving and not by receiving favors. Yet, of course, the doer of the favor is the firmer friend of the two, in order by continued kindness to keep the recipient in his debt; the debtor, in contrast, feels less keenly because the return he makes will be a payment, not a free gift. Only Athenians confer their benefits not from calculations of expediency, but in the confidence of liberality.

"In short, as a city we are the school of Greece; I doubt if the world can produce a man who on his own is equal to so many emergencies and possesses such versatility as the Athenian. The power of the city, acquired by these habits, proves that this is no mere boast thrown out for the occasion, but plain matter of fact. For Athens alone of her contemporaries is found, when tested, to be greater than her reputation. With Athens alone there is no reason for her assailants to feel shame when they are overcome by her, nor for her subjects to complain that his rulers are not worthy of ruling. The admiration of the present and succeeding ages will be ours, since we have not left our power without witness, but have shown it by mighty proofs. Far from needing a Homer to sing our praises, or some other of his craft whose verses might charm for the moment only to melt away at the touch of hard facts, we Athenians have forced even sea and land to be the highway of our daring, and everywhere, whether for evil or for good, have left imperishable monuments behind us. Such is the Athens for which these men, in the assertion of their resolve not to lose her, nobly fought and died; and well may every one of their survivors be ready to suffer in her cause.

"If I have dwelt at some length upon the character of our city, it has been to show that our stake in warfare is not the same as for those who have no such blessings to lose, and also that the praiseworthiness of the men over whom I am now speaking might be by definite proofs established. That panegyric is now in great measure complete; for the Athens that I have celebrated is only what the heroism of these and their like have made her, men whose fame, unlike that of most Greeks, will be found to match their actions. I think that the way these men met their end is a proof of their virtues; and not only for hardened veterans who set the final seal upon their merit, but also for those who gave the first hint of their valor. For there is justice in the claim that steadfastness in his nation's battles provides a cloak to cover a man's other imperfections; the good action blots out the bad, and his merit as a citizen more than outweighs his faults as an individual. None of these men allowed wealth with its prospect of future enjoyment to unnerve his spirit; none permitted poverty with its hope of a day of freedom and riches to tempt him to shrink from danger. No, holding vengeance upon their enemies more dear than any personal blessings, and reckoning this the most glorious of hazards, they joyfully accepted the risk, to pursue their vengeance and to postpone their wishes. They acted boldly and trusted in themselves while committing to hope the uncertainty in the business before them. Choosing to die resisting, rather than to live submitting, they fled only from dishonor, but met danger face to face; in one brief moment, while at the summit of their fortune, they escaped from fear and embraced their glory.

"So died these men as became Athenians. You, their survivors, must determine to have as unaltering a resolve in the field, though you may pray for a happier issue. Do not be content with ideas derived only from words about these advantages in defending your country (though these furnish a valuable text to a speaker before an audience so alive to him as the present). Realize for yourself the power of Athens, and feed your eyes upon her day after day, till you become her devoted lover. Then, when all her greatness breaks upon you, reflect that it was by courage, sense of duty, and a keen feeling of honor in action that men were enabled to win all this, and that no personal failure in an enterprise could make them consent to deprive their country of their valor, but they laid it at her feet as the most glorious contribution they could offer. By this mutual offering of their lives made by them all, they each of them individually received that renown which never grows old. For a sepulchre they have won not so much that tomb in which their bones are here deposited, but that noblest of shrines wherein their glory is laid up to be eternally remembered upon every occasion on which deed or story shall fall for its commemoration. For heroes have the whole earth for their tomb. In lands far from their own, where the column with its epitaph declares it, there is enshrined in every breast a record unwritten with no tablet to preserve it, except that of the heart. These heroes take as your model, and, judging happiness to be the fruit of freedom and freedom of valor, never decline the dangers of war. For it is not the miserable that would most justly be unsparing of their lives; these have nothing to hope for: it is rather they to whom continued life may bring reverses as yet unknown, and to whom a fall, if it came, would be most tremendous in its consequences. And surely, to a man of spirit, the degradation of cowardice must be immeasurably more grievous than the unfelt death which strikes him in the midst of his strength.

"Comfort, therefore, not condolence, is what I have to offer to the parents of the dead who may be here. Numberless are the chances to which, as they know, the life of man is subject; but fortunate indeed are they who draw for their lot a death so glorious as that which has caused your mourning, and to whom life has been so exactly measured as to terminate in the happiness in which it has been passed. Still I know that this is a hard saying, especially in regard to those of whom you will constantly be reminded by seeing, in the homes of others, blessings of which once you also boasted: for grief is felt not so much for the want of what we have never known, as for the loss of that to which we have been long accustomed. Yet you who are still of an age to beget children must bear up in the hope of having others in their stead; not only will they help you to forget those whom you have lost, but they will be to our city at once a reinforcement and a security. Never can a fair or just policy be expected of the citizen who does not, like his fellows, bring to the decision the fears and concerns of a father. Those of you who have passed your prime must congratulate yourselves with the thought that the best part of your life was fortunate, and that the brief span that remains will be cheered by the fame of the departed. For it is only the love of honor that never grows old; and honor it is, not gain, as some would have it, that rejoices the heart of the aged and infirm.

"Turning to the sons or brothers of the dead, I see an arduous struggle before you. When a man is gone, all will praise him, and were your merit ever so transcendent, you will still find it difficult not merely to overtake, but even to approach their renown. The living have envy to contend with, while those who are no longer in our path are honored with a goodwill where rivalry does not enter. On the other hand, if I must say anything on the subject of female excellence to those now in widowhood, it will be all comprised in

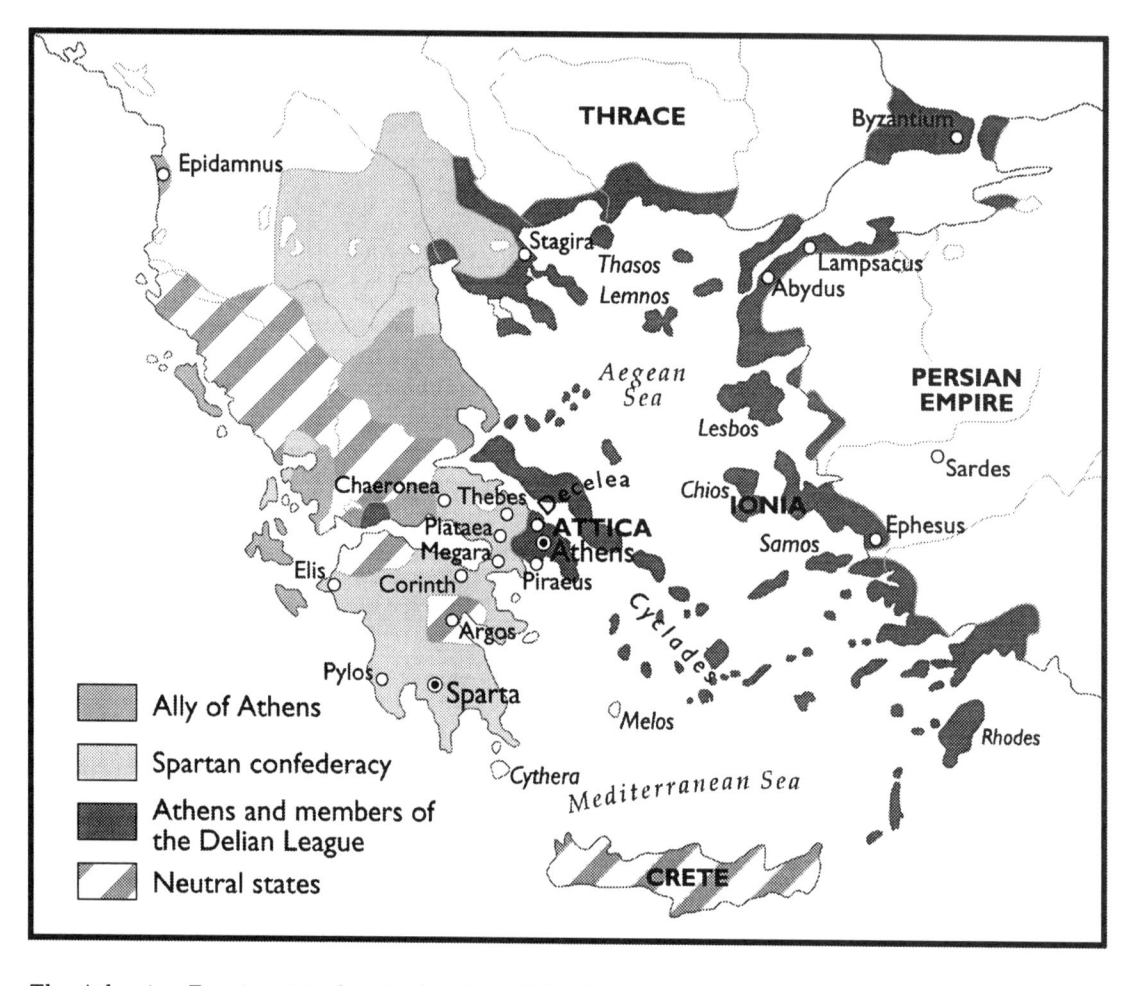

The Athenian Empire at its height dominated the Eastern Mediterranean. Although a democracy, Athens was aggressive in subjecting others to its will. Its imperialistic daring led to fears among its more powerful neighbors and ultimately to the Peloponnesian War.

this brief exhortation: Great will be your glory in not falling short of your natural character; and greatest will be hers who is least talked of among the men whether for good or for bad.

"My task is now finished. I have performed it to the best of my ability, and in words, at least, the requirements of the law are now satisfied. If deeds be in question, those who are here interred have received a part of their honors already, and for the rest, their children will be brought up till manhood at the public expense: our city thus offers a valuable prize as the garland of victory in this race of valor, for the reward both of those who have fallen and their survivors. And where the rewards for merit are greatest, there are found the best citizens.

"And now that you have brought to a close your lamentations for your relatives, you may depart."

Bust of Athenian Statesman, Pericles. CORBIS/Bettmann

Gettysburg Address

Abraham Lincoln

November 19, 1863

Lincoln's Gettysburg Address is similar in occasion and intent to the "Funeral Oration" of Pericles. Many believe that Lincoln consulted Pericles' speech when writing his own. What similarities do you notice?

Fourscore and seven years ago our fathers brought forth on this continent a new nation, conceived in liberty, and dedicated to the proposition that all men are created equal.

Now we are engaged in a great civil war, testing whether that nation, or any nation so conceived and so dedicated can long endure. We are met on a great battlefield of that war. We have come to dedicate a portion of that field as a final resting-place for those who here gave their lives that that nation might live. It is altogether fitting and proper that we should do this.

But, in a larger sense, we cannot dedicate—we cannot consecrate—we cannot hallow—this ground. The brave men, living and dead, who struggled here, have consecrated it far above our poor power to add or detract. The world will little note nor long remember what we say here, but it can never forget what they did here. It is for us, the living, rather, to be dedicated here to the unfinished work which they who fought here have thus far so nobly advanced. It is rather for us to be here dedicated to the great task remaining before us—that from these honored dead we take increased devotion to that cause for which they gave the last full measure of devotion; that we here highly resolve that these dead shall not have died in vain; that this nation, under God, shall have a new birth of freedom; and that government of the people, by the people, for the people, shall not perish from the earth.

Statue of Abraham Lincoln inside the Lincoln Memorial, Washington, D.C. CORBIS/Bettmann

Oedipus

Oedipus, the King is the second of the so-called Three Theban Plays. These plays are not really a trilogy in the Greek theatrical sense because although they all treat material that is closely related in the story sources, the plays were written at very different times and treat diverse subjects. They all do, however, focus upon the stories associated with the troubled family of Oedipus, and *Oedipus, the King* tells us about these troubles in a stark and horrifying way.

The fate that befalls poor Oedipus—to murder his father, marry his mother, and father children with her—violates the most serious taboos we know. Yet, intriguingly, Oedipus himself has this imposed upon him even before he is born and with no evident justification. What could anyone do to merit such evil treatment by the gods? And if such things can come about, then where is the justice of the gods?

Sophocles chooses to retell this "fairy tale" in a moment of deep crisis for his beloved Athens. In the midst of a ruinous war, Athens is struck by a plague, while its citizens are gathered within the city's walls. Perhaps as many as one-third of the people die (the plague may have been smallpox), and the Athenians, until that time proud of their ability to obey the law and confident of their destiny, begin to lose their faith in the gods and in the city. Sophocles means to rally the spirits of his fellow citizens.

How can such a morbid tale ever serve this purpose? We learn that no person knows his destiny, no matter how clever he may be. Nor can any person withhold fate, no matter how good he is, or even how much his community needs him. The gods have purposes in history beyond our knowledge, and it is our responsibility to hold up against the blows of a seemingly meaningless fate, maintaining the faith that the gods see a larger purpose to which we are blind. Oedipus does not know (though his audience does) that he is destined to experience great suffering, and through that suffering to become the protector of the city of Athens and even, in the end, to be taken up bodily into heaven. He earns this heroic regard by standing up against his destiny and maintaining, even in the depth of his agonies, a belief that the gods rule and rule well. Sophocles is teaching his fellow citizens a lesson in faith and endurance, even as they suffer the worst hardships.

Oedipus, the King has a special modern significance since it is the source of Freud's ideas about the "Oedipus Complex." Freud was, of course, most interested in the rivalries within the family. However, he was also interested in the odd structures of mind that allow us at the same time to know and not to know something. The process by which Oedipus—otherwise so clever and able to solve the most challenging riddle—comes to realize what has happened, half-blind always to the obvious clues, has been interesting to anyone who wants to know how we function.

Finally, *Oedipus, the King* is an example of perfect dramatic construction. The play observes the three unities as described by Aristotle—it takes place at one time, at one place, and in one continuous action. In addition, the rising current of a mystery to be solved, and the tense dramatic irony for the audience of knowing what is happening when the characters obviously do not, makes for great tension and forceful release when the horrible truth is revealed. In Aristotle's view, the play arouses pity and fear in the audience, which, when it is released through discovery, produces a powerful emotional catharsis. This, Aristotle contended, was a source of great satisfaction for audiences of this and other works of imagination. Whether we accept Aristotle's account or not, we can agree easily that this play by Sophocles is an example of excellent art in service of profound thinking about our destiny and our lives.

Oedipus the King

Sophocles

Characters

OEDIPUS, king of Thebes
A PRIEST of Zeus
CREON, brother of Jocasta
A CHORUS of Theban citizens and their
    LEADER
TIRESIAS, a Blind prophet
JOCASTA, the queen, wife of Oedipus
A MESSENGER from Corinth
A SHEPHERD
A MESSENGER from inside the palace
ANTIGONE, ISMENE, daughters of Oedipus
    and Jocasta
Guards and attendants
Priests of Thebes

Time and Scene: The royal house of Thebes. Double doors dominate the façade; a stone altar stands at the center of the stage.

Many years have passed since OEDIPUS *solved the riddle of the Sphinx and ascended the throne of Thebes, and now a plague has struck the city. A procession of priests enters; suppliants, broken and despondent, they carry branches wound in wool and lay them on the altar.*

The doors open. Guards assemble. OEDIPUS *comes forward, majestic but for a telltale limp, and slowly views the condition of his people.*

OEDIPUS:
Oh my children, the new blood of ancient
    Thebes,
why are you here? Huddling at my altar,
praying before me, your branches wound
    in wool.
Our city reeks with the smoke of burning
    incense,
rings with cries for the Healer and wailing
    for the dead.   5
I thought it wrong, my children, to hear
    the truth
from others, messengers. Here I am myself—
you all know me, the world knows my fame:
I am Oedipus.

Helping a Priest to his feet.

  Speak up, old man. Your years,
your dignity—you should speak for the
    others.   10
Why here and kneeling, what preys upon
    you so?
Some sudden fear? some strong desire?
You can trust me. I am ready to help,
I'll do anything. I would be blind to misery
not to pity my people kneeling at my feet.   15

PRIEST:
Oh Oedipus, king of the land, our greatest
    power!
You see us before you now, men of all ages
clinging to your altars. Here are boys,
still too weak to fly from the nest,
and here the old, bowed down with the
    years,   20
the holy ones—a priest of Zeus myself—
    and here
the picked, unmarried men, the young
    hope of Thebes.
And all the rest, your great family gathers
    now,
branches wreathed, massing in the squares,
kneeling before the two temples of queen
    Athena   25

From *Three Theban Plays by Sophocles*, translated by Robert Fagles. Translation copyright © 1982 by Robert Fagles. Used by permission of Viking Penguin, a division of Penguin Putnam Inc.

or the river-shrine where the embers glow
   and die
and Apollo sees the future in the ashes.
                              Our city—
look around you, see with your own
   eyes—
our ship pitches wildly, cannot lift her
   head
from the depths, the red waves of death
   . . .   30
Thebes is dying. A blight on the fresh
   crops
and the rich pastures, cattle sicken and
   die,
and the women die in labor, children
   stillborn,
and the plague, the fiery god of fever
   hurls down
on the city, his lightning slashing through
   us—   35
raging plague in all its vengeance,
   devastating
the house of Cadmus! And black Death
   luxuriates
in the raw, wailing miseries of Thebes.
Now, we pray to you. You cannot equal
   the gods,
your children know that, bending at your
   altar.   40
But we do rate you first of men,
both in the common crises of our lives
and face-to-face encounters with the gods.
You freed us from the Sphinx, you came
   to Thebes
and cut us loose from the bloody tribute
   we had paid   45
that harsh, brutal singer. We taught you
   nothing,
no skill, no extra knowledge, still you
   triumphed.
A god was with you, so they say, and we
   believe it—
you lifted up our lives.
                         So now again,
Oedipus, king, we bend to you, your
   power—   50
we implore you, all of us on our knees:
find us strength, rescue! Perhaps you've
   heard
the voice of a god or something from
   other men,
Oedipus . . . what do you know?
The man of experience—you see it every
   day—   55
his plans will work in a crisis, his first of
   all.

Act now—we beg you, best of men, raise
   up our city!
Act, defend yourself, your former glory!
Your country calls you savior now
for your zeal, your action years ago.   60
Never let us remember of your reign:
you helped us stand, only to fall once
   more.
Oh raise up our city, set us on our feet.
The omens were good that day you
   brought us joy—
be the same man today!   65
Rule our land, you know you have the
   power,
but rule a land of the living, not a
   wasteland.
Ship and towered city are nothing,
   stripped of men
alive within it, living all as one.

OEDIPUS:
                    My children,
I pity you. I see—how could I fail to see   70
what longings bring you here? Well I
   know
you are sick to death, all of you,
but sick as you are, not one is sick as I.
Your pain strikes each of you alone, each
in the confines of himself, no other. But
   my spirit   75
grieves for the city, for myself and all of
   you.
I wasn't asleep, dreaming. You haven't
   wakened me—
I have wept through the nights, you must
   know that,
groping, laboring over many paths of
   thought.
After a painful search I found one cure: 80
I acted at once. I sent Creon,
my wife's own brother, to Delphi—
Apollo the Prophet's oracle—to learn
what I might do or say to save our city.
Today's the day. When I count the days
   gone by   85
it torments me . . . what is he doing?
Strange, he's late, he's gone too long.
But once he returns, then, then I'll be a
   traitor
if I do not do all the god makes clear.

PRIEST:
Timely words. The men over there   90
are signaling—Creon's just arriving.

OEDIPUS:

Sighting CREON, then turning to the altar.

                        Lord Apollo,
let him come with a lucky word of rescue,
shining like his eyes!

PRIEST:
Welcome news, I think—he's crowned, look,
and the laurel wreath is bright with berries.   95

OEDIPUS:
We'll soon see. He's close enough to hear—

Enter CREON from the side; his face is shaded with a wreath.

Creon, prince, my kinsman, what do you bring us?
What message from the god?

CREON:
                      Good news.
I tell you even the hardest things to bear,
if they should turn out well, all would be well.   100

OEDIPUS:
Of course but what were the god's *words*? There's no hope
and nothing to fear in what you've said so far.

CREON:
If you want my report in the presence of these people . . .

Pointing to the priests while drawing OEDIPUS toward the palace.

I'm ready now, or we might go inside.

OEDIPUS:
                      Speak out,
speak to us all. I grieve for these, my people,   105
far more than I fear for my own life.

CREON:
                      Very well,
I will tell you what I heard from the god.
Apollo commands us—he was quite clear—
"Drive the corruption from the land,
don't harbor it any longer past all cure,   110
don't nurse it in your soil—root it out!"

OEDIPUS:
How can we cleanse ourselves—what rites?
What's the source of the trouble?

CREON:
Banish the man, or pay back blood with blood.
Murder sets the plague-storm on the city.

OEDIPUS:
                      Whose murder?   115
Whose fate does Apollo bring to light?

CREON:
                      Our leader,
my lord, was once a man named Laius,
before you came and put us straight on course.

OEDIPUS:
     I know—
or so I've heard. I never saw the man myself

CREON:
Well, he was killed and Apollo commands us now—   120
he could not be more clear,
"Pay the killers back—whoever is responsible."

OEDIPUS:
Where on earth are they? Where to find it now,
the trail of the ancient guilt so hard to trace?

CREON:
"Here in Thebes," he said.   125
Whatever is sought for can be caught, you know,
whatever is neglected slips away.

OEDIPUS:
                      But where,
in the palace, the fields or foreign soil,
where did Laius meet his bloody death?

CREON:
He went to consult an oracle, Apollo said,   130
and he set out and never came home again.

OEDIPUS:
No messenger, no fellow-traveler saw what happened?
Someone to cross-examine?

CREON:
                    No,
they were all killed but one. He escaped,
terrified, he could tell us nothing clearly,   135
nothing of what he saw—just one thing.

OEDIPUS:
                    What's that?
One thing could hold the key to it all,
a small beginning give us grounds for hope.

CREON:
He said thieves attacked them—a whole band,
not single-handed, cut King Laius down.

OEDIPUS:
                    A thief   140
so daring, so wild, he'd kill a king?
    Impossible,
unless conspirators paid him off in Thebes.

CREON:
We suspected as much. But with Laius dead
no leader appeared to help us in our troubles.

OEDIPUS:
Trouble? Your *king* was murdered—royal blood!   145
What stopped you from tracking down the killer
then and there?

CREON:
          The singing, riddling Sphinx.
She . . . persuaded us to let the mystery go
and concentrate on what lay at our feet.

OEDIPUS:
                    No,
I'll start again—I'll bring it all to light myself   150
Apollo is right, and so are you, Creon,
to turn our attention back to the murdered man.
Now you have *me* to fight for you, you'll see:
I am the land's avenger by all rights,
and Apollo's champion too.   155
But not to assist some distant kinsman, no,
for my own sake I'll rid us of this corruption.
Whoever killed the king may decide to kill me too,
with the same violent hand—by avenging Laius
I defend myself

                    To the priests.

          Quickly, my children.   160
Up from the steps, take up your branches now.

                    To the guards.

One of you summon the city here before us,
tell them I'll do everything. God help us,
we will see our triumph—or our fall.

OEDIPUS and CREON enter the palace, followed by the guards.

PRIEST:
Rise, my sons. The kindness we came for   165
Oedipus volunteers himself.
Apollo has sent his word, his oracle—
Come down, Apollo, save us, stop the plague.

The priests rise, remove their branches and exit to the side.

Enter a CHORUS, the citizens of Thebes, who have not heard the news that CREON brings. They march around the altar, chanting.

CHORUS:
          Zeus!
Great welcome voice of Zeus, what do you bring?
What word from the gold vaults of Delphi   170
comes to brilliant Thebes? Racked with terror—
          terror shakes my heart
and I cry your wild cries, Apollo, Healer of Delos

I worship you in dread . . . what now,
    what is your price?
some new sacrifice? some ancient rite
    from the past 175
come round again each spring?—
        what will you bring to birth?
Tell me, child of golden Hope
warm voice that never dies!
You are the first I call, daughter of Zeus 180
deathless Athena—I call your sister
    Artemis,
heart of the market place enthroned in
    glory,
        guardian of our earth—
I call Apollo, Archer astride the
    thunderheads of heaven—
O triple shield against death, shine before
    me now! 185
If ever, once in the past, you stopped
    some ruin
launched against our walls
        you hurled the flame of pain
far, far from Thebes—you gods
come now, come down once more!
        No, no 190
the miseries numberless, grief on grief, no
    end—
too much to bear, we are all dying
O my people . . .
    Thebes like a great army dying
and there is no sword of thought to save
    us, no 195
and the fruits of our famous earth, they
    will not ripen
no and the women cannot scream their
    pangs to birth—
screams for the Healer, children dead in
    the womb
        and life on life goes down
            you can watch them go 200
like seabirds winging west, outracing the
    day's fire
down the horizon, irresistibly
    streaking on to the shores of Evening
        Death
so many deaths, numberless deaths on
    deaths, no end—
Thebes is dying, look, her children 205
stripped of pity . . .
    generations strewn on the ground
unburied, unwept, the dead spreading
    death
and the young wives and gray-haired
    mothers with them
cling to the altars, trailing in from all over
    the city— 210

Thebes, city of death, one long cortege
    and the suffering rises
        wails for mercy rise
and the wild hymn for the Healer
    blazes out
clashing with our sobs our cries of
    mourning— 215
    O golden daughter of god, send rescue
radiant as the kindness in your eyes!
Drive him back!—the fever, the god of
    death
        that raging god of war
not armored in bronze, not shielded now,
    he burns me, 220
battle cries in the onslaught burning on—
O rout him from our borders!
Sail him, blast him out to the Sea-queen's
    chamber
        the black Atlantic gulfs
or the northern harbor, death to all 225
where the Thracian surf comes crashing,
Now what the night spares he comes by
    day and kills—
the god of death.
        O lord of the stormcloud,
you who twirl the lightning, Zeus, Father,
thunder Death to nothing! 230
Apollo, lord of the light, I beg you—
    whip your longbow's golden cord
showering arrows on our enemies—shafts
    of power
champions strong before us rushing on!
Artemis, Huntress, 235
torches flaring over the eastern ridges—
        ride Death down in pain!
God of the headdress gleaming gold, I cry
    to you—
your name and ours are one, Dionysus—
    come with your face aflame with wine 240
        your raving women's cries
your army on the march! Come with the
    lightning
come with torches blazing, eyes ablaze
    with glory!
Burn that god of death that all gods hate!

*OEDIPUS enters from the palace to address the CHO-
RUS, as if addressing the entire city of Thebes.*

OEDIPUS:
You pray to the gods? Let me grant your
    prayers. 245
Come, listen to me—do what the plague
    demands:
you'll find relief and lift your head from
    the depths.

I will speak out now as a stranger to the story,
a stranger to the crime. If I'd been present then,
there would have been no mystery, no long hunt 250
without a clue in hand. So now, counted
a native Theban years after the murder,
to all of Thebes I make this proclamation:
if any one of you knows who murdered Laius,
the son of Labdacus, I order him to reveal 255
the whole truth to me. Nothing to fear,
even if he must denounce himself,
let him speak up
and so escape the brunt of the charge—
he will suffer no unbearable punishment, 260
nothing worse than exile, totally unharmed.

OEDIPUS pauses, waiting for a reply.

                Next,
if anyone knows the murderer is a stranger,
a man from alien soil, come, speak up.
I will give him a handsome reward, and lay up
gratitude in my heart for him besides. 265

Silence again, no reply.

But if you keep silent, if anyone panicking,
trying to shield himself or friend or kin,
rejects my offer, then hear what I will do.
I order you, every citizen of the state
where I hold throne and power: banish this man— 270
whoever he may be—never shelter him, never
speak a word to him, never make him partner
to your prayers, your victims burned to the gods.
Never let the holy water touch his hands.
Drive him out, each of you, from every home. 275
He is the plague, the heart of our corruption,
as Apollo's oracle has just revealed to me.
So I honor my obligations:
I fight for the god and for the murdered man.
Now my curse on the murderer. Whoever he is, 280
a lone man unknown in his crime
or one among many, let that **man drag out**
his life in agony, step by painful step—
I curse myself as well . . . **if by any chance**
he proves to be an intimate of **our house,** 285
here at my hearth, with my full knowledge,
may the curse I just called down on him strike me!
These are your orders: perform them to the last.
I command you, for my sake, for Apollo's, for this country
blasted root and branch by the angry heavens. 290
Even if god had never urged you **on to act**
how could you leave the crime
uncleansed so long?
A man so noble—your king, brought down in blood—
you should have searched. But I am the king now,
I hold the throne that he held then, possess his bed 295
and a wife who shares our seed . . . why, our seed
might be the same, children born of the same mother
might have created blood-bonds **between** us
if his hope of offspring had not met disaster—
but fate swooped at his head and cut him short. 300
So I will fight for him as if he were my father,
stop at nothing, search the world
to lay my hands on the man who shed his blood,
the son of Labdacus descended of Polydorus,
Cadmus of old and Agenor, founder of the line: 305
their power and mine are one.
                Oh dear gods,
my curse on those who disobey **these** orders!
Do no crops grow out of the earth for them—
shrivel their women, kill their sons,
burn them to nothing in this plague 310
that hits us now, or something **even worse.**
But you, loyal men of Thebes who approve my actions,
may our champion, justice, may all the gods
be with us, fight beside us to the end!

LEADER:
In the grip of your curse, my king, I swear   315
I'm not the murderer, I cannot point him out.
As for the search, Apollo pressed it on us—
he should name the killer.

OEDIPUS:
                    Quite right,
but to force the gods to act against their will—
no man has the power.

LEADER:
            Then if I might mention   320
the next best thing . . .

OEDIPUS:
            The third best too—
don't hold back, say it.

LEADER:
            I still believe . . .
Lord Tiresias sees with the eyes of Lord Apollo.
Anyone searching for the truth, my king,
might learn it from the prophet, clear as day.   325

OEDIPUS:
I've not been slow with that. On Creon's cue
I sent the escorts, twice, within the hour.
I'm surprised he isn't here.

LEADER:
            We need him—
without him we have nothing but old, useless rumors.

OEDIPUS:
Which rumors? I'll search out every word.   330

LEADER:
Laius was killed, they say, by, certain travelers.

OEDIPUS:
I know—but no one can find the murderer.

LEADER:
If the man has a trace of fear in him
he won't stay silent long,
not with your curses ringing in his ears.   335

OEDIPUS:
He didn't flinch at murder,
he'll never flinch at words.

Enter Tiresias, the blind prophet, led by a boy with escorts in attendance. He remains at a distance.

LEADER:
Here is the one who will convict him, look,
they bring him on at last, the seer, the man of god.
The truth lives inside him, him alone.

OEDIPUS:
            O Tiresias,   340
master of all the mysteries of our life,
all you teach and all you dare not tell,
signs in the heavens, signs that walk the earth!
Blind as you are, you can feel all the more
what sickness haunts our city. You, my lord,   345
are the one shield, the one savior we can find.
We asked Apollo—perhaps the messengers
haven't told you—he sent his answer back:
"Relief from the plague can only come one way.
Uncover the murderers of Laius,   350
put them to death or drive them into exile."
So I beg you, grudge us nothing now, no voice,
no message plucked from the birds, the embers
or the other mantic ways within your grasp.
Rescue yourself, your city, rescue me—   355
rescue everything infected by the dead.
We are in your hands. For a man to help others
with all his gifts and native strength:
that is the noblest work.

TIRESIAS:
            How terrible—to see the truth
when the truth is only pain to him who sees!   360
I knew it well, but I put it from my mind,
else I never would have come.

OEDIPUS:
What's this? Why so grim, so dire?

TIRESIAS:
just send me home. You bear your burdens,
I'll bear mine. It's better that way, 365
please believe me.

OEDIPUS:
    Strange response . . . unlawful,
unfriendly too to the state that bred and reared you—
you withhold the word of god.

TIRESIAS:
    I fail to see
that your own words are so well-timed.
I'd rather not have the same thing said of me . . . 370

OEDIPUS:
For the love of god, don't turn away,
not if you know something. We beg you,
all of us on our knees.

TIRESIAS:
    None of you knows—
and I will never reveal my dreadful secrets,
not to say your own. 375

OEDIPUS:
What? You know and you won't tell?
You're bent on betraying us, destroying Thebes?

TIRESIAS:
I'd rather not cause pain for you or me.
So why this . . . useless interrogation?
You'll get nothing from me.

OEDIPUS:
    Nothing! You, 380
you scum of the earth, you'd enrage a heart of stone!
You won't talk? Nothing moves you?
Out with it, once and for all!

TIRESIAS:
You criticize my temper . . . unaware
of the one *you* live with, you revile me. 385

OEDIPUS:
Who could restrain his anger hearing you?
What outrage—you spurn the city!

TIRESIAS:
What will come will come.
Even if I shroud it all in silence.

OEDIPUS:
What will come? You're bound to *tell* me that. 390

TIRESIAS:
I will say no more. Do as you like, build your anger
to whatever pitch you please, rage your worst—

OEDIPUS:
Oh, I'll let loose, I have such fury in me—
now I see it all. You helped hatch the plot
you did the work, yes, short of killing him 395
with your own hands—and given eyes I'd say
you did the killing single-handed!

TIRESIAS:
    Is that so!
I charge you, then, submit to that decree
you just laid down: from this day onward
speak to no one, not these citizens, not myself 400
You are the curse, the corruption of the land!

OEDIPUS:
You, shameless—
aren't you appalled to start up such a story?
You think you can get away with this?

TIRESIAS:
    I have already.
The truth with all its power lives inside me. 405

OEDIPUS:
Who primed you for this? Not your prophet's trade.

TIRESIAS:
You did, you forced me, twisted it out of me.

OEDIPUS:
What? Say it again—I'll understand it better.

TIRESIAS:
Didn't you understand, just now?
Or are you tempting me to talk? 410

OEDIPUS:
No, I can't say I grasped your meaning.
Out with it, again!

TIRESIAS:
I say you are the murderer you hunt.

OEDIPUS:
That obscenity, twice—by god, you'll pay.

TIRESIAS:
Shall I say more, so you can really rage?   415

OEDIPUS:
Much as you want. Your words are nothing—
futile.

TIRESIAS:
You cannot imagine . . . I tell you,
you and your loved ones live together in infamy,
you cannot see how far you've gone in guilt.

OEDIPUS:
You think you can keep this up and never suffer?   420

TIRESIAS:
Indeed, if the truth has any power.

OEDIPUS:
                    It does
but not for you, old man. You've lost your power,
stone-blind, stone-deaf—senses, eyes blind as stone!

TIRESIAS:
I pity you, flinging at me the very insults
each man here will fling at you so soon.

OEDIPUS:
                    Blind,   425
lost in the night, endless night that nursed you!
You can't hurt me or anyone else who sees the light—
you can never touch me.

TIRESIAS:
                    True, it is not your fate
to fall at my hand, Apollo is quite enough;
and he will take some pains to work this out.   430

OEDIPUS:
Creon! Is this conspiracy his or yours?

TIRESIAS:
Creon is not your downfall, no, you are your own.

OEDIPUS:
O power—
wealth and empire, skill outstripping skill
in the heady rivalries of life,
what envy lurks inside you! Just for this,   435
the crown the city gave me—I never sought it,
they laid it in my hands—for this alone, Creon,
the soul of trust, my loyal friend from the start
steals against me . . . so hungry to overthrow me
he sets this wizard on me, this scheming quack,   440
this fortune-teller peddling lies, eyes peeled
for his own profit—seer blind in his craft!
Come here, you pious fraud. Tell me,
when did you ever prove yourself a prophet?
When the Sphinx, that chanting Fury kept her deathwatch here,
why silent then, not a word to set our people free?
There was a riddle, not for some passer-by to solve—
it cried out for a prophet. Where were you?
Did you rise to the crisis? Not a word,
you and your birds, your gods—nothing.   450
No, but I came by, Oedipus the ignorant,
I stopped the Sphinx! With no help from the birds,
the flight of my own intelligence hit the mark.
And this is the man you'd try to overthrow?
You think you'll stand by Creon when he's king?   455
You and the great mastermind—
you'll pay in tears, I promise you, for this,
this witch-hunt. If you didn't look so senile
the lash would teach you what your scheming means!

LEADER:
I would suggest his words were spoken in
    anger, 460
Oedipus . . . yours too, and it isn't what
    we need.
The best solution to the oracle, the riddle
posed by god—we should look for that.

TIRESIAS:
You are the king no doubt, but in one
    respect,
at least, I am your equal: the right to reply. 465
I claim that privilege too.
I am not your slave. I serve Apollo.
I don't need Creon to speak for me in
    public.
                              So,
you mock my blindness? Let me tell you
    this.
You with your precious eyes, 470
you're blind to the corruption of your life,
to the home you live in, those you live
    with—
who are your parents? Do you know? All
    unknowing
you are the scourge of your own flesh and
    blood,
the dead below the earth and the living
    here above, 475
and the double lash of your mother and
    your father's curse
will whip you from this land one day,
    their footfall
treading you down in terror, darkness
    shrouding
your eyes that now can see the light!
                          Soon, soon
you'll scream aloud—what haven won't
    reverberate? 480
What rock of Cithaeron won't scream
    back in echo?
That day you learn the truth about your
    marriage,
the wedding-march that sang you into
    your halls,
the lusty voyage home to the fatal harbor!
And a crowd of other horrors you'd never
    dream 485
will level you with yourself and all your
    children.
There. Now smear us with insults—
    Creon, myself
and every word I've said. No man will
    ever
be rooted from the earth as brutally as
    you.

OEDIPUS:
Enough! Such filth from him? Insufferable— 490
what, still alive? Get out—
faster, back where you came
    from—vanish!

TIRESIAS:
I would never have come if you hadn't
    called me here.

OEDIPUS:
If I thought you would blurt out such
    absurdities,
you'd have died waiting before I'd had
    you summoned. 495

TIRESIAS:
Absurd, am I! To you, not to your parents:
the ones who bore you found me sane
    enough.

OEDIPUS:
Parents—who? Wait . . . who is my father?

TIRESIAS:
This day will bring your birth and your
    destruction.

OEDIPUS:
Riddles—all you can say are riddles,
    murk and darkness. 500

TIRESIAS:
Ah, but aren't you the best man alive at
    solving riddles?

OEDIPUS:
Mock me for that, go on, and you'll reveal
    my greatness.

TIRESIAS:
Your great good fortune, true, it was your
    ruin.

OEDIPUS:
Not if I saved the city—what do I care?

TIRESIAS:
Well then, I'll be going.

To his attendant.

                      Take me home, boy. 505

OEDIPUS:
Yes, take him away. You're a nuisance here.
Out of the way, the irritation's gone.

Turning his back on TIRESIAS, moving toward the palace.

TIRESIAS:
                            I will go,
once I have said what I came here to say.
I will never shrink from the anger in your eyes—
you can't destroy me. Listen to me closely: 510
the man you've sought so long, proclaiming,
cursing up and down, the murderer of Laius—
he is here. A stranger,
you may think, who lives among you,
he soon will be revealed a native Theban   515
but he will take no joy in the revelation.
Blind who now has eyes, beggar who now is rich,
he will grope his way toward a foreign soil,
a stick tapping before him step by step.

OEDIPUS enters the palace.

Revealed at last, brother and father both   520
to the children he embraces, to his mother
son and husband both—he sowed the loins
his father sowed, he spilled his father's blood!
Go in and reflect on that, solve that.
And if you find I've lied   525
from this day onward call the prophet blind.

TIRESIAS and the boy exit to the side.

CHORUS:
                        Who—
who is the man the voice of god denounces
resounding out of the rocky gorge of Delphi?
The horror too dark to tell,
whose ruthless bloody hands have done the work?   530
His time has come to fly
to outrace the stallions of the storm
his feet a streak of speed—
Cased in armor, Apollo son of the Father
lunges on him, lightning-bolts afire!   535
And the grim unerring Furies
closing for the kill.

                        Look,
the word of god has just come blazing
flashing off Parnassus' snowy heights!
That man who left no trace—   540
after him, hunt him down with all our strength!
Now under bristling timber
up through rocks and caves he stalks
like the wild mountain bull—
cut off from men, each step an agony,
frenzied, racing blind   545
but he cannot outrace the dread voices of Delphi
ringing out of the heart of Earth,
the dark wings beating around him shrieking doom
the doom that never dies, the terror—
The skilled prophet scans the birds and shatters me with terror!   550
I can't accept him, can't deny him, don't know what to say,
I'm lost, and the wings of dark foreboding beating—
I cannot see what's come, what's still to come . . .
and what could breed a blood feud between
Laius' house and the son of Polybus?   555
I know of nothing, not in the past and not now,
no charge to bring against our king, no cause
to attack his fame that rings throughout Thebes—
not without proof—not for the ghost of Laius,
not to avenge a murder gone without a trace.   560
Zeus and Apollo know, they know, the great masters
of all the dark and depth of human life.
But whether a mere man can know the truth,
whether a seer can fathom more than I—
there is no test, no certain proof   565
though matching skill for skill
a man can outstrip a rival. No, not till I see
these charges proved will I side with his accusers.
We saw him then, when the she-hawk swept against him,
saw with our own eyes his skill, his brilliant triumph—   570
there was the test—he was the joy of Thebes!

Never will I convict my king, never in my heart.

Enter CREON from the side.

CREON:
My fellow-citizens, I hear King Oedipus levels terrible charges at me. I had to come.
I resent it deeply. If, in the present crisis, 575
he thinks he suffers any abuse from me,
anything I've done or said that offers him
the slightest injury, why, I've no desire
to linger out this life, my reputation in ruins.
The damage I'd face from such an accusation 580
is nothing simple. No, there's nothing worse:
branded a traitor in the city, a traitor
to all of you and my good friends.

LEADER:
                                                    True,
but a slur might have been forced out of him,
by anger perhaps, not any firm conviction. 585

CREON:
The charge was made in public, wasn't it?
I put the prophet up to spreading lies?

LEADER:
Such things were said . . .
I don't know, with what intent, if any.

CREON:
Was his glance steady, his mind right 590
when the charge was brought against me?

LEADER:
I really couldn't say. I never look
to judge the ones in power.

The doors open. OEDIPUS enters.

                                                    Wait,
here's Oedipus now.

OEDIPUS:
            You—here? You have the gall
to show your face before the palace gates? 595
You, plotting to kill me, kill the king—
I see it all, the marauding thief himself
scheming to steal my crown and power!
                                                    Tell me,
in god's name, what did you take me for,
coward or fool, when you spun out your plot? 600
Your treachery—you think I'd never detect it
creeping against me in the dark? Or sensing it,
not defend myself? Aren't you the fool,
you and your high adventure. Lacking numbers,
powerful friends, out for the big game of empire— 605
you need riches, armies to bring that quarry down!

CREON:
Are you quite finished? It's your turn to listen
for just as long as you've . . . instructed me.
Hear me out, then judge me on the facts.

OEDIPUS:
You've a wicked way with words, Creon, 610
but I'll be slow to learn—from you.
I find you a menace, a great burden to me.

CREON:
Just one thing, hear me out in this.

OEDIPUS:
                                                    Just one thing,
don't tell *me* you're not the enemy, the traitor.

CREON:
Look, if you think crude, mindless stubbornness 615
such a gift, you've lost your sense of balance.

OEDIPUS:
If you think you can abuse a kinsman,
then escape the penalty, you're insane.

CREON:
Fair enough, I grant you. But this injury
you say I've done you, what is it? 620

OEDIPUS:
Did you induce me, yes or no,
to send for that sanctimonious prophet?

CREON:
I did. And I'd do the same again.

OEDIPUS:
All right then, tell me, how long is it now
since Laius . . .

CREON:
    Laius—what did *he* do?

OEDIPUS:
                              Vanished,   625
swept from sight, murdered in his tracks.

CREON:
The count of the years would run you far
    back . . .

OEDIPUS:
And that far back, was the prophet at his
    trade?

CREON:
Skilled as he is today, and just as honored.

OEDIPUS:
Did he ever refer to me then, at that time?

CREON:
                                    No,   630
never, at least, when I was in his presence.

OEDIPUS:
But you did investigate the murder, didn't
    you?

CREON:
We did our best, of course, discovered
    nothing.

OEDIPUS:
But the great seer never accused me
    then—why not?

CREON:
I don't know. And when I don't, *I* keep
    quiet.   635

OEDIPUS:
You do know this, you'd tell it too—
if you had a shred of decency.

CREON:
                                 What?
If I know, I won't hold back.

OEDIPUS:
                        Simply this:
if the two of you had never put heads
    together,
we would never have heard about *my*
    killing Laius.   640

CREON:
If that's what he says . . . well, you know
    best
But now I have a right to learn from you
as you just learned from me.

OEDIPUS:
                         Learn your fill,
you never will convict me of the murder.

CREON:
Tell me, you're married to my sister,
    aren't you?   645

OEDIPUS:
A genuine discovery—there's no denying
    that.

CREON:
And you rule the land with her, with
    equal power?

OEDIPUS:
She receives from me whatever she
    desires.

CREON:
And I am the third, all of us are equals?

OEDIPUS:
Yes, and it's there you show your stripes—   650
you betray a kinsman.

CREON:
                      Not at all.
Not if you see things calmly, rationally,
as I do. Look at it this way first:
who in his right mind would rather rule
and live in anxiety than sleep in peace?   655
Particularly if he enjoys the same
    authority.
Not I, I'm not the man to yearn for
    kingship,
not with a king's power in my hands.
    Who would?
No one with any sense of self-control.
Now, as it is, you offer me all I need,   660
not a fear in the world. But if I wore the
    crown . . .
there'd be many painful duties to perform,
hardly to my taste.

How could kingship
please me more than influence, power
without a qualm? I'm not that deluded yet, 665
to reach for anything but privilege outright,
profit free and clear.
Now all men sing my praises, all salute me,
now all who request your favors curry mine.
I am their best hope: success rests in me. 670
Why give up that, I ask you, and borrow trouble?
A man of sense, someone who sees things clearly
would never resort to treason.
No, I have no lust for conspiracy in me,
nor could I ever suffer one who does. 675
Do you want proof? Go to Delphi yourself,
examine the oracle and see if I've reported
the message word-for-word. This too:
if you detect that I and the clairvoyant
have plotted anything in common, arrest me, 680
execute me. Not on the strength of one vote,
two in this case, mine as well as yours.
But don't convict me on sheer unverified surmise.
How wrong it is to take the good for bad,
purely at random, or take the bad for good. 685
But reject a friend, a kinsman? I would as soon
tear out the life within us, priceless life itself.
You'll learn this well, without fail, in time.
Time alone can bring the just man to light—
the criminal you can spot in one short day. 690

LEADER:
                              Good advice,
my lord, for anyone who wants to avoid disaster.
Those who jump to conclusions may go wrong.

OEDIPUS:
When my enemy moves against me quickly,
plots in secret, I move quickly too, I must,
I plot and pay him back. Relax my guard a moment, 695
waiting his next move—he wins his objective,
I lose mine.

CREON:
                What do you want?
You want me banished?

OEDIPUS:
                      No, I want you dead.

CREON:
Just to show how ugly a grudge can . . .

OEDIPUS:
                              So,
still stubborn? you don't think I'm serious? 700

CREON:
I think you're insane.

OEDIPUS:
                    Quite sane—in my behalf.

CREON:
Not just as much in mine?

OEDIPUS:
                      You—my mortal enemy?

CREON:
What if you're wholly wrong?

OEDIPUS:
                     No matter—I must rule.

CREON:
Not if you rule unjustly.

OEDIPUS:
                  Hear him, Thebes, my city!

CREON:
My city too, not yours alone! 705

LEADER:
Please, my lords.

Enter JOCASTA from the palace.

                  Look, Jocasta's coming,
and just in time too. With her help
you must put this fighting of yours to rest.

JOCASTA:
Have you no sense? Poor misguided men,
such shouting—why this public outburst? 710

Aren't you ashamed, with the land so sick,
to stir up private quarrels?

To OEDIPUS.

Into the palace now. And Creon, you go
   home.
Why make such a furor over nothing?

CREON:
My sister, it's dreadful . . . Oedipus, your
   husband, 715
he's bent on a choice of punishments for
   me,
banishment from the fatherland or death.

OEDIPUS:
Precisely. I caught him in the act, Jocasta,
plotting, about to stab me in the back.

CREON:
Never—curse me, let me die and be
   damned 720
if I've done you any wrong you charge me
   with.

JOCASTA:
Oh god, believe it, Oedipus,
honor the solemn oath he swears to
   heaven.
Do it for me, for the sake of all your
   people.

The CHORUS begins to chant.

CHORUS:
   Believe it, be sensible 725
   give way, my king, I beg you!

OEDIPUS:
   What do you want from me,
   concessions?

CHORUS:
   Respect him—he's been no fool in the
     past
   and now he's strong with the oath he
     swears to god.

OEDIPUS:
You know what you're asking? 730

CHORUS:
                 I do.

OEDIPUS:
                 Then out with it!

CHORUS:
   The man's your friend, your kin, he's
     under oath—
   don't cast him out, disgraced
   branded with guilt on the strength of
     hearsay only.

OEDIPUS:
Know full well, if that is what you want
you want me dead or banished from the
   land. 735

CHORUS:
                 Never—
   no, by the blazing Sun, first god of the
     heavens!
   Stripped of the gods, stripped of loved
     ones,
   let me die by inches if that ever crossed
     my mind.
   But the heart inside me sickens, dies as
     the land dies
   and now on top of the old griefs you
     pile this, 740
   your fury—both of you!

OEDIPUS:
                 Then let him go,
even if it does lead to my ruin, my death
or my disgrace, driven from Thebes for
   life.
It's you, not him I pity—your words move
   me.
He, wherever he goes, my hate goes with
   him. 745

CREON:
Look at you, sullen in yielding, brutal in
   your rage—
you will go too far. It's perfect justice:
natures like yours are hardest on
   themselves.

OEDIPUS:
Then leave me alone—get out!

CREON:
                 I'm going.
You're wrong, so wrong. These men know
   I'm right. 750

Exit to the side. The CHORUS turns to JOCASTA.

CHORUS:
Why do you hesitate, my lady
why not help him in?

JOCASTA:
Tell me what's happened first.

CHORUS:
Loose, ignorant talk started dark
  suspicions
and a sense of injustice cut deeply too.   755

JOCASTA:
On both sides?

CHORUS:
          Oh yes.

JOCASTA:
          What did they say?

CHORUS:
Enough, please, enough! The land's so
  racked already
or so it seems to me . . .
End the trouble here, just where they left
  it.

OEDIPUS:
You see what comes of your good
  intentions now?   760
And all because you tried to blunt my
  anger.

CHORUS:
              My king,
I've said it once, I'll say it time and
  again—
I'd be insane, you know it,
senseless, ever to turn my back on you.
You who set our beloved
  land—storm-tossed, shattered—   765
straight on course. Now again, good
  helmsman,
steer us through the storm!

*The CHORUS draws away, leaving
OEDIPUS and JOCASTA side by side.*

JOCASTA:
              For the love of god,
Oedipus, tell me too, what is it?
Why this rage? You're so unbending.

OEDIPUS:
I will tell you. I respect you, Jocasta,   770
much more than these men here . . .

Glancing at the CHORUS.

Creon's to blame, Creon schemes against
  me.

JOCASTA:
Tell me clearly, how did the quarrel start?

OEDIPUS:
He says *I* murdered Laius—I am guilty.

JOCASTA:
How does he know? Some secret
  knowledge   775
or simple hearsay?

OEDIPUS:
Oh, he sent his prophet in
to do his dirty work. You know Creon,
Creon keeps his own lips clean.

JOCASTA:
              A prophet?
Well then, free yourself of every charge!
Listen to me and learn some peace of
  mind: 780
no skill in the world,
nothing human can penetrate the future.
Here is proof, quick and to the point.
An oracle came to Laius one fine day
(I won't say from Apollo himself   785
  but his underlings, his priests) and it
  declared
that doom would strike him down at the
  hands of a son,
our son, to be born of our own flesh and
  blood. But Laius,
so the report goes at least, was killed by
  strangers,
thieves, at a place where three roads meet
  . . . my son—   790
he wasn't three days old and the boy's
  father
fastened his ankles, had a henchman fling
  him away
on a barren, trackless mountain.
              There, you see?
Apollo brought neither thing to pass. My
  baby
no more murdered his father than Laius
  suffered—   795
his wildest fear—death at his own son's
  hands.

That's how the seers and all their revelations
mapped out the future. Brush them from your mind.
Whatever the god needs and seeks
he'll bring to light himself, with ease.   800

OEDIPUS:
                                Strange,
hearing you just now . . . my mind wandered,
my thoughts racing back and forth.

JOCASTA:
What do you mean? Why so anxious, startled?

OEDIPUS:
I thought I heard you say that Laius
was cut down at a place where three roads meet.   805

JOCASTA:
That was the story. It hasn't died out yet.

OEDIPUS:
Where did this thing happen? Be precise.

JOCASTA:
A place called Phocis, where two branching roads,
one from Daulia, one from Delphi,
come together—a crossroads.   810

OEDIPUS:
When? How long ago?

JOCASTA:
The heralds no sooner reported Laius dead
than you appeared and they hailed you king of Thebes.

OEDIPUS:
My god, my god—what have you planned to do to me?

JOCASTA:
What, Oedipus? What haunts you so?

OEDIPUS:
                                Not yet.   815
Laius—how did he look? Describe him.
Had he reached his prime?

JOCASTA:
                                He was swarthy,
and the gray had just begun to streak his temples,
and his build . . . wasn't far from yours.

OEDIPUS:
                                Oh no no,
I think I've just called down a dreadful curse   820
upon myself—I simply didn't know!

JOCASTA:
What are you saying? I shudder to look at you.

OEDIPUS:
I have a terrible fear the blind seer can see.
I'll know in a moment. One thing more—

JOCASTA:
                                Anything,
afraid as I am—ask, I'll answer, all I can.   825

OEDIPUS:
Did he go with a light or heavy escort,
several men-at-arms, like a lord, a king?

JOCASTA:
There were five in the party, a herald among them,
and a single wagon carrying Laius.

OEDIPUS:
                                Ai—
now I can see it all, clear as day.   830
Who told you all this at the time, Jocasta?

JOCASTA:
A servant who reached home, the lone survivor.

OEDIPUS:
So, could he still be in the palace—even now?

JOCASTA:
No indeed. Soon as he returned from the scene
and saw you on the throne with Laius dead and gone,   835
he knelt and clutched my hand, pleading with me
to send him into the hinterlands, to pasture,
far as possible, out of sight of Thebes.
I sent him away. Slave though he was,
he'd earned that favor—and much more.   840

OEDIPUS:
Can we bring him back, quickly?

JOCASTA:
Easily. Why do you want him so?

OEDIPUS:
                I am afraid,
Jocasta, I have said too much already.
That man—I've got to see him.

JOCASTA:
                Then he'll come.
But even I have a right, I'd like to think,   845
to know what's torturing you, my lord.

OEDIPUS:
And so you shall—I can hold nothing back from you,
now I've reached this pitch of dark foreboding.
Who means more to me than you? Tell me,
whom would I turn toward but you   850
as I go through all this?
My father was Polybus, king of Corinth.
My mother, a Dorian, Merope. And I was held
the prince of the realm among the people there,
till something struck me out of nowhere,   855
something strange . . . worth remarking perhaps,
hardly worth the anxiety I gave it.
Some man at a banquet who had drunk too much
shouted out—he was far gone, mind you—
that I am not my father's son. Fighting words!   860
I barely restrained myself that day
but early the next I went to mother and father,
questioned them closely, and they were enraged
at the accusation and the fool who let it fly.
So as for my parents I was satisfied,   865
but still this thing kept gnawing at me,
the slander spread—I had to make my move.
                              And so,
unknown to mother and father I set out for Delphi,
and the god Apollo spurned me, sent me away
denied the facts I came for,   870
but first he flashed before my eyes a future
great with pain, terror, disaster—I can hear him cry,
"You are fated to couple with your mother, you will bring
a breed of children into the light no man can bear to see—
you will kill your father, the one who gave you life!"   875
I heard all that and ran. I abandoned Corinth,
from that day on I gauged its landfall only
by the stars, running, always running
toward some place where I would never see
the shame of all those oracles come true.   880
And as I fled I reached that very spot
where the great king, you say, met his death.
Now, Jocasta, I will tell you all.
Making my way toward this triple crossroad
I began to see a herald, then a brace of colts   885
drawing a wagon, and mounted on the bench . . . a man,
just as you've described him, coming face-to-face,
and the one in the lead and the old man himself
were about to thrust me off the road—brute force—
and the one shouldering me aside, the driver,   890
I strike him in anger!—and the old man, watching me
coming up along his wheels—he brings down
his prod, two prongs straight at my head!
I paid him back with interest!
Short work, by god—with one blow of the staff   895
in this right hand I knock him out of his high seat,
roll him out of the wagon, sprawling headlong—
I killed them all—every mother's son!
Oh, but if there is any blood-tie
between Laius and this stranger . . .   900
what man alive more miserable than I?
More hated by the gods? *I* am the man
no alien, no citizen welcomes to his house,
law forbids it—not a word to me in public,
driven out of every hearth and home.   905
And all these curses I—no one but I
brought down these piling curses on myself!

And you, his wife, I've touched your body with these,
the hands that killed your husband cover you with blood.
Wasn't I born for torment? Look me in the eyes! 910
I am abomination—heart and soul!
I must be exiled, and even in exile
never see my parents, never set foot
on native ground again. Else I am doomed
to couple with my mother and cut my father down ... 915
Polybus who reared me, gave me life.
 But why, why?
Wouldn't a man of judgment say—and wouldn't he be right—
some savage power has brought this down upon my head?
Oh no, not that, you pure and awesome gods,
never let me see that day! Let me slip 920
from the world of men, vanish without a trace
before I see myself stained with such corruption,
stained to the heart.

LEADER:
My lord, you fill our hearts with fear.
But at least until you question the witness, 925
do take hope.

OEDIPUS:
 Exactly. He is my last hope—
I am waiting for the shepherd. He is crucial.

JOCASTA:
And once he appears, what then? Why so urgent?

OEDIPUS:
I will tell you. If it turns out that his story
matches yours, I've escaped the worst. 930

JOCASTA:
What did I say? What struck you so?

OEDIPUS:
 You said *thieves*—
he told you a whole band of them murdered Laius.
So, if he still holds to the same number,
I cannot be the killer. One can't equal many.
But if he refers to one man, one alone, 935
clearly the scales come down on me:
I am guilty.

JOCASTA:
 Impossible. Trust me,
I told you precisely what he said,
and he can't retract it now;
the whole city heard it, not just I. 940
And even if he should vary his first report
by one man more or less, still, my lord,
he could never make the murder of Laius
truly fit the prophecy. Apollo was explicit:
my son was doomed to kill my husband ... my son, 945
poor defenseless thing, he never had a chance
to kill his father. They destroyed him first.
So much for prophecy. It's neither here nor there.
From this day on, I wouldn't look right or left.

OEDIPUS:
True, true. Still, that shepherd, 950
someone fetch him—now!

JOCASTA:
I'll send at once. But do let's go inside.
I'd never displease you, least of all in this.

OEDIPUS and JOCASTA enter the palace.

CHORUS:
Destiny guide me always
Destiny find me filled with reverence 955
 pure in word and deed.
Great laws tower above us, reared on high
born for the brilliant vault of heaven—
 Olympian Sky their only father,
nothing mortal, no man gave them birth, 960
their memory deathless, never lost in sleep:
within them lives a mighty god, the god does not grow old.
Pride breeds the tyrant
violent pride, gorging, crammed to bursting with all that is overripe and rich with ruin— 965
clawing up to the heights, headlong pride
crashes down the abyss—sheer doom!
 No footing helps, all foothold lost and gone.

But the healthy strife that makes the
   city strong—
I pray that god will never end that
   wrestling: 970
god, my champion, I will never let you
   go.
But if any man comes striding, high
   and mighty in all he says and does,
no fear of justice, no reverence
for the temples of the gods—   975
   let a rough doom tear him down,
repay his pride, breakneck, ruinous
   pride!
If he cannot reap his profits fairly
   cannot restrain himself from
   outrage—
mad, laying hands on the holy things
   untouchable!   980

   Can such a man, so desperate, still
   boast
he can save his life from the flashing
   bolts of god?
   If all such violence goes with
honor now
      why join the sacred dance?

Never again will I go reverent to
   Delphi,   985
   the inviolate heart of Earth
or Apollo's ancient oracle at Abae
or Olympia of the fires—
   unless these prophecies all come true
for all mankind to point toward in
   wonder.   990
   King of kings, if you deserve your titles
      Zeus, remember, never forget!
You and your deathless, everlasting
   reign.

   They are dying, the old oracles sent
   to Laius,
   now our masters strike them off the
   rolls.   995
      Nowhere Apollo's golden glory
   now—
      the gods, the gods go down.

Enter JOCASTA from the palace, carrying a suppliant's branch wound in wool.

JOCASTA:
Lords of the realm, it occurred to me,
just now, to visit the temples of the gods,
so I have my branch in hand and incense
   too.   1000
Oedipus is beside himself. Racked with
   anguish,
no longer a man of sense, he won't admit
the latest prophecies are hollow as the
   old—
he's at the mercy of every passing voice
if the voice tells of terror.   1005
I urge him gently, nothing seems to help,
so I turn to you, Apollo, you are nearest.

Placing her branch on the altar, while an old herdsman enters from the side, not the one just summoned by the King but an unexpected MESSENGER from Corinth.

I come with prayers and offerings . . . I
   beg you,
cleanse us, set us free of defilement!
Look at us, passengers in the grip of fear,   1010
watching the pilot of the vessel go to
   pieces.

MESSENGER:

   Approaching JOCASTA and the CHORUS.

Strangers, please, I wonder if you could
   lead us
to the palace of the king . . . I think it's
   Oedipus.
Better, the man himself—you know where
   he is?

LEADER:
This is his palace, stranger. He's inside.   1015
But here is his queen, his wife and mother
of his children.

MESSENGER:
      Blessings on you, noble queen,
queen of Oedipus crowned with all your
   family—
blessings on you always!

JOCASTA:
And the same to you, stranger, you
   deserve it . . .   1020
such a greeting. But what have you come
   for?
Have you brought us news?

MESSENGER:
      Wonderful news—
for the house my lady, for your husband
   too.

JOCASTA:
Really, what? Who sent you?

MESSENGER:
              Corinth.
I'll give you the message in a moment.   1025
You'll be glad of it—how could you help it?—
though it costs a little sorrow in the bargain.

JOCASTA:
What can it be, with such a double edge?

MESSENGER:
The people there, they want to make your Oedipus
king of Corinth, so they're saying now.   1030

JOCASTA:
Why? Isn't old Polybus still in power?

MESSENGER:
No more. Death has got him in the tomb.

JOCASTA:
What are you saying? Polybus, dead?—dead?

MESSENGER:
                  If not,
if I'm not telling the truth, strike me dead too.

JOCASTA:

To a servant.

Quickly, go to your master, tell him this!   1035
You prophecies of the gods, where are you now?
This is the man that Oedipus feared for years,
he fled him, not to kill him—and now he's dead,
quite by chance, a normal, natural death,
not murdered by his son.   1040

OEDIPUS:

Emerging from the palace.

              Dearest,
what now? Why call me from the palace?

JOCASTA:

Bringing the MESSENGER closer.

Listen to him, see for yourself what all
those awful prophecies of god have come to.

OEDIPUS:
And who is he? What can he have for me?

JOCASTA:
He's from Corinth, he's come to tell you   1045
your father is no more—Polybus—he's dead!

OEDIPUS:

Wheeling on the MESSENGER.

What? Let me have it from your lips.

MESSENGER:
                  Well,
if that's what you want first, then here it is:
make no mistake, Polybus is dead and gone.

OEDIPUS:
How—murder? sickness?—what? what killed him?   1050

MESSENGER:
A light tip of the scales can put old bones to rest.

OEDIPUS:
Sickness then—poor man, it wore him down.

MESSENGER:
       That,
and the long count of years he'd measured out.

OEDIPUS:
       So!
Jocasta, why, why look to the Prophet's hearth,
the fires of the future? Why scan the birds   1055
that scream above our heads? They winged me on
to the murder of my father, did they? That was my doom?

Well look, he's dead and buried,
   hidden—under the earth,
and here I am in Thebes, I never put hand
   to sword—
unless some longing for me wasted him
   away,   1060
then in a sense you'd say I caused his
   death.
But now, all those prophecies I
   feared—Polybus
packs them off to sleep with him in hell!
They're nothing, worthless.

JOCASTA:
                       There.
Didn't I tell you from the start?   1065

OEDIPUS:
So you did. I was lost in fear.

JOCASTA:
No more, sweep it from your mind
   forever.

OEDIPUS:
But my mother's bed, surely I must fear—

JOCASTA:
                          Fear?
What should a man fear? It's all chance,
chance rules our lives. Not a man on earth   1070
can see a day ahead, groping through the
   dark.
Better to live at random, best we can.
And as for this marriage with your
   mother—
have no fear. Many a man before you,
in his dreams, has shared his mother's
   bed.   1075
Take such things for shadows, nothing at
   all—
Live, Oedipus,
as if there's no tomorrow!

OEDIPUS:
                     Brave words,
and you'd persuade me if mother weren't
   alive.
But mother lives, so for all your
   reassurances   1080
I live in fear, I must.

JOCASTA:
                 But your father's death,
that, at least, is a great blessing, joy to the
   eyes!

OEDIPUS:
Great, I know . . . but I fear *her*—she's still
   alive.

MESSENGER:
Wait, who is this woman, makes you so
   afraid?

OEDIPUS:
Merope, old man. The wife of Polybus.   1085

MESSENGER:
The queen? What's there to fear in her?

OEDIPUS:
A dreadful prophecy, stranger, sent by the
   gods.

MESSENGER:
Tell me, could you? Unless it's forbidden
other ears to hear.

OEDIPUS:
                         Not at all.
Apollo told me once—it is my fate—   1090
I must make love with my own mother,
shed my father's blood with my own
   hands.
So for years I've given Corinth a wide
   berth,
and it's been my good fortune too. But
   still,
to see one's parents and look into their
   eyes   1095
is the greatest joy I know.

MESSENGER:
                   You're afraid of that?
That kept you out of Corinth?

OEDIPUS:
                   My *father*, old man—
so I wouldn't kill my father.

MESSENGER:
                      So that's it.
Well then, seeing I came with such good
   will, my king,
why don't I rid you of that old worry
   now?   1100

OEDIPUS:
What a rich reward you'd have for that!

MESSENGER:
What do you think I came for, majesty?

So you'd come home and I'd be better off.

OEDIPUS:
Never, I will never go near my parents.

MESSENGER:
My boy, it's clear you don't know what you're doing. 1105

OEDIPUS:
What do you mean, old man? For god's sake, explain.

MESSENGER:
If you ran from *them*, always dodging home . . .

OEDIPUS:
Always, terrified Apollo's oracle might come true—

MESSENGER:
And you'd be covered with guilt, from both your parents.

OEDIPUS:
That's right, old man, that fear is always with me. 1110

MESSENGER:
Don't you know? You've really nothing to fear.

OEDIPUS:
But why? If I'm their son—Merope, Polybus?

MESSENGER:
Polybus was nothing to you, that's why, not in blood.

OEDIPUS:
What are you saying—Polybus was not my father?

MESSENGER:
No more than I am. He and I are equals. 1115

OEDIPUS:
                  My father—
how can my father equal nothing? You're nothing to me!

MESSENGER:
Neither was he, no more your father than I am.

OEDIPUS:
Then why did he call me his son?

MESSENGER:
                  You were a gift,
years ago—know for a fact he took you from my hands.

OEDIPUS:
                  No, from another's hands? 1120
Then how could he love me so? He loved me, deeply . . .

MESSENGER:
True, and his early years without a child made him love you all the more.

OEDIPUS:
                  And you, did you . . .
buy me? find me by accident?

MESSENGER:
                  I stumbled on you,
down the woody flanks of Mount Cithaeron.

OEDIPUS:
            So close, 1125
what were you doing here, just passing through?

MESSENGER:
Watching over my flocks, grazing them on the slopes.

OEDIPUS:
A herdsman, were you? A vagabond, scraping for wages?

MESSENGER:
Your savior too, my son, in your worst hour.

OEDIPUS:
                  Oh—
when you picked me up, was I in pain? What exactly? 1130

MESSENGER:
Your ankles . . . they tell the story. Look at them.

OEDIPUS:
Why remind me of that, that old affliction?

MESSENGER:
Your ankles were pinned together. I set you free.

OEDIPUS:
That dreadful mark—I've had it from the cradle.

MESSENGER:
And you got your name from that misfortune too, 1135
the name's still with you.

OEDIPUS:
　　　　　　Dear god, who did it?—
mother? father? Tell me.

MESSENGER:
　　　　　　I don't know.
The one who gave you to me, he'd know more.

OEDIPUS:
What? You took me from someone else?
You didn't find me yourself?

MESSENGER:
　　　　　　No sir, 1140
another shepherd passed you on to me.

OEDIPUS:
Who? Do you know? Describe him.

MESSENGER:
He called himself a servant of . . .
if I remember rightly—Laius.

JOCASTA turns sharply.

OEDIPUS:
The king of the land who ruled here long ago? 1145

MESSENGER:
That's the one. That herdsman was his man.

OEDIPUS:
Is he still alive? Can I see him?

MESSENGER:
They'd know best, the people of these parts.

OEDIPUS and the MESSENGER turn to the CHORUS.

OEDIPUS:
Does anyone know that herdsman,
the one he mentioned? Anyone seen him 1150
in the fields, here in the city? Out with it!
The time has come to reveal this once for all.

LEADER:
I think he's the very shepherd you wanted to see,
a moment ago. But the queen, Jocasta,
she's the one to say.

OEDIPUS:
　　　　　　Jocasta, 1155
you remember the man we just sent for?
Is *that* the one he means?

JOCASTA:
　　　　　　That man . . .
why ask? Old shepherd, talk, empty nonsense,
don't give it another thought, don't even think—

OEDIPUS:
What—give up now, with a clue like this? 1160
Fail to solve the mystery of my birth?
Not for all the world!

JOCASTA:
　　　　　　Stop—in the name of god,
if you love your own life, call off this search!
My suffering is enough.

OEDIPUS:
　　　　　　Courage!
Even if my mother turns out to be a slave, 1165
and I a slave, three generations back,
you would not seem common.

JOCASTA:
　　　　　　Oh no,
listen to me, I beg you, don't do this.

OEDIPUS:
Listen to you? No more. I must know it all,
must see the truth at last.

JOCASTA:
　　　　　　No, please— 1170
for your sake—I want the best for you!

OEDIPUS:
Your best is more than I can bear.

JOCASTA:
You're doomed—
may you never fathom who you are!

OEDIPUS:

To a servant.

Hurry, fetch me the herdsman, now!
Leave her to glory in her royal birth.   1175

JOCASTA:
Aieeeeee—
    man of agony—
that is the only name I have for you,
that, no other—ever, ever, ever!

Flinging through the palace doors. A long, tense silence follows.

LEADER:
Where's she gone, Oedipus?
Rushing off, such wild grief . . .   1180
I'm afraid that from this silence
something monstrous may come bursting
    forth.

OEDIPUS:
Let it burst! Whatever will, whatever
    must!
I must know my birth, no matter how
    common
it may be—I must see my origins
    face-to-face.   1185
She perhaps, she with her woman's pride
may well be mortified by my birth,
but I, I count myself the son of Chance,
the great goddess, giver of all good
    things—
I'll never see myself disgraced. She is my
    mother!   1190
And the moons have marked me out, my
    blood-brothers,
one moon on the wane, the next moon
    great with power.
That is my blood, my nature—I will never
    betray it,
never fail to search and learn my birth!

CHORUS:
Yes—if I am a true prophet   1195
    if I can grasp the truth,
by the boundless skies of Olympus,
at the full moon of tomorrow, Mount
    Cithaeron
you will know how Oedipus glories in
    you—
you, his birthplace, nurse, his
    mountain-mother!   1200
And we will sing you, dancing out your
    praise—
you lift our monarch's heart!
Apollo, Apollo, god of the wild cry
    may our dancing please you!
        Oedipus—
    son, dear child, who bore you?   1205
Who of the nymphs who seem to live
    forever
mated with Pan, the mountain-striding
    Father?
Who was your mother? who, some bride
    of Apollo
the god who loves the pastures spreading
    toward the sun?
Or was it Hermes, king of the lightning
    ridges?   1210
Or Dionysus, lord of frenzy, lord of the
    barren peaks—
did he seize you in his hands, dearest of
    all his lucky finds?—
found by the nymphs, their warm eyes
    dancing, gift
to the lord who loves them dancing out
    his joy!

OEDIPUS strains to see a figure coming from the distance. Attended by palace guards, an old SHEPHERD enters slowly, reluctant to approach the king.

OEDIPUS:
I never met the man, my friends . . . still,   1215
if I had to guess, I'd say that's the
    shepherd,
the very one we've looked for all along.
Brothers in old age, two of a kind,
he and our guest here. At any rate
the ones who bring him in are my own
    men,   1220
I recognize them.

Turning to the LEADER.

But you know more than I,
you should, you've seen the man before.

LEADER:
I know him, definitely. One of Laius' men,
a trusty shepherd, if there ever was one.

OEDIPUS:
You, I ask you first, stranger,   1225
you from Corinth—is this the one you
    mean?

MESSENGER:
You're looking at him. He's your man.

OEDIPUS:

                To the SHEPHERD.

You, old man, come over here—
look at me. Answer all my questions.
Did you ever serve King Laius?

SHEPHERD:
              So I did . . .   1230
a slave, not bought on the block though,
born and reared in the palace.

OEDIPUS:
Your duties, your kind of work?

SHEPHERD:
Herding the flocks, the better part of my
    life.

OEDIPUS:
Where, mostly? Where did you do your
    grazing?   1235

SHEPHERD:
      Well,
Cithaeron sometimes, or the foothills
    round about.

OEDIPUS:
This man—you know him? ever see him
    there?

SHEPHERD:

Confused, glancing from the MESSENGER to the King.

Doing what?—what man do you mean?

OEDIPUS:

Pointing to the MESSENGER.

This one here—ever have dealings with
    him?

SHEPHERD:
Not so I could say, but give me a chance,   1240
my memory's bad . . .

MESSENGER:
No wonder he doesn't know me, master.
But let me refresh his memory for him.
I'm sure he recalls old times we had
on the slopes of Mount Cithaeron;   1245
he and I, grazing our flocks, he with two
and I with one—we both struck up
    together,
three whole seasons, six months at a
    stretch
from spring to the rising of Arcturus in
    the fall,
then with winter coming on I'd drive my
    herds   1250
to my own pens, and back he'd go with his
to Laius' folds.

To the SHEPHERD.

          Now that's how it was,
wasn't it—yes or no?

SHEPHERD:
             Yes, I suppose . . .
it's all so long ago.

MESSENGER:
          Come, tell me,
you gave me a child back then, a boy,
    remember?   1255
A little fellow to rear, my very own.

SHEPHERD:
What? Why rake up that again?

MESSENGER:
Look, here he is, my fine old friend—
the same man who was just a baby then.

SHEPHERD:
Damn you, shut your mouth—quiet!   1260

OEDIPUS:
Don't lash out at him, old man—
you need lashing more than he does.

SHEPHERD:
                Why,
master, majesty—what have I done
    wrong?

OEDIPUS:
You won't answer his question about the boy.

SHEPHERD:
He's talking nonsense, wasting his breath. 1265

OEDIPUS:
So, you won't talk willingly—
then you'll talk with pain.

The guards seize the SHEPHERD.

SHEPHERD:
No, dear god, don't torture an old man!

OEDIPUS:
Twist his arms back, quickly!

SHEPHERD:
         God help us, why?—
what more do you need to know? 1270

OEDIPUS:
Did you give him that child? He's asking.

SHEPHERD:
I did . . . I wish to god I'd died that day.

OEDIPUS:
You've got your wish if you don't tell the truth.

SHEPHERD:
The more I tell, the worse the death I'll die.

OEDIPUS:
Our friend here wants to stretch things out, does he? 1275

Motioning to his men for torture.

SHEPHERD:
No, no, I gave it to him—I just said so.

OEDIPUS:
Where did you get it? Your house?
   Someone else's?

SHEPHERD:
It wasn't mine, no, I got it from . . . someone.

OEDIPUS:
Which one of them?

Looking at the citizens.

     Whose house?

SHEPHERD:
                    No—
god's sake, master, no more questions! 1280

OEDIPUS:
You're a dead man if I have to ask again.

SHEPHERD:
Then—the child came from the house . . .
of Laius.

OEDIPUS:
    A slave? or born of his own blood?

SHEPHERD:
                      Oh no,
I'm right at the edge, the horrible
   truth—I've got to say it!

OEDIPUS:
And I'm at the edge of hearing horrors,
   yes, but I must hear!

SHEPHERD:
All right! His son, they said it was—his son!
But the one inside, your wife,
she'd tell it best.

OEDIPUS:
My wife—
she gave it to you? 1290

SHEPHERD:
Yes, yes, my king.

OEDIPUS:
Why, what for?

SHEPHERD:
To kill it.

OEDIPUS:
Her own child,
how could she? 1295

SHEPHERD:
She was afraid—
frightening prophecies.

OEDIPUS:
What?

SHEPHERD:
    They said—
he'd kill his parents.

OEDIPUS:
But you gave him to this old man—why?   1300

SHEPHERD:
I pitied the little baby, master,
hoped he'd take him off to his own
        country,
far away, but he saved him for this, this
        fate.
If you are the man he says you are,
        believe me,
you were born for pain.   1305

OEDIPUS:
            O god—
all come true, all burst to light!
O light—now let me look: my last on you!
I stand revealed at last—
cursed in my birth, cursed in marriage,
cursed in the lives I cut down with these
        hands!   1310

Rushing through the doors with a great cry. The Corinthian MESSENGER, the SHEPHERD and attendants exit slowly to the side.

CHORUS:
    O the generations of men
the dying generations—adding the total
of all your lives I find they come to
        nothing...
    does there exist, is there a man on earth
who seizes more joy than just a dream, a
        vision?   1315
And the vision no sooner dawns than dies
blazing into oblivion.
You are my great example, you, your life
your destiny, Oedipus, man of misery—
I count no man blest.
            You outranged all men!   1320
    Bending your bow to the breaking-point
you captured priceless glory, O dear god,
and the Sphinx came crashing down,
            the virgin, claws hooked
like a bird of omen singing, shrieking
        death—   1325
like a fortress reared in the face of death
you rose and saved our land.
From that day on we called you king
we crowned you with honors, Oedipus,
        towering over all—
mighty king of the seven gates of Thebes.   1330
But now to hear your story—is there a
        man more agonized?
More wed to pain and frenzy? Not a man
        on earth,
the joy of your life ground down to
        nothing
O Oedipus, name for the ages—
    one and the same wide harbor served
        you   1335
            son and father both
son and father came to rest in the same
        bridal chamber.
How, how could the furrows your father
        plowed
bear you, your agony, harrowing on
in silence O so long?
            But now for all your power   1340
Time, all-seeing Time has dragged you to
        the light,
judged your marriage monstrous from the
        start—
the son and the father tangling, both one—
O child of Laius, would to god
    I'd never seen you, never never!   1345
    Now I weep like a man who wails the
        dead
and the dirge comes pouring forth with
        all my heart
I tell you the truth, you gave me life
my breath leapt up in you
and now you bring down night upon my
        eyes.   1350

Enter a MESSENGER from the palace.

MESSENGER:
Men of Thebes always first in honor,
what horrors you will hear, what you will
        see,
what a heavy weight of sorrow you will
        shoulder...
if you are true to your birth, if you still
        have
some feeling for the royal house of Thebes.   1355
I tell you neither the waters of the Danube
nor the Nile can wash this palace clean.
Such things it hides, it soon will bring to
        light—
terrible things, and none done blindly
        now,
all done with a will. The pains   1360
we inflict upon ourselves hurt most of all.

LEADER:
God knows we have pains enough already.
What can you add to them?

MESSENGER:
The queen is dead.

LEADER:
        Poor lady—how?

MESSENGER:
By her own hand. But you are spared the worst, 1365
you never had to watch . . . I saw it all,
and with all the memory that's in me
you will learn what that poor woman suffered.
Once she'd broken in through the gates,
dashing past us, frantic, whipped to fury, 1370
ripping her hair out with both hands—
straight to her rooms she rushed, flinging herself
across the bridal-bed, doors slamming behind her—
once inside, she wailed for Laius, dead so long,
remembering how she bore his child long ago, 1375
the life that rose up to destroy him, leaving
its mother to mother living creatures
with the very son she'd borne.
Oh how she wept, mourning the marriage-bed
where she let loose that double brood—monsters— 1380
husband by her husband, children by her child.
    And then—
but how she died is more than I can say. Suddenly
Oedipus burst in, screaming, he stunned us so
we couldn't watch her agony to the end,
our eyes were fixed on him. Circling 1385
like a maddened beast, stalking, here, there,
crying out to us—
    Give him a sword! His wife,
no wife, his mother, where can he find the mother earth
that cropped two crops at once, himself and all his children?
He was raging—one of the dark powers pointing the way, 1390
none of us mortals crowding around him, no,
with a great shattering cry—someone, something leading him on—
he hurled at the twin doors and bending the bolts back
out of their sockets, crashed through the chamber.
And there we saw the woman hanging by the neck, 1395
cradled high in a woven noose, spinning,
swinging back and forth. And when he saw her,
giving a low, wrenching sob that broke our hearts,
slipping the halter from her throat, he eased her down,
in a slow embrace he laid her down, poor thing . . . 1400
then, what came next, what horror we beheld!
He rips off her brooches, the long gold pins
holding her robes—and lifting them high,
looking straight up into the points,
he digs them down the sockets of his eyes, crying, "You, 1405
you'll see no more the pain I suffered, all the pain I caused!
Too long you looked on the ones you never should have seen,
blind to the ones you longed to see, to know! Blind
from this hour on! Blind in the darkness—blind!"
His voice like a dirge, rising, over and over 1410
raising the pins, raking them down his eyes.
And at each stroke blood spurts from the roots,
splashing his beard, a swirl of it, nerves and clots—
black hail of blood pulsing, gushing down.
These are the griefs that burst upon them both, 1415
coupling man and woman. The joy they had so lately,
the fortune of their old ancestral house
was deep joy indeed. Now, in this one day,
wailing, madness and doom, death, disgrace,
all the griefs in the world that you can name, 1420
all are theirs forever.

LEADER:
    Oh poor man, the misery—
has he any rest from pain now?

A voice within, in torment.

MESSENGER:
     He's shouting,
"Loose the bolts, someone, show me to all of Thebes!
My father's murderer, my mother's—"
No, I can't repeat it, it's unholy. 1425
Now he'll tear himself from his native earth,
not linger, curie the house with his own curse.
But he needs strength, and a guide to lead him on.
This is sickness more than he can bear.

The palace doors open.

    Look,
he'll show you himself. The great doors are opening— 1430
you are about to see a sight, a horror
even his mortal enemy would pity.

Enter OEDIPUS, blinded, led by a boy. He stands at the palace steps, as if surveying his people once again.

CHORUS:
     O the terror—
the suffering, for all the world to see,
the worst terror that ever met my eyes.
What madness swept over you? What god, 1435
what dark power leapt beyond all bounds,
beyond belief, to crush your wretched life?—
godforsaken, cursed by the gods!
I pity you but I can't bear to look.
I've much to ask, so much to learn, 1440
so much fascinates my eyes,
but you . . . I shudder at the sight.

OEDIPUS:
    Oh, Ohh—
the agony! I am agony—
where am I going? where on earth?
 where does all this agony hurl me? 1445
where's my voice!—
 winging, swept away on a dark tide—
My destiny, my dark power, what a leap
 you made!

CHORUS:
To the depths of terror, too dark to hear, to see.

OEDIPUS:
 Dark, horror of darkness 1450
my darkness, drowning, swirling around me
crashing wave on wave—unspeakable, irresistible
 headwind, fatal harbor! Oh again,
the misery, all at once, over and over
the stabbing daggers, stab of memory 1455
raking me insane.

CHORUS:
   No wonder you suffer
twice over, the pain of your wounds,
the lasting grief of pain.

OEDIPUS:
   Dear friend, still hem?
Standing by me, still with a care for me,
the blind man? Such compassion, 1460
loyal to the last. Oh it's you,
I know you're here, dark as it is
I'd know you anywhere, your voice—
it's yours, clearly yours.

CHORUS:
   Dreadful, what you've done . . .
how could you bear it, gouging out your eyes? 1465
What superhuman power drove you on?

OEDIPUS:
 Apollo, friends, Apollo—
he ordained my agonies—these, my pains on pains!
But the hand that struck my eyes was mine,
mine alone—no one else— 1470
 I did it all myself!
What good were eyes to me?
Nothing I could see could bring me joy.

CHORUS:
No, no, exactly as you say.

OEDIPUS:
   What can I ever see?
What love, what call of the heart 1475

can touch my ears with joy? Nothing,
    friends.
    Take me away, far, far from Thebes,
        quickly, cast me away, my friends—
this great murderous ruin, this man
    cursed to heaven,
    the man the deathless gods hate most
        of all!   1480

CHORUS:
Pitiful, you suffer so, you understand so
    much . . .
I wish you had never known.

OEDIPUS:
                Die, die—
whoever he was that day in the wilds
who cut my ankles free of the ruthless
    pins,
he pulled me clear of death, he saved
    my life   1485
for this, this kindness—
            Curse him, kill him!
If I'd died then, I'd never have dragged
    myself,
my loved ones through such hell.

CHORUS:
Oh if only . . . would to god.

OEDIPUS:
            I'd never have come to this,
my father's murderer—never been
    branded
mother's husband, all men see me now!
    Now,
loathed by the gods, son of the mother I
    defiled
coupling in my father's bed, spawning
    lives in the loins
that spawned my wretched life. What
    grief can crown this grief?
    It's mine alone, my destiny—I am
        Oedipus!

CHORUS:
How can I say you've chosen for the best?
Better to die than be alive and blind.

OEDIPUS:
What I did was best—don't lecture me,
no more advice. I, with *my* eyes,   1500
how could I look my father in the eyes
when I go down to death? Or mother, so
    abused . . .
I have done such things to the two of
    them,
crimes too huge for hanging.
                Worse yet
the sight of my children, born as they
    were born,   1505
how could I long to look into their eyes?
No, not with these eyes of mine, never.
Not this city either, her high towers,
the sacred glittering images of her gods—
I am misery! I, her best son, reared   1510
as no other son of Thebes was ever reared,
I've stripped myself, I gave the command
    myself
All men must cast away the great
    blasphemer,
the curse now brought to light by the
    gods,
the son of Laius—I, my father's son!   1515

Now I've exposed my guilt, horrendous
    guilt,
could I train a level glance on you, my
    countrymen?
Impossible! No, if I could just block off
    my ears,
the springs of hearing, I would stop at
    nothing—
I'd wall up my loathsome body like a
    prison,   1520
blind to the sound of life, not just the
    sight.
Oblivion—what a blessing . . .
for the mind to dwell a world away from
    pain.

O Cithaeron, why did you give me shelter?
Why didn't you take me, crush my life out
    on the spot?   1525
I'd never have revealed my birth to all
    mankind.

O Polybus, Corinth, the old house of my
    fathers,
so I believed—what a handsome prince
    you raised—
under the skin, what sickness to the core.
Look at me! Born of outrage, outrage to
    the core.   1530

O triple roads—it all comes back, the
    secret,
dark ravine, and the oaks closing in
where the three roads join . . .
You drank my father's blood, my own
    blood

spilled by my own hands—you still
    remember me? 1535
What things you saw me do? Then, I came
    here
and did them all once more!
                    Marriages! O marriage,
you gave me birth, and once you brought
    me into the world
you brought my sperm rising back,
    springing to light
fathers, brothers, sons—one murderous
    breed— 1540
brides, wives, mothers. The blackest things
a man can do, I have done them all!
                       No more—
it's wrong to name what's wrong to do.
    Quickly,
for the love of god, hide me somewhere,
kill me, hurl me into the sea 1545
where you can never look on me again.

Beckoning to the CHORUS as they shrink away.

                              Closer,
it's all right. Touch the man of grief.
Do. Don't be afraid. My troubles are mine
and I am the only man alive who can
    sustain them.

Enter CREON from the palace, attended by palace guards.

LEADER:
Put your requests to Creon. Here he is, 1550
just when we need him. He'll have a plan,
    he'll act.
Now that he's the sole defense of the
    country
in your place.

OEDIPUS:
              Oh no, what can I say to him?
How can I ever hope to win his trust?
I wronged him so, just now, in every way. 1555
You must see that—I was so wrong, so
    wrong.

CREON:
I haven't come to mock you, Oedipus,
or to criticize your former failings.

Turning to the guards.

                        You there,
have you lost all respect for human
    feelings?
At least revere the Sun, the holy fire 1560
that keeps us all alive. Never expose a
    thing
of guilt and holy dread so great it appalls
the earth, the rain from heaven, the light
    of day!
Get him into the halls—quickly as you can.
Piety demands no less. Kindred alone 1565
should see a kinsman's shame. This is
    obscene.

OEDIPUS:
Please, in god's name . . . you wipe my
    fears away,
coming so generously to me the worst of
    men.
Do one thing more, for your sake, not
    mine.

CREON:
What do you want? Why so insistent? 1570

OEDIPUS:
Drive me out of the land at once, far from
    sight,
where I can never hear a human voice.

CREON:
I'd have done that already, I promise you.
First I wanted the god to clarify my duties.

OEDIPUS:
The god? His command was clear, every
    word: 1575
death for the father-killer, the curse—
he said destroy me!

CREON:
So he did. Still, in such a crisis
it's better to ask precisely what to do.

OEDIPUS:
                       So miserable—
you would consult the god about a man
    like me? 1580

CREON:
By all means. And this time, I assume,
even you will obey the god's decrees.

OEDIPUS:
                           I will.
I will. And you, I command you—I beg
    you . . .
the woman inside, bury her as you see fit.
It's the only decent thing, 1585

to give your own the last rites. As for me,
never condemn the city of my fathers
to house my body, not while I'm alive, no,
let me live on the mountains, on Cithaeron,
my favorite haunt, I have made it famous. 1590
Mother and father marked out that rock
to be my everlasting tomb—buried alive.
Let me die there, where they tried to kill me.
Oh but this I know: no sickness can destroy me,
nothing can. I would never have been saved 1595
from death—I have been saved
for something great and terrible, something strange.
Well let my destiny come and take me on its way!
About my children, Creon, the boys at least,
don't burden yourself. They're men, 1600
wherever they go, they'll find the means to live.
But my two daughters, my poor helpless girls,
clustering at our table, never without me
hovering near them . . . whatever I touched,
they always had their share. Take care of them, 1605
I beg you. Wait, better—permit me, would you?
Just to touch them with my hands and take
our fill of tears. Please . . . my king.
Grant it, with all your noble heart.
If I could hold them, just once, I'd think 1610
I had them with me, like the early days
when I could see their eyes.

ANTIGONE and ISMENE, two small children, are led in from the palace by a nurse.

What's that?
O god! Do I really hear you sobbing?—
my two children. Creon, you've pitied me?
Sent me my darling girls, my own flesh and blood! 1615
Am I right?

CREON:
Yes, it's my doing.
I know the joy they gave you all these years,
the joy you must feel now.

OEDIPUS:
Bless you, Creon!
May god watch over you for this kindness,
better than he ever guarded me.
Children, where are you?
Here, come quickly—

Groping for ANTIGONE and ISMENE, who approach their father cautiously, then embrace him.

Come to these hands of mine,
your brother's hands, your own father's hands
that served his once bright eyes so well—
that made them blind. Seeing nothing, children,
knowing nothing, I became your father, 1625
I fathered you in the soil that gave me life.

How I weep for you—I cannot see you now . . .
just thinking of all your days to come, the bitterness,
the life that rough mankind will thrust upon you.
Where are the public gatherings you can join, 1630
the banquets of the clans? Home you'll come,
in tears, cut off from the sight of it all,
the brilliant rites unfinished.
And when you reach perfection, ripe for marriage,
who will he be, my dear ones? Risking all 1635
to shoulder the curse that weighs down my parents,
yes and you too—that wounds us all together.
What more misery could you want?
Your father killed his father, sowed his mother,
one, one and the selfsame woman sprang you— 1640
he cropped the very roots of his existence.
Such disgrace, and you must bear it all!
Who will marry you then? Not a man on earth.
Your doom is clear: you'll wither away to nothing,
single, without a child.

Turning to CREON.

Oh Creon, 1645
you are the only father they have now . . .
we who brought them into the world

are gone, both gone at a stroke—
Don't let them go begging, abandoned,
women without men. Your own flesh and
    blood! 1650
Never bring them down to the level of my
    pains.
Pity them. Look at them, so young, so
    vulnerable,
shorn of everything—you're their only
    hope.
Promise me, noble Creon, touch my hand!

Reaching toward CREON, who draws back.

You, little ones, if you were old enough 1655
to understand, there is much I'd tell you.
Now, as it is, I'd have you say a prayer.
Pray for life, my children,
live where you are free to grow and
    season.
Pray god you find a better life than mine, 1660
the father who begot you.

CREON:
                                        Enough.
You've wept enough. Into the palace now.

OEDIPUS:
I must, but I find it very hard.

CREON:
Time is the great healer, you will see.

OEDIPUS:
I am going—you know on what condition? 1665

CREON:
Tell me. I'm listening.

OEDIPUS:
Drive me out of Thebes, in exile.

CREON:
Not I. Only the gods can give you that.

OEDIPUS:
Surely the gods hate me so much—

CREON:
You'll get your wish at once.

OEDIPUS:
                          You consent? 1670

CREON:
I try to say what I mean; it's my habit.

OEDIPUS:
Then take me away. It's time.

CREON:
Come along, let go of the children.

OEDIPUS:
                                    No—
don't take them away from me, not now!
    No no no!

*Clutching his daughters as the guards wrench them
loose and take them through the palace doors.*

CREON:
Still the king, the master of all things? 1675
No more: here your power ends.
None of your power follows you through
    life.

*Exit OEDIPUS and CREON to the palace. The CHO-
RUS comes forward to address the audience directly.*

CHORUS:
People of Thebes, my countrymen, look
    on Oedipus.
He solved the famous riddle with his
    brilliance,
he rose to power, a man beyond all power. 1680
Who could behold his greatness without
    envy?
Now what a black sea of terror has
    overwhelmed him.
Now as we keep our watch and wait the
    final day,
count no man happy till he dies, free of
    pain at last.

Exit in procession.

Study Guide for Sophocles' *Oedipus the King*

—R.M.B.

Preliminary Background

Oedipus rules over Thebes, a city whose mythological background is important to understanding the play. Oedipus even begins the play by calling its residents the "new blood of ancient Cadmus" (not "ancient Thebes," as Fagles' liberally translates the Greek). In short, Cadmus founded the city of Thebes after he killed a dragon, and he sowed the dragon's teeth into the ground, from which sprang Thebes' first inhabitants. Thus, Thebes' current residents are mainly descended either from a hero who tamed the wild beast, or from the beast itself. Think about the relation of this background to the larger theme of civilization and savagery in this drama.

Look for references in the first scenes to Oedipus' conquest of the Sphinx, who had been plaguing Thebes before his arrival with a riddle: "What moves on four feet in the morning, two at noon and three in the evening, yet speaks with one voice?" The answer was man. Sophocles' play never explicitly tells the riddle of the Sphinx. How else are feet significant in this play? Look for this later.

In what way does this victory recall Cadmus' slaughter of the dragon?

Throughout the play you will need to consider the relationship between Oedipus and the gods. Why are the gods doing this to him, or at least allowing this to happen? Why should Apollo be so concerned about finding the murderer of Laius?

Also, what is the relationship in this play between fate and free will? Try to distinguish between the oracle of Apollo, which issued the prophecy that Oedipus would kill his father and marry his mother, and the events of the play.

Note that the Greek term for fate, *moira*, merely means "lot" or "share." It is much more impersonal and unguided than our normal associations of "fate."

Prologue (1–168)

Thebes turns to Oedipus to save them again by ridding them of a terrible plague. Sophocles may have written this play shortly after a great plague which struck Athens; Thucydides' *History* presents a powerful depiction of this plague, which struck soon after Pericles' speech.

All call upon the Healer Apollo. What does Apollo have to do with healing? Why should Oedipus consult this god's oracle?

Consider: does Oedipus strike you as arrogant in this scene and others, or is Oedipus a case of the saying of that great philosopher Muhammed Ali—"It ain't bragging if you can do it"?

Pay close attention to any references to sight, eyes or blindness, as vision is an important metaphor in this play.

After Creon enters and tells the words of Apollo, note the discrepancy between the number of outlaws in the account of each character. Why do you think Oedipus says "thief" while Creon says "thieves"? This will happen again later.

If you have read Pericles' Funeral Oration, consider the extent to which Oedipus embodies the characteristics of the ideal Athenian as described by Pericles.

Parodos (169–525)

The Chorus calls on a series of gods for help. Why invoke these gods in particular?

First Scene (245–526)

This scene is filled with many instances of dramatic irony, which is defined as a situation where the audience knows more than the characters so that the characters' words mean something different than they intend. Find at least three examples of this.

Tiresias is a blind seer who serves the god Apollo. Why does Tiresias refuse to help Oedipus? Do you find any fault with the extreme anger Oedipus displays with him?

Why can't Oedipus understand the information Tiresias does give to him at the end of the scene?

Note the complexity of Oedipus' character, a mixture of paranoia and an earnest desire to save the city.

First Stasimon (527–572)

The Chorus is completely confused by the accusations of Tiresias. Consider the images of hunting and wildness here, as they will return later.

Second Scene (573–953)

Arguably, this is the key scene. Is Creon especially admirable here? Compare his actions and wishes to those of Oedipus. Why would Oedipus be so suspicious of him?

Read carefully Jocasta's account of her lost child which begins at 783, and then Oedipus' reaction to it. Does anything in his reaction strike you as strange? Consider this especially in light of the almost identical story he tells later in the same scene. Why doesn't Oedipus make a connection?

Pay close attention to Jocasta's denunciation of oracles. Jocasta expresses a fundamental doubt in the gods because oracles are the means gods use to communicate with mortals.

Second Stasimon (954–996)

The Chorus describe a wild, impious, violent man. Whom do they mean? What is the connection between this wild man and "the sacred dance" (984) ?

Third Scene (998–1214):

Consider the general force of Jocasta's on-going aspersion of oracles in the light of what is about to happen. Note: lines 1074–75 are underlined in the German translation of this play which Freud had in the library of books he kept when he fled the Nazis.
   1135: why is the connection between Oedipus' name and his ankles so important?
   At what point do you think that Jocasta begins to suspect the truth?
   When the Shepherd arrives, why won't he talk willingly?
   When Jocasta runs off the stage, Oedipus thinks she is afraid he will be proven a peasant. Why does this idea make him so happy (1182–1194)? What does it mean to be the "Child of Luck?" The Greek word here, *tuche*, means something more like "chance," which lacks the positive connotations of luck.

Third Stasimon (1195–1214)

The Chorus takes Oedipus' hope and runs with it, imagining him to be the foundling son of a god.

Fourth Scene (1215–1310)

Aristotle believed this was the finest tragedy because the protagonist's recognition of the truth coincides with the reversal of his fortunes. Where, exactly, does this occur in the play?

Fourth Stasimon (1311–1350)

Oedipus is now a paradigm of misfortune, and not the son of a god.

Fifth Scene (1351–1432)

What was Oedipus trying to do when he finds his wife-mother dead?
   Is blinding an appropriate punishment? Why does he not kill himself?

Kommos (1433–1499)

A *kommos* is a scene of lamentation in lyrical meters between actor and chorus.
    How would you describe Oedipus' state of mind and attitude here? Does anything surprise you about the way he views his disaster? How does he see himself with respect to his lot in life and the gods?

Sixth Scene and Exodus (1499–end)

The last question applies even more here. Is Creon fair to Oedipus? Consider especially his admonition at 1675.
    Why are Oedipus' daughters in particular so special to him?
    What effect has blindness had on his knowledge?
    Of what, exactly, is Oedipus guilty? Should he be punished to this extent?

Thucydides and the Plague in Athens

—S.Z.

In his account of the Peloponnesian War, Thucydides describes the terrible plague that fell upon Athens when the Athenian people were gathered inside their walled city in a defensive strategy meant to frustrate the Spartans. Reading these passages we can better understand Sophocles' *Oedipus the King* and the urgency with which the playwright addresses his fellow citizens. Where Pericles, in his "Funeral Oration," celebrated the self-sufficiency of man and never once mentioned the gods as a source of the city's grandeur and accomplishment, Sophocles reminds his audience that man is not the measure of all things and that catastrophes must be understood, through faith, as part of a larger story that human beings cannot know. As Thucydides notes, the Athenians had lost their faith in the gods and in the law as a result of their sufferings:

The most terrible thing of all was the despair into which people fell when they realized that they had caught the plague; for they would immediately adopt an attitude of utter hopelessness, and, by giving in in this way, would lose their powers of resistance. Terrible, too, was the sight of people dying like sheep through having caught the disease as a result of nursing others. . . . When they did visit the sick, they lost their own lives, and this was particularly true of those who made it a point of honor to act properly.

Not only was it the case that the very best people died for no apparent reason, leading to a despair of reason and of faith, but the proud Athenians also lost their vaunted respect for honor and behaved in a shameful manner:

. . . The bodies of the dying were heaped one on top of the other, and half-dead creatures could be seen staggering about in the streets or flocking around the fountains in their desire for water . . . The catastrophe was so overwhelming that men, not knowing what would happen next to them, became indifferent to every rule of religion or of law. All the funeral ceremonies which used to be observed were now disorganized, and they buried the dead as best they could. Many people, lacking the necessary means of burial because so many deaths had already occurred in their households, adopted the most shameless methods. They would arrive first at a funeral pyre that had been made by others, put their own dead upon it and set it alight; or, finding another pyre, they would throw the corpse that they were carrying on top of the other one and go away.

The historian tells us also, that under these terrible events, the Athenians adopted a carelessness and nihilism that destroyed their devotion to law and order:

Seeing how quick and abrupt were the changes of fortune which came to the rich who suddenly died and to those who had previously been penniless . . . people began openly to venture on acts of self-indulgence which before they used to keep in the dark. . . . No fear of god or law of man had a restraining influence. As for the gods, it seemed to be the same thing whether one worshiped them or not, when one saw the good and bad dying indiscriminately.

Reading *Oedipus the King* against this background helps us understand the urgency with which Sophocles reminds his people of the power of the gods and the mystery of fate and the need to keep ones faith in the face of great misery.

Athens after the Oration: Realism vs. Idealism

—R.M.B.

A mere three decades after Pericles praised the Athens that loved tolerance, equality and freedom, its citizens freely voted to kill Socrates for practicing philosophy. Clearly, something had drastically changed. Thucydides, after preserving Pericles' vision of Athens at its zenith, also depicted the decline of Greek civilization under war and epidemic. Like the tragedians, this historian studied not just human virtue, but also how humans respond to adversity, and while Athens heroically resisted for twenty-seven years both the collected forces of the Greek world and a plague that killed about a quarter of its population (including Pericles himself), the pressures of empire took its toll. Throughout *Oedipus the King* Sophocles evokes the desperation Athens felt while gripped by disease. The plague itself, which hit Athens a few months after Pericles' oration, was seen by Thucydides as "the beginnings of a state of unprecedented lawlessness" because it deprived Athenians of their confidence in the future and in the ability of the "polis" (the Greek citystate) to safeguard their well-being. This free, moderate, and open society thus proved difficult to sustain. Athens first lost its democracy in a bloody coup and then lost the war; when democracy returned, Athens was not quite the same.

"War," wrote Thucydides, "is a violent teacher," and once its hardships deprived civilized Greeks of basic securities and comforts "there was a general deterioration of character throughout the Greek world." Faced with turmoil spreading throughout the Greek world, Thucydides came to the conclusion, just as Freud recognized 2,400 years later in *Civilization and Its Discontents*, that only societal constraints keep humans from lapsing into savagery: "Then, with ordinary conventions of human life thrown into confusion, human nature, always ready to offend even when laws exist, showed itself proudly in its true colors, as something incapable of controlling passion, insubordinate to the idea of justice, the enemy to anything superior to itself." Thus, the Athenians discovered a pragmatism about politics whose brutality matched its earlier Periclean idealism.

Roughly fifteen years after Pericles' speech, Thucydides records that Athenian generals responded thus to the residents of the small island of Melos who refused to join the Athenian empire: "the standard of justice depends on the equality of power to compel and that in fact the strong do what they have the power to do and the weak accept what they have to accept." If you read Plato's *Republic*, you will recognize these ideas in the assertion by Thrasymachus that justice is the advantage of the stronger. Later, Machiavelli's *The Prince* will similarly argue the irrelevance of ethics to politics. This shift does not diminish the ideals of Pericles' vision, but it should help us recognize that the Greeks themselves realized that a stable, democratic society is an extraordinary but fragile achievement and that civilization depends on maintaining a balance between private and public needs. The tensions of preserving this equilibrium are fundamental themes in the works of Sophocles, Aeschylus, Sappho and Plato.

On Aristotle's Poetics

—J.S.L.

Aristotle (384–322 B.C.E.) was Plato's student. Plato was interested in how and why all things were the same. Aristotle, however, developed a philosophy to explain how and why things are different.

To Aristotle the difference between Nature and Art was crucial. Nature moved itself while art was moved by humans. We grow bigger; we move our arms. We are, essentially, natural. In contrast, art—for example, a tragedy by Sophocles—does not grow because something like genes within the play program the growth. An artist puts the play together; a play is not natural, but artificial.

Yet, for Aristotle, art imitates nature; it is like nature. For example, a tragic play reminds us of human life; the artist imitates "actions, with agents who are necessarily good men or bad—the diversities of human character being nearly always derivative from this primary distinction . . ." (Poetics 2, 1148a2–3).

Aristotle thought that our pleasure in art rested partially on our perception of such likenesses: "The reason of delight in seeing the picture is that one is . . . learning—gathering the meaning of things; e.g., that the man [in the picture] is so-and-so" (4, 1448b15). Aristotle knew that humans seem also to enjoy some media simply by nature. We are pleased by colors, harmonies, and rhythms even before they are used to imitate (4, 1448b19–22). Our pleasures in media and learning combine so that humans are the most imitative animals. Think of children's delight in "dressing up" or in their drawings.

When adults make plays, they also imitate. Like children, adults act and use costumes, make-up, a stage, and painted scenery. In short, a playwright dramatizes the imitation. A video director would, to Aristotle, cinematize. A novelist would narrate. Thus, artists "may either speak at one moment in narrative and at another in an assumed character . . . or the imitators may represent the whole story dramatically, as though they were actually doing the things described" (3, 1448a21-23).

In this natural human delight and the clever use of media, in particular language, Aristotle thought invention arose: "Imitation, then, being natural to us—as also the sense of harmony and rhythm, the metres, being obviously species of rhythms—it was through their original aptitude, and by a series of improvements . . . that [humans] created poetry out of improvisations" (4, 1448b20–24). Art completes processes which nature never started or which require human intervention to end. This process of completion marks the most important difference between Plato and Aristotle's view of art; for Plato, art always falls short of real beauty, goodness, or truth. For Aristotle, art makes beautiful, useful, and even better things to exist that otherwise would not.

We can see this inventiveness and completion in his Poetics. It begins: "Epic poetry and Tragedy, as also Comedy, Dithyrambic poetry, and most flute-playing and lyre-playing, are all, viewed as a whole, modes of imitation." (1447a14–16). Tragedy, as a form of art, was a Greek invention. Aristotle found that Greek inventors—artists—had abandoned narrative epic and gravitated toward the theatre where they dramatized tragedy (4, 1449a1–6). Aristotle's Poetics was an explanation of how tragedy and comedy arose and of what they really were as forms of art. (The book on comedy has been lost.)

For Aristotle, the purpose or aim of something did the best job of explaining what it really was, because a purpose always needs some means to accomplish it. Unlike humans, who Aristotle thought naturally shared one aim—happiness, art had many aims or ends; hence, there were many species of art. According to Aristotle, tragedy aimed at a "catharsis" (or "purgation") of pity and fear.

So, why produce pity and fear? Comedy pleases us, but where is the pleasure in pity and fear? To begin to understand, look at the parts, the means, Aristotle thought tragedy used to accomplish a catharsis of pity and fear. There were six: plot, character, thought, diction, music, spectacle. Why six? Since a tragedy imitates through actors and musicians on stage [spectacle and music], that's two. Since it uses language [diction], that's one more. Finally, since tragedy imitates actions done by characters who think and feel, that's the final three: plot (or action), character (or traits, purposes, and choices), and thought (argument and feeling).

For Aristotle tragedy is primarily an "imitation of an action that is serious," and plot (or action) is the "soul . . . of Tragedy" (6, 1449b24 and 1450a38). Action is more important than character, or anything else: "All human happiness or misery takes the form of action; the end for which we live is a certain kind of activity . . . it is in our actions—what we do—that we are happy or the reverse." In tragedy, the agents "do not act in order to portray character." Rather, the dramatists "include character for the sake of the action" (1450a16–21). This implies that our hopes and fears, our satisfactions and pity—in short, our pleasure—depends on what happens to the good and bad characters.

The most important actions that affect characters are reversals (or *peripeties*) of their happiness or misery (their fortunes), their discoveries (or recognitions), and their suffering (or pathos). How an art work uses reversals, discoveries, and suffering makes a difference to what happens to the characters and, thus, how we feel.

These actions had to be properly arranged, and they had to be as numerous and large as was consistent with producing pity and fear (7, 1451a2–6 and 9, 1452a1). Aristotle called this the plot's size or magnitude. If a play had the right parts, with the right size, in the right order, and all of these worked together to produce pity and fear, then, Aristotle thought, the play would be beautiful, powerful, and good.

Above all, these actions should unite. Did you ever own a baseball glove that fell apart or a dress where the lining pulled out of the skirt? A play cannot fall apart like this, so the way to know if it holds together is to ask whether the parts fit each other to make one well-designed, good-functioning product. This Aristotle calls "unity":

> *The Unity of a Plot does not consist, as some suppose, in its having one man as its subject, [since] an infinity of things befall one man, some of which is impossible to reduce to a unity. The story, as an imitation of action, must represent one action, a complete whole, with its several incidents so closely connected that the transposal or withdrawal of any one of them will disjoin or dislocate the whole (8, 1451a1–3; 16–35).*

Later critics added two other unities of "time" (all action in a single day) and "place" (all action in one place), thus forming the three unities. But for Aristotle, unity in action was the important consideration.

Think of *Oedipus the King*. What makes it so good? It's nearly impossible to move anything around or take anything out without changing the plot and, thus, our emotional reaction to the play. Students think about how the gods seemed to have trapped Oedipus. But think of the plot. If Sophocles leaves out Oedipus's concern for Thebes and his pride in his know-how, Oedipus will not try to solve the murder mystery. If Oedipus does not strive to perform justice, his fortune will not reverse from happiness to misery. If Sophocles leaves out the curse, Oedipus's suffering would be much less. If Sophocles makes Oedipus call for the shepherd before the messenger comes, Oedipus never discovers that his father was Laius nor that Jocasta was his mother. If Jocasta does not kill herself, Oedipus will not suffer blindness. And without blinding himself, he will not discover how much he needs his remaining family—his children.

In this unity the completion of an imitation combines with the pleasure Aristotle thought we took in tragedy to produce catharsis. In a well-made tragedy we recognize the use of all the means available-action, character, and thought—in a likely, sequential order which permits the maximum impact on the tragic hero. So doing, we feel, to the fullest, pity or fear over something we had never before seen. However, we will not feel pity for the tragic hero unless what happens to him is undeserved, nor will we feel fear unless he or she is like us—in the sense that we could imagine that they, too, could become miserable. What best leads to undeserved misery? Aristotle finds three chief ways.

A hamartia—a mistake in action—by the tragic hero (sometimes called the protagonist) which brings on his or her own destruction will be pitiable and fearful if the hero/ine is good enough so that we can see that s/he is trying to do the right thing, but in error enough so that his/her mistake is irretrievable. Oedipus's curse is like that. He tries to perform justice that the gods demand, but mistakenly makes the justice so severe and inescapable that it destroys him, his wife, and his family. Oedipus's mistaken curse reverses his fortune from relative happiness to fearful and pitiful misery. It is a mistake we too could make.

Another way is a tragic deed, like Oedipus's killing his father. Laius suffered at Oedipus's hands. Even if we were justified, would that killing be a burden we would wish to carry? Would we want to sleep with our mothers, even inadvertently? The tragic deed should be such that we can, at least, see why the hero would wish to avoid it.

Aristotle thinks the third way is to use the best form of discovery in the right place in the plot (14, 1453b26). Though a character can discover what he or she did, the most tragic form of discovery is to learn to whom one is related (11, 1452a33–b8). Oedipus does the tragic deed in ignorance and discovers his relation afterward. We would normally expect enemies, not friends or family, to fight. Oedipus, however, kills another in the heat of battle and later on discovers that he slew his father. The discovery destroys and reverses the emotions of Oedipus's life. Where before he was angry and, then, confident in his self-defense, now he loathes himself for killing a man he ought to have loved. Would we want this discovery for ourselves?

So, Aristotle thought that as these tragic actions come together in the plot the artist makes something that might be, not something that already is, pitiable and fearful. Ultimately, the tragic artist aims at pity and fear because in pity our sense of human injury is weighed against our sense of justice. And in fear our sense of injury and justice is cast into the future for someone who never existed, but whom we care deeply about. For Aristotle, this was "philosophical" (9, 1451b4–6). Tragedy takes what we know or recognize—whether an old story (or myth) or a historical fact makes no difference—and turns it into something new, something possible (9, 1451b27–33). Art was important to Aristotle, not because it "expressed" what the Greeks were to themselves; the Greeks already knew that and had figures like Pericles to tell them if they forgot. Instead, the importance of artistic invention rested in its broadening of experience beyond Athens, or—even—the sweep of Greek history.

Therefore, Aristotle wrote the Poetics not only to explain tragedy and comedy, but to protect art from critics—especially specialists-who would limit or bend invention to their purposes. He writes "It is to be remembered, too, that there is not the same kind of correctness in poetry as in politics, or indeed any other art" (25, 1460b13). The goodness of a work rests not in its subservience to political, religious, or scientific aims, but to its own: "Impossibilities . . . are justifiable, if they serve the end of poetry itself—if . . . they make the work or some portion of it more astounding" (25, 1460b23–27). Thus, in a society which had no constitutional concept of rights, the Poetics was a treatise in defense of freedom, especially of the emotions and artistic invention. Finally, then, the Poetics served to challenge philosophers and politicians who in their systems and educational plans always tied art to the truth: "If the poet's description be criticized as not true . . . one may urge perhaps that the object ought to be as described—an answer like that of Sophocles, who said that he drew men as they ought to be . . ." (33–35). In this the Poetics fits Intellectual Heritage, for IH is less a study of the truth, than of the possibilities humans have invented and made for themselves.

Source: Aristotle. *The Basic Works of Aristotle*. Ed. Richard McKeon. NY: Random House, 1941.

The Hero

—S.Z.

Anthropologists have long been interested in the stories different cultures fashion to explain themselves and their history. Studying "hero stories," the anthropologists observe certain basic elements that seem to be common in many of these stories, even across very distant societies. The elements of the hero story, as studied by Lord Raglan in his book *The Hero* (New York, 1937) can be seen as present in several of the texts we study (we will supply the analysis for Oedipus). How close is this pattern in the stories of the lives of Moses, Jesus, Sundiata?

The Pattern of the Hero:

1. The Hero's mother is a royal virgin;
2. His father is a king, and
3. Often a near relative of his mother, but
4. The circumstances of his conception are unusual, and
5. He is also reputed to be the son of a god.
6. At birth an attempt is made, usually by his father or his maternal grandfather, to kill him, but
7. He is spirited away, and
8. Reared by foster-parents in a far country.
9. We are told nothing of his childhood, but
10. On reaching manhood he returns or goes to his future kingdom.
11. After a victory over the king and/or a giant, dragon, or wild beast,
12. He marries a princess, often the daughter of his predecessor, and
13. Becomes king.
14. For a time he reigns uneventfully, and
15. Prescribes laws, but
16. Later he loses favour with the gods and/or his subjects, and
17. Is driven from the throne and city, after which
18. He meets with a mysterious death,
19. Often at the top of a hill.
20. His children, if any, do not succeed him.
21. His body is not buried, but nevertheless
22. He has one or more holy sepulchres.

The Oedipus Story's Hero Elements:

His mother, Jocasta, is
1. a princess, and his father is
2. King Laius, who, like her, is
3. of the line of Cadmus. He was sworn to have no connection with her but
4. does so when drunk, probably
5. in the character of Dionysus. Laius
6. tries to kill Oedipus at birth, but
7. he is spirited away, and
8. reared by the King of Corinth.
9. We hear nothing of his childhood, but
10. on reaching manhood he returns to Thebes, after
11. gaining victories over his father and the Sphinx. He
12. marries Jocasta, and
13. becomes king. For some years he
14. reigns uneventfully, but
16. later comes to be regarded as the cause of a plague, and
17. is deposed and driven into exile. He meets with
18. a mysterious death at
19. a place near Athens called the Steep Pavement. He is succeeded by
20. Creon, through whom he was deposed, and though
21. the place of his burial is uncertain, he has
22. several holy sepulchres.

60

Antigone

Sophocles had his play *Antigone* performed in 440 B.C.E., and this play has intrigued readers and audiences ever since. The materials for the play are drawn from a story well known to its audience. Clearly, Sophocles meant to use this ancient story of the Oedipus family, a story of Thebes, to explore questions in his contemporary Athens.

Looked at from this perspective, we can begin to appreciate the political themes that animate this play. The city, or *polis* (a Greek name for city that provides us with the word "political"), is still emerging at the time of Sophocles, as it is emerging even today in some places in the world. Athens, like many early cities, is made up of people who had previous allegiances to family groups, clans or tribes. In those previous organizations, the law was traditional, upheld by the concept of the wishes of the gods, and enforced by elders of the blood group.

The new city, however, asserts a law that is political, that is, reflects the wishes of the people of the city, as interpreted by the ruling political authority. In the new city, blood relations are being replaced with friendships (free associations of individuals). The law must be respected by people from all backgrounds, even when their traditions vary. Political power is either enforced by force or is to some degree consensual, as would be the case in democratic Athens.

In *Antigone*, Sophocles explores the problems that belong to this transition of authority. How is the law to be made so that it can become a force for stability and mutual agreement? What is the relation between man-made law and the ancient traditions associated with the dictates of the gods? And what problems might emerge when men, or a single leader, attempt to make and enforce the law, even though such a person or persons are still "mere mortals"?

Creon is the "new man for the new day," and represents the political authority of the *polis*. Antigone, his niece, speaks for ancient traditions associated with heaven's wishes. It is interesting to note that Creon has much to say in arguing his rational case for obedience to his law; Antigone can only proclaim her truth. The new politics is discussive and rational; the old world follows its way without argumentation or doubt.

Still, it is Creon who goes badly wrong in defining and asserting the law. He seems to fail in two distinct ways. First, he cannot separate his personal desires from the issue of what is good for the city. They become the same things, a sure recipe for tyranny. Second, Creon lacks a proper respect for the gods, and ends by rejecting their clear signs when these do not agree with his own desires. And finally, Creon demonstrates, for all his rationality or perhaps because of it, a shocking ignorance of the dark forces and passions that rule men's lives.

Antigone has long since come to represent a heroine who speaks truth to power. Even if all the city is against her, she holds out for the truth as she knows it. Antigone has been held as an example during World War II in France when patriots wished to rally the people against the Nazi regime whose brutal law was imposed upon them. She was alive, too, in the battles against Jim Crow laws in the American South when individuals opposed laws they knew to be wrong.

How can a law be wrong when the political authority has proclaimed it? This is the question at the heart of Sophocles' play. And perhaps more important, how can the law, how can politics, build for the *polis* a stronger foundation so that such confrontations between law and opposing claims for justice can be averted? Is there a boundary to the laws of the state? And if so, where is it, and how can citizens assert themselves when the boundary is breached?

Many readers have preferred to experience *Antigone* as a confrontation between two tragically stubborn individuals, and the play is certainly that. However, *Antigone* remains one of the great philosophical explorations in our literature. The questions it raises are as timely as recent events in Rwanda, in Bosnia, in Jerusalem and in every American city.

Antigone

Sophocles

Characters

ANTIGONE, daughter of Oedipus and Jocasta
ISMENE, sister of Antigone
A CHORUS of old Theban citizens and their LEADER
CREON, king of Thebes, uncle of Antigone and Ismene
A SENTRY
HAEMON, son of Creon and Eurydice
TIRESIAS, a blind prophet
A MESSENGER
EURYDICE, wife of Creon
Guards, attendants, and a boy

TIME AND SCENE: The royal house of Thebes. It is still night, and the invading armies of Argos have just been driven from the city. Fighting on opposite sides, the sons of Oedipus, Eteocles and Polynices, have killed each other in combat. Their uncle, CREON, is now king of Thebes. Enter ANTIGONE, slipping through the central doors of the palace. She motions to her sister, ISMENE, who follows her cautiously toward an altar at the center of the stage.

ANTIGONE:
My own flesh and blood—dear sister, dear Ismene,
how many griefs our father Oedipus handed down!
Do you know one, I ask you, one grief
that Zeus will not perfect for the two of us
while we still live and breathe? There's nothing, 5
no pain—our lives are pain—no private shame,
no public disgrace, nothing I haven't seen
in your griefs and mine. And now this:
an emergency decree, they say, the Commander
has just now declared for all of Thebes. 10
What, haven't you heard? Don't you see?
The doom reserved for enemies
marches on the ones we love the most.

ISMENE:
Not I, I haven't heard a word, Antigone.
Nothing of loved ones, 15
no joy or pain has come my way, not since
the two of us were robbed of our two brothers,
both gone in a day, a double blow—
not since the armies of Argos vanished,
just this very night. I know nothing more, 20
whether our luck's improved or ruin's still to come.

ANTIGONE:
I thought so. That's why I brought you out here,
past the gates, so you could hear in private.

ISMENE:
What's the matter? Trouble, clearly . . .
you sound so dark, so grim. 25

ANTIGONE:
Why not? Our own brothers' burial!
Hasn't Creon graced one with all the rites,
disgraced the other? Eteocles, they say,
has been given full military honors,
rightly so—Creon has laid him in the earth 30
and he goes with glory down among the dead.

From *Three Theban Plays by Sophocles*, translated by Robert Fagles. Translation copyright © 1982 by Robert Fagles. Used by permission of Viking Penguin, a division of Penguin Putnam Inc.

But the body of Polynices, who died miserably—
why, a city-wide proclamation, rumor has it,
forbids anyone to bury him, even mourn him.
He's to be left unwept, unburied, a lovely treasure 35
for birds that scan the field and feast to their heart's content.
Such, I hear, is the martial law our good Creon
lays down for you and me—yes, me, I tell you—
and he's coming here to alert the uninformed
in no uncertain terms, 40
and he won't treat the matter lightly. Whoever
disobeys in the least will die, his doom is sealed:
stoning to death inside the city walls!
There you have it. You'll soon show what you are,
worth your breeding, Ismene, or a coward— 45
for all your royal blood.

ISMENE:
My poor sister, if things have come to this,
who am I to make or mend them, tell me,
what good am I to you?

ANTIGONE:
            Decide.
Will you share the labor, share the work? 50
ISMENE
What work, what's the risk? What do you mean?

ANTIGONE:

Raising her hands.

Will you lift up his body with these bare hands
and lower it with me?

ISMENE:
            What? You'd bury him—
when a law forbids the city?

ANTIGONE:
            Yes!
He is my brother and—deny it as you will—
your brother too. 55
No one will ever convict me for a traitor.

ISMENE:
So desperate, and Creon has expressly—

ANTIGONE:
            No,
he has no right to keep me from my own.

ISMENE:
Oh my sister, think— 60
think how our own father died, hated,
his reputation in ruins, driven on
by the crimes he brought to light himself
to gouge out his eyes with his own hands—
then mother . . . his mother and wife, both in one, 65
mutilating her life in the twisted noose—
and last, our two brothers dead in a single day,
both shedding their own blood, poor suffering boys,
battling out their common destiny hand-to-hand.
Now look at the two of us, left so alone . . . 70
think what a death we'll die, the worst of all
if we violate the laws and override
the fixed decree of the throne, its power—
we must be sensible. Remember we are women,
we're not born to contend with men. Then too, 75
we're underlings, ruled by much stronger hands,
so we must submit in this, and things still worse.
I, for one, I'll beg the dead to forgive me—
I'm forced, I have no choice—I must obey
the ones who stand in power. Why rush to extremes? 80
It's madness, madness.

ANTIGONE:
            I won't insist,
no, even if you should have a change of heart,
I'd never welcome you in the labor, not with me.
So, do as you like, whatever suits you best—
I will bury him myself. 85
And even if I die in the act, that death will be a glory.
I will lie with the one I love and loved by him—

an outrage sacred to the gods! I have longer
to please the dead than please the living here:
in the kingdom down below I'll lie forever. 90
Do as you like, dishonor the laws
the gods hold in honor.

ISMENE:
        I'd do them no dishonor . . .
but defy the city? I have no strength for that.

ANTIGONE:
You have your excuses. I am on my way,
I will raise a mound for him, for my dear brother. 95

ISMENE:
Oh Antigone, you're so rash—I'm so afraid for you!

ANTIGONE:
Don't fear for me. Set your own life in order.

ISMENE:
Then don't, at least, blurt this out to anyone.
Keep it a secret. I'll join you in that, I promise.

ANTIGONE:
Dear god, shout it from the rooftops. I'll hate you 100
all the more for silence—tell the world!

ISMENE:
So fiery—and it ought to chill your heart.

ANTIGONE:
I know I please where I must please the most.

ISMENE:
Yes, if you can, but you're in love with impossibility.

ANTIGONE:
Very well then, once my strength gives out 105
I will be done at last.

ISMENE:
        You're wrong from the start,
you're off on a hopeless quest.

ANTIGONE:
If you say so, you will make me hate you,
and the hatred of the dead by all rights,
will haunt you night and day. 110
But leave me to my own absurdity, leave me
to suffer this—dreadful thing. I will suffer
nothing as great as death without glory.

Exit to the side.

ISMENE:
Then go if you must, but rest assured,
wild, irrational as you are, my sister, 115
you are truly dear to the ones who love you.

Withdrawing to the palace.
Enter a CHORUS, *the old citizens of Thebes, chanting as the sun begins to rise.*

CHORUS:
Glory!—great beam of the sun, brightest of all
that ever rose on the seven gates of Thebes,
    you burn through night at last!
        Great eye of the golden day, 120
mounting the Dirce's banks you throw him back—
the enemy out of Argos, the white shield, the man of bronze—
he's flying headlong now
    the bridle of fate stampeding him with pain!

    And he had driven against our borders, 125
    launched by the warring claims of Polynices—
like an eagle screaming, winging havoc
over the land, wings of armor
shielded white as snow,
    a huge army massing, 130
    crested helmets bristling for assault.

He hovered above our roofs, his vast maw gaping
closing down around our seven gates,
    his spears thirsting for the kill
        but now he's gone, look, 135
before he could glut his jaws with Theban blood
or the god of fire put our crown of towers to the torch.

He grappled the Dragon none can
    master—Thebes—
        the clang of our arms like thunder at
            his back!

    Zeus hates with a vengeance all
        bravado,   140
    the mighty boasts of men. He watched
        them
    coming on in a rising flood, the pride
    of their golden armor ringing shrill—
    and brandishing his lightning
    blasted the fighter just at the goal,   145
        rushing to shout his triumph from our
            walls.

Down from the heights he crashed,
    pounding down on the earth!
And a moment ago, blazing torch in
    hand—
        mad for attack, ecstatic
he breathed his rage, the storm   150
    of his fury hurling at our heads!
But now his high hopes have laid him low
and down the enemy ranks the iron god
    of war
deals his rewards, his stunning
        blows—Ares
rapture of battle, our right arm in the
    crisis.   155

    Seven captains marshaled at seven gates
    seven against their equals, gave
    their brazen trophies up to Zeus,
    god of the breaking rout of battle,
    all but two: those blood brothers,   160
        one father, one mother—matched in
            rage,
    spears matched for the twin conquest—
    clashed and won the common prize of
        death.

But now for Victory! Glorious in the
    morning,
joy in her eyes to meet our joy   165
    she is winging down to Thebes,
our fleets of chariots wheeling in her
    wake—
    Now let us win oblivion from the wars,
    thronging the temples of the gods
    in singing, dancing choirs through the
        night!   170
        Lord Dionysus, god of the dance
        that shakes the land of Thebes, now
            lead the way!

Enter CREON from the palace, attended by his guard.

    But look, the king of the realm is
        coming,
    Creon, the new man for the new day,
    whatever the gods are sending now . . .   175
    what new plan will he launch?
    Why this, this special session?
    Why this sudden call to the old men
    summoned at one command?

CREON:
                My countrymen,
the ship of state is safe. The gods who
    rocked her,   180
after a long, merciless pounding in the
    storm,
have righted her once more.
                Out of the whole city
I have called you here alone. Well I know,
first, your undeviating respect
for the throne and royal power of King
    Laius.   185
Next, while Oedipus steered the land of
    Thebes,
and even after he died, your loyalty was
    unshakable,
you still stood by their children. Now
    then,
since the two sons are dead—two blows
    of fate
in the same day, cut down by each other's
    hands,   190
both killers, both brothers stained with
    blood—
as I am next in kin to the dead,
I now possess the throne and all its
    powers.
Of course you cannot know a man
    completely,
his character, his principles, sense of
    judgment,   195
not till he's shown his colors, ruling the
    people,
making laws. Experience, there's the test.
As I see it, whoever assumes the task,
the awesome task of setting the city's
    course,
and refuses to adopt the soundest policies   200
but fearing someone, keeps his lips locked
    tight,
he's utterly worthless. So I rate him now,
I always have. And whoever places a
    friend
above the good of his own country, he is
    nothing:

I have no use for him. Zeus my witness, 205
Zeus who sees all things, always—
I could never stand by silent, watching destruction
march against our city, putting safety to rout,
nor could I ever make that man a friend of mine
who menaces our country. Remember this: 210
our country is our safety.
Only while she voyages true on course
can we establish friendships, truer than blood itself.
Such are my standards. They make our city great.
Closely akin to them I have proclaimed, 215
just now, the following decree to our people
concerning the two sons of Oedipus.
Eteocles, who died fighting for Thebes,
excelling all in arms: he shall be buried,
crowned with a hero's honors, the cups we pour 220
to soak the earth and reach the famous dead.
But as for his blood brother, Polynices,
who returned from exile, home to his father-city
and the gods of his race, consumed with one desire—
to burn them roof to roots—who thirsted to drink 225
his kinsmen's blood and sell the rest to slavery:
that man—a proclamation has forbidden the city
to dignify him with burial, mourn him at all.
No, he must be left unburied, his corpse
carrion for the birds and dogs to tear, 230
an obscenity for the citizens to behold!
These are my principles. Never at my hands
will the traitor be honored above the patriot.
But whoever proves his loyalty to the state—
I'll prize that man in death as well as life. 235

LEADER:
If this is your pleasure, Creon, treating
our city's enemy and our friend this way
The power is yours, I suppose, to enforce it
with the laws, both for the dead and all of us,
the living.

CREON:
        Follow my orders closely then, 240
be on your guard.

LEADER:
               We are too old.
Lay that burden on younger shoulders.

CREON:
                      No, no,
I don't mean the body—I've posted guards already.

LEADER:
What commands for us then? What other service?

CREON:
See that you never side with those who break my orders. 245

LEADER:
Never. Only a fool could be in love with death.

CREON:
Death is the price—you're right. But all too often
the mere hope of money has ruined many men.

A SENTRY enters from the side.

SENTRY:
                    My lord,
I can't say I'm winded from running, or set out
with any spring in my legs either—no sir, 250
I was lost in thought, and it made me stop, often,
dead in my tracks, wheeling, turning back,
and all the time a voice inside me muttering,
"Idiot, why? You're going straight to your death."
Then muttering, "Stopped again, poor fool? 255
If somebody gets the news to Creon first,
what's to save your neck?"
                      And so,
mulling it over, on I trudged, dragging my feet,
you can make a short road take forever...
but at last, look, common sense won out, 260

I'm here, and I'm all yours,
and even though I come empty-handed
I'll tell my story just the same, because
I've come with a good grip on one hope,
what will come will come, whatever fate— 265

CREON:
Come to the point!
What's wrong—why so afraid?

SENTRY:
First, myself, I've got to tell you,
I didn't do it, didn't see who did—
Be fair, don't take it out on me. 270

CREON:
You're playing it safe, soldier,
barricading yourself from any trouble.
It's obvious, you've something strange to tell.

SENTRY:
Dangerous too, and danger makes you delay
for all you're worth. 275

CREON:
Out with it—then dismiss!

SENTRY:
All right, here it comes. The body—
someone's just buried it, then run off.
sprinkled some dry dust on the flesh,
given it proper rites.

CREON:
        What? 280
What man alive would dare—

SENTRY:
        I've no idea, I swear it.
There was no mark of a spade, no pickaxe there,
no earth turned up, the ground packed hard and dry,
unbroken, no tracks, no wheelruts, nothing,
the workman left no trace. Just at sunup 285
the first watch of the day points it out—
it was a wonder! We were stunned . . .
a terrific burden too, for all of us, listen:
you can't see the corpse, not that it's buried,
really, just a light cover of road-dust on it, 290
as if someone meant to lay the dead to rest
and keep from getting cursed.

Not a sign in sight that dogs or wild beasts
had worried the body, even torn the skin.
But what came next! Rough talk flew thick and fast, 295
guard grilling guard—we'd have come to blows
at last, nothing to stop it; each man for himself
and each the culprit, no one caught red-handed,
all of us pleading ignorance, dodging the charges,
ready to take up red-hot iron in our fists, 300
go through fire, swear oaths to the gods—
"I didn't do it, I had no hand in it either,
not in the plotting, not the work itself!"
Finally, after all this wrangling came to nothing,
one man spoke out and made us stare at the ground, 305
hanging our heads in fear. No way to counter him,
no way to take his advice and come through
safe and sound. Here's what he said:
"Look, we've got to report the facts to Creon,
we can't keep this hidden." Well, that won out, 310
and the lot fell to me, condemned me,
unlucky as ever, I got the prize. So here I am,
against my will and yours too, well I know—
no one wants the man who brings bad news.

LEADER:
    My king,
ever since he began I've been debating in my mind, 315
could this possibly be the work of the gods?

CREON:
    Stop—
before you make me choke with anger—the gods!
You, you're senile, must you be insane?
You say—why it's intolerable—say the gods
could have the slightest concern for that corpse? 320
Tell me, was it for meritorious service
they proceeded to bury him, prized him so? The hero

who came to burn their temples ringed with pillars,
their golden treasures—scorch their hallowed earth
and fling their laws to the winds. 325
Exactly when did you last see the gods
celebrating traitors? Inconceivable!
No, from the first there were certain citizens
who could hardly stand the spirit of my regime,
grumbling against me in the dark, heads together, 330
tossing wildly, never keeping their necks beneath
the yoke, loyally submitting to their king.
These are the instigators, I'm convinced—
they've perverted my own guard, bribed them
to do their work.
           Money! Nothing worse 335
in our lives, so current, rampant, so corrupting
Money—you demolish cities, root men from their homes,
you train and twist good minds and set them on
to the most atrocious schemes. No limit,
you make them adept at every kind of outrage, 340
every godless crime—money!
                Everyone—
the whole crew bribed to commit this crime,
they've made one thing sure at least:
sooner or later they will pay the price.

Wheeling on the SENTRY.

                You—
I swear to Zeus as I still believe in Zeus, 345
if you don't find the man who buried that corpse,
the very man, and produce him before my eyes,
simple death won't be enough for you,
not till we string you up alive
and wring the immorality out of you. 350
Then you can steal the rest of your day,
better informed about where to make a killing.
You'll have learned, at last, it doesn't pay
to itch for rewards from every hand that beckons.
Filthy profits wreck most men, you'll see— 355
they'll never save your life.

SENTRY:
           Please,
may I say a word or two, or just turn and go?

CREON:
Can't you tell? Everything you say offends me.

SENTRY:
Where does it hurt you, in the ears or in the heart?

CREON:
And who are you to pinpoint my displeasure? 360

SENTRY:
The culprit grates on your feelings,
I just annoy your ears.

CREON:
           Still talking?
You talk too much! A born nuisance—

SENTRY:
                Maybe so,
but I never did this thing, so help me!

CREON:
                Yes you did—
what's more, you squandered your life for silver! 365

SENTRY:
Oh it's terrible when the one who does the judging
judges things all wrong.

CREON:
           Well now,
you just be clever about your judgments—
if you fail to produce the criminals for me,
you'll swear your dirty money brought you pain. 370

Turning sharply, reentering the palace.

SENTRY:
I hope he's found. Best thing by far.
But caught or not, that's in the lap of fortune:
I'll never come back, you've seen the last of me.
I'm saved, even now, and I never thought,
I never hoped— 375

dear gods, I owe you all my thanks!

Rushing out.

CHORUS:
              Numberless wonders
terrible wonders walk the world but none the match for man—
that great wonder crossing the heaving gray sea,
    driven on by the blasts of winter
on through breakers crashing left and right, 380
    holds his steady course
and the oldest of the gods he wears away—
the Earth, the immortal, the inexhaustible—
as his plows go back and forth, year in, year out
with the breed of stallions turning up the furrows. 385
And the blithe, lightheaded race of birds he snares,
the tribes of savage beasts, the life that swarms the depths—
        with one fling of his nets
woven and coiled tight, he takes them all,
man the skilled, the brilliant! 390
He conquers all, taming with his techniques
the prey that roams the cliffs and wild lairs,
training the stallion, clamping the yoke across
his shaggy neck, and the tireless mountain bull.
And speech and thought, quick as the wind 395
and the mood and mind for law that rules the city—
all these he has taught himself
and shelter from the arrows of the frost
when there's rough lodging under the cold clear sky
and the shafts of lashing rain— 400
    ready, resourceful man!
        Never without resources
never an impasse as he marches on the future—
only Death, from Death alone he will find no rescue
but from desperate plagues he has plotted his escapes. 405

Man the master, ingenious past all measure
past all dreams, the skills within his grasp—
he forges on, now to destruction
now again to greatness. When he weaves in
the laws of the land, and the justice of the gods 410
that binds his oaths together
    he and his city rise high—
        but the city casts out
that man who weds himself to inhumanity
thanks to reckless daring. Never share my hearth 415
never think my thoughts, whoever does such things.

Enter ANTIGONE from the side, accompanied by the SENTRY.

    Here is a dark sign from the gods—
what to make of this? I know her,
how can I deny it? That young girl's Antigone!
Wretched, child of a wretched father, 420
Oedipus. Look, is it possible?
They bring you in like a prisoner—
why? did you break the king's laws?
Did they take you in some act of mad defiance?

SENTRY:
She's the one, she did it single-handed— 425
we caught her burying the body. Where's Creon?

Enter CREON from the palace.

LEADER:
Back again just in time when you need him.

CREON:
In time for what? What is it?

SENTRY:
              My king,
there's nothing you can swear you'll never do—
second thoughts make liars of us all. 430
I could have sworn I wouldn't hurry back
(what with your threats, the buffeting I just took),
but a stroke of luck beyond our wildest hopes,

what a joy, there's nothing like it. So,
back I've come, breaking my oath, who cares?   435
I'm bringing in our prisoner—this young girl—
we took her giving the dead the last rites.
But no casting lots this time; this is *my* luck,
my prize, no one else's.
                Now, my lord,
here she is. Take her, question her,   440
cross-examine her to your heart's content.
But set me free, it's only right—
I'm rid of this dreadful business once for all.

CREON:
Prisoner! Her? You took her—where, doing what?

SENTRY:
Burying the man. That's the whole story.

CREON:
                    What?   445
You mean what you say, you're telling me the truth?

SENTRY:
She's the one. With my own eyes I saw her
bury the body, just what you've forbidden.
There. Is that plain and clear?

CREON:
What did you see? Did you catch her in the act?   450

SENTRY:
Here's what happened. We went back to our post,
those threats of yours breathing down our necks—
we brushed the corpse clean of the dust that covered it,
stripped it bare . . . it was slimy, going soft,
and we took to high ground, backs to the wind   455
so the stink of him couldn't hit us;
jostling, baiting each other to keep awake,
shouting back and forth—no napping on the job,
not this time. And so the hours dragged by
until the sun stood dead above our heads,   460
a huge white ball in the noon sky, beating,
blazing down, and then it happened—
suddenly, a whirlwind!
Twisting a great dust-storm up from the earth,
a black plague of the heavens, filling the plain,   465
ripping the leaves off every tree in sight,
choking the air and sky. We squinted hard
and took our whipping from the gods.
And after the storm passed—it seemed endless—
there, we saw the girl!   470
And she cried out a sharp, piercing cry,
like a bird come back to an empty nest,
peering into its bed, and all the babies gone.
Just so, when she sees the corpse bare
she bursts into a long, shattering wail   475
and calls down withering curses on the heads
of all who did the work. And she scoops up dry dust,
handfuls, quickly, and lifting a fine bronze urn,
lifting it high and pouring, she crowns the dead
with three full libations.
                    Soon as we saw   480
we rushed her, closed on the kill like hunters,
and she, she didn't flinch. We interrogated her,
charging her with offenses past and present—
she stood up to it all, denied nothing. I tell you,
it made me ache and laugh in the same breath.   485
It's pure joy to escape the worst yourself,
it hurts a man to bring down his friends.
But all that, I'm afraid, means less to me
than my own skin. That's the way I'm made.

CREON:

Wheeling on ANTIGONE.

      You,
with your eyes fixed on the ground—speak up.   490
Do you deny you did this, yes or no?

ANTIGONE:
I did it. I don't deny a thing.

CREON:

> *To the SENTRY.*

You, get out, wherever you please—
you're clear of a very heavy charge.

> *He leaves; CREON turns back to ANTIGONE.*

You, tell me briefly, no long speeches— 495
were you aware a decree had forbidden this?

ANTIGONE:
Well aware. How could I avoid it? It was public.

CREON:
And still you had the gall to break this law?

ANTIGONE:
Of course I did. It wasn't Zeus, not in the least,
who made this proclamation—not to me. 500
Nor did that justice, dwelling with the gods
beneath the earth, ordain such laws for men.
Nor did I think your edict had such force
that you, a mere mortal, could override the gods,
the great unwritten, unshakable traditions. 505
They are alive, not just today or yesterday:
they live forever, from the first of time,
and no one knows when they first saw the light.
These laws—I was not about to break them,
not out of fear of some man's wounded pride, 510
and face the retribution of the gods.
Die I must, I've known it all my life—
how could I keep from knowing?—even without
your death-sentence ringing in my ears.
And if I am to die before my time 515
I consider that a gain. Who on earth,
alive in the midst of so much grief as I,
could fail to find his death a rich reward?
So for me, at least, to meet this doom of yours
is precious little pain. But if I had allowed 520
my own mother's son to rot, an unburied corpse—
that would have been an agony! This is nothing.
And if my present actions strike you as foolish,
let's just say I've been accused of folly
by a fool.

LEADER:
> Like father like daughter, 525
passionate, wild . . .
she hasn't learned to bend before adversity.

CREON:
No? Believe me, the stiffest stubborn wills
fall the hardest; the toughest iron,
tempered strong in the white-hot fire, 530
you'll see it crack and shatter first of all.
And I've known spirited horses you can break
with a light bit—proud, rebellious horses.
There's no room for pride, not in a slave,
not with the lord and master standing by. 535
This girl was an old hand at insolence
when she overrode the edicts we made public.
But once she had done it—the insolence,
twice over—to glory in it, laughing,
mocking us to our face with what she'd done. 540
I am not the man, not now: she is the man
if this victory goes to her and she goes free.
Never! Sister's child or closer in blood
than all my family clustered at my altar
worshiping Guardian Zeus—she'll never escape, 545
she and her blood sister, the most barbaric death.
Yes, I accuse her sister of an equal part
in scheming this, this burial.

> *To his attendants.*

> Bring her here!
I just saw her inside, hysterical, gone to pieces.
It never fails: the mind convicts itself 550
in advance, when scoundrels are up to no good,
plotting in the dark. Oh but I hate it more
when a traitor, caught red-handed,
tries to glorify his crimes.

ANTIGONE:
Creon, what more do you want 555

than my arrest and execution?

CREON:
Nothing. Then I have it all.

ANTIGONE:
Then why delay? Your moralizing repels me,
every word you say—pray god it always will.
So naturally all I say repels you too.
                              Enough.   560
Give me glory! What greater glory could I win
than to give my own brother decent burial?
These citizens here would all agree,

To the CHORUS.

they would praise me too
if their lips weren't locked in fear.   565

Pointing to CREON.

Lucky tyrants—the perquisites of power!
Ruthless power to do and say whatever pleases *them*.

CREON:
You alone, of all the people in Thebes,
see things that way.

ANTIGONE:
                    They see it just that way
but defer to you and keep their tongues in leash.   570

CREON:
And you, aren't you ashamed to differ so from them?
So disloyal!

ANTIGONE:
            Not ashamed for a moment,
not to honor my brother, my own flesh and blood.

CREON:
Wasn't Eteocles a brother too—cut down, facing him?

ANTIGONE:
Brother, yes, by the same mother, the same father.   575

CREON:
Then how can you render his enemy such honors,
such impieties in his eyes?

ANTIGONE:
He will never testify to that,
Eteocles dead and buried.

CREON:
                    He will—
if you honor the traitor just as much as him.   580

ANTIGONE:
But it was his brother, not some slave that died—

CREON:
Ravaging our country!—
but Eteocles died fighting in our behalf.

ANTIGONE:
No matter—Death longs for the same rites for all.

CREON:
Never the same for the patriot and the traitor.   585

ANTIGONE:
Who, Creon, who on earth can say the ones below
don't find this pure and uncorrupt?

CREON:
Never. Once an enemy, never a friend,
not even after death.

ANTIGONE:
I was born to join in love, not hate—   590
that is my nature.

CREON:
            Go down below and love,
if love you must—love the dead! While I'm alive,
no woman is going to lord it over me.

Enter ISMENE from the palace, under guard.

CHORUS:
                    Look,
Ismene's coming, weeping a sister's tears,
loving sister, under a cloud . . .   595
her face is flushed, her cheeks streaming.

Sorrow puts her lovely radiance in the
    dark.

CREON:
                      You—
in my own house, you viper, slinking
    undetected,
sucking my life-blood! I never knew
I was breeding twin disasters, the two of
    you   600
rising up against my throne. Come, tell
    me,
will you confess your part in the crime or
    not?
Answer me. Swear to me.

ISMENE:
                   I did it, yes—
if only she consents—I share the guilt,
the consequences too.

ANTIGONE:
              No,   605
justice will never suffer that—not you,
you were unwilling. I never brought you
    in.

ISMENE:
But now, you face such dangers . . . I'm
    not ashamed
to sail through trouble with you,
make your troubles mine.

ANTIGONE:
                    Who did the work?   610
Let the dead and the god of death bear
    witness!
I have no love for a friend who loves in
    words alone.

ISMENE:
Oh no, my sister, don't reject me, please,
let me die beside you, consecrating
the dead together.

ANTIGONE:
              Never share my dying,   615
don't lay claim to what you never touched.
My death will be enough.

ISMENE:
What do I care for life, cut off from you?

ANTIGONE:
Ask Creon. Your concern is all for him.

ISMENE:
Why abuse me so? It doesn't help you
    now.

ANTIGONE:
         You're right—   620
if I mock you, I get no pleasure from it,
only pain.

ISMENE:
         Tell me, dear one,
what can I do to help you, even now?

ANTIGONE:
Save yourself. I don't grudge you your
    survival.

ISMENE:
Oh no, no, denied my portion in your
    death?   625

ANTIGONE:
You chose to live, I chose to die.

ISMENE:
                          Not, at least,
without every kind of caution I could
    voice.

ANTIGONE:
Your wisdom appealed to one
    world—mine, another.

ISMENE:
But look, we're both guilty, both
    condemned to death.

ANTIGONE:
Courage! live your life. I gave myself to
    death,   630
long ago, so I might serve the dead.

CREON:
They're both mad, I tell you, the two of
    them.
One's just shown it, the other's been that
    way
since she was born.

ISMENE:
          True, my king,
the sense we were born with cannot last
    forever . . .   635
commit cruelty on a person long enough
and the mind begins to go.

CREON:
                    Yours did,
when you chose to commit your crimes with her.

ISMENE:
How can I live alone, without her?

CREON:
                            Her?
Don't even mention her—she no longer exists.   640

ISMENE:
What? You'd kill your own son's bride?

CREON:
                             Absolutely:
there are other fields for him to plow.

ISMENE:
                        Perhaps,
but never as true, as close a bond as theirs.

CREON:
A worthless woman for my son? It repels me.

ISMENE:
Dearest Haemon, your father wrongs you so!   645

CREON:
Enough, enough—you and your talk of marriage!

ISMENE:
Creon—you're really going to rob your son of Antigone?

CREON:
Death will do it for me—break their marriage off.

LEADER:
So, it's settled then? Antigone must die?

CREON:
Settled, yes—we both know that.   650

To the guards.

Stop wasting time. Take them in.
From now on they'll act like women.
Tie them up, no more running loose;
even the bravest will cut and run,
once they see Death coming for their lives.   655

The guards escort ANTIGONE *and* ISMENE *into the palace.* CREON *remains while the old citizens form their* CHORUS.

CHORUS:
Blest, they are the truly blest who all their lives
    have never tasted devastation. For others, once
the gods have rocked a house to its foundations
    the ruin will never cease, cresting on and on
from one generation on throughout the race—   660
like a great mounting tide
driven on by savage northern gales,
    surging over the dead black depths
roiling up from the bottom dark heaves of sand
and the headlands, taking the storm's onslaught full-force,   665
roar, and the low moaning
    echoes on and on
        and now
as in ancient times I see the sorrows of the house,
the living heirs of the old ancestral kings,
piling on the sorrows of the dead
    and one generation cannot free the next—   670
some god will bring them crashing down,
the race finds no release.
And now the light, the hope
    springing up from the late last root
in the house of Oedipus, that hope's cut down in turn   675
by the long, bloody knife swung by the gods of death
by a senseless word
    by fury at the heart.
        Zeus,
yours is the power, Zeus, what man on earth
can override it, who can hold it back?
Power that neither Sleep, the all-ensnaring   680
no, nor the tireless months of heaven
can ever overmaster—young through all time,
mighty lord of power, you hold fast
    the dazzling crystal mansions of Olympus.
And throughout the future, late and soon   685
as through the past, your law prevails:

no towering form of greatness
    enters into the lives of mortals
        free and clear of ruin.
                True,
our dreams, our high hopes voyaging far and wide   690
    bring sheer delight to many, to many others
        delusion, blithe, mindless lusts
and the fraud steals on one slowly . . . unaware
till he trips and puts his foot into the fire.
    He was a wise old man who coined   695
the famous saying: "Sooner or later
foul is fair, fair is foul
to the man the gods will ruin?—
    He goes his way for a moment only
        free of blinding ruin.   700

Enter HAEMON from the palace.

    Here's Haemon now, the last of all your sons.
    Does he come in tears for his bride,
    his doomed bride, Antigone—
    bitter at being cheated of their marriage?

CREON:
We'll soon know, better than seers could tell us.   705

                Turning to HAEMON.

Son, you've heard the final verdict on your bride?
Are you coming now, raving against your father?
Or do you love me, no matter what I do?

HAEMON:
Father, I'm your *son* . . . you in your wisdom
set my bearings for me—I obey you.   710
No marriage could ever mean more to me than you,
whatever good direction you may offer.

CREON:
            Fine, Haemon.
That's how you ought to feel within your heart,
subordinate to your father's will in every way.
That's what a man prays for: to produce good sons—   715
a household full of them, dutiful and attentive,
so they can pay his enemy back with interest
and match the respect their father shows his friend.
But the man who rears a brood of useless children,
what has he brought into the world, I ask you?   720
Nothing but trouble for himself, and mockery
from his enemies laughing in his face.
                Oh Haemon,
never lose your sense of judgment over a woman.
The warmth, the rush of pleasure, it all goes cold
in your arms, I warn you . . . a worthless woman   725
in your house, a misery in your bed.
What wound cuts deeper than a loved one
turned against you? Spit her out,
like a mortal enemy—let the girl go.
Let her find a husband down among the dead.   730
Imagine it: I caught her in naked rebellion,
the traitor, the only one in the whole city.
I'm not about to prove myself a liar,
not to my people, no, I'm going to kill her!
That's right—so let her cry for mercy, sing her hymns   735
to Zeus who defends all bonds of kindred blood.
Why, if I bring up my own kin to be rebels,
think what I'd suffer from the world at large.
Show me the man who rules his household well:
I'll show you someone fit to rule the state.   740
That good man, my son,
I have every confidence he and he alone
can give commands and take them too. Staunch
in the storm of spears he'll stand his ground,
a loyal, unflinching comrade at your side.   745
But whoever steps out of line, violates the laws
or presumes to hand out orders to his superiors,
he'll win no praise from me. But that man
the city places in authority, his orders
must be obeyed, large and small,   750
right and wrong.

                    Anarchy—
show me a greater crime in all the earth!
She, she destroys cities, rips up houses,
breaks the ranks of spearmen into
     headlong rout.
But the ones who last it out, the great
     mass of them   755
owe their lives to discipline. Therefore
we must defend the men who live by law,
never let some woman triumph over us.
Better to fall from power, if fall we must,
at the hands of a man—never be rated   760
inferior to a woman, never.

LEADER:
                              To us,
unless old age has robbed us of our wits,
you seem to say what you have to say
     with sense.

HAEMON:
Father, only the gods endow a man with
     reason,
the finest of all their gifts, a treasure.   765
Far be it from me—I haven't the skill,
and certainly no desire, to tell you when,
if ever, you make a slip in speech . . .
     though
someone else might have a good
     suggestion.
Of course it's not for you,   770
in the normal run of things, to watch
whatever men say or do, or find to
     criticize.
The man in the street, you know, dreads
     your glance,
he'd never say anything displeasing to
     your face.
But it's for me to catch the murmurs in the
     dark,   775
the way the city mourns for this young
     girl.
"No woman," they say, "ever deserved
     death less,
and such a brutal death for such a
     glorious action.
She, with her own dear brother lying in
     his blood—
she couldn't bear to leave him dead,
     unburied,   780
food for the wild dogs or wheeling
     vultures.
Death? She deserves a glowing crown of
     gold!"
So they say, and the rumor spreads in
     secret,
darkly . . .
          I rejoice in your success, father—
nothing more precious to me in the world.   785
What medal of honor brighter to his
     children
than a father's growing glory? Or a child's
to his proud father? Now don't, please,
be quite so single-minded, self-involved,
or assume the world is wrong and you are
     right.   790
Whoever thinks that he alone possesses
     intelligence,
the gift of eloquence, he and no one else,
and character too . . . such men, I tell you,
spread them open—you will find them
     empty.
                              No,
it's no disgrace for a man, even a wise
     man,   795
to learn many things and not to be too
     rigid.
You've seen trees by a raging winter
     torrent,
how many sway with the flood and
     salvage every twig,
but not the stubborn—they're ripped out,
     roots and all.
Bend or break. The same when a man is
     sailing: 800
haul your sheets too taut, never give an
     inch,
you'll capsize, and go the rest of the
     voyage
keel up and the rowing-benches under.
Oh give way. Relax your anger—change!
I'm young, I know, but let me offer this: 805
it would be best by far, I admit,
if a man were born infallible, right by
     nature.
If not—and things don't often go that way,
it's best to learn from those with good
     advice.

LEADER:
You'd do well, my lord, if he's speaking
     to the point,   810
to learn from him,

Turning to HAEMON.

                    and you, my boy, from him.
You both are talking sense.

CREON:
                              So,

men our age, we're to be lectured, are we?—
schooled by a boy his age?

HAEMON:
Only in what is right. But if I seem young, 815
look less to my years and more to what I do.

CREON:
Do? Is admiring rebels an achievement?

HAEMON:
I'd never suggest that you admire treason.

CREON:
         Oh?—
isn't that just the sickness that's attacked her?

HAEMON:
The whole city of Thebes denies it, to a man. 820

CREON:
And is Thebes about to tell me how to rule?

HAEMON:
Now, you see? Who's talking like a child?

CREON:
Am I to rule this land for others—or myself?

HAEMON:
It's no city at all, owned by one man alone.

CREON:
What? The city *is* the king's—that's the law! 825

HAEMON:
What a splendid king you'd make of a desert island—
you and you alone.

CREON:

To the CHORUS.

    This boy, I do believe,
is fighting on her side, the woman's side.

HAEMON:
If you are a woman, yes—
my concern is all for you. 830

CREON:
Why, you degenerate—bandying accusations,
threatening me with justice, your own father!

HAEMON:
I see my father offending justice—wrong.

CREON:
           Wrong?
To protect my royal rights?

HAEMON:
        Protect your rights?
When you trample down the honors of the gods? 835

CREON:
You, you soul of corruption, rotten through—
woman's accomplice!

HAEMON:
         That may be,
but you will never find me accomplice to a criminal.

CREON:
That's what *she* is,
and every word you say is a blatant appeal for her— 840

HAEMON:
And you, and me, and the gods beneath the earth.

CREON:
You will never marry her, not while she's alive.

HAEMON:
Then she will die . . . but her death will kill another.

CREON:
What, brazen threats? You go too far!

HAEMON:
         What threat?
Combating your empty, mindless judgments with a word? 845

CREON:
You'll suffer for your sermons, you and
   your empty wisdom!

HAEMON:
If you weren't my father, I'd say you were
   insane.

CREON:
Don't flatter me with Father—you
   woman's slave!

HAEMON:
You really expect to fling abuse at me
and not receive the same?

CREON:
                    Is that so!   850
Now, by heaven, I promise you, you'll
   pay—
taunting, insulting me! Bring her out,
that hateful—she'll die now, here,
in front of his eyes, beside her groom!

HAEMON:
No, no, she will never die beside me—   855
don't delude yourself. And you will never
see me, never set eyes on my face again.
Rage your heart out, rage with friends
who can stand the sight of you.

Rushing out.

LEADER:
Gone, my king, in a burst of anger.   860
A temper young as his . . . hurt him once,
he may do something violent.

CREON:
                    Let him do—
dream up something desperate, past all
   human limit!
Good riddance. Rest assured,
he'll never save those two young girls
   from death.   865

LEADER:
Both of them, you really intend to kill
   them both?

CREON:
No, not her, the one whose hands are
   clean—
you're quite right.

LEADER:
                But Antigone—
what sort of death do you have in mind
   for her?

CREON:
I will take her down some wild, desolate
   path   870
never trod by men, and wall her up alive
in a rocky vault, and set out short rations,
just the measure piety demands
to keep the entire city free of defilement.
There let her pray to the one god she
   worships: 875
Death—who knows?—may just reprieve
   her from death.
Or she may learn at last, better late than
   never,
what a waste of breath it is to worship
   Death.

Exit to the palace.

CHORUS:
Love, never conquered in battle
Love the plunderer laying waste the rich!   880
Love standing the night-watch
              guarding a girl's soft cheek,
you range the seas, the shepherds'
   steadings off in the wilds—
not even the deathless gods can flee your
   onset,
nothing human born for a day—   885
whoever feels your grip is driven mad.
                        Love!—
you wrench the minds of the righteous
   into outrage,
swerve them to their ruin—you have
   ignited this,
this kindred strife, father and son at war
              and Love alone the victor—   890
warm glance of the bride triumphant,
   burning with desire!
Throned in power, side-by-side with the
   mighty laws!
Irresistible Aphrodite, never conquered—
Love, you mock us for your sport.

ANTIGONE is brought from the palace under guard.

    But now, even I would rebel against the
       king,   895
    I would break all bounds when I see
       this—

I fill with tears, I cannot hold them
   back,
  not any more . . . I see Antigone make
     her way
   to the bridal vault where all are laid to
     rest.

ANTIGONE:
Look at me, men of my fatherland,   900
setting out on the last road
looking into the last light of day
the last I will ever see . . .
the god of death who puts us all to bed
takes me down to the banks of Acheron
   alive—   905
denied my part in the wedding-songs,
no wedding-song in the dusk has
   crowned my marriage—
I go to wed the lord of the dark waters.

CHORUS:
  Not crowned with glory or with a dirge,
  you leave for the deep pit of the dead.   910
  No withering illness laid you low,
   no strokes of the sword—a law to
     yourself,
   alone, no mortal like you, ever, you go
     down
   to the halls of Death alive and
     breathing.

ANTIGONE:
But think of Niobe—well I know her
   story—   915
   think what a living death she died,
Tantalus' daughter, stranger queen from
   the east:
there on the mountain heights, growing
   stone
binding as ivy, slowly walled her round
and the rains will never cease, the legends
   say   920
the snows will never leave her . . .
   wasting away, under her brows the
     tears
showering down her breasting ridge and
   slopes—
a rocky death like hers puts me to sleep.

CHORUS:
  But she was a god, born of gods,   925
  and we are only mortals born to die.
  And yet, of course, it's a great thing
  for a dying girl to hear, even to hear
  she shares a destiny equal to the gods,
  during life and later, once she's dead.

ANTIGONE:
           O you mock me!
Why, in the name of all my fathers' gods
why can't you wait till I am gone—
   must you abuse me to my face?
O my city, all your fine rich sons!
And you, you springs of the Dirce,   935
holy grove of Thebes where the chariots
   gather,
       you at least, you'll bear me witness,
         look,
unmourned by friends and forced by such
   crude laws
I go to my rockbound prison, strange new
   tomb—
     always a stranger, O dear god,   940
   I have no home on earth and none
     below,
     not with the living, not with the
       breathless dead.

CHORUS:
  You went too far, the last limits of
     daring—
  smashing against the high throne of
     justice!
  Your life's in ruins, child—I wonder . . .   945
  do you pay for your father's terrible
     ordeal?

ANTIGONE:
There—at last you've touched it, the
   worst pain
the worst anguish! Raking up the grief for
   father
   three times over, for all the doom
that's struck us down, the brilliant house
   of Laius.   950
O mother, your marriage-bed
the coiling horrors, the coupling there—
   you with your own son, my
     father—doomstruck mother!
Such, such were my parents, and I their
   wretched child,
I go to them now, cursed, unwed, to share
   their home—   955
   I am a stranger! O dear brother, doomed
   in your marriage—your marriage
     murders mine,
     your dying drags me down to death
       alive!

Enter Creon.

CHORUS:
Reverence asks some reverence in return—
but attacks on power never go unchecked, 960
not by the man who holds the reins of power.
Your own blind will, your passion has destroyed you.

ANTIGONE:
No one to weep for me, my friends,
no wedding-song—they take me away
in all my pain . . . the road lies open, waiting. 965
Never again, the law forbids me to see
the sacred eye of day. I am agony!
No tears for the destiny that's mine,
no loved one mourns my death.

CREON:
                    Can't you see?
If a man could wail his own dirge *before* he dies, 970
he'd never finish.

To the guards.

                    Take her away, quickly!
Wall her up in the tomb, you have your orders.
Abandon her there, alone, and let her choose—
death or a buried life with a good roof for shelter.
As for myself, my hands are clean. This young girl— 975
dead or alive, she will be stripped of her rights,
her stranger's rights, here in the world above.

ANTIGONE:
O tomb, my bridal-bed—my house, my prison
cut in the hollow rock, my everlasting watch!
I'll soon be there, soon embrace my own, 980
the great growing family of our dead
Persephone has received among her ghosts.
                    I,
the last of them all, the most reviled by far,
go down before my destined time's run out.
But still I go, cherishing one good hope: 985
my arrival may be dear to father,
dear to you, my mother,
dear to you, my loving brother, Eteocles—
When you died I washed you with my hands,
I dressed you all, I poured the sacred cups 990
across your tombs. But now, Polynices,
because I laid your body out as well,
this, this is my reward. Nevertheless
I honored you—the decent will admit it—
well and wisely too.
                    Never, I tell you, 995
if I had been the mother of children
or if my husband died, exposed and rotting—
I'd never have taken this ordeal upon myself,
never defied our people's will. What law,
you ask, do I satisfy with what I say? 1000
A husband dead, there might have been another.
A child by another too, if I had lost the first.
But mother and father both lost in the halls of Death,
no brother could ever spring to light again.
For this law alone I held you first in honor. 1005
For this, Creon, the king, judges me a criminal
guilty of dreadful outrage, my dear brother!
And now he leads me off, a captive in his hands,
with no part in the bridal-song, the bridal-bed,
denied all joy of marriage, raising children— 1010
deserted so by loved ones, struck by fate,
I descend alive to the caverns of the dead.
What law of the mighty gods have I transgressed?
Why look to the heavens any more, tormented as I am?
Whom to call, what comrades now? Just think, 1015
my reverence only brands me for irreverence!
Very well: if this is the pleasure of the gods,
once I suffer I will know that I was wrong.
But if these men are wrong, let them suffer
nothing worse than they mete out to me— 1020
these masters of injustice!

LEADER:
Still the same rough winds, the wild
   passion
raging through the girl.

CREON:

                   To the guards.

    Take her away.
You're wasting time—you'll pay for it too.

ANTIGONE:
Oh god, the voice of death. It's come, it's
   here.   1025

CREON:
True. Not a word of hope—your doom is
   sealed.

ANTIGONE:
   Land of Thebes, city of all my fathers—
   O you gods, the first gods of the race!
   They drag me away, now, no more
      delay.
   Look on me, you noble sons of Thebes— 1030
   the last of a great line of kings,
   I alone, see what I suffer now
   at the hands of what breed of men—
   all for reverence, my reverence for the
      gods!

   She leaves under guard: the CHORUS gathers.

CHORUS:
      Danaë, Danaë—   1035
even she endured a fate like yours,
   in all her lovely strength she traded
the light of day for the bolted brazen
      vault—
buried within her tomb, her
   bridal-chamber,
wed to the yoke and broken.   1040
      But she was of glorious birth
         my child, my child
and treasured the seed of Zeus within her
   womb,
the cloudburst streaming gold!
     The power of fate is a wonder,   1045
      dark, terrible wonder—
   neither wealth nor armies
     towered walls nor ships
      black hulls lashed by the salt
      can save us from that force.   1050
The yoke tamed him too

young Lycurgus flaming in anger
king of Edonia, all for his mad taunts
Dionysus clamped him down, encased
in the chain-mail of rock   1055
   and there his rage
       his terrible flowering rage burst—
sobbing, dying away . . . at last that
   madman
came to know his god—
   the power he mocked, the power   1060
   he taunted in all his frenzy
   trying to stamp out
   the women strong with the god—
   the torch, the raving sacred cries—
   enraging the Muses who adore the flute. 1065
And far north where the Black Rocks
   cut the sea in half
and murderous straits
split the coast of Thrace
   a forbidding city stands   1070
where once, hard by the walls
the savage Ares thrilled to watch
a king's new queen, a Fury rearing in rage
   against his two royal sons—
     her bloody hands, her dagger-shuttle 1075
stabbing out their eyes—cursed, blinding
   wounds—
their eyes blind sockets screaming for
   revenge!
They wailed in agony, cries echoing cries
   the princes doomed at birth . . .
and their mother doomed to chains,   1080
walled up in a tomb of stone—
   but she traced her own birth back
to a proud Athenian line and the high
   gods
and off in caverns half the world away,
born of the wild North Wind   1085
   she sprang on her father's gales,
     racing stallions up the leaping cliffs—
child of the heavens. But even on her the
   Fates
the gray everlasting Fates rode hard
my child, my child.
   Enter TIRESIAS, the blind prophet, led by a boy.

TIRESIAS:
      Lords of Thebes,   1090
I and the boy have come together,
hand in hand. Two see with the eyes of
   one . . .
so the blind must go, with a guide to lead
   the way.

CREON:
What is it, old Tiresias? What news now?

TIRESIAS:
I will teach you. And you obey the seer.

CREON:
                                    I will, 1095
I've never wavered from your advice
   before.

TIRESIAS:
And so you kept the city straight on
   course.

CREON:
I owe you a great deal, I swear to that.

TIRESIAS:
Then reflect, my son: you are poised,
once more, on the razor-edge of fate. 1100

CREON:
What is it? I shudder to hear you.

TIRESIAS:
                        You will learn
when you listen to the warnings of my
   craft.
As I sat on the ancient seat of augury,
in the sanctuary where every bird I know
will hover at my hands—suddenly I heard
   it, 1105
a strange voice in the wingbeats,
   unintelligible,
barbaric, a mad scream! Talons flashing,
   ripping,
they were killing each other—that much I
   knew—
the murderous fury whirring in those
   wings
made that much clear!
                          I was afraid, 1110
I turned quickly, tested the burnt-sacrifice,
ignited the altar at all points—but no fire,
the god in the fire never blazed.
Not from those offerings . . . over the
   embers
slid a heavy ooze from the long
   thighbones, 1115
smoking, sputtering out, and the bladder
puffed and burst—spraying gall into the
   air—
and the fat wrapping the bones slithered
   off
and left them glistening white. No fire!
The rites failed that might have blazed the
   future 1120
with a sign. So I learned from the boy
   here:
he is my guide, as I am guide to others.
                           And it is you—
your high resolve that sets this plague on
   Thebes.
The public altars and sacred hearths are
   fouled,
one and all, by the birds and dogs with
   carrion 1125
torn from the corpse, the doomstruck son
   of Oedipus!
And so the gods are deaf to our prayers,
   they spurn
the offerings in our hands, the flame of
   holy flesh.
No birds cry out an omen clear and true—
they're gorged with the murdered
   victim's blood and fat. 1130
Take these things to heart, my son, I warn
   you.
All men make mistakes, it is only human.
But once the wrong is done, a man
can turn his back on folly, misfortune too,
if he tries to make amends, however low
   he's fallen, 1135
and stops his bullnecked ways.
   Stubbornness
brands you for stupidity—pride is a crime.
No, yield to the dead!
Never stab the fighter when he's down.
Where's the glory, killing the dead twice
   over? 1140
I mean you well. I give you sound advice.
It's best to learn from a good adviser
when he speaks for your own good:
it's pure gain.

CREON:
                Old man—all of you! So,
you shoot your arrows at my head like
   archers at the target—
I even have *him* loosed on me, this
   fortune-teller.
Oh his ilk has tried to sell me short
and ship me off for years. Well,
drive your bargains, traffic—much as you
   like—
in the gold of India, silver-gold of Sardis. 1150
You'll never bury that body in the grave,
not even if Zeus's eagles rip the corpse
and wing their rotten pickings off to the
   throne of god!
Never, not even in fear of such defilement
will I tolerate his burial, that traitor. 1155
Well I know, we can't defile the gods—

no mortal has the power.
                    No,
reverend old Tiresias, all men fall,
it's only human, but the wisest fall obscenely
when they glorify obscene advice with rhetoric— 1160
all for their own gain.

TIRESIAS:
Oh god, is there a man alive
who knows, who actually believes . . .

CREON:
                    What now?
What earth-shattering truth are you about to utter?

TIRESIAS:
. . . just how much a sense of judgment, wisdom 1165
is the greatest gift we have?

CREON:
          Just as much, I'd say,
as a twisted mind is the worst affliction known.

TIRESIAS:
You are the one who's sick, Creon, sick to death.

CREON:
I am in no mood to trade insults with a seer.

TIRESIAS:
You have already, calling my prophecies a lie.

CREON:
    Why not? 1170
You and the whole breed of seers are mad for money!

TIRESIAS:
And the whole race of tyrants lusts for filthy gain.

CREON:
This slander of yours—
are you aware you're speaking to the king?

TIRESIAS:
Well aware. Who helped you save the city?

CREON:
          You—T 1175
you have your skills, old seer, but you lust for injustice!

TIRESIAS:
You will drive me to utter the dreadful secret in my heart.

CREON:
Spit it out! Just don't speak it out for profit.

TIRESIAS:
Profit? No, not a bit of profit, not for you.

CREON:
Know full well, you'll never buy off my resolve. 1180

TIRESIAS:
Then know this too, learn this by heart!
The chariot of the sun will not race through
so many circuits more, before you have surrendered,
one born of your own loins, your own flesh and blood,
a corpse for corpses given in return, since you have thrust 1185
to the world below a child sprung for the world above,
ruthlessly lodged a living soul within the grave—
then you've robbed the gods below the earth,
keeping a dead body here in the bright air,
unburied, unsung, unhallowed by the rites. 1190
You, you have no business with the dead,
nor do the gods above—this is violence
you have forced upon the heavens.
And so the avengers, the dark destroyers late
but true to the mark, now lie in wait for you, 1195
the Furies sent by the gods and the god of death
to strike you down with the pains that you perfected!
There. Reflect on that, tell me I've been bribed.
The day comes soon, no long test of time, not now,
when the mourning cries for men and women break 1200

throughout your halls. Great hatred rises
  against you—
cities in tumult, all whose mutilated sons
the dogs have graced with burial, or the
  wild beasts
or a wheeling crow that wings the
  ungodly stench of carrion
back to each city, each warrior's hearth
  and home.   1205
These arrows for your heart! Since you've
  raked me
I loose them like an archer in my anger,
arrows deadly true. You'll never escape
their burning, searing force.

                    Motioning to his escort.

Come, boy, take me home.   1210
So he can vent his rage on younger men,
and learn to keep a gentler tongue in his
  head
and better sense than what he carries now.

                         Exit to the side.

LEADER:
The old man's gone, my king—
terrible prophecies. Well I know,   1215
since the hair on this old head went gray,
he's never lied to Thebes.

CREON:
I know it myself—I'm shaken, torn.
It's a dreadful thing to yield . . . but resist
  now?
Lay my pride bare to the blows of ruin?   1220
That's dreadful too.

LEADER:
             But good advice,
Creon, take it now, you must.

CREON:
What should I do? Tell me . . . I'll obey.

LEADER:
Go! Free the girl from the rocky vault
and raise a mound for the body you
  exposed.   1225

CREON:
That's your advice? You think I should
  give in?

LEADER:
Yes, my king, quickly. Disasters sent by
  the gods
cut short our follies in a flash;

CREON:
                         Oh it's hard,
giving up the heart's desire . . . but I will
  do it—
no more fighting a losing battle with
  necessity.   1230

LEADER:
Do it now, go, don't leave it to others.

CREON:
Now—I'm on my way! Come, each of you,
take up axes, make for the high ground,
over there, quickly! I and my better
  judgment
have come round to this—I shackled her,   1235
I'll set her free myself. I am afraid . . .
it's best to keep the established laws
to the very day we die.

Rushing out, followed by his entourage. The CHORUS clusters around the altar.

CHORUS:
God of a hundred names!
                    Great Dionysus—
  Son and glory of Semele! Pride of
                    Thebes—T1240
Child of Zeus whose thunder rocks the
  clouds—
Lord of the famous lands of evening—
King of the Mysteries!
         King of Eleusis, Demeter's plain
her breasting hills that welcome in the
  world—
Great Dionysus!
             Bacchus, living in Thebes   1245
the mother-city of all your frenzied
  women—
                    Bacchus
  living along the Ismenus' rippling
    waters
standing over the field sown with the
  Dragon's teeth!
You—we have seen you through the
  flaring smoky fires,
  your torches blazing over the twin
    peaks   1250
where nymphs of the hallowed cave climb
  onward

fired with you, your sacred rage—
we have seen you at Castalia's running spring
and down from the heights of Nysa crowned with ivy
the greening shore rioting vines and grapes   1255
    down you come in your storm of wild women
        ecstatic, mystic cries—
            Dionysus—
down to watch and ward the roads of Thebes!
First of all cities, Thebes you honor first
you and your mother, bride of the lightning—   1260
come, Dionysus! now your people lie
in the iron grip of plague,
come in your racing, healing stride
        down Parnassus' slopes
or across the moaning straits.
            Lord of the dancing—   1265
dance, dance the constellations breathing fire!
Great master of the voices of the night!
Child of Zeus, God's offspring, come, come forth!
Lord, king, dance with your nymphs, swirling, raving
arm-in-arm in frenzy through the night   1270
    they dance you, Iacchus—
        Dance, Dionysus
giver of all good things!

Enter a MESSENGER from the side.

MESSENGER:
            Neighbors,
friends of the house of Cadmus and the kings,
there's not a thing in this mortal life of ours
I'd praise or blame as settled once for all.   1275
Fortune lifts and Fortune fells the lucky
and unlucky every day. No prophet on earth
can tell a man his fate. Take Creon:
there was a man to rouse your envy once,
as I see it. He saved the realm from enemies,   1280
taking power, he alone, the lord of the fatherland,
he set us true on course—he flourished like a tree
with the noble line of sons he bred and reared . . .
and now it's lost, all gone.
            Believe me,
when a man has squandered his true joys,   1285
he's good as dead, I tell you, a living corpse.
Pile up riches in your house, as much as you like—
live like a king with a huge show of pomp,
but if real delight is missing from the lot,
I wouldn't give you a wisp of smoke for it,   1290
not compared with joy.

LEADER:
            What now?
What new grief do you bring the house of kings?

MESSENGER:
Dead, dead—and the living are guilty of their death!

LEADER:
Who's the murderer? Who is dead? Tell us.

MESSENGER:
Haemon's gone, his blood spilled by the very hand—   1295

LEADER:
His father's or his own?

MESSENGER:
            His own . . .
raging mad with his father for the death—

LEADER:
Oh great seer,
you saw it all, you brought your word to birth!

MESSENGER:
Those are the facts. Deal with them as you will.

As he turns to go, EURYDICE enters from the palace.

LEADER:
Look, Eurydice. Poor woman, Creon's wife,   1300
so close at hand. By chance perhaps,
unless she's heard the news about her son.

EURYDICE:
            My countrymen,

All of you—I caught the sound of your words
as I was leaving to do my part,
to appeal to queen Athena with my prayers. 1305
I was just loosing the bolts, opening the doors,
when a voice filled with sorrow, family sorrow,
struck my ears, and I fell back, terrified,
into the women's arms—everything went black.
Tell me the news, again, whatever it is . . . 1310
sorrow and I are hardly strangers.
I can bear the worst.

MESSENGER:
                     I—dear lady,
I'll speak as an eye-witness. I was there.
And I won't pass over one word of the truth.
Why should I try to soothe you with a story, 1315
only to prove a liar in a moment?
Truth is always best.
         So,
I escorted your lord, I guided him
to the edge of the plain where the body lay,
Polynices, torn by the dogs and still unmourned. 1320
And saying a prayer to Hecate of the Crossroads,
Pluto too, to hold their anger and be kind,
we washed the dead in a bath of holy water
and plucking some fresh branches, gathering . . .
what was left of him, we burned them all together 1325
and raised a high mound of native earth, and then
we turned and made for that rocky vault of hers,
the hollow, empty bed of the bride of Death.
And far off, one of us heard a voice,
a long wail rising, echoing 1330
out of that unhallowed wedding-chamber,
he ran to alert the master and Creon pressed on,
closer—the strange, inscrutable cry came sharper,
throbbing around him now, and he let loose
a cry of his own, enough to wrench the heart, 1335
"Oh god, am I the prophet now? going down
the darkest road I've ever gone? My son—
it's *his* dear voice, he greets me! Go, men,
closer, quickly! Go through the gap,
the rocks are dragged back— 1340
right to the tomb's very mouth—and look,
see if it's Haemon's voice I think I hear,
or the gods have robbed me of my senses."
The king was shattered. We took his orders,
went and searched, and there in the deepest, 1345
dark recesses of the tomb we found her . . .
hanged by the neck in a fine linen noose,
strangled in her veils—and the boy,
his arms flung around her waist,
clinging to her, wailing for his bride, 1350
dead and down below, for his father's crimes
and the bed of his marriage blighted by misfortune.
When Creon saw him, he gave a deep sob,
he ran in, shouting, crying out to him,
"Oh my child—what have you done? what seized you, 1355
what insanity? what disaster drove you mad?
Come out, my son! I beg you on my knees!"
But the boy gave him a wild burning glance,
spat in his face, not a word in reply,
he drew his sword—his father rushed out, 1360
running as Haemon lunged and missed!—
and then, doomed, desperate with himself,
suddenly leaning his full weight on the blade,
he buried it in his body, halfway to the hilt.
And still in his senses, pouring his arms around her, 1365
he embraced the girl and breathing hard,
released a quick rush of blood,
bright red on her cheek glistening white.
And there he lies, body enfolding body . . .
he has won his bride at last, poor boy, 1370
not here but in the houses of the dead.
Creon shows the world that of all the ills
afflicting men the worst is lack of judgment.

EURYDICE turns and reenters the palace.

LEADER:
What do you make of that? The lady's gone,
without a word, good or bad.

MESSENGER:
              I'm alarmed too   1375
but here's my hope—faced with her son's death
she finds it unbecoming to mourn in public.
Inside, under her roof, she'll set her women
to the task and wail the sorrow of the house.
She's too discreet. She won't do something rash.   1380

LEADER:
I'm not so sure. To me, at least,
a long heavy silence promises danger,
just as much as a lot of empty outcries.

MESSENGER:
We'll see if she's holding something back,
hiding some passion in her heart.   1385
I'm going in. You may be right—who knows?
Even too much silence has its dangers.

Exit to the palace. Enter CREON from the side, escorted by attendants carrying HAEMON's body on a bier.

LEADER:
  The king himself! Coming toward us,
  look, holding the boy's head in his hands.
  Clear, damning proof, if it's right to say so—   1390
    proof of his own madness, no one else's,
    no, his own blind wrongs.

CREON:
              Ohhh,
so senseless, so insane . . . my crimes,
my stubborn, deadly—
Look at us, the killer, the killed,   1395
father and son, the same blood—the misery!
My plans, my mad fanatic heart,
my son, cut off so young!
Ai, dead, lost to the world,
not through your stupidity, no, my own.

LEADER:
              Too late,   1400
too late, you see what justice means.

CREON:
              Oh I've learned
  through blood and tears! Then, it was then,
  when the god came down and struck me—a great weight
  shattering, driving me down that wild savage path,
  ruining, trampling down my joy. Oh the agony,   1405
    the heartbreaking agonies of our lives.

Enter the MESSENGER from the palace.

MESSENGER:
              Master,
what a hoard of grief you have, and you'll have more.
The grief that lies to hand you've brought yourself—

Pointing to HAEMON's body.

the rest, in the house, you'll see it all too soon.

CREON:
What now? What's worse than this?

MESSENGER:
              The queen is dead.   1410
The mother of this dead boy . . . mother to the end—
poor thing, her wounds are fresh.

CREON:
              No, no,
harbor of Death, so choked, so hard to cleanse!—
why me? why are you killing me?
Herald of pain, more words, more grief?   1415
I died once, you kill me again and again!
What's the report, boy . . . some news for me?
My wife dead? O dear god!
Slaughter heaped on slaughter?

The doors open; the body of EURYDICE is brought out on her bier.

MESSENGER:
                    See for yourself:
now they bring her body from the palace.

CREON:
                            Oh no,   1420
    another, a second loss to break the
        heart.
    What next, what fate still waits for me?
    I just held my son in my arms and now,
    look, a new corpse rising before my
        eyes—
        wretched, helpless mother—O my son! 1425

MESSENGER:
She stabbed herself at the altar,
then her eyes went dark, after she'd raised
a cry for the noble fate of Megareus, the
    hero
killed in the first assault, then for Haemon,
then with her dying breath she called
    down   1430
torments on your head—you killed her
    sons.

CREON:
                        Oh the dread,
    I shudder with dread! Why not kill me
        too?—
    run me through with a good sharp
        sword?
    Oh god, the misery, anguish—
    I, I'm churning with it, going under.   1435

MESSENGER:
Yes, and the dead, the woman lying there,
piles the guilt of all their deaths on you.

CREON:
How did she end her life, what bloody
    stroke?

MESSENGER:
She drove home to the heart with her own
    hand,
once she learned her son was dead . . .
    that agony.   1440

CREON:
    And the guilt is all mine—
    can never be fixed on another man,
    no escape for me. I killed you,
    I, god help me, I admit it all!

To his attendants.

Take me away, quickly, out of sight.   1445
I don't even exist—I'm no one. Nothing.

LEADER:
Good advice, if there's any good in
    suffering.
Quickest is best when troubles block the
    way.

CREON:

Kneeling in prayer.

Come, let it come!—that best of fates
    for me
that brings the final day, best fate of all. 1450
Oh quickly, now—
so I never have to see another sunrise.

LEADER:
That will come when it come,
we must deal with all that lies before us.
The future rests with the ones who tend
    the future.   1455

CREON:
That prayer—I poured my heart into that
    prayer!

LEADER:
No more prayers now. For mortal men
there is no escape from the doom we must
    endure.

CREON:
    Take me away, I beg you, out of sight.
    A rash, indiscriminate fool!   1460
    I murdered you, my son, against my
        will—
    you too, my wife . . .
                    Wailing wreck of a man,
    whom to look to? where to lean for
        support?

Desperately turning from HAEMON to EURYDICE on their biers.

    Whatever I touch goes wrong—once
        more
    a crushing fate's come down upon my
        head!   1465

The MESSENGER and attendants lead CREON into the palace.

CHORUS:
Wisdom is by far the greatest part of joy,
and reverence toward the gods must be
 safeguarded.
The mighty words of the proud are paid
 in full
with mighty blows of fate, and at long last
those blows will teach us wisdom. 1470

The old citizens exit to the side.

Greek Theater at Dodona. Greek theaters were quite large, seating up to 15,000 people. Performances could go on all day for several days, including festive processions in which the audience would take part. The majestic settings for these open-air theaters provided a special grandeur for the plays themselves. Roger Wood/© Corbis.

Study Guide for Sophocles' *Antigone*

—*R.M.B.*

This guide is keyed to the translation by Robert Fagles (Penguin Press).

Setting

The drama begins at dawn, after a night in which there has been a war in Thebes between armies led by the two sons of Oedipus. Keep in mind that the Greek theater was in the open air, and that the first performances of the day would begin at daybreak. Thus, imagine that the time of day of the setting would be identical to the performance time.

Polynices, the elder son of Oedipus, had been expelled from Thebes by his brother Eteocles. As with the fraternal rivalries in *Genesis*, the first-born son believes he has the right to rule. He returned to Thebes with an army from Argos after having married the daughter of that city's king. He desired not just victory, but the destruction of his homeland.

1–116

As you read the first scene, consider the gravity of the city's condition and how aware Antigone seems of it. Throughout the play, Antigone and Creon will talk much about friends and enemies. Think about what each means by these terms. In general, Antigone and Creon tend to use the same words but mean different things by them. For example, consider Antigone's reference to being a "traitor" (57). This is a political term; does Antigone mean a traitor to the city, or to something else? Compare with Creon at 580.

Why does Antigone assume that Creon's order is directed against her and Ismene? When Creon appears later, consider whether his conduct and language in fact support her assumption.

Do you sympathize at all with Ismene's caution? Does Antigone treat her fairly?

Why is Antigone so concerned with glory (113)? Should she be? Think about what Pericles said about glory and women.

How old do you think Antigone is?

117–78

After the initial dialogue the Chorus emerges for their first choral ode (stasimon), which concerns the previous night's battle. Contrast the picture of Polynices drawn there with Antigone's earlier discussion of her brother; does your opinion of him, and of Antigone's position, change at all? The chorus evokes Dionysus (171), the first of several times this god is mentioned. Why should the chorus call upon Dionysus?

179–376

Creon enters. It is very important that you do not project Creon's later conduct back into his first speech. Read this speech carefully, consider his values and beliefs, and ask yourself whether there is anything wrong with his principles, whether in Greek terms or your own. Later, compare Creon's subsequent actions with the principles he articulates here. Throughout this scene, pay close attention to the assumptions Creon makes about gender.

When Creon talks about the gods and the law (317ff), is he talking about the same types of gods as Antigone does? The Greeks distinguished between the Olympian gods and the chthonic gods (chthonic means "of the earth"). The chthonic gods oversaw the most basic and earliest customs such as blood ties and burial rites.

How would you compare Creon's speech with Pericles' Funeral Oration? Do Creon's ideas resemble Pericles? (And is Antigone more like her father or Sappho?)

377–416

Second stasimon, perhaps the most famous choral ode in Greek tragedy. What image of man does this ode present? In this vision, what is human greatness? What are the limits of human ability and action? When can a daring man get into trouble? Choral odes often generalize a given problem specific to the play's action into a statement about human life as a whole. Is that the case here? If so, then is the chorus alluding to Antigone, or to Creon, or to both?

417–655

Why is Creon so surprised when the Sentry brings in Antigone? Antigone is compared to a mother bird (471ff), not the last time she is referred to as maternal in this play. Is there anything strange or ironic about Antigone being represented as a mother?

Antigone's defense to Creon (499–524) is very important, so read it carefully.

Ismene defends Antigone and asks Creon how he could kill his own son's bride (641). Has there been any reference to this relationship before? Antigone is engaged to Creon's son. Why doesn't she ever mention him? Note that Sophocles was limited to three actors, so practical considerations could rule out Haemon appearing here; Haemon and Antigone were likely played by the same actor.

656–700

Contrast this stasimon with the previous one. Is this ode's thought and tone similar or different? What, if anything, has changed?

701–878

Compare the Creon in this scene with the one who first entered the play. Has he changed at all in language or conduct? To what does Haemon appeal in his attempt to save Antigone?

Does Haemon threaten his father, as Creon thinks (842)?

Why does Creon choose the particular method of execution that he does (870–8)? What does it say about him?

879–94

The ancient Greeks had two words for "love"; *philia*, meaning something like "friendship," and *eros*, which has more to do with passion. When the chorus talks about "love" in the ode, which of the two do they mean? And why is the chorus generalizing about love here?

895–1034

Note the chorus' reference to Antigone's "bridal vault" (899). What do they mean by referring to a wedding chamber? This will be an important image in the last part of the play. Antigone becomes a "Bride of Death" (or "Bride of Hades"). This alludes to the myth of Demeter and Persephone. Persephone was taken by Hades to be his bride, and her mother Demeter, the harvest goddess, withdrew the earth's fertility to punish the Olympians for their treachery. Ultimately a deal was struck to allow Persephone to spend part of the year on earth, and part in the underworld, which the Greeks used to explain the change of the seasons. Any girl who died unmarried was thought to have "married death."

Strangely, the maternal imagery as well continues with Antigone, as she tries to compare herself with Niobe (915), another "grieving mother" figure, whose children were killed by Apollo and Artemis. Can she represent both the grieving mother and the lost daughter?

How would you characterize the chorus' exchange with Antigone here?

Consider Antigone's speech which begins at line 978. Is this speech consistent with what she has argued before? Does her logic remind you at all of Creon at any point in the drama?

Is Antigone's faith in the gods wavering here?

1035–89

Consider what these myths have in common with each other, and with the story of the play at this point.

1090–1237

What does the failure of Tiresias' sacrifice have to do with Polynices and Antigone? What, specifically, in Tiresias' warnings leads Creon to change his mind?

1238–72

Why does the chorus call on Dionysus in this ode?

1273–End

Why does Antigone choose to commit suicide? Does it suggest her mother's death, or is there an important difference?

Creon's wife is only on stage momentarily, yet she plays a key role in Creon's disaster. What does her suicide mean to him?

Is Creon a tragic figure? Do you feel sympathy for him at the end as someone who initially tried to do good yet was overwhelmed by circumstance, or do you believe that he is a bullying, misogynistic control-freak who gets what he deserves? Try to come up with arguments for both sides. Could the play have been called Creon, instead?

Conversely, what, specifically, makes Antigone a tragic figure? Think about what, exactly, you mean by such words as "tragedy" and "tragic."

Finally, if Antigone is right, why do the gods not save her? If Creon is wrong, is Antigone necessarily right?

A Brief Biography of Plato (circa 428–c. 347 BCE)

Plato was born an aristocrat. His father, who was named Ariston, may well have been a descendent of the early kings of Athens. His mother was related to Solon, the famous 6th century BCE lawmaker. Plato's father died when he was young, and his mother married Pyrilampes an associate of Pericles, the leading statesman of Athens.

Fitting his class heritage, Plato had political ambitions as a young man. However, he became disillusioned by the politics of Athens, and especially its political leaders. He became a disciple of Socrates, adopting his pursuit of truth through asking questions in the dialectical fashion. The death sentence delivered upon Socrates by democratic Athens sent Plato into exile in 399 BCE.

Plato began the Academy (we still have that name for institutions of higher learning) in 387 BCE. In the Academy, students learned astronomy, physical science, mathematics, political theory, and philosophy. Its most famous student was the philosopher Aristotle.

At one point Plato attempted to influence an actual ruler to model himself after the philosopher king, described in the *Republic*. In 367 BCE, Plato traveled to Sicily to tutor Dionysus the Younger, the new ruler of Syracuse. Plato, unfortunately, had little success in marrying philosophy to politics directly.

Plato spent his last days lecturing and writing. He died near the age of 80 in Athens.

During his lifetime Plato wrote many dialogues, of which the *Republic* is only the best known. His dialogues explore such topics as education, the law, the qualities of the statesman, the nature of rhetoric, love, piety, friendship, and, always, the nature and forms of knowledge. The central character in many of these dialogues is his beloved teacher, Socrates.

Alfred North Whitehead, a noted philosopher of the 20th century, commented that the history of philosophy was simply "a series of footnotes to Plato." The Academy continued in existence until 529 CE, almost nine hundred years. Plato's influence can be seen most dramatically in the thinking of early Christian theologians, and also in the thinking of Jewish and Muslim thinkers of the medieval period. His writings remain a precious legacy for all who love to think about the subjects that matter most.

Bust of Plato. Some depictions of Plato are grand and almost mythic; this one presents a man with a strong face and rough features. Plato was the son of an aristocratic family. However, he did not lead a pampered life. Tradition says he excelled as a wrestler, which would be appropriate for a man who fought so many tangled intellectual battles in his writings. Gianni Dagli Orti/© Corbis.

Outline for Plato's *Republic*

Part I. Some Current Views of Justice

1. Cephalus. Justice as Honesty in Word and Deed (327a–331d)
2. Polemarchus. Justice as Helping Friends and Harming Enemies (331e–336a)
3. Thrasymachus. Justice as the Interest of the Stronger (336b–347e)
4. Thrasymachus. Is Injustice More Profitable than Justice? (347e–354c)

Part II. Justice in the State and in the Individual

5. The Problem Stated (357a–367e)
6. The Rudiments of Social Organization (367e–372a)
7. The Luxurious State (372a–375a)
8. The Guardian's Temperament (375a–376d)
   Primary Education of the Guardians
9. Censorship of Literature for School Use (376d–392c)
10. The Influence of Dramatic Recitation (392c–398b)
11. Musical Accompaniment and Meter (398c–400c)
12. The Aim of Education in Poetry and Music (400c–403c)
13. Physical Training. Physicians and Judges (403c–412b)
14. Selection of Rulers: The Guardian's Manner of Living (412b–421c)
15. The Guardian's Duties (421c–427c)
16. The Virtues in the State (427d–434d)
17. The Three Parts of the Soul (434d–441c)
18. The Virtues in the Individual (441c–445b)

Part II. (Appendix) The Position of Women and the Usages of War

19. The Equality of Women (445b–457b)
20. Abolition of the Family for the Guardians (457b–466d)
21. Usages of War (466d–471c)

Part III. The Philosopher King

22. The Paradox: Philosophers Must Be Kings (471c–474b)
23. Definition of the Philosopher. The Two Worlds (474b–480a)
24. The Philosopher's Fitness to Rule (484a–487a)
25. Why the Philosophic Nature Is Useless or Corrupted in Existing Society (487b–497a)
26. A Philosophic Ruler Is Not an Impossibility (497a–502c)
27. The Good as the Highest Object of Knowledge (502c–509c)
28. Four Stages of Cognition. The Line (509d–511e)
29. The Allegory of the Cave (514a–521b)
30. Higher Education (521c–531c)

31. Dialectic (531c–535a)
32. Programme of Study (535a–541b)

Part IV. The Decline of Society and of the Soul. Comparison of the Just and Unjust Lives

33. The Fall of the Ideal State. Timocracy and the Timocratic Man (543a–550c)
34. Oligarchy (Plutocracy) and the Oligarchic Man (550c–555b)
35. Democracy and the Democratic Man (555b–562a)
36. Despotism and the Despotic Man (562a–576b)
37. The Just and Unjust Lives Compared in Respect of Happiness (576b–588a)
38. Justice, Not Injustice, Is Profitable (588b–592b)

Part V. The Quarrel Between Philosophy and Poetry

39. How Representation in Art Is Related to Truth (595a–602b)
40. Dramatic Poetry Appeals to the Emotions, Not to the Reason (602c–605c)
41. The Effect of Dramatic Poetry on Character (605c–608b)

Part VI. Immortality and the Rewards of Justice

42. A Proof of Immortality (608c–612a)
43. The Rewards of Justice in this Life (612a–613e)
44. The Rewards of Justice after Death. The Myth of Er (613e–621d)

The Republic*

Plato
—Comments by E.N.

> **327a–328d The setting and dramatis personae of the dialogue**
> Note that Adeimantus and Glaucon are Plato's brothers, and that Thrasymachus expresses views generally associated with the Sophists.

I went down to the Piraeus yesterday with Glaucon, the son of Ariston. I wanted to say a prayer to the goddess,** and I was also curious to see how they would manage the festival, since they were holding it for the first time. I thought the procession of the local residents was a fine one and that the one conducted by the Thracians was no less outstanding. After we had said our prayer and seen the procession, we started back towards Athens. Polemarchus saw us from a distance as we were setting off for home and told his slave to run and ask us to wait for him. The slave caught hold of my cloak from behind: Polemarchus wants you to wait, he said. I turned around and asked where Polemarchus was. He's coming up behind you, he said, please wait for him. And Glaucon replied: All right, we will.

Just then Polemarchus caught up with us. Adeimantus, Glaucon's brother,*** was with him and so were Niceratus, the son of Nicias, and some others, all of whom were apparently on their way from the procession.

Polemarchus said: It looks to me, Socrates, as if you two are starting off for Athens.

It looks the way it is, then, I said.
Do you see how many we are? he said.
S. I do.
P. Well, you must either prove stronger than we are, or you will have to stay here.
S. Isn't there another alternative, namely, that we persuade you to let us go?
P. But could you persuade us, if we won't listen?
Certainly not, Glaucon said.
P. Well, we won't listen; you'd better make up your mind to that.
Don't you know, Adeimantus said, that there is to be a torch race on horseback for the goddess tonight?
On horseback? I said. That's something new. Are they going to race on horseback and hand the torches on in relays, or what?
In relays, Polemarchus said, and there will be an all-night festival that will be well worth seeing. After dinner, we'll go out to look at it. We'll be joined there by many of the young men, and we'll talk. So don't go; stay.
It seems, Glaucon said, that we'll have to stay.
If you think so, I said, then we must.
So we went to Polemarchus' house, and there we found Lysias and Euthydemus, the brothers of Polemarchus, Thrasymachus of Chalcedon, Charmantides of Paiania, and Cleitophon the son of Aristonymus.**** Polemarchus' father, Cephalus, was also there, and I thought he looked quite old, as I hadn't

---

Reprinted from *The Republic by Plato*, translated by G.M.A. Grube, revised by C.D.C. Reeve, by permission of Hackett Publishing. Copyright © 1992 by Hackett Publishing. All rights reserved.

* Note the traditional Greek title, *Politeia* (=The Polity/The Organization of the City), and subtitle, *Peri Dikaion, Politikos* (= Of the Just/On Justice, Political Dialogue).
** The Thracian goddess Bendis, whose cult had recently been introduced in the Piraeus, the harbor area near Athens.
*** Glaucon and Adeimantus were Plato's brothers. They are Socrates' chief interlocutors after Book I.
**** Lysias was a well-known writer of speeches for use in legal trials. Socrates discusses a speech attributed to him in the *Phaedrus*. Thrasymachus was a sophist, a paid teacher of oratory and virtue. The few fragments

seen him for some time. He was sitting on a sort of cushioned chair with a wreath on his head, as he had been offering a sacrifice in the courtyard. There was a circle of chairs, and we sat down by him.

As soon as he saw me, Cephalus welcomed me and said: Socrates, you don't come down to the Piraeus to see us as often as you should. If it were still easy for me to walk to town, you wouldn't have to come here; we'd come to you. But, as it is, you ought to come here more often. Or you should know that as the physical pleasures wither away, my desire for conversation and its pleasures grows. So do as I say: Stay with these young men now, but come regularly to see us, just as you would to friends or relatives.

...

331b–332c (A fine sentiment, Cephalus ... giving him what is owed to him), 334b–336b (I don't know any more what I did mean ... as if to tear us to pieces)

These selections provide:

(i) The main question posed: What is Justice?

Socrates appears to be searching for an essential definition of justice, rather than for some partial or fragmentary understanding of it (the possibility of Justice having a form is thus assumed from the outset.)

(ii) A brief discussion of the concept of *arete*

(*Arete* is usually translated as "virtue," sometimes as "excellence."). The *arete* of something is related to its function: it is that aspect of a thing that enables it to perform its function excellently.

(iii) A good example of the Socratic "dialectic" (or the so-called maieutic method)

Repeatedly, a definition is put forward by an interlocutor, criticized by Socrates, then amended by the interlocutor, in what seems to be an attempt by Socrates to draw step by step the essential knowledge of the thing discussed from the interlocutor.

However, Socrates' attempt is here abortive; Thrasymachus, then Glaucon, interrupt the process to proffer a defence of injustice, after which Socrates switches to, on the whole, an exposition of the definition of justice and of the implications of this definition. Thus, if time is short, section 3 may be skipped.

S. A fine sentiment, Cephalus, but, speaking of this very thing itself, namely, justice, are we to say unconditionally that it is speaking the truth and paying whatever debts one has incurred? Or is doing these things sometimes just, sometimes unjust? I mean this sort of thing, for example: Everyone would surely agree that if a sane man lends weapons to a friend and then asks for them back when he is out of his mind, the friend shouldn't return them, and wouldn't be acting justly if he did. Nor should anyone be willing to tell the whole truth to someone who is out of his mind.

C. That's true.

S. Then the definition of justice isn't speaking the truth and repaying what one has borrowed.

It certainly is, Socrates, said Polemarchus, interrupting, if indeed we're to trust Simonides at all.[*]

Well, then, Cephalus said, I'll hand over the argument to you, as I have to look after the sacrifice.

So, Polemarchus said, am I then to be your heir in everything?

You certainly are, Cephalus said, laughing, and off he went to the sacrifice.

Then tell us, heir to the argument, I said, just what Simonides stated about justice that you consider correct.

---

of his writings that survive are translated in Freeman, *Ancilla to the Pre-Socratic Philosophers* (Cambridge: Harvard University Press, 1977). Charmantides is otherwise unknown.

[*] Simonides (c. 548–468 B.C.), a lyric and elegiac poet, was born in the Aegean island of Ceos.

P. He stated that it is just to give to each what is owed to him. And it's a fine saying, in my view.

S. Well, now, it isn't easy to doubt Simonides, for he's a wise and godlike man. But what exactly does he mean? Perhaps you know, Polemarchus, but I don't understand him. Clearly, he doesn't mean what we said a moment ago, that it is just to give back whatever a person has lent to you, even if he's out of his mind when he asks for it. And yet what he has lent to you is surely something that's owed to him, isn't it?

P. Yes.

S. But is absolutely not to be given to him when he's out of his mind?

P. That's true.

S. Then it seems that Simonides must have meant something different when he says that to return what is owed is just.

P. Something different indeed, by god. He means that friends owe it to their friends to do good for them, never harm.

S. I follow you. Someone doesn't give a lender back what he's owed by giving him gold, if doing so would be harmful, and both he and the lender are friends. Isn't that what you think Simonides meant?

P. It is.

S. But what about this? Should one also give one's enemies whatever is owed to them?

P. By all means, one should give them what is owed to them. And in my view what enemies owe to each other is appropriately and precisely—something bad.

S. It seems then that Simonides was speaking in riddles—just like a poet!—when he said what justice is, for he thought it just to give to each what is appropriate to him, and this is what he called giving him what is owed to him.

. . .

P. No, by god, it isn't. I don't know any more what I did mean but I still believe that to benefit one's friends and harm one's enemies is justice.

S. Speaking of friends, do you mean those a person believes to be good and useful to him or those who actually are good and useful, even if he doesn't think they are, and similarly with enemies?

P. Probably, one loves those one considers good and useful and hates those one considers bad and harmful.

S. But surely people often make mistakes about this, believing many people to be good and useful when they aren't, and making the opposite mistake about enemies?

P. They do indeed.

S. And then good people are their enemies and bad ones their friends?

P. That's right.

S. And so it's just to benefit bad people and harm good ones?

P. Apparently.

S. But good people are just and able to do no wrong?

P. True.

S. Then, according to your account, it's just to do bad things to those who do no injustice.

P. No, that's not just at all, Socrates; my account must be a bad one.

S. It's just, then, is it, to harm unjust people and benefit just ones?

P. That's obviously a more attractive view than the other one, anyway.

S. Then, it follows, Polemarchus, that it is just for the many, who are mistaken in their judgment, to harm their friends, who are bad, and benefit their enemies, who are good. And so we arrive at a conclusion opposite to what we said Simonides meant.

P. That certainly follows. But let's change our definition, for it seems that we didn't define friends and enemies correctly.

S. How did we define them, Polemarchus?

P. We said that a friend is someone who is believed to be useful.

S. And how are we to change that now?

P. Someone who is both believed to be useful and is useful is a friend; someone who is believed to be useful but isn't, is believed to be a friend but isn't. And the same for the enemy.

S. According to this account, then, a good person will be a friend and a bad one an enemy.

P. Yes.

S. So you want us to add something to what we said before about justice, when we said that it is just to treat friends well and enemies badly. You want us to add to this that it is just to treat well a friend who is good and to harm an enemy who is bad?

P. Right. That seems fine to me.

S. Is it, then, the role of a just man to harm anyone?

P. Certainly, he must harm those who are both bad and enemies.

S. Do horses become better or worse when they are harmed?

P. Worse.

S. With respect to the virtue*

P. The one that makes horses good.

S. And when dogs are harmed, they become worse in the virtue that makes dogs good, not horses?

P. Necessarily.

S. Then won't we say the same about human beings, too, that when they are harmed they become worse in human virtue?

P. Indeed.

S. But isn't justice human virtue?

P. Yes, certainly.

S. Then people who are harmed must become more unjust?

P. So it seems.

S. Can musicians make people unmusical through music?

P. They cannot.

S. Or horsemen make people unhorsemanlike through horsemanship?

P. No.

S. Well, then can those who are just make people unjust through justice? In a word, can those who are good make people bad through virtue?

P. They cannot.

S. It isn't the function of heat to cool things but of its opposite?

P. Yes.

S. Nor the function of dryness to make things wet but of its opposite?

P. Indeed.

S. Nor the function of goodness to harm but of its opposite?

P. Apparently.

S. And a just person is good?

P. Indeed.

S. Then, Polemarchus, it isn't the function of a just person to harm a friend or anyone else, rather it is the function of his opposite, an unjust person?

P. In my view that's completely true, Socrates.

S. If anyone tells us, then, that it is just to give to each what he's owed and understands by this that a just man should harm his enemies and benefit his friends, he isn't wise to say it, since what he says isn't true, for it has become clear to us that it is never just to harm anyone?

P. I agree.

S. You and I shall fight as partners, then, against anyone who tells us that Simonides, Bias, Pittacus, or any of our other wise and blessedly happy men said this.**

P. I, at any rate, am willing to be your partner in the battle.

S. Do you know to whom I think the saying belongs that it is just to benefit friends and harm enemies?

P. Who?

S. I think it belongs to Periander, or Perdiccas, or Xerxes, or Ismenias of Corinth, or some other wealthy man who believed himself to have great power.***

P. That's absolutely true.

S. All right, since it has become apparent that justice and the just aren't what such people say they are, what else could they be?

While we were speaking, Thrasymachus had tried many times to take over the discussion but was restrained by those sitting near him, who wanted to hear our argument to the end. When we paused after what I'd just said, however, he couldn't keep quiet any longer. He coiled himself up like a wild beast about to spring, and he hurled himself at us as if to tear us to pieces.

. . .

---

* If something is a knife (say) or a man, its *aretē* or virtue as a knife or a man is that state or property of it that makes it a good knife or a good man. See Charmides 161a8–9; Euthyphro 6d9–e1; Gorgias 506d2–4; Protagoras 332b4–6; Republic 353d9–354a2. The *aretē* of a knife might include having a sharp blade; the *aretē* of a man might include being intelligent, well-born, just, or courageous. *Aretē* is thus broader than our notion of moral virtue. It applies to things (such as knives) which are not moral agents. And it applies to aspects of moral agents (such as intelligence or family status) which are not normally considered to be moral aspects of them. For these reasons it is sometimes more appropriate to render *aretē* that makes dogs go

** Bias of Priene in Ionia (now the region of Turkey bordering on the eastern shore of the Aegean) and Pittacus of Mytilene (on the island of Lesbos in the eastern Aegean), both sixth century B.C., were two of the legendary seven sages of Greece.

*** Periander was tyrant of the city of Corinth (650–570 B.C.). Perdiccas is probably Perdiccas II, King of Macedon (c. 450–413 B.C.), who is also mentioned in the Gorgias 471a–e. Xerxes was the king of Persia who invaded Greece in the second Persian war (begun in 480 B.C.). Ismenias is mentioned in the Meno 90a. All four are either notorious tyrants or men famous for their wealth.

> 338a–339b (It was obvious that Thrasymachus … We'll have look into it), 342d–345b (Surely then, no doctor … is more profitable than justice.), 358b–362cd (I'll renew the argument … than for just ones).
>
> **The case in favor of injustice**
>
> As Socrates himself notices in respect of Thrasymachus' argument (354b), Thrasymachus' and Glaucon's interventions shift the debate to the connection between justice and happiness. From this point on, Socrates is thus faced with the challenge of providing a definition of justice that, contrary to the claims of Thrasymachus and Glaucon, would show justice to be intimately connected to happiness.
>
> However, the definition (or theory) of justice which Socrates will propose rests entirely on the theory of the forms, in two ways. First, if the theory of forms is true, then what is required is to discover the form of justice; second, the particular form of justice presupposes the truth of the theory of forms, since in essence justice turns out to be a state in which the part which knows the forms (including the form of justice), whether in the city or in the individual, is the part that rules. Hence a reconstruction of Socrates' argument requires at this point an exposition and a defence of the theory of the forms.

While I was saying this, Glaucon and the others begged him to speak. It was obvious that Thrasymachus thought he had a fine answer and that he wanted to earn their admiration by giving it, but he pretended that he wanted to indulge his love of victory by forcing me to answer. However, he agreed in the end, and then said: There you have Socrates' wisdom; he himself isn't willing to teach, but he goes around learning from others and isn't even grateful to them.

S. When you say that I learn from others you are right, Thrasymachus, but when you say that I'm not grateful, that isn't true. I show what gratitude I can, but since I have no money, I can give only praise. But just how enthusiastically I give it when someone seems to me to speak well, you'll know as soon as you've answered, for I think that you will speak well.

T. Listen, then. I say that justice is nothing other than the advantage of the stronger. Well, why don't you praise me? But then you'd do anything to avoid having to do that.

S. I must first understand you, for I don't yet know what you mean. The advantage of the stronger, you say, is just. What do you mean, Thrasymachus? Surely you don't mean something like this: Polydamus, the pancratist,* is stronger than we are; it is to his advantage to eat beef to build up his physical strength; therefore, this food is also advantageous and just for us who are weaker than he is?

T. You disgust me, Socrates. Your trick is to take hold of the argument at the point where you can do it the most harm.

S. Not at all, but tell us more clearly what you mean.

T. Don't you know that some cities are ruled by a tyranny, some by a democracy, and some by an aristocracy?

S. Of course.

T. And in each city this element is stronger, namely, the ruler?

S. Certainly.

T. And each makes laws to its own advantage. Democracy makes democratic laws, tyranny makes tyrannical laws, and so on with the others. And they declare what they have made—what is to their own advantage—to be just for their subjects, and they punish anyone who goes against this as lawless and unjust. This, then, is what I say justice is, the same in all cities, the advantage of the established rule. Since the established rule is surely stronger, anyone who reasons correctly will conclude that the just is the same everywhere, namely, the advantage of the stronger.

S. Now I see what you mean. Whether it's true or not, I'll try to find out. But you yourself have answered that the just is the advantageous, Thrasymachus, whereas you forbade that answer to me. True, you've added "of the stronger" to it.

---

* Pancration was a mixture of boxing and wrestling combined with kicking and strangling. Biting and gouging were forbidden, but pretty well everything else, including breaking and dislocating limbs, was permitted.

S. And I suppose you think that's an insignificant addition.

T. It isn't clear yet whether it's significant. But it is clear that we must investigate to see whether or not it's true. I agree that the just is some kind of advantage. But you add that it's *of the stronger*. I don't know about that. We'll have to look into it.

. . .

S. Surely, then, no doctor, insofar as he is a doctor, seeks or orders what is advantageous to himself, but what is advantageous to his patient? We agreed that a doctor in the precise sense is a ruler of bodies, not a money-maker. Wasn't that agreed?

T. Yes.

S. So a ship's captain in the precise sense is a ruler of sailors, not a sailor?

T. That's what we agreed.

S. Doesn't it follow that a ship's captain or ruler won't seek and order what is advantageous to himself, but what is advantageous to a sailor?

He reluctantly agreed.

S. So, then, Thrasymachus, no one in any position of rule, insofar as he is a ruler, seeks or orders what is advantageous to himself, but what is advantageous to his subjects; the ones of whom he is himself the craftsman. It is to his subjects and what is advantageous and proper to them that he looks, and everything he says and does he says and does for them.

When we reached this point in the argument, and it was clear to all that his account of justice had turned into its opposite, instead of answering, Thrasymachus said: Tell me, Socrates, do you still have a wet nurse?

S. What's this? Hadn't you better answer *my* questions rather than asking *me* such things?

T. Because she's letting you run around with a snotty nose, and doesn't wipe it when she needs to! Why, for all she cares, you don't even know about sheep and shepherds.

S. Just what is it I don't know?

T. You think that shepherds and cowherds seek the good of their sheep and cattle, and fatten them and take care of them, looking to something other than their master's good and their own. Moreover, you believe that rulers in cities—true rulers, that is—think about their subjects differently than one does about sheep, and that night and day they think of something besides their own advantage. You are so far from understanding about justice and what's just, about injustice and what's unjust, that you don't realize that justice is really the good of another, the advantage of the stronger and the ruler, and harmful to the one who obeys and serves. Injustice is the opposite, it rules the truly simple and just, and those it rules do what is to the advantage of the other and stronger, and they make the one they serve happy, but themselves not at all. You must look at it as follows, my most simple Socrates: A just man always gets less than an unjust one. First, in their contracts with one another, you'll never find, when the partnership ends, that a just partner has got more than an unjust one, but less. Second, in matters relating to the city, when taxes are to be paid, a just man pays more on the same property, an unjust one less, but when the city is giving out refunds, a just man gets nothing, while an unjust one makes a large profit. Finally, when each of them holds a ruling position in some public office, a just person, even if he isn't penalized in other ways, finds that his private affairs deteriorate because he has to neglect them, that he gains no advantage from the public purse because of his justice, and that he's hated by his relatives and acquaintances when he's unwilling to do them an unjust favor. The opposite is true of an unjust man in every respect. Therefore, I repeat what I said before: A person of great power outdoes everyone else.* Consider him if you want to figure out how much more advantageous it is for the individual to be just rather than unjust. You'll understand this most easily if you turn your thoughts to the most complete injustice, the one that makes the doer of injustice happiest and the sufferers of it, who are unwilling to do injustice, most wretched. This is tyranny, which through stealth or force appropriates the property of others, whether sacred or profane, public or private, not little by little, but all at once. If someone commits only one part of injustice and is caught, he's punished and

---

* Outdoing (*pleonektein*) is an important notion in the remainder of the *Republic*. It is connected to *pleonexia*, which is what one succumbs to when one always wants to outdo everyone else by getting and having more and more. *Pleonexia* is, or is the cause of, injustice (359c), since always wanting to outdo others leads one to try to get what belongs to them, what isn't *one's own*. It is contrasted with *doing or having one's own*, which is, or is the cause of, justice (434a, 441e).

greatly reproached—such partly unjust people are called temple-robbers,* kidnappers, housebreakers, robbers, and thieves when they commit these crimes. But when someone, in addition to appropriating their possessions, kidnaps and enslaves the citizens as well, instead of these shameful names he is called happy and blessed, not only by the citizens themselves, but by all who learn that he has done the whole of injustice. Those who reproach injustice do so because they are afraid not of doing it but of suffering it. So, Socrates, injustice, if it is on a large enough scale, is stronger, freer, and more masterly than justice. And, as I said from the first, justice is what is advantageous to the stronger, while injustice is to one's own profit and advantage.

Having emptied this great flood of words into our ears all at once like a bath attendant, Thrasymachus intended to leave. But those present didn't let him and made him stay to give an account of what he had said. I too begged him to stay, and I said to him: After hurling such a speech at us, Thrasymachus, do you intend to leave before adequately instructing us or finding out whether you are right or not? Or do you think it a small matter to determine which whole way of life would make living most worthwhile for each of us?

Is *that* what I seem to you to think? Thrasymachus said.

S. Either that, or else you care nothing for us and aren't worried about whether we'll live better or worse lives because of our ignorance of what you say you know. So show some willingness to teach it to us. It wouldn't be a bad investment for you to be the benefactor of a group as large as ours. For my own part, I'll tell you that I am not persuaded. I don't believe that injustice is more profitable than justice, not even if you give it full scope and put no obstacles in its way. Suppose that there *is* an unjust person, and suppose he *does* have the power to do injustice, whether by trickery or open warfare—nonetheless, he doesn't persuade me that injustice is more profitable than justice.

. . .

G. I'll renew the argument of Thrasymachus. First, I'll state what kind of thing people consider justice to be and what its origins are. Second, I'll argue that all who practice it do so unwillingly, as something necessary, not as something good. Third, I'll argue that they have good reason to act as they do, for the life of an unjust person is, they say, much better than that of a just one.

It isn't, Socrates, that I believe any of that myself. I'm perplexed, indeed, and my ears are deafened listening to Thrasymachus and countless others. But I've yet to hear anyone defend justice in the way I want, proving that it is better than injustice. I want to hear it praised *by itself*, and I think that I'm most likely to hear this from you. Therefore, I'm going to speak at length in praise of the unjust life, and in doing so I'll show you the way I want to hear you praising justice and denouncing injustice. But see whether you want me to do that or not.

S. I want that most of all. Indeed, what subject could someone with any understanding enjoy discussing more often?

G. Excellent. Then let's discuss the first subject I mentioned—what justice is and what its origins are.

G. They say that to do injustice is naturally good and to suffer injustice bad, but that the badness of suffering it so far exceeds the goodness of doing it that those who have done and suffered injustice and tasted both, but who lack the power to do it and avoid suffering it, decide that it is profitable to come to an agreement with each other neither to do injustice nor to suffer it. As a result, they begin to make laws and covenants, and what the law commands they call lawful and just. This, they say, is the origin and essence of justice. It is intermediate between the best and the worst. The best is to do injustice without paying the penalty; the worst is to suffer it without being able to take revenge. Justice is a mean between these two extremes. People value it not as a good but because they are too weak to do injustice with impunity. Someone who has the power to do this, however, and is a true man wouldn't make an agreement with anyone not to do injustice in order not to suffer it. For him that would be madness. This is the nature of justice, according to the argument, Socrates, and these are its natural origins.

G. We can see most clearly that those who practice justice do it unwillingly and because

---

* The temples acted as public treasuries, so that a temple robber is the equivalent of a present-day bank robber.

they lack the power to do injustice, if in our thoughts we grant to a just and an unjust person the freedom to do whatever they like. We can then follow both of them and see where their desires would lead. And we'll catch the just person red-handed travelling the same road as the unjust. The reason for this is the desire to outdo others and get more and more. This is what anyone's nature naturally pursues as good, but nature is forced by law into the perversion of treating fairness with respect.

G. The freedom I mentioned would be most easily realized if both people had the power they say the ancestor of Gyges of Lydia possessed. The story goes that he was a shepherd in the service of the ruler of Lydia. There was a violent thunderstorm, and an earthquake broke open the ground and created a chasm at the place where he was tending his sheep. Seeing this, he was filled with amazement and went down into it. And there, in addition to many other wonders of which we're told, he saw a hollow bronze horse. There were windowlike openings in it, and, peeping in, he saw a corpse, which seemed to be of more than human size, wearing nothing but a gold ring on its finger. He took the ring and came out of the chasm. He wore the ring at the usual monthly meeting that reported to the king on the state of the flocks. And as he was sitting among the others, he happened to turn the setting of the ring towards himself to the inside of his hand. When he did this, he became invisible to those sitting near him, and they went on talking as if he had gone. He wondered at this, and, fingering the ring, he turned the setting outwards again and became visible. So he experimented with the ring to test whether it indeed had this power—and it did. If he turned the setting inward, he became invisible; if he turned it outward, he became visible again. When he realized this, he at once arranged to become one of the messengers sent to report to the king. And when he arrived there, he seduced the king's wife, attacked the king with her help, killed him, and took over the kingdom.

G. Let's suppose, then, that there were two such rings, one worn by a just and the other by an unjust person. Now, no one, it seems, would be so incorruptible that he would stay on the path of justice or stay away from other people's property, when he could take whatever he wanted from the marketplace with impunity, go into people's houses and have sex with anyone he wished, kill or release from prison anyone he wished, and do all the other things that would make him like a god among humans. Rather his actions would be in no way different from those of an unjust person, and both would follow the same path. This, some would say, is a great proof that one is never just willingly but only when compelled to be. No one believes justice to be a good when it is kept private, since, wherever either person thinks he can do injustice with impunity, he does it. Indeed, every man believes that injustice is far more profitable to himself than justice. And any exponent of this argument will say he's right, for someone who didn't want to do injustice, given this sort of opportunity, and who didn't touch other people's property would be thought wretched and stupid by everyone aware of the situation, though, of course, they'd praise him in public, deceiving each other for fear of suffering injustice. So much for my second topic.

G. As for the choice between the lives we're discussing, we'll be able to make a correct judgment about that only if we separate the most just and the most unjust. Otherwise we won't be able to do it. Here's the separation I have in mind. We'll subtract nothing from the injustice of an unjust person and nothing from the justice of a just one, but we'll take each to be complete in his own way of life. First, therefore, we must suppose that an unjust person will act as clever craftsmen do: A first-rate captain or doctor, for example, knows the difference between what his craft can and can't do. He attempts the first but lets the second go by, and if he happens to slip, he can put things right. In the same way, an unjust person's successful attempts at injustice must remain undetected, if he is to be fully unjust. Anyone who is caught should be thought inept, for the extreme of injustice is to be believed to be just without being just. And our completely unjust person must be given complete injustice; nothing may be subtracted from it. We must allow that, while doing the greatest injustice, he has nonetheless provided himself with the greatest reputation for justice. If he happens to make a slip, he must be able to put it right. If any of his unjust activities should be discovered, he must be able to speak persuasively or to use force. And if force is needed, he must have the help of courage and strength and of the substantial wealth and friends with which he has provided himself.

G. Having hypothesized such a person, let's now in our argument put beside him a just man, who is simple and noble and who, as Aeschylus says, doesn't want to be believed to be good but to be so.* We must take away his reputation, for a reputation for justice would bring him honor and rewards, so that it wouldn't be clear whether he is just for the sake of justice itself or for the sake of those honors and rewards. We must strip him of everything except justice and make his situation the opposite of an unjust person's. Though he does no injustice, he must have the greatest reputation for it, so that his justice may be tested full-strength and not diluted by wrong-doing and what comes from it. Let him stay like that unchanged until he dies—just, but all his life believed to be unjust. In this way, both will reach the extremes, the one of justice and the other of injustice, and we'll be able to judge which of them is happier.

S. Whew! Glaucon, I said, how vigorously you've scoured each of the men for our competition, just as you would a pair of statues for an art competition.

G. I do the best I can, he replied. Since the two are as I've described, in any case, it shouldn't be difficult to complete the account of the kind of life that awaits each of them, but it must be done. And if what I say sounds crude, Socrates, remember that it isn't I who speak but those who praise injustice at the expense of justice. They'll say that a just person in such circumstances will be whipped, stretched on a rack, chained, blinded with fire, and, at the end, when he has suffered every kind of evil, he'll be impaled, and will realize then that one shouldn't want to be just but to be believed to be just. Indeed, Aeschylus' words are far more correctly applied to unjust people than to just ones, for the supporters of injustice will say that a really unjust person, having a way of life based on the truth about things and not living in accordance with opinion, doesn't want simply to be believed to be unjust but actually to be so—

*Harvesting a deep furrow in his mind,
Where wise counsels propagate.*

G. He rules his city because of his reputation for justice; he marries into any family he wishes; he gives his children in marriage to anyone he wishes; he has contracts and partnerships with anyone he wants; and besides benefiting himself in all these ways, he profits because he has no scruples about doing injustice. In any contest, public or private, he's the winner and outdoes his enemies. And by outdoing them, he becomes wealthy, benefiting his friends and harming his enemies. He makes adequate sacrifices to the gods and sets up magnificent offerings to them. He takes better care of the gods, therefore, (and, indeed, of the human beings he's fond of) than a just person does. Hence it's likely that the gods, in turn, will take better care of him than of a just person. That's what they say, Socrates, that gods and humans provide a better life for unjust people than for just ones.

. . .

514a–517e (Imagine human beings ... wouldn't they kill him?), 508b–509d (What the good is ... visible and intelligible), 517b–517c (This whole image ... must see it.), 518c–518d (But our present ... isn't that right?)
The theory of forms:
The allegory of the cave and its metaphysical meaning

These selections provide an understanding of the theory of forms, metaphorically through the famous allegory of the cave (514a–517e), then directly through a brief—too brief—explanation of the metaphysical doctrine of the forms which the allegory illustrates (508b–509d, 517b–517c and 518c–518d). If time permits, it would be advisable at this point to introduce short extracts from other dialogues (notably from the *Phaedo*, *Meno*, *Cratylus* and *Parmenides*), as well as the simile of the divided line (509e–511e)—if students appear to be keeping up with the text—in order to further clarify this doctrine.

---

* In *Seven Against Thebes*, 592–94, it is said of Amphiaraus that "he did not wish to be believed to be the best but to be it." The passage continues with the words Glaucon quotes below at 362a–b.

S. Imagine human beings living in an underground, cavelike dwelling, with an entrance a long way up, which is both open to the light and as wide as the cave itself. They've been there since childhood, fixed in the same place, with their necks and legs fettered, able to see only in front of them, because their bonds prevent them from turning their heads around. Light is provided by a fire burning far above and behind them. Also behind them, but on higher ground, there is a path stretching between them and the fire. Imagine that along this path a low wall has been built, like the screen in front of puppeteers above which they show their puppets. 514

G. I'm imagining it.

S. Then also imagine that there are people along the wall, carrying all kinds of artifacts that project above it—statues of people and other animals, made out of stone, wood, and every material. And, as you'd expect, some of the carriers are talking, and some are silent. 515

G. It's a strange image you're describing, and strange prisoners.

S. They're like us. Do you suppose, first of all, that these prisoners see anything of themselves and one another besides the shadows that the fire casts on the wall in front of them?

G. How could they, if they have to keep their heads motionless throughout life?

S. What about the things being carried along the wall? Isn't the same true of them?

G. Of course.

S. And if they could talk to one another, don't you think they'd suppose that the names they used applied to the things they see passing before them?*

G. They'd have to.

S. And what if their prison also had an echo from the wall facing them? Don't you think they'd believe that the shadows passing in front of them were talking whenever one of the carriers passing along the wall was doing so?

G. I certainly do.

S. Then the prisoners would in every way believe that the truth is nothing other than the shadows of those artifacts.

G. They must surely believe that.

S. Consider, then, what being released from their bonds and cured of their ignorance would naturally be like. When one of them was freed and suddenly compelled to stand up, turn his head, walk, and look up toward the light, he'd be pained and dazzled and unable to see the things whose shadows he'd seen before. What do you think he'd say, if we told him that what he'd seen before was inconsequential, but that now—because he is a bit closer to the things that are and is turned towards things that are more—he sees more correctly? Or, to put it another way, if we pointed to each of the things passing by, asked him what each of them is, and compelled him to answer, don't you think he'd be at a loss and that he'd believe that the things he saw earlier were truer than the ones he was now being shown?

G. Much truer.

S. And if someone compelled him to look at the light itself, wouldn't his eyes hurt, and wouldn't he turn around and flee towards the things he's able to see, believing that they're really clearer than the ones he's being shown?

G. He would.

S. And if someone dragged him away from there by force, up the rough, steep path, and didn't let him go until he had dragged him into the sunlight, wouldn't he be pained and irritated at being treated that way? And when he came into the light, with the sun filling his eyes, wouldn't he be unable to see a single one of the things now said to be true? 516

G. He would be unable to see them, at least at first.

S. I suppose, then, that he'd need time to get adjusted before he could see things in the world above. At first, he'd see shadows most easily, then images of men and other things in water, then the things themselves. Of these, he'd be able to study the things in the sky and the sky itself more easily at night, looking at the light of the stars and the moon, than during the day, looking at the sun and the light of the sun.

G. Of course.

S. Finally, I suppose, he'd be able to see the sun, not images of it in water or some alien place, but the sun itself, in its own place, and be able to study it.

G. Necessarily so.

S. And at this point he would infer and conclude that the sun provides the seasons

---

* Reading *parionta autous nomizein onomazein*. E.g., they would think that the name "human being" applied to the shadow of a statue of a human being.

and the years, governs everything in the visible world, and is in some way the cause of all the things that he used to see.

G. It's clear that would be his next step.

S. What about when he reminds himself of his first dwelling place, his fellow prisoners, and what passed for wisdom there? Don't you think that he'd count himself happy for the change and pity the others?

G. Certainly.

S. And if there had been any honors, praises, or prizes among them for the one who was sharpest at identifying the shadows as they passed by and who best remembered which usually came earlier, which later, and which simultaneously, and who could thus best divine the future, do you think that our man would desire these rewards or envy those among the prisoners who were honored and held power? Instead, wouldn't he feel, with Homer, that he'd much prefer to "work the earth as a serf to another, one without possessions,"* and go through any sufferings, rather than share their opinions and live as they do?

G. I suppose he would rather suffer anything than live like that.

S. Consider this too. If this man went down into the cave again and sat down in his same seat, wouldn't his eyes—coming suddenly out of the sun like that—be filled with darkness?

G. They certainly would.

S. And before his eyes had recovered—and the adjustment would not be quick—while his vision was still dim, if he had to compete again with the perpetual prisoners in recognizing the shadows, wouldn't he invite ridicule? Wouldn't it be said of him that he'd returned from his upward journey with his eyesight ruined and that it isn't worthwhile even to try to travel upward? And, as for anyone who tried to free them and lead them upward, if they could somehow get their hands on him, wouldn't they kill him?

. . .

S. What the good itself is in the intelligible realm, in relation to understanding and intelligible things, the sun is in the visible realm, in relation to sight and visible things.

G. How? Explain a bit more.

S. You know that, when we turn our eyes to things whose colors are no longer in the light of day but in the gloom of night, the eyes are dimmed and seem nearly blind, as if clear vision were no longer in them.

G. Of course.

S. Yet whenever one turns them on things illuminated by the sun, they see clearly, and vision appears in those very same eyes?

G. Indeed.

S. Well, understand the soul in the same way: When it focuses on something illuminated by truth and what is, it understands, knows, and apparently possesses understanding, but when it focuses on what is mixed with obscurity, on what comes to be and passes away, it opines and is dimmed, changes its opinions this way and that, and seems bereft of understanding.

G. It does seem that way.

S. So that what gives truth to the things known and the power to know to the knower is the form of the good. And though it is the cause of knowledge and truth, it is also an object of knowledge. Both knowledge and truth are beautiful things, but the good is other and more beautiful than they. In the visible realm, light and sight are rightly considered sunlike, but it is wrong to think that they are the sun, so here it is right to think of knowledge and truth as goodlike but wrong to think that either of them is the good—for the good is yet more prized.

G. This is an inconceivably beautiful thing you're talking about, if it provides both knowledge and truth and is superior to them in beauty. You surely don't think that a thing like that could be pleasure.

S. Hush! Let's examine its image in more detail as follows.

G. How?

S. You'll be willing to say, I think, that the sun not only provides visible things with the power to be seen but also with coming to be, growth, and nourishment, although it is not itself coming to be.

G. How could it be?

S. Therefore, you should also say that not only do the objects of knowledge owe their being known to the good, but their being is also due to it, although the good is not being, but superior to it in rank and power.

G. And Glaucon facetiously said: By Apollo, what a daimonic superiority!

---

* *Odyssey* 11.489–90. The shade of the dead Achilles speaks these words to Odysseus, who is visiting Hades. Plato is, therefore, likening the cave dwellers to the dead.

S. It's your own fault; you forced me to tell you my opinion about it.

G. And I don't want you to stop either. So continue to explain its similarity to the sun, if you've omitted anything.

S. I'm certainly omitting a lot.

G. Well, don't, not even the smallest thing.

S. I think I'll have to omit a fair bit, but, as far as is possible at the moment, I won't omit anything voluntarily.

G. Don't.

S. Understand, then, that, as we said, there are these two things, one sovereign of the intelligible kind and place, the other of the visible (I don't say "of heaven" so as not to seem to you to be playing the sophist with the name*). In any case, you have two kinds of thing, visible and intelligible.

. . .

S. This whole image, Glaucon, must be fitted together with what we said before. The visible realm should be likened to the prison dwelling, and the light of the fire inside it to the power of the sun. And if you interpret the upward journey and the study of things above as the upward journey of the soul to the intelligible realm, you'll grasp what I hope to convey, since that is what you wanted to hear about. Whether it's true or not, only the god knows. But this is how I see it: In the knowable realm, the form of the good is the last thing to be seen, and it is reached only with difficulty. Once one has seen it, however, one must conclude that it is the cause of all that is correct and beautiful in anything, that it produces both light and its source in the visible realm, and that in the intelligible realm it controls and provides truth and understanding, so that anyone who is to act sensibly in private or public must see it.

. . .

S. But our present discussion, on the other hand, shows that the power to learn is present in everyone's soul and that the instrument with which each learns is like an eye that cannot be turned around from darkness to light without turning the whole body. This instrument cannot be turned around from that which is coming into being without turning the whole soul until it is able to study that which is and the brightest thing that is, namely, the one we call the good. Isn't that right?

. . .

> **427d–434d (Well, son of Ariston . . . that and nothing else)**
> **The form of justice in the City (The just city)**
>
> This selection outlines the main features of the Kallipolis (the ideal, just City) without explaining yet why an individual comes to belong to one of the three groups that constitute such a city. Provisionally, Socrates' main claim at this point is that in the just city the wise (philosopher kings/guardians) rule over the auxiliaries (soldiers), and the workers. When this condition obtains, the city possesses the traditional virtues of wisdom, courage and self-control, and so justice.

S. Well, son of Ariston, your city might now be said to be established. The next step is to get an adequate light somewhere and to call upon your brother as well as Polemarchus and the others, so as to look inside it and see where the justice and the injustice might be in it, what the difference between them is, and which of the two the person who is to be happy should possess, whether its possession is unnoticed by all the gods and human beings or not.

G. You're talking nonsense, Glaucon said. You promised to look for them yourself because you said it was impious for you not to come to the rescue of justice in every way you could.

S. That's true, and I must do what I promised, but you'll have to help.

G. We will.

S. I hope to find it in this way. I think our city, if indeed it has been correctly founded, is completely good.

G. Necessarily so.

---

* The play may be on the similarity of sound between ouranou ("of heaven") and *horatou* ("of the visible"). But it is more likely that Socrates is referring the fact that *ouranou* seems to contain the word *nou*, the genitive case of *nous* ("understanding"), and relative of *noētou* ("of the intelligible"). Hence if he said that the sun was sovereign of heaven, he might be taken to suggest in sophistical fashion that it was sovereign of the intelligible and that there was no real difference between the good and the sun.

S. Clearly, then, it is wise, courageous, moderate, and just.

G. Clearly.

S. Then, if we find any of these in it, what's left over will be the ones we haven't found?

G. Of course.

S. Therefore, as with any other four things, if we were looking for any one of them in something and recognized it first, that would be enough for us, but if we recognized the other three first, this itself would be sufficient to enable us to recognize what we are looking for. Clearly it couldn't be anything other than what's left over.

G. That's right.

S. Therefore, since there are four virtues, mustn't we look for them in the same way?

G. Clearly.

S. Now, the first thing I think I can see clearly in the city is wisdom, and there seems to be something odd about it.

G. What's that?

S. I think that the city we described is really wise. And that's because it has good judgment, isn't it?

G. Yes.

S. Now, this very thing, good judgment, is clearly some kind of knowledge, for it's through knowledge, not ignorance, that people judge well.

G. Clearly.

S. But there are many kinds of knowledge in the city.

G. Of course.

S. Is it because of the knowledge possessed by its carpenters, then, that the city is to be called wise and sound in judgment?

G. Not at all. It's called skilled in carpentry because of that.

S. Then it isn't to be called wise because of the knowledge by which it arranges to have the best wooden implements.

G. No, indeed.

S. What about the knowledge of bronze items or the like?

G. It isn't because of any knowledge of that sort.

S. Nor because of the knowledge of how to raise a harvest from the earth, for it's called skilled in farming because of that.

G. I should think so.

S. Then, is there some knowledge possessed by some of the citizens in the city we just founded that doesn't judge about any particular matter but about the city as a whole and the maintenance of good relations, both internally and with other cities?

G. There is indeed.

S. What is this knowledge, and who has it?

G. It is guardianship, and it is possessed by those rulers we just now called complete guardians.

S. Then, what does this knowledge entitle you to say about the city?

G. That it has good judgment and is really wise.

S. Who do you think that there will be more of in our city, metal-workers or these true guardians?

G. There will be far more metal-workers.

S. Indeed, of all those who are called by a certain name because they have some kind of knowledge, aren't the guardians the least numerous?

G. By far.

S. Then, a whole city established according to nature would be wise because of the smallest class and part in it, namely, the governing or ruling one. And to this class, which seems to be by nature the smallest, belongs a share of the knowledge that alone among all the other kinds of knowledge is to be called wisdom.

G. That's completely true.

S. Then we've found one of the four virtues, as well as its place in the city, though I don't know how we found it.

G. Our way of finding it seems good enough to me.

S. And surely courage and the part of the city it's in, the part on account of which the city is called courageous, aren't difficult to see.

G. How is that?

S. Who, in calling the city cowardly or courageous, would look anywhere other than to the part of it that fights and does battle on its behalf?

G. No one would look anywhere else.

S. At any rate, I don't think that the courage or cowardice of its other citizens would cause the city itself to be called either courageous or cowardly.

G. No, it wouldn't

S. The city is courageous, then, because of a part of itself that has the power to preserve through everything its belief about what things are to be feared, namely, that they are the things and kinds of things that the lawgiver declared to be such in the course of educating it. Or don't you call that courage?

G. I don't completely understand what you mean. Please, say it again.

S. I mean that courage is a kind of preservation.

G. What sort of preservation?

S. That preservation of the belief that has been inculcated by the law through education about what things and sorts of things are to be feared. And by preserving this belief "through everything," I mean preserving it and not abandoning it because of pains, pleasures, desires, or fears. If you like, I'll compare it to something I think it resembles.

G. I'd like that.

S. You know that dyers, who want to dye wool purple, first pick out from the many colors of wool the one that is naturally white, then they carefully prepare this in various ways, so that it will absorb the color as well as possible, and only at that point do they apply the purple dye. When something is dyed in this way, the color is fast—no amount of washing, whether with soap or without it, can remove it. But you also know what happens to material if it hasn't been dyed in this way, but instead is dyed purple or some other color without careful preparation.

G. I know that it looks washed out and ridiculous.

S. Then, you should understand that, as far as we could, we were doing something similar when we selected our soldiers and educated them in music and physical training. What we were contriving was nothing other than this: That because they had the proper nature and upbringing, they would absorb the laws in the finest possible way, just like a dye, so that their belief about what they should fear and all the rest would become so fast that even such extremely effective detergents as pleasure, pain, fear, and desire wouldn't wash it out—and pleasure is much more potent than any powder, washing soda, or soap. This power to preserve through everything the correct and law-inculcated belief about what is to be feared and what isn't is what I call courage, unless, of course, you say otherwise.

G. I have nothing different to say, for I assume that you don't consider the correct belief about these same things, which you find in animals and slaves, and which is not the result of education, to be inculcated by law, and that you don't call it courage but something else.

S. That's absolutely true.

G. Then I accept your account of courage.

S. Accept it instead as my account of *civic* courage, and you will be right. We'll discuss courage more fully some other time, if you like. At present, our inquiry concerns not it but justice. And what we've said is sufficient for that purpose.

G. You're quite right.

S. There are now two things left for us to find in the city, namely, moderation[*] and—the goal of our entire inquiry—justice.

G. That's right.

S. Is there a way we could find justice so as not to have to bother with moderation any further?

G. I don't know any, and I wouldn't want justice to appear first if that means that we won't investigate moderation. So if you want to please me, look for the latter first.

S. I'm certainly willing. It would be wrong not to be.

G. Look, then.

S. We will. Seen from here, it is more like a kind of consonance and harmony than the previous ones.

G. In what way?

S. Moderation is surely a kind of order, the mastery of certain kinds of pleasures and desires. People indicate as much when they use the phrase "self-control" and other similar phrases. I don't know just what they mean by them, but they are, so to speak, like tracks or clues that moderation has left behind in language. Isn't that so?

G. Absolutely.

S. Yet isn't the expression "self-control" ridiculous? The stronger self that does the controlling is the same as the weaker self that gets controlled, so that only one person is referred to in all such expressions.

G. Of course.

S. Nonetheless, the expression is apparently trying to indicate that, in the soul of that very person, there is a better part and a worse one and that, whenever the naturally better part is in control of the worse, this is ex-

---

[*] The Greek term is *sōphrosunē*. It has a very wide meaning: self-control, good sense, reasonableness, temperance, and (in some contexts) chastity. Someone who keeps his head under pressure or temptation possesses *sōphrosunē*.

pressed by saying that the person is self-controlled or master of himself. At any rate, one praises someone by calling him self-controlled. But when, on the other hand, the smaller and better part is overpowered by the larger, because of bad upbringing or bad company, this is called being self-defeated or licentious and is a reproach.

G. Appropriately so.

S. Take a look at our new city, and you'll find one of these in it. You'll say that it is rightly called self-controlled, if indeed something in which the better rules the worse is properly called moderate and self-controlled.

G. I am looking, and what you say is true.

S. Now, one finds all kinds of diverse desires, pleasures, and pains, mostly in children, women, household slaves, and in those of the inferior majority who are called free.

G. That's right.

S. But you meet with the desires that are simple, measured, and directed by calculation in accordance with understanding and correct belief only in the few people who are born with the best natures and receive the best education.

G. That's true.

S. Then, don't you see that in your city, too, the desires of the inferior many are controlled by the wisdom and desires of the superior few?

G. I do.

S. Therefore, if any city is said to be in control of itself and of its pleasures and desires, it is this one.

G. Absolutely.

S. And isn't it, therefore, also moderate because of all this?

G. It is.

S. And further, if indeed the ruler and the ruled in any city share the same belief about who should rule, it is in this one. Or don't you agree?

G. I agree entirely.

S. And when the citizens agree in this way, in which of them do you say moderation is located? In the ruler or the ruled?

G. I suppose in both.

S. Then, you see how right we were to divine that moderation resembles a kind of harmony?

G. How so?

S. Because, unlike courage and wisdom, each of which resides in one part, making the city brave and wise respectively, moderation spreads throughout the whole. It makes the weakest, the strongest, and those in between—whether in regard to reason, physical strength, numbers, wealth, or anything else—all sing the same song together. And this unanimity, this agreement between the naturally worse and the naturally better as to which of the two is to rule both in the city and in each one, is rightly called moderation.

G. I agree completely.

S. All right. We've now found, at least from the point of view of our present beliefs, three out of the four virtues in our city. So what kind of virtue is left, then, that makes the city share even further in virtue? Surely, it's clear that it is justice.

G. That is clear.

S. Then, Glaucon, we must station ourselves like hunters surrounding a wood and focus our understanding, so that justice doesn't escape us and vanish into obscurity, for obviously it's around here somewhere. So look and try eagerly to catch sight of it, and if you happen to see it before I do, you can tell me about it.

G. I wish I could, but you'll make better use of me if you take me to be a follower who can see things when you point them out to him.

S. Follow, then, and join me in a prayer.

G. I'll do that, just so long as you lead.

S. I certainly will, though the place seems to be impenetrable and full of shadows. It is certainly dark and hard to search though. But all the same, we must go on.

G. Indeed we must.

S. And then I caught sight of something. Ah ha! Glaucon, it looks as though there's a track here, so it seems that our quarry won't altogether escape us.

G. That's good news.

S. Either that, or we've just been stupid.

G. In what way?

S. Because what we are looking for seems to have been rolling around at our feet from the very beginning, and we didn't see it, which was ridiculous of us. Just as people sometimes search for the very thing they are holding in their hands, so we didn't look in the right direction but gazed off into the distance, and that's probably why we didn't notice it.

G. What do you mean?

S. I mean that, though we've been talking and hearing about it for a long time, I think we didn't understand what we were saying or that, in a way, we were talking about justice.

G. That's a long prelude for someone who wants to hear the answer.

S. Then listen and see whether there's anything in what I say. Justice, I think, is exactly what we said must be established throughout the city when we were founding it—either that or some form of it. We stated, and often repeated, if you remember, that everyone must practice one of the occupations in the city for which he is naturally best suited.

G. Yes, we did keep saying that.

S. Moreover, we've heard many people say and have often said ourselves that justice is doing one's own work and not meddling with what isn't one's own.

G. Yes, we have.

S. Then, it turns out that this doing one's own work—provided that it comes to be in a certain way—is justice. And do you know what I take as evidence of this?

G. No, tell me

S. I think that this is what was left over in the city when moderation, courage, and wisdom have been found. It is the power that makes it possible for them to grow in the city and that preserves them when they've grown for as long as it remains there itself. And of course we said that justice would be what was left over when we had found the other three.

G. Yes, that must be so.

S. And surely, if we had to decide which of the four will make the city good by its presence, it would be a hard decision. Is it the agreement in belief between the rulers and the ruled? Or the preservation among the soldiers of the law-inspired belief about what is to be feared and what isn't? Or the wisdom and guardianship of the rulers? Or is it, above all, the fact that every child, woman, slave, freeman, craftsman, ruler, and ruled each does his own work and doesn't meddle with what is other people's?

G. How could this fail to be a hard decision?

S. It seems, then, that the power that consists in everyone's doing his own work rivals wisdom, moderation, and courage in its contribution to the virtue of the city.

G. It certainly does.

S. And wouldn't you call this rival to the others in its contribution to the city's virtue justice?

G. Absolutely.

S. Look at it this way if you want to be convinced. Won't you order your rulers to act as judges in the city's courts?

G. Of course.

S. And won't their sole aim in delivering judgments be that no citizen should have what belongs to another or be deprived of what is his own?

G. They'll have no aim but that.

S. Because that is just?

G. Yes.

S. Therefore, from this point of view also, the having and doing of one's own would be accepted as justice.

G. That's right.

S. Consider, then, and see whether you agree with me about this. If a carpenter attempts to do the work of a cobbler, or a cobbler that of a carpenter, or they exchange their tools or honors with one another, or if the same person tries to do both jobs, and all other such exchanges are made, do you think that does any great harm to the city?

G. Not much.

S. But I suppose that when someone, who is by nature a craftsman or some other kind of money-maker, is puffed up by wealth, or by having a majority of votes, or by his own strength, or by some other such thing, and attempts to enter the class of soldiers, or one of the unworthy soldiers tries to enter that of the judges and guardians, and these exchange their tools and honors, or when the same person tries to do all these things at once, then I think you'll agree that these exchanges and this sort of meddling bring the city to ruin.

G. Absolutely.

S. Meddling and exchange between these three classes, then, is the greatest harm that can happen to the city and would rightly be called the worst thing someone could do to it.

G. Exactly.

S. And wouldn't you say that the worst thing that someone could do to his city is injustice?

G. Of course.

S. Then, that exchange and meddling is injustice. Or to put it the other way around: For the money-making, auxiliary, and guardian classes each to do its own work in the city, is the opposite. That's justice, isn't it, and makes the city just?

G. I see justice is that and nothing else.

. . .

> 434d–436d (Let's not take ... Isn't that so?) 439a–444b (Hence the soul ... That's what they are)
> **The form of justice in the individual (The just individual)**
>
> In these extracts the three-part theory of the soul is explained and (briefly) argued for, then used in claiming that the just individual is one in whom the rational part rules over the spirited and appetitive parts. When this condition is realized, the individual can be said to be wise, courageous and self-controlled, hence just. Thus the form of justice is the same in both the city and the individual. It now remains to see how Socrates connects the just individual and the just city.

434 d

S. Let's not take that as secure just yet, but if we find that the same form, when it comes to be in each individual person, is accepted as justice there as well, we can assent to it. What else can we say? But if that isn't what we find, we must look for something else to be justice. For the moment, however, let's complete the present inquiry. We thought that, if we first tried to observe justice in some larger thing that possessed it, this would make it easier to observe in a single individual. We agreed that this larger thing is a city, and so we established the best city we could, knowing well that justice would be in one that was good. So, let's apply what has come to light in the city to an individual, and if it is accepted there, all will be well. But if something different is found in the individual, then we must go back and test that on the city. And if we do this, and compare them side by side, we might well make justice light up as if we were rubbing fire-sticks together. And, when it has come to light, we can get a secure grip on it for ourselves.

e

435

G. You're following the road we set, and we must do as you say.

S. Well, then, are things called by the same name, whether they are bigger or smaller than one another, like or unlike with respect to that to which that name applies?

G. Alike.

S. Then a just man won't differ at all from a just city in respect to the form of justice; rather he'll be like the city.

b

G. He will.

S. But a city was thought to be just when each of the three natural classes within it did its own work, and it was thought to be moderate, courageous, and wise because of certain other conditions and states of theirs.

G. That's true.

S. Then, if an individual has these same three parts in his soul, we will expect him to be correctly called by the same names as the city if he has the same conditions in them.

c

G. Necessarily so.

S. Then once again we've come upon an easy question, namely, does the soul have these three parts in it or not?

G. It doesn't look easy to me. Perhaps, Socrates, there's some truth in the old saying that everything fine is difficult.

S. Apparently so. But you should know, Glaucon, that, in my opinion, we will never get a precise answer using our present methods of argument—although there is another longer and fuller road that does lead to such an answer. But perhaps we can get an answer that's up to the standard of our previous statements and inquiries.

d

G. Isn't that satisfactory? It would be enough for me at present.

S. In that case, it will be fully enough for me too.

G. Then don't weary, but go on with the inquiry.

S. Well, then, we are surely compelled to agree that each of us has within himself the same parts and characteristics as the city? Where else would they come from? It would be ridiculous for anyone to think that spiritedness didn't come to be in cities from such individuals as the Thracians, Scythians, and others who live to the north of us who are held to possess spirit, or that the same isn't true of the love of learning, which is mostly associated with our part of the world, or of the love of money, which one might say is conspicuously displayed by the Phoenicians and Egyptians.

e

436

G. It would.

S. That's the way it is, anyway, and it isn't hard to understand.

G. Certainly not.

S. But this is hard. Do we do these things with the same part of ourselves, or do we do them with three different parts? Do we learn with one part, get angry with another, and with some third part desire the pleasures of food, drink, sex, and the others that are closely akin to them? Or, when we set out after something, do we act with the whole of our soul, in each case? This is what's hard to determine in a way that's up to the standards of our argument.

G. I think so too.

S. Well, then, let's try to determine in that way whether these parts are the same or different.

G. How?

S. It is obvious that the same thing will not be willing to do or undergo opposites in the same part of itself, in relation to the same thing, at the same time. So, if we ever find this happening in the soul, we'll know that we aren't dealing with one thing but many.

G. All right.

S. Then consider what I'm about to say.

G. Say on.

S. Is it possible for the same thing to stand still and move at the same time in the same part of itself?

G. Not at all.

S. Let's make our agreement more precise in order to avoid disputes later on. If someone said that a person who is standing still but moving his hands and head is moving and standing still at the same time, we wouldn't consider, I think, that he ought to put it like that. What he ought to say is that one part of the person is standing still and another part is moving. Isn't that so?

...

S. Hence the soul of the thirsty person, insofar as he's thirsty, doesn't wish anything else but to drink, and it wants this and is impelled towards it.

G. Clearly.

S. Therefore, if something draws it back when it is thirsting, wouldn't that be something different in it from whatever thirsts and drives it like a beast to drink? It can't be, we say, that the same thing, with the same part of itself, in relation to the same, at the same time, does opposite things.

G. No, it can't.

S. In the same way, I suppose, it's wrong to say of the archer that his hands at the same time push the bow away and draw it towards him. We ought to say that one hand pushes it away and the other draws it towards him.

G. Absolutely.

S. Now, would we assert that sometimes there are thirsty people who don't wish to drink?

G. Certainly, it happens often to many different people.

S. What, then, should one say about them? Isn't it that there is something in their soul, bidding them to drink, and something different, forbidding them to do so, that overrules the thing that bids?

G. I think so.

S. Doesn't that which forbids in such cases come into play—if it comes into play at all—as a result of rational calculation, while what drives and drags them to drink is a result of feelings and diseases?

G. Apparently.

S. Hence it isn't unreasonable for us to claim that they are two, and different from one another. We'll call the part of the soul with which it calculates the rational part and the part with which it lusts, hungers, thirsts, and gets excited by other appetites the irrational appetitive part, companion of certain indulgences and pleasures.

G. Yes. Indeed, that's a reasonable thing to think.

S. Then, let these two parts be distinguished in the soul. Now, is the spirited part by which we get angry a third part or is it of the same nature as either of the other two?

G. Perhaps it's like the appetitive part.

S. But I've heard something relevant to this, and I believe it. Leontius, the son of Aglaion, was going up from the Piraeus along the outside of the North Wall when he saw some corpses lying at the executioner's feet. He had an appetite to look at them but at the same time he was disgusted and turned away. For a time he struggled with himself and covered his face, but, finally, overpowered by the appetite, he pushed his eyes wide open and rushed towards the corpses, saying, "Look for yourselves, you evil wretches, take your fill of the beautiful sight!"*

G. I've heard that story myself.

S. It certainly proves that anger sometimes makes war against the appetites, as one thing against another.

G. Besides, don't we often notice in other cases that when appetite forces someone contrary to rational calculation, he reproaches

---

* Leontius' desire to look at the corpses is sexual in nature, for a fragment of contemporary comedy tells us that Leontius was known for his love of boys as pale as corpses.

himself and gets angry with that in him that's doing the forcing, so that of the two factions that are fighting a civil war, so to speak, spirit allies itself with reason? But I don't think you can say that you've ever seen spirit, either in yourself or anyone else, ally itself with an appetite to do what reason has decided must not be done.

G. No, by god, I haven't

S. What happens when a person thinks that he has done something unjust? Isn't it true that the nobler he is, the less he resents it if he suffers hunger, cold, or the like at the hands of someone whom he believes to be inflicting this on him justly, and won't his spirit, as I say, refuse to be aroused?

G. That's true.

S. But what happens if, instead, he believes that someone has been unjust to him? Isn't the spirit within him boiling and angry, fighting for what he believes to be just? Won't it endure hunger, cold, and the like and keep on till it is victorious, not ceasing from noble actions until it either wins, dies, or calms down, called to heel by the reason within him, like a dog by its shepherd?

G. Spirit is certainly like that. And, of course, we made the auxiliaries in our city like dogs obedient to the rulers, who are themselves like shepherds of a city.

S. You well understand what I'm trying to say. But also reflect on this further point.

G. What?

S. The position of the spirited part seems to be the opposite of what we thought before. Then we thought of it as something appetitive, but now we say that it is far from being that, for in the civil war in the soul it aligns itself far more with the rational part.

G. Absolutely.

S. Then is it also different from the rational part, or is it some form of it, so that there are two parts in the soul—the rational and the appetitive—instead of three? Or rather, just as there were three classes in the city that held it together, the money-making, the auxiliary, and the deliberative, is the spirited part a third thing in the soul that is by nature the helper of the rational part, provided that it hasn't been corrupted by a bad upbringing?

G. It must be a third.

S. Yes, provided that we can show it is different from the rational part, as we saw earlier it was from the appetitive one.

G. It isn't difficult to show that it is different. Even in small children, one can see that they are full of spirit right from birth, while as far as rational calculation is concerned, some never seem to get a share of it, while the majority do so quite late.

S. That's really well put. And in animals too one can see that what you say is true. Besides, our earlier quotation from Homer bears it out, where he says,

He struck his chest and spoke to his heart.

For here Homer clearly represents the part that has calculated about better and worse as different from the part that is angry without calculation.

G. That's exactly right.

S. Well, then, we've now made our difficult way through a sea of argument. We are pretty much agreed that the same number and the same kinds of classes as are in the city are also in the soul of each individual.

G. That's true.

S. Therefore, it necessarily follows that the individual is wise in the same way and in the same part of himself as the city.

G. That's right.

S. And isn't the individual courageous in the same way and in the same part of himself as the city? And isn't everything else that has to do with virtue the same in both?

G. Necessarily.

S. Moreover, Glaucon, I suppose we'll say that a man is just in the same way as a city.

G. That too is entirely necessary.

S. And we surely haven't forgotten that the city was just because each of the three classes in it was doing its own work.

G. I don't think we could forget that.

S. Then we must also remember that each one of us in whom each part is doing its own work will himself be just and do his own.

G. Of course, we must.

S. Therefore, isn't it appropriate for the rational part to rule, since it is really wise and exercises foresight on behalf of the whole soul, and for the spirited part to obey it and be its ally?

G. It certainly is.

S. And isn't it, as we were saying, a mixture of music and poetry, on the one hand, and physical training, on the other, that makes the two parts harmonious, stretching and nurturing the rational part with fine words and learning, relaxing the other part through soothing stories, and making it gentle by means of harmony and rhythm?

G. That's precisely it.

S. And these two, having been nurtured in this way, and having truly learned their own roles and been educated in them, will govern the appetitive part, which is the largest part in each person's soul and is by nature most insatiable for money. They'll watch over it to see that it isn't filled with the so-called pleasures of the body and that it doesn't become so big and strong that it no longer does its own work but attempts to enslave and rule over the classes it isn't fitted to rule, thereby overturning everyone's whole life.

G. That's right.

S. Then, wouldn't these two parts also do the finest job of guarding the whole soul and body against external enemies—reason by planning, spirit by fighting, following its leader, and carrying out the leader's decisions through its courage?

G. Yes, that's true.

S. And it is because of the spirited part, I suppose, that we call a single individual courageous, namely, when it preserves through pains and pleasures the declarations of reason about what is to be feared and what isn't.

G. That's right.

S. And we'll call him wise because of that small part of himself that rules in him and makes those declarations and has within it the knowledge of what is advantageous for each part and for the whole soul, which is the community of all three parts.

G. Absolutely.

S. And isn't he moderate because of the friendly and harmonious relations between these same parts, namely, when the ruler and the ruled believe in common that the rational part should rule and don't engage in civil war against it?

G. Moderation is surely nothing other than that, both in the city and in the individual.

S. And, of course, a person will be just because of what we've so often mentioned, and in that way.

G. Necessarily.

S. Well, then, is the justice in us at all indistinct? Does it seem to be something different from what we found in the city?

G. It doesn't seem so to me.

S. If there are still any doubts in our soul about this, we could dispel them altogether by appealing to ordinary cases.

G. Which ones?

S. For example, if we had to come to an agreement about whether someone similar in nature and training to our city had embezzled a deposit of gold or silver that he had accepted, who do you think would consider him to have done it rather than someone who isn't like him?

G. No one.

S. And would he have anything to do with temple robberies, thefts, betrayals of friends in private life or of cities in public life?

G. No, nothing.

S. And he'd be in no way untrustworthy in keeping an oath or other agreement.

G. How could he be?

S. And adultery, disrespect of parents, and neglect of the gods would be more in keeping with every other kind of character than his.

G. With every one.

S. And isn't the cause of all this that every part within him does its own work, whether it's ruling or being ruled?

G. Yes, that and nothing else.

S. Then, are you still looking for justice to be something other than this power, the one that produces men and cities of the sort we've described?

G. No, I certainly am not.

S. Then the dream we had has been completely fulfilled—our suspicion that, with the help of some god, we had hit upon the origin and pattern of justice right at the beginning in founding our city.

G. Absolutely.

S. Indeed, Glaucon, the principle that it is right for someone who is by nature a cobbler to practice cobblery and nothing else, for the carpenter to practice carpentry, and the same for the others is a sort of image of justice—that's why it's beneficial.

G. Apparently.

S. And in truth justice is, it seems, something of this sort. However, it isn't concerned with someone's doing his own externally, but with what is inside him, with what is truly himself and his own. One who is just does not allow any part of himself to do the work of another part or allow the various classes within him to meddle with each other. He regulates well what is really his own and rules himself. He puts himself in order, is his own friend, and harmonizes the three parts of himself like three limiting notes in a musical scale—high, low, and middle. He binds together those parts and any others there may be in between, and from having been many things he becomes entirely one, moderate and harmonious. Only then does he act.

And when he does anything, whether acquiring wealth, taking care of his body, engaging in politics, or in private contracts—in all of these, he believes that the action is just and fine that preserves this inner harmony and helps achieve it, and calls it so, and regards as wisdom the knowledge that oversees such actions. And he believes that the action that destroys this harmony is unjust, and calls it so, and regards the belief that oversees it as ignorance.

G. That's absolutely true, Socrates.

S. Well, then, if we claim to have found the just man, the just city, and what the justice is that is in them, I don't suppose that we'll seem to be telling a complete falsehood.

G. No, we certainly won't.

S. Shall we claim it, then?

G. We shall.

S. So be it. Now, I suppose we must look for injustice.

G. Clearly.

S. Surely, it must be a kind of civil war between the three parts, a meddling and doing of another's work, a rebellion by some part against the whole soul in order to rule it inappropriately. The rebellious part is by nature suited to be a slave, while the other part is not a slave but belongs to the ruling class. We'll say something like that, I suppose, and that the turmoil and straying of these parts are injustice, licentiousness, cowardice, ignorance, and, in a word, the whole of vice.

That's what they are.

. . .

> **484b–485b (What's our next topic . . . coming to be and decaying), 519b–521b (And what about . . . No one.)**
> **The just individual in the just City (Why philosophers should rule)**
>
> These selections finally weave together the main strands of Socrates' argument so far. In the just city philosophers rule because they know the forms (the form of justice in particular), and they know the forms because of the kind of soul they have (or were made to acquire through the proper education); such a soul is one in which the rational part dominates. Other individuals occupy the place they do also because of the kind of soul they have. Thus, a just city is a city in which each individual occupies a station commensurate with the kind of soul they have; and, conversely, a just individual is one whose soul plays its apposite role in the city. (An interesting consequence of this view, which Socrates clarifies in respect of Guardians, is that there could be no just individuals outside a political association.) Harmony and happiness result from this just condition.

G. What's our next topic?

S. What else but the one that's next in order? Since those who are able to grasp what is always the same in all respects are philosophers, while those who are not able to do so and who wander among the many things that vary in every sort of way are not philosophers, which of the two should be the leaders in a city?

G. What would be a sensible answer to that?

S. We should establish as guardians those who are clearly capable of guarding the laws and the ways of life of the city.

G. That's right.

S. And isn't it clear that the guardian who is to keep watch over everything should be keen-sighted rather than blind?

G. Of course it's clear.

S. Do you think, then, that there's any difference between the blind and those who are really deprived of the knowledge of each thing that is? The latter have no clear model in their souls, and so they cannot—in the manner of painters—look to what is most true, make constant reference to it, and study it as exactly as possible. Hence they cannot establish here on earth conventions about what is fine or just or good, when they need to be established, or guard and preserve them, once they have been established.

G. No, by god, there isn't much difference between them.

S. Should we, then, make these blind people our guardians or rather those who know each thing that is and who are not inferior to the others, either in experience or in any other part of virtue?

G. It would be absurd to choose anyone but philosophers, if indeed they're not inferior in these ways, for the respect in which they are superior is pretty well the most important one.

S. Then shouldn't we explain how it is possible for someone to have both these sorts of qualities? 485

G. Certainly.

S. Then, as we said at the beginning of this discussion, it is necessary to understand the nature of philosophers first, for I think that, if we can reach adequate agreement about that, we'll also agree that the same people *can* have both qualities and that no one but they should be leaders in cities.

G. How so?

S. Let's agree that philosophic natures always love the sort of learning that makes clear to them some feature of the being that always is and does not wander around between coming to be and decaying. *b*

. . .

S. And what about the uneducated who have no experience of truth? Isn't it likely—indeed, doesn't it follow necessarily from what was said before—that they will never adequately govern a city? But neither would those who've been allowed to spend their whole lives being educated. The former would fail because they don't have a single goal at which all their actions, public and private, inevitably aim; the latter would fail because they'd refuse to act, thinking that they had settled while still alive in the faraway Isles of the Blessed.* 519 *b* *c*

G. That's true.

S. It is our task as founders, then, to compel the best natures to reach the study we said before is the most important, namely, to make the ascent and see the good. But when they've made it and looked sufficiently, we mustn't allow them to do what they're allowed to do today. *d*

G. What's that?

S. To stay there and refuse to go down again to the prisoners in the cave and share their labors and honors, whether they are of less worth or of greater.

G. Then are we to do them an injustice by making them live a worse life when they could live a better one?

S. You are forgetting again that it isn't the law's concern to make any one class in the city outstandingly happy but to contrive to spread happiness throughout the city by bringing the citizens into harmony with each other through persuasion or compulsion and by making them share with each other the benefits that each class can confer on the community. The law produces such people in the city, not in order to allow them to turn in whatever direction they want, but to make use of them to bind the city together. 520 *e*

G. That's true, I had forgotten.

S. Observe, then, Glaucon, that we won't be doing an injustice to those who've become philosophers in our city and that what we'll say to them, when we compel them to guard and care for the others, will be just. We'll say: "When people like you come to be in other cities, they're justified in not sharing in their city's labors, for they've grown there spontaneously, against the will of the constitution. And what grows of its own accord and owes no debt for its upbringing has justice on its side when it isn't keen to pay anyone for that upbringing. But we've made you kings in our city and leaders of the swarm, as it were, both for yourselves and for the rest of the city. You're better and more completely educated than the others and are better able to share in both types of life.** Therefore each of you in turn must go down to live in the common dwelling place of the others and grow accustomed to seeing in the dark. When you are used to it, you'll see vastly better than the people there. And because you've seen the truth about fine, just, and good things, you'll know each image for what it is and also that of which it is the image. Thus, for you and for us, the city will be governed, not like the majority of cities nowadays, by people who fight over shadows and struggle against one another in order to rule—as if that were a great good—but by people who are awake rather than dreaming, for the truth is surely this: A city whose prospective rulers are least eager to rule must of necessity be most free from civil war, whereas a city with the opposite kind of rulers is governed in the opposite way." *b* *c* *d*

G. Absolutely.

S. Then do you think that those we've nurtured will disobey us and refuse to share the labors of the city, each in turn, while living the greater part of their time with one another in the pure realm?

---

* A place where good people are said to live in eternal happiness, normally after death.
** I.e., the practical life of ruling the city and the theoretical life of studying the good itself.

G. It isn't possible, for we'll be giving just orders to just people. Each of them will certainly go to rule as to something compulsory, however, which is exactly the opposite of what's done by those who now rule in each city. This is how it is. If you can find a way of life that's better than ruling for the prospective rulers, your well-governed city will become a possibility, for only in it will the truly rich rule—not those who are rich in gold but those who are rich in the wealth that the happy must have, namely, a good and rational life. But if beggars hungry for private goods go into public life, thinking that the good is there for the seizing, then the well-governed city is impossible, for then ruling is something fought over, and this civil and domestic war destroys these people and the rest of the city as well.

S. That's very true.

G. Can you name any life that despises political rule besides that of the true philosopher?

S. No, by god, I can't.

G. But surely it is those who are not lovers of ruling who must rule, for if they don't, the lovers of it, who are rivals, will fight over it.

S. Of course.

G. Then who will you compel to become guardians of the city, if not those who have the best understanding of what matters for good government and who have other honors than political ones, and a better life as well?

S. No one.

. . .

> **414b–415d (How then . . . come after them)**
> **Maintaining the just city**
> In this passage Socrates proposes the noble lie (the myth of the earthborn) as one way to prevent meddling between the social strata.

S. How, then, could we devise one of those useful falsehoods we were talking about a while ago, one noble falsehood that would, in the best case, persuade even the rulers, but if that's not possible, then the others in the city?

G. What sort of falsehood?

S. Nothing new, but a Phoenician story which describes something that has happened in many places. At least, that's what the poets say, and they've persuaded many people to believe it too. It hasn't happened among us, and I don't even know if it could. It would certainly take a lot of persuasion to get people to believe it.

G. You seem hesitant to tell the story.

S. When you hear it, you'll realize that I have every reason to hesitate.

G. Speak, and don't be afraid.

S. I'll tell it, then, though I don't know where I'll get the audacity or even what words I'll use. I'll first try to persuade the rulers and the soldiers and then the rest of the city that the upbringing and the education we gave them, and the experiences that went with them, were a sort of dream, that in fact they themselves, their weapons, and the other craftsmen's tools were at that time really being fashioned and nurtured inside the earth, and that when the work was completed, the earth, who is their mother, delivered all of them up into the world. Therefore, if anyone attacks the land in which they live, they must plan on its behalf and defend it as their mother and nurse and think of the other citizens as their earthborn brothers.

G. It isn't for nothing that you were so shy about telling your falsehood.

S. Appropriately so. Nevertheless, listen to the rest of the story. "All of you in the city are brothers," we'll say to them in telling our story, "but the god who made you mixed some gold into those who are adequately equipped to rule, because they are most valuable. He put silver in those who are auxiliaries and iron and bronze in the farmers and other craftsmen. For the most part you will produce children like yourselves, but, because you are all related, a silver child will occasionally be born from a golden parent, and vice versa, and all the others from each other. So the first and most important command from the god to the rulers is that there is nothing that they must guard better or watch more carefully than the mixture of metals in the souls of the next generation. If an offspring of theirs should be found to have a mixture of iron or bronze, they must not pity him in any way, but give him the rank appropriate to his nature and drive him out to join the craftsmen and farmers. But if an offspring of these people is found to have a mixture of gold or silver, they will honor him and take him up to join the guardians or the auxiliaries, for there is an oracle which says that the city will be ruined if it ever has an iron or a bronze guardian."

G. So, do you have any device that will make our citizens believe this story?

S. I can't see any way to make them believe it themselves, but perhaps there is one in the case of their sons and later generations and all the other people who come after them.

...

> **559d–562a (Let's go back ... rightly called democratic)**
> **The critique of democratic man**
> This last selection criticizes democratic man (N.B. Pericles' funeral oration) on the basis of the theory of justice. On Socrates' argument, democracy turns out to be a variety of injustice, since in a democracy the City and individual are ruled by the most ignorant part of the soul (the appetitive part).

S. Let's go back, then, and explain how the democratic man develops out of the oligarchic one. It seems to me as though it mostly happens as follows.

G. How?

S. When a young man, who is reared in the miserly and uneducated manner we described, tastes the honey of the drones and associates with wild and dangerous creatures who can provide every variety of multicolored pleasure in every sort of way, this, as you might suppose, is the beginning of his transformation from having an oligarchic constitution within him to having a democratic one.

G. It's inevitable that this is how it starts.

S. And just as the city changed when one party received help from like-minded people outside, doesn't the young man change when one party of his desires receives help from external desires that are akin to them and of the same form?

G. Absolutely.

S. And I suppose that, if any contrary help comes to the oligarchic party within him, whether from his father or from the rest of his household, who exhort and reproach him, then there's civil war and counterrevolution within him, and he battles against himself.

G. That's right.

S. Sometimes the democratic party yields to the oligarchic, so that some of the young man's appetites are overcome, others are expelled, a kind of shame rises in his soul, and order is restored.

G. That does sometimes happen.

S. But I suppose that, as desires are expelled, others akin to them are being nurtured unawares, and because of his father's ignorance about how to bring him up, they grow numerous and strong.

G. That's what tends to happen.

S. These desires draw him back into the same bad company and in secret intercourse breed a multitude of others.

G. Certainly.

S. And, seeing the citadel of the young man's soul empty of knowledge, fine ways of living, and words of truth (which are the best watchmen and guardians of the thoughts of those men whom the gods love), they finally occupy that citadel themselves.

G. They certainly do.

S. And in the absence of these guardians, false and boastful words and beliefs rush up and occupy this part of him.

G. Indeed, they do.

S. Won't he then return to these lotus-eaters and live with them openly? And if some help comes to the thrifty part of his soul from his household, won't these boastful words close the gates of the royal wall within him to prevent these allies from entering and refuse even to receive the words of older private individuals as ambassadors? Doing battle and controlling things themselves, won't they call reverence foolishness and moderation cowardice, abusing them and casting them out beyond the frontiers like disenfranchised exiles? And won't they persuade the young man that measured and orderly expenditure is boorish and mean, and, joining with many useless desires, won't they expel it across the border?

G. They certainly will.

S. Having thus emptied and purged these from the soul of the one they've possessed and initiated in splendid rites, they proceed to return insolence, anarchy, extravagance, and shamelessness from exile in a blaze of torchlight, wreathing them in garlands and accompanying them with a vast chorus of followers. They praise the returning exiles and give them fine names, calling insolence good breeding, anarchy freedom, extravagance magnificence, and shamelessness courage. Isn't it in some such way as this that someone who is young changes, after being brought up with necessary desires, to the liberation and release of useless and unnecessary pleasures?

G. Yes, that's clearly the way it happens.

S. And I suppose that after that he spends as much money, effort, and time on unnecessary pleasures as on necessary ones. If he's lucky, and his frenzy doesn't go too far, when he grows older, and the great tumult within him has spent itself, he welcomes back some of the exiles, ceases to surrender himself completely to the newcomers, and puts his pleasures on an equal footing. And so he lives, always surrendering rule over himself to whichever desire comes along, as if it were chosen by lot.* And when that is satisfied, he surrenders the rule to another, not disdaining any but satisfying them all equally.

G. That's right.

S. And he doesn't admit any word of truth into the guardhouse, for if someone tells him that some pleasures belong to fine and good desires and others to evil ones and that he must pursue and value the former and restrain and enslave the latter, he denies all this and declares that all pleasures are equal and must be valued equally.

G. That's just what someone in that condition would do.

S. And so he lives on, yielding day by day to the desire at hand. Sometimes he drinks heavily while listening to the flute; at other times, he drinks only water and is on a diet; sometimes he goes in for physical training; at other times, he's idle and neglects everything; and sometimes he even occupies himself with what he takes to be philosophy. He often engages in politics, leaping up from his seat and saying and doing whatever comes into his mind. If he happens to admire soldiers, he's carried in that direction, if money-makers, in that one. There's neither order nor necessity in his life, but he calls it pleasant, free, and blessedly happy, and he follows it for as long as he lives.

G. You've perfectly described the life of a man who believes in legal equality.

S. I also suppose that he's a complex man, full of all sorts of characters, fine and multi-colored, just like the democratic city, and that many men and women might envy his life, since it contains the most models of constitutions and ways of living. That's right.

G. Then shall we set this man beside democracy as one who is rightly called democratic?

---

* Many public officials were elected by lot in Athens. Socrates seems to have been opposed to this practice. See Aristotle, *Rhetoric* 1393b5–9 and Xenophon, *Memorabilia* I.ii.9–10.

Six Major Themes in Plato's *Republic*

1. In the generation before Plato's there began to be some very serious interest among Greek thinkers about mathematics. You probably know about Pythagoras and his theorem describing the relations of the sides of right triangles. The Pythagoreans were amazed by the discovery of this constant, and they were also amazed by the relations of parts of circles (all that business with "pi" that helps us get to an understanding of radii, diameters, circumferences, and volume), another set of constant relationships. These discoveries led into the metaphysical realm, thoughts about things that can't be seen and measured and counted—honor, justice, beauty, goodness, etc. Can it be that there are constants—i.e., basic forms, of these things, too?

2. Plato's teacher Socrates claimed he was compelled to find out the answer to this question by a Divine Voice. So, he went into the streets of Athens to inquire among his fellow citizens after the bases on which they acted and believed.

    What he found was surprising. Questioning many of the leading persons of his day—statesmen, poets, craftsmen—he found that they could not give an adequate account for their beliefs or for the principles upon which they acted. It was indeed as if they were blindmen describing a world they had come to know only by rumors and made-up stories.

    In his "Allegory of the Cave," Socrates likens this to people shackled on the floor of a cave, able to see only shadows of things and making up stories about those shadows. But what would it be like to see the sources of the shadows, and seek beyond them to an understanding of the "real forms" of things?

    One way for us to understand this is to ask where we have gotten our understanding of the world. Most people would agree that we are taught by others (and perhaps by our culture itself) what to pay attention to and how to understand it. We don't really learn by experience (though most people believe they do); instead, we learn a great deal from rumor (traditional wisdom), from a kind of agreement our community enters into to understand the world (that's why communities have very different understandings of things, even though members of those communities come to believe that their particular orientation is the truth). And we learn, within our own culture, what is true for that time in history.

    What a philosopher like Plato tries to do is discover basic truths that are trans-cultural and trans-historical—i.e., in the very nature of things.

3. One of the methods employed by Socrates, and re-enacted by Plato, has come to be called *dialectic*. This is a procedure in which thinkers engage in a questioning discussion in order to arrive at clear and sturdy definitions. Some say this project gave birth to academic habits of the university as we have come to know it. After all, in most "real world" discussions, participants are happy to agree with one another without putting every statement to the test of reasoning and clarity and counter instances; or worse yet, when there is debate, the main interest is in who wins the argument.

    The academic world alone, some say, is happy with this annoying process of questioning everything to get things clear (and not to win an argument, which would be a corruption of Plato's dialectic). One can see this annoyance in the Platonic dialogues, as most interlocutors (those who speak with Socrates) become exasperated, not only with the tenacity of the questioning but by the growing realization that they don't know what they are talking about (for example Thrasymachus).

4. The philosopher puts himself at great risk in Plato's accounts. Plato, after all, had experienced the public trial and condemnation to death of Socrates, his beloved teacher. People do not like being put into situations that reveal their ignorance, especially ignorance of their most deeply held beliefs.

5. In his trial (*Apology*), the Athenian court brings three charges against Socrates: (1) inventing new gods; (2) corrupting the young; and (3) making the worse argument appear to be the better one (a kind of wizardly magic). Without question, Socrates is guilty of all three things (except the third really means, "destroying our hallowed beliefs by subjecting them to tough, logical scrutiny").

    A democratic court, with 501 jurors from all walks of life, chooses to put their philosopher to death. This experience makes Plato hostile to democracy, which he sees as a mob directed by mass thinking that is illusory.

    Nonetheless, it is the obligation of the philosopher to tell the truth (after Socrates, with some caution for the consequences). Plato compares the philosopher to a "stinging fly" that keeps awake the great sleepy horse that is society. In *Republic* Plato sees the philosopher as the man who has come to know the true forms of things and returns to the cave to liberate his fellow humans from their shadows of confusion (and risks injury or worse in the process).

    Plato teaches that "the unexamined life is not worth living." This is the other side of "ignorance is bliss." What do you think?

6. Plato's dialogues continue to be a great challenge to us. They suggest that everything we think we know may well be wrong, or at least may be understood in a confused way. They invite us to question everything in a rational way and to seek not only clear definitions and understanding but the true good, which Plato believes is always linked to the "true forms" of things. For Plato, divinity is found in the discovery of the well-made forms of reality that lie behind the broken and confused world we know.

    While all this may seem very mysterious at first, we encounter this break between the world as it is and the better world that we have a notion of whenever we look at "what is" and instantly know this is wrong and that there must be a better way. We are somehow aware, perhaps in a hazy way, that there is another world of "should" and "ought" that the real world aspires to, only to fall short of, and often tragically so. The effort to describe clearly what that other world of "true forms" is constitutes the project of Plato's philosophy. The love for that pursuit and the desire for these clear understandings is for Plato, like a lover's pursuit of the object of love.

    That is why it is called "philosophy" in the first place, which means literally "the love for wisdom."

> *Philos* (love), as in "Philadelphia"
>   (City of Brotherly Love)
> *Sophia* (wisdom)

Introduction to *The Apology*

The *Apology* is Plato's attempt to present an account of the trial of Socrates by recording the speech Socrates made in his own defense. This major piece lays out several key themes: Plato's hostility to democracy, a model of a perfect devotion to truth, and an account of the role of the philosopher in society.

From the opening remarks, we see Socrates' sarcasm directed against the mob thinking of his neighbors. He is on trial before 501 citizens, a group appointed by the Assembly. So there is no doubt that his trial and condemnation are directly at the hands of the citizens of Athens. Socrates explains, for example, that he could induce them to set him free by appealing to their sentiments; all he need do is bring his young sons with him and beg for his life on their behalf. His point is abusive but clarifying. The democracy has passions but cannot think straight. Democratic justice is a kind of soap opera. He refuses to meet the law at this level and chooses instead to educate, even at the risk of his life.

Why risk his life for a citizenry that is so unworthy? Socrates is devoted to an ethics of perfection; he must never do that which produces harm to others, and that includes harm to the community itself. By addressing the law through reason and not through emotion, Socrates presents a sobering lesson for his fellow citizens. To appeal to their sentiments would only further corrupt them. He must be at all times a model of integrity or risk the collapse of his authority in all matters. His inward voice demands the truth of him; and he follows this voice even at the risk of his life. There are things worse than death, and dishonoring oneself by bending to the popular will is one of them.

The third major theme of the *Apology* addresses the role of the philosopher. Why does a society need the constant criticism of this wise man? Societies are lazy and stupid, like great workhorses. They require a "stinging fly" to keep them alert and thinking. The philosopher must not only investigate the truth but also arouse his neighbors to think clearly. By condemning and killing its philosopher, Athens has caused itself to suffer a grievous loss. In Plato's view, it is the sort of thing that democracies do, in their mistaken confidence that the great many represents a superior power of mind and will.

The *Apology* is a powerful piece of writing, and no less so because it challenges many of our most deeply held beliefs.

The Last Days of Socrates

Plato

The Apology

Introduction: Socrates starts in rhetorical fashion, answering his opponent's claim that he will try to mislead the jury. He promises the truth, and begs to be allowed to speak in his own conversational style, into which he now slips.

What effect my accusers have had upon you, gentlemen, I do not know, but for my own part I was almost carried away by them; their arguments were so convincing. On the other hand, scarcely a word of what they said was true. I was especially astonished at one of their many misrepresentations: the point where they told you that you must be careful not to let me deceive you, implying that I am a skilful speaker. I thought that it was peculiarly brazen of them to have the nerve to tell you this, only just before events must prove them wrong, when it becomes obvious that I have not the slightest skill as a speaker—unless, of course, by a skilful speaker they mean one who speaks the truth. If that is what they mean, I would agree that I am an orator, and quite out of their class.

My accusers, then, as I maintain, have said little or nothing that is true, but from me you shall hear the whole truth; not, I can assure you, gentlemen, in flowery language like theirs, decked out with fine words and phrases; no, what you will hear will be improvised thoughts in the first words that occur to me, confident as I am in the justice of my cause; and I do not want any of you to expect anything different. It would hardly be suitable, gentlemen, for a man of my age to address you in the artificial language of a student exercise. One thing, however, I do most earnestly beg and entreat of you: if you hear me defending myself in the same language which it has been my habit to use, both around the trading stalls of be market-place (where many of you have heard me) and elsewhere, do not be surprised, and do not make a fuss because of it. My situation, you see, is as follows: this is my first appearance in a court of law, at the age of seventy; and so I am a complete stranger to the language of this place. Now if I were really from another country, you would assuredly excuse me if I spoke in the manner and dialect in which I had been brought up; and so in the present case I make this request of you, which I think is only reasonable: to disregard the manner of my speech—it doesn't matter how it compares—and to consider and concentrate your attention upon this one question, whether my claims are just or not. That is the first duty of the juryman, and it is the pleader's duty to speak the truth.

Section A: Ignoring the court charges for the moment, Socrates talks of the origins of his unpopularity in people's belief (i) that he is one of those who seek physical explanations rather than divine ones for everyday phenomena (i.e., a typical Presocratic philosopher), and (ii) that he is adept at pleading the poorer case more powerfully than the better one (i.e., a typical sophist).

The proper course for me, gentlemen of the jury, is to deal first with the earliest charges that have been falsely brought against me, and with my earliest accusers; and then with the later ones. I make this distinction because I have already been accused in your hearing by a great many people for a great many years, though without a word of truth; and I am more afraid of

---

From *The Last Days of Socrates* by Plato, translated by Hugh Tredennick (Penguin Classics 1954, Second revised edition 1969). Copyright © Hugh Tredennick, 1954, 1959, 1969. Reproduced by permission of Penguin Books Ltd.

those people than I am of Anytus and his colleagues, although they are formidable enough. But the others are still more formidable; I mean the people who took hold of so many of you when you were children and tried to fill your minds with untrue accusations against me, saying, "There is a clever man called Socrates who has theories about the heavens and has investigated everything below the earth, and can make the weaker argument defeat the stronger." It is these people, gentlemen, the disseminators of these rumours, who are my dangerous accusers; because those who hear them suppose that anyone who inquires into such matters does not also believe in gods. Besides, there are a great many of these accusers, and they have been accusing me now for a great many years; and what is more, they approached you at the most impressionable age, when some of you were children or adolescents; and they literally won their case by default, because there was no one to defend me. And the most problematic thing of all is that it is impossible for me even to know and tell you their names, unless one of them happens to be a playwright. All these people, who have tried to stir up convictions against me out of envy and love of slander and some too merely passing on what they have been told by others—all these are very difficult to deal with. It is impossible to bring them here for cross-examination; one simply has to conduct one's defence and argue one's case against an invisible opponent, because there is no one to answer. So I ask you to accept my statement that my critics fall into two classes: on the one hand my immediate accusers, and on the other those earlier ones whom I have mentioned; and you must suppose that I have first to defend myself against the latter. After all, you heard them accusing me at an earlier date and much more vehemently than these more recent accusers.

Very well, then; I must begin my defence, gentlemen, and I must try, in the short time that I have, to rid your minds of a false impression which is the work of many years. I should like this to be the result, gentlemen, assuming it to be for your advantage and my own; and I should like to be successful in my defence; but I think that it will be difficult, and I am quite aware of the nature of my task. However, let that turn out as God wills; I must obey the law and make my defence.

Let us go back to the beginning and consider what the charge is that has made people so critical of me, and has encouraged Meletus to draw up this indictment. Very well; what did my critics say in attacking my character? I must read out their affidavit, so to speak, as though they were my legal accusers. "Socrates is committing an injustice, in that he inquires into things below the earth and in the sky, and makes the weaker argument defeat the stronger, and teaches others to follow his example." It runs something like that. You have seen it for yourselves in the play by Aristophanes, where Socrates is lifted around, proclaiming that he is walking on air, and uttering a great deal of other nonsense about things of which I know nothing whatsoever. I mean no disrespect for such knowledge, if anyone really is versed in it—I do not want any more lawsuits brought against me by Meletus—but the fact is, gentlemen, that I take no interest in these things. What is more, I call upon the greater part of you as witnesses to my statement, and I appeal to all of you who have ever listened to me talking (and there are a great many to whom this applies) to reassure one another on this point. Tell one another whether any one of you has ever heard me discuss such questions briefly or at length; and then you will realize that the other popular reports about me are equally unreliable.

Section B: Socrates denies that he is a professional teacher.

The fact is that there is nothing in any of these charges; and if you have heard anyone say that I try to educate people and charge a fee, there is no truth in that either—though I think that it is a fine thing if a man has the ability to teach, as in the case of Gorgias of Leontini, Prodicus of Ceos and Hippias of Elis. Each one of these is perfectly capable of going into any city and actually persuading the young men to leave the company of their fellow citizens, with any of whom they can associate for nothing, attach themselves to him, pay money for the privilege, and be grateful into the bargain. There is another expert too from Paros who I discovered was here on a visit. I happened to meet a man who has paid more in sophists' fees than all the rest put together—I mean Callias, the son of Hipponicus; so I asked him (he has two sons, you see): "Callias," I said, "if your sons had been colts or calves, we should have had no difficulty in finding and engaging a trainer to make them excel in the appropriate qualities; and this trainer would have been some sort of horse-dealer or agriculturalist. But seeing that they are human beings, whom do you intend to get as their instructor? Who is the expert in perfecting the virtues of people in a society? I assume from the fact of your having sons that you must have considered the question. Is there such a person or not?" "Certainly," said he. "Who is he, and where does he come from?" said I, "and what does he charge?" "Evenus of Paros, Socrates," said he, "and his fee is 500 drachmae." I felt that Evenus was to be congratulated if he really was a master of this art and taught it at such a moderate fee. I should certainly become a proud and gentlemanly figure if I understood these things; but in fact, gentlemen, I do not.

Section C: Socrates explains what his own activity has been. The oracle of Apollo has declared that he is the wisest of men, and he has been trying to find men wiser than he is as part of his search for the god's meaning. The section begins in Socrates' conversational manner, but the narrative which follows is stylistically very like that of other Athenian speeches for the law-courts.

Here perhaps one of you might interrupt me and say, "But what is it that you do, Socrates? How is it that you have been misrepresented like this? Surely all this talk and gossip about you would never have arisen if you had confined yourself to ordinary activities, but only if your behaviour was abnormal. Give us the explanation, if you do not want us to draw our own conclusions." This seems to me to be a reasonable request, and I will try to explain to you what it is that has given me this false notoriety; so please give me your attention. Perhaps some of you will think that I am not being serious; but I assure you that I am going to tell you the whole truth.

I have gained this reputation, gentlemen, from nothing more or less than a kind of wisdom. What kind of wisdom do I mean? Human wisdom, I suppose. It seems that I really am wise in this limited sense. Presumably the geniuses whom I mentioned just now are wise in a wisdom that is more than human—I do not know how else to account for it, because I certainly do not have this knowledge, and anyone who says that I have is lying and just saying it to slander me. Now, gentlemen please do not interrupt me even if I seem to make an extravagant claim; for what I am going to tell you is not a tale of my own; I am going to refer you to an unimpeachable authority. I shall call as witness to my wisdom (such as it is) the god at Delphi.

You know Chaerephon, I presume. He was a friend of mine from boyhood, and a good democrat who played his part with the rest of you in the recent expulsion and restoration. And you know what he was like; how enthusiastic he was over anything that he had once undertaken. Well, one day he actually went to Delphi and asked this question of the god—as I said before, gentlemen, please do not interrupt—what he asked was whether there was anyone wiser than myself. The Pythian priestess replied that there was no one. As Chaerephon is dead, the evidence for my statement will be supplied by his brother here.

Please consider my object in telling you this. I want to explain to you how the attack on my reputation first started. When I heard about the oracle's answer, I said to myself, "What is the god saying, and what is his hidden meaning? I am only too conscious that I have no claim to wisdom, great or small; so what can he mean by asserting that I am the wisest man in the world? He cannot be telling a lie; that would not be right for him."

After puzzling about it for some time, I set myself at last with considerable reluctance to check the truth of it in the following way. I went to interview a man with a high reputation for wisdom, because I felt that here if anywhere I should succeed in disproving the oracle and pointing out to my divine authority, "You said that I was the wisest of men, but here is a man who is wiser than I am."

Well, I gave a thorough examination to this person—I need not mention his name, but it was one of our politicians that I was studying when I had this experience—and in conversation with him I formed the impression that although in many people's opinion, and especially in his own, he appeared to be wise, in fact he was not. Then when I began to try to show him that he only thought he was wise and was not really so, my efforts were resented both by him and by many of the other people present. However, I reflected as I walked away: "Well, I am certainly wiser than this man. It is only too likely that neither of us has any knowledge to boast of; but he thinks that he knows something which he does not know, whereas I am quite conscious of my ignorance. At any rate it seems that I am wiser than he is to this small extent, that I do not think that I know what I do not know."

After this I went on to interview a man with an even greater reputation for wisdom, and I formed the same impression again; and here too I incurred the resentment of the man himself and a number of others.

From that time on I interviewed one person after another. I realized with distress and alarm that I was making myself unpopular, but I felt compelled to put the god's business first; since I was trying to find out the meaning of the oracle, I was bound to interview everyone who had a reputation for knowledge. And by God, gentlemen (for I must be frank with you), my honest impression was thus: it seemed to me, as I pursued my investigation at the god's command, that the people with the greatest reputations were almost entirely deficient, while others who were supposed to be their inferiors were much more noteworthy for their general good sense.

I want you to think of my adventures as a cycle of labours undertaken to establish the truth of the oracle once for all. After I had finished with the politicians I turned to the poets, dramatic, lyric, and all the rest, in the belief that here I should expose myself as a comparative ignoramus. I used to pick up what I thought were some of their most polished works and question them closely about the meaning of what they had written, in the hope of incidentally enlarging my own knowledge. Well, gentlemen, I hesitate to tell you the truth, but it must be told. It is hardly an exaggeration to say that any of the bystanders could have explained those poems better than their actual authors. So I soon made up my mind about the poets too: I decided that it was not wisdom that enabled them to write their poetry, but a kind of instinct or inspiration, such as you find in seers and prophets who deliver all their sublime messages without knowing in the least what they mean. It seemed clear to me that the poets were in much the same case; and I also observed that the very fact that they were poets made them think that they had a perfect understanding of all other subjects, of which they were totally ignorant. So I left that line of inquiry too with the same sense of advantage that I had felt in the case of the politicians.

Last of all I turned to the skilled craftsmen. I knew quite well that I had practically no understanding myself, and I was sure that I should find them full of impressive knowledge. In this I was not disappointed; they understood things which I did not, and to that extent they were wiser than I was. However, gentlemen, these professional experts seemed to share the same failing which I had noticed in the poets; I mean that on the strength of their technical proficiency they claimed a perfect understanding of every other subject, however important; and I felt that this error eclipsed their positive wisdom. So I made myself spokesman for the oracle, and asked myself whether I would rather be as I was—neither wise with their wisdom nor ignorant with their ignorance—or possess both qualities as they did. I replied through myself to the oracle that it was best for me to be as I was.

Section D: The results of Socrates' interrogations: odium, poverty, wealthy youths who enjoy imitating him, and charges that he is responsible for corrupting them.

The effect of these investigations of mine, gentlemen, has been to arouse against me a great deal of hostility, and hostility of a particularly bitter and persistent kind, which has resulted in various malicious suggestions, and in having that term "wise" applied to me. This is due to the fact that whenever I succeed in disproving another person's claim to wisdom in a given subject, the bystanders assume that I know everything about that subject myself. But the truth of the matter, gentlemen, is likely to be this: that real wisdom is the property of the god, and this oracle is his way of telling us that human wisdom has little or no value. It seems to me that he is not referring literally to Socrates, but has merely taken my name as an example, as if he would say to us, "The wisest of you men is he who has realized, like Socrates, that in respect of wisdom he is really worthless."

That is why I still go about seeking and searching in obedience to the divine command, if I think that anyone is wise, whether citizen or stranger; and when I decide that he is not wise, I try to assist the god by proving that he is not. This occupation has kept me too busy to do much either in politics or in my own affairs; in fact, my service to God has reduced me to extreme poverty.

Furthermore the young men—those with wealthy fathers and plenty of leisure—have of their own accord attached themselves to me because they enjoy hearing other people cross-questioned. These often take me as their model, and go on to try to question other persons; whereupon, I suppose, they find an unlimited number of people who think that they know something, but really know little or nothing. Consequently their victims become annoyed, not with themselves but with me; and they complain that there is a pestilential busybody called Socrates who fills young people's heads with wrong ideas. If you ask them what he does, and what he teaches that has this effect, they have no answer, not knowing what to say; but as they do not want to admit their confusion, they fall back on the stock charges against any seeker after wisdom: that he teaches his pupils about things in the heavens and below the earth, and to disbelieve in gods, and to make the weaker argument defeat the stronger. They would be very loath, I fancy, to admit the truth: which is that they are being convicted of pretending to knowledge when they are entirely ignorant. They were so jealous, I suppose, for their own reputation, and also energetic and numerically strong, and spoke about me with such vigour and persuasiveness, that their harsh criticisms have for a long time now been monopolizing your ears.

Section E: Conclusion of the narrative concerned with Socrates' activities and of Socrates' reply to the "Old Accusers."

There you have the causes which led to the attack upon me by Meletus and Anytus and Lycon, Meletus being aggrieved on behalf of the poets, Anytus on behalf of the professional men and politicians, and Lycon on behalf of the orators. So, as I said at the beginning, I should be surprised if I were able, in the short time that I have, to rid your minds of a misconception so deeply implanted.

There, gentlemen, you have the true facts, which I present to you without any concealment or suppression, great or small. I am fairly certain that this plain speaking of mine is the cause of my unpopularity; and this really goes to prove that my statements are true, and that I have described correctly the nature and the grounds of the calumny which has been brought against me. Whether you inquire into them now or later, you will find the facts as I have just described them.

Section F: The cross-examination, part I. Socrates here proceeds to lose any sympathy which he may have gained in describing his activity by giving the jury a demonstration of how it works. Meletus's lack of thought for the upbringing of young men is exposed.

So much for my defence against the charges brought by the first group of my accusers. I shall now try to defend myself against Meletus—high-principled and patriotic as he claims to be—and after that against the rest.

Let us first consider their affidavit again, as though it represented a fresh prosecution. It runs something like this: "Socrates is guilty of corrupting the minds of the young, and of believing in supernatural things of his own invention instead of the gods recognized by the State." Such is the charge; let us examine its points one by one.

Now it claims that I am guilty of corrupting the young. But I say, gentlemen, that Meletus is guilty of treating a serious matter with levity, since he summons people to stand their trial on frivolous grounds, and professes concern and keen anxiety in matters to which he has never given the slightest attention. I will try to prove this to your satisfaction.

Come now, Meletus, tell me this. You regard it as supremely important, do you not, that our young people should be exposed to the best possible influence?

"I do."

Very well, then; tell these gentlemen who it is that influences the young for the better. Obviously you must know, if you pay it so much attention. You have discovered the vicious influence, as you say, in myself, and you are now prosecuting me before these gentlemen; speak up and inform them who it is that has a good influence upon the young—You see, Meletus, that you are tongue-tied and cannot answer. Do you not feel that this is discreditable, and a sufficient proof in itself of what I said, that you have not paid attention to the subject? Tell me, my friend, who is it that makes the young good?

"The laws."

That is not what I mean, my dear sir; I am asking you to name the person whose first business it is to know the laws.

"These gentlemen here, Socrates, the members of the jury."

Do you mean, Meletus, that they have the ability to educate the young, and to make them better?

"Certainly."

Does this apply to all jurymen, or only to some?

"To all of them."

Excellent! a generous supply of benefactors. Well, then, do these spectators who are present in court have an improving influence, or no?

"Yes, they do."

And what about the members of the Council?

"Yes, the Councillors too."

But surely, Meletus, the members of the Assembly do not corrupt the young? Or do all of them too exert an improving influence?

"Yes, they do."

Then it would seem that the whole population of Athens has a refining effect upon the young, except myself; and I alone corrupt them. Is that your meaning?

"Most emphatically, yes."

A great misfortune, indeed, you've damned me for! Well, let me put another question to you. Take the case of horses; do you believe that those who improve them make up the whole of mankind, and that there is only one person who has a bad effect on them? Or is the truth just the opposite, that the ability to improve them belongs to one person or to very few persons, who are horse-trainers, whereas most people, if they have to do with horses and make use of them, do them harm? Is not this the case, Meletus, both with horses and with all other animals? Of course it is, whether you and Anytus deny it or not. It would be a singular dispensation of fortune for our young people if there were only one person who corrupted them, while all the rest had a beneficial effect. Well then, Meletus, you've given ample proof that you have never bothered your head about the young; and you make it perfectly clear that you have never paid the slightest attention to the matters over which you are now indicting me.

Here is another point. Tell me seriously, Meletus, is it better to live in a good or in a bad community? Answer my question, like a good fellow; there is nothing difficult about it. Is it not true that wicked people do harm to those with whom they are in the closest contact, and that good people have a good effect?

"Quite true."

Is there anyone who prefers to be harmed rather than benefited by his associates? Answer me, please; the law commands you to answer. Is there anyone who prefers to be harmed?

"Of course not."

Well, then, when you summon me before this court for corrupting the young and making their characters worse, do you mean that I do so intentionally or unintentionally?"

"I mean intentionally."

Why, Meletus, are you at your age so much wiser than I at mine? You have discovered that bad people always have a bad effect, and good people a good effect, upon their nearest neighbours; am I so hopelessly ignorant as not even to realize that by spoiling the character of one of my companions I shall run the risk of getting some harm from him? So ignorant as to commit this grave offence intentionally, as you claim? No, I do not believe it, Meletus, and I do not suppose that anyone else does. Either I have not a bad influence, or it is unintentional; so in either case what you claim is false. And if I unintentionally have a bad influence, the correct procedure in cases of such involuntary misdemeanours is not to summon the culprit before this court, but to take him aside privately for instruction and reproof; because obviously if my eyes are opened, I shall stop doing what I do not intend to do. But you deliberately avoided my company in the past and refused to enlighten me, and now you bring me before this court, which is the place appointed for those who need punishment, not for those who need enlightenment.

Section G: The cross-examination, part II. With a suspicious-sounding argument Socrates tries to show that Meletus's formal charge contradicts itself. Meletus is made to claim that Socrates believes in no gods whatever, and, after confusing Socrates with Anaxagoras, is finally made to assent to the notion that the supernatural things referred to in the charge could only be believed in by one who believed in gods.

It is quite clear by now, gentlemen, that Meletus, as I said before, has never paid the slightest attention to this subject. However, I invite you to tell us, Meletus, in what sense you make out that I corrupt the minds of the young. Surely the terms of your indictment make it clear that you accuse me of teaching them to believe in new deities instead of the gods recognized by the state; isn't that the teaching of mine which you say has this demoralizing effect?

"That is precisely what I maintain."

Then I appeal to you, Meletus, in the name of these same gods about whom we are speaking, to explain yourself a little more clearly to myself and to the jury, because I cannot make out what your point is. Is it that I teach people to believe in some gods (which implies that I myself believe in gods, and am not a complete atheist, and so not guilty on that score), but in different gods from those recognized by the state, so that your accusation rests upon the fact that they are different? Or do you assert that I believe in no gods at all, and teach others to do the same?

"Yes; I say that you disbelieve in gods altogether."

You surprise me, Meletus; what is your object in saying that? Do you suggest that I do not believe that the sun and moon are gods, like other men do?

"He certainly does not, gentlemen of the jury, since he says that the sun is a stone and the moon a mass of earth."

Do you imagine that you are prosecuting Anaxagoras, my dear Meletus? Have you so poor an opinion of these gentlemen, and do you assume them to be so illiterate as not to know that the writings of Anaxagoras of Clazomenae are full of theories like these? And do you seriously suggest that it is from me that the young get these ideas, when they can buy them on occasion in the orchestra for a drachma at most, and so have the laugh on Socrates if he claims them for his own, especially when they are so peculiar? Tell me honestly, Meletus, is that your opinion of me? Do I believe in no god?

"No, none at all; not in the slightest degree."

You are not at all convincing, Meletus; not even to yourself, I suspect. In my opinion, gentlemen, this man is quite unable to restrain his insolence, and it is simply this which makes him bring this action against me—a kind of insolence or lack of restraint or youthful aggression. He seems to be devising a sort of riddle for me, saying to himself, "Will the infallible Socrates realize that I am contradicting myself for my own amusement, or shall I succeed in deceiving him and the rest of my audience?" It certainly seems to me that he is contradicting himself in this indictment, which might just as well run: "Socrates is guilty of not believing in the gods, but believing in the gods." And this is pure flippancy.

I ask you to examine with me, gentlemen, the line of reasoning which leads me to this conclusion. You, Meletus, will please answer my questions. And will the rest of you all please remember, as I requested at the beginning, not to interrupt if I conduct the discussion in my customary way?

Is there anyone in the world, Meletus, who believes in human matters, and not in human beings? Make him answer, gentlemen, and don't let him keep on making these continual objections. Is there anyone who does not believe in horses, but believes in equine matters? Or who does not believe in musicians, but believes in musical matters? No, there is not, my worthy friend. If you do not want to answer, I will supply it for you and for these gentlemen too. But the next question you must answer: Is there anyone who believes in supernatural matters and not in supernatural beings?"

"No."

How good of you to give a bare answer under compulsion by the court! Well, do you assert that I believe and teach others to believe in supernatural matters? It does not matter whether they are new or old; the fact remains that I believe in them according to your statement; indeed you solemnly swore as much in your affidavit. But if I believe in supernatural matters, it follows inevitably that I also believe in supernatural beings. Is not that so? It is; I assume your assent, since you do not answer. Do we not hold that supernatural beings are either gods or the children of gods? Do you agree or not?

"Certainly."

Then if I believe in supernatural beings, as you assert, if these supernatural beings are gods in any sense, we shall reach the conclusion which I mentioned just now when I said that you were testing me with riddles for your own amusement, by stating first that I do not believe in gods, and then again that I do, since I believe in supernatural beings. If on the other hand these supernatural beings are bastard children of the gods by nymphs or other mothers, as they are reputed to be, who in the world would believe in the children of gods and not in the gods themselves? It would be as ridiculous as to believe in the young of horses or donkeys and not in horses and donkeys themselves. No, Meletus; there is no avoiding the conclusion that you brought this charge against me to try me out, or else in despair of finding a genuine offence of which to accuse me. As for your prospect of convincing any living person with even a smattering of intelligence that belief in the supernatural does not imply belief in the divine, and again that non-belief in gods does not imply non-belief in supernatural beings and heroes, it is outside all the bounds of possibility.

Section H: Socrates is committed to his activities as if to his position in battle; he will not be prevailed upon to give them up. The section is important, in that Socrates puts his obligation to Apollo (based on a dubious personal interpretation of the oracle) ahead of a hypothetical command from the city that he should stop philosophizing. This section is more rhetorical at first, becoming chatty later.

As a matter of fact, gentlemen, I do not feel that it requires much defence to clear myself of Meletus's accusation; what I have said already is enough. But you know very well the truth of what I said in an earlier part of my speech, that I have incurred a great deal of bitter hostility; and this is what will bring about my destruction, if anything does; not Meletus or Anytus, but the slander and jealousy of a very large section of the people. They have been fatal to a great many other innocent men, and I suppose will continue to be so; there is no likelihood that they will stop at me. But perhaps someone will say, "Do you feel no compunction, Socrates, at having pursued an activity which puts you in danger of the death penalty?" I might fairly reply to him, "You are mistaken, my friend, if you think that a man who is worth anything ought to spend his time weighing up the prospects of life and death. He has only one thing to consider in performing any action; that is, whether he is acting justly or unjustly, like a good man or a bad one. On your view the heroes who died at Troy would be poor creatures, especially the son of Thetis. He, if you remember, made so light of danger in comparison with incurring dishonour that when his goddess mother warned him, eager as he was to kill Hector, in some such words as these, I fancy, 'My son, if you avenge your comrade Patroclus's death and kill Hector, you will die yourself;

Next after Hector is thy fate prepared,'

—when he heard this warning, he made light of his death and danger, being much more afraid of an ignoble life and of failing to avenge his friends. 'Let me die forthwith,' said he, 'when I have requited the villain, rather than remain here by the beaked ships to be mocked, a burden on the ground.' Do you suppose that he gave a thought to death and danger?"

The truth of the matter is this, gentlemen. Where a man has once taken up his stand, either because it seems best to him or in obedience to his orders, there I believe he is bound to remain and face the danger, taking no account of death or anything else before dishonour.

This being so, it would be shocking inconsistency on my part, gentlemen, if when the officers whom you chose to command me assigned me my position at Potidaea and Amphipolis and Delium, I remained at my post like anyone else and faced death, and yet afterwards, when God appointed me, as I supposed and believed, to the duty of leading the philosophic life, examining myself and others, I were then through fear of death or of any other danger to desert my post. That would indeed be shocking, and then I might really with justice be summoned to court for not believing in the gods, and disobeying the oracle, and being afraid of death, and thinking that I am wise when I am not. For let me tell you, gentlemen, that to be afraid of death is only another form of thinking that one is wise when one is not; it is to think that one knows what one does not know. No one knows with regard to death whether it is not really the greatest blessing that can happen to a man; but people dread it as though they were certain that it is the greatest evil; and this ignorance, which thinks that it knows what it does not, must surely be ignorance most culpable. This, I take it, gentlemen, is the extent, and this the nature of my superiority over the rest of mankind; and if I were to claim to be wiser than my neighbour in any respect, it would be in this: that not possessing any real knowledge of what awaits us in Hades, I am also conscious that I do not possess it. But I do know that to do wrong and to disobey my superior, whether god or man, is bad and dishonourable; and so I shall never feel more fear or aversion for something which, for all I know, may really be a blessing than for those evils which I know to be evils.

Suppose, then, that you acquit me, and pay no attention to Anytus, who has said that either I should not have appeared before this court at all, or, since I have appeared here, I must be put to death, because if I once escaped your sons would all immediately become utterly corrupted by putting the teaching of Socrates into practice. Suppose that, in view of this, you said to me, "Socrates, on this occasion we shall disregard Anytus and acquit you, but only on one condition: that you give up spending your time on this quest and stop philosophizing. If we catch you going on in the same way, you shall be put to death." Well, supposing, as I said, that you should offer to acquit me on these terms, I should reply, "Gentlemen, I am your very grateful and devoted servant, but I owe a greater obedience to God than to you; and so long as I draw breath and have my faculties, I shall never stop practising philosophy and exhorting you and indicating the truth for everyone that I meet. I shall go on saying, in my usual way, 'My very good friend, you are an Athenian and belong to a city which is the greatest and most famous in the world for its wisdom and strength. Are you not ashamed that you give your attention to acquiring as much money as possible, and similarly with reputation and honour, and give no attention or thought to truth and understanding and the perfection of your soul?' And if any of you disputes this and professes to care about these things, I shall not at once let him go or leave him; no, I shall question him and examine him and put him to the test; and if it appears that in spite of his profession he has made no real progress towards goodness, I shall reprove him for neglecting what is of supreme importance, and giving his attention to trivialities. I shall do this to everyone that I meet, young or old, foreigner or fellow-citizen; but especially to you my fellow-citizens, inasmuch as you are closer to me in kinship. This, I do assure you, is what my god commands; and it is my belief that no greater good has ever befallen you in this city than my service to my god; for I spend all my time going about trying to persuade you, young and old, to make your first and chief concern not for your bodies or for your possessions, but for the highest welfare of your souls, proclaiming as I go, 'Wealth does not bring goodness, but goodness brings wealth and every other blessing, both to the individual and to the state.' Now if I corrupt the young by this message, the message would seem to be harmful; but if anyone says that my message is different from this he is talking nonsense. And so, gentlemen," I would say, "You can please yourselves whether you listen to Anytus or not, and whether you acquit me or not; you know that I am not going to alter my conduct, not even if I have to die a hundred deaths."

Section I: Socrates represents his activity as a benefaction to the city. This is presented more like an old man's story than as a piece of court oratory.

Order, please, gentlemen! Abide by my request to give me a hearing without interruption; besides, I believe that it will be to your advantage to listen. I am going to tell you something else which may provoke a clamour; but please restrain yourselves. I assure you that if I am what I claim to be, and you put me to death, you will harm yourselves more than me. Neither Meletus nor Anytus can do me any harm at all; they would not have the power, because I do not believe that the law of God permits a better man to be harmed by a worse. No doubt my accuser might put me to death or have me banished or deprived of civic rights; but even if he thinks, as he probably does (and others too, I dare say), that these are great calamities, I do not think so; I believe that it is far worse to do what he is doing now, trying to put a man to death unjustly. For this reason, gentlemen, far from pleading on my own behalf, as might be supposed, I am really pleading on yours, to save you from misusing the gift of God by condemning me. If you put me to death, you will not easily find anyone to take my place. To put it bluntly (even if it sounds rather comical) God has assigned me to this city, as if to a large thoroughbred horse which because of its great size is inclined to be lazy and needs the stimulation of some stinging fly. It seems to me that God has attached me to this city to perform the office of such a fly; and all day long I never cease to settle here, there, and everywhere, rousing, persuading, reproving every one of you. You will not easily find another like me, gentlemen, and if you take my advice you will spare my life. But perhaps before long you may awake from your drowsing, and in your annoyance take Anytus's advice and finish me off thoughtlessly with a single slap; and then you could go on sleeping till the end of your days, unless God in his care for you sends someone to take my place.

If you doubt whether I am really the sort of person who would have been sent to this city as a gift from God, you can convince yourselves by looking at it in this way. Does it seem human that I should have neglected my own affairs and endured the humiliation of allowing my family to be neglected for all these years, while I busied myself all the time on your behalf, going like a father or an elder brother to see each one of you privately, and urging you to set your thoughts on goodness? if I had got any enjoyment from it, or if I had been paid for my good advice, there would have been some explanation for my conduct; but as it is you can see for yourselves that although my accusers unblushingly charge me with all sorts of other crimes, there is one thing that they have not had the impudence to pretend on any testimony, and that is that I have ever exacted or asked a fee from anyone. The witness that I can offer to prove the truth of my statement is good enough, I think—my poverty.

Section J: Socrates' failure to participate in public affairs is attributed to the timely intervention of his supernatural sign. Euthyphro (3b) shows how the very existence of such a sign could have been held against Socrates, and he might have been better advised not to introduce it. Similarly he would have been better advised not to suggest in a fiercely democratic court that any person committed to justice could not survive if he played a full part in the political life of his city. He also reprovingly draws attention to the time when he opposed unconstitutional action favoured by the people, and recalls a similar incident when he was given orders by the notorious Thirty. Neither story could have improved his standing with the jurors very much.

It may seem curious that I should go round giving advice like this and busying myself in people's private affairs, and yet never venture publicly to address you as a whole and advise on matters of state. The reason for this is what you have often heard me say before on many other occasions: that I am subject to a divine or supernatural experience, which Meletus saw fit to travesty in his indictment. It began in my early childhood—a sort of voice which comes to me; and when it comes it always dissuades me from what I am proposing to do, and never urges me on. It is this that debars me from entering public life, and a very good thing too, in my opinion; because you may be quite sure, gentlemen, that if I had tried long ago to engage in politics, I should long ago have lost my life, without doing any good either to you or to myself. Please do not be offended if I tell you the truth. No man on earth who conscientiously opposes either you or any other organized democracy, and flatly prevents a great many wrongs and illegalities from taking place in the state to which he belongs, can possibly escape with his life. The true champion of justice, if he intends to survive even for a short time, must necessarily confine himself to private life and leave politics alone.

I will offer you substantial proofs of what I have said; not theories, but what you better appreciate, facts. Listen while I describe my actual experiences, so that you may know that I would never submit wrongly to any authority through fear of death, but would refuse at any cost—even that of my life. It will be a commonplace story, such as you often hear in the courts; but it is true.

The only office which I have ever held in our city, gentlemen, was when I served on the Council. It so happened that our tribe Antiochis was presiding when you decided that the ten commanders who had failed to rescue the men who were lost in the naval engagement should be tried *en bloc*; which was illegal, as you all recognized later. On this occasion I was the only member of the executive who opposed your acting in any way unconstitutionally, and voted against the proposal; and although the public speakers were all ready to denounce and arrest me, and you were all urging them on at the top of your voices, I thought that it was my duty to face it out on the side of law and justice rather than support you, through fear of prison or death, in your wrong decision.

This happened while we were still under a democracy. When the oligarchy came into power, the Thirty Commissioners in their turn summoned me and four others to the Round Chamber and instructed us to go and fetch Leon of Salamis from his home for execution. This was of course only one of many instances in which they issued such instructions, their object being to implicate as many people as possible in their crimes. On this occasion, however, I again made it clear, not by my words but by my actions, that the attention I paid to death was zero (if that is not too unrefined a claim); but that I gave all my attention to avoiding doing anything unjust or unholy. Powerful as it was, that government did not terrify me into doing a wrong action; when we came out of the Round Chamber the other four went off to Salamis and arrested Leon, and I went home. I should probably have been put to death for this, if the government had not fallen soon afterwards. There are plenty of people who will testify to these statements.

Section K: A transitional passage (somewhat dogmatic and rhetorical) leads into further consideration of the effect that Socrates has had upon young men. Socrates explains why he has always made himself freely available to them, and observes that Meletus has failed to call any of his followers—or their relatives—as witnesses to the corruption charge.

Do you suppose that I should have lived as long as I have if I had moved in the sphere of public life, and conducting myself in that sphere like an honourable man, had always upheld the cause of right, and conscientiously set this end above all other things? Not by a very long way, gentlemen; neither would any other man. You will find that throughout my life I have been consistent in any public duties that I have performed, and the same also in my personal dealings: I have never countenanced any action that was incompatible with justice on the part of any person, including those whom some people maliciously call my pupils. I have never set up as any man's teacher; but if anyone, young or old, is eager to hear me conversing and carrying out my private mission, I never grudge him the opportunity; nor do I charge a fee for talking to him, and refuse to talk without one; I am ready to answer questions for rich and poor alike, and I am equally ready if anyone prefers to listen to what I have to say and answer my questions. If any given one of these people becomes a good citizen or a bad one, I cannot with justice be held responsible, since I have never promised or imparted any teaching to anybody; and if anyone asserts that he has ever learned or heard from me privately anything which was not open to everyone else, you may be quite sure that he is not telling the truth.

But how is it that some people enjoy spending a great deal of time in my company? You have heard the reason, gentlemen; I told you quite frankly. It is because they enjoy hearing me examine those who think that they are wise when they are not; an experience which has its amusing side. This duty I have accepted, as I said, in obedience to God's commands given in oracles and dreams and in every way that any other divine dispensation has ever impressed a duty upon man. This is a true statement, gentlemen, and easy to verify.

If it is a fact that I am in process of corrupting some of the young, and have succeeded already in corrupting others; and if it were a fact that some of the latter, being now grown up, had discovered that I had ever given them bad advice when they were young, surely they ought now to be coming forward to denounce and punish me; and if they did not like to do it themselves, you would expect some of their families—their fathers and brothers and other near relations—to remember it now, if their own flesh and blood had suffered any harm from me. Certainly a great many of them have found their way into this court, as I can see for myself: first Crito over there, my contemporary and near neighbour, the father of this young man Critobulus; and then Lysanias of Sphettus, the father of Aeschines here; and next Antiphon of Cephisia, over there, the father of Epigenes. Then besides there are all those whose brothers have been members of our circle: Nicostratus the son of Theozotides, the brother of Theodotus but Theodotus is dead, so he cannot appeal to his brother and Paralius here, the son of Demodocus; his brother was Theages. And here is Adimantus the son of Ariston, whose brother Plato is over there; and Aeantodorus, whose brother Apollodorus is here on this side. I can name many more besides, some of whom Meletus most certainly ought to have produced as witnesses in the course of his speech. If he forgot to do so then, let him do it now I'll make a concession; let him state whether he has any such evidence to offer. On the contrary, gentlemen, you will find that they are all prepared to help me—the corrupter and evil genius of their nearest and dearest relatives, as Meletus and Anytus say. The actual victims of my corrupting influence might perhaps be excused for helping me; but as for the uncorrupted, their relations of mature age, what other reason can they have for helping me except the just and proper one, that they know Meletus is lying and I am telling the truth?

Section L: Socrates excuses himself from the common practice of making pitiful appeals to the jurors. He does so on three grounds: that it would be dishonourable, that it would be inviting injustice, and that in inviting an unjust decision contrary to the juryman's oath, it would be impious. Being impious, he observes, it would be the way of one who does not believe in the gods. Socrates' tone has become that of a moral campaigner, lecturing the Athenians about their discreditable court practices. Socrates, on trial for his life, is virtually condemning the de facto procedures of the Athenian courts!

There, gentlemen: that, and perhaps a little more to the same effect, is the substance of what I can say in my defence. It may be that some one of you, remembering his own case, will be annoyed that whereas he, in standing his trial upon a less serious charge than this, made pitiful appeals to the jury with floods of tears, and had his infant children produced in court to excite the maximum of sympathy, and many of his relatives and friends as well, I on the contrary intend to do nothing of the sort, and that although I am facing (as it might appear) the utmost danger. It may be that one of you, reflecting on these facts, will harden himself against me, and being irritated by his reflections, will give his vote in anger. If one of you is so disposed—I do not expect it of you, but there is the possibility—I think that I should be quite justified in saying to him, "My dear sir, of course I have some relatives. To quote the very words of Homer, even I am not sprung 'from an oak or from a rock,' but from human parents, and consequently I have relatives; yes, and sons too, gentlemen, three of them, one almost grown up and the other two only children; but all the same I am not going to produce them here and beseech you to acquit me."

Why do I not intend to do anything of this kind? Not out of perversity, gentlemen, nor out of contempt for you; whether I am brave or not in the face of death has nothing to do with it; the point is that for my own credit and yours and for the credit of the state as a whole, I do not think that it is honourable for me to use any of these methods at my age and with my reputation—which may be true or it may be false, but at any rate the view is established that Socrates is different from the common run of mankind. Now if those of you who are supposed to be distinguished for wisdom or courage or any other virtue were to behave in this way, it would be a disgrace. I have often noticed that some people of this type, for all their high standing, go to extraordinary lengths when they come up for trial, which shows that they think it will be a dreadful thing to lose their lives; as though they would be immortal if you did not put them to death! In my opinion these people bring disgrace upon our city. Any of our visitors might be excused for thinking that the finest specimens of Athenian manhood, whom their fellow-citizens choose in preference to themselves for archonships and other high positions, are no better than women. If you have even the smallest reputation, gentlemen, you ought not to descend to these methods; and if we do so, you must not give us licence. On the contrary, you must make it clear that anyone who stages these pathetic scenes and so brings ridicule upon our city is far more likely to be condemned than if he kept perfectly quiet.

But apart from all question of appearances, gentlemen, I do not think that it is *just* for a man to appeal to the jury or to get himself acquitted by doing so; he ought to inform them of the facts and convince them by argument. The jury does not sit to dispense justice as a favour, but to decide where justice lies; and the oath which they have sworn is not to show favour at their own discretion, but to return a just and lawful verdict. It follows that we must not develop in you, nor you allow to grow in yourselves, the habit of perjury; that would be impious for us both. Therefore you must not expect me, gentlemen, to behave towards you in a way which I consider neither reputable nor just nor consistent with my religious duty; and above all you must not expect it when I stand charged with impiety by Meletus here. Surely it is obvious that if I tried to persuade you and prevail upon you by my entreaties to go against your solemn oath, I should be teaching you contempt for religion; and by my very defence I should be virtually accusing myself of having no religious belief. But that is very far from the truth. I have a more sincere belief, gentlemen, than any of my accusers; and I leave it to you and to God to judge me in whatever way shall be best for me and for yourselves.

The verdict is "Guilty"

Section M: Socrates, having now been convicted by a comparatively narrow margin of sixty votes, has to propose a penalty as an alternative to the death penalty claimed by the prosecution. He still adheres to some of the bolder theses of his defence speech, something which Plato is able to use to draw the threads of his Picture of Socrates together. But the jurors would probably have been dismayed to see how little his attitude has changed. Socrates argues that he deserves to be sentenced to dining at public expense like victors at the Games. After firmly rejecting prison or exile, he offers a fine, firstly one within his means, and secondly thirty times that after his friends offer to help.

There are a great many reasons, gentlemen, why I am not distressed by this result—I mean your condemnation of me—but the chief reason is that the result was not unexpected. What does surprise me is the number of votes cast on the two sides. I should never have believed that it would be such a close thing; but now it seems that if a mere thirty votes had gone the other way, I should have been acquitted. Even as it is, I feel that so far as Meletus's part is concerned I have been acquitted; and not only that, but anyone can see that if Anytus and Lycon had not come forward to accuse me, Meletus would actually have lost a thousand drachmae for not having obtained one fifth of the votes.

However, we must face the fact that he demands the death penalty. Very good. What alternative penalty shall I propose to you, gentlemen? Obviously it must be what's deserved. Well, what penalty do I deserve to pay or suffer, in view of what I have done?

I have never lived an ordinary quiet life. I did not care for the things that most people care about: making money, having a comfortable home, high military or civil rank, and all the other activities—political appointments, secret societies, party organizations—which go on in our city; I thought that I was really too fair-minded to survive if I went in for this sort of thing. So instead of taking a course which would have done no good either to you or to me, I set myself to do you individually in private what I hold to be the greatest possible service: I tried to persuade each one of you not to think more of practical advantages than of his mental and moral well-being, or in general to think more of advantage than of well-being, in the case of the state or of anything else. What do I deserve for behaving in this way? Some reward, gentlemen, if I am bound to suggest what I really deserve; and what is more, a reward which would be appropriate for myself. Well, what is appropriate for a poor man who is a public benefactor and who requires leisure for the purpose of giving you moral encouragement? Nothing could be more appropriate for such a person than free dining in the Prytaneum. He deserves it much more than any victor in the races at Olympia, whether he wins with a single horse or a pair or a team of four. These people give you the semblance of success, but I give you the reality; they do not need maintenance, but I do. So if I am to suggest an appropriate penalty which is strictly in accordance with justice, I suggest free maintenance by the state.

Perhaps when I say this I may give you the impression, as I did in my remarks about exciting sympathy and making passionate appeals, that I am showing a stubborn perversity. That is not so, gentlemen; the real position is this. I am convinced that I never wrong anyone intentionally, but I cannot convince you of this, because we have had so little time for discussion. If it was your practice, as it is with other nations, to give not one day but several to the hearing of capital trials, I believe that you might have been convinced; but under present conditions it is not easy to dispose of grave allegations in a short space of time. So being convinced that I do no wrong to anybody, I can hardly be expected to wrong myself by asserting that I deserve something bad, or by proposing a corresponding penalty. Why should I? For fear of suffering this penalty proposed by Meletus, when, as I said, I do not know whether it is a good thing or a bad? Do you expect me to choose something which I know very well is bad by making my counter-proposal? Imprisonment? Why should I spend my days in prison, in subjection to whichever Eleven hold office? A fine, with imprisonment until it is paid? In my case the effect would be just the same, because I have no money to pay a fine. Or shall I suggest banishment? You would very likely accept the suggestion.

I should have to be desperately in love with life to do that, gentlemen. I am not so blind that I cannot see that you, my fellow-citizens, have come to the end of your patience with my discussions and conversations; you have found them too irksome and irritating, and now you are trying to get rid of them. Will any other people find them easy to put up with? That is most unlikely, gentlemen. A fine life I should have if I left this country at my age and spent the rest of my days trying one city after another and being turned out every time! I know very well that wherever I go the young people will listen to my conversation just as they do here; and if I try to keep them off, they themselves will prevail upon their elders and have me thrown out, while if I do not, the fathers and other relatives will drive me out of their own accord for the sake of the young.

Perhaps someone may say, "But surely, Socrates, after you have left us you can spend the rest of your life in quietly minding your own business." This is the hardest thing of all to make some of you understand. If I say that this would be disobedience to God, and that is why I cannot "mind my own business," you will not believe me—you'll think I'm pulling your leg. If on the other hand I tell you that to let no day pass without discussing goodness and all the other subjects about which you hear me talking and examining both myself and others is really the very best thing that a man can do, and that life without this sort of examination is not worth living, you will be even less inclined to believe me. Nevertheless that is how it is, gentlemen, as I maintain; though it is not easy to convince you of it. Besides, I am not accustomed to think of myself as deserving punishment. If I had money, I would have suggested a fine that I could afford, because that would not have done me any harm. As it is, I cannot, because I have none; unless of course you like to fix the penalty at what I could pay. I suppose I could probably afford a hundred drachmae and I suggest a fine of that amount.

One moment, gentlemen. Plato here, and Crito and Critobulus and Apollodorus, want me to propose three thousand drachmae on their security. Very well, I agree to this sum, and you can rely upon these gentlemen for its payment.

The penalty is death

Section N: Socrates converses with the jurymen after being sentenced by an increased majority of jurors (over two-thirds) to death rather than a fine.

Well, gentlemen, for the sake of a very small gain in time you are going to earn the reputation—and the blame from those who wish to disparage our city—of having put Socrates to death, "that wise man," because they will say I am wise even if I am not, these people who want to find fault with you. If you had waited just a little while, you would have had your way in the course of nature. You can see that I am well on in life and near to death. I am saying this not to all of you but to those who voted for my execution, and I have something else to say to them as well.

No doubt you think, gentlemen, that I have been condemned for lack of the arguments which I could have used if I had thought it right to leave nothing unsaid or undone to secure my acquittal. But that is very far from the truth. It is not a lack of arguments that has caused my condemnation, but a lack of effrontery and impudence, and the fact that I have refused to address you in the way which would give you most pleasure. You would have liked to hear me weep and wail, doing and saying all sorts of things which I declare to be unworthy of myself, but which you are used to hearing from other people. But I did not think then that I ought to stoop to servility because I was in danger, and I do not regret now the way in which I pleaded my case; I would much rather die as the result of this defence than live as the result of the other sort. In a court of law, just as in warfare, neither I nor any other ought to use his wits to escape death by any means. In battle it is often obvious that you could escape being killed by giving up your arms and throwing yourself upon the mercy of your pursuers; and in every kind of danger there are plenty of devices for avoiding death if you are unscrupulous enough to stop at nothing. But I suggest, gentlemen, that the difficulty is not so much to escape death; the real difficulty is to escape from wickedness, which is far more fleet of foot. In this present instance I, the slow old man, have been overtaken by the slower of the two, but my accusers, who are clever and quick, have been overtaken by the faster: by iniquity. When I leave this court I shall go away condemned by you to death, but they will go away convicted by Truth herself of depravity and injustice. And they accept their sentence even as I accept mine. No doubt it was bound to be so, and I think that the result is fair enough.

Having said so much, I feel moved to prophesy to you who have given your vote against me; for I am now at that point where the gift of prophecy comes most readily to men: at the point of death. I tell you, my executioners, that as soon as I am dead, vengeance shall fall upon you with a punishment far more painful than your killing of me. You have brought about my death in the belief that through it you will be delivered from submitting the conduct of your lives to criticism; but I say that the result will be just the opposite. You will have more critics, whom up till now I have restrained without your knowing it; and being younger they will be harsher to you and will cause you more annoyance.

If you expect to stop denunciation of your wrong way of life by putting people to death, there is something amiss with your reasoning. This way of escape is neither possible nor creditable; the best and easiest way is not to stop the mouths of others, but to make yourselves as well behaved as possible. This is my last message to you who voted for my condemnation.

As for you who voted for my acquittal, I should very much like to say a few words to reconcile you to this result, while the officials are busy and I am not yet on my way to the place where I must die. I ask you, gentlemen, to spare me these few moments; there is no reason why we should not exchange a few words while the law permits. I look upon you as my friends, and I want to show you the meaning of what has now happened to me.

Gentlemen of the jury—for you deserve to be so called—I have had a remarkable experience. In the past the prophetic voice to which I have become accustomed has always been my constant companion, opposing me even in quite trivial things if I was going to take the wrong course. Now something has happened to me, as you can see, which might be thought and is commonly considered to be a supreme calamity; yet neither when I left home this morning, nor when I was taking my place here in the court, nor at any point in any part of my speech, did the divine sign oppose me. In other discussions it has often checked me in the middle of a sentence; but this time it has never opposed me in any part of this business in anything that I have said or done. What do I suppose to be the explanation? I will tell you, I suspect that this thing that has happened to me is a blessing, and we are quite mistaken in supposing death to be an evil. I have good grounds for thinking this, because my accustomed sign could not have failed to oppose me if what I was doing had not been sure to bring some good result.

We should reflect that there is much reason to hope for a good result on other grounds as well. Death is one of two things. Either it is annihilation, and the dead have no consciousness of anything; or, as we are told, it is really a change: a migration of the soul from this place to another. Now if there is no consciousness but only a dreamless sleep, death must be a marvelous gain. I suppose that if anyone were told to pick out the night on which he slept so soundly as not even to dream, and then to compare it with all the other nights and days of his life, and then were told to say, after due consideration, how many better and happier days and nights than this he had spent in the course of his life—well, I think that the Great King himself, to say nothing of any private person, would find these days and nights easy to count in comparison with the rest. If death is like this, then, I call it gain; because the whole of time, if you look at it in this way, can be regarded as no more than one single night. If on the other hand death is a removal from here to some other place, and if what we are told is true, that all the dead are there, what greater blessing could there be than this, gentlemen of the jury? If on arrival in the other world, beyond the reach of these so-called jurors here, one will find there the true jurors who are said to preside in those courts, Minos and Rhadamanthys and Aeacus and Triptolemus and all those other demi-gods who were upright in their earthly life, would that be an unrewarding place to settle? Put it in this way; how much would one of you give to meet Orpheus and Musaeus, Hesiod and Homer? I am willing to die ten times over if this account is true. For me at least it would be a wonderful personal experience to join them there, to meet Palamedes and Ajax the son of Telamon and any other heroes of the old days who met their death through an unjust trial, and to compare my fortunes with theirs—it would be rather amusing, I think—and above all I should like to spend my time there, as here, in examining and searching people's minds, to find out who is really wise among them, and who only thinks that he is. What would one not give, gentlemen, to be able to scrutinize the leader of that great host against Troy, or Odysseus, or Sisyphus, or the thousands of other men and women whom one could mention, their company and conversation—like the chance to examine them—would be unimaginable happiness? At any rate I presume that they do not put one to death there for such conduct; because apart from the other happiness in which their world surpasses ours, they are now immortal for the rest of time, if what we are told is true.

You too, gentlemen of the jury, must look forward to death with confidence, and fix your minds on this one belief, which is certain: that nothing can harm a good man either in life or after death, and his fortunes are not a matter of indifference to the gods. This present experience of mine does not result from mere earthly causes; I am quite clear that the time had come when it was better for me to die and be released from my distractions. That is why my sign never turned me back. For my own part I bear no grudge at all against those who condemned me and accused me, although it was not with this kind intention that they did so, but because they thought that they were hurting me; and that is culpable of them. However, I ask them to grant me one favour. When my sons grow up, gentlemen, if you think that they are putting money or anything else before goodness, take your revenge by plaguing them as I plagued you; and if they fancy themselves for no reason, you must scold them just as I scolded you, for neglecting the important things and thinking that they are good for something when they are good for nothing. If you do this, I shall have had justice at your hands—I and my children.

Well, now it is time to be off, I to die and you to live; but which of us has the happier prospect is unknown to anyone but God.

GREEK FOUNDATIONS

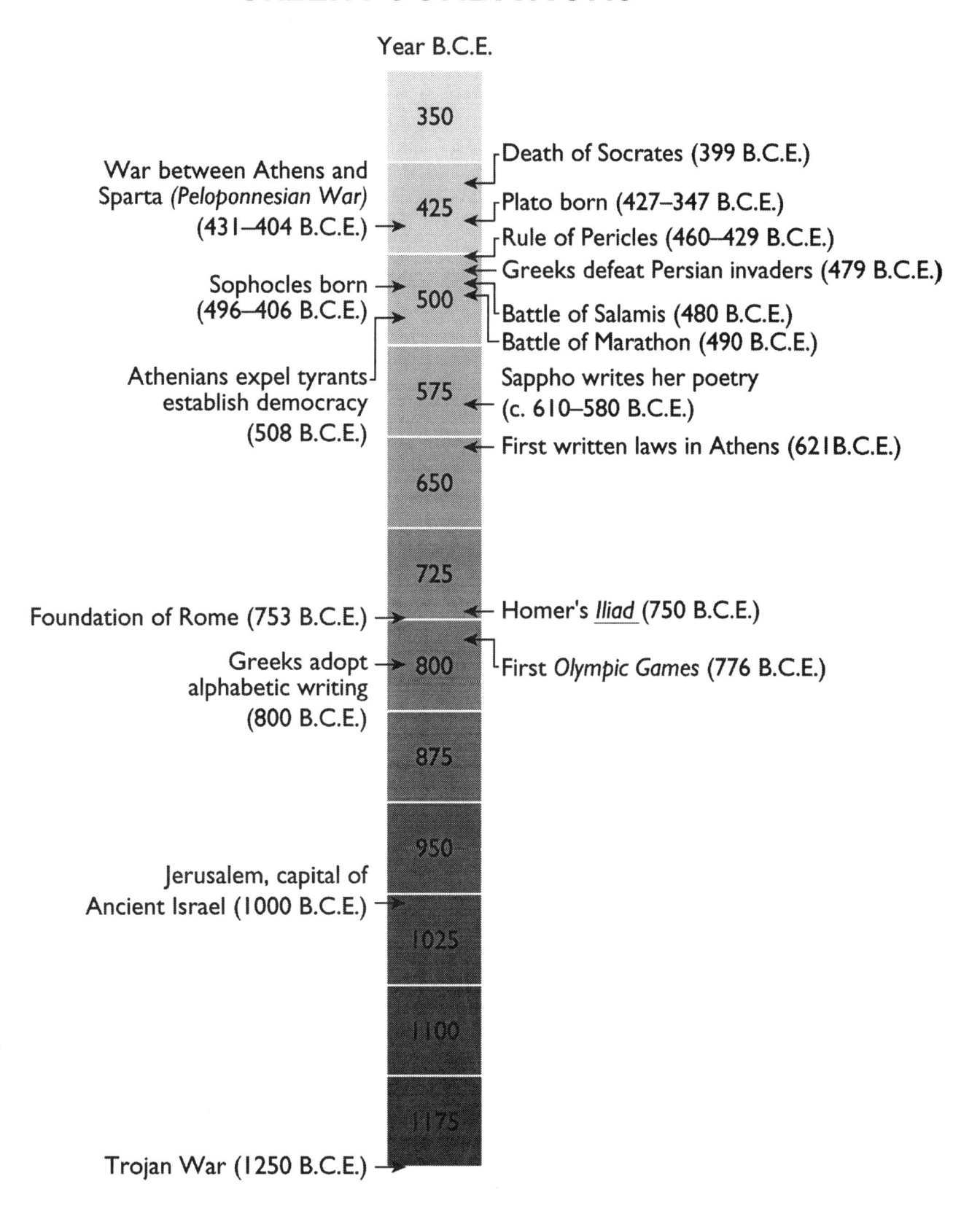

Year B.C.E.

Year	Left Events	Right Events
350		
425	War between Athens and Sparta *(Peloponnesian War)* (431–404 B.C.E.)	Death of Socrates (399 B.C.E.) Plato born (427–347 B.C.E.) Rule of Pericles (460–429 B.C.E.)
500	Sophocles born (496–406 B.C.E.)	Greeks defeat Persian invaders (479 B.C.E.) Battle of Salamis (480 B.C.E.) Battle of Marathon (490 B.C.E.)
575	Athenians expel tyrants establish democracy (508 B.C.E.)	Sappho writes her poetry (c. 610–580 B.C.E.) First written laws in Athens (621 B.C.E.)
650		
725		
	Foundation of Rome (753 B.C.E.)	Homer's *Iliad* (750 B.C.E.)
800	Greeks adopt alphabetic writing (800 B.C.E.)	First *Olympic Games* (776 B.C.E.)
875		
950		
	Jerusalem, capital of Ancient Israel (1000 B.C.E.)	
1025		
1100		
1175		
	Trojan War (1250 B.C.E.)	

Religious Foundations

No account of our Intellectual Heritage would be adequate that left out the religious traditions and their key texts. The *Hebrew Bible* and the *New Testament* have had a profound impact upon the public sphere and, of course, upon people's private lives. Many modern people would have no reluctance in saying that they guide their lives upon the teachings of these ancient works. The *Qur'an* is the source of guidance for Muslims, and Islam is the fastest growing religion in the United States, both because of immigration and of conversions. In addition, the *Qur'an* provides further discussion of the laws and beliefs announced in the Judeo-Christian tradition. We include also the *Sundiata: an Epic of Old Mali*. While this work is not a religious scripture at all, it does provide some insight into beliefs and practices of a non-Western source.

The Greeks trusted in reason and to the cleverness of humankind. Pericles praises the accomplishments of his fellow Athenians and looks to no divine source to account for the grandeur of their city. The "numberless wonders" speech in *Antigone*, even though it leads to the recognition of the importance of the gods, celebrates the powers of human beings to command the forces of nature and their own inward chaos. Plato hears a mysterious voice within, but it is a voice that urges him to employ his reason to delve into the mysteries of his being and of justice in his city. Intellect is praised as the source of man's greatness.

The religious tradition starts in an entirely different place. From *Genesis* on, it is clear that human beings are wretched when they are left to their own powers. Adam and Eve are foolish and disloyal, pathetic and even ridiculous. Early inventions include such glories as the Tower of Babel and Sodom and Gomorrah. In Noah's time, God can find only one man who is pious and remembers his Creator. In *Exodus*, the Israelites in slavery forget their Lord and His promises and slip into a slavery of mind and spirit far more profound than their physical enslavement. The first two-thirds of *Exodus* portrays a stubbornly ignorant people, disobedient, dishonorable, and enslaved to their appetites and fears.

The contrast with the Greeks could not be more startling. For religious traditions of monotheism, humankind are helpless and wicked without the powerful presence and guiding hand of God. Human nature is weak and wayward; our mind is endlessly inventive and misleading, our will is weak, our appetites are uncontrolled; our behavior towards one another is lawless and aggressive. The Ten Commandments are not made to prohibit what we do not do, but what we are avid to do and do constantly—murder, steal, lie, dishonor parents, commit adultery, covet neighbors' goods and wives; that is where our nature leads us. Our only help is the firm hand of God, the source of law and of the punishments that keep us on the correct path in life.

The source of information is entirely different from the Greeks. The traditions of monotheism do not rely on reason but on revelation. The authority for the truth is not some man-made argument that can stand against all logical challenge, but the authority of God Himself. Although the laws of God are surely meant to construct the dignity of humankind and our freedom within a lawful community in which human life will flourish and find happiness, the process by which the law becomes known and established is not democratic. God is not another citizen convincing us of the truth of his arguments by reasoning with us. He announces what is good for us and promises stern punishments should we choose to disobey. Given our willfulness and moral confusion—as depicted relentlessly in the Bible—we require this authoritative guidance and are incapable of self-guidance by reason.

The scriptures show also God's powerful hand in history. God chooses whom he will to be his instrument. The Israelites are chosen in *Exodus* despite (but also because of) their slavish nature. God will make them a into a "priestly kingdom" and a "holy nation"—surely one of His greatest miracles—in order to show His power and love to all the world. The Israelites must bear this burden of being God's "chosen people" and often fall short. In *Isaiah* we learn of the terrible consequences for them when they forget their obligations to God but also of God's long-term promise that they will produce the Messiah who will redeem the world.

One book of the Hebrew Bible should remind of Greek art and thought, and that is the *Book of Job*. Here a mortal man must suffer what appears to be the injustice of God and sustain his faith against all reason. Job should remind us of Oedipus, and how universal certain questions are.

The *New Testament*, produced by and for the Jews of the first century of our era, fulfills this ancient promise. Jesus comes to renew the law, to announce a religion of universal brotherhood, to conquer death with the promise of life eternal, to announce eternal justice to those who experience none of it in this corrupted world, and to establish love and not law as the center of all human affairs. God's sacrifice of His son in the form of human flesh is a bond to redeem humankind from the original sin and fall, and to offer humankind the promise of eternal salvation for those who can give themselves wholly to God. Seven hundred years after the promise in *Isaiah*, the *New Testament* fulfills God's pledge.

For Muslims, God announces Himself again six hundreds years after the coming of the prophet Jesus. Muhammad, himself a prophet and not divine, hears directly from the angel Gabriel the last and most complete account from God of what humankind must be and do. Considered by Muslims to be the final revelation, the *Qur'an* contains yet another powerful expression of how human beings are to live so as to honor God and the best that is in them. Like Christianity, there is a strong emphasis upon God's Judgment at the Last Day and the final justice that will reward those who obeyed God's law and punish those who did as they pleased. Like the Hebrew Bible, the *Qur'an* provides a thorough guide to life, in this world and towards the next.

Finally, the *Sundiata* introduces us to animism, an outlook where the world is composed of spiritual presences. Here, nature contains god-like beings whose influence upon human beings is profound. Like the Greeks, ancient Africans have many spiritual presences, and they are near to us in everyday dealings. They are not by any means exclusively concerned with morality. However, they do guide us towards our destinies, both individual and national. Sundiata himself should remind us of Moses, a national liberator who draws strength from supernatural sources and brings the law that makes us able to fulfill the promise of goodness that is in us.

Introduction to the Bible

—G.W.

Jewish and Christian Bibles

The English word "Bible" comes from the Greek *ta biblia* which means "The Books," a name well chosen since the Bible is a collection of individual works from numerous authors over a long period of time (from approximately 1225 B.C.E. to 200 C.E.). For the Jewish community, the Bible is composed of twenty-four books divided into three sections: Torah (Law), Prophets (divided into Former and Latter Prophets), and Writings. The term "Hebrew Bible" will be used to refer to this collection.

Some Christian denominations (Roman Catholics, Eastern Orthodox) add six or seven additional books (plus additions to the books of Esther and Daniel). These additional books are called *Deuterocanonicals* (second canon) by these groups and the *Apocrypha* by most Protestants whose Old Testament has the same contents as the Hebrew Bible although in a different order. Table 1 illustrates these differences.

The Christian community added twenty-seven early Christian writings to the Hebrew Bible, which became known as the New Testament, with the Hebrew Bible becoming known as the Old Testament to Christians. All Christian Bibles agree on the number and order of the books of the New Testament.

For ease of use in finding sections of the Bible, the books were divided into chapters and verses (e.g., Genesis 1:3 refers to the third verse in the first chapter of Genesis).

The Hebrew Bible

The Torah has a narrative framework. The narrative includes a prehistory (Genesis 1–11) that sets the stage for the story of Israel's origins; the adventures of the Patriarchs of Israel; and an account of Moses, the Exodus, Israel at Mount Sinai, and forty years of journeying that ends with Israel on the border of the Promised Land. Almost all of ancient Israel's surviving rituals, legal materials, and customs have been collected together into the Moses/Mount Sinai setting in Exodus, Leviticus, Numbers, and Deuteronomy

The Prophets in the Hebrew Bible are divided into two sections. The Former Prophets recount Israel's history from the death of Moses through the entrance into Canaan; the rise and fall of first one, then two Israelite kingdoms; and the Babylonian conquest of the Southern kingdom, Judah, the longest surviving Israelite kingdom. This history is interpreted in the light of the basic prophetic religious conviction that when Israel obeyed God they prospered and when they did not, disaster was imminent. The Latter Prophets contain collections of the words of Israel's prophets, many in poetic form, from the eighth through the fifth centuries B.C.E.

The Writings are a varied collection of literary types. There is religious poetry (Psalms, Lamentations), love poetry (Song of Songs), and wisdom writings (Job, Proverbs, Ecclesiastes). Chronicles, Ezra, and Nehemiah are, like the Former Prophets, history interpreted in religious terms. Ruth and Esther are short works of edifying fiction. Daniel is the only apocalyptic* book

---

* Apocalyptic literature is a genre of literature that comes in response to an extreme crisis in faith. Its primary focus is on a future triumph of faith, perhaps in a new age, a new world by those who remain constant in their faith during that crisis. Daniel, for example, comes out of an attempt to erase Judaism under the reign of Antiochus Epiphanes IV and makes use of numerology and images which are not always clear to modem interpreters of the Bible.

Table 1. The Books of the Hebrew Bible/Old Testament

Hebrew Bible	*Protestant Bible*	*Catholic Bible*
THE LAW	PENTATEUCH	PENTATEUCH
Genesis	Genesis	Genesis
Exodus	Exodus	Exodus
Leviticus	Leviticus	Leviticus
Numbers	Numbers	Numbers
Deuteronomy	Deuteronomy	Deuteronomy
THE PROPHETS	HISTORICAL BOOKS	HISTORICAL BOOKS
Former Prophets	Joshua	Joshua
Joshua	Judges	Judges
Judges	Ruth	Ruth
Samuel	I & II Samuel	I & II Samuel
Kings	I & II Kings	I & II Kings
Latter Prophets	I & II Chronicles	I & II Chronicles
Isaiah	Ezra	Ezra
Jeremiah	Nehemiah	Nehemiah
Ezekiel	Esther	Tobit
(The Twelve)	POETRY & WISDOM	Judith
Hosea	Job	Esther (with
Joel	Psalms	additions)
Amos	Proverbs	I & II Maccabees
Obadiah	Ecclesiastes	POETRY & WISDOM
Jonah	Song of Solomon	Job
Micah	MAJOR PROPHETS	Pslams
Nahum	Isaiah	Proverbs
Habakkuk	Jeremiah &	Ecclesiastes
Zephaniah	Lamentations	Song of Songs
Haggai	Ezekiel	Wisdom of Solomon
Zechariah	MINOR PROPHETS	Ecclesiasticus
Malachi	Daniel	(Wisdom of
THE WRITINGS	Hosea	ben Sira)
Psalms	Joel	MAJOR PROPHETS
Proverbs	Amos	Isaiah
Job	Obadiah	Jeremiah &
Song of Songs	Jonah	Lamentations
(or Solomon)	Micah	Baruch
Ruth	Nahum	Ezekiel
Lamentations	Habakkuk	MINOR PROPHETS
Ecclesiastes (or	Zephaniah	Daniel (with
ben Sira, or Sirach)	Haggai	additions)
Esther	Zechariah	Hosea
Daniel	Malachi	Joel
Ezra		Amos
Nehemiah		Obadiah
Chronicles		Jonah
		Micah
		Nahum
		Habakkuk
		Zephaniah
		Haggai
		Zechariah
		Malachi

in the Hebrew Bible (along with Revelation in the New Testament); it is only in the Christian tradition that Daniel is placed among the prophets.

The apocryphal (or deuterocanonical) books contain the same variety and many of the same literary types as the Hebrew Bible. Ecclesiasticus and Wisdom of Solomon are Jewish wisdom books of high quality. I and II Maccabees are historical books from the period between the Hebrew Bible and the New Testament. Tobith and Judith are short stories. Susanna and Bel and the Dragon are edifying tales appended to Daniel. The Prayer of Azariah and the Song of the Three Young Men are psalm poetry added to Daniel. The additions to Esther provide a more explicit religious piety to the Hebrew Bible version.

The New Testament

The gospels (Matthew, Mark, Luke, and John) are narrative works offering teachings of Jesus and accounts of events in his life. They were a new literary form driven by their purposes of convincing readers that Jesus was the messiah, encouraging conversions to Christianity, and instructing the converted. They were not written in their present form until a generation or two after Jesus' death.[*] The Acts of the Apostles is also a narrative work, taking up where the gospels leave off. It gives a schematic history of the early spread of Christianity.

The letter is the most common literary form in the New Testament. Thirteen or fourteen letters have been attributed to the most important figure in the early church, the Apostle Paul. Others are attributed to the apostles Peter and John, and James and Jude (brothers of Jesus). Some works that most scholars do not regard as letters have been included as such in the New Testament (e.g., Hebrews, First John, James). The Revelation (to John) is the only apocalyptic book to be included.

Outline of Bible History

Table 2, gives the historical contexts in which the various books of the Bible were produced, and approximate dates. Writings did not originate in a vacuum but out of the events in the history of Judaism and Christianity which they are often a response to. Some sense of date and events is helpful in understanding the message of the various writings of the Bible.

The Development of the Bible

Using the resources of the biblical scholarship of the last several centuries, it is possible to describe the process that brought the different portions of the Bible into their final form. The following section provides a general overview of that process. Dates listed, unless otherwise noted, mark the beginning of the process.

The Hebrew Bible

Oral tradition preserved much of the early traditions within the Hebrew community for centuries. Contained within that tradition were the stories that are included in Genesis 1–11, the material about the Patriarchs, and the story of Moses and the exodus, as well as others. (1900 B.C.E.)

About the time of Moses, the first written traditions began to develop, probably very limited. Possibly many of the laws of the Pentateuch were included as they began to be collected around the Ten Commandments. (1290 B.C.E.)

The oral tradition continued to grow simultaneously with a primitive written tradition. These traditions were preserved by special persons in the community and interpreted current history from the religious belief that Yahweh, God, was active in that history, indeed was revealed in his actions in their history. (1250 B.C.E.)

With the establishment of monarchy, most of the existing oral material was written down and court histories began to be kept. Some oral tradition continued as well. (1020 B.C.E.) When Israel

---

[*] See, for example, Matthew 18 in the New Revised Standard Version, where several references to "the church" are attributed to Jesus. The church had not come into existence until some time after Jesus' life and death.

Table 2. Outline of Bible History

Event or Period	Approximate Date	Biblical Reference
Abraham & the Patriarchs	1900–1700 B.C.E.	Genesis 11–50
Moses & the Exodus	1275–1225 B.C.E.	Exodus–Deuteronomy
Joshua & the conquest of Canaan	1200 B.C.E.	Joshua
The Judges (tribal confederacy)	1200–1020 B.C.E.	Judges
The Monarchy	1020–587 B.C.E.	Kings & Chronicles
The Prophets	1250–450 B.C.E.	Prophetic Books
Division of Israel & Judah	922 B.C.E.	II Kings
The Babylonian Exile	587–539 B.C.E.	Ezra–Nehemiah, Prophets
The Postexilic Period	539 B.C.E.–135 C.E.	
The Hellenistic Period	323–165 B.C.E.	Daniel
The Maccabean Period	165–63 B.C.E.	Maccabees
The Roman Period	63–135 C.E.	
The Birth of Jesus	8–4 B.C.E.	Gospels
The Founding of Christianity	30 C.E.	Acts
Paul's Ministry	33–65 C.E.	Acts & Letters of Paul
Development of Christian Literature	50–120 C.E.	
Completion of the Bible	After 200 C.E.	

was divided into two kingdoms (Judah and Israel), each community developed and maintained its own traditions, both oral and written, and these traditions preserved the point of view of the South and the North. (922 B.C.E.)

In both the Northern and Southern kingdoms, prophets began to play a central role. The traditions surrounding a prophet were, at first, maintained orally. By about 750 B.C.E. the prophets or their disciples began to record their prophecies in poetic form and these were preserved by the religious communities of both kingdoms. (922 B.C.E.) In addition, in the Southern kingdom (Judah) the priests (the most prominent religious group) began to preserve and shape the religious tradition. (922 B.C.E.)

Following the fall of the Northern kingdom (Israel) to Assyria in 722/21 B.C.E., some of those who preserved the religious traditions of the North escaped to Judah and the process of the merger of the two traditions began. (700 B.C.E.) The combined religious traditions of Israel and Judah were introduced into the community of Judah during the reign of King Josiah. Portions of the Hebrew Bible, most likely the Pentateuch, began to assume the authority of scripture. (521 B.C.E.)

The fall of the Southern Kingdom to Babylon and the period of exile which followed brought a further merger of the two traditions. Prophetic and priestly traditions were woven together and the religious point of view of both these traditions were preserved. Synagogues began to develop in this period and the preserved religious traditions became central to the community of faith. (587 B.C.E.)

The literary traditions, the written texts, began to replace the living prophets as Judaism sought to understand the events in their history and the theological interpretation of those events was extremely important to the editors/redactors who shaped the Hebrew Bible. With Hellenization this process was intensified as Israel looked to the past to understand and live out its relationship with the God of Israel. By 165 B.C.E. religious authority was rooted in the literary traditions of the Hebrew Bible and by the end of the first century C.E., the Hebrew Bible which survives today had emerged from the community.

In the nineteenth century, the Graf-Wellhausen hypothesis argued for four primary sources for the Pentateuch (and in subsequent sections of the Hebrew Bible, also). Noting different names for God in stories told two or more times, lists of kings that had not appeared yet in the time of Moses, the repetition of the phrase, "until this day," etc., the authors suggested that at least the first five books of the Bible were composed of four separate sources identified as J (the Southern tradition), E (the Northern tradition), P (the Priestly tradition) and D (Deuteronomy). While there is currently a great deal of debate over the specific identification of the sources, that there are numerous sources woven together in the Hebrew Bible is not being questioned in the discussion.

The New Testament

Christianity began with a scripture, the Hebrew Bible which they accepted. The process of the shaping of the New Testament began as stories about Jesus, as well as sayings of Jesus, some oral, some written, were preserved among those who believed that Jesus was the messiah. (33 C.E.) Included was the development of the traditions concerning his death and resurrection.

Paul, a convert to Christianity after the death of Christ and a major figure in the rise and spread of Christianity, wrote letters to communities where the early churches had been established (either by him or other Christians) and had begun to grow. Jesus' sayings began to be applied with the authority of scripture. (49 C.E.) As the eyewitnesses to many of the events of Jesus' life began to die, the stories about, and the sayings of, Jesus were placed into a written form, a primitive, early form of what would come to be the gospels.* Further letters and other accounts about Jesus were produced, also. (80 C.E.) The only apocalyptic work in the New Testament was produced probably under the influence of persecution by the Romans. (100 C.E.) Paul's letters were also being used with the authority of scripture by this time.

By 150 C.E., in addition to the Gospels and letters of Paul, some of the other works now in the New Testament were being used, with the Hebrew Bible, as scripture. Other works which are not included in the New Testament also continued to be used, but by 393 C.E. the twenty-seven books which make up the New Testament in its present form were universally agreed upon.

Textual History

The textual history of the Bible focuses on the preservation and transmission of the Bible in the original languages (Hebrew, Aramaic, and Greek) and the translation of the Bible into other languages. Since we have no "original" texts, we are dependent on manuscripts copied and passed on and early translations from original languages into other ancient languages.

Until the late 1940s, with the discovery of the Dead Sea Scrolls, the oldest complete Hebrew manuscript available for textual study dated from around 1000 C.E. The discovery of the Dead Sea Scrolls in caves along the shores of the Dead Sea gave us manuscripts from ca. 200–100 B.C.E., over 1000 years older than the previous manuscripts. Portions of every book of the Hebrew Bible except Esther were discovered there and illustrated the high degree of accuracy of the transmission of the text from 200 B.C.E. to 1000 C.E.

The textual history of the New Testament is also complex, with at least 5,000 known handwritten manuscripts, no two of which are exactly alike. Fortunately, most of the differences are of minor significance in determining the basic meaning of the texts. Again, almost all good modern translations will indicate in the notes at the bottom of the page the readings of other manuscripts and versions where there is disagreement. Good modern translations rest on the study of these manuscripts and versions and it's highly likely that the first author-editors of the biblical books would recognize these texts as close to those they worked with or produced.

---

* Most New Testament scholars accept that the gospels are composed of several sources. The most widely recognized theory argues for Mark as the first gospel, followed by Matthew and Luke, who based their gospels on Mark, and also shared a common sayings of Jesus source called Q (from the German *quelle*, "source"). They included material from independent sources called M and L, respectively. When the gospels in their present form were completed and by whom cannot be determined with any real certainty.

Translation of the Bible into English

Because most students in IH are dependent upon English translations, following is a brief survey of the basic stages in the development of the English Bible. The first complete translation into English was by John Wycliffe in ca. 1382 and while enthusiastically received by the people in England, church and state authorities banned the translation, condemning to death any who used it.

About 150 years later, William Tyndale translated the New Testament from Greek into English. Because of pressure from the church, he finished his work in Germany and when the translation reached England it was attacked by church authorities, who complained that it would lead to vice, corruption, and moral depravity. Tyndale was later executed for having translated the Bible into the vernacular. The first complete English Bible to be printed was translated by Miles Coverdale and published in 1535. As with the previous version and the subsequent versions based on Coverdale's translation, there was great debate over the worth of such translations, with the church hierarchy generally opposed.

In response to the growing popularity of the English translations, the Roman Catholic leaders joined together in support of a new English version, the result being the Douay Version (1606–1610). This would remain the official Catholic Bible until the twentieth century. Its Protestant equivalent, the King James Version (Authorized Version, 1611), was ordered by King James in an attempt to bring unity to a divided church in England. While there was initial resistance, this translation would become the most widely used Bible among Protestants well into the twentieth century.

In the nineteenth century important new manuscripts of the Bible in the original languages were discovered, making new translations desirable. A revision of the Authorized version (AV), based on the new evidence, was produced by an interdenominational group of scholars in England and published in 1885. An American revision, the American Standard Version, appeared in 1901.

A revision of the 1885 and 1901 versions was done in America in the 1930s and 1940s and published in 1952 as the Revised Standard Version. The Bible that IH uses is the New Revised Standard Version, a recent revision of the Revised Standard Bible. These two versions are widely used today in America.

Other modern translations include the New English Bible (1970), prepared by British scholars; the New American Bible (1970), prepared by the Catholic Biblical Association and sponsored by the American Bishops, which replaced the Douay Version as the Catholic Bible; the Jerusalem Bible, a translation into English from the French version produced by Catholic scholars; the New American Standard (1975), another revision of the 1901 Authorized version; the Good News for Modern Man, or Today's English Version as it is known in the American Bible Society's version, (1976) perhaps the most readable translation into English; and the New International Version (1978), a bible meant to replace the New King James Version among conservative Protestants.

For students not familiar with the original languages, it is often a good idea to compare several alternative readings of difficult passages in modern translations to see the possible range of meanings.

Why So Many Translations?

This is a frequently asked question, along with "Why are they so different?" and "Which one is best?" There are a number of reasons: new, better manuscripts are discovered and new translations make use of them; English language continues to develop and as the meanings of words change (e.g., the meaning of "gay" in the last few years) and new idioms come into a language, new translations become necessary; we also have increasing knowledge of the original languages in which the Bible was written that improves our understanding and results in new translations.

Translations do not always agree and to some extent every translation involves interpretation. Hebrew originally had no vowels and no word division. Try making sense, in English, of the following by adding vowels and dividing it into words:

GDSNWHR

You could have come up with "God is now here" or "God is nowhere," two radically different points of view. In most instances, context would determine the choice of which meaning was intended by the original translation. In the Bible, the former would be more likely; while in a reading from Freud or Marx, one might opt for the second phrase.

In addition, words in the original languages often carry multiple meanings and the translator has to decide which meaning to choose in the translation. In Genesis 1:2 the Hebrew word *ruach* means both "spirit" and "wind" and either would fit the context. Modern translations are about evenly divided as to which meaning was intended here.

Which translation is best? Out of the recent translations, IH has selected the New Revised Standard Version of the Bible as the one for IH. You can, of course, always read your favorite version in addition to this translation.

Why Read the Bible in IH Anyway?

Year after year the Bible remains the world's best selling book with perhaps one hundred and fifty billion sold since Gutenberg invented the printing press in 1453 and made the Bible his first project. As a best seller the Bible would seem to have a great deal against it—it is a collection that at times does not seem to have a great deal of unity, its size is overwhelming, the names and places are often strange and difficult to pronounce, and the ideas belong to a world that has long since passed away.

If the task of reading the Bible is so difficult, why should it be considered a worthwhile part of Intellectual Heritage? There are a number of possible reasons for its inclusion: it contains a vast literature of wisdom and knowledge that has guided numerous generations before us; it contains profound insights into the meaning of human life; it is the single most important source for Western culture, especially the words and phrases we commonly use; it has had the most profound influence on modern religious thought; it offers us the most complete history of the ancient past that we possess and for millions of Christians, Jews, and, to a lesser extent, Muslims it is authoritative in their faith. To understand their faiths and the importance of those faiths in world history, a knowledge of the works of the Bible is necessary. No survey of literature that has had a profound effect on our society and our world would be complete without the inclusion of the Bible.

Hebrew Bible

The Hebrew Bible is an immense text which includes many kinds of literature from mythic tales, to songs and poems, to philosophical dramas, to historical chronicles, and prophecy. Our attempt is to allow you to sample some of this richness while we explore several of the most important themes.

Many Christian readers are surprised that the Hebrew Bible is about Hebrews at all. Christianity adopted, and in some cases adapted the Hebrew Bible and named it the "Old Testament" both to indicate the priority of their own *New Testament* and to appropriate the book of the Jews as their own. However, there is no mistaking the fact that the Hebrew Bible is written in Hebrew, by Jews, and primarily about Jewish law and history. This is, at the same time, not to deny that the *New Testament* is built upon this earlier collection of sacred materials and forms a development out of those Jewish materials. For our purposes, we will consider the Hebrew Bible as the basis of Judaism and explore the religion, history, law, and wisdom of that people.

We begin, of course, with *Genesis*, and look closely at the creation story in the first chapter and at its continuation in the Story of the Garden of Eden. The story of Adam and Eve, so well known to most readers, on a mature reading reveals subtleties. What is freedom? Why do they (and we) mistake blessings for injuries? What is our marital relation meant to be? Why is life so difficult for us? How do we tame our will? All these questions and more wind out of this remarkable story of our first parents.

Genesis is rich with stories—the tower of Babel, Sodom and Gomorrah, Noah and the Flood, Abraham and Isaac, Jacob's theft of his brother's birthright, and Joseph of his remarkable life. We cannot treat all of these stories, but we do some of them, and in close detail.

Exodus recounts the liberation of the Israelites who had been enslaved in Egypt for 430 years. Their enslavement is not only physical but moral, as we see them behave crudely towards the Lord, despite His many miracles and blessings. The greatest miracle of God is the task of transforming this "stiff-necked" crowd into a "priestly kingdom and a holy nation." As we see, this is not so easily done and requires not only the giving of the law but bloody slaughter. Moses emerges as something more than a simple lawgiver or the vehicle for God's miracles as we witness the desperate choices that he makes.

In *Psalms* we hear some of the mature expression of Israel, celebrating victories, suffering the doubts of power and conquest, agonizing affliction while maintaining a hard faith. These songs and poems remind us, especially the famous Psalm 23, of how religion and life became inseparable for "God's Chosen."

Job is a remarkable philosophical drama in which Satan and the Almighty test the faith of a good man by showering miseries upon his life. Although the tradition maintains that Job is patient under his afflictions, the story may make us doubt that conclusion. Job, as any of us would, loses his balance and raises doubts about God and his justice. He debates his fears with his companions and is by no means consoled by argument and discussion. When God appears to him in a whirlwind, it is to conquer Job's dwindling faith in an amazing show of power. The entire drama may well remind us of Oedipus and his struggle under the assault of his gods. *Job* continues to speak to modern people who by no means live their lives without suffering and pain and an unsteady faith in God.

Isaiah represents what the bulk of the Hebrew Bible treats. When the Jews forget God, largely because of their success and their growing wealth, God brings down upon them the harshest of punishments. The "Chosen People" are made to lose their kingdom and suffer the humiliation of being conquered and scattered by their neighbors. Prophets like Isaiah explain why the Jews have earned this hard treatment and offer a promise of return. In the case of *Isaiah* we are offered a vision of a Messianic future world where God's love and justice will reign supreme. Much of this material, written 700 years before the birth of Christ, is appropriated within the Christian vision of the messiah come to change the world. *Isaiah* also offers a vision of Zion, the Jewish version of the "Good City" that Plato constructs in his *Republic*.

The Hebrew Bible material is probably known to many student readers from earlier reading, especially in childhood. Our goal is to explore the Bible in an adult way and show how thoughtful and challenging a book it really is for mature readers.

The creation of heaven and earth in Genesis provides a fascinating account. The Sun and Moon, created on Day Four, provide light. Yet light has already been provided on Day One. The stars provide "signs and seasons", that is, they offer a calendar and astrological assistance. Corbis-Bettmann.

Genesis

Six Days of Creation and the Sabbath

1 In the beginning when God created the heavens and the earth, ²the earth was a formless void and darkness covered the face of the deep, while a wind from God swept over the face of the waters. ³Then God said, "Let there be light"; and there was light. ⁴And God saw that the light was good; and God separated the light from the darkness. ⁵God called the light Day, and the darkness he called Night. And there was evening and there was morning, the first day.

6 And God said, "Let there be a dome in the midst of the waters, and let it separate the waters from the waters." ⁷So God made the dome and separated the waters that were under the dome from the waters that were above the dome. And it was so. ⁸God called the dome Sky. And there was evening and there was morning, the second day.

9 And God said, "Let the waters under the sky be gathered together into one place, and let the dry land appear." And it was so. ¹⁰God called the dry land Earth, and the waters that were gathered together he called Seas. And God saw that it was good. ¹¹Then God said, "Let the earth put forth vegetation: plants yielding seed, and fruit trees of every kind on earth that bear fruit with the seed in it." And it was so. ¹²The earth brought forth vegetation: plants yielding seed of every kind, and trees of every kind bearing fruit with the seed in it. And God saw that it was good. ¹³And there was evening and there was morning, the third day.

14 And God said, "Let there be lights in the dome of the sky to separate the day from the night; and let them be for signs and for seasons and for days and years, ¹⁵and let them be lights in the dome of the sky to give light upon the earth." And it was so. ¹⁶God made the two great lights—the greater light to rule the day and the lesser light to rule the night—and the stars. ¹⁷God set them in the dome of the sky to give light upon the earth, ¹⁸to rule over the day and over the night, and to separate the light from the darkness. And God saw that it was good. ¹⁹And there was evening and there was morning, the fourth day.

20 And God said, "Let the waters bring forth swarms of living creatures, and let birds fly above the earth across the dome of the sky." ²¹So God created the great sea monsters and every living creature that moves, of every kind, with which the waters swarm, and every winged bird of every kind. And God saw that it was good. ²²God blessed them, saying, "Be fruitful and multiply and fill the waters in the seas, and let birds multiply on the earth." ²³And there was evening and there was morning, the fifth day.

24 And God said, "Let the earth bring forth living creatures of every kind: cattle and creeping things and wild animals of the earth of every kind." And it was so. ²⁵God made the wild animals of the earth of every kind, and the cattle of every kind, and everything that creeps upon the ground of every kind. And God saw that it was good.

26 Then God said, "Let us make humankind in our image, according to our likeness; and let them have dominion over the fish of the sea, and over the birds of the air, and over the cattle, and

---

Scripture quotations are from the *New Revised Standard Version of the Bible*, copyright 1989 by the Division of Christian Education of the National Council of the Churches of Christ in the USA. Used by permission. All rights reserved.

over all the wild animals of the earth, and over every creeping thing that creeps upon the earth." ²⁷ So God created humankind in his image,
in the image of God he created them;
male and female he created them.
²⁸God blessed them, and God said to them, "Be fruitful and multiply, and fill the earth and subdue it; and have dominion over the fish of the sea and over the birds of the air and over every living thing that moves upon the earth." ²⁹God said, "See, I have given you every plant yielding seed that is upon the face of all the earth, and every tree with seed in its fruit; you shall have them for food. ³⁰And to every beast of the earth, and to every bird of the air, and to everything that creeps on the earth, everything that has the breath of life, I have given every green plant for food." And it was so. ³¹God saw everything that he had made, and indeed, it was very good. And there was evening and there was morning, the sixth day.

2 Thus the heavens and the earth were finished, and all their multitude. ²And on the seventh day God finished the work that he had done, and he rested on the seventh day from all the work that he had done. ³So God blessed the seventh day and hallowed it, because on it God rested from all the work that he had done in creation.

4 These are the generations of the heavens and the earth when they were created.

Another Account of the Creation

In the day that the LORD God made the earth and the heavens, ⁵when no plant of the field was yet in the earth and no herb of the field had yet sprung up—for the LORD God had not caused it to rain upon the earth, and there was no one to till the ground; ⁶but a stream would rise from the earth, and water the whole face of the ground—⁷then the LORD God formed man from the dust of the ground, and breathed into his nostrils the breath of life; and the man became a living being. ⁸And the LORD God planted a garden in Eden, in the east; and there he put the man whom he had formed. ⁹Out of the ground the LORD God made to grow every tree that is pleasant to the sight and good for food, the tree of life also in the midst of the garden, and the tree of the knowledge of good and evil.

10 A river flows out of Eden to water the garden, and from there it divides and becomes four branches. ¹¹The name of the first is Pishon; it is the one that flows around the whole land of Havilah, where there is gold; ¹²and the gold of that land is good; bdellium and onyx stone are there. ¹³The name of the second river is Gihon; it is the one that flows around the whole land of Cush. ¹⁴The name of the third river is Tigris, which flows east of Assyria. And the fourth river is the Euphrates.

15 The LORD God took the man and put him in the garden of Eden to till it and keep it. ¹⁶And the LORD God commanded the man, "You may freely eat of every tree of the garden; ¹⁷but of the tree of the knowledge of good and evil you shall not eat, for in the day that you eat of it you shall die."

18 Then the LORD God said, "It is not good that the man should be alone; I will make him a helper as his partner." ¹⁹So out of the ground the LORD God formed every animal of the field and every bird of the air, and brought them to the man to see what he would call them; and whatever the man called every living creature, that was its name. ²⁰The man gave names to all cattle, and to the birds of the air, and to every animal of the field; but for the man there was not found a helper as his partner. ²¹So the LORD God caused a deep sleep to fall upon the man, and he slept; then he took one of his ribs and closed up its place with flesh. ²²And the rib that the LORD God had taken from the man he made into a woman and brought her to the man. ²³Then the man said,

"This at last is bone of my bones
and flesh of my flesh;
this one shall be called Woman,
for out of Man this one was taken."

24 Therefore a man leaves his father and his mother and clings to his wife, and they become one flesh. ²⁵And the man and his wife were both naked, and were not ashamed.

The First Sin and Its Punishment

3 Now the serpent was more crafty than any other wild animal that the LORD God had made. He said to the woman, "Did God say, 'You shall not eat from any tree in the garden'?" ²The woman said to the serpent, "We may eat of the

fruit of the trees in the garden; ³but God said, 'You shall not eat of the fruit of the tree that is in the middle of the garden, nor shall you touch it, or you shall die.'" ⁴But the serpent said to the woman, "You will not die; ⁵for God knows that when you eat of it your eyes will be opened, and you will be like God, knowing good and evil." ⁶So when the woman saw that the tree was good for food, and that it was a delight to the eyes, and that the tree was to be desired to make one wise, she took of its fruit and ate; and she also gave some to her husband, who was with her, and he ate. ⁷Then the eyes of both were opened, and they knew that they were naked; and they sewed fig leaves together and made loincloths for themselves.

8 They heard the sound of the LORD God walking in the garden at the time of the evening breeze, and the man and his wife hid themselves from the presence of the LORD God among the trees of the garden. ⁹But the LORD God called to the man, and said to him, "Where are you?" ¹⁰He said, "I heard the sound of you in the garden, and I was afraid, because I was naked; and I hid myself." ¹¹He said, "Who told you that you were naked? Have you eaten from the tree of which I commanded you not to eat?" ¹²The man said, "The woman whom you gave to be with me, she gave me fruit from the tree, and I ate." ¹³Then the LORD God said to the woman, "What is this that you have done?" The woman said, "The serpent tricked me, and I ate." ¹⁴The LORD God said to the serpent,

"Because you have done this,
 cursed are you among all animals
 and among all wild creatures;
upon your belly you shall go,
 and dust you shall eat
all the days of your life.
¹⁵ I will put enmity between you and the woman,
 and between your offspring and hers;
he will strike your head,
 and you will strike your heel."

¹⁶To the woman he said,

"I will greatly increase your pangs in childbearing;
 in pain you shall bring forth children,
yet your desire shall be for your husband,
 and he shall rule over you."

¹⁷And to the man he said,

"Because you have listened to the voice of your wife,
 and have eaten of the tree
about which I commanded you,
 'You shall not eat of it,'
cursed is the ground because of you;
 in toil you shall eat of it all the days of your life;
¹⁸ thorns and thistles it shall bring forth for you;
 and you shall eat the plants of the field.
¹⁹ By the sweat of your face
 you shall eat bread
until you return to the ground,
 for out of it you were taken;
you are dust,
 and to dust you shall return."

20 The man named his wife Eve, because she was the mother of all living. ²¹And the LORD God made garments of skins for the man and for his wife, and clothed them.

22 Then the LORD God said, "See, the man has become like one of us, knowing good and evil; and now, he might reach out his hand and take also from the tree of life, and eat, and live forever"— ²³therefore the LORD God sent him forth from the garden of Eden, to till the ground from which he was taken. ²⁴He drove out the man; and at the east of the garden of Eden he placed the cherubim, and a sword flaming and turning to guard the way to the tree of life.

Cain Murders Abel

4 Now the man knew his wife Eve, and she conceived and bore Cain, saying, "I have produced a man with the help of the LORD." ²Next she bore his brother Abel. Now Abel was a keeper of sheep, and Cain a tiller of the ground. ³In the course of time Cain brought to the LORD an offering of the fruit of the ground, ⁴and Abel for his part brought of the firstlings of his flock, their fat portions. And the LORD had regard for Abel and his offering, ⁵but for Cain and his offering he had no regard. So Cain was very angry, and his countenance fell. ⁶The LORD said to Cain, "Why are you angry, and why has your countenance fallen? ⁷If you do well, will you not be accepted? And if you do not do well, sin is lurking at the door; its desire is for you, but you must master it."

8 Cain said to his brother Abel, "Let us go out to the field." And when they were in the field, Cain rose up against his brother Abel, and killed him. ⁹Then the LORD said to Cain, "Where is your brother Abel?" He said, "I do not know; am I my brother's keeper?" ¹⁰And the LORD said, "What have you done? Listen; your brother's

blood is crying out to me from the ground! ¹¹And now you are cursed from the ground, which has opened its mouth to receive your brother's blood from your hand. ¹²When you till the ground, it will no longer yield to you its strength; you will be a fugitive and a wanderer on the earth." ¹³Cain said to the LORD, "My punishment is greater than I can bear! ¹⁴Today you have driven me away from the soil, and I shall be hidden from your face; I shall be a fugitive and a wanderer on the earth, and anyone who meets me may kill me." ¹⁵Then the LORD said to him, "Not so! Whoever kills Cain will suffer a sevenfold vengeance." And the LORD put a mark on Cain, so that no one who came upon him would kill him. ¹⁶Then Cain went away from the presence of the LORD, and settled in the land of Nod, east of Eden.

Beginnings of Civilization

17 Cain knew his wife, and she conceived and bore Enoch; and he built a city, and named it Enoch after his son Enoch. ¹⁸To Enoch was born Irad; and Irad was the father of Mehujael, and Mehujael the father of Methushael, and Methushael the father of Lamech. ¹⁹Lamech took two wives; the name of the one was Adah, and the name of the other Zillah. ²⁰Adah bore Jabal; he was the ancestor of those who live in tents and have livestock. ²¹His brother's name was Jubal; he was the ancestor of all those who play the lyre and pipe. ²²Zillah bore Tubal-cain, who made all kinds of bronze and iron tools. The sister of Tubal-cain was Naamah.

23 Lamech said to his wives:

"Adah and Zillah, hear my voice;
  you wives of Lamech, listen to what I say:
I have killed a man for wounding me,
  a young man for striking me.
²⁴ If Cain is avenged sevenfold,
  truly Lamech seventy-sevenfold."

25 Adam knew his wife again, and she bore a son and named him Seth, for she said, "God has appointed for me another child instead of Abel, because Cain killed him." ²⁶To Seth also a son was born, and he named him Enosh. At that time people began to invoke the name of the LORD.

The Wickedness of Humankind

6 When people began to multiply on the face of the ground, and daughters were born to them, ²the sons of God saw that they were fair; and they took wives for themselves of all that they chose. ³Then the LORD said, "My spirit shall not abide in mortals forever, for they are flesh; their days shall be one hundred twenty years." ⁴The Nephilim were on the earth in those days—and also afterward—when the sons of God went in to the daughters of humans, who bore children to them. These were the heroes that were of old, warriors of renown.

5 The LORD saw that the wickedness of humankind was great in the earth, and that every inclination of the thoughts of their hearts was only evil continually. ⁶And the LORD was sorry that he had made humankind on the earth, and it grieved him to his heart. ⁷So the LORD said, "I will blot out from the earth the human beings I have created—people together with animals and creeping things and birds of the air, for I am sorry that I have made them." ⁸But Noah found favor in the sight of the LORD.

Noah Pleases God

9 These are the descendants of Noah. Noah was a righteous man, blameless in his generation; Noah walked with God. ¹⁰And Noah had three sons, Shem, Ham, and Japheth.

11 Now the earth was corrupt in God's sight, and the earth was filled with violence. ¹²And God saw that the earth was corrupt; for all flesh had corrupted its ways upon the earth. ¹³And God said to Noah, "I have determined to make an end of all flesh, for the earth is filled with violence because of them; now I am going to destroy them along with the earth. ¹⁴Make yourself an ark of cypress wood; make rooms in the ark, and cover it inside and out with pitch. ¹⁵This is how you are to make it: the length of the ark three hundred cubits, its width fifty cubits, and its height thirty cubits. ¹⁶Make a roof for the ark, and finish it to a cubit above; and put the door of the ark in its side; make it with lower, second, and third decks. ¹⁷For my part, I am going to bring a flood of waters on the earth, to destroy from under heaven all flesh in which is the breath of life;

everything that is on the earth shall die. ¹⁸But I will establish my covenant with you; and you shall come into the ark, you, your sons, your wife, and your sons' wives with you. ¹⁹And of every living thing, of all flesh, you shall bring two of every kind into the ark, to keep them alive with you; they shall be male and female. ²⁰Of the birds according to their kinds, and of the animals according to their kinds, of every creeping thing of the ground according to its kind, two of every kind shall come in to you, to keep them alive. ²¹Also take with you every kind of food that is eaten, and store it up; and it shall serve as food for you and for them." ²²Noah did this; he did all that God commanded him.

The Great Flood

7 Then the LORD said to Noah, "Go into the ark, you and all your household, for I have seen that you alone are righteous before me in this generation. ²Take with you seven pairs of all clean animals, the male and its mate; and a pair of the animals that are not clean, the male and its mate; ³and seven pairs of the birds of the air also, male and female, to keep their kind alive on the face of all the earth. ⁴For in seven days I will send rain on the earth for forty days and forty nights; and every living thing that I have made I will blot out from the face of the ground." ⁵And Noah did all that the LORD had commanded him.

6 Noah was six hundred years old when the flood of waters came on the earth. ⁷And Noah with his sons and his wife and his sons' wives went into the ark to escape the waters of the flood. ⁸Of clean animals, and of animals that are not clean, and of birds, and of everything that creeps on the ground, ⁹two and two, male and female, went into the ark with Noah, as God had commanded Noah. ¹⁰And after seven days the waters of the flood came on the earth.

11 In the six hundredth year of Noah's life, in the second month, on the seventeenth day of the month, on that day all the fountains of the great deep burst forth, and the windows of the heavens were opened. ¹²The rain fell on the earth forty days and forty nights. ¹³On the very same day Noah with his sons, Shem and Ham and Japheth, and Noah's wife and the three wives of his sons entered the ark, ¹⁴they and every wild animal of every kind, and all domestic animals of every kind, and every creeping thing that creeps on the earth, and every bird of every kind—every bird, every winged creature. ¹⁵They went into the ark with Noah, two and two of all flesh in which there was the breath of life. ¹⁶And those that entered, male and female of all flesh, went in as God had commanded him; and the LORD shut him in.

17 The flood continued forty days on the earth; and the waters increased, and bore up the ark, and it rose high above the earth. ¹⁸The waters swelled and increased greatly on the earth; and the ark floated on the face of the waters. ¹⁹The waters swelled so mightily on the earth that all the high mountains under the whole heaven were covered; ²⁰the waters swelled above the mountains, covering them fifteen cubits deep. ²¹And all flesh died that moved on the earth, birds, domestic animals, wild animals, all swarming creatures that swarm on the earth, and all human beings; ²²everything on dry land in whose nostrils was the breath of life died. ²³He blotted out every living thing that was on the face of the ground, human beings and animals and creeping things and birds of the air; they were blotted out from the earth. Only Noah was left, and those that were with him in the ark. ²⁴And the waters swelled on the earth for one hundred fifty days.

The Flood Subsides

8 But God remembered Noah and all the wild animals and all the domestic animals that were with him in the ark. And God made a wind blow over the earth, and the waters subsided; ²the fountains of the deep and the windows of the heavens were closed, the rain from the heavens was restrained, ³and the waters gradually receded from the earth. At the end of one hundred fifty days the waters had abated; ⁴and in the seventh month, on the seventeenth day of the month, the ark came to rest on the mountains of Ararat. ⁵The waters continued to abate until the tenth month; in the tenth month, on the first day of the month, the tops of the mountains appeared.

6 At the end of forty days Noah opened the window of the ark that he had made ⁷and sent out the raven; and it went to and fro until the waters were dried up from the earth. ⁸Then he sent out the dove from him, to see if the waters had subsided from the face of the ground; ⁹but

the dove found no place to set its foot, and it returned to him to the ark, for the waters were still on the face of the whole earth. So he put out his hand and took it and brought it into the ark with him. [10]He waited another seven days, and again he sent out the dove from the ark; [11]and the dove came back to him in the evening, and there in its beak was a freshly plucked olive leaf; so Noah knew that the waters had subsided from the earth. [12]Then he waited another seven days, and sent out the dove; and it did not return to him any more.

13 In the six hundred first year, in the first month, the first day of the month, the waters were dried up from the earth; and Noah removed the covering of the ark, and looked, and saw that the face of the ground was drying. [14]In the second month, on the twenty-seventh day of the month, the earth was dry. [15]Then God said to Noah, [16]"Go out of the ark, you and your wife, and your sons and your sons' wives with you. [17]Bring out with you every living thing that is with you of all flesh—birds and animals and every creeping thing that creeps on the earth—so that they may abound on the earth, and be fruitful and multiply on the earth." [18]So Noah went out with his sons and his wife and his sons' wives. [19]And every animal, every creeping thing, and every bird, everything that moves on the earth, went out of the ark by families.

God's Promise to Noah

20 Then Noah built an altar to the LORD, and took of every clean animal and of every clean bird, and offered burnt offerings on the altar. [21]And when the LORD smelled the pleasing odor, the LORD said in his heart, "I will never again curse the ground because of humankind, for the inclination of the human heart is evil from youth; nor will I ever again destroy every living creature as I have done.
[22] As long as the earth endures,
    seedtime and harvest, cold and heat,
    summer and winter, day and night,
        shall not cease."

The Covenant with Noah

9 God blessed Noah and his sons, and said to them, "Be fruitful and multiply, and fill the earth. [2]The fear and dread of you shall rest on every animal of the earth, and on every bird of the air, on everything that creeps on the ground, and on all the fish of the sea; into your hand they are delivered. [3]Every moving thing that lives shall be food for you; and just as I gave you the green plants, I give you everything. [4]Only, you shall not eat flesh with its life, that is, its blood. [5]For your own lifeblood I will surely require a reckoning: from every animal I will require it and from human beings, each one for the blood of another, I will require a reckoning for human life.
[6] Whoever sheds the blood of a human,
    by a human shall that person's blood be shed;
for in his own image
    God made humankind.
[7]And you, be fruitful and multiply, abound on the earth and multiply in it."

8 Then God said to Noah and to his sons with him, [9]"As for me, I am establishing my covenant with you and your descendants after you, [10]and with every living creature that is with you, the birds, the domestic animals, and every animal of the earth with you, as many as came out of the ark. [11]I establish my covenant with you, that never again shall all flesh be cut off by the waters of a flood, and never again shall there be a flood to destroy the earth." [12]God said, "This is the sign of the covenant that I make between me and you and every living creature that is with you, for all future generations: [13]I have set my bow in the clouds, and it shall be a sign of the covenant between me and the earth. [14]When I bring clouds over the earth and the bow is seen in the clouds, [15]I will remember my covenant that is between me and you and every living creature of all flesh; and the waters shall never again become a flood to destroy all flesh. [16]When the bow is in the clouds, I will see it and remember the everlasting covenant between God and every living creature of all flesh that is on the earth." [17]God said to Noah, "This is the sign of the covenant that I have established between me and all flesh that is on the earth."

Noah and His Sons

18 The sons of Noah who went out of the ark were Shem, Ham, and Japheth. Ham was the father of Canaan. ¹⁹These three were the sons of Noah; and from these the whole earth was peopled.

20 Noah, a man of the soil, was the first to plant a vineyard. ²¹He drank some of the wine and became drunk, and he lay uncovered in his tent. ²²And Ham, the father of Canaan, saw the nakedness of his father, and told his two brothers outside. ²³Then Shem and Japheth took a garment, laid it on both their shoulders, and walked backward and covered the nakedness of their father; their faces were turned away, and they did not see their father's nakedness. ²⁴When Noah awoke from his wine and knew what his youngest son had done to him, ²⁵he said,

"Cursed be Canaan;
 lowest of slaves shall he be to his brothers."

²⁶He also said,

"Blessed by the LORD my God be Shem;
 and let Canaan be his slave.
²⁷ May God make space for Japheth,
 and let him live in the tents of Shem;
 and let Canaan be his slave."

28 After the flood Noah lived three hundred fifty years. ²⁹All the days of Noah were nine hundred fifty years; and he died.

Nations Descended from Noah

10 These are the descendants of Noah's sons, Shem, Ham, and Japheth; children were born to them after the flood.

2 The descendants of Japheth: Gomer, Magog, Madai, Javan, Tubal, Meshech, and Tiras. ³The descendants of Gomer: Ashkenaz, Riphath, and Togarmah. ⁴The descendants of Javan: Elishah, Tarshish, Kittim, and Rodanim. ⁵From these the coastland peoples spread. These are the descendants of Japheth in their lands, with their own language, by their families, in their nations.

6 The descendants of Ham: Cush, Egypt, Put, and Canaan. ⁷The descendants of Cush: Seba, Havilah, Sabtah, Raamah, and Sabteca. The descendants of Raamah: Sheba and Dedan. ⁸Cush became the father of Nimrod; he was the first on earth to become a mighty warrior. ⁹He was a mighty hunter before the LORD; therefore it is said, "Like Nimrod a mighty hunter before the LORD." ¹⁰The beginning of his kingdom was Babel, Erech, and Accad, all of them in the land of Shinar. ¹¹From that land he went into Assyria, and built Nineveh, Rehoboth-ir, Calah, and ¹²Resen between Nineveh and Calah; that is the great city. ¹³Egypt became the father of Ludim, Anamim, Lehabim, Naphtuhim, ¹⁴Pathrusim, Casluhim, and Caphtorim, from which the Philistines come.

15 Canaan became the father of Sidon his firstborn, and Heth, ¹⁶and the Jebusites, the Amorites, the Girgashites, ¹⁷the Hivites, the Arkites, the Sinites, ¹⁸the Arvadites, the Zemarites, and the Hamathites. Afterward the families of the Canaanites spread abroad. ¹⁹And the territory of the Canaanites extended from Sidon, in the direction of Gerar, as far as Gaza, and in the direction of Sodom, Gomorrah, Admah, and Zeboiim, as far as Lasha. ²⁰These are the descendants of Ham, by their families, their languages, their lands, and their nations.

21 To Shem also, the father of all the children of Eber, the elder brother of Japheth, children were born. ²²The descendants of Shem: Elam, Asshur, Arpachshad, Lud, and Aram. ²³The descendants of Aram: Uz, Hul, Gether, and Mash. ²⁴Arpachshad became the father of Shelah; and Shelah became the father of Eber. ²⁵To Eber were born two sons: the name of the one was Peleg, for in his days the earth was divided, and his brother's name was Joktan. ²⁶Joktan became the father of Almodad, Sheleph, Hazarmaveth, Jerah, ²⁷Hadoram, Uzal, Diklah, ²⁸Obal, Abimael, Sheba, ²⁹Ophir, Havilah, and Jobab; all these were the descendants of Joktan. ³⁰The territory in which they lived extended from Mesha in the direction of Sephar, the hill country of the east. ³¹These are the descendants of Shem, by their families, their languages, their lands, and their nations.

32 These are the families of Noah's sons, according to their genealogies, in their nations; and from these the nations spread abroad on the earth after the flood.

The Tower of Babel

11 Now the whole earth had one language and the same words. ²And as they migrated from the east, they came upon a plain in the land of

Shinar and settled there. ³And they said to one another, "Come, let us make bricks, and burn them thoroughly." And they had brick for stone, and bitumen for mortar. ⁴Then they said, "Come, let us build ourselves a city, and a tower with its top in the heavens, and let us make a name for ourselves; otherwise we shall be scattered abroad upon the face of the whole earth." ⁵The LORD came down to see the city and the tower, which mortals had built. ⁶And the LORD said, "Look, they are one people, and they have all one language; and this is only the beginning of what they will do; nothing that they propose to do will now be impossible for them. ⁷Come, let us go down, and confuse their language there, so that they will not understand one another's speech." ⁸So the LORD scattered them abroad from there over the face of all the earth, and they left off building the city. ⁹Therefore it was called Babel, because there the LORD confused the language of all the earth; and from there the LORD scattered them abroad over the face of all the earth.

Descendants of Shem

10 These are the descendants of Shem. When Shem was one hundred years old, he became the father of Arpachshad two years after the flood; ¹¹and Shem lived after the birth of Arpachshad five hundred years, and had other sons and daughters.

12 When Arpachshad had lived thirty-five years, he became the father of Shelah; ¹³and Arpachshad lived after the birth of Shelah four hundred three years, and had other sons and daughters.

14 When Shelah had lived thirty years, he became the father of Eber; ¹⁵and Shelah lived after the birth of Eber four hundred three years, and had other sons and daughters.

16 When Eber had lived thirty-four years, he became the father of Peleg; ¹⁷and Eber lived after the birth of Peleg four hundred thirty years, and had other sons and daughters.

18 When Peleg had lived thirty years, he became the father of Reu; ¹⁹and Peleg lived after the birth of Reu two hundred nine years, and had other sons and daughters.

20 When Reu had lived thirty-two years, he became the father of Serug; ²¹and Reu lived after the birth of Serug two hundred seven years, and had other sons and daughters.

22 When Serug had lived thirty years, he became the father of Nahor; ²³and Serug lived after the birth of Nahor two hundred years, and had other sons and daughters.

24 When Nahor had lived twenty-nine years, he became the father of Terah; ²⁵and Nahor lived after the birth of Terah one hundred nineteen years, and had other sons and daughters.

26 When Terah had lived seventy years, he became the father of Abram, Nahor, and Haran.

Descendants of Terah

27 Now these are the descendants of Terah. Terah was the father of Abram, Nahor, and Haran; and Haran was the father of Lot. ²⁸Haran died before his father Terah in the land of his birth, in Ur of the Chaldeans. ²⁹Abram and Nahor took wives; the name of Abram's wife was Sarai, and the name of Nahor's wife was Milcah. She was the daughter of Haran the father of Milcah and Iscah. ³⁰Now Sarai was barren; she had no child.

31 Terah took his son Abram and his grandson Lot son of Haran, and his daughter-in-law Sarai, his son Abram's wife, and they went out together from Ur of the Chaldeans to go into the land of Canaan; but when they came to Haran, they settled there. ³²The days of Terah were two hundred five years; and Terah died in Haran.

The Call of Abram

12 Now the LORD said to Abram, "Go from your country and your kindred and your father's house to the land that I will show you. ²I will make of you a great nation, and I will bless you, and make your name great, so that you will be a blessing. ³I will bless those who bless you, and the one who curses you I will curse; and in you all the families of the earth shall be blessed."

4 So Abram went, as the LORD had told him; and Lot went with him. Abram was seventy-five years old when he departed from Haran. ⁵Abram took his wife Sarai and his brother's son Lot, and all the possessions that they had gathered, and the persons whom they had acquired in Haran; and they set forth to go to the land of Canaan. When they had come to the land of Canaan,

⁶Abram passed through the land to the place at Shechem, to the oak of Moreh. At that time the Canaanites were in the land. ⁷Then the LORD appeared to Abram, and said, "To your offspring I will give this land." So he built there an altar to the LORD, who had appeared to him. ⁸From there he moved on to the hill country on the east of Bethel, and pitched his tent, with Bethel on the west and Ai on the east; and there he built an altar to the LORD and invoked the name of the LORD. ⁹And Abram journeyed on by stages toward the Negeb.

Abram and Sarai in Egypt

10 Now there was a famine in the land. So Abram went down to Egypt to reside there as an alien, for the famine was severe in the land. ¹¹When he was about to enter Egypt, he said to his wife Sarai, "I know well that you are a woman beautiful in appearance; ¹²and when the Egyptians see you, they will say, 'This is his wife'; then they will kill me, but they will let you live. ¹³Say you are my sister, so that it may go well with me because of you, and that my life may be spared on your account." ¹⁴When Abram entered Egypt the Egyptians saw that the woman was very beautiful. ¹⁵When the officials of Pharaoh saw her, they praised her to Pharaoh. And the woman was taken into Pharaoh's house. ¹⁶And for her sake he dealt well with Abram; and he had sheep, oxen, male donkeys, male and female slaves, female donkeys, and camels.

17 But the LORD afflicted Pharaoh and his house with great plagues because of Sarai, Abram's wife. ¹⁸So Pharaoh called Abram, and said, "What is this you have done to me? Why did you not tell me that she was your wife? ¹⁹Why did you say, 'She is my sister,' so that I took her for my wife? Now then, here is your wife, take her, and be gone." ²⁰And Pharaoh gave his men orders concerning him; and they set him on the way, with his wife and all that he had.

Abram and Lot Separate

13 So Abram went up from Egypt, he and his wife, and all that he had, and Lot with him, into the Negeb.

2 Now Abram was very rich in livestock, in silver, and in gold. ³He journeyed on by stages from the Negeb as far as Bethel, to the place where his tent had been at the beginning, between Bethel and Ai, ⁴to the place where he had made an altar at the first; and there Abram called on the name of the LORD. ⁵Now Lot, who went with Abram, also had flocks and herds and tents, ⁶so that the land could not support both of them living together; for their possessions were so great that they could not live together, ⁷and there was strife between the herders of Abram's livestock and the herders of Lot's livestock. At that time the Canaanites and the Perizzites lived in the land.

8 Then Abram said to Lot, "Let there be no strife between you and me, and between your herders and my herders; for we are kindred. ⁹Is not the whole land before you? Separate yourself from me. If you take the left hand, then I will go to the right; or if you take the right hand, then I will go to the left." ¹⁰Lot looked about him, and saw that the plain of the Jordan was well watered everywhere like the garden of the LORD, like the land of Egypt, in the direction of Zoar; this was before the LORD had destroyed Sodom and Gomorrah. ¹¹So Lot chose for himself all the plain of the Jordan, and Lot journeyed eastward; thus they separated from each other. ¹²Abram settled in the land of Canaan, while Lot settled among the cities of the Plain and moved his tent as far as Sodom. ¹³Now the people of Sodom were wicked, great sinners against the LORD.

14 The LORD said to Abram, after Lot had separated from him, "Raise your eyes now, and look from the place where you are, northward and southward and eastward and westward; ¹⁵for all the land that you see I will give to you and to your offspring forever. ¹⁶I will make your offspring like the dust of the earth; so that if one can count the dust of the earth, your offspring also can be counted. ¹⁷Rise up, walk through the length and the breadth of the land, for I will give it to you." ¹⁸So Abram moved his tent, and came and settled by the oaks of Mamre, which are at Hebron; and there he built an altar to the LORD.

Lot's Captivity and Rescue

14 In the days of King Amraphel of Shinar, King Arioch of Ellasar, King Chedorlaomer of Elam, and King Tidal of Goiim, ²these kings

made war with King Bera of Sodom, King Birsha of Gomorrah, King Shinab of Admah, King Shemeber of Zeboiim, and the king of Bela (that is, Zoar). ³All these joined forces in the Valley of Siddim (that is, the Dead Sea). ⁴Twelve years they had served Chedorlaomer, but in the thirteenth year they rebelled. ⁵In the fourteenth year Chedorlaomer and the kings who were with him came and subdued the Rephaim in Ashteroth-karnaim, the Zuzim in Ham, the Emim in Shaveh-kiriathaim, ⁶and the Horites in the hill country of Seir as far as El-paran on the edge of the wilderness; ⁷then they turned back and came to En-mishpat (that is, Kadesh), and subdued all the country of the Amalekites, and also the Amorites who lived in Hazazon-tamar. ⁸Then the king of Sodom, the king of Gomorrah, the king of Admah, the king of Zeboiim, and the king of Bela (that is, Zoar) went out, and they joined battle in the Valley of Siddim ⁹with King Chedorlaomer of Elam, King Tidal of Goiim, King Amraphel of Shinar, and King Arioch of Ellasar, four kings against five. ¹⁰Now the Valley of Siddim was full of bitumen pits; and as the kings of Sodom and Gomorrah fled, some fell into them, and the rest fled to the hill country. ¹¹So the enemy took all the goods of Sodom and Gomorrah, and all their provisions, and went their way; ¹²they also took Lot, the son of Abram's brother, who lived in Sodom, and his goods, and departed.

13 Then one who had escaped came and told Abram the Hebrew, who was living by the oaks of Mamre the Amorite, brother of Eshcol and of Aner; these were allies of Abram. ¹⁴When Abram heard that his nephew had been taken captive, he led forth his trained men, born in his house, three hundred eighteen of them, and went in pursuit as far as Dan. ¹⁵He divided his forces against them by night, he and his servants, and routed them and pursued them to Hobah, north of Damascus. ¹⁶Then he brought back all the goods, and also brought back his nephew Lot with his goods, and the women and the people.

Abram Blessed by Melchizedek

17 After his return from the defeat of Chedorlaomer and the kings who were with him, the king of Sodom went out to meet him at the Valley of Shaveh (that is, the King's Valley). ¹⁸And King Melchizedek of Salem brought out bread and wine; he was priest of God Most High. ¹⁹He blessed him and said,

"Blessed be Abram by God Most High,
   maker of heaven and earth;
²⁰ and blessed be God Most High,
   who has delivered your enemies into your hand!"

And Abram gave him one tenth of everything. ²¹Then the king of Sodom said to Abram, "Give me the persons, but take the goods for yourself." ²²But Abram said to the king of Sodom, "I have sworn to the LORD, God Most High, maker of heaven and earth, ²³that I would not take a thread or a sandal-thong or anything that is yours, so that you might not say, 'I have made Abram rich.' ²⁴I will take nothing but what the young men have eaten, and the share of the men who went with me—Aner, Eshcol, and Mamre. Let them take their share."

God's Covenant with Abram

15 After these things the word of the LORD came to Abram in a vision, "Do not be afraid, Abram, I am your shield; your reward shall be very great." ²But Abram said, "O Lord GOD, what will you give me, for I continue childless, and the heir of my house is Eliezer of Damascus?" ³And Abram said, "You have given me no offspring, and so a slave born in my house is to be my heir." ⁴But the word of the LORD came to him, "This man shall not be your heir; no one but your very own issue shall be your heir." ⁵He brought him outside and said, "Look toward heaven and count the stars, if you are able to count them." Then he said to him, "So shall your descendants be." ⁶And he believed the LORD; and the LORD reckoned it to him as righteousness.

7 Then he said to him, "I am the LORD who brought you from Ur of the Chaldeans, to give you this land to possess." ⁸But he said, "O Lord GOD, how am I to know that I shall possess it?" ⁹He said to him, "Bring me a heifer three years old, a female goat three years old, a ram three years old, a turtledove, and a young pigeon." ¹⁰He brought him all these and cut them in two, laying each half over against the other; but he did not cut the birds in two. ¹¹And when birds of prey came down on the carcasses, Abram drove them away.

12 As the sun was going down, a deep sleep fell upon Abram, and a deep and terrifying darkness descended upon him. ¹³Then the LORD said

to Abram, "Know this for certain, that your offspring shall be aliens in a land that is not theirs, and shall be slaves there, and they shall be oppressed for four hundred years; ¹⁴but I will bring judgment on the nation that they serve, and afterward they shall come out with great possessions. ¹⁵As for yourself, you shall go to your ancestors in peace; you shall be buried in a good old age. ¹⁶And they shall come back here in the fourth generation; for the iniquity of the Amorites is not yet complete."

17 When the sun had gone down and it was dark, a smoking fire pot and a flaming torch passed between these pieces. ¹⁸On that day the LORD made a covenant with Abram, saying, "To your descendants I give this land, from the river of Egypt to the great river, the river Euphrates, ¹⁹the land of the Kenites, the Kenizzites, the Kadmonites, ²⁰the Hittites, the Perizzites, the Rephaim, ²¹the Amorites, the Canaanites, the Girgashites, and the Jebusites."

The Birth of Ishmael

16 Now Sarai, Abram's wife, bore him no children. She had an Egyptian slave-girl whose name was Hagar, ²and Sarai said to Abram, "You see that the LORD has prevented me from bearing children; go in to my slave-girl; it may be that I shall obtain children by her." And Abram listened to the voice of Sarai. ³So, after Abram had lived ten years in the land of Canaan, Sarai, Abram's wife, took Hagar the Egyptian, her slave-girl, and gave her to her husband Abram as a wife. ⁴He went in to Hagar, and she conceived; and when she saw that she had conceived, she looked with contempt on her mistress. ⁵Then Sarai said to Abram, "May the wrong done to me be on you! I gave my slave-girl to your embrace, and when she saw that she had conceived, she looked on me with contempt. May the LORD judge between you and me!" ⁶But Abram said to Sarai, "Your slave-girl is in your power; do to her as you please." Then Sarai dealt harshly with her, and she ran away from her.

7 The angel of the LORD found her by a spring of water in the wilderness, the spring on the way to Shur. ⁸And he said, "Hagar, slave-girl of Sarai, where have you come from and where are you going?" She said, "I am running away from my mistress Sarai." ⁹The angel of the LORD said to her, "Return to your mistress, and submit to her." ¹⁰The angel of the LORD also said to her, "I will so greatly multiply your offspring that they cannot be counted for multitude." ¹¹And the angel of the LORD said to her,

"Now you have conceived and shall bear a son;
you shall call him Ishmael,
for the LORD has given heed to your affliction.

¹² He shall be a wild ass of a man,
with his hand against everyone,
and everyone's hand against him;
and he shall live at odds with all his kin."

¹³So she named the LORD who spoke to her, "You are El-roi"; for she said, "Have I really seen God and remained alive after seeing him?" ¹⁴Therefore the well was called Beer-lahai-roi; it lies between Kadesh and Bered.

15 Hagar bore Abram a son; and Abram named his son, whom Hagar bore, Ishmael. ¹⁶Abram was eighty-six years old when Hagar bore him Ishmael.

The Sign of the Covenant

17 When Abram was ninety-nine years old, the LORD appeared to Abram, and said to him, "I am God Almighty; walk before me, and be blameless. ²And I will make my covenant between me and you, and will make you exceedingly numerous." ³Then Abram fell on his face; and God said to him, ⁴"As for me, this is my covenant with you: You shall be the ancestor of a multitude of nations. ⁵No longer shall your name be Abram, but your name shall be Abraham; for I have made you the ancestor of a multitude of nations. ⁶I will make you exceedingly fruitful; and I will make nations of you, and kings shall come from you. ⁷I will establish my covenant between me and you, and your offspring after you throughout their generations, for an everlasting covenant, to be God to you and to your offspring after you. ⁸And I will give to you, and to your offspring after you, the land where you are now an alien, all the land of Canaan, for a perpetual holding; and I will be their God."

9 God said to Abraham, "As for you, you shall keep my covenant, you and your offspring after you throughout their generations. ¹⁰This is my covenant, which you shall keep, between me and you and your offspring after you: Every male

among you shall be circumcised. ¹¹You shall circumcise the flesh of your foreskins, and it shall be a sign of the covenant between me and you. ¹²Throughout your generations every male among you shall be circumcised when he is eight days old, including the slave born in your house and the one bought with your money from any foreigner who is not of your offspring. ¹³Both the slave born in your house and the one bought with your money must be circumcised. So shall my covenant be in your flesh an everlasting covenant. ¹⁴Any uncircumcised male who is not circumcised in the flesh of his foreskin shall be cut off from his people; he has broken my covenant."

15 God said to Abraham, "As for Sarai your wife, you shall not call her Sarai, but Sarah shall be her name. ¹⁶I will bless her, and moreover I will give you a son by her. I will bless her, and she shall give rise to nations; kings of peoples shall come from her." ¹⁷Then Abraham fell on his face and laughed, and said to himself, "Can a child be born to a man who is a hundred years old? Can Sarah, who is ninety years old, bear a child?" ¹⁸And Abraham said to God, "O that Ishmael might live in your sight!" ¹⁹God said, "No, but your wife Sarah shall bear you a son, and you shall name him Isaac. I will establish my covenant with him as an everlasting covenant for his offspring after him. ²⁰As for Ishmael, I have heard you; I will bless him and make him fruitful and exceedingly numerous; he shall be the father of twelve princes, and I will make him a great nation. ²¹But my covenant I will establish with Isaac, whom Sarah shall bear to you at this season next year." ²²And when he had finished talking with him, God went up from Abraham.

23 Then Abraham took his son Ishmael and all the slaves born in his house or bought with his money, every male among the men of Abraham's house, and he circumcised the flesh of their foreskins that very day, as God had said to him. ²⁴Abraham was ninety-nine years old when he was circumcised in the flesh of his foreskin. ²⁵And his son Ishmael was thirteen years old when he was circumcised in the flesh of his foreskin. ²⁶That very day Abraham and his son Ishmael were circumcised; ²⁷and all the men of his house, slaves born in the house and those bought with money from a foreigner, were circumcised with him.

A Son Promised to Abraham and Sarah

18 The LORD appeared to Abraham by the oaks of Mamre, as he sat at the entrance of his tent in the heat of the day. ²He looked up and saw three men standing near him. When he saw them, he ran from the tent entrance to meet them, and bowed down to the ground. ³He said, "My lord, if I find favor with you, do not pass by your servant. ⁴Let a little water be brought, and wash your feet, and rest yourselves under the tree. ⁵Let me bring a little bread, that you may refresh yourselves, and after that you may pass on— since you have come to your servant." So they said, "Do as you have said." ⁶And Abraham hastened into the tent to Sarah, and said, "Make ready quickly three measures of choice flour, knead it, and make cakes." ⁷Abraham ran to the herd, and took a calf, tender and good, and gave it to the servant, who hastened to prepare it. ⁸Then he took curds and milk and the calf that he had prepared, and set it before them; and he stood by them under the tree while they ate.

9 They said to him, "Where is your wife Sarah?" And he said, "There, in the tent." ¹⁰Then one said, "I will surely return to you in due season, and your wife Sarah shall have a son." And Sarah was listening at the tent entrance behind him. ¹¹Now Abraham and Sarah were old, advanced in age; it had ceased to be with Sarah after the manner of women. ¹²So Sarah laughed to herself, saying, "After I have grown old, and my husband is old, shall I have pleasure?" ¹³The LORD said to Abraham, "Why did Sarah laugh, and say, 'Shall I indeed bear a child, now that I am old?' ¹⁴Is anything too wonderful for the LORD? At the set time I will return to you, in due season, and Sarah shall have a son." ¹⁵But Sarah denied, saying, "I did not laugh"; for she was afraid. He said, "Oh yes, you did laugh."

Judgment Pronounced on Sodom

16 Then the men set out from there, and they looked toward Sodom; and Abraham went with them to set them on their way. ¹⁷The LORD said, "Shall I hide from Abraham what I am about to do, ¹⁸seeing that Abraham shall become a great and mighty nation, and all the nations of the

earth shall be blessed in him? ¹⁹No, for I have chosen him, that he may charge his children and his household after him to keep the way of the LORD by doing righteousness and justice; so that the LORD may bring about for Abraham what he has promised him." ²⁰Then the LORD said, "How great is the outcry against Sodom and Gomorrah and how very grave their sin! ²¹I must go down and see whether they have done altogether according to the outcry that has come to me; and if not, I will know."

22 So the men turned from there, and went toward Sodom, while Abraham remained standing before the LORD. ²³Then Abraham came near and said, "Will you indeed sweep away the righteous with the wicked? ²⁴Suppose there are fifty righteous within the city; will you then sweep away the place and not forgive it for the fifty righteous who are in it? ²⁵Far be it from you to do such a thing, to slay the righteous with the wicked, so that the righteous fare as the wicked! Far be that from you! Shall not the Judge of all the earth do what is just?" ²⁶And the LORD said, "If I find at Sodom fifty righteous in the city, I will forgive the whole place for their sake." ²⁷Abraham answered, "Let me take it upon myself to speak to the Lord, I who am but dust and ashes. ²⁸Suppose five of the fifty righteous are lacking? Will you destroy the whole city for lack of five?" And he said, "I will not destroy it if I find forty-five there." ²⁹Again he spoke to him, "Suppose forty are found there." He answered, "For the sake of forty I will not do it." ³⁰Then he said, "Oh do not let the Lord be angry if I speak. Suppose thirty are found there." He answered, "I will not do it, if I find thirty there." ³¹He said, "Let me take it upon myself to speak to the Lord. Suppose twenty are found there." He answered, "For the sake of twenty I will not destroy it." ³²Then he said, "Oh do not let the Lord be angry if I speak just once more. Suppose ten are found there." He answered, "For the sake of ten I will not destroy it." ³³And the LORD went his way, when he had finished speaking to Abraham; and Abraham returned to his place.

The Depravity of Sodom

19 The two angels came to Sodom in the evening, and Lot was sitting in the gateway of Sodom. When Lot saw them, he rose to meet them, and bowed down with his face to the ground. ²He said, "Please, my lords, turn aside to your servant's house and spend the night, and wash your feet; then you can rise early and go on your way." They said, "No; we will spend the night in the square." ³But he urged them strongly; so they turned aside to him and entered his house; and he made them a feast, and baked unleavened bread, and they ate. ⁴But before they lay down, the men of the city, the men of Sodom, both young and old, all the people to the last man, surrounded the house; ⁵and they called to Lot, "Where are the men who came to you tonight? Bring them out to us, so that we may know them." ⁶Lot went out of the door to the men, shut the door after him, ⁷and said, "I beg you, my brothers, do not act so wickedly. ⁸Look, I have two daughters who have not known a man; let me bring them out to you, and do to them as you please; only do nothing to these men, for they have come under the shelter of my roof." ⁹But they replied, "Stand back!" And they said, "This fellow came here as an alien, and he would play the judge! Now we will deal worse with you than with them." Then they pressed hard against the man Lot, and came near the door to break it down. ¹⁰But the men inside reached out their hands and brought Lot into the house with them, and shut the door. ¹¹And they struck with blindness the men who were at the door of the house, both small and great, so that they were unable to find the door.

Sodom and Gomorrah Destroyed

12 Then the men said to Lot, "Have you anyone else here? Sons-in-law, sons, daughters, or anyone you have in the city—bring them out of the place. ¹³For we are about to destroy this place, because the outcry against its people has become great before the LORD, and the LORD has sent us to destroy it." ¹⁴So Lot went out and said to his sons-in-law, who were to marry his daughters, "Up, get out of this place; for the LORD is about to destroy the city." But he seemed to his sons-in-law to be jesting.

15 When morning dawned, the angels urged Lot, saying, "Get up, take your wife and your two daughters who are here, or else you will be consumed in the punishment of the city." ¹⁶But he lingered; so the men seized him and his wife and his two daughters by the hand, the LORD being merciful to him, and they brought him out and left him outside the city. ¹⁷When they had

brought them outside, they said, "Flee for your life; do not look back or stop anywhere in the Plain; flee to the hills, or else you will be consumed." ¹⁸And Lot said to them, "Oh, no, my lords; ¹⁹your servant has found favor with you, and you have shown me great kindness in saving my life; but I cannot flee to the hills, for fear the disaster will overtake me and I die. ²⁰Look, that city is near enough to flee to, and it is a little one. Let me escape there—is it not a little one?—and my life will be saved!" ²¹He said to him, "Very well, I grant you this favor too, and will not overthrow the city of which you have spoken. ²²Hurry, escape there, for I can do nothing until you arrive there." Therefore the city was called Zoar. ²³The sun had risen on the earth when Lot came to Zoar.

24 Then the LORD rained on Sodom and Gomorrah sulfur and fire from the LORD out of heaven; ²⁵and he overthrew those cities, and all the Plain, and all the inhabitants of the cities, and what grew on the ground. ²⁶But Lot's wife, behind him, looked back, and she became a pillar of salt.

27 Abraham went early in the morning to the place where he had stood before the LORD; ²⁸and he looked down toward Sodom and Gomorrah and toward all the land of the Plain and saw the smoke of the land going up like the smoke of a furnace.

29 So it was that, when God destroyed the cities of the Plain, God remembered Abraham, and sent Lot out of the midst of the overthrow, when he overthrew the cities in which Lot had settled.

The Shameful Origin of Moab and Ammon

30 Now Lot went up out of Zoar and settled in the hills with his two daughters, for he was afraid to stay in Zoar; so he lived in a cave with his two daughters. ³¹And the firstborn said to the younger, "Our father is old, and there is not a man on earth to come in to us after the manner of all the world. ³²Come, let us make our father drink wine, and we will lie with him, so that we may preserve offspring through our father." ³³So they made their father drink wine that night; and the firstborn went in, and lay with her father; he did not know when she lay down or when she rose. ³⁴On the next day, the firstborn said to the younger, "Look, I lay last night with my father; let us make him drink wine tonight also; then you go in and lie with him, so that we may preserve offspring through our father." ³⁵So they made their father drink wine that night also; and the younger rose, and lay with him; and he did not know when she lay down or when she rose. ³⁶Thus both the daughters of Lot became pregnant by their father. ³⁷The firstborn bore a son, and named him Moab; he is the ancestor of the Moabites to this day. ³⁸The younger also bore a son and named him Ben-ammi; he is the ancestor of the Ammonites to this day.

Abraham and Sarah at Gerar

20 From there Abraham journeyed toward the region of the Negeb, and settled between Kadesh and Shur. While residing in Gerar as an alien, ²Abraham said of his wife Sarah, "She is my sister." And King Abimelech of Gerar sent and took Sarah. ³But God came to Abimelech in a dream by night, and said to him, "You are about to die because of the woman whom you have taken; for she is a married woman." ⁴Now Abimelech had not approached her; so he said, "Lord, will you destroy an innocent people? ⁵Did he not himself say to me, 'She is my sister'? And she herself said, 'He is my brother.' I did this in the integrity of my heart and the innocence of my hands." ⁶Then God said to him in the dream, "Yes, I know that you did this in the integrity of your heart; furthermore it was I who kept you from sinning against me. Therefore I did not let you touch her. ⁷Now then, return the man's wife; for he is a prophet, and he will pray for you and you shall live. But if you do not restore her, know that you shall surely die, you and all that are yours."

8 So Abimelech rose early in the morning, and called all his servants and told them all these things; and the men were very much afraid. ⁹Then Abimelech called Abraham, and said to him, "What have you done to us? How have I sinned against you, that you have brought such great guilt on me and my kingdom? You have done things to me that ought not to be done." ¹⁰And Abimelech said to Abraham, "What were you thinking of, that you did this thing?" ¹¹Abraham said, "I did it because I thought, There is no fear of God at all in this place, and they will kill me because of my wife. ¹²Besides, she is indeed my sister, the daughter of my father but not the

daughter of my mother; and she became my wife. [13]And when God caused me to wander from my father's house, I said to her, 'This is the kindness you must do me: at every place to which we come, say of me, He is my brother.'" [14]Then Abimelech took sheep and oxen, and male and female slaves, and gave them to Abraham, and restored his wife Sarah to him. [15]Abimelech said, "My land is before you; settle where it pleases you." [16]To Sarah he said, "Look, I have given your brother a thousand pieces of silver; it is your exoneration before all who are with you; you are completely vindicated." [17]Then Abraham prayed to God; and God healed Abimelech, and also healed his wife and female slaves so that they bore children. [18]For the LORD had closed fast all the wombs of the house of Abimelech because of Sarah, Abraham's wife.

The Birth of Isaac

21 The LORD dealt with Sarah as he had said, and the LORD did for Sarah as he had promised. [2]Sarah conceived and bore Abraham a son in his old age, at the time of which God had spoken to him. [3]Abraham gave the name Isaac to his son whom Sarah bore him. [4]And Abraham circumcised his son Isaac when he was eight days old, as God had commanded him. [5]Abraham was a hundred years old when his son Isaac was born to him. [6]Now Sarah said, "God has brought laughter for me; everyone who hears will laugh with me." [7]And she said, "Who would ever have said to Abraham that Sarah would nurse children? Yet I have borne him a son in his old age."

Hagar and Ishmael Sent Away

8 The child grew, and was weaned; and Abraham made a great feast on the day that Isaac was weaned. [9]But Sarah saw the son of Hagar the Egyptian, whom she had borne to Abraham, playing with her son Isaac. [10]So she said to Abraham, "Cast out this slave woman with her son; for the son of this slave woman shall not inherit along with my son Isaac." [11]The matter was very distressing to Abraham on account of his son. [12]But God said to Abraham, "Do not be distressed because of the boy and because of your slave woman; whatever Sarah says to you, do as she tells you, for it is through Isaac that offspring shall be named for you. [13]As for the son of the slave woman, I will make a nation of him also, because he is your offspring." [14]So Abraham rose early in the morning, and took bread and a skin of water, and gave it to Hagar, putting it on her shoulder, along with the child, and sent her away. And she departed, and wandered about in the wilderness of Beer-sheba.

15 When the water in the skin was gone, she cast the child under one of the bushes. [16]Then she went and sat down opposite him a good way off, about the distance of a bowshot; for she said, "Do not let me look on the death of the child." And as she sat opposite him, she lifted up her voice and wept. [17]And God heard the voice of the boy; and the angel of God called to Hagar from heaven, and said to her, "What troubles you, Hagar? Do not be afraid; for God has heard the voice of the boy where he is. [18]Come, lift up the boy and hold him fast with your hand, for I will make a great nation of him." [19]Then God opened her eyes and she saw a well of water. She went, and filled the skin with water, and gave the boy a drink.

20 God was with the boy, and he grew up; he lived in the wilderness, and became an expert with the bow. [21]He lived in the wilderness of Paran; and his mother got a wife for him from the land of Egypt.

Abraham and Abimelech Make a Covenant

22 At that time Abimelech, with Phicol the commander of his army, said to Abraham, "God is with you in all that you do; [23]now therefore swear to me here by God that you will not deal falsely with me or with my offspring or with my posterity, but as I have dealt loyally with you, you will deal with me and with the land where you have resided as an alien." [24]And Abraham said, "I swear it."

25 When Abraham complained to Abimelech about a well of water that Abimelech's servants had seized, [26]Abimelech said, "I do not know who has done this; you did not tell me, and I have not heard of it until today." [27]So Abraham took sheep and oxen and gave them to Abimelech, and the two men made a covenant. [28]Abraham set apart seven ewe lambs of the flock. [29]And Abimelech said to Abraham, "What is the meaning of these seven ewe lambs that you have set apart?"

[30]He said, "These seven ewe lambs you shall accept from my hand, in order that you may be a witness for me that I dug this well." [31]Therefore that place was called Beer-sheba; because there both of them swore an oath. [32]When they had made a covenant at Beer-sheba, Abimelech, with Phicol the commander of his army, left and returned to the land of the Philistines. [33]Abraham planted a tamarisk tree in Beer-sheba, and called there on the name of the LORD, the Everlasting God. [34]And Abraham resided as an alien many days in the land of the Philistines.

The Command to Sacrifice Isaac

22 After these things God tested Abraham. He said to him, "Abraham!" And he said, "Here I am." [2]He said, "Take your son, your only son Isaac, whom you love, and go to the land of Moriah, and offer him there as a burnt offering on one of the mountains that I shall show you." [3]So Abraham rose early in the morning, saddled his donkey, and took two of his young men with him, and his son Isaac; he cut the wood for the burnt offering, and set out and went to the place in the distance that God had shown him. [4]On the third day Abraham looked up and saw the place far away. [5]Then Abraham said to his young men, "Stay here with the donkey; the boy and I will go over there; we will worship, and then we will come back to you." [6]Abraham took the wood of the burnt offering and laid it on his son Isaac, and he himself carried the fire and the knife. So the two of them walked on together. [7]Isaac said to his father Abraham, "Father!" And he said, "Here I am, my son." He said, "The fire and the wood are here, but where is the lamb for a burnt offering?" [8]Abraham said, "God himself will provide the lamb for a burnt offering, my son." So the two of them walked on together.

9 When they came to the place that God had shown him, Abraham built an altar there and laid the wood in order. He bound his son Isaac, and laid him on the altar, on top of the wood. [10]Then Abraham reached out his hand and took the knife to kill his son. [11]But the angel of the LORD called to him from heaven, and said, "Abraham, Abraham!" And he said, "Here I am." [12]He said, "Do not lay your hand on the boy or do anything to him; for now I know that you fear God, since you have not withheld your son, your only son, from me." [13]And Abraham looked up and saw a ram, caught in a thicket by its horns. Abraham went and took the ram and offered it up as a burnt offering instead of his son. [14]So Abraham called that place "The LORD will provide"; as it is said to this day, "On the mount of the LORD it shall be provided."

15 The angel of the LORD called to Abraham a second time from heaven, [16]and said, "By myself I have sworn, says the LORD: Because you have done this, and have not withheld your son, your only son, [17]I will indeed bless you, and I will make your offspring as numerous as the stars of heaven and as the sand that is on the seashore. And your offspring shall possess the gate of their enemies, [18]and by your offspring shall all the nations of the earth gain blessing for themselves, because you have obeyed my voice." [19]So Abraham returned to his young men, and they arose and went together to Beer-sheba; and Abraham lived at Beer-sheba.

Sarah's Death and Burial

23 Sarah lived one hundred twenty-seven years; this was the length of Sarah's life. [2]And Sarah died at Kiriath-arba (that is, Hebron) in the land of Canaan; and Abraham went in to mourn for Sarah and to weep for her. [3]Abraham rose up from beside his dead, and said to the Hittites, [4]"I am a stranger and an alien residing among you; give me property among you for a burying place, so that I may bury my dead out of my sight." [5]The Hittites answered Abraham, [6]"Hear us, my lord; you are a mighty prince among us. Bury your dead in the choicest of our burial places; none of us will withhold from you any burial ground for burying your dead." [7]Abraham rose and bowed to the Hittites, the people of the land. [8]He said to them, "If you are willing that I should bury my dead out of my sight, hear me, and entreat for me Ephron son of Zohar, [9]so that he may give me the cave of Machpelah, which he owns; it is at the end of his field. For the full price let him give it to me in your presence as a possession for a burying place." [10]Now Ephron was sitting among the Hittites; and Ephron the Hittite answered Abraham in the hearing of the Hittites, of all who went in at the gate of his city, [11]"No, my lord, hear me; I give you the field, and I give you the cave that is in it; in the presence of my people I give it to you; bury your dead." [12]Then Abraham bowed down before the people of the land.

¹³He said to Ephron in the hearing of the people of the land, "If you only will listen to me! I will give the price of the field; accept it from me, so that I may bury my dead there." ¹⁴Ephron answered Abraham, ¹⁵"My lord, listen to me; a piece of land worth four hundred shekels of silver—what is that between you and me? Bury your dead." ¹⁶Abraham agreed with Ephron; and Abraham weighed out for Ephron the silver that he had named in the hearing of the Hittites, four hundred shekels of silver, according to the weights current among the merchants.

17 So the field of Ephron in Machpelah, which was to the east of Mamre, the field with the cave that was in it and all the trees that were in the field, throughout its whole area, passed ¹⁸to Abraham as a possession in the presence of the Hittites, in the presence of all who went in at the gate of his city. ¹⁹After this, Abraham buried Sarah his wife in the cave of the field of Machpelah facing Mamre (that is, Hebron) in the land of Canaan. ²⁰The field and the cave that is in it passed from the Hittites into Abraham's possession as a burying place.

The Marriage of Isaac and Rebekah

24 Now Abraham was old, well advanced in years; and the LORD had blessed Abraham in all things. ²Abraham said to his servant, the oldest of his house, who had charge of all that he had, "Put your hand under my thigh ³and I will make you swear by the LORD, the God of heaven and earth, that you will not get a wife for my son from the daughters of the Canaanites, among whom I live, ⁴but will go to my country and to my kindred and get a wife for my son Isaac." ⁵The servant said to him, "Perhaps the woman may not be willing to follow me to this land; must I then take your son back to the land from which you came?" ⁶Abraham said to him, "See to it that you do not take my son back there. ⁷The LORD, the God of heaven, who took me from my father's house and from the land of my birth, and who spoke to me and swore to me, 'To your offspring I will give this land,' he will send his angel before you, and you shall take a wife for my son from there. ⁸But if the woman is not willing to follow you, then you will be free from this oath of mine; only you must not take my son back there." ⁹So the servant put his hand under the thigh of Abraham his master and swore to him concerning this matter.

10 Then the servant took ten of his master's camels and departed, taking all kinds of choice gifts from his master; and he set out and went to Aram-naharaim, to the city of Nahor. ¹¹He made the camels kneel down outside the city by the well of water; it was toward evening, the time when women go out to draw water. ¹²And he said, "O LORD, God of my master Abraham, please grant me success today and show steadfast love to my master Abraham. ¹³I am standing here by the spring of water, and the daughters of the townspeople are coming out to draw water. ¹⁴Let the girl to whom I shall say, 'Please offer your jar that I may drink,' and who shall say, 'Drink, and I will water your camels'—let her be the one whom you have appointed for your servant Isaac. By this I shall know that you have shown steadfast love to my master."

15 Before he had finished speaking, there was Rebekah, who was born to Bethuel son of Milcah, the wife of Nahor, Abraham's brother, coming out with her water jar on her shoulder. ¹⁶The girl was very fair to look upon, a virgin, whom no man had known. She went down to the spring, filled her jar, and came up. ¹⁷Then the servant ran to meet her and said, "Please let me sip a little water from your jar." ¹⁸"Drink, my lord," she said, and quickly lowered her jar upon her hand and gave him a drink. ¹⁹When she had finished giving him a drink, she said, "I will draw for your camels also, until they have finished drinking." ²⁰So she quickly emptied her jar into the trough and ran again to the well to draw, and she drew for all his camels. ²¹The man gazed at her in silence to learn whether or not the LORD had made his journey successful.

22 When the camels had finished drinking, the man took a gold nose-ring weighing a half shekel, and two bracelets for her arms weighing ten gold shekels, ²³and said, "Tell me whose daughter you are. Is there room in your father's house for us to spend the night?" ²⁴She said to him, "I am the daughter of Bethuel son of Milcah, whom she bore to Nahor." ²⁵She added, "We have plenty of straw and fodder and a place to spend the night." ²⁶The man bowed his head and worshiped the LORD ²⁷and said, "Blessed be the LORD, the God of my master Abraham, who has not forsaken his steadfast love and his faithfulness toward my master. As for me, the LORD has led me on the way to the house of my master's kin."

28 Then the girl ran and told her mother's household about these things. ²⁹Rebekah had a brother whose name was Laban; and Laban ran out to the man, to the spring. ³⁰As soon as he had seen the nose-ring, and the bracelets on his sister's arms, and when he heard the words of his sister Rebekah, "Thus the man spoke to me," he went to the man; and there he was, standing by the camels at the spring. ³¹He said, "Come in, O blessed of the LORD. Why do you stand outside when I have prepared the house and a place for the camels?" ³²So the man came into the house; and Laban unloaded the camels, and gave him straw and fodder for the camels, and water to wash his feet and the feet of the men who were with him. ³³Then food was set before him to eat; but he said, "I will not eat until I have told my errand." He said, "Speak on."

34 So he said, "I am Abraham's servant. ³⁵The LORD has greatly blessed my master, and he has become wealthy; he has given him flocks and herds, silver and gold, male and female slaves, camels and donkeys. ³⁶And Sarah my master's wife bore a son to my master when she was old; and he has given him all that he has. ³⁷My master made me swear, saying, 'You shall not take a wife for my son from the daughters of the Canaanites, in whose land I live; ³⁸but you shall go to my father's house, to my kindred, and get a wife for my son.' ³⁹I said to my master, 'Perhaps the woman will not follow me.' ⁴⁰But he said to me, 'The LORD, before whom I walk, will send his angel with you and make your way successful. You shall get a wife for my son from my kindred, from my father's house. ⁴¹Then you will be free from my oath, when you come to my kindred; even if they will not give her to you, you will be free from my oath.'

42 "I came today to the spring, and said, 'O LORD, the God of my master Abraham, if now you will only make successful the way I am going! ⁴³I am standing here by the spring of water; let the young woman who comes out to draw, to whom I shall say, "Please give me a little water from your jar to drink," ⁴⁴and who will say to me, "Drink, and I will draw for your camels also"— let her be the woman whom the LORD has appointed for my master's son.'

45 "Before I had finished speaking in my heart, there was Rebekah coming out with her water jar on her shoulder; and she went down to the spring, and drew. I said to her, 'Please let me drink.' ⁴⁶She quickly let down her jar from her shoulder, and said, 'Drink, and I will also water your camels.' So I drank, and she also watered the camels. ⁴⁷Then I asked her, 'Whose daughter are you?' She said, 'The daughter of Bethuel, Nahor's son, whom Milcah bore to him.' So I put the ring on her nose, and the bracelets on her arms. ⁴⁸Then I bowed my head and worshiped the LORD, and blessed the LORD, the God of my master Abraham, who had led me by the right way to obtain the daughter of my master's kinsman for his son. ⁴⁹Now then, if you will deal loyally and truly with my master, tell me; and if not, tell me, so that I may turn either to the right hand or to the left."

50 Then Laban and Bethuel answered, "The thing comes from the LORD; we cannot speak to you anything bad or good. ⁵¹Look, Rebekah is before you, take her and go, and let her be the wife of your master's son, as the LORD has spoken."

52 When Abraham's servant heard their words, he bowed himself to the ground before the LORD. ⁵³And the servant brought out jewelry of silver and of gold, and garments, and gave them to Rebekah; he also gave to her brother and to her mother costly ornaments. ⁵⁴Then he and the men who were with him ate and drank, and they spent the night there. When they rose in the morning, he said, "Send me back to my master." ⁵⁵Her brother and her mother said, "Let the girl remain with us a while, at least ten days; after that she may go." ⁵⁶But he said to them, "Do not delay me, since the LORD has made my journey successful; let me go that I may go to my master." ⁵⁷They said, "We will call the girl, and ask her." ⁵⁸And they called Rebekah, and said to her, "Will you go with this man?" She said, "I will." ⁵⁹So they sent away their sister Rebekah and her nurse along with Abraham's servant and his men. ⁶⁰And they blessed Rebekah and said to her,

"May you, our sister, become
thousands of myriads;
may your offspring gain possession
of the gates of their foes."

⁶¹Then Rebekah and her maids rose up, mounted the camels, and followed the man; thus the servant took Rebekah, and went his way.

62 Now Isaac had come from Beer-lahai-roi, and was settled in the Negeb. ⁶³Isaac went out in the evening to walk in the field; and looking up, he saw camels coming. ⁶⁴And Rebekah looked up, and when she saw Isaac, she slipped quickly from the camel, ⁶⁵and said to the servant, "Who is the man over there, walking in the field to meet us?" The servant said, "It is my master." So she took her veil and covered herself. ⁶⁶And the servant told Isaac all the things that he had done. ⁶⁷Then Isaac brought her into his mother Sarah's tent. He took Rebekah, and she became his wife;

and he loved her. So Isaac was comforted after his mother's death.

Abraham Marries Keturah

25 Abraham took another wife, whose name was Keturah. [2]She bore him Zimran, Jokshan, Medan, Midian, Ishbak, and Shuah. [3]Jokshan was the father of Sheba and Dedan. The sons of Dedan were Asshurim, Letushim, and Leummim. [4]The sons of Midian were Ephah, Epher, Hanoch, Abida, and Eldaah. All these were the children of Keturah. [5]Abraham gave all he had to Isaac. [6]But to the sons of his concubines Abraham gave gifts, while he was still living, and he sent them away from his son Isaac, eastward to the east country.

The Death of Abraham

7 This is the length of Abraham's life, one hundred seventy-five years. [8]Abraham breathed his last and died in a good old age, an old man and full of years, and was gathered to his people. [9]His sons Isaac and Ishmael buried him in the cave of Machpelah, in the field of Ephron son of Zohar the Hittite, east of Mamre, [10]the field that Abraham purchased from the Hittites. There Abraham was buried, with his wife Sarah. [11]After the death of Abraham God blessed his son Isaac. And Isaac settled at Beer-lahai-roi.

Ishmael's Descendants

12 These are the descendants of Ishmael, Abraham's son, whom Hagar the Egyptian, Sarah's slave-girl, bore to Abraham. [13]These are the names of the sons of Ishmael, named in the order of their birth: Nebaioth, the firstborn of Ishmael; and Kedar, Adbeel, Mibsam, [14]Mishma, Dumah, Massa, [15]Hadad, Tema, Jetur, Naphish, and Kedemah. [16]These are the sons of Ishmael and these are their names, by their villages and by their encampments, twelve princes according to their tribes. [17](This is the length of the life of Ishmael, one hundred thirty-seven years; he breathed his last and died, and was gathered to his people.) [18]They settled from Havilah to Shur, which is opposite Egypt in the direction of Assyria; he settled down alongside of all his people.

The Birth and Youth of Esau and Jacob

19 These are the descendants of Isaac, Abraham's son: Abraham was the father of Isaac, [20]and Isaac was forty years old when he married Rebekah, daughter of Bethuel the Aramean of Paddan-aram, sister of Laban the Aramean. [21]Isaac prayed to the LORD for his wife, because she was barren; and the LORD granted his prayer, and his wife Rebekah conceived. [22]The children struggled together within her; and she said, "If it is to be this way, why do I live?" So she went to inquire of the LORD. [23]And the LORD said to her,

"Two nations are in your womb,
and two peoples born of you shall be divided;
the one shall be stronger than the other,
the elder shall serve the younger."

[24]When her time to give birth was at hand, there were twins in her womb. [25]The first came out red, all his body like a hairy mantle; so they named him Esau. [26]Afterward his brother came out, with his hand gripping Esau's heel; so he was named Jacob. Isaac was sixty years old when she bore them.

27 When the boys grew up, Esau was a skillful hunter, a man of the field, while Jacob was a quiet man, living in tents. [28]Isaac loved Esau, because he was fond of game; but Rebekah loved Jacob.

Esau Sells His Birthright

29 Once when Jacob was cooking a stew, Esau came in from the field, and he was famished. [30]Esau said to Jacob, "Let me eat some of that red stuff, for I am famished!" (Therefore he was called Edom.) [31]Jacob said, "First sell me your birthright." [32]Esau said, "I am about to die; of what use is a birthright to me?" [33]Jacob said, "Swear to me first." So he swore to him, and sold his birthright to Jacob. [34]Then Jacob gave Esau bread and lentil stew, and he ate and drank, and rose and went his way. Thus Esau despised his birthright.

Issac and Abimelech

26 Now there was a famine in the land, besides the former famine that had occurred in the days of Abraham. And Isaac went to Gerar, to King Abimelech of the Philistines. 2The LORD appeared to Isaac and said, "Do not go down to Egypt; settle in the land that I shall show you. 3Reside in this land as an alien, and I will be with you, and will bless you; for to you and to your descendants I will give all these lands, and I will fulfill the oath that I swore to your father Abraham. 4I will make your offspring as numerous as the stars of heaven, and will give to your offspring all these lands; and all the nations of the earth shall gain blessing for themselves through your offspring, 5because Abraham obeyed my voice and kept my charge, my commandments, my statutes, and my laws."

6 So Isaac settled in Gerar. 7When the men of the place asked him about his wife, he said, "She is my sister"; for he was afraid to say, "My wife," thinking, "or else the men of the place might kill me for the sake of Rebekah, because she is attractive in appearance." 8When Isaac had been there a long time, King Abimelech of the Philistines looked out of a window and saw him fondling his wife Rebekah. 9So Abimelech called for Isaac, and said, "So she is your wife! Why then did you say, 'She is my sister'?" Isaac said to him, "Because I thought I might die because of her." 10Abimelech said, "What is this you have done to us? One of the people might easily have lain with your wife, and you would have brought guilt upon us." 11So Abimelech warned all the people, saying, "Whoever touches this man or his wife shall be put to death."

12 Isaac sowed seed in that land, and in the same year reaped a hundredfold. The LORD blessed him, 13and the man became rich; he prospered more and more until he became very wealthy. 14He had possessions of flocks and herds, and a great household, so that the Philistines envied him. 15(Now the Philistines had stopped up and filled with earth all the wells that his father's servants had dug in the days of his father Abraham.) 16And Abimelech said to Isaac, "Go away from us; you have become too powerful for us."

17 So Isaac departed from there and camped in the valley of Gerar and settled there. 18Isaac dug again the wells of water that had been dug in the days of his father Abraham; for the Philistines had stopped them up after the death of Abraham; and he gave them the names that his father had given them. 19But when Isaac's servants dug in the valley and found there a well of spring water, 20the herders of Gerar quarreled with Isaac's herders, saying, "The water is ours." So he called the well Esek, because they contended with him. 21Then they dug another well, and they quarreled over that one also; so he called it Sitnah. 22He moved from there and dug another well, and they did not quarrel over it; so he called it Rehoboth, saying, "Now the LORD has made room for us, and we shall be fruitful in the land."

23 From there he went up to Beer-sheba. 24And that very night the LORD appeared to him and said, "I am the God of your father Abraham; do not be afraid, for I am with you and will bless you and make your offspring numerous for my servant Abraham's sake." 25So he built an altar there, called on the name of the LORD, and pitched his tent there. And there Isaac's servants dug a well.

26 Then Abimelech went to him from Gerar, with Ahuzzath his adviser and Phicol the commander of his army. 27Isaac said to them, "Why have you come to me, seeing that you hate me and have sent me away from you?" 28They said, "We see plainly that the LORD has been with you; so we say, let there be an oath between you and us, and let us make a covenant with you 29so that you will do us no harm, just as we have not touched you and have done to you nothing but good and have sent you away in peace. You are now the blessed of the LORD." 30So he made them a feast, and they ate and drank. 31In the morning they rose early and exchanged oaths; and Isaac set them on their way, and they departed from him in peace. 32That same day Isaac's servants came and told him about the well that they had dug, and said to him, "We have found water!" 33He called it Shibah; therefore the name of the city is Beer-sheba to this day.

Esau's Hittite Wives

34 When Esau was forty years old, he married Judith daughter of Beeri the Hittite, and Basemath daughter of Elon the Hittite; 35and they made life bitter for Isaac and Rebekah.

Issac Blesses Jacob

27 When Isaac was old and his eyes were dim so that he could not see, he called his elder son Esau and said to him, "My son"; and he answered, "Here I am." ²He said, "See, I am old; I do not know the day of my death. ³Now then, take your weapons, your quiver and your bow, and go out to the field, and hunt game for me. ⁴Then prepare for me savory food, such as I like, and bring it to me to eat, so that I may bless you before I die."

5 Now Rebekah was listening when Isaac spoke to his son Esau. So when Esau went to the field to hunt for game and bring it, ⁶Rebekah said to her son Jacob, "I heard your father say to your brother Esau, ⁷'Bring me game, and prepare for me savory food to eat, that I may bless you before the LORD before I die.' ⁸Now therefore, my son, obey my word as I command you. ⁹Go to the flock, and get me two choice kids, so that I may prepare from them savory food for your father, such as he likes; ¹⁰and you shall take it to your father to eat, so that he may bless you before he dies." ¹¹But Jacob said to his mother Rebekah, "Look, my brother Esau is a hairy man, and I am a man of smooth skin. ¹²Perhaps my father will feel me, and I shall seem to be mocking him, and bring a curse on myself and not a blessing." ¹³His mother said to him, "Let your curse be on me, my son; only obey my word, and go, get them for me." ¹⁴So he went and got them and brought them to his mother; and his mother prepared savory food, such as his father loved. ¹⁵Then Rebekah took the best garments of her elder son Esau, which were with her in the house, and put them on her younger son Jacob; ¹⁶and she put the skins of the kids on his hands and on the smooth part of his neck. ¹⁷Then she handed the savory food, and the bread that she had prepared, to her son Jacob.

18 So he went in to his father, and said, "My father"; and he said, "Here I am; who are you, my son?" ¹⁹Jacob said to his father, "I am Esau your firstborn. I have done as you told me; now sit up and eat of my game, so that you may bless me." ²⁰But Isaac said to his son, "How is it that you have found it so quickly, my son?" He answered, "Because the LORD your God granted me success." ²¹Then Isaac said to Jacob, "Come near, that I may feel you, my son, to know whether you are really my son Esau or not." ²²So Jacob went up to his father Isaac, who felt him and said, "The voice is Jacob's voice, but the hands are the hands of Esau." ²³He did not recognize him, because his hands were hairy like his brother Esau's hands; so he blessed him. ²⁴He said, "Are you really my son Esau?" He answered, "I am." ²⁵Then he said, "Bring it to me, that I may eat of my son's game and bless you." So he brought it to him, and he ate; and he brought him wine, and he drank. ²⁶Then his father Isaac said to him, "Come near and kiss me, my son." ²⁷So he came near and kissed him; and he smelled the smell of his garments, and blessed him, and said,

"Ah, the smell of my son
    is like the smell of a field that the
        LORD has blessed.
²⁸ May God give you of the dew of heaven,
    and of the fatness of the earth,
    and plenty of grain and wine.
²⁹ Let peoples serve you,
    and nations bow down to you.
    Be lord over your brothers,
        and may your mother's sons bow
            down to you.
    Cursed be everyone who curses you,
        and blessed be everyone who blesses
            you!"

Esau's Lost Blessing

30 As soon as Isaac had finished blessing Jacob, when Jacob had scarcely gone out from the presence of his father Isaac, his brother Esau came in from his hunting. ³¹He also prepared savory food, and brought it to his father. And he said to his father, "Let my father sit up and eat of his son's game, so that you may bless me." ³²His father Isaac said to him, "Who are you?" He answered, "I am your firstborn son, Esau." ³³Then Isaac trembled violently, and said, "Who was it then that hunted game and brought it to me, and I ate it all before you came, and I have blessed him?—yes, and blessed he shall be!" ³⁴When Esau heard his father's words, he cried out with an exceedingly great and bitter cry, and said to his father, "Bless me, me also, father!" ³⁵But he said, "Your brother came deceitfully, and he has taken away your blessing." ³⁶Esau said, "Is he not rightly named Jacob? For he has supplanted me these two times. He took away my birthright; and look, now he has taken away my blessing." Then he said, "Have you not reserved a blessing for me?" ³⁷Isaac answered Esau, "I have already made him your lord, and I

have given him all his brothers as servants, and with grain and wine I have sustained him. What then can I do for you, my son?" ³⁸Esau said to his father, "Have you only one blessing, father? Bless me, me also, father!" And Esau lifted up his voice and wept.

39 Then his father Isaac answered him:
"See, away from the fatness of the
    earth shall your home be,
and away from the dew of heaven
    on high.
⁴⁰ By your sword you shall live,
    and you shall serve your brother;
but when you break loose,
    you shall break his yoke from your
        neck."

Jacob Escapes Esau's Fury

41 Now Esau hated Jacob because of the blessing with which his father had blessed him, and Esau said to himself, "The days of mourning for my father are approaching; then I will kill my brother Jacob." ⁴²But the words of her elder son Esau were told to Rebekah; so she sent and called her younger son Jacob and said to him, "Your brother Esau is consoling himself by planning to kill you. ⁴³Now therefore, my son, obey my voice; flee at once to my brother Laban in Haran, ⁴⁴and stay with him a while, until your brother's fury turns away— ⁴⁵until your brother's anger against you turns away, and he forgets what you have done to him; then I will send, and bring you back from there. Why should I lose both of you in one day?"

46 Then Rebekah said to Isaac, "I am weary of my life because of the Hittite women. If Jacob marries one of the Hittite women such as these, one of the women of the land, what good will my life be to me?"

28 Then Isaac called Jacob and blessed him, and charged him, "You shall not marry one of the Canaanite women. ²Go at once to Paddan-aram to the house of Bethuel, your mother's father; and take as wife from there one of the daughters of Laban, your mother's brother. ³May God Almighty bless you and make you fruitful and numerous, that you may become a company of peoples. ⁴May he give to you the blessing of Abraham, to you and to your offspring with you, so that you may take possession of the land where you now live as an alien—land that God gave to Abraham." ⁵Thus Isaac sent Jacob away; and he went to Paddan-aram, to Laban son of Bethuel the Aramean, the brother of Rebekah, Jacob's and Esau's mother.

Esau Marries Ishmael's Daughter

6 Now Esau saw that Isaac had blessed Jacob and sent him away to Paddan-aram to take a wife from there, and that as he blessed him he charged him, "You shall not marry one of the Canaanite women," ⁷and that Jacob had obeyed his father and his mother and gone to Paddan-aram. ⁸So when Esau saw that the Canaanite women did not please his father Isaac, ⁹Esau went to Ishmael and took Mahalath daughter of Abraham's son Ishmael, and sister of Nebaioth, to be his wife in addition to the wives he had.

Jacob's Dream at Bethel

10 Jacob left Beer-sheba and went toward Haran. ¹¹He came to a certain place and stayed there for the night, because the sun had set. Taking one of the stones of the place, he put it under his head and lay down in that place. ¹²And he dreamed that there was a ladder set up on the earth, the top of it reaching to heaven; and the angels of God were ascending and descending on it. ¹³And the LORD stood beside him and said, "I am the LORD, the God of Abraham your father and the God of Isaac; the land on which you lie I will give to you and to your offspring; ¹⁴and your offspring shall be like the dust of the earth, and you shall spread abroad to the west and to the east and to the north and to the south; and all the families of the earth shall be blessed in you and in your offspring. ¹⁵Know that I am with you and will keep you wherever you go, and will bring you back to this land; for I will not leave you until I have done what I have promised you." ¹⁶Then Jacob woke from his sleep and said, "Surely the LORD is in this place—and I did not know it!" ¹⁷And he was afraid, and said, "How awesome is this place! This is none other than the house of God, and this is the gate of heaven."

18 So Jacob rose early in the morning, and he took the stone that he had put under his head and set it up for a pillar and poured oil on the top of it. ¹⁹He called that place Bethel; but the name of

the city was Luz at the first. [20]Then Jacob made a vow, saying, "If God will be with me, and will keep me in this way that I go, and will give me bread to eat and clothing to wear, [21]so that I come again to my father's house in peace, then the LORD shall be my God, [22]and this stone, which I have set up for a pillar, shall be God's house; and of all that you give me I will surely give one tenth to you."

Jacob Meets Rachel

29 Then Jacob went on his journey, and came to the land of the people of the east. [2]As he looked, he saw a well in the field and three flocks of sheep lying there beside it; for out of that well the flocks were watered. The stone on the well's mouth was large, [3]and when all the flocks were gathered there, the shepherds would roll the stone from the mouth of the well, and water the sheep, and put the stone back in its place on the mouth of the well.

4 Jacob said to them, "My brothers, where do you come from?" They said, "We are from Haran." [5]He said to them, "Do you know Laban son of Nahor?" They said, "We do." [6]He said to them, "Is it well with him?" "Yes," they replied, "and here is his daughter Rachel, coming with the sheep." [7]He said, "Look, it is still broad daylight; it is not time for the animals to be gathered together. Water the sheep, and go, pasture them." [8]But they said, "We cannot until all the flocks are gathered together, and the stone is rolled from the mouth of the well; then we water the sheep."

9 While he was still speaking with them, Rachel came with her father's sheep; for she kept them. [10]Now when Jacob saw Rachel, the daughter of his mother's brother Laban, and the sheep of his mother's brother Laban, Jacob went up and rolled the stone from the well's mouth, and watered the flock of his mother's brother Laban. [11]Then Jacob kissed Rachel, and wept aloud. [12]And Jacob told Rachel that he was her father's kinsman, and that he was Rebekah's son; and she ran and told her father.

13 When Laban heard the news about his sister's son Jacob, he ran to meet him; he embraced him and kissed him, and brought him to his house. Jacob told Laban all these things, [14]and Laban said to him, "Surely you are my bone and my flesh!" And he stayed with him a month.

Jacob Marries Laban's Daughters

15 Then Laban said to Jacob, "Because you are my kinsman, should you therefore serve me for nothing? Tell me, what shall your wages be?" [16]Now Laban had two daughters; the name of the elder was Leah, and the name of the younger was Rachel. [17]Leah's eyes were lovely, and Rachel was graceful and beautiful. [18]Jacob loved Rachel; so he said, "I will serve you seven years for your younger daughter Rachel." [19]Laban said, "It is better that I give her to you than that I should give her to any other man; stay with me." [20]So Jacob served seven years for Rachel, and they seemed to him but a few days because of the love he had for her.

21 Then Jacob said to Laban, "Give me my wife that I may go in to her, for my time is completed." [22]So Laban gathered together all the people of the place, and made a feast. [23]But in the evening he took his daughter Leah and brought her to Jacob; and he went in to her. [24](Laban gave his maid Zilpah to his daughter Leah to be her maid.) [25]When morning came, it was Leah! And Jacob said to Laban, "What is this you have done to me? Did I not serve with you for Rachel? Why then have you deceived me?" [26]Laban said, "This is not done in our country—giving the younger before the firstborn. [27]Complete the week of this one, and we will give you the other also in return for serving me another seven years." [28]Jacob did so, and completed her week; then Laban gave him his daughter Rachel as a wife. [29](Laban gave his maid Bilhah to his daughter Rachel to be her maid.) [30]So Jacob went in to Rachel also, and he loved Rachel more than Leah. He served Laban for another seven years.

31 When the LORD saw that Leah was unloved, he opened her womb; but Rachel was barren. [32]Leah conceived and bore a son, and she named him Reuben; for she said, "Because the LORD has looked on my affliction; surely now my husband will love me." [33]She conceived again and bore a son, and said, "Because the LORD has heard that I am hated, he has given me this son also"; and she named him Simeon. [34]Again she conceived and bore a son, and said, "Now this time my husband will be joined to me, because I have borne him three sons"; therefore he was named Levi. [35]She conceived again and bore a son, and said, "This time I will praise the LORD"; therefore she named him Judah; then she ceased bearing.

30 When Rachel saw that she bore Jacob no children, she envied her sister; and she said to Jacob, "Give me children, or I shall die!" ²Jacob became very angry with Rachel and said, "Am I in the place of God, who has withheld from you the fruit of the womb?" ³Then she said, "Here is my maid Bilhah; go in to her, that she may bear upon my knees and that I too may have children through her." ⁴So she gave him her maid Bilhah as a wife; and Jacob went in to her. ⁵And Bilhah conceived and bore Jacob a son. ⁶Then Rachel said, "God has judged me, and has also heard my voice and given me a son"; therefore she named him Dan. ⁷Rachel's maid Bilhah conceived again and bore Jacob a second son. ⁸Then Rachel said, "With mighty wrestlings I have wrestled with my sister, and have prevailed"; so she named him Naphtali.

9 When Leah saw that she had ceased bearing children, she took her maid Zilpah and gave her to Jacob as a wife. ¹⁰Then Leah's maid Zilpah bore Jacob a son. ¹¹And Leah said, "Good fortune!" so she named him Gad. ¹²Leah's maid Zilpah bore Jacob a second son. ¹³And Leah said, "Happy am I! For the women will call me happy"; so she named him Asher.

14 In the days of wheat harvest Reuben went and found mandrakes in the field, and brought them to his mother Leah. Then Rachel said to Leah, "Please give me some of your son's mandrakes." ¹⁵But she said to her, "Is it a small matter that you have taken away my husband? Would you take away my son's mandrakes also?" Rachel said, "Then he may lie with you tonight for your son's mandrakes." ¹⁶When Jacob came from the field in the evening, Leah went out to meet him, and said, "You must come in to me; for I have hired you with my son's mandrakes." So he lay with her that night. ¹⁷And God heeded Leah, and she conceived and bore Jacob a fifth son. ¹⁸Leah said, "God has given me my hire because I gave my maid to my husband"; so she named him Issachar. ¹⁹And Leah conceived again, and she bore Jacob a sixth son. ²⁰Then Leah said, "God has endowed me with a good dowry; now my husband will honor me, because I have borne him six sons"; so she named him Zebulun. ²¹Afterwards she bore a daughter, and named her Dinah.

22 Then God remembered Rachel, and God heeded her and opened her womb. ²³She conceived and bore a son, and said, "God has taken away my reproach"; ²⁴and she named him Joseph, saying, "May the LORD add to me another son!"

Jacob Prospers at Laban's Expense

25 When Rachel had borne Joseph, Jacob said to Laban, "Send me away, that I may go to my own home and country. ²⁶Give me my wives and my children for whom I have served you, and let me go; for you know very well the service I have given you." ²⁷But Laban said to him, "If you will allow me to say so, I have learned by divination that the LORD has blessed me because of you; ²⁸name your wages, and I will give it." ²⁹Jacob said to him, "You yourself know how I have served you, and how your cattle have fared with me. ³⁰For you had little before I came, and it has increased abundantly; and the LORD has blessed you wherever I turned. But now when shall I provide for my own household also?" ³¹He said, "What shall I give you?" Jacob said, "You shall not give me anything; if you will do this for me, I will again feed your flock and keep it: ³²let me pass through all your flock today, removing from it every speckled and spotted sheep and every black lamb, and the spotted and speckled among the goats; and such shall be my wages. ³³So my honesty will answer for me later, when you come to look into my wages with you. Every one that is not speckled and spotted among the goats and black among the lambs, if found with me, shall be counted stolen." ³⁴Laban said, "Good! Let it be as you have said." ³⁵But that day Laban removed the male goats that were striped and spotted, and all the female goats that were speckled and spotted, every one that had white on it, and every lamb that was black, and put them in charge of his sons; ³⁶and he set a distance of three days' journey between himself and Jacob, while Jacob was pasturing the rest of Laban's flock.

37 Then Jacob took fresh rods of poplar and almond and plane, and peeled white streaks in them, exposing the white of the rods. ³⁸He set the rods that he had peeled in front of the flocks in the troughs, that is, the watering places, where the flocks came to drink. And since they bred when they came to drink, ³⁹the flocks bred in front of the rods, and so the flocks produced young that were striped, speckled, and spotted. ⁴⁰Jacob separated the lambs, and set the faces of the flocks toward the striped and the completely black animals in the flock of Laban; and he put

his own droves apart, and did not put them with Laban's flock. ⁴¹Whenever the stronger of the flock were breeding, Jacob laid the rods in the troughs before the eyes of the flock, that they might breed among the rods, ⁴²but for the feebler of the flock he did not lay them there; so the feebler were Laban's, and the stronger Jacob's. ⁴³Thus the man grew exceedingly rich, and had large flocks, and male and female slaves, and camels and donkeys.

Jacob Flees with Family and Flocks

31 Now Jacob heard that the sons of Laban were saying, "Jacob has taken all that was our father's; he has gained all this wealth from what belonged to our father." ²And Jacob saw that Laban did not regard him as favorably as he did before. ³Then the LORD said to Jacob, "Return to the land of your ancestors and to your kindred, and I will be with you." ⁴So Jacob sent and called Rachel and Leah into the field where his flock was, ⁵and said to them, "I see that your father does not regard me as favorably as he did before. But the God of my father has been with me. ⁶You know that I have served your father with all my strength; ⁷yet your father has cheated me and changed my wages ten times, but God did not permit him to harm me. ⁸If he said, 'The speckled shall be your wages,' then all the flock bore speckled; and if he said, 'The striped shall be your wages,' then all the flock bore striped. ⁹Thus God has taken away the livestock of your father, and given them to me.

10 During the mating of the flock I once had a dream in which I looked up and saw that the male goats that leaped upon the flock were striped, speckled, and mottled. ¹¹Then the angel of God said to me in the dream, 'Jacob,' and I said, 'Here I am!' ¹²And he said, 'Look up and see that all the goats that leap on the flock are striped, speckled, and mottled; for I have seen all that Laban is doing to you. ¹³I am the God of Bethel, where you anointed a pillar and made a vow to me. Now leave this land at once and return to the land of your birth.'" ¹⁴Then Rachel and Leah answered him, "Is there any portion or inheritance left to us in our father's house? ¹⁵Are we not regarded by him as foreigners? For he has sold us, and he has been using up the money given for us. ¹⁶All the property that God has taken away from our father belongs to us and to our children; now then, do whatever God has said to you."

17 So Jacob arose, and set his children and his wives on camels; ¹⁸and he drove away all his livestock, all the property that he had gained, the livestock in his possession that he had acquired in Paddan-aram, to go to his father Isaac in the land of Canaan.

19 Now Laban had gone to shear his sheep, and Rachel stole her father's household gods. ²⁰And Jacob deceived Laban the Aramean, in that he did not tell him that he intended to flee. ²¹So he fled with all that he had; starting out he crossed the Euphrates, and set his face toward the hill country of Gilead.

Laban Overtakes Jacob

22 On the third day Laban was told that Jacob had fled. ²³So he took his kinsfolk with him and pursued him for seven days until he caught up with him in the hill country of Gilead. ²⁴But God came to Laban the Aramean in a dream by night, and said to him, "Take heed that you say not a word to Jacob, either good or bad."

25 Laban overtook Jacob. Now Jacob had pitched his tent in the hill country, and Laban with his kinsfolk camped in the hill country of Gilead. ²⁶Laban said to Jacob, "What have you done? You have deceived me, and carried away my daughters like captives of the sword. ²⁷Why did you flee secretly and deceive me and not tell me? I would have sent you away with mirth and songs, with tambourine and lyre. ²⁸And why did you not permit me to kiss my sons and my daughters farewell? What you have done is foolish. ²⁹It is in my power to do you harm; but the God of your father spoke to me last night, saying, 'Take heed that you speak to Jacob neither good nor bad.' ³⁰Even though you had to go because you longed greatly for your father's house, why did you steal my gods?" ³¹Jacob answered Laban, "Because I was afraid, for I thought that you would take your daughters from me by force. ³²But anyone with whom you find your gods shall not live. In the presence of our kinsfolk, point out what I have that is yours, and take it." Now Jacob did not know that Rachel had stolen the gods.

33 So Laban went into Jacob's tent, and into Leah's tent, and into the tent of the two maids,

but he did not find them. And he went out of Leah's tent, and entered Rachel's. ³⁴Now Rachel had taken the household gods and put them in the camel's saddle, and sat on them. Laban felt all about in the tent, but did not find them. ³⁵And she said to her father, "Let not my lord be angry that I cannot rise before you, for the way of women is upon me." So he searched, but did not find the household gods.

36 Then Jacob became angry, and upbraided Laban. Jacob said to Laban, "What is my offense? What is my sin, that you have hotly pursued me? ³⁷Although you have felt about through all my goods, what have you found of all your household goods? Set it here before my kinsfolk and your kinsfolk, so that they may decide between us two. ³⁸These twenty years I have been with you; your ewes and your female goats have not miscarried, and I have not eaten the rams of your flocks. ³⁹That which was torn by wild beasts I did not bring to you; I bore the loss of it myself; of my hand you required it, whether stolen by day or stolen by night. ⁴⁰It was like this with me: by day the heat consumed me, and the cold by night, and my sleep fled from my eyes. ⁴¹These twenty years I have been in your house; I served you fourteen years for your two daughters, and six years for your flock, and you have changed my wages ten times. ⁴²If the God of my father, the God of Abraham and the Fear of Isaac, had not been on my side, surely now you would have sent me away empty-handed. God saw my affliction and the labor of my hands, and rebuked you last night."

Laban and Jacob Make a Covenant

43 Then Laban answered and said to Jacob, "The daughters are my daughters, the children are my children, the flocks are my flocks, and all that you see is mine. But what can I do today about these daughters of mine, or about their children whom they have borne? ⁴⁴Come now, let us make a covenant, you and I; and let it be a witness between you and me." ⁴⁵So Jacob took a stone, and set it up as a pillar. ⁴⁶And Jacob said to his kinsfolk, "Gather stones," and they took stones, and made a heap; and they ate there by the heap. ⁴⁷Laban called it Jegar-sahadutha: but Jacob called it Galeed. ⁴⁸Laban said, "This heap is a witness between you and me today." Therefore he called it Galeed, ⁴⁹and the pillar Mizpah, for he said, "The LORD watch between you and me, when we are absent one from the other. ⁵⁰If you ill-treat my daughters, or if you take wives in addition to my daughters, though no one else is with us, remember that God is witness between you and me."

51 Then Laban said to Jacob, "See this heap and see the pillar, which I have set between you and me. ⁵²This heap is a witness, and the pillar is a witness, that I will not pass beyond this heap to you, and you will not pass beyond this heap and this pillar to me, for harm. ⁵³May the God of Abraham and the God of Nahor"—the God of their father—" judge between us." So Jacob swore by the Fear of his father Isaac, ⁵⁴and Jacob offered a sacrifice on the height and called his kinsfolk to eat bread; and they ate bread and tarried all night in the hill country.

55 Early in the morning Laban rose up, and kissed his grandchildren and his daughters and blessed them; then he departed and returned home.

32 Jacob went on his way and the angels of God met him; ²and when Jacob saw them he said, "This is God's camp!" So he called that place Mahanaim.

Jacob Sends Presents to Appease Esau

3 Jacob sent messengers before him to his brother Esau in the land of Seir, the country of Edom, ⁴instructing them, "Thus you shall say to my lord Esau: Thus says your servant Jacob, 'I have lived with Laban as an alien, and stayed until now; ⁵and I have oxen, donkeys, flocks, male and female slaves; and I have sent to tell my lord, in order that I may find favor in your sight.'"

6 The messengers returned to Jacob, saying, "We came to your brother Esau, and he is coming to meet you, and four hundred men are with him." ⁷Then Jacob was greatly afraid and distressed; and he divided the people that were with him, and the flocks and herds and camels, into two companies, ⁸thinking, "If Esau comes to the one company and destroys it, then the company that is left will escape."

9 And Jacob said, "O God of my father Abraham and God of my father Isaac, O LORD who said to me, 'Return to your country and to your

kindred, and I will do you good,' ¹⁰I am not worthy of the least of all the steadfast love and all the faithfulness that you have shown to your servant, for with only my staff I crossed this Jordan; and now I have become two companies. ¹¹Deliver me, please, from the hand of my brother, from the hand of Esau, for I am afraid of him; he may come and kill us all, the mothers with the children. ¹²Yet you have said, 'I will surely do you good, and make your offspring as the sand of the sea, which cannot be counted because of their number.'"

13 So he spent that night there, and from what he had with him he took a present for his brother Esau, ¹⁴two hundred female goats and twenty male goats, two hundred ewes and twenty rams, ¹⁵thirty milch camels and their colts, forty cows and ten bulls, twenty female donkeys and ten male donkeys. ¹⁶These he delivered into the hand of his servants, every drove by itself, and said to his servants, "Pass on ahead of me, and put a space between drove and drove." ¹⁷He instructed the foremost, "When Esau my brother meets you, and asks you, 'To whom do you belong? Where are you going? And whose are these ahead of you?' ¹⁸then you shall say, 'They belong to your servant Jacob; they are a present sent to my lord Esau; and moreover he is behind us.'" ¹⁹He likewise instructed the second and the third and all who followed the droves, "You shall say the same thing to Esau when you meet him, ²⁰and you shall say, 'Moreover your servant Jacob is behind us.'" For he thought, "I may appease him with the present that goes ahead of me, and afterwards I shall see his face; perhaps he will accept me." ²¹So the present passed on ahead of him; and he himself spent that night in the camp.

Jacob Wrestles at Peniel

22 The same night he got up and took his two wives, his two maids, and his eleven children, and crossed the ford of the Jabbok. ²³He took them and sent them across the stream, and likewise everything that he had. ²⁴Jacob was left alone; and a man wrestled with him until daybreak. ²⁵When the man saw that he did not prevail against Jacob, he struck him on the hip socket; and Jacob's hip was put out of joint as he wrestled with him. ²⁶Then he said, "Let me go, for the day is breaking." But Jacob said, "I will not let you go, unless you bless me." ²⁷So he said to him, "What is your name?" And he said, "Jacob." ²⁸Then the man said, "You shall no longer be called Jacob, but Israel, for you have striven with God and with humans, and have prevailed." ²⁹Then Jacob asked him, "Please tell me your name." But he said, "Why is it that you ask my name?" And there he blessed him. ³⁰So Jacob called the place Peniel, saying, "For I have seen God face to face, and yet my life is preserved." ³¹The sun rose upon him as he passed Penuel, limping because of his hip. ³²Therefore to this day the Israelites do not eat the thigh muscle that is on the hip socket, because he struck Jacob on the hip socket at the thigh muscle.

Exodus

The Law

The passages we read are very important for understanding the basic thrust of the Hebrew Bible and many of its key themes. In these passages we have the giving of the law. This code of law is certainly the most complete that we have of any ancient people, rivalled only by the Code of Hammurabi of Sumeria. It emphasizes the reliance on law to liberate the people from their enslavement to passion and desire (something Plato discusses, too). More important, it forms the basis for the law we live under, even today.

It is important to note that the law in *Exodus* goes much further than the Ten Commandments and that other books of the *Torah* (which translates as "the Law" or "The Guide") complete it.

I think it helps to conceive of the law in a few distinct categories:

1. law governing our relation to God and the expression of that relation through ritual practice;
2. law governing our relations to one another (our social behavior);
3. law governing our disposition toward one another (against coveting, for example, which may never find actual expression as social behavior but is a matter of the heart); and
4. law governing our daily practical lives (regarding cleanliness, for example, or carrying out boundary disputes, or how best to accomplish a marriage)—a Guide to Living.

However the list might be made, the law delivered in *Exodus* is a remarkable human achievement and lays the basis for the *New Testament* law and the law delivered in the *Qur'an*.

The Birth of Politics

The Israelites are portrayed as in desperate need of law. They are lawless to the point of being ridiculous. Even after they have witnessed the power of the Lord God to produce miracles on their behalf (the parting of the Sea, Manna from Heaven, etc.), they continue to hold onto their doubts and their slave ways (they wish to return to the "fleshpots of Egypt"—i.e., to have something guaranteed them to eat, even if they are slaves). Very soon after they have taken an oath to obey God's law following a dramatic demonstration of God's power at Mt. Sinai, they revert to fertility religions (the Golden Calf) and to drunkenness and revelry (and what do you suppose "revelry" means?).

Recall that God has made Moses a promise which Moses relates to the people. In *Exodus* 19, God makes the Israelites His "Chosen People." He promises that if they obey His law, he will make them a beacon for all other nations, an example of holiness for all the world.

This helps us understand the remarkable act of Moses in bringing about a civil war in which 3,000 people are killed for their refusal to honor their pledge to obey God's law. There are several important observations to make about this bloody event.

Some students believe they find a contradiction between the Commandment forbidding killing and this bloody slaughter of the revelers. Others remind that the Commandment is directed against murder and not killing (the Hebrew word makes this distinction clear).

Exodus provides a clear example of the failure of democracy (again think of Plato) in the laughable figure of Aaron. Aaron leads by following the people's wishes. Moses provides a very different example of leadership.

Many have commented that Moses takes matters into his own hands here after appearing to have talked God out of His desire to destroy them all. God appears never to have told Moses to say and do what he does—Moses seems to have invented some things (is this Plato's "Noble Lie," justified by necessity?). Was this slaughter necessary? What would have happened to the Israelites and God's Plan if the revelers were allowed to continue to misdirect the people from their goal? The text tells us that other peoples would hold them in derision, and isn't this a promise that they will be destroyed by the many hostile peoples that surround them? How can the people make their way unless they are purified from their slave history and condition? These are some of the arguments advanced to justify Moses and his direction of slaughter against the "stiff-necked" element of his people.

So some say that *Exodus* gives us both the birth of law and also the dawning of politics and the obligation of leaders to consider what must be done in accord both with the general good and with the goal of building an honorable people.

You might notice that this last sentence describes a great deal you have already read in IH and more that you will read.

Exodus

1 These are the names of the sons of Israel who came to Egypt with Jacob, each with his household: ²Reuben, Simeon, Levi, and Judah, ³Issachar, Zebulun, and Benjamin, ⁴Dan and Naphtali, Gad and Asher. ⁵The total number of people born to Jacob was seventy. Joseph was already in Egypt. ⁶Then Joseph died, and all his brothers, and that whole generation. ⁷But the Israelites were fruitful and prolific; they multiplied and grew exceedingly strong, so that the land was filled with them.

The Israelites Are Oppressed

8 Now a new king arose over Egypt, who did not know Joseph. ⁹He said to his people, "Look, the Israelite people are more numerous and more powerful than we. ¹⁰Come, let us deal shrewdly with them, or they will increase and, in the event of war, join our enemies and fight against us and escape from the land." ¹¹Therefore they set taskmasters over them to oppress them with forced labor. They built supply cities, Pithom and Rameses, for Pharaoh. ¹²But the more they were oppressed, the more they multiplied and spread, so that the Egyptians came to dread the Israelites. ¹³The Egyptians became ruthless in imposing tasks on the Israelites, ¹⁴and made their lives bitter with hard service in mortar and brick and in every kind of field labor. They were ruthless in all the tasks that they imposed on them.

15 The king of Egypt said to the Hebrew midwives, one of whom was named Shiphrah and the other Puah, ¹⁶"When you act as midwives to the Hebrew women, and see them on the birthstool, if it is a boy, kill him; but if it is a girl, she shall live." ¹⁷But the midwives feared God; they did not do as the king of Egypt commanded them, but they let the boys live. ¹⁸So the king of Egypt summoned the midwives and said to them, "Why have you done this, and allowed the boys to live?" ¹⁹The midwives said to Pharaoh, "Because the Hebrew women are not like the Egyptian women; for they are vigorous and give birth before the midwife comes to them." ²⁰So God dealt well with the midwives; and the people multiplied and became very strong. ²¹And because the midwives feared God, he gave them families. ²²Then Pharaoh commanded all his people, "Every boy that is born to the Hebrews you shall throw into the Nile, but you shall let every girl live."

Birth and Youth of Moses

2 Now a man from the house of Levi went and married a Levite woman. ²The woman conceived and bore a son; and when she saw that he was a fine baby, she hid him three months. ³When she could hide him no longer she got a papyrus basket for him, and plastered it with bitumen and pitch; she put the child in it and placed it among the reeds on the bank of the river. ⁴His sister stood at a distance, to see what would happen to him.

5 The daughter of Pharaoh came down to bathe at the river, while her attendants walked beside the river. She saw the basket among the reeds and sent her maid to bring it. ⁶When she opened it, she saw the child. He was crying, and she took pity on him, "This must be one of the Hebrews' children," she said. ⁷Then his sister said to Pharaoh's daughter, "Shall I go and get you a nurse from the Hebrew women to nurse the child for you?" ⁸Pharaoh's daughter said to her, "Yes." So the girl went and called the child's

mother. ⁹Pharaoh's daughter said to her, "Take this child and nurse it for me, and I will give you your wages." So the woman took the child and nursed it. ¹⁰When the child grew up, she brought him to Pharaoh's daughter, and she took him as her son. She named him Moses, "because," she said, "I drew him out of the water."

Moses Flees to Midian

11 One day, after Moses had grown up, he went out to his people and saw their forced labor. He saw an Egyptian beating a Hebrew, one of his kinsfolk. ¹²He looked this way and that, and seeing no one he killed the Egyptian and hid him in the sand. ¹³When he went out the next day, he saw two Hebrews fighting; and he said to the one who was in the wrong, "Why do you strike your fellow Hebrew?" ¹⁴He answered, "Who made you a ruler and judge over us? Do you mean to kill me as you killed the Egyptian?" Then Moses was afraid and thought, "Surely the thing is known." ¹⁵When Pharaoh heard of it, he sought to kill Moses.

But Moses fled from Pharaoh. He settled in the land of Midian, and sat down by a well. ¹⁶The priest of Midian had seven daughters. They came to draw water, and filled the troughs to water their father's flock. ¹⁷But some shepherds came and drove them away. Moses got up and came to their defense and watered their flock. ¹⁸When they returned to their father Reuel, he said, "How is it that you have come back so soon today?" ¹⁹They said, "An Egyptian helped us against the shepherds; he even drew water for us and watered the flock." ²⁰He said to his daughters, "Where is he? Why did you leave the man? Invite him to break bread." ²¹Moses agreed to stay with the man, and he gave Moses his daughter Zipporah in marriage. ²²She bore a son, and he named him Gershom; for he said, "I have been an alien residing in a foreign land."

23 After a long time the king of Egypt died. The Israelites groaned under their slavery, and cried out. Out of the slavery their cry for help rose up to God. ²⁴God heard their groaning, and God remembered his covenant with Abraham, Isaac, and Jacob. ²⁵God looked upon the Israelites, and God took notice of them.

Moses at the Burning Bush

3 Moses was keeping the flock of his father-in-law Jethro, the priest of Midian; he led his flock beyond the wilderness, and came to Horeb, the mountain of God. ²There the angel of the LORD appeared to him in a flame of fire out of a bush; he looked, and the bush was blazing, yet it was not consumed. ³Then Moses said, "I must turn aside and look at this great sight, and see why the bush is not burned up." ⁴When the LORD saw that he had turned aside to see, God called to him out of the bush, "Moses, Moses!" And he said, "Here I am." ⁵Then he said, "Come no closer! Remove the sandals from your feet, for the place on which you are standing is holy ground." ⁶He said further, "I am the God of your father, the God of Abraham, the God of Isaac, and the God of Jacob." And Moses hid his face, for he was afraid to look at God.

"Moses" by Michelangelo (1475-1564) presents a powerful figure, as befits the man who liberated his people against such odds and brought them the law most forcefully. Corbis-Bettmann.

7 Then the LORD said, "I have observed the misery of my people who are in Egypt; I have heard their cry on account of their taskmasters. Indeed, I know their sufferings, ⁸and I have come down to deliver them from the Egyptians, and to bring them up out of that land to a good and broad land, a land flowing with milk and honey, to the country of the Canaanites, the Hittites, the Amorites, the Perizzites, the Hivites, and the Jebusites. ⁹The cry of the Israelites has now come to me; I have also seen how the Egyptians oppress them. ¹⁰So come, I will send you to Pharaoh to bring my people, the Israelites, out of Egypt." ¹¹But Moses said to God, "Who am I that I should go to Pharaoh, and bring the Israelites out of Egypt?" ¹²He said, "I will be with you; and this shall be the sign for you that it is I who sent you: when you have brought the people out of Egypt, you shall worship God on this mountain."

The Divine Name Revealed

13 But Moses said to God, "If I come to the Israelites and say to them, 'The God of your ancestors has sent me to you,' and they ask me, 'What is his name?' what shall I say to them?" ¹⁴God said to Moses, "I AM WHO I AM." He said further, "Thus you shall say to the Israelites, 'I AM has sent me to you.'" ¹⁵God also said to Moses, "Thus you shall say to the Israelites, 'The LORD, the God of your ancestors, the God of Abraham, the God of Isaac, and the God of Jacob, has sent me to you':

This is my name forever,
and this my title for all generations.

16 Go and assemble the elders of Israel, and say to them, 'The LORD, the God of your ancestors, the God of Abraham, of Isaac, and of Jacob, has appeared to me, saying: I have given heed to you and to what has been done to you in Egypt. ¹⁷I declare that I will bring you up out of the misery of Egypt, to the land of the Canaanites, the Hittites, the Amorites, the Perizzites, the Hivites, and the Jebusites, a land flowing with milk and honey.' ¹⁸They will listen to your voice; and you and the elders of Israel shall go to the king of Egypt and say to him, 'The LORD, the God of the Hebrews, has met with us; let us now go a three days' journey into the wilderness, so that we may sacrifice to the LORD our God.' ¹⁹I know, however, that the king of Egypt will not let you go unless compelled by a mighty hand. ²⁰So I will stretch out my hand and strike Egypt with all my wonders that I will perform in it; after that he will let you go. ²¹I will bring this people into such favor with the Egyptians that, when you go, you will not go empty-handed; ²²each woman shall ask her neighbor and any woman living in the neighbor's house for jewelry of silver and of gold, and clothing, and you shall put them on your sons and on your daughters; and so you shall plunder the Egyptians."

Moses' Miraculous Power

4 Then Moses answered, "But suppose they do not believe me or listen to me, but say, 'The LORD did not appear to you.'" ²The LORD said to him, "What is that in your hand?" He said, "A staff." ³And he said, "Throw it on the ground." So he threw the staff on the ground, and it became a snake; and Moses drew back from it. ⁴Then the LORD said to Moses, "Reach out your hand, and seize it by the tail"—so he reached out his hand and grasped it, and it became a staff in his hand— ⁵"so that they may believe that the LORD, the God of their ancestors, the God of Abraham, the God of Isaac, and the God of Jacob, has appeared to you."

6 Again, the LORD said to him, "Put your hand inside your cloak." He put his hand into his cloak; and when he took it out, his hand was leprous, as white as snow. ⁷Then God said, "Put your hand back into your cloak"—so he put his hand back into his cloak, and when he took it out, it was restored like the rest of his body— ⁸"If they will not believe you or heed the first sign, they may believe the second sign. ⁹If they will not believe even these two signs or heed you, you shall take some water from the Nile and pour it on the dry ground; and the water that you shall take from the Nile will become blood on the dry ground."

10 But Moses said to the LORD, "O my Lord, I have never been eloquent, neither in the past nor even now that you have spoken to your servant; but I am slow of speech and slow of tongue." ¹¹Then the LORD said to him, "Who gives speech to mortals? Who makes them mute or deaf, seeing or blind? Is it not I, the LORD? ¹²Now go, and I will be with your mouth and teach you what you are to speak." ¹³But he said, "O my Lord, please send someone else." ¹⁴Then the anger of the LORD was kindled against Moses and he said, "What of your brother Aaron,

the Levite? I know that he can speak fluently; even now he is coming out to meet you, and when he sees you his heart will be glad. [15]You shall speak to him and put the words in his mouth; and I will be with your mouth and with his mouth, and will teach you what you shall do. [16]He indeed shall speak for you to the people; he shall serve as a mouth for you, and you shall serve as God for him. [17]Take in your hand this staff, with which you shall perform the signs."

Moses Returns to Egypt

18 Moses went back to his father-in-law Jethro and said to him, "Please let me go back to my kindred in Egypt and see whether they are still living." And Jethro said to Moses, "Go in peace." [19]The LORD said to Moses in Midian, "Go back to Egypt; for all those who were seeking your life are dead." [20]So Moses took his wife and his sons, put them on a donkey and went back to the land of Egypt; and Moses carried the staff of God in his hand.

21 And the LORD said to Moses, "When you go back to Egypt, see that you perform before Pharaoh all the wonders that I have put in your power; but I will harden his heart, so that he will not let the people go. [22]Then you shall say to Pharaoh, 'Thus says the LORD: Israel is my firstborn son. [23]I said to you, "Let my son go that he may worship me." But you refused to let him go; now I will kill your firstborn son.'"

24 On the way, at a place where they spent the night, the LORD met him and tried to kill him. [25]But Zipporah took a flint and cut off her son's foreskin, and touched Moses' feet with it, and said, "Truly you are a bridegroom of blood to me!" [26]So he let him alone. It was then she said, "A bridegroom of blood by circumcision."

27 The LORD said to Aaron, "Go into the wilderness to meet Moses." So he went; and he met him at the mountain of God and kissed him. [28]Moses told Aaron all the words of the LORD with which he had sent him, and all the signs with which he had charged him. [29]Then Moses and Aaron went and assembled all the elders of the Israelites. [30]Aaron spoke all the words that the LORD had spoken to Moses, and performed the signs in the sight of the people. [31]The people believed; and when they heard that the LORD had given heed to the Israelites and that he had seen their misery, they bowed down and worshiped.

Bricks without Straw

5 Afterward Moses and Aaron went to Pharaoh and said, "Thus says the LORD, the God of Israel, 'Let my people go, so that they may celebrate a festival to me in the wilderness.'" [2]But Pharaoh said, "Who is the LORD, that I should heed him and let Israel go? I do not know the LORD, and I will not let Israel go." [3]Then they said, "The God of the Hebrews has revealed himself to us; let us go a three days' journey into the wilderness to sacrifice to the LORD our God, or he will fall upon us with pestilence or sword." [4]But the king of Egypt said to them, "Moses and Aaron, why are you taking the people away from their work? Get to your labors!" [5]Pharaoh continued, "Now they are more numerous than the people of the land and yet you want them to stop working!" [6]That same day Pharaoh commanded the taskmasters of the people, as well as their supervisors, [7]"You shall no longer give the people straw to make bricks, as before; let them go and gather straw for themselves. [8]But you shall require of them the same quantity of bricks as they have made previously; do not diminish it, for they are lazy; that is why they cry, 'Let us go and offer sacrifice to our God.' [9]Let heavier work be laid on them; then they will labor at it and pay no attention to deceptive words."

10 So the taskmasters and the supervisors of the people went out and said to the people, "Thus says Pharaoh, 'I will not give you straw. [11]Go and get straw yourselves, wherever you can find it; but your work will not be lessened in the least.'" [12]So the people scattered throughout the land of Egypt, to gather stubble for straw. [13]The taskmasters were urgent, saying, "Complete your work, the same daily assignment as when you were given straw." [14]And the supervisors of the Israelites, whom Pharaoh's taskmasters had set over them, were beaten, and were asked, "Why did you not finish the required quantity of bricks yesterday and today, as you did before?"

15 Then the Israelite supervisors came to Pharaoh and cried, "Why do you treat your servants like this? [16]No straw is given to your servants, yet they say to us, 'Make bricks!' Look how your servants are beaten! You are unjust to your own people." [17]He said, "You are lazy, lazy; that is why you say, 'Let us go and sacrifice to the LORD.' [18]Go now, and work; for no straw shall be given you, but you shall still deliver the same number of bricks." [19]The Israelite supervisors

saw that they were in trouble when they were told, "You shall not lessen your daily number of bricks." ²⁰As they left Pharaoh, they came upon Moses and Aaron who were waiting to meet them. ²¹They said to them, "The LORD look upon you and judge! You have brought us into bad odor with Pharaoh and his officials, and have put a sword in their hand to kill us."

22 Then Moses turned again to the LORD and said, "O LORD, why have you mistreated this people? Why did you ever send me? ²³Since I first came to Pharaoh to speak in your name, he has mistreated this people, and you have done nothing at all to deliver your people."

Israel's Deliverance Assured

6 Then the LORD said to Moses, "Now you shall see what I will do to Pharaoh: Indeed, by a mighty hand he will let them go; by a mighty hand he will drive them out of his land."

2 God also spoke to Moses and said to him: "I am the LORD. ³I appeared to Abraham, Isaac, and Jacob as God Almighty, but by my name 'The LORD' I did not make myself known to them. ⁴I also established my covenant with them, to give them the land of Canaan, the land in which they resided as aliens. ⁵I have also heard the groaning of the Israelites whom the Egyptians are holding as slaves, and I have remembered my covenant. ⁶Say therefore to the Israelites, 'I am the LORD, and I will free you from the burdens of the Egyptians and deliver you from slavery to them. I will redeem you with an outstretched arm and with mighty acts of judgment. ⁷I will take you as my people, and I will be your God. You shall know that I am the LORD your God, who has freed you from the burdens of the Egyptians. ⁸I will bring you into the land that I swore to give to Abraham, Isaac, and Jacob; I will give it to you for a possession. I am the LORD.'" ⁹Moses told this to the Israelites; but they would not listen to Moses, because of their broken spirit and their cruel slavery.

10 Then the LORD spoke to Moses, ¹¹"Go and tell Pharaoh king of Egypt to let the Israelites go out of his land." ¹²But Moses spoke to the LORD, "The Israelites have not listened to me; how then shall Pharaoh listen to me, poor speaker that I am?" ¹³Thus the LORD spoke to Moses and Aaron, and gave them orders regarding the Israelites and Pharaoh king of Egypt, charging them to free the Israelites from the land of Egypt.

Genealogy of Moses and Aaron

14 The following are the heads of their ancestral houses: the sons of Reuben, the firstborn of Israel: Hanoch, Pallu, Hezron, and Carmi; these are the families of Reuben. ¹⁵The sons of Simeon: Jemuel, Jamin, Ohad, Jachin, Zohar, and Shaul, the son of a Canaanite woman; these are the families of Simeon. ¹⁶The following are the names of the sons of Levi according to their genealogies: Gershon, Kohath, and Merari, and the length of Levi's life was one hundred thirty-seven years. ¹⁷The sons of Gershon: Libni and Shimei, by their families. ¹⁸The sons of Kohath: Amram, Izhar, Hebron, and Uzziel, and the length of Kohath's life was one hundred thirty-three years. ¹⁹The sons of Merari: Mahli and Mushi. These are the families of the Levites according to their genealogies. ²⁰Amram married Jochebed his father's sister and she bore him Aaron and Moses, and the length of Amram's life was one hundred thirty-seven years. ²¹The sons of Izhar: Korah, Nepheg, and Zichri. ²²The sons of Uzziel: Mishael, Elzaphan, and Sithri. ²³Aaron married Elisheba, daughter of Amminadab and sister of Nahshon, and she bore him Nadab, Abihu, Eleazar, and Ithamar. ²⁴The sons of Korah: Assir, Elkanah, and Abiasaph; these are the families of the Korahites. ²⁵Aaron's son Eleazar married one of the daughters of Putiel, and she bore him Phinehas. These are the heads of the ancestral houses of the Levites by their families.

26 It was this same Aaron and Moses to whom the LORD said, "Bring the Israelites out of the land of Egypt, company by company." ²⁷It was they who spoke to Pharaoh king of Egypt to bring the Israelites out of Egypt, the same Moses and Aaron.

Moses and Aaron Obey God's Commands

28 On the day when the LORD spoke to Moses in the land of Egypt, ²⁹he said to him, "I am the LORD; tell Pharaoh king of Egypt all that I am speaking to you." ³⁰But Moses said in the Lord's

presence, "Since I am a poor speaker, why would Pharaoh listen to me?"

7 The LORD said to Moses, "See, I have made you like God to Pharaoh, and your brother Aaron shall be your prophet. ²You shall speak all that I command you, and your brother Aaron shall tell Pharaoh to let the Israelites go out of his land. ³But I will harden Pharaoh's heart, and I will multiply my signs and wonders in the land of Egypt. ⁴When Pharaoh does not listen to you, I will lay my hand upon Egypt and bring my people the Israelites, company by company, out of the land of Egypt by great acts of judgment. ⁵The Egyptians shall know that I am the LORD, when I stretch out my hand against Egypt and bring the Israelites out from among them." ⁶Moses and Aaron did so; they did just as the LORD commanded them. ⁷Moses was eighty years old and Aaron eighty-three when they spoke to Pharaoh.

Aaron's Miraculous Rod

8 The LORD said to Moses and Aaron, ⁹"When Pharaoh says to you, 'Perform a wonder,' then you shall say to Aaron, 'Take your staff and throw it down before Pharaoh, and it will become a snake.'" ¹⁰So Moses and Aaron went to Pharaoh and did as the LORD had commanded; Aaron threw down his staff before Pharaoh and his officials, and it became a snake. ¹¹Then Pharaoh summoned the wise men and the sorcerers; and they also, the magicians of Egypt, did the same by their secret arts. ¹²Each one threw down his staff, and they became snakes; but Aaron's staff swallowed up theirs. ¹³Still Pharaoh's heart was hardened, and he would not listen to them, as the LORD had said.

The First Plague: Water Turned to Blood

14 Then the LORD said to Moses, "Pharaoh's heart is hardened; he refuses to let the people go. ¹⁵Go to Pharaoh in the morning, as he is going out to the water; stand by at the river bank to meet him, and take in your hand the staff that was turned into a snake. ¹⁶Say to him, 'The LORD, the God of the Hebrews, sent me to you to say, "Let my people go, so that they may worship me in the wilderness." But until now you have not listened.' ¹⁷Thus says the LORD, "By this you shall know that I am the LORD." See, with the staff that is in my hand I will strike the water that is in the Nile, and it shall be turned to blood. ¹⁸The fish in the river shall die, the river itself shall stink, and the Egyptians shall be unable to drink water from the Nile.'" ¹⁹The LORD said to Moses, "Say to Aaron, 'Take your staff and stretch out your hand over the waters of Egypt—over its rivers, its canals, and its ponds, and all its pools of water—so that they may become blood; and there shall be blood throughout the whole land of Egypt, even in vessels of wood and in vessels of stone.'"

20 Moses and Aaron did just as the LORD commanded. In the sight of Pharaoh and of his officials he lifted up the staff and struck the water in the river, and all the water in the river was turned into blood, ²¹and the fish in the river died. The river stank so that the Egyptians could not drink its water, and there was blood throughout the whole land of Egypt. ²²But the magicians of Egypt did the same by their secret arts; so Pharaoh's heart remained hardened, and he would not listen to them; as the LORD had said. ²³Pharaoh turned and went into his house, and he did not take even this to heart. ²⁴And all the Egyptians had to dig along the Nile for water to drink, for they could not drink the water of the river.

25 Seven days passed after the LORD had struck the Nile.

The Second Plague: Frogs

8 Then the LORD said to Moses, "Go to Pharaoh and say to him, 'Thus says the LORD: Let my people go, so that they may worship me. ²If you refuse to let them go, I will plague your whole country with frogs. ³The river shall swarm with frogs; they shall come up into your palace, into your bedchamber and your bed, and into the houses of your officials and of your people, and into your ovens and your kneading bowls. ⁴The frogs shall come up on you and on your people and on all your officials.'" ⁵And the LORD said to Moses, "Say to Aaron, 'Stretch out your hand with your staff over the rivers, the canals, and the pools, and make frogs come up on the land of Egypt.'" ⁶So Aaron stretched out his hand over the waters of Egypt; and the frogs came up and

covered the land of Egypt. ⁷But the magicians did the same by their secret arts, and brought frogs up on the land of Egypt.

8 Then Pharaoh called Moses and Aaron, and said, "Pray to the LORD to take away the frogs from me and my people, and I will let the people go to sacrifice to the LORD." ⁹Moses said to Pharaoh, "Kindly tell me when I am to pray for you and for your officials and for your people, that the frogs may be removed from you and your houses and be left only in the Nile." ʸAnd he said, "Tomorrow." Moses said, "As you say! So that you may know that there is no one like the LORD our God, ¹¹the frogs shall leave you and your houses and your officials and your people; they shall be left only in the Nile." ¹²Then Moses and Aaron went out from Pharaoh; and Moses cried out to the LORD concerning the frogs that he had brought upon Pharaoh. ¹³And the LORD did as Moses requested: the frogs died in the houses, the courtyards, and the fields. ¹⁴And they gathered them together in heaps, and the land stank. ¹⁵But when Pharaoh saw that there was a respite, he hardened his heart, and would not listen to them, just as the LORD had said.

The Third Plague: Gnats

16 Then the LORD said to Moses, "Say to Aaron, 'Stretch out your staff and strike the dust of the earth, so that it may become gnats throughout the whole land of Egypt.'" ¹⁷And they did so; Aaron stretched out his hand with his staff and struck the dust of the earth, and gnats came on humans and animals alike; all the dust of the earth turned into gnats throughout the whole land of Egypt. ¹⁸The magicians tried to produce gnats by their secret arts, but they could not. There were gnats on both humans and animals. ¹⁹And the magicians said to Pharaoh, "This is the finger of God!" But Pharaoh's heart was hardened, and he would not listen to them, just as the LORD had said.

The Fourth Plague: Flies

20 Then the LORD said to Moses, "Rise early in the morning and present yourself before Pharaoh, as he goes out to the water, and say to him, 'Thus says the LORD: Let my people go, so that they may worship me. ²¹For if you will not let my people go, I will send swarms of flies on you, your officials, and your people, and into your houses; and the houses of the Egyptians shall be filled with swarms of flies; so also the land where they live. ²²But on that day I will set apart the land of Goshen, where my people live, so that no swarms of flies shall be there, that you may know that I the LORD am in this land. ²³Thus I will make a distinction between my people and your people. This sign shall appear tomorrow.'" ²⁴The LORD did so, and great swarms of flies came into the house of Pharaoh and into his officials' houses; in all of Egypt the land was ruined because of the flies.

25 Then Pharaoh summoned Moses and Aaron, and said, "Go, sacrifice to your God within the land." ²⁶But Moses said, "It would not be right to do so; for the sacrifices that we offer to the LORD our God are offensive to the Egyptians. If we offer in the sight of the Egyptians sacrifices that are offensive to them, will they not stone us? ²⁷We must go a three days' journey into the wilderness and sacrifice to the LORD our God as he commands us." ²⁸So Pharaoh said, "I will let you go to sacrifice to the LORD your God in the wilderness, provided you do not go very far away. Pray for me." ²⁹Then Moses said, "As soon as I leave you, I will pray to the LORD that the swarms of flies may depart tomorrow from Pharaoh, from his officials, and from his people; only do not let Pharaoh again deal falsely by not letting the people go to sacrifice to the LORD."

30 So Moses went out from Pharaoh and prayed to the LORD. ³¹And the LORD did as Moses asked: he removed the swarms of flies from Pharaoh, from his officials, and from his people; not one remained. ³²But Pharaoh hardened his heart this time also, and would not let the people go.

The Fifth Plague: Livestock Diseased

9 Then the LORD said to Moses, "Go to Pharaoh, and say to him, 'Thus says the LORD, the God of the Hebrews: Let my people go, so that they may worship me. ²For if you refuse to let them go and still hold them, ³the hand of the LORD will strike with a deadly pestilence your livestock in the field: the horses, the donkeys, the camels, the herds, and the flocks. ⁴But the LORD

will make a distinction between the livestock of Israel and the livestock of Egypt, so that nothing shall die of all that belongs to the Israelites.'" ⁵The LORD set a time, saying, "Tomorrow the LORD will do this thing in the land." ⁶And on the next day the LORD did so; all the livestock of the Egyptians died, but of the livestock of the Israelites not one died. ⁷Pharaoh inquired and found that not one of the livestock of the Israelites was dead. But the heart of Pharaoh was hardened, and he would not let the people go.

The Sixth Plague: Boils

8 Then the LORD said to Moses and Aaron, "Take handfuls of soot from the kiln, and let Moses throw it in the air in the sight of Pharaoh. ⁹It shall become fine dust all over the land of Egypt, and shall cause festering boils on humans and animals throughout the whole land of Egypt." ¹⁰So they took soot from the kiln, and stood before Pharaoh, and Moses threw it in the air, and it caused festering boils on humans and animals. ¹¹The magicians could not stand before Moses because of the boils, for the boils afflicted the magicians as well as all the Egyptians. ¹²But the LORD hardened the heart of Pharaoh, and he would not listen to them, just as the LORD had spoken to Moses.

The Seventh Plague: Thunder and Hail

13 Then the LORD said to Moses, "Rise up early in the morning and present yourself before Pharaoh, and say to him, 'Thus says the LORD, the God of the Hebrews: Let my people go, so that they may worship me. ¹⁴For this time I will send all my plagues upon you yourself, and upon your officials, and upon your people, so that you may know that there is no one like me in all the earth. ¹⁵For by now I could have stretched out my hand and struck you and your people with pestilence, and you would have been cut off from the earth. ¹⁶But this is why I have let you live: to show you my power, and to make my name resound through all the earth. ¹⁷You are still exalting yourself against my people, and will not let them go. ¹⁸Tomorrow at this time I will cause the heaviest hail to fall that has ever fallen in Egypt from the day it was founded until now. ¹⁹Send, therefore, and have your livestock and everything that you have in the open field brought to a secure place; every human or animal that is in the open field and is not brought under shelter will die when the hail comes down upon them.'" ²⁰Those officials of Pharaoh who feared the word of the LORD hurried their slaves and livestock off to a secure place. ²¹Those who did not regard the word of the LORD left their slaves and livestock in the open field.

22 The LORD said to Moses, "Stretch out your hand toward heaven so that hail may fall on the whole land of Egypt, on humans and animals and all the plants of the field in the land of Egypt." ²³Then Moses stretched out his staff toward heaven, and the LORD sent thunder and hail, and fire came down on the earth. And the LORD rained hail on the land of Egypt; ²⁴there was hail with fire flashing continually in the midst of it, such heavy hail as had never fallen in all the land of Egypt since it became a nation. ²⁵The hail struck down everything that was in the open field throughout all the land of Egypt, both human and animal; the hail also struck down all the plants of the field, and shattered every tree in the field. ²⁶Only in the land of Goshen, where the Israelites were, there was no hail.

27 Then Pharaoh summoned Moses and Aaron, and said to them, "This time I have sinned; the LORD is in the right, and I and my people are in the wrong. ²⁸Pray to the LORD! Enough of God's thunder and hail! I will let you go; you need stay no longer." ²⁹Moses said to him, "As soon as I have gone out of the city, I will stretch out my hands to the LORD; the thunder will cease, and there will be no more hail, so that you may know that the earth is the Lord's. ³⁰But as for you and your officials, I know that you do not yet fear the LORD God." ³¹(Now the flax and the barley were ruined, for the barley was in the ear and the flax was in bud. ³²But the wheat and the spelt were not ruined, for they are late in coming up.) ³³So Moses left Pharaoh, went out of the city, and stretched out his hands to the LORD; then the thunder and the hail ceased, and the rain no longer poured down on the earth. ³⁴But when Pharaoh saw that the rain and the hail and the thunder had ceased, he sinned once more and hardened his heart, he and his officials. ³⁵So the heart of Pharaoh was hardened, and he would not let the Israelites go, just as the LORD had spoken through Moses.

The Eighth Plague: Locusts

10 Then the LORD said to Moses, "Go to Pharaoh; for I have hardened his heart and the heart of his officials, in order that I may show these signs of mine among them, ²and that you may tell your children and grandchildren how I have made fools of the Egyptians and what signs I have done among them—so that you may know that I am the LORD."

3 So Moses and Aaron went to Pharaoh, and said to him, "Thus says the LORD, the God of the Hebrews, 'How long will you refuse to humble yourself before me? Let my people go, so that they may worship me. ⁴For if you refuse to let my people go, tomorrow I will bring locusts into your country. ⁵They shall cover the surface of the land, so that no one will be able to see the land. They shall devour the last remnant left you after the hail, and they shall devour every tree of yours that grows in the field. ⁶They shall fill your houses, and the houses of all your officials and of all the Egyptians—something that neither your parents nor your grandparents have seen, from the day they came on earth to this day.'" Then he turned and went out from Pharaoh.

7 Pharaoh's officials said to him, "How long shall this fellow be a snare to us? Let the people go, so that they may worship the LORD their God; do you not yet understand that Egypt is ruined?" ⁸So Moses and Aaron were brought back to Pharaoh, and he said to them, "Go, worship the LORD your God! But which ones are to go?" ⁹Moses said, "We will go with our young and our old; we will go with our sons and daughters and with our flocks and herds, because we have the Lord's festival to celebrate." ¹⁰He said to them, "The LORD indeed will be with you, if ever I let your little ones go with you! Plainly, you have some evil purpose in mind. ¹¹No, never! Your men may go and worship the LORD, for that is what you are asking." And they were driven out from Pharaoh's presence.

12 Then the LORD said to Moses, "Stretch out your hand over the land of Egypt, so that the locusts may come upon it and eat every plant in the land, all that the hail has left." ¹³So Moses stretched out his staff over the land of Egypt, and the LORD brought an east wind upon the land all that day and all that night; when morning came, the east wind had brought the locusts. ¹⁴The locusts came upon all the land of Egypt and settled on the whole country of Egypt, such a dense swarm of locusts as had never been before, nor ever shall be again. ¹⁵They covered the surface of the whole land, so that the land was black; and they ate all the plants in the land and all the fruit of the trees that the hail had left; nothing green was left, no tree, no plant in the field, in all the land of Egypt. ¹⁶Pharaoh hurriedly summoned Moses and Aaron and said, "I have sinned against the LORD your God, and against you. ¹⁷Do forgive my sin just this once, and pray to the LORD your God that at the least he remove this deadly thing from me." ¹⁸So he went out from Pharaoh and prayed to the LORD. ¹⁹The LORD changed the wind into a very strong west wind, which lifted the locusts and drove them into the Red Sea; not a single locust was left in all the country of Egypt. ²⁰But the LORD hardened Pharaoh's heart, and he would not let the Israelites go.

The Ninth Plague: Darkness

21 Then the LORD said to Moses, "Stretch out your hand toward heaven so that there may be darkness over the land of Egypt, a darkness that can be felt." ²²So Moses stretched out his hand toward heaven, and there was dense darkness in all the land of Egypt for three days. ²³People could not see one another, and for three days they could not move from where they were; but all the Israelites had light where they lived. ²⁴Then Pharaoh summoned Moses, and said, "Go, worship the LORD. Only your flocks and your herds shall remain behind. Even your children may go with you." ²⁵But Moses said, "You must also let us have sacrifices and burnt offerings to sacrifice to the LORD our God. ²⁶Our livestock also must go with us; not a hoof shall be left behind, for we must choose some of them for the worship of the LORD our God, and we will not know what to use to worship the LORD until we arrive there." ²⁷But the LORD hardened Pharaoh's heart, and he was unwilling to let them go. ²⁸Then Pharaoh said to him, "Get away from me! Take care that you do not see my face again, for on the day you see my face you shall die." ²⁹Moses said, "Just as you say! I will never see your face again."

Warning of the Final Plague

11 The LORD said to Moses, "I will bring one more plague upon Pharaoh and upon Egypt; afterwards he will let you go from here; indeed, when he lets you go, he will drive you away. ²Tell the people that every man is to ask his neighbor and every woman is to ask her neighbor for objects of silver and gold." ³The LORD gave the people favor in the sight of the Egyptians. Moreover, Moses himself was a man of great importance in the land of Egypt, in the sight of Pharaoh's officials and in the sight of the people.

4 Moses said, "Thus says the LORD: About midnight I will go out through Egypt. ⁵Every firstborn in the land of Egypt shall die, from the firstborn of Pharaoh who sits on his throne to the firstborn of the female slave who is behind the handmill, and all the firstborn of the livestock. ⁶Then there will be a loud cry throughout the whole land of Egypt, such as has never been or will ever be again. ⁷But not a dog shall growl at any of the Israelites—not at people, not at animals—so that you may know that the LORD makes a distinction between Egypt and Israel. ⁸Then all these officials of yours shall come down to me, and bow low to me, saying, 'Leave us, you and all the people who follow you.' After that I will leave." And in hot anger he left Pharaoh.

9 The LORD said to Moses, "Pharaoh will not listen to you, in order that my wonders may be multiplied in the land of Egypt." ¹⁰Moses and Aaron performed all these wonders before Pharaoh; but the LORD hardened Pharaoh's heart, and he did not let the people of Israel go out of his land.

The First Passover Initiated

12 The LORD said to Moses and Aaron in the land of Egypt: ²This month shall mark for you the beginning of months; it shall be the first month of the year for you. ³Tell the whole congregation of Israel that on the tenth of this month they are to take a lamb for each family, a lamb for each household. ⁴If a household is too small for a whole lamb, it shall join its closest neighbor in obtaining one; the lamb shall be divided in proportion to the number of people who eat of it. ⁵Your lamb shall be without blemish, a year-old male; you may take it from the sheep or from the goats. ⁶You shall keep it until the fourteenth day of this month; then the whole assembled congregation of Israel shall slaughter it at twilight. ⁷They shall take some of the blood and put it on the two doorposts and the lintel of the houses in which they eat it. ⁸They shall eat the lamb that same night; they shall eat it roasted over the fire with unleavened bread and bitter herbs. ⁹Do not eat any of it raw or boiled in water, but roasted over the fire, with its head, legs, and inner organs. ¹⁰You shall let none of it remain until the morning; anything that remains until the morning you shall burn. ¹¹This is how you shall eat it: your loins girded, your sandals on your feet, and your staff in your hand; and you shall eat it hurriedly. It is the passover of the LORD. ¹²For I will pass through the land of Egypt that night, and I will strike down every firstborn in the land of Egypt, both human beings and animals; on all the gods of Egypt I will execute judgments: I am the LORD. ¹³The blood shall be a sign for you on the houses where you live: when I see the blood, I will pass over you, and no plague shall destroy you when I strike the land of Egypt.

14 This day shall be a day of remembrance for you. You shall celebrate it as a festival to the LORD; throughout your generations you shall observe it as a perpetual ordinance. ¹⁵Seven days you shall eat unleavened bread; on the first day you shall remove leaven from your houses, for whoever eats leavened bread from the first day until the seventh day shall be cut off from Israel. ¹⁶On the first day you shall hold a solemn assembly, and on the seventh day a solemn assembly; no work shall be done on those days; only what everyone must eat, that alone may be prepared by you. ¹⁷You shall observe the festival of unleavened bread, for on this very day I brought your companies out of the land of Egypt: you shall observe this day throughout your generations as a perpetual ordinance. ¹⁸In the first month, from the evening of the fourteenth day until the evening of the twenty-first day, you shall eat unleavened bread. ¹⁹For seven days no leaven shall be found in your houses; for whoever eats what is leavened shall be cut off from the congregation of Israel, whether an alien or a native of the land. ²⁰You shall eat nothing leavened; in all your settlements you shall eat unleavened bread.

21 Then Moses called all the elders of Israel and said to them, "Go, select lambs for your families, and slaughter the passover lamb. ²²Take a bunch of hyssop, dip it in the blood that is in

the basin, and touch the lintel and the two doorposts with the blood in the basin. None of you shall go outside the door of your house until morning. 23For the LORD will pass through to strike down the Egyptians; when he sees the blood on the lintel and on the two doorposts, the LORD will pass over that door and will not allow the destroyer to enter your houses to strike you down. 24You shall observe this rite as a perpetual ordinance for you and your children. 25When you come to the land that the LORD will give you, as he has promised, you shall keep this observance. 26And when your children ask you, 'What do you mean by this observance?' 27you shall say, 'It is the passover sacrifice to the LORD, for he passed over the houses of the Israelites in Egypt, when he struck down the Egyptians but spared our houses.'" And the people bowed down and worshiped.

28 The Israelites went and did just as the LORD had commanded Moses and Aaron.

The Tenth Plague: Death of the Firstborn

29 At midnight the LORD struck down all the firstborn in the land of Egypt, from the firstborn of Pharaoh who sat on his throne to the firstborn of the prisoner who was in the dungeon, and all the firstborn of the livestock. 30Pharaoh arose in the night, he and all his officials and all the Egyptians; and there was a loud cry in Egypt, for there was not a house without someone dead. 31Then he summoned Moses and Aaron in the night, and said, "Rise up, go away from my people, both you and the Israelites! Go, worship the LORD, as you said. 32Take your flocks and your herds, as you said, and be gone. And bring a blessing on me too!"

The Exodus: From Ramses to Succoth

33 The Egyptians urged the people to hasten their departure from the land, for they said, "We shall all be dead." 34So the people took their dough before it was leavened, with their kneading bowls wrapped up in their cloaks on their shoulders. 35The Israelites had done as Moses told them; they had asked the Egyptians for jewelry of silver and gold, and for clothing, 36and the LORD had given the people favor in the sight of the Egyptians, so that they let them have what they asked. And so they plundered the Egyptians.

37 The Israelites journeyed from Rameses to Succoth, about six hundred thousand men on foot, besides children. 38A mixed crowd also went up with them, and livestock in great numbers, both flocks and herds. 39They baked unleavened cakes of the dough that they had brought out of Egypt; it was not leavened, because they were driven out of Egypt and could not wait, nor had they prepared any provisions for themselves.

40 The time that the Israelites had lived in Egypt was four hundred thirty years. 41At the end of four hundred thirty years, on that very day, all the companies of the LORD went out from the land of Egypt. 42That was for the LORD a night of vigil, to bring them out of the land of Egypt. That same night is a vigil to be kept for the LORD by all the Israelites throughout their generations.

Directions for the Passover

43 The LORD said to Moses and Aaron: This is the ordinance for the passover: no foreigner shall eat of it, 44but any slave who has been purchased may eat of it after he has been circumcised; 45no bound or hired servant may eat of it. 46It shall be eaten in one house; you shall not take any of the animal outside the house, and you shall not break any of its bones. 47The whole congregation of Israel shall celebrate it. 48If an alien who resides with you wants to celebrate the passover to the LORD, all his males shall be circumcised; then he may draw near to celebrate it; he shall be regarded as a native of the land. But no uncircumcised person shall eat of it; 49there shall be one law for the native and for the alien who resides among you.

50 All the Israelites did just as the LORD had commanded Moses and Aaron. 51That very day the LORD brought the Israelites out of the land of Egypt, company by company.

13 The LORD said to Moses: 2Consecrate to me all the firstborn; whatever is the first to open the womb among the Israelites, of human beings and animals, is mine.

The Festival of Unleavened Bread

3 Moses said to the people, "Remember this day on which you came out of Egypt, out of the house of slavery, because the LORD brought you out from there by strength of hand; no leavened bread shall be eaten. [4]Today, in the month of Abib, you are going out. [5]When the LORD brings you into the land of the Canaanites, the Hittites, the Amorites, the Hivites, and the Jebusites, which he swore to your ancestors to give you, a land flowing with milk and honey, you shall keep this observance in this month. [6]Seven days you shall eat unleavened bread, and on the seventh day there shall be a festival to the LORD. [7]Unleavened bread shall be eaten for seven days; no leavened bread shall be seen in your possession, and no leaven shall be seen among you in all your territory. [8]You shall tell your child on that day, 'It is because of what the LORD did for me when I came out of Egypt.' [9]It shall serve for you as a sign on your hand and as a reminder on your forehead, so that the teaching of the LORD may be on your lips; for with a strong hand the LORD brought you out of Egypt. [10]You shall keep this ordinance at its proper time from year to year.

The Consecration of the First Born

11 "When the LORD has brought you into the land of the Canaanites, as he swore to you and your ancestors, and has given it to you, [12]you shall set apart to the LORD all that first opens the womb. All the firstborn of your livestock that are males shall be the Lord's. [13]But every firstborn donkey you shall redeem with a sheep; if you do not redeem it, you must break its neck. Every firstborn male among your children you shall redeem. [14]When in the future your child asks you, 'What does this mean?' you shall answer, 'By strength of hand the LORD brought us out of Egypt, from the house of slavery. [15]When Pharaoh stubbornly refused to let us go, the LORD killed all the firstborn in the land of Egypt, from human firstborn to the firstborn of animals. Therefore I sacrifice to the LORD every male that first opens the womb, but every firstborn of my sons I redeem.' [16]It shall serve as a sign on your hand and as an emblem on your forehead that by strength of hand the LORD brought us out of Egypt."

The Pillars of Clouds and Fire

17 When Pharaoh let the people go, God did not lead them by way of the land of the Philistines, although that was nearer; for God thought, "If the people face war, they may change their minds and return to Egypt." [18]So God led the people by the roundabout way of the wilderness toward the Red Sea. The Israelites went up out of the land of Egypt prepared for battle. [19]And Moses took with him the bones of Joseph who had required a solemn oath of the Israelites, saying, "God will surely take notice of you, and then you must carry my bones with you from here." [20]They set out from Succoth, and camped at Etham, on the edge of the wilderness. [21]The LORD went in front of them in a pillar of cloud by day, to lead them along the way, and in a pillar of fire by night, to give them light, so that they might travel by day and by night. [22]Neither the pillar of cloud by day nor the pillar of fire by night left its place in front of the people.

Crossing the Red Sea

14 Then the LORD said to Moses: [2]Tell the Israelites to turn back and camp in front of Pi-hahiroth, between Migdol and the sea, in front of Baal-zephon; you shall camp opposite it, by the sea. [3]Pharaoh will say of the Israelites, 'They are wandering aimlessly in the land; the wilderness has closed in on them.' [4]I will harden Pharaoh's heart, and he will pursue them, so that I will gain glory for myself over Pharaoh and all his army; and the Egyptians shall know that I am the LORD. And they did so.

5 When the king of Egypt was told that the people had fled, the minds of Pharaoh and his officials were changed toward the people, and they said, "What have we done, letting Israel leave our service?" [6]So he had his chariot made ready, and took his army with him; [7]he took six hundred picked chariots and all the other chariots of Egypt with officers over all of them. [8]The LORD hardened the heart of Pharaoh king of

Egypt and he pursued the Israelites, who were going out boldly. ⁹The Egyptians pursued them, all Pharaoh's horses and chariots, his chariot drivers and his army; they overtook them camped by the sea, by Pi-hahiroth, in front of Baal-zephon.

10 As Pharaoh drew near, the Israelites looked back, and there were the Egyptians advancing on them. In great fear the Israelites cried out to the LORD. ¹¹They said to Moses, "Was it because there were no graves in Egypt that you have taken us away to die in the wilderness? What have you done to us, bringing us out of Egypt? ¹²Is this not the very thing we told you in Egypt, 'Let us alone and let us serve the Egyptians'? For it would have been better for us to serve the Egyptians than to die in the wilderness." ¹³But Moses said to the people, "Do not be afraid, stand firm, and see the deliverance that the LORD will accomplish for you today; for the Egyptians whom you see today you shall never see again. ¹⁴The LORD will fight for you, and you have only to keep still."

15 Then the LORD said to Moses, "Why do you cry out to me? Tell the Israelites to go forward. ¹⁶But you lift up your staff, and stretch out your hand over the sea and divide it, that the Israelites may go into the sea on dry ground. ¹⁷Then I will harden the hearts of the Egyptians so that they will go in after them; and so I will gain glory for myself over Pharaoh and all his army, his chariots, and his chariot drivers. ¹⁸And the Egyptians shall know that I am the LORD, when I have gained glory for myself over Pharaoh, his chariots, and his chariot drivers."

19 The angel of God who was going before the Israelite army moved and went behind them; and the pillar of cloud moved from in front of them and took its place behind them. ²⁰It came between the army of Egypt and the army of Israel. And so the cloud was there with the darkness, and it lit up the night; one did not come near the other all night.

21 Then Moses stretched out his hand over the sea. The LORD drove the sea back by a strong east wind all night, and turned the sea into dry land; and the waters were divided. ²²The Israelites went into the sea on dry ground, the waters forming a wall for them on their right and on their left. ²³The Egyptians pursued, and went into the sea after them, all of Pharaoh's horses, chariots, and chariot drivers. ²⁴At the morning watch the LORD in the pillar of fire and cloud looked down upon the Egyptian army, and threw the Egyptian army into panic. ²⁵He clogged their chariot wheels so that they turned with difficulty. The Egyptians said, "Let us flee from the Israelites, for the LORD is fighting for them against Egypt."

The Pursuers Drowned

26 Then the LORD said to Moses, "Stretch out your hand over the sea, so that the water may come back upon the Egyptians, upon their chariots and chariot drivers." ²⁷So Moses stretched out his hand over the sea, and at dawn the sea returned to its normal depth. As the Egyptians fled before it, the LORD tossed the Egyptians into the sea. ²⁸The waters returned and covered the chariots and the chariot drivers, the entire army of Pharaoh that had followed them into the sea; not one of them remained. ²⁹But the Israelites walked on dry ground through the sea, the waters forming a wall for them on their right and on their left.

30 Thus the LORD saved Israel that day from the Egyptians; and Israel saw the Egyptians dead on the seashore. ³¹Israel saw the great work that the LORD did against the Egyptians. So the people feared the LORD and believed in the LORD and in his servant Moses.

The Song of Moses

15 Then Moses and the Israelites sang this song to the LORD:
"I will sing to the LORD, for he has triumphed gloriously;
   horse and rider he has thrown into the sea.
2 The LORD is my strength and my might, and he has become my salvation;
   this is my God, and I will praise him,
   my father's God, and I will exalt him.
3 The LORD is a warrior;
   the LORD is his name.
4 "Pharaoh's chariots and his army he cast into the sea;
   his picked officers were sunk in the Red Sea.
5 The floods covered them;
   they went down into the depths like a stone.
6 Your right hand, O LORD, glorious in power—
   your right hand, O LORD, shattered the enemy.
7 In the greatness of your majesty you overthrew your adversaries;

you sent out your fury, it consumed them like stubble.
8 At the blast of your nostrils the waters piled up,
the floods stood up in a heap;
the deeps congealed in the heart of the sea.
9 The enemy said, 'I will pursue, I will overtake,
I will divide the spoil, my desire shall have its fill of them.
I will draw my sword, my hand shall destroy them.'
10 You blew with your wind, the sea covered them;
they sank like lead in the mighty waters.
11 "Who is like you, O LORD, among the gods?
Who is like you, majestic in holiness, awesome in splendor, doing wonders?
12 You stretched out your right hand,
the earth swallowed them.
13 "In your steadfast love you led the people whom you redeemed;
you guided them by your strength to your holy abode.
14 The peoples heard, they trembled;
pangs seized the inhabitants of Philistia.
15 Then the chiefs of Edom were dismayed;
trembling seized the leaders of Moab;
all the inhabitants of Canaan melted away.
16 Terror and dread fell upon them;
by the might of your arm, they became still as a stone
until your people, O LORD, passed by,
until the people whom you acquired passed by.
17 You brought them in and planted them on the mountain of your own possession,
the place, O LORD, that you made your abode,
the sanctuary, O LORD, that your hands have established.
18 The LORD will reign forever and ever."

19 When the horses of Pharaoh with his chariots and his chariot drivers went into the sea, the LORD brought back the waters of the sea upon them; but the Israelites walked through the sea on dry ground.

The Song of Miriam

20 Then the prophet Miriam, Aaron's sister, took a tambourine in her hand; and all the women went out after her with tambourines and with dancing. 21And Miriam sang to them:

"Sing to the LORD, for he has triumphed gloriously;
horse and rider he has thrown into the sea."

Bitter Water Made Sweet

22 Then Moses ordered Israel to set out from the Red Sea, and they went into the wilderness of Shur. They went three days in the wilderness and found no water. 23When they came to Marah, they could not drink the water of Marah because it was bitter. That is why it was called Marah. 24And the people complained against Moses, saying, "What shall we drink?" 25He cried out to the LORD; and the LORD showed him a piece of wood; he threw it into the water, and the water became sweet.

There the LORD made for them a statute and an ordinance and there he put them to the test. 26He said, "If you will listen carefully to the voice of the LORD your God, and do what is right in his sight, and give heed to his commandments and keep all his statutes, I will not bring upon you any of the diseases that I brought upon the Egyptians; for I am the LORD who heals you."

27 Then they came to Elim, where there were twelve springs of water and seventy palm trees; and they camped there by the water.

Bread from Heaven

16 The whole congregation of the Israelites set out from Elim; and Israel came to the wilderness of Sin, which is between Elim and Sinai, on the fifteenth day of the second month after they had departed from the land of Egypt. 2The whole congregation of the Israelites complained against Moses and Aaron in the wilderness. 3The Israelites said to them, "If only we had died by the hand of the LORD in the land of Egypt, when we sat by the fleshpots and ate our fill of bread; for you have brought us out into this wilderness to kill this whole assembly with hunger."

4 Then the LORD said to Moses, "I am going to rain bread from heaven for you, and each day the people shall go out and gather enough for that day. In that way I will test them, whether they will follow my instruction or not. 5On the sixth day, when they prepare what they bring in,

it will be twice as much as they gather on other days." ⁶So Moses and Aaron said to all the Israelites, "In the evening you shall know that it was the LORD who brought you out of the land of Egypt, ⁷and in the morning you shall see the glory of the LORD, because he has heard your complaining against the LORD. For what are we, that you complain against us?" ⁸And Moses said, "When the LORD gives you meat to eat in the evening and your fill of bread in the morning, because the LORD has heard the complaining that you utter against him—what are we? Your complaining is not against us but against the LORD."

9 Then Moses said to Aaron, "Say to the whole congregation of the Israelites, 'Draw near to the LORD, for he has heard your complaining.'" ¹⁰And as Aaron spoke to the whole congregation of the Israelites, they looked toward the wilderness, and the glory of the LORD appeared in the cloud. ¹¹The LORD spoke to Moses and said, ¹²"I have heard the complaining of the Israelites; say to them, 'At twilight you shall eat meat, and in the morning you shall have your fill of bread; then you shall know that I am the LORD your God.'"

13 In the evening quails came up and covered the camp; and in the morning there was a layer of dew around the camp. ¹⁴When the layer of dew lifted, there on the surface of the wilderness was a fine flaky substance, as fine as frost on the ground. ¹⁵When the Israelites saw it, they said to one another, "What is it?" For they did not know what it was. Moses said to them, "It is the bread that the LORD has given you to eat. ¹⁶This is what the LORD has commanded: 'Gather as much of it as each of you needs, an omer to a person according to the number of persons, all providing for those in their own tents.'" ¹⁷The Israelites did so, some gathering more, some less. ¹⁸But when they measured it with an omer, those who gathered much had nothing over, and those who gathered little had no shortage; they gathered as much as each of them needed. ¹⁹And Moses said to them, "Let no one leave any of it over until morning." ²⁰But they did not listen to Moses; some left part of it until morning, and it bred worms and became foul. And Moses was angry with them. ²¹Morning by morning they gathered it, as much as each needed; but when the sun grew hot, it melted.

22 On the sixth day they gathered twice as much food, two omers apiece. When all the leaders of the congregation came and told Moses, ²³he said to them, "This is what the LORD has commanded: 'Tomorrow is a day of solemn rest, a holy sabbath to the LORD; bake what you want to bake and boil what you want to boil, and all that is left over put aside to be kept until morning.'" ²⁴So they put it aside until morning, as Moses commanded them; and it did not become foul, and there were no worms in it. ²⁵Moses said, "Eat it today, for today is a sabbath to the LORD; today you will not find it in the field. ²⁶Six days you shall gather it; but on the seventh day, which is a sabbath, there will be none."

27 On the seventh day some of the people went out to gather, and they found none. ²⁸The LORD said to Moses, "How long will you refuse to keep my commandments and instructions? ²⁹See! The LORD has given you the sabbath, therefore on the sixth day he gives you food for two days; each of you stay where you are; do not leave your place on the seventh day." ³⁰So the people rested on the seventh day.

31 The house of Israel called it manna; it was like coriander seed, white, and the taste of it was like wafers made with honey. ³²Moses said, "This is what the LORD has commanded: 'Let an omer of it be kept throughout your generations, in order that they may see the food with which I fed you in the wilderness, when I brought you out of the land of Egypt.'" ³³And Moses said to Aaron, "Take a jar, and put an omer of manna in it, and place it before the LORD, to be kept throughout your generations." ³⁴As the LORD commanded Moses, so Aaron placed it before the covenant, for safekeeping. ³⁵The Israelites ate manna forty years, until they came to a habitable land; they ate manna, until they came to the border of the land of Canaan. ³⁶An omer is a tenth of an ephah.

Water from the Rock

17 From the wilderness of Sin the whole congregation of the Israelites journeyed by stages, as the LORD commanded. They camped at Rephidim, but there was no water for the people to drink. ²The people quarreled with Moses, and said, "Give us water to drink." Moses said to them, "Why do you quarrel with me? Why do you test the LORD?" ³But the people thirsted there for water; and the people complained against Moses and said, "Why did you bring us out of Egypt, to kill us and our children and livestock with thirst?" ⁴So Moses cried out to the LORD, "What shall I do with this people? They are almost ready to stone me." ⁵The LORD said

to Moses, "Go on ahead of the people, and take some of the elders of Israel with you; take in your hand the staff with which you struck the Nile, and go. ⁶I will be standing there in front of you on the rock at Horeb. Strike the rock, and water will come out of it, so that the people may drink." Moses did so, in the sight of the elders of Israel. ⁷He called the place Massah and Meribah, because the Israelites quarreled and tested the LORD, saying, "Is the LORD among us or not?"

Amalek Attacks Israel and Is Defeated

8 Then Amalek came and fought with Israel at Rephidim. ⁹Moses said to Joshua, "Choose some men for us and go out, fight with Amalek. Tomorrow I will stand on the top of the hill with the staff of God in my hand." ¹⁰So Joshua did as Moses told him, and fought with Amalek, while Moses, Aaron, and Hur went up to the top of the hill. ¹¹Whenever Moses held up his hand, Israel prevailed; and whenever he lowered his hand, Amalek prevailed. ¹²But Moses' hands grew weary; so they took a stone and put it under him, and he sat on it. Aaron and Hur held up his hands, one on one side, and the other on the other side; so his hands were steady until the sun set. ¹³And Joshua defeated Amalek and his people with the sword.

14 Then the LORD said to Moses, "Write this as a reminder in a book and recite it in the hearing of Joshua: I will utterly blot out the remembrance of Amalek from under heaven." ¹⁵And Moses built an altar and called it, The LORD is my banner. ¹⁶He said, "A hand upon the banner of the LORD! The LORD will have war with Amalek from generation to generation."

Jethro's Advice

18 Jethro, the priest of Midian, Moses' father-in-law, heard of all that God had done for Moses and for his people Israel, how the LORD had brought Israel out of Egypt. ²After Moses had sent away his wife Zipporah, his father-in-law Jethro took her back, ³along with her two sons. The name of the one was Gershom (for he said, "I have been an alien in a foreign land"), ⁴and the name of the other, Eliezer (for he said, "The God of my father was my help, and delivered me from the sword of Pharaoh"). ⁵Jethro, Moses' father-in-law, came into the wilderness where Moses was encamped at the mountain of God, bringing Moses' sons and wife to him. ⁶He sent word to Moses, "I, your father-in-law Jethro, am coming to you, with your wife and her two sons." ⁷Moses went out to meet his father-in-law; he bowed down and kissed him; each asked after the other's welfare, and they went into the tent. ⁸Then Moses told his father-in-law all that the LORD had done to Pharaoh and to the Egyptians for Israel's sake, all the hardship that had beset them on the way, and how the LORD had delivered them. ⁹Jethro rejoiced for all the good that the LORD had done to Israel, in delivering them from the Egyptians.

10 Jethro said, "Blessed be the LORD, who has delivered you from the Egyptians and from Pharaoh. ¹¹Now I know that the LORD is greater than all gods, because he delivered the people from the Egyptians, when they dealt arrogantly with them." ¹²And Jethro, Moses' father-in-law, brought a burnt offering and sacrifices to God; and Aaron came with all the elders of Israel to eat bread with Moses' father-in-law in the presence of God.

13 The next day Moses sat as judge for the people, while the people stood around him from morning until evening. ¹⁴When Moses' father-in-law saw all that he was doing for the people, he said, "What is this that you are doing for the people? Why do you sit alone, while all the people stand around you from morning until evening?" ¹⁵Moses said to his father-in-law, "Because the people come to me to inquire of God. ¹⁶When they have a dispute, they come to me and I decide between one person and another, and I make known to them the statutes and instructions of God." ¹⁷Moses' father-in-law said to him, "What you are doing is not good. ¹⁸You will surely wear yourself out, both you and these people with you. For the task is too heavy for you; you cannot do it alone. ¹⁹Now listen to me. I will give you counsel, and God be with you! You should represent the people before God, and you should bring their cases before God; ²⁰teach them the statutes and instructions and make known to them the way they are to go and the things they are to do. ²¹You should also look for able men among all the people, men who fear God, are trustworthy, and hate dishonest gain; set such men over them as officers over thousands, hundreds, fifties and tens. ²²Let them sit as judges for the people at all times; let them

bring every important case to you, but decide every minor case themselves. So it will be easier for you, and they will bear the burden with you. ²³If you do this, and God so commands you, then you will be able to endure, and all these people will go to their home in peace."

24 So Moses listened to his father-in-law and did all that he had said. ²⁵Moses chose able men from all Israel and appointed them as heads over the people, as officers over thousands, hundreds, fifties, and tens. ²⁶And they judged the people at all times; hard cases they brought to Moses, but any minor case they decided themselves. ²⁷Then Moses let his father-in-law depart, and he went off to his own country.

The Israelites Reach Mount Sinai

19 On the third new moon after the Israelites had gone out of the land of Egypt, on that very day, they came into the wilderness of Sinai. ²They had journeyed from Rephidim, entered the wilderness of Sinai, and camped in the wilderness; Israel camped there in front of the mountain. ³Then Moses went up to God; the LORD called to him from the mountain, saying, "Thus you shall say to the house of Jacob, and tell the Israelites: ⁴You have seen what I did to the Egyptians, and how I bore you on eagles' wings and brought you to myself. ⁵Now therefore, if you obey my voice and keep my covenant, you shall be my treasured possession out of all the peoples. Indeed, the whole earth is mine, ⁶but you shall be for me a priestly kingdom and a holy nation. These are the words that you shall speak to the Israelites."

7 So Moses came, summoned the elders of the people, and set before them all these words that the LORD had commanded him. ⁸The people all answered as one: "Everything that the LORD has spoken we will do." Moses reported the words of the people to the LORD. ⁹Then the LORD said to Moses, "I am going to come to you in a dense cloud, in order that the people may hear when I speak with you and so trust you ever after."

The People Consecrated

When Moses had told the words of the people to the LORD, ¹⁰the LORD said to Moses: "Go to the people and consecrate them today and tomorrow. Have them wash their clothes ¹¹and prepare for the third day, because on the third day the LORD will come down upon Mount Sinai in the sight of all the people. ¹²You shall set limits for the people all around, saying, 'Be careful not to go up the mountain or to touch the edge of it. Any who touch the mountain shall be put to death. ¹³No hand shall touch them, but they shall be stoned or shot with arrows; whether animal or human being, they shall not live.' When the trumpet sounds a long blast, they may go up on the mountain." ¹⁴So Moses went down from the mountain to the people. He consecrated the people, and they washed their clothes. ¹⁵And he said to the people, "Prepare for the third day; do not go near a woman."

16 On the morning of the third day there was thunder and lightning, as well as a thick cloud on the mountain, and a blast of a trumpet so loud that all the people who were in the camp trembled. ¹⁷Moses brought the people out of the camp to meet God. They took their stand at the foot of the mountain. ¹⁸Now Mount Sinai was wrapped in smoke, because the LORD had descended upon it in fire; the smoke went up like the smoke of a kiln, while the whole mountain shook violently. ¹⁹As the blast of the trumpet grew louder and louder, Moses would speak and God would answer him in thunder. ²⁰When the LORD descended upon Mount Sinai, to the top of the mountain, the LORD summoned Moses to the top of the mountain, and Moses went up. ²¹Then the LORD said to Moses, "Go down and warn the people not to break through to the LORD to look; otherwise many of them will perish. ²²Even the priests who approach the LORD must consecrate themselves or the LORD will break out against them." ²³Moses said to the LORD, "The people are not permitted to come up to Mount Sinai; for you yourself warned us, saying, 'Set limits around the mountain and keep it holy.'" ²⁴The LORD said to him, "Go down, and come up bringing Aaron with you; but do not let either the priests or the people break through to come up to the LORD; otherwise he will break out against them." ²⁵So Moses went down to the people and told them.

The Ten Commandments

20 Then God spoke all these words:

2 I am the LORD your God, who brought you out of the land of Egypt, out of the house of slavery; ³you shall have no other gods before me.

4 You shall not make for yourself an idol, whether in the form of anything that is in heaven above, or that is on the earth beneath, or that is in the water under the earth. ⁵You shall not bow down to them or worship them; for I the LORD your God am a jealous God, punishing children for the iniquity of parents, to the third and the fourth generation of those who reject me, ⁶but showing steadfast love to the thousandth generation of those who love me and keep my commandments.

7 You shall not make wrongful use of the name of the LORD your God, for the LORD will not acquit anyone who misuses his name.

8 Remember the sabbath day, and keep it holy. ⁹Six days you shall labor and do all your work. ¹⁰But the seventh day is a sabbath to the LORD your God; you shall not do any work—you, your son or your daughter, your male or female slave, your livestock, or the alien resident in your towns. ¹¹For in six days the LORD made heaven and earth, the sea, and all that is in them, but rested the seventh day; therefore the LORD blessed the sabbath day and consecrated it.

12 Honor your father and your mother, so that your days may be long in the land that the LORD your God is giving you.

13 You shall not murder.

14 You shall not commit adultery.

15 You shall not steal.

16 You shall not bear false witness against your neighbor.

17 You shall not covet your neighbor's house; you shall not covet your neighbor's wife, or male or female slave, or ox, or donkey, or anything that belongs to your neighbor.

18 When all the people witnessed the thunder and lightning, the sound of the trumpet, and the mountain smoking, they were afraid and trembled and stood at a distance, ¹⁹and said to Moses, "You speak to us, and we will listen; but do not let God speak to us, or we will die." ²⁰Moses said to the people, "Do not be afraid; for God has come only to test you and to put the fear of him upon you so that you do not sin." ²¹Then the people stood at a distance, while Moses drew near to the thick darkness where God was.

The Law concerning the Altar

22 The LORD said to Moses: Thus you shall say to the Israelites: "You have seen for yourselves that I spoke with you from heaven. ²³You shall not make gods of silver alongside me, nor shall you make for yourselves gods of gold. ²⁴You need make for me only an altar of earth and sacrifice on it your burnt offerings and your offerings of well-being, your sheep and your oxen; in every place where I cause my name to be remembered I will come to you and bless you. ²⁵But if you make for me an altar of stone, do not build it of hewn stones; for if you use a chisel upon it you profane it. ²⁶You shall not go up by steps to my altar, so that your nakedness may not be exposed on it."

The Law concerning Slaves

21 These are the ordinances that you shall set before them:

2 When you buy a male Hebrew slave, he shall serve six years, but in the seventh he shall go out a free person, without debt. ³If he comes in single, he shall go out single; if he comes in married, then his wife shall go out with him. ⁴If his master gives him a wife and she bears him sons or daughters, the wife and her children shall be her master's and he shall go out alone. ⁵But if the slave declares, "I love my master, my wife, and my children; I will not go out a free person," ⁶then his master shall bring him before God. He shall be brought to the door or the doorpost; and his master shall pierce his ear with an awl; and he shall serve him for life.

7 When a man sells his daughter as a slave, she shall not go out as the male slaves do. ⁸If she does not please her master, who designated her for himself, then he shall let her be redeemed; he shall have no right to sell her to a foreign people, since he has dealt unfairly with her. ⁹If he designates her for his son, he shall deal with her as with a daughter. ¹⁰If he takes another wife to himself, he shall not diminish the food, clothing, or marital rights of the first wife. ¹¹And if he does not do these three things for her, she shall go out without debt, without payment of money.

The Law concerning Violence

12 Whoever strikes a person mortally shall be put to death. ¹³If it was not premeditated, but came about by an act of God, then I will appoint for you a place to which the killer may flee. ¹⁴But if someone willfully attacks and kills another by treachery, you shall take the killer from my altar for execution.

15 Whoever strikes father or mother shall be put to death.

16 Whoever kidnaps a person, whether that person has been sold or is still held in possession, shall be put to death.

17 Whoever curses father or mother shall be put to death.

18 When individuals quarrel and one strikes the other with a stone or fist so that the injured party, though not dead, is confined to bed, ¹⁹but recovers and walks around outside with the help of a staff, then the assailant shall be free of liability, except to pay for the loss of time, and to arrange for full recovery.

20 When a slaveowner strikes a male or female slave with a rod and the slave dies immediately, the owner shall be punished. ²¹But if the slave survives a day or two, there is no punishment; for the slave is the owner's property.

22 When people who are fighting injure a pregnant woman so that there is a miscarriage, and yet no further harm follows, the one responsible shall be fined what the woman's husband demands, paying as much as the judges determine. ²³If any harm follows, then you shall give life for life, ²⁴eye for eye, tooth for tooth, hand for hand, foot for foot, ²⁵burn for burn, wound for wound, stripe for stripe.

26 When a slaveowner strikes the eye of a male or female slave, destroying it, the owner shall let the slave go, a free person, to compensate for the eye. ²⁷If the owner knocks out a tooth of a male or female slave, the slave shall be let go, a free person, to compensate for the tooth.

The Law concerning Property

28 When an ox gores a man or a woman to death, the ox shall be stoned, and its flesh shall not be eaten; but the owner of the ox shall not be liable. ²⁹If the ox has been accustomed to gore in the past, and its owner has been warned but has not restrained it, and it kills a man or a woman, the ox shall be stoned, and its owner also shall be put to death. ³⁰If a ransom is imposed on the owner, then the owner shall pay whatever is imposed for the redemption of the victim's life. ³¹If it gores a boy or a girl, the owner shall be dealt with according to this same rule. ³²If the ox gores a male or female slave, the owner shall pay to the slaveowner thirty shekels of silver, and the ox shall be stoned.

33 If someone leaves a pit open, or digs a pit and does not cover it, and an ox or a donkey falls into it, ³⁴the owner of the pit shall make restitution, giving money to its owner, but keeping the dead animal.

35 If someone's ox hurts the ox of another, so that it dies, then they shall sell the live ox and divide the price of it; and the dead animal they shall also divide. ³⁶But if it was known that the ox was accustomed to gore in the past, and its owner has not restrained it, the owner shall restore ox for ox, but keep the dead animal.

Laws of Restitution

22 When someone steals an ox or a sheep, and slaughters it or sells it, the thief shall pay five oxen for an ox, and four sheep for a sheep. The thief shall make restitution, but if unable to do so, shall be sold for the theft.

2 If a thief is found breaking in, and is beaten to death, no bloodguilt is incurred; ³but if it happens after sunrise, bloodguilt is incurred. ⁴When the animal, whether ox or donkey or sheep, is found alive in the thief's possession, the thief shall pay double.

5 When someone causes a field or vineyard to be grazed over, or lets livestock loose to graze in someone else's field, restitution shall be made from the best in the owner's field or vineyard.

6 When fire breaks out and catches in thorns so that the stacked grain or the standing grain or the field is consumed, the one who started the fire shall make full restitution.

7 When someone delivers to a neighbor money or goods for safekeeping, and they are stolen from the neighbor's house, then the thief, if caught, shall pay double. ⁸If the thief is not caught, the owner of the house shall be brought before God, to determine whether or not the owner had laid hands on the neighbor's goods.

9 In any case of disputed ownership involving ox, donkey, sheep, clothing, or any other loss, of

which one party says, "This is mine," the case of both parties shall come before God; the one whom God condemns shall pay double to the other.

10 When someone delivers to another a donkey, ox, sheep, or any other animal for safekeeping, and it dies or is injured or is carried off, without anyone seeing it, [11]an oath before the LORD shall decide between the two of them that the one has not laid hands on the property of the other; the owner shall accept the oath, and no restitution shall be made. [12]But if it was stolen, restitution shall be made to its owner. [13]If it was mangled by beasts, let it be brought as evidence; restitution shall not be made for the mangled remains.

14 When someone borrows an animal from another and it is injured or dies, the owner not being present, full restitution shall be made. [15]If the owner was present, there shall be no restitution; if it was hired, only the hiring fee is due.

Social and Religious Laws

16 When a man seduces a virgin who is not engaged to be married, and lies with her, he shall give the bride-price for her and make her his wife. [17]But if her father refuses to give her to him, he shall pay an amount equal to the bride-price for virgins.

18 You shall not permit a female sorcerer to live.

19 Whoever lies with an animal shall be put to death.

20 Whoever sacrifices to any god, other than the LORD alone, shall be devoted to destruction.

21 You shall not wrong or oppress a resident alien, for you were aliens in the land of Egypt. [22]You shall not abuse any widow or orphan. [23]If you do abuse them, when they cry out to me, I will surely heed their cry; [24]my wrath will burn, and I will kill you with the sword, and your wives shall become widows and your children orphans.

25 If you lend money to my people, to the poor among you, you shall not deal with them as a creditor; you shall not exact interest from them. [26]If you take your neighbor's cloak in pawn, you shall restore it before the sun goes down; [27]for it may be your neighbor's only clothing to use as cover; in what else shall that person sleep? And if your neighbor cries out to me, I will listen, for I am compassionate.

28 You shall not revile God, or curse a leader of your people.

29 You shall not delay to make offerings from the fullness of your harvest and from the outflow of your presses. The firstborn of your sons you shall give to me. [30]You shall do the same with your oxen and with your sheep: seven days it shall remain with its mother; on the eighth day you shall give it to me.

31 You shall be people consecrated to me; therefore you shall not eat any meat that is mangled by beasts in the field; you shall throw it to the dogs.

Justice for All

23 You shall not spread a false report. You shall not join hands with the wicked to act as a malicious witness. [2]You shall not follow a majority in wrongdoing; when you bear witness in a lawsuit, you shall not side with the majority so as to pervert justice; [3]nor shall you be partial to the poor in a lawsuit.

4 When you come upon your enemy's ox or donkey going astray, you shall bring it back.

5 When you see the donkey of one who hates you lying under its burden and you would hold back from setting it free, you must help to set it free.

6 You shall not pervert the justice due to your poor in their lawsuits. [7]Keep far from a false charge, and do not kill the innocent and those in the right, for I will not acquit the guilty. [8]You shall take no bribe, for a bribe blinds the officials, and subverts the cause of those who are in the right.

9 You shall not oppress a resident alien; you know the heart of an alien, for you were aliens in the land of Egypt.

Sabbatical Year and Sabbath

10 For six years you shall sow your land and gather in its yield; [11]but the seventh year you shall let it rest and lie fallow, so that the poor of your people may eat; and what they leave the wild animals may eat. You shall do the same with your vineyard, and with your olive orchard.

12 Six days you shall do your work, but on the seventh day you shall rest, so that your ox and your donkey may have relief, and your homeborn slave and the resident alien may be refreshed. ¹³Be attentive to all that I have said to you. Do not invoke the names of other gods; do not let them be heard on your lips.

The Annual Festivals

14 Three times in the year you shall hold a festival for me. ¹⁵You shall observe the festival of unleavened bread; as I commanded you, you shall eat unleavened bread for seven days at the appointed time in the month of Abib, for in it you came out of Egypt. No one shall appear before me empty-handed.

16 You shall observe the festival of harvest, of the first fruits of your labor, of what you sow in the field. You shall observe the festival of ingathering at the end of the year, when you gather in from the field the fruit of your labor. ¹⁷Three times in the year all your males shall appear before the Lord GOD.

18 You shall not offer the blood of my sacrifice with anything leavened, or let the fat of my festival remain until the morning.

19 The choicest of the first fruits of your ground you shall bring into the house of the LORD your God. You shall not boil a kid in its mother's milk.

20 I am going to send an angel in front of you, to guard you on the way and to bring you to the place that I have prepared. ²¹Be attentive to him and listen to his voice; do not rebel against him, for he will not pardon your transgression; for my name is in him.

22 But if you listen attentively to his voice and do all that I say, then I will be an enemy to your enemies and a foe to your foes.

23 When my angel goes in front of you, and brings you to the Amorites, the Hittites, the Perizzites, the Canaanites, the Hivites, and the Jebusites, and I blot them out, ²⁴you shall not bow down to their gods, or worship them, or follow their practices, but you shall utterly demolish them and break their pillars in pieces. ²⁵You shall worship the LORD your God, and I will bless your bread and your water; and I will take sickness away from among you. ²⁶No one shall miscarry or be barren in your land; I will fulfill the number of your days. ²⁷I will send my terror in front of you, and will throw into confusion all the people against whom you shall come, and I will make all your enemies turn their backs to you. ²⁸And I will send the pestilence in front of you, which shall drive out the Hivites, the Canaanites, and the Hittites from before you. ²⁹I will not drive them out from before you in one year, or the land would become desolate and the wild animals would multiply against you. ³⁰Little by little I will drive them out from before you, until you have increased and possess the land. ³¹I will set your borders from the Red Sea to the sea of the Philistines, and from the wilderness to the Euphrates; for I will hand over to you the inhabitants of the land, and you shall drive them out before you. ³²You shall make no covenant with them and their gods. ³³They shall not live in your land, or they will make you sin against me; for if you worship their gods, it will surely be a snare to you.

The Blood of the Covenant

24 Then he said to Moses, "Come up to the LORD, you and Aaron, Nadab, and Abihu, and seventy of the elders of Israel, and worship at a distance. ²Moses alone shall come near the LORD; but the others shall not come near, and the people shall not come up with him."

3 Moses came and told the people all the words of the LORD and all the ordinances; and all the people answered with one voice, and said, "All the words that the LORD has spoken we will do." ⁴And Moses wrote down all the words of the LORD. He rose early in the morning, and built an altar at the foot of the mountain, and set up twelve pillars, corresponding to the twelve tribes of Israel. ⁵He sent young men of the people of Israel, who offered burnt offerings and sacrificed oxen as offerings of well-being to the LORD. ⁶Moses took half of the blood and put it in basins, and half of the blood he dashed against the altar. ⁷Then he took the book of the covenant, and read it in the hearing of the people; and they said, "All that the LORD has spoken we will do, and we will be obedient." ⁸Moses took the blood and dashed it on the people, and said, "See the blood of the covenant that the LORD has made with you in accordance with all these words."

On the Mountain with God

9 Then Moses and Aaron, Nadab, and Abihu, and seventy of the elders of Israel went up, ¹⁰and they saw the God of Israel. Under his feet there was something like a pavement of sapphire stone, like the very heaven for clearness. ¹¹God did not lay his hand on the chief men of the people of Israel; also they beheld God, and they ate and drank.

12 The LORD said to Moses, "Come up to me on the mountain, and wait there; and I will give you the tablets of stone, with the law and the commandment, which I have written for their instruction." ¹³So Moses set out with his assistant Joshua, and Moses went up into the mountain of God. ¹⁴To the elders he had said, "Wait here for us, until we come to you again; for Aaron and Hur are with you; whoever has a dispute may go to them."

15 Then Moses went up on the mountain, and the cloud covered the mountain. ¹⁶The glory of the LORD settled on Mount Sinai, and the cloud covered it for six days; on the seventh day he called to Moses out of the cloud. ¹⁷Now the appearance of the glory of the LORD was like a devouring fire on the top of the mountain in the sight of the people of Israel. ¹⁸Moses entered the cloud, and went up on the mountain. Moses was on the mountain for forty days and forty nights.

. . . .

The Sabbath Law

31 12 The LORD said to Moses: ¹³You yourself are to speak to the Israelites: "You shall keep my sabbaths, for this is a sign between me and you throughout your generations, given in order that you may know that I, the LORD, sanctify you. ¹⁴You shall keep the sabbath, because it is holy for you; everyone who profanes it shall be put to death; whoever does any work on it shall be cut off from among the people. ¹⁵Six days shall work be done, but the seventh day is a sabbath of solemn rest, holy to the LORD; whoever does any work on the sabbath day shall be put to death. ¹⁶Therefore the Israelites shall keep the sabbath, observing the sabbath throughout their generations, as a perpetual covenant. ¹⁷It is a sign forever between me and the people of Israel that in six days the LORD made heaven and earth, and on the seventh day he rested, and was refreshed."

The Two Tablets of the Covenant

18 When God finished speaking with Moses on Mount Sinai, he gave him the two tablets of the covenant, tablets of stone, written with the finger of God.

The Golden Calf

32 When the people saw that Moses delayed to come down from the mountain, the people gathered around Aaron, and said to him, "Come, make gods for us, who shall go before us; as for this Moses, the man who brought us up out of the land of Egypt, we do not know what has become of him." ²Aaron said to them, "Take off the gold rings that are on the ears of your wives, your sons, and your daughters, and bring them to me." ³So all the people took off the gold rings from their ears, and brought them to Aaron. ⁴He took the gold from them, formed it in a mold, and cast an image of a calf; and they said, "These are your gods, O Israel, who brought you up out of the land of Egypt!" ⁵When Aaron saw this, he built an altar before it; and Aaron made proclamation and said, "Tomorrow shall be a festival to the LORD." ⁶They rose early the next day, and offered burnt offerings and brought sacrifices of well-being; and the people sat down to eat and drink, and rose up to revel.

7 The LORD said to Moses, "Go down at once! Your people, whom you brought up out of the land of Egypt, have acted perversely; ⁸they have been quick to turn aside from the way that I commanded them; they have cast for themselves an image of a calf, and have worshiped it and sacrificed to it, and said, 'These are your gods, O Israel, who brought you up out of the land of Egypt!'" ⁹The LORD said to Moses, "I have seen this people, how stiff-necked they are. ¹⁰Now let me alone, so that my wrath may burn hot against them and I may consume them; and of you I will make a great nation."

11 But Moses implored the LORD his God, and said, "O LORD, why does your wrath burn hot against your people, whom you brought out of the land of Egypt with great power and with a mighty hand? ¹²Why should the Egyptians say, 'It was with evil intent that he brought them out to kill them in the mountains, and to consume them from the face of the earth'? Turn from your fierce wrath; change your mind and do not bring disaster on your people. ¹³Remember Abraham, Isaac, and Israel, your servants, how you swore to them by your own self, saying to them, 'I will multiply your descendants like the stars of heaven, and all this land that I have promised I will give to your descendants, and they shall inherit it forever.'" ¹⁴And the LORD changed his mind about the disaster that he planned to bring on his people.

15 Then Moses turned and went down from the mountain, carrying the two tablets of the covenant in his hands, tablets that were written on both sides, written on the front and on the back. ¹⁶The tablets were the work of God, and the writing was the writing of God, engraved upon the tablets. ¹⁷When Joshua heard the noise of the people as they shouted, he said to Moses, "There is a noise of war in the camp." ¹⁸But he said,

"It is not the sound made by victors, or the sound made by losers; it is the sound of revelers that I hear."

19 As soon as he came near the camp and saw the calf and the dancing, Moses' anger burned hot, and he threw the tablets from his hands and broke them at the foot of the mountain. ²⁰He took the calf that they had made, burned it with fire, ground it to powder, scattered it on the water, and made the Israelites drink it.

21 Moses said to Aaron, "What did this people do to you that you have brought so great a sin upon them?" ²²And Aaron said, "Do not let the anger of my lord burn hot; you know the people, that they are bent on evil. ²³They said to me, 'Make us gods, who shall go before us; as for this Moses, the man who brought us up out of the land of Egypt, we do not know what has become of him.' ²⁴So I said to them, 'Whoever has gold, take it off'; so they gave it to me, and I threw it into the fire, and out came this calf!"

25 When Moses saw that the people were running wild (for Aaron had let them run wild, to the derision of their enemies), ²⁶then Moses stood in the gate of the camp, and said, "Who is on the Lord's side? Come to me!" And all the sons of Levi gathered around him. ²⁷He said to them, "Thus says the LORD, the God of Israel, 'Put your sword on your side, each of you! Go back and forth from gate to gate throughout the camp, and each of you kill your brother, your friend, and your neighbor.'" ²⁸The sons of Levi did as Moses commanded, and about three thousand of the people fell on that day. ²⁹Moses said, "Today you have ordained yourselves for the service of the LORD, each one at the cost of a son or a brother, and so have brought a blessing on yourselves this day."

30 On the next day Moses said to the people, "You have sinned a great sin. But now I will go up to the LORD; perhaps I can make atonement for your sin." ³¹So Moses returned to the LORD and said, "Alas, this people has sinned a great sin; they have made for themselves gods of gold. ³²But now, if you will only forgive their sin—but if not, blot me out of the book that you have written." ³³But the LORD said to Moses, "Whoever has sinned against me I will blot out of my book. ³⁴But now go, lead the people to the place about which I have spoken to you; see, my angel shall go in front of you. Nevertheless, when the day comes for punishment, I will punish them for their sin."

35 Then the LORD sent a plague on the people, because they made the calf—the one that Aaron made.

The Command to Leave Sinai

33 The LORD said to Moses, "Go, leave this place, you and the people whom you have brought up out of the land of Egypt, and go to the land of which I swore to Abraham, Isaac, and Jacob, saying, 'To your descendants I will give it.' ²I will send an angel before you, and I will drive out the Canaanites, the Amorites, the Hittites, the Perizzites, the Hivites, and the Jebusites. ³Go up to a land flowing with milk and honey; but I will not go up among you, or I would consume you on the way, for you are a stiff-necked people."

4 When the people heard these harsh words, they mourned, and no one put on ornaments. ⁵For the LORD had said to Moses, "Say to the Israelites, 'You are a stiff-necked people; if for a single moment I should go up among you, I would consume you. So now take off your ornaments, and I will decide what to do to you.'" ⁶Therefore the Israelites stripped themselves of their ornaments, from Mount Horeb onward.

The Tent outside the Camp

7 Now Moses used to take the tent and pitch it outside the camp, far off from the camp; he called it the tent of meeting. And everyone who sought the LORD would go out to the tent of meeting, which was outside the camp. [8]Whenever Moses went out to the tent, all the people would rise and stand, each of them, at the entrance of their tents and watch Moses until he had gone into the tent. [9]When Moses entered the tent, the pillar of cloud would descend and stand at the entrance of the tent, and the LORD would speak with Moses. [10]When all the people saw the pillar of cloud standing at the entrance of the tent, all the people would rise and bow down, all of them, at the entrance of their tent. [11]Thus the LORD used to speak to Moses face to face, as one speaks to a friend. Then he would return to the camp; but his young assistant, Joshua son of Nun, would not leave the tent.

Moses' Intercession

12 Moses said to the LORD, "See, you have said to me, 'Bring up this people'; but you have not let me know whom you will send with me. Yet you have said, 'I know you by name, and you have also found favor in my sight.' [13]Now if I have found favor in your sight, show me your ways, so that I may know you and find favor in your sight. Consider too that this nation is your people." [14]He said, "My presence will go with you, and I will give you rest." [15]And he said to him, "If your presence will not go, do not carry us up from here. [16]For how shall it be known that I have found favor in your sight, I and your people, unless you go with us? In this way, we shall be distinct, I and your people, from every people on the face of the earth."

17 The LORD said to Moses, "I will do the very thing that you have asked; for you have found favor in my sight, and I know you by name." [18]Moses said, "Show me your glory, I pray." [19]And he said, "I will make all my goodness pass before you, and will proclaim before you the name, 'The LORD'; and I will be gracious to whom I will be gracious, and will show mercy on whom I will show mercy. [20]But," he said, "you cannot see my face; for no one shall see me and live." [21]And the LORD continued, "See, there is a place by me where you shall stand on the rock; [22]and while my glory passes by I will put you in a cleft of the rock, and I will cover you with my hand until I have passed by; [23]then I will take away my hand, and you shall see my back; but my face shall not be seen."

Moses Makes New Tablets

34 The LORD said to Moses, "Cut two tablets of stone like the former ones, and I will write on the tablets the words that were on the former tablets, which you broke. [2]Be ready in the morning, and come up in the morning to Mount Sinai and present yourself there to me, on the top of the mountain. [3]No one shall come up with you, and do not let anyone be seen throughout all the mountain; and do not let flocks or herds graze in front of that mountain." [4]So Moses cut two tablets of stone like the former ones; and he rose early in the morning and went up on Mount Sinai, as the LORD had commanded him, and took in his hand the two tablets of stone. [5]The LORD descended in the cloud and stood with him there, and proclaimed the name, "The LORD." [6]The LORD passed before him, and proclaimed,

"The LORD, the LORD,
a God merciful and gracious,
slow to anger,
and abounding in steadfast love and faithfulness,
[7] keeping steadfast love for the thousandth generation,
forgiving iniquity and transgression and sin,
yet by no means clearing the guilty,
but visiting the iniquity of the parents
upon the children
and the children's children,
to the third and the fourth generation."

[8]And Moses quickly bowed his head toward the earth, and worshiped. [9]He said, "If now I have found favor in your sight, O Lord, I pray, let the Lord go with us. Although this is a stiff-necked people, pardon our iniquity and our sin, and take us for your inheritance."

The Covenant Renewed

10 He said: I hereby make a covenant. Before all your people I will perform marvels, such as have not been performed in all the earth or in any nation; and all the people among whom you live shall see the work of the LORD; for it is an awesome thing that I will do with you.

11 Observe what I command you today. See, I will drive out before you the Amorites, the Canaanites, the Hittites, the Perizzites, the Hivites, and the Jebusites. ¹²Take care not to make a covenant with the inhabitants of the land to which you are going, or it will become a snare among you. ¹³You shall tear down their altars, break their pillars, and cut down their sacred poles ¹⁴(for you shall worship no other god, because the LORD, whose name is Jealous, is a jealous God). ¹⁵You shall not make a covenant with the inhabitants of the land, for when they prostitute themselves to their gods and sacrifice to their gods, someone among them will invite you, and you will eat of the sacrifice. ¹⁶And you will take wives from among their daughters for your sons, and their daughters who prostitute themselves to their gods will make your sons also prostitute themselves to their gods.

17 You shall not make cast idols.

18 You shall keep the festival of unleavened bread. Seven days you shall eat unleavened bread, as I commanded you, at the time appointed in the month of Abib; for in the month of Abib you came out from Egypt.

19 All that first opens the womb is mine, all your male livestock, the firstborn of cow and sheep. ²⁰The firstborn of a donkey you shall redeem with a lamb, or if you will not redeem it you shall break its neck. All the firstborn of your sons you shall redeem.

No one shall appear before me empty-handed.

21 Six days you shall work, but on the seventh day you shall rest; even in plowing time and in harvest time you shall rest. ²²You shall observe the festival of weeks, the first fruits of wheat harvest, and the festival of ingathering at the turn of the year. ²³Three times in the year all your males shall appear before the LORD God, the God of Israel. ²⁴For I will cast out nations before you, and enlarge your borders; no one shall covet your land when you go up to appear before the LORD your God three times in the year.

25 You shall not offer the blood of my sacrifice with leaven, and the sacrifice of the festival of the passover shall not be left until the morning.

26 The best of the first fruits of your ground you shall bring to the house of the LORD your God.

You shall not boil a kid in its mother's milk.

27 The LORD said to Moses: Write these words; in accordance with these words I have made a covenant with you and with Israel. ²⁸He was there with the LORD forty days and forty nights; he neither ate bread nor drank water. And he wrote on the tablets the words of the covenant, the ten commandments.

The Shining Face of Moses

29 Moses came down from Mount Sinai. As he came down from the mountain with the two tablets of the covenant in his hand, Moses did not know that the skin of his face shone because he had been talking with God. ³⁰When Aaron and all the Israelites saw Moses, the skin of his face was shining, and they were afraid to come near him. ³¹But Moses called to them; and Aaron and all the leaders of the congregation returned to him, and Moses spoke with them. ³²Afterward all the Israelites came near, and he gave them in commandment all that the LORD had spoken with him on Mount Sinai. ³³When Moses had finished speaking with them, he put a veil on his face; ³⁴but whenever Moses went in before the LORD to speak with him, he would take the veil off, until he came out; and when he came out, and told the Israelites what he had been commanded, ³⁵the Israelites would see the face of Moses, that the skin of his face was shining; and Moses would put the veil on his face again, until he went in to speak with him.

Sabbath Regulations

35 Moses assembled all the congregation of the Israelites and said to them: These are the things that the LORD has commanded you to do:

2 Six days shall work be done, but on the seventh day you shall have a holy sabbath of solemn rest to the LORD; whoever does any work on it shall be put to death. ³You shall kindle no fire in all your dwellings on the sabbath day.

Preparations for Making the Tabernacle

4 Moses said to all the congregation of the Israelites: This is the thing that the LORD has commanded: ⁵Take from among you an offering to the LORD; let whoever is of a generous heart bring the Lord's offering: gold, silver, and bronze; ⁶blue, purple, and crimson yarns, and fine linen; goats' hair, ⁷tanned rams' skins, and fine leather; acacia wood, ⁸oil for the light, spices for the anointing oil and for the fragrant incense, ⁹and onyx stones and gems to be set in the ephod and the breastpiece.

10 All who are skillful among you shall come and make all that the LORD has commanded: the tabernacle, ¹¹its tent and its covering, its clasps and its frames, its bars, its pillars, and its bases; ¹²the ark with its poles, the mercy seat, and the curtain for the screen; ¹³the table with its poles and all its utensils, and the bread of the Presence; ¹⁴the lampstand also for the light, with its utensils and its lamps, and the oil for the light; ¹⁵and the altar of incense, with its poles, and the anointing oil and the fragrant incense, and the screen for the entrance, the entrance of the tabernacle; ¹⁶the altar of burnt offering, with its grating of bronze, its poles, and all its utensils, the basin with its stand; ¹⁷the hangings of the court, its pillars and its bases, and the screen for the gate of the court; ¹⁸the pegs of the tabernacle and the pegs of the court, and their cords; ¹⁹the finely worked vestments for ministering in the holy place, the holy vestments for the priest Aaron, and the vestments of his sons, for their service as priests.

Offerings for the Tabernacle

20 Then all the congregation of the Israelites withdrew from the presence of Moses. ²¹And they came, everyone whose heart was stirred, and everyone whose spirit was willing, and brought the Lord's offering to be used for the tent of meeting, and for all its service, and for the sacred vestments. ²²So they came, both men and women; all who were of a willing heart brought brooches and earrings and signet rings and pendants, all sorts of gold objects, everyone bringing an offering of gold to the LORD. ²³And everyone who possessed blue or purple or crimson yarn or fine linen or goats' hair or tanned rams' skins or fine leather, brought them. ²⁴Everyone who could make an offering of silver or bronze brought it as the Lord's offering; and everyone who possessed acacia wood of any use in the work, brought it. ²⁵All the skillful women spun with their hands, and brought what they had spun in blue and purple and crimson yarns and fine linen; ²⁶all the women whose hearts moved them to use their skill spun the goats' hair. ²⁷And the leaders brought onyx stones and gems to be set in the ephod and the breastpiece, ²⁸and spices and oil for the light, and for the anointing oil, and for the fragrant incense. ²⁹All the Israelite men and women whose hearts made them willing to bring anything for the work that the LORD had commanded by Moses to be done, brought it as a freewill offering to the LORD.

Bezalel and Oholiab

30 Then Moses said to the Israelites: See, the LORD has called by name Bezalel son of Uri son of Hur, of the tribe of Judah; ³¹he has filled him with divine spirit, with skill, intelligence, and knowledge in every kind of craft, ³²to devise artistic designs, to work in gold, silver, and bronze, ³³in cutting stones for setting, and in carving wood, in every kind of craft. ³⁴And he has inspired him to teach, both him and Oholiab son of Ahisamach, of the tribe of Dan. ³⁵He has filled them with skill to do every kind of work done by an artisan or by a designer or by an embroiderer in blue, purple, and crimson yarns, and in fine linen, or by a weaver—by any sort of artisan or skilled designer.

Job

Job and His Family

1 There was once a man in the land of Uz whose name was Job. That man was blameless and upright, one who feared God and turned away from evil. ²There were born to him seven sons and three daughters. ³He had seven thousand sheep, three thousand camels, five hundred yoke of oxen, five hundred donkeys, and very many servants; so that this man was the greatest of all the people of the east. ⁴His sons used to go and hold feasts in one another's houses in turn; and they would send and invite their three sisters to eat and drink with them. ⁵And when the feast days had run their course, Job would send and sanctify them, and he would rise early in the morning and offer burnt offerings according to the number of them all; for Job said, "It may be that my children have sinned, and cursed God in their hearts." This is what Job always did.

Attack on Job's Character

6 One day the heavenly beings came to present themselves before the LORD, and Satan also came among them. ⁷The LORD said to Satan, "Where have you come from?" Satan answered the LORD, "From going to and fro on the earth, and from walking up and down on it." ⁸The LORD said to Satan, "Have you considered my servant Job? There is no one like him on the earth, a blameless and upright man who fears God and turns away from evil." ⁹Then Satan answered the LORD, "Does Job fear God for nothing? ¹⁰Have you not put a fence around him and his house and all that he has, on every side? You have blessed the work of his hands, and his possessions have increased in the land. ¹¹But stretch out your hand now, and touch all that he has, and he will curse you to your face." ¹²The LORD said to Satan, "Very well, all that he has is in your power; only do not stretch out your hand against him!" So Satan went out from the presence of the LORD.

Job Loses Property and Children

13 One day when his sons and daughters were eating and drinking wine in the eldest brother's house, ¹⁴a messenger came to Job and said, "The oxen were plowing and the donkeys were feeding beside them, ¹⁵and the Sabeans fell on them and carried them off, and killed the servants with the edge of the sword; I alone have escaped to tell you." ¹⁶While he was still speaking, another came and said, "The fire of God fell from heaven and burned up the sheep and the servants, and consumed them; I alone have escaped to tell you." ¹⁷While he was still speaking, another came and said, "The Chaldeans formed three columns, made a raid on the camels and carried them off, and killed the servants with the edge of the sword; I alone have escaped to tell you." ¹⁸While he was still speaking, another came and said, "Your sons and daughters were eating and drinking wine in their eldest brother's house, ¹⁹and suddenly a great wind came across the desert, struck the four corners of the house, and it fell on the young people, and they are dead; I alone have escaped to tell you."

20 Then Job arose, tore his robe, shaved his head, and fell on the ground and worshiped. ²¹He said, "Naked I came from my mother's womb, and naked shall I return there; the LORD gave, and the LORD has taken away; blessed be the name of the LORD."

22 In all this Job did not sin or charge God with wrongdoing.

Attack on Job's Health

2 One day the heavenly beings came to present themselves before the LORD, and Satan also came among them to present himself before the LORD. ²The LORD said to Satan, "Where have you come from?" Satan answered the LORD, "From going to and fro on the earth, and from walking up and down on it." ³The LORD said to Satan, "Have you considered my servant Job? There is no one like him on the earth, a blameless and upright man who fears God and turns away from evil. He still persists in his integrity, although you incited me against him, to destroy him for no reason." ⁴Then Satan answered the LORD, "Skin for skin! All that people have they will give to save their lives. ⁵But stretch out your hand now and touch his bone and his flesh, and he will curse you to your face." ⁶The LORD said to Satan, "Very well, he is in your power; only spare his life."

7 So Satan went out from the presence of the LORD, and inflicted loathsome sores on Job from the sole of his foot to the crown of his head. ⁸Job took a potsherd with which to scrape himself, and sat among the ashes.

9 Then his wife said to him, "Do you still persist in your integrity? Curse God, and die." ¹⁰But he said to her, "You speak as any foolish woman would speak. Shall we receive the good at the hand of God, and not receive the bad?" In all this Job did not sin with his lips.

Job's Three Friends

11 Now when Job's three friends heard of all these troubles that had come upon him, each of them set out from his home—Eliphaz the Temanite, Bildad the Shuhite, and Zophar the Naamathite. They met together to go and console and comfort him. ¹²When they saw him from a distance, they did not recognize him, and they raised their voices and wept aloud; they tore their robes and threw dust in the air upon their heads. ¹³They sat with him on the ground seven days and seven nights, and no one spoke a word to him, for they saw that his suffering was very great.

Job Curses the Day He Was Born

3 After this Job opened his mouth and cursed the day of his birth. ²Job said:
3 "Let the day perish in which I was born,
   and the night that said,
   'A man-child is conceived.'
4 Let that day be darkness!
   May God above not seek it,
   or light shine on it.
5 Let gloom and deep darkness claim it.
   Let clouds settle upon it;
   let the blackness of the day terrify it.
6 That night—let thick darkness seize it!
   let it not rejoice among the days of the year;
   let it not come into the number of the months.
7 Yes, let that night be barren;
   let no joyful cry be heard in it.
8 Let those curse it who curse the Sea,
   those who are skilled to rouse up Leviathan.
9 Let the stars of its dawn be dark;
   let it hope for light, but have none;
   may it not see the eyelids of the morning—
10 because it did not shut the doors of my mother's womb,
   and hide trouble from my eyes.
11 "Why did I not die at birth,
   come forth from the womb and expire?
12 Why were there knees to receive me,
   or breasts for me to suck?
13 Now I would be lying down and quiet;
   I would be asleep; then I would be at rest
14 with kings and counselors of the earth
   who rebuild ruins for themselves,
15 or with princes who have gold,
   who fill their houses with silver.
16 Or why was I not buried like a stillborn child,
   like an infant that never sees the light?
17 There the wicked cease from troubling,
   and there the weary are at rest.
18 There the prisoners are at ease together;
   they do not hear the voice of the taskmaster.
19 The small and the great are there,
   and the slaves are free from their masters.
20 "Why is light given to one in misery,
   and life to the bitter in soul,
21 who long for death, but it does not come,
   and dig for it more than for hidden treasures;
22 who rejoice exceedingly,

and are glad when they find the grave?
23 Why is light given to one who cannot see the way,
  whom God has fenced in?
24 For my sighing comes like my bread,
  and my groanings are poured out like water.
25 Truly the thing that I fear comes upon me,
  and what I dread befalls me.
26 I am not at ease, nor am I quiet;
  I have no rest; but trouble comes."

Eliphaz Speaks: Job Has Sinned

4

Then Eliphaz the Temanite answered:
2 "If one ventures a word with you, will you be offended?
  But who can keep from speaking?
3 See, you have instructed many;
  you have strengthened the weak hands.
4 Your words have supported those who were stumbling,
  and you have made firm the feeble knees.
5 But now it has come to you, and you are impatient;
  it touches you, and you are dismayed.
6 Is not your fear of God your confidence,
  and the integrity of your ways your hope?
7 "Think now, who that was innocent ever perished?
  Or where were the upright cut off?
8 As I have seen, those who plow iniquity
  and sow trouble reap the same.
9 By the breath of God they perish,
  and by the blast of his anger they are consumed.
10 The roar of the lion, the voice of the fierce lion,
  and the teeth of the young lions are broken.
11 The strong lion perishes for lack of prey,
  and the whelps of the lioness are scattered.

12 "Now a word came stealing to me,
  my ear received the whisper of it.
13 Amid thoughts from visions of the night,
  when deep sleep falls on mortals,
14 dread came upon me, and trembling,
  which made all my bones shake.
15 A spirit glided past my face;
  the hair of my flesh bristled.
16 It stood still,
  but I could not discern its appearance.
  A form was before my eyes;
  there was silence, then I heard a voice:
17 'Can mortals be righteous before God?
  Can human beings be pure before their Maker?
18 Even in his servants he puts no trust,
  and his angels he charges with error;
19 how much more those who live in houses of clay,
  whose foundation is in the dust,
  who are crushed like a moth.
20 Between morning and evening they are destroyed;
  they perish forever without any regarding it.
21 Their tent-cord is plucked up within them,
  and they die devoid of wisdom.'

Job Is Corrected by God

5

"Call now; is there anyone who will answer you?
  To which of the holy ones will you turn?
2 Surely vexation kills the fool,
  and jealousy slays the simple.
3 I have seen fools taking root,
  but suddenly I cursed their dwelling.
4 Their children are far from safety,
  they are crushed in the gate,
  and there is no one to deliver them.
5 The hungry eat their harvest,
  and they take it even out of the thorns;
  and the thirsty pant after their wealth.
6 For misery does not come from the earth,
  nor does trouble sprout from the ground;
7 but human beings are born to trouble
  just as sparks fly upward.
8 "As for me, I would seek God,
  and to God I would commit my cause.
9 He does great things and unsearchable,
  marvelous things without number.
10 He gives rain on the earth
  and sends waters on the fields;
11 he sets on high those who are lowly,
  and those who mourn are lifted to safety.
12 He frustrates the devices of the crafty,
  so that their hands achieve no success.
13 He takes the wise in their own craftiness;
  and the schemes of the wily are brought to a quick end.

¹⁴ They meet with darkness in the daytime,
 and grope at noonday as in the night.
¹⁵ But he saves the needy from the sword of their mouth,
 from the hand of the mighty.
¹⁶ So the poor have hope,
 and injustice shuts its mouth.
¹⁷ "How happy is the one whom God reproves;
 therefore do not despise the discipline of the Almighty.
¹⁸ For he wounds, but he binds up;
 he strikes, but his hands heal.
¹⁹ He will deliver you from six troubles;
 in seven no harm shall touch you.
²⁰ In famine he will redeem you from death,
 and in war from the power of the sword.
²¹ You shall be hidden from the scourge of the tongue,
 and shall not fear destruction when it comes.
²² At destruction and famine you shall laugh,
 and shall not fear the wild animals of the earth.
²³ For you shall be in league with the stones of the field,
 and the wild animals shall be at peace with you.
²⁴ You shall know that your tent is safe,
 you shall inspect your fold and miss nothing.
²⁵ You shall know that your descendants will be many,
 and your offspring like the grass of the earth.
²⁶ You shall come to your grave in ripe old age,
 as a shock of grain comes up to the threshing floor in its season.
²⁷ See, we have searched this out; it is true.
 Hear, and know it for yourself."

Job Replies: My Complaint is Just

6

Then Job answered:
² "O that my vexation were weighed,
 and all my calamity laid in the balances!
³ For then it would be heavier than the sand of the sea;
 therefore my words have been rash.
⁴ For the arrows of the Almighty are in me;
 my spirit drinks their poison;
 the terrors of God are arrayed against me.
⁵ Does the wild ass bray over its grass,
 or the ox low over its fodder?
⁶ Can that which is tasteless be eaten without salt,
 or is there any flavor in the juice of mallows?
⁷ My appetite refuses to touch them;
 they are like food that is loathsome to me.
⁸ "O that I might have my request,
 and that God would grant my desire;
⁹ that it would please God to crush me,
 that he would let loose his hand and cut me off!
¹⁰ This would be my consolation;
 I would even exult in unrelenting pain;
 for I have not denied the words of the Holy One.
¹¹ What is my strength, that I should wait?
 And what is my end, that I should be patient?
¹² Is my strength the strength of stones,
 or is my flesh bronze?
¹³ In truth I have no help in me,
 and any resource is driven from me.

¹⁴ "Those who withhold kindness from a friend
 forsake the fear of the Almighty.
¹⁵ My companions are treacherous like a torrent-bed,
 like freshets that pass away,
¹⁶ that run dark with ice,
 turbid with melting snow.
¹⁷ In time of heat they disappear;
 when it is hot, they vanish from their place.
¹⁸ The caravans turn aside from their course;
 they go up into the waste, and perish.
¹⁹ The caravans of Tema look,
 the travelers of Sheba hope.
²⁰ They are disappointed because they were confident;
 they come there and are confounded.
²¹ Such you have now become to me;
 you see my calamity, and are afraid.
²² Have I said, 'Make me a gift'?
 Or, 'From your wealth offer a bribe for me'?
²³ Or, 'Save me from an opponent's hand'?
 Or, 'Ransom me from the hand of oppressors'?

²⁴ "Teach me, and I will be silent;
 make me understand how I have gone wrong.
²⁵ How forceful are honest words!
 But your reproof, what does it reprove?

26 Do you think that you can reprove words,
  as if the speech of the desperate were wind?
27 You would even cast lots over the orphan,
  and bargain over your friend.
28 "But now, be pleased to look at me;
  for I will not lie to your face.
29 Turn, I pray, let no wrong be done.
  Turn now, my vindication is at stake.
30 Is there any wrong on my tongue?
  Cannot my taste discern calamity?

Job: My Suffering Is Without End

7

"Do not human beings have a hard service on earth,
  and are not their days like the days of a laborer?
2 Like a slave who longs for the shadow,
  and like laborers who look for their wages,
3 so I am allotted months of emptiness,
  and nights of misery are apportioned to me.
4 When I lie down I say, 'When shall I rise?'
  But the night is long,
  and I am full of tossing until dawn.
5 My flesh is clothed with worms and dirt;
  my skin hardens, then breaks out again.
6 My days are swifter than a weaver's shuttle,
  and come to their end without hope.

7 "Remember that my life is a breath;
  my eye will never again see good.
8 The eye that beholds me will see me no more;
  while your eyes are upon me, I shall be gone.
9 As the cloud fades and vanishes,
  so those who go down to Sheol do not come up;
10 they return no more to their houses,
  nor do their places know them any more.

11 "Therefore I will not restrain my mouth;
  I will speak in the anguish of my spirit;
  I will complain in the bitterness of my soul.
12 Am I the Sea, or the Dragon,
  that you set a guard over me?
13 When I say, 'My bed will comfort me,
  my couch will ease my complaint,'
14 then you scare me with dreams
  and terrify me with visions,
15 so that I would choose strangling
  and death rather than this body.
16 I loathe my life; I would not live forever.
  Let me alone, for my days are a breath.
17 What are human beings, that you make so much of them,
  that you set your mind on them,
18 visit them every morning,
  test them every moment?
19 Will you not look away from me for a while,
  let me alone until I swallow my spittle?
20 If I sin, what do I do to you, you watcher of humanity?
  Why have you made me your target?
  Why have I become a burden to you?
21 Why do you not pardon my transgression
  and take away my iniquity?
  For now I shall lie in the earth;
  you will seek me, but I shall not be."

Bildad Speaks: Job Should Repent

8

Then Bildad the Shuhite answered:
2 "How long will you say these things,
  and the words of your mouth be a great wind?
3 Does God pervert justice?
  Or does the Almighty pervert the right?
4 If your children sinned against him,
  he delivered them into the power of their transgression.
5 If you will seek God
  and make supplication to the Almighty,
6 if you are pure and upright,
  surely then he will rouse himself for you
  and restore to you your rightful place.
7 Though your beginning was small,
  your latter days will be very great.

8 "For inquire now of bygone generations,
  and consider what their ancestors have found;
9 for we are but of yesterday, and we know nothing,
  for our days on earth are but a shadow.
10 Will they not teach you and tell you
  and utter words out of their understanding?

11 "Can papyrus grow where there is no marsh?

Can reeds flourish where there is no water?
12 While yet in flower and not cut down,
 they wither before any other plant.
13 Such are the paths of all who forget God;
 the hope of the godless shall perish.
14 Their confidence is gossamer,
 a spider's house their trust.
15 If one leans against its house, it will not stand;
 if one lays hold of it, it will not endure.
16 The wicked thrive before the sun,
 and their shoots spread over the garden.
17 Their roots twine around the stoneheap;
 they live among the rocks.
18 If they are destroyed from their place,
 then it will deny them, saying, 'I have never seen you.'
19 See, these are their happy ways,
 and out of the earth still others will spring.

20 "See, God will not reject a blameless person,
 nor take the hand of evildoers.
21 He will yet fill your mouth with laughter,
 and your lips with shouts of joy.
22 Those who hate you will be clothed with shame,
 and the tent of the wicked will be no more."

Job Replies: There Is No Mediator

9

Then Job answered:
2 "Indeed I know that this is so;
 but how can a mortal be just before God?
3 If one wished to contend with him,
 one could not answer him once in a thousand.
4 He is wise in heart, and mighty in strength
 —who has resisted him, and succeeded?—
5 he who removes mountains, and they do not know it,
 when he overturns them in his anger;
6 who shakes the earth out of its place,
 and its pillars tremble;
7 who commands the sun, and it does not rise;
 who seals up the stars;
8 who alone stretched out the heavens
 and trampled the waves of the Sea;
9 who made the Bear and Orion,
 the Pleiades and the chambers of the south;
10 who does great things beyond understanding,
 and marvelous things without number.
11 Look, he passes by me, and I do not see him;
 he moves on, but I do not perceive him.
12 He snatches away; who can stop him?
 Who will say to him, 'What are you doing?'

13 "God will not turn back his anger;
 the helpers of Rahab bowed beneath him.
14 How then can I answer him,
 choosing my words with him?
15 Though I am innocent, I cannot answer him;
 I must appeal for mercy to my accuser.
16 If I summoned him and he answered me,
 I do not believe that he would listen to my voice.
17 For he crushes me with a tempest,
 and multiplies my wounds without cause;
18 he will not let me get my breath,
 but fills me with bitterness.
19 If it is a contest of strength, he is the strong one!
 If it is a matter of justice, who can summon him?
20 Though I am innocent, my own mouth would condemn me;
 though I am blameless, he would prove me perverse.
21 I am blameless; I do not know myself;
 I loathe my life.
22 It is all one; therefore I say,
 he destroys both the blameless and the wicked.
23 When disaster brings sudden death,
 he mocks at the calamity of the innocent.
24 The earth is given into the hand of the wicked;
 he covers the eyes of its judges—
 if it is not he, who then is it?

25 "My days are swifter than a runner;
 they flee away, they see no good.
26 They go by like skiffs of reed,
 like an eagle swooping on the prey.
27 If I say, 'I will forget my complaint;
 I will put off my sad countenance and be of good cheer,'
28 I become afraid of all my suffering,
 for I know you will not hold me innocent.
29 I shall be condemned;
 why then do I labor in vain?
30 If I wash myself with soap
 and cleanse my hands with lye,
31 yet you will plunge me into filth,
 and my own clothes will abhor me.
32 For he is not a mortal, as I am, that I might answer him,

that we should come to trial together.
33 There is no umpire between us,
    who might lay his hand on us both.
34 If he would take his rod away from me,
    and not let dread of him terrify me,
35 then I would speak without fear of him,
    for I know I am not what I am thought to be.

Job: I Loathe My Life

10

"I loathe my life;
    I will give free utterance to my complaint;
    I will speak in the bitterness of my soul.
2 I will say to God, Do not condemn me;
    let me know why you contend against me.
3 Does it seem good to you to oppress,
    to despise the work of your hands
    and favor the schemes of the wicked?
4 Do you have eyes of flesh?
    Do you see as humans see?
5 Are your days like the days of mortals,
    or your years like human years,
6 that you seek out my iniquity
    and search for my sin,
7 although you know that I am not guilty,
    and there is no one to deliver out of your hand?
8 Your hands fashioned and made me;
    and now you turn and destroy me.
9 Remember that you fashioned me like clay;
    and will you turn me to dust again?
10 Did you not pour me out like milk
    and curdle me like cheese?
11 You clothed me with skin and flesh,
    and knit me together with bones and sinews.
12 You have granted me life and steadfast love,
    and your care has preserved my spirit.
13 Yet these things you hid in your heart;
    I know that this was your purpose.
14 If I sin, you watch me,
    and do not acquit me of my iniquity.
15 If I am wicked, woe to me!
    If I am righteous, I cannot lift up my head,
    for I am filled with disgrace
    and look upon my affliction.
16 Bold as a lion you hunt me;
    you repeat your exploits against me.
17 You renew your witnesses against me,
    and increase your vexation toward me;
    you bring fresh troops against me.

18 "Why did you bring me forth from the womb?
    Would that I had died before any eye had seen me,
19 and were as though I had not been,
    carried from the womb to the grave.
20 Are not the days of my life few?
    Let me alone, that I may find a little comfort
21 before I go, never to return,
    to the land of gloom and deep darkness,
22 the land of gloom and chaos,
    where light is like darkness."

Zophar Speaks: Job's Guilt Deserves Punishment

11

Then Zophar the Naamathite answered:
2 "Should a multitude of words go unanswered,
    and should one full of talk be vindicated?
3 Should your babble put others to silence,
    and when you mock, shall no one shame you?
4 For you say, 'My conduct is pure,
    and I am clean in God's sight.'
5 But oh, that God would speak,
    and open his lips to you,
6 and that he would tell you the secrets of wisdom!
    For wisdom is many-sided.
Know then that God exacts of you less
    than your guilt deserves.

7 "Can you find out the deep things of God?
    Can you find out the limit of the Almighty?
8 It is higher than heaven—what can you do?
    Deeper than Sheol—what can you know?
9 Its measure is longer than the earth,
    and broader than the sea.
10 If he passes through, and imprisons,
    and assembles for judgment, who can hinder him?
11 For he knows those who are worthless;
    when he sees iniquity, will he not consider it?
12 But a stupid person will get understanding,
    when a wild ass is born human.

13 "If you direct your heart rightly,
    you will stretch out your hands toward him.
14 If iniquity is in your hand, put it far away,

and do not let wickedness reside in your tents.
15 Surely then you will lift up your face without blemish;
   you will be secure, and will not fear.
16 You will forget your misery;
   you will remember it as waters that have passed away.
17 And your life will be brighter than the noonday;
   its darkness will be like the morning.
18 And you will have confidence, because there is hope;
   you will be protected and take your rest in safety.
19 You will lie down, and no one will make you afraid;
   many will entreat your favor.
20 But the eyes of the wicked will fail;
   all way of escape will be lost to them,
   and their hope is to breathe their last."

Job Replies: I Am a Laughingstock

12

Then Job answered:
2 "No doubt you are the people,
   and wisdom will die with you.
3 But I have understanding as well as you;
   I am not inferior to you.
   Who does not know such things as these?
4 I am a laughingstock to my friends;
   I, who called upon God and he answered me,
   a just and blameless man, I am a laughingstock.
5 Those at ease have contempt for misfortune,
   but it is ready for those whose feet are unstable.
6 The tents of robbers are at peace,
   and those who provoke God are secure,
   who bring their god in their hands.

7 "But ask the animals, and they will teach you;
   the birds of the air, and they will tell you;
8 ask the plants of the earth, and they will teach you;
   and the fish of the sea will declare to you.
9 Who among all these does not know
   that the hand of the LORD has done this?

10 In his hand is the life of every living thing
   and the breath of every human being.
11 Does not the ear test words
   as the palate tastes food?
12 Is wisdom with the aged,
   and understanding in length of days?

13 "With God are wisdom and strength;
   he has counsel and understanding.
14 If he tears down, no one can rebuild;
   if he shuts someone in, no one can open up.
15 If he withholds the waters, they dry up;
   if he sends them out, they overwhelm the land.
16 With him are strength and wisdom;
   the deceived and the deceiver are his.
17 He leads counselors away stripped,
   and makes fools of judges.
18 He looses the sash of kings,
   and binds a waistcloth on their loins.
19 He leads priests away stripped,
   and overthrows the mighty.
20 He deprives of speech those who are trusted,
   and takes away the discernment of the elders.
21 He pours contempt on princes,
   and looses the belt of the strong.
22 He uncovers the deeps out of darkness,
   and brings deep darkness to light.
23 He makes nations great, then destroys them;
   he enlarges nations, then leads them away.
24 He strips understanding from the leaders of the earth,
   and makes them wander in a pathless waste.
25 They grope in the dark without light;
   he makes them stagger like a drunkard.

13

"Look, my eye has seen all this,
   my ear has heard and understood it.
2 What you know, I also know;
   I am not inferior to you.
3 But I would speak to the Almighty,
   and I desire to argue my case with God.
4 As for you, you whitewash with lies;
   all of you are worthless physicians.
5 If you would only keep silent,
   that would be your wisdom!
6 Hear now my reasoning,
   and listen to the pleadings of my lips.
7 Will you speak falsely for God,
   and speak deceitfully for him?
8 Will you show partiality toward him,

will you plead the case for God?
9 Will it be well with you when he searches you out?
Or can you deceive him, as one person deceives another?
10 He will surely rebuke you
if in secret you show partiality.
11 Will not his majesty terrify you,
and the dread of him fall upon you?
12 Your maxims are proverbs of ashes,
your defenses are defenses of clay.

13 "Let me have silence, and I will speak,
and let come on me what may.
14 I will take my flesh in my teeth,
and put my life in my hand.
15 See, he will kill me; I have no hope;
but I will defend my ways to his face.
16 This will be my salvation,
that the godless shall not come before him.
17 Listen carefully to my words,
and let my declaration be in your ears.
18 I have indeed prepared my case;
I know that I shall be vindicated.
19 Who is there that will contend with me?
For then I would be silent and die.

Job's Despondent Prayer

20 Only grant two things to me,
then I will not hide myself from your face:
21 withdraw your hand far from me,
and do not let dread of you terrify me.
22 Then call, and I will answer;
or let me speak, and you reply to me.
23 How many are my iniquities and my sins?
Make me know my transgression and my sin.
24 Why do you hide your face,
and count me as your enemy?
25 Will you frighten a windblown leaf
and pursue dry chaff?
26 For you write bitter things against me,
and make me reap the iniquities of my youth.
27 You put my feet in the stocks,
and watch all my paths;
you set a bound to the soles of my feet.
28 One wastes away like a rotten thing,
like a garment that is moth-eaten.

14

"A mortal, born of woman, few of
days and full of trouble,
2 comes up like a flower and withers,
flees like a shadow and does not last.
3 Do you fix your eyes on such a one?
Do you bring me into judgment with you?
4 Who can bring a clean thing out of an unclean?
No one can.
5 Since their days are determined,
and the number of their months is known to you, and you have appointed the bounds that they cannot pass,
6 look away from them, and desist,
that they may enjoy, like laborers, their days.

7 "For there is hope for a tree,
if it is cut down, that it will sprout again,
and that its shoots will not cease.
8 Though its root grows old in the earth,
and its stump dies in the ground,
9 yet at the scent of water it will bud
and put forth branches like a young plant.
10 But mortals die, and are laid low;
humans expire, and where are they?
11 As waters fail from a lake,
and a river wastes away and dries up,
12 so mortals lie down and do not rise again;
until the heavens are no more, they will not awake
or be roused out of their sleep.
13 Oh that you would hide me in Sheol,
that you would conceal me until your wrath is past,
that you would appoint me a set time, and remember me!
14 If mortals die, will they live again?
All the days of my service I would wait
until my release should come.
15 You would call, and I would answer you;
you would long for the work of your hands.
16 For then you would not number my steps,
you would not keep watch over my sin;
17 my transgression would be sealed up in a bag,
and you would cover over my iniquity.

18 "But the mountain falls and crumbles away,
and the rock is removed from its place;
19 the waters wear away the stones;
the torrents wash away the soil of the earth;
so you destroy the hope of mortals.

²⁰ You prevail forever against them, and they pass away;
 you change their countenance, and send them away.
²¹ Their children come to honor, and they do not know it;
 they are brought low, and it goes unnoticed.
²² They feel only the pain of their own bodies,
 and mourn only for themselves."

Eliphaz Speaks: Job Undermines Religion

15

Then Eliphaz the Temanite answered:
² "Should the wise answer with windy knowledge,
 and fill themselves with the east wind?
³ Should they argue in unprofitable talk,
 or in words with which they can do no good?
⁴ But you are doing away with the fear of God,
 and hindering meditation before God.
⁵ For your iniquity teaches your mouth,
 and you choose the tongue of the crafty.
⁶ Your own mouth condemns you, and not I;
 your own lips testify against you.

⁷ "Are you the firstborn of the human race?
 Were you brought forth before the hills?
⁸ Have you listened in the council of God?
 And do you limit wisdom to yourself?
⁹ What do you know that we do not know?
 What do you understand that is not clear to us?
¹⁰ The gray-haired and the aged are on our side,
 those older than your father.
¹¹ Are the consolations of God too small for you,
 or the word that deals gently with you?
¹² Why does your heart carry you away,
 and why do your eyes flash,
¹³ so that you turn your spirit against God,
 and let such words go out of your mouth?
¹⁴ What are mortals, that they can be clean?
 Or those born of woman, that they can be righteous?
¹⁵ God puts no trust even in his holy ones,
 and the heavens are not clean in his sight;
¹⁶ how much less one who is abominable and corrupt,
 one who drinks iniquity like water!
¹⁷ "I will show you; listen to me;
 what I have seen I will declare—
¹⁸ what sages have told,
 and their ancestors have not hidden,
¹⁹ to whom alone the land was given,
 and no stranger passed among them.
²⁰ The wicked writhe in pain all their days,
 through all the years that are laid up for the ruthless.
²¹ Terrifying sounds are in their ears;
 in prosperity the destroyer will come upon them.
²² They despair of returning from darkness,
 and they are destined for the sword.
²³ They wander abroad for bread, saying, 'Where is it?'
 They know that a day of darkness is ready at hand;
²⁴ distress and anguish terrify them;
 they prevail against them, like a king prepared for battle.
²⁵ Because they stretched out their hands against God,
 and bid defiance to the Almighty,
²⁶ running stubbornly against him
 with a thick-bossed shield;
²⁷ because they have covered their faces with their fat,
 and gathered fat upon their loins,
²⁸ they will live in desolate cities,
 in houses that no one should inhabit,
 houses destined to become heaps of ruins;
²⁹ they will not be rich, and their wealth will not endure,
 nor will they strike root in the earth;
³⁰ they will not escape from darkness;
 the flame will dry up their shoots,
 and their blossom will be swept away by the wind.
³¹ Let them not trust in emptiness, deceiving themselves;
 for emptiness will be their recompense.
³² It will be paid in full before their time,
 and their branch will not be green.
³³ They will shake off their unripe grape, like the vine,
 and cast off their blossoms, like the olive tree.
³⁴ For the company of the godless is barren,
 and fire consumes the tents of bribery.
³⁵ They conceive mischief and bring forth evil
 and their heart prepares deceit."

Job Reaffirms His Innocence

16

Then Job answered:
2 "I have heard many such things;
 miserable comforters are you all.
3 Have windy words no limit?
 Or what provokes you that you keep on talking?
4 I also could talk as you do,
 if you were in my place;
 I could join words together against you,
 and shake my head at you.
5 I could encourage you with my mouth,
 and the solace of my lips would assuage your pain.

6 "If I speak, my pain is not assuaged,
 and if I forbear, how much of it leaves me?
7 Surely now God has worn me out;
 he has made desolate all my company.
8 And he has shriveled me up,
 which is a witness against me;
 my leanness has risen up against me,
 and it testifies to my face.
9 He has torn me in his wrath, and hated me;
 he has gnashed his teeth at me;
 my adversary sharpens his eyes against me.
10 They have gaped at me with their mouths;
 they have struck me insolently on the cheek;
 they mass themselves together against me.
11 God gives me up to the ungodly,
 and casts me into the hands of the wicked.
12 I was at ease, and he broke me in two;
 he seized me by the neck and dashed me to pieces;
 he set me up as his target;
13 his archers surround me.
 He slashes open my kidneys, and shows no mercy;
 he pours out my gall on the ground.
14 He bursts upon me again and again;
 he rushes at me like a warrior.
15 I have sewed sackcloth upon my skin,
 and have laid my strength in the dust.
16 My face is red with weeping,
 and deep darkness is on my eyelids,
17 though there is no violence in my hands,
 and my prayer is pure.
18 "O earth, do not cover my blood;
 let my outcry find no resting place.
19 Even now, in fact, my witness is in heaven,
 and he that vouches for me is on high.
20 My friends scorn me;
 my eye pours out tears to God,
21 that he would maintain the right of a mortal with God,
 as one does for a neighbor.
22 For when a few years have come,
 I shall go the way from which I shall not return.

Job Prays for Relief

17

My spirit is broken, my days are extinct, the grave is ready for me.
2 Surely there are mockers around me,
 and my eye dwells on their provocation.

3 "Lay down a pledge for me with yourself;
 who is there that will give surety for me?
4 Since you have closed their minds to understanding,
 therefore you will not let them triumph.
5 Those who denounce friends for reward—
 the eyes of their children will fail.
6 "He has made me a byword of the peoples,
 and I am one before whom people spit.
7 My eye has grown dim from grief,
 and all my members are like a shadow.
8 The upright are appalled at this,
 and the innocent stir themselves up against the godless.
9 Yet the righteous hold to their way,
 and they that have clean hands grow stronger and stronger.
10 But you, come back now, all of you,
 and I shall not find a sensible person among you.
11 My days are past, my plans are broken off,
 the desires of my heart.
12 They make night into day;
 'The light,' they say, 'is near to the darkness.'
13 If I look for Sheol as my house,
 if I spread my couch in darkness,
14 if I say to the Pit, 'You are my father,'
 and to the worm, 'My mother,' or 'My sister,'
15 where then is my hope?
 Who will see my hope?
16 Will it go down to the bars of Sheol?
 Shall we descend together into the dust?"

. . . .

Elihu Rebukes Job's Friends

32 So these three men ceased to answer Job, because he was righteous in his own eyes. ²Then Elihu son of Barachel the Buzite, of the family of Ram, became angry. He was angry at Job because he justified himself rather than God; ³he was angry also at Job's three friends because they had found no answer, though they had declared Job to be in the wrong. ⁴Now Elihu had waited to speak to Job, because they were older than he. ⁵But when Elihu saw that there was no answer in the mouths of these three men, he became angry.

⁶ Elihu son of Barachel the Buzite answered:
"I am young in years,
    and you are aged;
therefore I was timid and afraid
    to declare my opinion to you.
⁷ I said, 'Let days speak,
    and many years teach wisdom.'
⁸ But truly it is the spirit in a mortal,
    the breath of the Almighty, that makes for understanding.
⁹ It is not the old that are wise,
    nor the aged that understand what is right.
¹⁰ Therefore I say, 'Listen to me;
    let me also declare my opinion.'

¹¹ "See, I waited for your words,
    I listened for your wise sayings,
    while you searched out what to say.
¹² I gave you my attention,
    but there was in fact no one that confuted Job,
    no one among you that answered his words.
¹³ Yet do not say, 'We have found wisdom;
    God may vanquish him, not a human.'
¹⁴ He has not directed his words against me,
    and I will not answer him with your speeches.

¹⁵ "They are dismayed, they answer no more;
    they have not a word to say.
¹⁶ And am I to wait, because they do not speak,
    because they stand there, and answer no more?
¹⁷ I also will give my answer;
    I also will declare my opinion.
¹⁸ For I am full of words;
    the spirit within me constrains me.
¹⁹ My heart is indeed like wine that has no vent;
    like new wineskins, it is ready to burst.
²⁰ I must speak, so that I may find relief;
    I must open my lips and answer.
²¹ I will not show partiality to any person
    or use flattery toward anyone.
²² For I do not know how to flatter—
    or my Maker would soon put an end to me!

Elihu Rebukes Job

33 "But now, hear my speech, O Job,
    and listen to all my words.
² See, I open my mouth;
    the tongue in my mouth speaks.
³ My words declare the uprightness of my heart,
    and what my lips know they speak sincerely.
⁴ The spirit of God has made me,
    and the breath of the Almighty gives me life.
⁵ Answer me, if you can;
    set your words in order before me; take your stand.
⁶ See, before God I am as you are;
    I too was formed from a piece of clay.
⁷ No fear of me need terrify you;
    my pressure will not be heavy on you.

⁸ "Surely, you have spoken in my hearing,
    and I have heard the sound of your words.
⁹ You say, 'I am clean, without transgression;
    I am pure, and there is no iniquity in me.
¹⁰ Look, he finds occasions against me,
    he counts me as his enemy;
¹¹ he puts my feet in the stocks,
    and watches all my paths.'

¹² "But in this you are not right. I will answer you:
    God is greater than any mortal.
¹³ Why do you contend against him,
    saying, 'He will answer none of my words'?
¹⁴ For God speaks in one way,
    and in two, though people do not perceive it.
¹⁵ In a dream, in a vision of the night,
    when deep sleep falls on mortals,
    while they slumber on their beds,
¹⁶ then he opens their ears,
    and terrifies them with warnings,
¹⁷ that he may turn them aside from their deeds,
    and keep them from pride,
¹⁸ to spare their souls from the Pit,

their lives from traversing the River.
19 They are also chastened with pain upon their beds,
and with continual strife in their bones,
20 so that their lives loathe bread,
and their appetites dainty food.
21 Their flesh is so wasted away that it cannot be seen;
and their bones, once invisible, now stick out.
22 Their souls draw near the Pit,
and their lives to those who bring death.
23 Then, if there should be for one of them an angel,
a mediator, one of a thousand,
one who declares a person upright,
24 and he is gracious to that person, and says,
'Deliver him from going down into the Pit;
I have found a ransom;
25 let his flesh become fresh with youth;
let him return to the days of his youthful vigor.'
26 Then he prays to God, and is accepted by him,
he comes into his presence with joy,
and God repays him for his righteousness.
27 That person sings to others and says,
'I sinned, and perverted what was right,
and it was not paid back to me.
28 He has redeemed my soul from going down to the Pit,
and my life shall see the light.'
29 "God indeed does all these things,
twice, three times, with mortals,
30 to bring back their souls from the Pit,
so that they may see the light of life.
31 Pay heed, Job, listen to me;
be silent, and I will speak.
32 If you have anything to say, answer me;
speak, for I desire to justify you.
33 If not, listen to me;
be silent, and I will teach you wisdom."

Elihu Proclaim's God's Justice

34

Then Elihu continued and said:
2 "Hear my words, you wise men,
and give ear to me, you who know;
3 for the ear tests words
as the palate tastes food.
4 Let us choose what is right;
let us determine among ourselves what is good.
5 For Job has said, 'I am innocent,
and God has taken away my right;
6 in spite of being right I am counted a liar;
my wound is incurable, though I am without transgression.'
7 Who is there like Job,
who drinks up scoffing like water,
8 who goes in company with evildoers
and walks with the wicked?
9 For he has said, 'It profits one nothing
to take delight in God.'

10 "Therefore, hear me, you who have sense,
far be it from God that he should do wickedness,
and from the Almighty that he should do wrong.
11 For according to their deeds he will repay them,
and according to their ways he will make it befall them.
12 Of a truth, God will not do wickedly,
and the Almighty will not pervert justice.
13 Who gave him charge over the earth
and who laid on him the whole world?
14 If he should take back his spirit to himself,
and gather to himself his breath,
15 all flesh would perish together,
and all mortals return to dust.
16 "If you have understanding, hear this;
listen to what I say.
17 Shall one who hates justice govern?
Will you condemn one who is righteous and mighty,
18 who says to a king, 'You scoundrel!'
and to princes, 'You wicked men!';
19 who shows no partiality to nobles,
nor regards the rich more than the poor,
for they are all the work of his hands?
20 In a moment they die;
at midnight the people are shaken and pass away,
and the mighty are taken away by no human hand.

21 "For his eyes are upon the ways of mortals,
and he sees all their steps.
22 There is no gloom or deep darkness
where evildoers may hide themselves.
23 For he has not appointed a time for anyone
to go before God in judgment.
24 He shatters the mighty without investigation,
and sets others in their place.
25 Thus, knowing their works,

he overturns them in the night, and they are crushed.
²⁶ He strikes them for their wickedness
while others look on,
²⁷ because they turned aside from following him,
and had no regard for any of his ways,
²⁸ so that they caused the cry of the poor to come to him,
and he heard the cry of the afflicted—
²⁹ When he is quiet, who can condemn?
When he hides his face, who can behold him,
whether it be a nation or an individual?—
³⁰ so that the godless should not reign,
or those who ensnare the people.

³¹ "For has anyone said to God,
'I have endured punishment; I will not offend any more;
³² teach me what I do not see;
if I have done iniquity, I will do it no more'?
³³ Will he then pay back to suit you,
because you reject it?
For you must choose, and not I; therefore declare what you know.
³⁴ Those who have sense will say to me,
and the wise who hear me will say,
³⁵ 'Job speaks without knowledge,
his words are without insight.'
³⁶ Would that Job were tried to the limit,
because his answers are those of the wicked.
³⁷ For he adds rebellion to his sin;
he claps his hands among us,
and multiplies his words against God."

Elihu Condemns Self-Righteousness

35

Elihu continued and said:
² "Do you think this to be just?
You say, 'I am in the right before God.'
³ If you ask, 'What advantage have I?
How am I better off than if I had sinned?'
⁴ I will answer you and your friends with you.
⁵ Look at the heavens and see;
observe the clouds, which are higher than you.
⁶ If you have sinned, what do you accomplish against him?
And if your transgressions are multiplied,
what do you do to him?
⁷ If you are righteous, what do you give to him;
or what does he receive from your hand?
⁸ Your wickedness affects others like you,
and your righteousness, other human beings.

⁹ "Because of the multitude of oppressions people cry out;
they call for help because of the arm of the mighty.
¹⁰ But no one says, 'Where is God my Maker,
who gives strength in the night,
¹¹ who teaches us more than the animals of the earth,
and makes us wiser than the birds of the air?'
¹² There they cry out, but he does not answer,
because of the pride of evildoers.
¹³ Surely God does not hear an empty cry,
nor does the Almighty regard it.
¹⁴ How much less when you say that you do not see him,
that the case is before him, and you are waiting for him!
¹⁵ And now, because his anger does not punish,
and he does not greatly heed transgression,
¹⁶ Job opens his mouth in empty talk,
he multiplies words without knowledge."

Elihu Exalts God's Goodness

36

Elihu continued and said:
² "Bear with me a little, and I will show you,
for I have yet something to say on God's behalf.
³ I will bring my knowledge from far away,
and ascribe righteousness to my Maker.
⁴ For truly my words are not false;
one who is perfect in knowledge is with you.

⁵ "Surely God is mighty and does not despise any;
he is mighty in strength of understanding.
⁶ He does not keep the wicked alive,
but gives the afflicted their right.
⁷ He does not withdraw his eyes from the righteous,
but with kings on the throne

he sets them forever, and they are exalted.
8 And if they are bound in fetters
and caught in the cords of affliction,
9 then he declares to them their work
and their transgressions, that they are behaving arrogantly.
10 He opens their ears to instruction,
and commands that they return from iniquity.
11 If they listen, and serve him,
they complete their days in prosperity, and their years in pleasantness.
12 But if they do not listen, they shall perish by the sword,
and die without knowledge.
13 "The godless in heart cherish anger;
they do not cry for help when he binds them.
14 They die in their youth,
and their life ends in shame.
15 He delivers the afflicted by their affliction,
and opens their ear by adversity.
16 He also allured you out of distress
into a broad place where there was no constraint, and what was set on your table was full of fatness.

17 "But you are obsessed with the case of the wicked;
judgment and justice seize you.
18 Beware that wrath does not entice you into scoffing,
and do not let the greatness of the ransom turn you aside.
19 Will your cry avail to keep you from distress,
or will all the force of your strength?
20 Do not long for the night,
when peoples are cut off in their place.
21 Beware! Do not turn to iniquity;
because of that you have been tried by affliction.
22 See, God is exalted in his power;
who is a teacher like him?
23 Who has prescribed for him his way,
or who can say, 'You have done wrong'?

Elihu Proclaims God's Majesty

24 "Remember to extol his work,
of which mortals have sung.
25 All people have looked on it;
everyone watches it from far away.
26 Surely God is great, and we do not know him;
the number of his years is unsearchable.
27 For he draws up the drops of water;
he distills his mist in rain,
28 which the skies pour down
and drop upon mortals abundantly.
29 Can anyone understand the spreading of the clouds,
the thunderings of his pavilion?
30 See, he scatters his lightning around him
and covers the roots of the sea.
31 For by these he governs peoples;
he gives food in abundance.
32 He covers his hands with the lightning,
and commands it to strike the mark.
33 Its crashing tells about him;
he is jealous with anger against iniquity.

37

"At this also my heart trembles, and leaps out of its place.
2 Listen, listen to the thunder of his voice
and the rumbling that comes from his mouth.
3 Under the whole heaven he lets it loose,
and his lightning to the corners of the earth.
4 After it his voice roars;
he thunders with his majestic voice
and he does not restrain the lightnings when his voice is heard.
5 God thunders wondrously with his voice;
he does great things that we cannot comprehend.
6 For to the snow he says, 'Fall on the earth';
and the shower of rain, his heavy shower of rain,
7 serves as a sign on everyone's hand,
so that all whom he has made may know it.
8 Then the animals go into their lairs
and remain in their dens.
9 From its chamber comes the whirlwind,
and cold from the scattering winds.
10 By the breath of God ice is given,
and the broad waters are frozen fast.
11 He loads the thick cloud with moisture;
the clouds scatter his lightning.
12 They turn round and round by his guidance,
to accomplish all that he commands them on the face of the habitable world.
13 Whether for correction, or for his land,
or for love, he causes it to happen.
14 "Hear this, O Job;
stop and consider the wondrous works of God.

¹⁵ Do you know how God lays his command upon them,
and causes the lightning of his cloud to shine?
¹⁶ Do you know the balancings of the clouds,
the wondrous works of the one whose knowledge is perfect,
¹⁷ you whose garments are hot
when the earth is still because of the south wind?
¹⁸ Can you, like him, spread out the skies,
hard as a molten mirror?
¹⁹ Teach us what we shall say to him;
we cannot draw up our case because of darkness.
²⁰ Should he be told that I want to speak?
Did anyone ever wish to be swallowed up?
²¹ Now, no one can look on the light
when it is bright in the skies, when the wind has passed and cleared them.
²² Out of the north comes golden splendor;
around God is awesome majesty.
²³ The Almighty—we cannot find him;
he is great in power and justice,
and abundant righteousness he will not violate.
²⁴ Therefore mortals fear him;
he does not regard any who are wise in their own conceit."

. . . .

40

And the LORD said to Job:
² "Shall a faultfinder contend with the Almighty?
Anyone who argues with God must respond."
³ Then Job answered the LORD:
⁴ "See, I am of small account; what shall I answer you?
I lay my hand on my mouth.
⁵ I have spoken once, and I will not answer;
twice, but will proceed no further."

God's Challenge to Job

⁶ Then the LORD answered Job out of the whirlwind:
⁷ "Gird up your loins like a man;
I will question you, and you declare to me.
⁸ Will you even put me in the wrong?
Will you condemn me that you may be justified?
⁹ Have you an arm like God,
and can you thunder with a voice like his?
¹⁰ "Deck yourself with majesty and dignity;
clothe yourself with glory and splendor.
¹¹ Pour out the overflowings of your anger,
and look on all who are proud, and abase them.
¹² Look on all who are proud, and bring them low;
tread down the wicked where they stand.
¹³ Hide them all in the dust together;
bind their faces in the world below.
¹⁴ Then I will also acknowledge to you
that your own right hand can give you victory.

¹⁵ "Look at Behemoth,
which I made just as I made you;
it eats grass like an ox.
¹⁶ Its strength is in its loins,
and its power in the muscles of its belly.
¹⁷ It makes its tail stiff like a cedar;
the sinews of its thighs are knit together.
¹⁸ Its bones are tubes of bronze,
its limbs like bars of iron.
¹⁹ "It is the first of the great acts of God—
only its Maker can approach it with the sword.
²⁰ For the mountains yield food for it
where all the wild animals play.
²¹ Under the lotus plants it lies,
in the covert of the reeds and in the marsh.
²² The lotus trees cover it for shade;
the willows of the wadi surround it.
²³ Even if the river is turbulent, it is not frightened;
it is confident though Jordan rushes against its mouth.
²⁴ Can one take it with hooks
or pierce its nose with a snare?

41

"Can you draw out Leviathan with a fishhook,
or press down its tongue with a cord?
² Can you put a rope in its nose,
or pierce its jaw with a hook?
³ Will it make many supplications to you?
Will it speak soft words to you?
⁴ Will it make a covenant with you
to be taken as your servant forever?
⁵ Will you play with it as with a bird,
or will you put it on leash for your girls?
⁶ Will traders bargain over it?

Will they divide it up among the merchants?
7 Can you fill its skin with harpoons,
or its head with fishing spears?
8 Lay hands on it;
think of the battle; you will not do it again!
9 Any hope of capturing it will be disappointed;
were not even the gods overwhelmed at the sight of it?
10 No one is so fierce as to dare to stir it up.
Who can stand before it?
11 Who can confront it and be safe?
—under the whole heaven, who?

12 "I will not keep silence concerning its limbs,
or its mighty strength, or its splendid frame.
13 Who can strip off its outer garment?
Who can penetrate its double coat of mail?
14 Who can open the doors of its face?
There is terror all around its teeth.
15 Its back is made of shields in rows,
shut up closely as with a seal.
16 One is so near to another
that no air can come between them.
17 They are joined one to another;
they clasp each other and cannot be separated.
18 Its sneezes flash forth light,
and its eyes are like the eyelids of the dawn.
19 From its mouth go flaming torches;
sparks of fire leap out.
20 Out of its nostrils comes smoke,
as from a boiling pot and burning rushes.
21 Its breath kindles coals,
and a flame comes out of its mouth.
22 In its neck abides strength,
and terror dances before it.
23 The folds of its flesh cling together;
it is firmly cast and immovable.
24 Its heart is as hard as stone,
as hard as the lower millstone.
25 When it raises itself up the gods are afraid;
at the crashing they are beside themselves.
26 Though the sword reaches it, it does not avail,
nor does the spear, the dart, or the javelin.
27 It counts iron as straw,
and bronze as rotten wood.
28 The arrow cannot make it flee;
slingstones, for it, are turned to chaff.
29 Clubs are counted as chaff;
it laughs at the rattle of javelins.
30 Its underparts are like sharp potsherds;
it spreads itself like a threshing sledge on the mire.
31 It makes the deep boil like a pot;
it makes the sea like a pot of ointment.
32 It leaves a shining wake behind it;
one would think the deep to be white-haired.
33 On earth it has no equal,
a creature without fear.
34 It surveys everything that is lofty;
it is king over all that are proud."

Job Is Humbled and Satisfied

42

Then Job answered the LORD:
2 "I know that you can do all things,
and that no purpose of yours can be thwarted.
3 'Who is this that hides counsel without knowledge?'
Therefore I have uttered what I did not understand,
things too wonderful for me, which I did not know.
4 'Hear, and I will speak;
I will question you, and you declare to me.'
5 I had heard of you by the hearing of the ear,
but now my eye sees you;
6 therefore I despise myself,
and repent in dust and ashes."

Job's Friends Are Humiliated

7 After the LORD had spoken these words to Job, the LORD said to Eliphaz the Temanite: "My wrath is kindled against you and against your two friends; for you have not spoken of me what is right, as my servant Job has. ⁸Now therefore take seven bulls and seven rams, and go to my servant Job, and offer up for yourselves a burnt offering; and my servant Job shall pray for you, for I will accept his prayer not to deal with you according to your folly; for you have not spoken of me what is right, as my servant Job has done." ⁹So Eliphaz the Temanite and Bildad the Shuhite and Zophar the Naamathite went and did what the LORD had told them; and the LORD accepted Job's prayer.

Job's Fortunes Are Restored Twofold

10 And the LORD restored the fortunes of Job when he had prayed for his friends; and the LORD gave Job twice as much as he had before. [11]Then there came to him all his brothers and sisters and all who had known him before, and they ate bread with him in his house; they showed him sympathy and comforted him for all the evil that the LORD had brought upon him; and each of them gave him a piece of money and a gold ring. [12]The LORD blessed the latter days of Job more than his beginning; and he had fourteen thousand sheep, six thousand camels, a thousand yoke of oxen, and a thousand donkeys. [13]He also had seven sons and three daughters. [14]He named the first Jemimah, the second Keziah, and the third Keren-happuch. [15]In all the land there were no women so beautiful as Job's daughters; and their father gave them an inheritance along with their brothers. [16]After this Job lived one hundred and forty years, and saw his children, and his children's children, four generations. [17]And Job died, old and full of days.

Psalms

Psalm 19

To the leader. A Psalm of David.

1 The heavens are telling the glory of God;
   and the firmament proclaims his handiwork.
2 Day to day pours forth speech,
   and night to night declares knowledge.
3 There is no speech, nor are there words;
   their voice is not heard;
4 yet their voice goes out through all the earth,
   and their words to the end of the world.
In the heavens he has set a tent for the sun,
5 which comes out like a bridegroom from his wedding canopy,
   and like a strong man runs its course with joy.
6 Its rising is from the end of the heavens,
   and its circuit to the end of them; and nothing is hid from its heat.

7 The law of the LORD is perfect,
   reviving the soul; the decrees of the LORD are sure, making wise the simple;
8 the precepts of the LORD are right,
   rejoicing the heart; the commandment of the LORD is clear, enlightening the eyes;
9 the fear of the LORD is pure,
   enduring forever; the ordinances of the LORD are true and righteous altogether.
10 More to be desired are they than gold,
    even much fine gold;
  sweeter also than honey,
    and drippings of the honeycomb.
11 Moreover by them is your servant warned;
    in keeping them there is great reward.
12 But who can detect their errors?
    Clear me from hidden faults.
13 Keep back your servant also from the insolent;
    do not let them have dominion over me.
  Then I shall be blameless, and innocent of great transgression.

14 Let the words of my mouth and the meditation of my heart
    be acceptable to you, O LORD, my rock and my redeemer.

Psalm 20

To the leader. A Psalm of David.

1 The LORD answer you in the day of trouble!
   The name of the God of Jacob protect you!
2 May he send you help from the sanctuary,
   and give you support from Zion.
3 May he remember all your offerings,
   and regard with favor your burnt sacrifices.
   Selah

4 May he grant you your heart's desire,
   and fulfill all your plans.
5 May we shout for joy over your victory,
   and in the name of our God set up our banners. May the LORD fulfill all your petitions.
6 Now I know that the LORD will help his anointed;
   he will answer him from his holy heaven with mighty victories by his right hand.
7 Some take pride in chariots, and some in horses,
   but our pride is in the name of the LORD our God.
8 They will collapse and fall,
   but we shall rise and stand upright.

⁹ Give victory to the king, O LORD;
　answer us when we call.

Psalm 21

To the leader. A Psalm of David.

¹ In your strength the king rejoices, O LORD,
　and in your help how greatly he exults!
² You have given him his heart's desire,
　and have not withheld the request of his lips. Selah
³ For you meet him with rich blessings;
　you set a crown of fine gold on his head.
⁴ He asked you for life; you gave it to him—
　length of days forever and ever.
⁵ His glory is great through your help;
　splendor and majesty you bestow on him.
⁶ You bestow on him blessings forever;
　you make him glad with the joy of your presence.
⁷ For the king trusts in the LORD,
　and through the steadfast love of the Most High he shall not be moved.
⁸ Your hand will find out all your enemies;
　your right hand will find out those who hate you.
⁹ You will make them like a fiery furnace
　when you appear.
　The LORD will swallow them up in his wrath,
　and fire will consume them.
¹⁰ You will destroy their offspring from the earth,
　and their children from among humankind.
¹¹ If they plan evil against you,
　if they devise mischief, they will not succeed.
¹² For you will put them to flight;
　you will aim at their faces with your bows.
¹³ Be exalted, O LORD, in your strength!
　We will sing and praise your power.

Psalm 22

*To the leader: according to The Deer of the Dawn.
A Psalm of David*

¹ My God, my God, why have you forsaken me?
　Why are you so far from helping me, from the words of my groaning?
² O my God, I cry by day, but you do not answer;
　and by night, but find no rest.
³ Yet you are holy,
　enthroned on the praises of Israel.
⁴ In you our ancestors trusted;
　they trusted, and you delivered them.
⁵ To you they cried, and were saved;
　in you they trusted, and were not put to shame.
⁶ But I am a worm, and not human;
　scorned by others, and despised by the people.
⁷ All who see me mock at me;
　they make mouths at me, they shake their heads;
⁸ "Commit your cause to the LORD; let him deliver—
　let him rescue the one in whom he delights!"
⁹ Yet it was you who took me from the womb;
　you kept me safe on my mother's breast.
¹⁰ On you I was cast from my birth,
　and since my mother bore me you have been my God.
¹¹ Do not be far from me,
　for trouble is near
　and there is no one to help.
¹² Many bulls encircle me,
　strong bulls of Bashan surround me;
¹³ they open wide their mouths at me,
　like a ravening and roaring lion.
¹⁴ I am poured out like water,
　and all my bones are out of joint;
　my heart is like wax;
　it is melted within my breast;
¹⁵ my mouth is dried up like a potsherd,
　and my tongue sticks to my jaws;
　you lay me in the dust of death.
¹⁶ For dogs are all around me;
　a company of evildoers encircles me.
　My hands and feet have shriveled;
¹⁷ I can count all my bones. They stare and gloat over me;
¹⁸ they divide my clothes among themselves,
　and for my clothing they cast lots.
¹⁹ But you, O LORD, do not be far away!
　O my help, come quickly to my aid!
²⁰ Deliver my soul from the sword,

my life from the power of the dog!
21 Save me from the mouth of the lion!

From the horns of the wild oxen you have rescued me.
22 I will tell of your name to my brothers and sisters;
in the midst of the congregation I will praise you:
23 You who fear the LORD, praise him!
All you offspring of Jacob, glorify him;
stand in awe of him,
all you offspring of Israel!
24 For he did not despise or abhor
the affliction of the afflicted;
he did not hide his face from me,
but heard when I cried to him.

25 From you comes my praise in the great congregation;
my vows I will pay before those who fear him.
26 The poor shall eat and be satisfied;
those who seek him shall praise the LORD.
May your hearts live forever!

27 All the ends of the earth shall remember
and turn to the LORD;
and all the families of the nations
shall worship before him.
28 For dominion belongs to the LORD,
and he rules over the nations.

29 To him, indeed, shall all who sleep in the earth bow down;
before him shall bow all who go down to the dust,
and I shall live for him.
30 Posterity will serve him;
future generations will be told about the Lord,
31 and proclaim his deliverance to a people yet unborn,
saying that he has done it.

Psalm 23

A Psalm of David

1 The LORD is my shepherd, I shall not want.
2 He makes me lie down in green pastures;
he leads me beside still waters;
3 he restores my soul.
He leads me in right paths
for his name's sake.
4 Even though I walk through the darkest valley,
I fear no evil;
for you are with me;
your rod and your staff—
they comfort me.
5 You prepare a table before me
in the presence of my enemies; you anoint my head with oil; my cup overflows.
6 Surely goodness and mercy shall follow me
all the days of my life,
and I shall dwell in the house of the LORD
my whole life long.

Psalm 24

Of David. A Psalm.

1 The earth is the Lord's and all that is in it,
the world, and those who live in it;
2 for he has founded it on the seas,
and established it on the rivers.
3 Who shall ascend the hill of the LORD?
And who shall stand in his holy place?
4 Those who have clean hands and pure hearts,
who do not lift up their souls to what is false,
and do not swear deceitfully.
5 They will receive blessing from the LORD,
and vindication from the God of their salvation.
6 Such is the company of those who seek him,
who seek the face of the God of Jacob. Selah

7 Lift up your heads, O gates!
and be lifted up, O ancient doors!
that the King of glory may come in.
8 Who is the King of glory?
The LORD, strong and mighty,
the LORD, mighty in battle.
9 Lift up your heads, O gates!
and be lifted up, O ancient doors!
that the King of glory may come in.
10 Who is this King of glory?
The LORD of hosts,
he is the King of glory. Selah

Psalm 25

Of David.

To you, O LORD, I lift up my soul.
2 O my God, in you I trust;
　　do not let me be put to shame;
　　do not let my enemies exult over me.
3 Do not let those who wait for you be put to shame;
　　let them be ashamed who are wantonly treacherous.

4 Make me to know your ways, O LORD;
　　teach me your paths.
5 Lead me in your truth, and teach me,
　　for you are the God of my salvation;
　　for you I wait all day long.

6 Be mindful of your mercy, O LORD, and of your steadfast love,
　　for they have been from of old.
7 Do not remember the sins of my youth or my transgressions;
　　according to your steadfast love remember me,
　　for your goodness' sake, O LORD!

8 Good and upright is the LORD;
　　therefore he instructs sinners in the way.
9 He leads the humble in what is right,
　　and teaches the humble his way.

10 All the paths of the LORD are steadfast love and faithfulness,
　　for those who keep his covenant and his decrees.
11 For your name's sake, O LORD,
　　pardon my guilt, for it is great.
12 Who are they that fear the LORD?
　　He will teach them the way that they should choose.

13 They will abide in prosperity,
　　and their children shall possess the land.
14 The friendship of the LORD is for those who fear him,
　　and he makes his covenant known to them.
15 My eyes are ever toward the LORD,
　　for he will pluck my feet out of the net.
16 Turn to me and be gracious to me,
　　for I am lonely and afflicted.
17 Relieve the troubles of my heart,
　　and bring me out of my distress.
18 Consider my affliction and my trouble,
　　and forgive all my sins.

19 Consider how many are my foes,
　　and with what violent hatred they hate me.
20 O guard my life, and deliver me;
　　do not let me be put to shame, for I take refuge in you.
21 May integrity and uprightness preserve me,
　　for I wait for you.

22 Redeem Israel, O God,
　　out of all its troubles.

Isaiah

1 The vision of Isaiah son of Amoz, which he saw concerning Judah and Jerusalem in the days of Uzziah, Jotham, Ahaz, and Hezekiah, kings of Judah.

The Wickedness of Judah

2 Hear, O heavens, and listen, O earth;
    for the LORD has spoken:
I reared children and brought them up,
    but they have rebelled against me.
3 The ox knows its owner,
    and the donkey its master's crib;
but Israel does not know,
    my people do not understand.

4 Ah, sinful nation, people
    laden with iniquity,
offspring who do evil,
    children who deal corruptly,
who have forsaken the LORD,
    who have despised the Holy One of Israel,
    who are utterly estranged!

5 Why do you seek further beatings?
    Why do you continue to rebel?
The whole head is sick,
    and the whole heart faint.
6 From the sole of the foot even to the head,
    there is no soundness in it,
but bruises and sores
    and bleeding wounds;
they have not been drained, or bound up,
    or softened with oil.

7 Your country lies desolate,
    your cities are burned with fire;
in your very presence
    aliens devour your land;
    it is desolate, as overthrown by foreigners.
8 And daughter Zion is left
    like a booth in a vineyard,
like a shelter in a cucumber field, like a besieged city.
9 If the LORD of hosts
    had not left us a few survivors,
we would have been like Sodom,
    and become like Gomorrah.

10 Hear the word of the LORD,
    you rulers of Sodom!
Listen to the teaching of our God,
    you people of Gomorrah!
11 What to me is the multitude of your sacrifices?
    says the LORD;
I have had enough of burnt offerings of rams
    and the fat of fed beasts;
I do not delight in the blood of bulls,
    or of lambs, or of goats.

12 When you come to appear before me,
    who asked this from your hand?
Trample my courts no more;
13 bringing offerings is futile;
    incense is an abomination to me.
New moon and sabbath and calling of convocation—
    I cannot endure solemn assemblies with iniquity.
14 Your new moons and your appointed festivals
    my soul hates;
they have become a burden to me,
    I am weary of bearing them.
15 When you stretch out your hands,
    I will hide my eyes from you;
even though you make many prayers,
    I will not listen;
    your hands are full of blood.
16 Wash yourselves; make yourselves clean;

remove the evil of your doings
from before my eyes;
cease to do evil,
^{17} learn to do good;
seek justice,
rescue the oppressed,
defend the orphan,
plead for the widow.

^{18} Come now, let us argue it out,
says the LORD:
though your sins are like scarlet,
they shall be like snow;
though they are red like crimson,
they shall become like wool.
^{19} If you are willing and obedient,
you shall eat the good of the land;
^{20} but if you refuse and rebel,
you shall be devoured by the sword;
for the mouth of the LORD has spoken.

The Degenerate City

^{21} How the faithful city
has become a whore!
She that was full of justice,
righteousness lodged in her—
but now murderers!
^{22} Your silver has become dross,
your wine is mixed with water.
^{23} Your princes are rebels
and companions of thieves.
Everyone loves a bribe and runs after gifts.
They do not defend the orphan,
and the widow's cause does not come before them.

^{24} Therefore says the Sovereign, the LORD of hosts, the Mighty One of Israel:
Ah, I will pour out my wrath on my enemies,
and avenge myself on my foes!
^{25} I will turn my hand against you;
I will smelt away your dross as with lye
and remove all your alloy.
^{26} And I will restore your judges as at the first,
and your counselors as at the beginning.
Afterward you shall be called the city of righteousness,
the faithful city.

^{27} Zion shall be redeemed by justice,
and those in her who repent, by righteousness.

^{28} But rebels and sinners shall be destroyed together,
and those who forsake the LORD shall be consumed.
^{29} For you shall be ashamed of the oaks
in which you delighted; and you shall blush
for the gardens that you have chosen.
^{30} For you shall be like an oak
whose leaf withers,
and like a garden without water.
^{31} The strong shall become like tinder,
and their work like a spark;
they and their work shall burn together,
with no one to quench them.

The Future House of God

2

The word that Isaiah son of Amoz saw concerning Judah and Jerusalem.

^{2} In days to come
the mountain of the Lord's house
shall be established as the highest of the mountains,
and shall be raised above the hills;
all the nations shall stream to it.
^{3} Many peoples shall come and say,
"Come, let us go up to the mountain of the LORD,
to the house of the God of Jacob;
that he may teach us his ways
and that we may walk in his paths."
For out of Zion shall go forth instruction,
and the word of the LORD from Jerusalem.
^{4} He shall judge between the nations,
and shall arbitrate for many peoples;
they shall beat their swords into plowshares,
and their spears into pruning hooks;
nation shall not lift up sword against nation,
neither shall they learn war any more.

Judgment Pronounced on Arrogance

^{5} O house of Jacob,
come, let us walk
in the light of the LORD!

6 For you have forsaken the ways of your people,
   O house of Jacob.
   Indeed they are full of diviners from the east
     and of soothsayers like the Philistines,
     and they clasp hands with foreigners.
7 Their land is filled with silver and gold,
     and there is no end to their treasures;
   their land is filled with horses,
     and there is no end to their chariots.
8 Their land is filled with idols;
     they bow down to the work of their hands,
     to what their own fingers have made.
9 And so people are humbled,
     and everyone is brought low—
     do not forgive them!
10 Enter into the rock,
     and hide in the dust
   from the terror of the LORD,
     and from the glory of his majesty.
11 The haughty eyes of people shall be brought low,
     and the pride of everyone shall be humbled;
   and the LORD alone will be exalted in that day.
12 For the LORD of hosts has a day
     against all that is proud and lofty,
     against all that is lifted up and high;
13 against all the cedars of Lebanon,
     lofty and lifted up;
     and against all the oaks of Bashan;
14 against all the high mountains,
     and against all the lofty hills;
15 against every high tower,
     and against every fortified wall;
16 against all the ships of Tarshish,
     and against all the beautiful craft.
17 The haughtiness of people shall be humbled,
     and the pride of everyone shall be brought low;
   and the LORD alone will be exalted on that day.
18 The idols shall utterly pass away.
19 Enter the caves of the rocks
     and the holes of the ground,
   from the terror of the LORD,
     and from the glory of his majesty,
     when he rises to terrify the earth.
20 On that day people will throw away
     to the moles and to the bats
   their idols of silver and their idols of gold,
     which they made for themselves to worship,
21 to enter the caverns of the rocks
     and the clefts in the crags,
   from the terror of the LORD,
     and from the glory of his majesty,
     when he rises to terrify the earth.
22 Turn away from mortals,
     who have only breath in their nostrils,
     for of what account are they?

3 For now the Sovereign, the LORD of hosts,
     is taking away from Jerusalem and from Judah
   support and staff—
     all support of bread,
     and all support of water—
2 warrior and soldier,
     judge and prophet,
     diviner and elder,
3 captain of fifty
     and dignitary,
   counselor and skillful magician and expert enchanter.
4 And I will make boys their princes,
     and babes shall rule over them.
5 The people will be oppressed,
     everyone by another
     and everyone by a neighbor;
   the youth will be insolent to the elder,
     and the base to the honorable.
6 Someone will even seize a relative,
     a member of the clan, saying,
   "You have a cloak;
     you shall be our leader,
   and this heap of ruins
     shall be under your rule."
7 But the other will cry out on that day, saying,
   "I will not be a healer;
     in my house there is neither bread nor cloak;
   you shall not make me
     leader of the people."
8 For Jerusalem has stumbled
     and Judah has fallen,
   because their speech and their deeds are against the LORD,
     defying his glorious presence.

9 The look on their faces bears witness against them;
     they proclaim their sin like Sodom,
     they do not hide it.
   Woe to them!
     For they have brought evil on themselves.
10 Tell the innocent how fortunate they are,
     for they shall eat the fruit of their labors.
11 Woe to the guilty! How unfortunate they are,
     for what their hands have done shall be done to them.
12 My people—children are their oppressors,

and women rule over them.
O my people, your leaders mislead you,
and confuse the course of your paths.
¹³ The LORD rises to argue his case;
he stands to judge the peoples.
¹⁴ The LORD enters into judgment
with the elders and princes of his people:
It is you who have devoured the vineyard;
the spoil of the poor is in your houses.
¹⁵ What do you mean by crushing my people,
by grinding the face of the poor? says the
Lord GOD of hosts.

¹⁶ The LORD said:
Because the daughters of Zion are haughty
and walk with outstretched necks,
glancing wantonly with their eyes,
mincing along as they go,
tinkling with their feet;
¹⁷ the Lord will afflict with scabs
the heads of the daughters of Zion,
and the LORD will lay bare their secret
parts.

18 In that day the Lord will take away the finery of the anklets, the headbands, and the crescents; ¹⁹the pendants, the bracelets, and the scarfs; ²⁰the headdresses, the armlets, the sashes, the perfume boxes, and the amulets; ²¹the signet rings and nose rings; ²²the festal robes, the mantles, the cloaks, and the handbags; ²³the garments of gauze, the linen garments, the turbans, and the veils.
²⁴ Instead of perfume there will be a stench;
and instead of a sash, a rope;
and instead of well-set hair, baldness;
and instead of a rich robe, a binding of sackcloth;
instead of beauty, shame.
²⁵ Your men shall fall by the sword
and your warriors in battle.
²⁶ And her gates shall lament and mourn;
ravaged, she shall sit upon the ground.

4

Seven women shall take hold of one man in
that day, saying,
"We will eat our own bread and wear our own
clothes;
just let us be called by your name;
take away our disgrace."

The Future Glory of the Survivors in Zion

2 On that day the branch of the LORD shall be beautiful and glorious, and the fruit of the land shall be the pride and glory of the survivors of Israel. ³Whoever is left in Zion and remains in Jerusalem will be called holy, everyone who has been recorded for life in Jerusalem, ⁴once the Lord has washed away the filth of the daughters of Zion and cleansed the bloodstains of Jerusalem from its midst by a spirit of judgment and by a spirit of burning. ⁵Then the LORD will create over the whole site of Mount Zion and over its places of assembly a cloud by day and smoke and the shining of a flaming fire by night. Indeed over all the glory there will be a canopy. ⁶It will serve as a pavilion, a shade by day from the heat, and a refuge and a shelter from the storm and rain.

The Song of the Unfruitful Vineyard

5

Let me sing for my beloved
my love-song concerning his vineyard:
My beloved had a vineyard
on a very fertile hill.
² He dug it and cleared it of stones,
and planted it with choice vines;
he built a watchtower in the midst of it,
and hewed out a wine vat in it;
he expected it to yield grapes,
but it yielded wild grapes.

³ And now, inhabitants of Jerusalem
and people of Judah,
judge between me
and my vineyard.
⁴ What more was there to do for my vineyard
that I have not done in it?
When I expected it to yield grapes,
why did it yield wild grapes?

⁵ And now I will tell you
what I will do to my vineyard.
I will remove its hedge,
and it shall be devoured;
I will break down its wall,

and it shall be trampled down.
6 I will make it a waste;
   it shall not be pruned or hoed,
   and it shall be overgrown with briers and thorns;
I will also command the clouds
   that they rain no rain upon it.
7 For the vineyard of the LORD of hosts
   is the house of Israel,
and the people of Judah
   are his pleasant planting;
he expected justice,
   but saw bloodshed;
righteousness,
   but heard a cry!

Social Injustice Denounced

8 Ah, you who join house to house,
   who add field to field,
until there is room for no one but you,
   and you are left to live alone
      in the midst of the land!
9 The LORD of hosts has sworn in my hearing:
Surely many houses shall be desolate,
   large and beautiful houses, without inhabitant.
10 For ten acres of vineyard shall yield but one bath,
   and a homer of seed shall yield a mere ephah.

11 Ah, you who rise early in the morning
      in pursuit of strong drink,
   who linger in the evening
      to be inflamed by wine,
12 whose feasts consist of lyre and harp,
      tambourine and flute and wine,
   but who do not regard the deeds of the LORD,
      or see the work of his hands!
13 Therefore my people go into exile without knowledge;
   their nobles are dying of hunger,
   and their multitude is parched with thirst.

14 Therefore Sheol has enlarged its appetite
      and opened its mouth beyond measure;
   the nobility of Jerusalem and her multitude go down,
      her throng and all who exult in her.
15 People are bowed down, everyone is brought low,
      and the eyes of the haughty are humbled.

16 But the LORD of hosts is exalted by justice,
      and the Holy God shows himself holy by righteousness.
17 Then the lambs shall graze as in their pasture,
      fatlings and kids shall feed among the ruins.

18 Ah, you who drag iniquity along with cords of falsehood,
      who drag sin along as with cart ropes,
19 who say, "Let him make haste,
      let him speed his work
         that we may see it;
   let the plan of the Holy One of Israel hasten to fulfillment,
      that we may know it!"
20 Ah, you who call evil good
      and good evil,
   who put darkness for light
      and light for darkness,
   who put bitter for sweet
      and sweet for bitter!
21 Ah, you who are wise in your own eyes,
      and shrewd in your own sight!
22 Ah, you who are heroes in drinking wine
      and valiant at mixing drink,
23 who acquit the guilty for a bribe,
      and deprive the innocent of their rights!

Foreign Invasion Predicted

24 Therefore, as the tongue of fire devours the stubble,
      and as dry grass sinks down in the flame,
   so their root will become rotten,
      and their blossom go up like dust;
   for they have rejected the instruction of the LORD of hosts,
      and have despised the word of the Holy One of Israel.

25 Therefore the anger of the LORD was kindled against his people,
      and he stretched out his hand against them and struck them;
   the mountains quaked,
      and their corpses were like refuse in the streets.
   For all this his anger has not turned away,
      and his hand is stretched out still.

26 He will raise a signal for a nation far away,
      and whistle for a people at the ends of the earth;

Here they come, swiftly, speedily!
27 None of them is weary, none stumbles,
none slumbers or sleeps,
not a loincloth is loose,
not a sandal-thong broken;
28 their arrows are sharp,
all their bows bent,
their horses' hoofs seem like flint,
and their wheels like the whirlwind.
29 Their roaring is like a lion,
like young lions they roar;
they growl and seize their prey,
they carry it off, and no one can rescue.
30 They will roar over it on that day,
like the roaring of the sea.
And if one look to the land—
only darkness and distress;
and the light grows dark with clouds.

A Vision of God in the Temple

6 In the year that King Uzziah died, I saw the Lord sitting on a throne, high and lofty; and the hem of his robe filled the temple. ²Seraphs were in attendance above him; each had six wings: with two they covered their faces, and with two they covered their feet, and with two they flew. ³And one called to another and said:

"Holy, holy, holy is the LORD of hosts;
the whole earth is full of his glory.

⁴The pivots on the thresholds shook at the voices of those who called, and the house filled with smoke. ⁵And I said: "Woe is me! I am lost, for I am a man of unclean lips, and I live among a people of unclean lips; yet my eyes have seen the King, the LORD of hosts!"

6 Then one of the seraphs flew to me, holding a live coal that had been taken from the altar with a pair of tongs. ⁷The seraph touched my mouth with it and said: "Now that this has touched your lips, your guilt has departed and your sin is blotted out." ⁸Then I heard the voice of the Lord saying, "Whom shall I send, and who will go for us?" And I said, "Here am I; send me!" ⁹And he said, "Go and say to this people: 'Keep listening, but do not comprehend; keep looking, but do not understand.'
10 Make the mind of this people dull,
and stop their ears,
and shut their eyes,
so that they may not look with their eyes,
and listen with their ears,
and comprehend with their minds,
and turn and be healed."
¹¹ Then I said, "How long, O Lord?" And he said:
"Until cities lie waste
without inhabitant,
and houses without people,
and the land is utterly desolate;
¹² until the LORD sends everyone far away,
and vast is the emptiness in the midst of the land.
¹³ Even if a tenth part remain in it,
it will be burned again, like a terebinth or an oak
whose stump remains standing
when it is felled."
The holy seed is its stump.

Isaiah Reassures King Ahaz

7 In the days of Ahaz son of Jotham son of Uzziah, king of Judah, King Rezin of Aram and King Pekah son of Remaliah of Israel went up to attack Jerusalem, but could not mount an attack against it. ²When the house of David heard that Aram had allied itself with Ephraim, the heart of Ahaz and the heart of his people shook as the trees of the forest shake before the wind.

3 Then the LORD said to Isaiah, Go out to meet Ahaz, you and your son Shear-jashub, at the end of the conduit of the upper pool on the highway to the Fuller's Field, ⁴and say to him, Take heed, be quiet, do not fear, and do not let your heart be faint because of these two smoldering stumps of firebrands, because of the fierce anger of Rezin and Aram and the son of Remaliah. ⁵Because Aram—with Ephraim and the son of Remaliah—has plotted evil against you, saying, ⁶Let us go up against Judah and cut off Jerusalem and conquer it for ourselves and make the son of Tabeel king in it; ⁷therefore thus says the Lord GOD:
It shall not stand,
and it shall not come to pass.
8 For the head of Aram is Damascus,
and the head of Damascus is Rezin.
(Within sixty-five years Ephraim will be shattered, no longer a people.)
9 The head of Ephraim is Samaria,
and the head of Samaria is the son of Remaliah.
If you do not stand firm in faith,
you shall not stand at all.

Isaiah Gives Ahaz the Sign of Immanuel

10 Again the LORD spoke to Ahaz, saying, ¹¹Ask a sign of the LORD your God; let it be deep as Sheol or high as heaven. ¹²But Ahaz said, I will not ask, and I will not put the LORD to the test. ¹³Then Isaiah said: "Hear then, O house of David! Is it too little for you to weary mortals, that you weary my God also? ¹⁴Therefore the Lord himself will give you a sign. Look, the young woman is with child and shall bear a son, and shall name him Immanuel. ¹⁵He shall eat curds and honey by the time he knows how to refuse the evil and choose the good. ¹⁶For before the child knows how to refuse the evil and choose the good, the land before whose two kings you are in dread will be deserted. ¹⁷The LORD will bring on you and on your people and on your ancestral house such days as have not come since the day that Ephraim departed from Judah—the king of Assyria."

18 On that day the LORD will whistle for the fly that is at the sources of the streams of Egypt, and for the bee that is in the land of Assyria. ¹⁹And they will all come and settle in the steep ravines, and in the clefts of the rocks, and on all the thornbushes, and on all the pastures.

20 On that day the Lord will shave with a razor hired beyond the River—with the king of Assyria—the head and the hair of the feet, and it will take off the beard as well.

21 On that day one will keep alive a young cow and two sheep, ²²and will eat curds because of the abundance of milk that they give; for everyone that is left in the land shall eat curds and honey.

23 On that day every place where there used to be a thousand vines, worth a thousand shekels of silver, will become briers and thorns. ²⁴With bow and arrows one will go there, for all the land will be briers and thorns; ²⁵and as for all the hills that used to be hoed with a hoe, you will not go there for fear of briers and thorns; but they will become a place where cattle are let loose and where sheep tread.

Isaiah's Son a Sign of the Assyrian Invasion

8 Then the LORD said to me, Take a large tablet and write on it in common characters, "Belonging to Maher-shalal-hash-baz," ²and have it attested for me by reliable witnesses, the priest Uriah and Zechariah son of Jeberechiah. ³And I went to the prophetess, and she conceived and bore a son. Then the LORD said to me, Name him Maher-shalal-hash-baz; ⁴for before the child knows how to call "My father" or "My mother," the wealth of Damascus and the spoil of Samaria will be carried away by the king of Assyria.

5 The LORD spoke to me again: ⁶Because this people has refused the waters of Shiloah that flow gently, and melt in fear before Rezin and the son of Remaliah; ⁷therefore, the Lord is bringing up against it the mighty flood waters of the River, the king of Assyria and all his glory; it will rise above all its channels and overflow all its banks; ⁸it will sweep on into Judah as a flood, and, pouring over, it will reach up to the neck; and its outspread wings will fill the breadth of your land, O Immanuel.

⁹ Band together, you peoples, and be dismayed;
    listen, all you far countries;
  gird yourselves and be dismayed;
    gird yourselves and be dismayed!
¹⁰ Take counsel together, but it shall be brought
    to naught;
  speak a word, but it will not stand,
    for God is with us.

11 For the LORD spoke thus to me while his hand was strong upon me, and warned me not to walk in the way of this people, saying: ¹²Do not call conspiracy all that this people calls conspiracy, and do not fear what it fears, or be in dread. ¹³But the LORD of hosts, him you shall regard as holy; let him be your fear, and let him be your dread. ¹⁴He will become a sanctuary, a stone one strikes against; for both houses of Israel he will become a rock one stumbles over—a trap and a snare for the inhabitants of Jerusalem. ¹⁵And many among them shall stumble; they shall fall and be broken; they shall be snared and taken.

Disciples of Isaiah

16 Bind up the testimony, seal the teaching among my disciples. [17]I will wait for the LORD, who is hiding his face from the house of Jacob, and I will hope in him. [18]See, I and the children whom the LORD has given me are signs and portents in Israel from the LORD of hosts, who dwells on Mount Zion. [19]Now if people say to you, "Consult the ghosts and the familiar spirits that chirp and mutter; should not a people consult their gods, the dead on behalf of the living, [20]for teaching and for instruction?" Surely, those who speak like this will have no dawn! [21]They will pass through the land, greatly distressed and hungry; when they are hungry, they will be enraged and will curse their king and their gods. They will turn their faces upward, [22]or they will look to the earth, but will see only distress and darkness, the gloom of anguish; and they will be thrust into thick darkness.

The Righteous Reign of the Coming King

9 But there will be no gloom for those who were in anguish. In the former time he brought into contempt the land of Zebulun and the land of Naphtali, but in the latter time he will make glorious the way of the sea, the land beyond the Jordan, Galilee of the nations.

2 The people who walked in darkness
    have seen a great light;
those who lived in a land of deep darkness—
    on them light has shined.
3 You have multiplied the nation,
    you have increased its joy;
they rejoice before you
    as with joy at the harvest,
    as people exult when dividing plunder.
4 For the yoke of their burden,
    and the bar across their shoulders,
    the rod of their oppressor,
    you have broken as on the day of Midian.
5 For all the boots of the tramping warriors
    and all the garments rolled in blood
    shall be burned as fuel for the fire.
6 For a child has been born for us,
    a son given to us;
authority rests upon his shoulders;
    and he is named
Wonderful Counselor, Mighty God,
    Everlasting Father, Prince of Peace.
7 His authority shall grow continually,
    and there shall be endless peace
for the throne of David and his kingdom.
    He will establish and uphold it
with justice and with righteousness
    from this time onward and forevermore.
The zeal of the LORD of hosts will do this.

Judgment on Arrogance and Oppression

8 The Lord sent a word against Jacob,
    and it fell on Israel;
9 and all the people knew it—
    Ephraim and the inhabitants of Samaria—
    but in pride and arrogance of heart they said:
10 "The bricks have fallen,
    but we will build with dressed stones;
the sycamores have been cut down,
    but we will put cedars in their place."
11 So the LORD raised adversaries against them,
    and stirred up their enemies,
12 the Arameans on the east and the Philistines on the west,
    and they devoured Israel with open mouth.
For all this his anger has not turned away;
    his hand is stretched out still.

13 The people did not turn to him who struck them,
    or seek the LORD of hosts.
14 So the LORD cut off from Israel head and tail,
    palm branch and reed in one day—
15 elders and dignitaries are the head,
    and prophets who teach lies are the tail;
16 for those who led this people led them astray,
    and those who were led by them were left in confusion.
17 That is why the Lord did not have pity on their young people,
    or compassion on their orphans and widows;
for everyone was godless and an evildoer,
    and every mouth spoke folly.
For all this his anger has not turned away,
    his hand is stretched out still.

18 For wickedness burned like a fire,
    consuming briers and thorns;

it kindled the thickets of the forest,
  and they swirled upward in a column of smoke.
19 Through the wrath of the LORD of hosts
  the land was burned,
and the people became like fuel for the fire;
  no one spared another.
20 They gorged on the right, but still were hungry,
  and they devoured on the left, but were not satisfied;
they devoured the flesh of their own kindred;
21 Manasseh devoured Ephraim,
  and Ephraim Manasseh, and together they were against Judah.
For all this his anger has not turned away;
  his hand is stretched out still.

10

Ah, you who make iniquitous decrees,
  who write oppressive statutes,
2 to turn aside the needy from justice
  and to rob the poor of my people of their right,
that widows may be your spoil,
  and that you may make the orphans your prey!
3 What will you do on the day of punishment,
  in the calamity that will come from far away?
To whom will you flee for help,
  and where will you leave your wealth,
4 so as not to crouch among the prisoners
  or fall among the slain?
For all this his anger has not turned away;
  his hand is stretched out still.

Arrogant Assyria Also Judged

5 Ah, Assyria, the rod of my anger—
  the club in their hands is my fury!
6 Against a godless nation I send him,
  and against the people of my wrath I command him,
to take spoil and seize plunder,
  and to tread them down like the mire of the streets.
7 But this is not what he intends,
  nor does he have this in mind;
but it is in his heart to destroy,
  and to cut off nations not a few.
8 For he says:
"Are not my commanders all kings?
9 Is not Calno like Carchemish?
  Is not Hamath like Arpad?
  Is not Samaria like Damascus?
10 As my hand has reached to the kingdoms of the idols
  whose images were greater than those of Jerusalem and Samaria,
11 shall I not do to Jerusalem and her idols
  what I have done to Samaria and her images?"

12 When the Lord has finished all his work on Mount Zion and on Jerusalem, he will punish the arrogant boasting of the king of Assyria and his haughty pride.
13 For he says: "By the strength of my hand I have done it,
  and by my wisdom, for I have understanding;
I have removed the boundaries of peoples,
  and have plundered their treasures;
like a bull I have brought down those who sat on thrones.
14 My hand has found, like a nest,
  the wealth of the peoples;
and as one gathers eggs that have been forsaken,
  so I have gathered all the earth;
and there was none that moved a wing,
  or opened its mouth, or chirped."
15 Shall the ax vaunt itself over the one who wields it,
  or the saw magnify itself against the one who handles it?
As if a rod should raise the one who lifts it up,
  or as if a staff should lift the one who is not wood!
16 Therefore the Sovereign, the LORD of hosts,
  will send wasting sickness among his stout warriors,
and under his glory a burning will be kindled,
  like the burning of fire.
17 The light of Israel will become a fire,
  and his Holy One a flame;
and it will burn and devour
  his thorns and briers in one day.
18 The glory of his forest and his fruitful land
  the LORD will destroy, both soul and body,
  and it will be as when an invalid wastes away.
19 The remnant of the trees of his forest will be so few
  that a child can write them down.

The Repentant Remnant of Israel

20 On that day the remnant of Israel and the survivors of the house of Jacob will no more lean on the one who struck them, but will lean on the LORD, the Holy One of Israel, in truth. ²¹A remnant will return, the remnant of Jacob, to the mighty God. ²²For though your people Israel were like the sand of the sea, only a remnant of them will return. Destruction is decreed, overflowing with righteousness. ²³For the Lord GOD of hosts will make a full end, as decreed, in all the earth.

24 Therefore thus says the Lord GOD of hosts: O my people, who live in Zion, do not be afraid of the Assyrians when they beat you with a rod and lift up their staff against you as the Egyptians did. ²⁵For in a very little while my indignation will come to an end, and my anger will be directed to their destruction. ²⁶The LORD of hosts will wield a whip against them, as when he struck Midian at the rock of Oreb; his staff will be over the sea, and he will lift it as he did in Egypt. ²⁷On that day his burden will be removed from your shoulder, and his yoke will be destroyed from your neck.

He has gone up from Rimmon,
28   he has come to Aiath;
    he has passed through Migron,
      at Michmash he stores his baggage;
29   they have crossed over the pass,
      at Geba they lodge for the night;
    Ramah trembles,
      Gibeah of Saul has fled.
30   Cry aloud, O daughter Gallim!
    Listen, O Laishah!
    Answer her, O Anathoth!
31   Madmenah is in flight,
      the inhabitants of Gebim flee for safety.
32   This very day he will halt at Nob,
    he will shake his fist
      at the mount of daughter Zion,
      the hill of Jerusalem.

33   Look, the Sovereign, the LORD of hosts,
    will lop the boughs with terrifying power;
    the tallest trees will be cut down,
      and the lofty will be brought low.
34   He will hack down the thickets of the
      forest with an ax,
    and Lebanon with its majestic trees
      will fall.

The Peaceful Kingdom

11
A shoot shall come out from the stump of Jesse,
    and a branch shall grow out of his roots.
2   The spirit of the LORD shall rest on him,
    the spirit of wisdom and understanding,
    the spirit of counsel and might,
    the spirit of knowledge and the fear of the
      LORD.
3   His delight shall be in the fear of the LORD.

He shall not judge by what his eyes see,
    or decide by what his ears hear;
4   but with righteousness he shall judge the poor,
    and decide with equity for the meek of the
      earth;
he shall strike the earth with the rod of his
    mouth,
    and with the breath of his lips he shall kill
      the wicked.
5   Righteousness shall be the belt around his
      waist,
    and faithfulness the belt around his loins.

6   The wolf shall live with the lamb,
    the leopard shall lie down with the kid,
  the calf and the lion and the fatling together,
    and a little child shall lead them.
7   The cow and the bear shall graze,
    their young shall lie down together;
    and the lion shall eat straw like the ox.
8   The nursing child shall play over the hole of
      the asp,
    and the weaned child shall put its hand on
      the adder's den.
9   They will not hurt or destroy
    on all my holy mountain;
for the earth will be full of the knowledge of
    the LORD
    as the waters cover the sea.

Return of the Remnant of Israel and Judah

10 On that day the root of Jesse shall stand as a signal to the peoples; the nations shall inquire of him, and his dwelling shall be glorious.

11 On that day the Lord will extend his hand yet a second time to recover the remnant that is left of his people, from Assyria, from Egypt, from Pathros, from Ethiopia, from Elam, from Shinar, from Hamath, and from the coastlands of the sea.

¹² He will raise a signal for the nations,
    and will assemble the outcasts of Israel,
and gather the dispersed of Judah
    from the four corners of the earth.
¹³ The jealousy of Ephraim shall depart,
    the hostility of Judah shall be cut off;
Ephraim shall not be jealous of Judah,
    and Judah shall not be hostile towards Ephraim.
¹⁴ But they shall swoop down on the backs of the Philistines in the west,
    together they shall plunder the people of the east.
They shall put forth their hand against Edom and Moab,
    and the Ammonites shall obey them.
¹⁵ And the LORD will utterly destroy
    the tongue of the sea of Egypt;
and will wave his hand over the River
    with his scorching wind;
and will split it into seven channels,
    and make a way to cross on foot;
¹⁶ so there shall be a highway from Assyria
    for the remnant that is left of his people,
as there was for Israel
    when they came up from the land of Egypt.

Thanksgiving and Praise

12

You will say in that day:
I will give thanks to you, O LORD,
    for though you were angry with me, your anger turned away,
and you comforted me.

² Surely God is my salvation;
    I will trust, and will not be afraid,
for the LORD GOD is my strength and my might;
    he has become my salvation.

3 With joy you will draw water from the wells of salvation. ⁴And you will say in that day:
Give thanks to the LORD,
    call on his name;
make known his deeds among the nations;
    proclaim that his name is exalted.

⁵ Sing praises to the LORD, for he has done gloriously;
    let this be known in all the earth.
⁶ Shout aloud and sing for joy, O royal Zion,
    for great in your midst is the Holy One of Israel.

Christ's Crucifixion is the central event of Christianity for most Christians. That God should suffer, through His son, the extreme agonies of humankind shows ultimate love for us. The sacrifice redeems us from our original sin and makes the heavenly kingdom and eternal life possible. Macduff Everton/© Corbis.

Introduction to the *Gospel of Matthew*

The "Fulfillment" of Mosaic Law

The question we might ask, moving into the *New Testament*, is what's new? I find that three items express what the "good news" (the literal translation of the term "Gospel") is about.

First, Jesus rewrites the Mosaic law. The "Sermon on the Mount" reinterprets the law as given to Moses at Mt. Sinai. In each case, when Jesus begins "You have heard it said," he refers to a specific law announced to the Israelites as reported in *Exodus*. This can be confusing since Jesus announces that he is not changing any of the ancient laws but instead is fulfilling them. How are we to understand this claim?

An excellent example is the law concerning divorce. In the Mosaic law divorce is permitted. Those seeking divorce must make a public announcement and receive an official certificate so that all in the community are aware that the divorce is real and has been officially sanctioned. Jesus, however, proclaims that divorce is forbidden, except in cases where the marriage partner has been unchaste (committed adultery). He explains that otherwise divorced persons are forced to find relationships that are adulterous.

In *Matthew* Jesus is questioned on this point by the Pharisees (Jewish Biblical purists) in Chapter 19. The Pharisees charge that Jesus has abolished the Law of God as given by Moses, something Jesus said he would never do. Jesus responds that the law reported to the Israelites by Moses is superseded by a statement that comes directly from God. Jesus refers to God's explanation to Adam and Eve in *Genesis* 2:24–45 that they have become one flesh and that no one can put them asunder. Jesus goes on to explain that Moses had to adjust the law given to the Israelites because those people were so brutish that they would have rebelled against Moses if he had not allowed them the liberality of easy divorce.

This is a bold move on the part of Jesus. He claims here that the law of Moses is incomplete (or "unfulfilled") because it is historically situated and that other portions of the Hebrew Bible provide a clearer understanding of God's laws for human beings.

Of course, throughout the "Sermon on the Mount" Jesus rewrites (his word is "fulfills") the law. Is murder forbidden? Not only that but anger (a form of murder accomplished in one's heart) is forbidden, and God will not accept the prayers of a person who has anger in his/her heart or even has someone angry at her/him. One must go and make peace with one's neighbor before God will hear one's prayers.

The typical fulfillment of the older law requires that we see our own hearts as the battleground between good and evil. It psychologizes, or makes inward, what previously was a civil law that commanded public behavior. There is a case to be made that the law of Moses already contains this inwardness since the Ten Commandments forbid "coveting" goods and the wives of neighbors (without mentioning any act that might follow from lust for goods or other persons). Thus, when Jesus teaches that there is such a thing as adultery of the heart (to look with lust upon a woman), he is simply restating one Mt. Sinai commandment to clarify another. As with the issue of divorce, Jesus sets one text from the Hebrew Bible against another in order to clarify and make perfect ("fulfill") God's law.

One part of the "Good News" or "Gospel," then, is that now, with Jesus, we have the law clarified, and just as God intended it to be known to His children.

Jesus is an excellent teacher with the power of putting things clearly. Thus, he reduces all the several hundred laws to two: "Love God with all your heart" and "Love your neighbor as yourself." This is a remarkable summary and an excellent example of what is meant when others comment in *Matthew* that Jesus teaches with authority.

Universalization

After the new version of the law, the second piece of good news is the creation of a universal religion. Judaism is for the Israelites and is not a missionary religion, i.e., does not actively seek converts. The covenant with the Jews is a national covenant and is exclusive (though *Exodus* 19:5–6 does raise some fascinating questions about what role the redemption of the Israelites is to play in the larger scheme of human history).

In *Matthew* Jesus is quite explicit that the new covenant is for all peoples (and even that the Jews are to be treated harshly for having been inattentive to the early covenant with God—the source, by the way, for much anti-semitic horror throughout European history). Thus, the incident with the Canaanite woman (*Matthew* 15:21–28) is meant to teach the disciples that Jesus' mission is to all people; as is the commission to the disciples in *Matthew* 28:16–20).

This turn to universal membership models very closely the Roman Empire itself, which extends across much of the known world at that time and includes many peoples. Christianity seems to be the first religious movement to embrace everyone and to emphasize that all human beings are brothers and sisters under God in precisely the same way and with the same status, so long as they accept Jesus.

Notable, too, is the role of women in the story of Jesus. Although none are disciples, many figure very prominently and take leading roles in events. The writings of Paul are not nearly so friendly to women, however.

An interesting question is whether it is more comfortable living next to a particularistic religious nation, such as the Jews or the Japanese (Shinto), or next to a Christian or Muslim nation (both aggressively missionary)? It may be unpleasant knowing that you are not wanted; however, it might be even more unpleasant to be preached at, and a good deal worse, by people who know what's best for you. The actual history here is not pretty!

Gospels—The Kingdom

This is the third of the items on "What's New with Christianity." As you recall, the first two are: (1) the "fulfillment" of the law—Jesus' teachings on the Mosaic law; (2) the covenant for all peoples (the universal religion); and the third (this message) the coming of the Kingdom.

You may recall that the Greeks have a different sense of the afterworld from the Christian account. For the Classical Greeks our souls take a journey to the underworld, where they remain for all eternity. This underworld is not reserved for good people only; all souls who have received the proper burial are released from this world to fly off (or sail off) to the next (you might recall what an issue this is in *Antigone*). In some extremely rare instances, a mortal may be lifted into the heavens by the gods (Hercules received such a gift, but he was partly a god to begin with; Oedipus in *Oedipus at Colonus*, the third of the Theban plays, also receives this rare blessing for the endurance of his faith in the gods). But in virtually all instances, the dead souls go down into the gloom (see the remarks of Achilles about all this in Homer's *Odyssey*).

The Israelites have a more shadowy version of what comes next. There is some mention of a place called "Sheol." But there isn't much done to specify what this is, who goes there, for how long, to experience what conditions, and so on. There is also mention of "Gehenna," a place associated with the stink of burning brimstone and sulfur (the actual place was the waste disposal site near Jerusalem). This would seem to be the origin of our notions of hell. But again there is no clear and consistent account of the afterlife there. There is also some mention of returning to the "Bosom of Abraham," which sounds rather like the return to one's family in the Greek tradition.

An interesting notation of this difference in the Hebrew tradition from what comes later is the King James translation of *Psalm* 23, where the Christian translator installs into the last line a notion of eternity that is not mentioned in the original Hebrew text.

All of this is written to emphasize the remarkable "Good News" in Christianity that death has been overcome (you recall the curse upon Adam) for those who abide by God's law. Not only is there a Heaven of eternal bliss for those who have lived the life God intended for us, but there is a Day of Judgment (or Doomsday—"Dome" the Anglo-Saxon word for "trial") for those who failed to do so.

While this world is certainly corrupted, a world where the best people suffer terribly at the hands of the power-hungry and sadistic, at the Day of Judgment all this will be reversed, and the "meek shall inherit the earth" and those who have refused to come to the banquet (see the "Parable of the Wedding Banquet"—*Matthew* 22) will be thrown "into the outer darkness, where there will be weeping and gnashing of teeth."

In *Matthew* this Judgment of the World seems imminent. There is a clear message of what to look for that will precede this Day of Judgment (*Matthew* 24) and even when readers of *Matthew* can expect this. *Matthew* 25 provides explicit information on hell, ". . . depart from me into the eternal fire prepared for the devil and his angels"; and on heaven for the righteous who receive "eternal life."

The "Good News" answers the terrors that human beings all face, the fear of death and obliteration, and with that the meaninglessness of an individual life. There have been, of course, other answers, but this one has captured the hearts of many.

It's too much to say that this "News" spread like wildfire. However, three centuries after the time of Jesus, the Roman Empire itself adopted Christianity as its state religion, when the Emperor Constantine, having been directed by visions of the Cross, conquered and converted Rome in 321 A.D. The power of Christianity to shape European history follows from that event.

Gospel of Matthew

The Genealogy of Jesus the Messiah

1 An account of the genealogy of Jesus the Messiah, the son of David, the son of Abraham.

2 Abraham was the father of Isaac, and Isaac the father of Jacob, and Jacob the father of Judah and his brothers, ³and Judah the father of Perez and Zerah by Tamar, and Perez the father of Hezron, and Hezron the father of Aram, ⁴and Aram the father of Aminadab, and Aminadab the father of Nahshon, and Nahshon the father of Salmon, ⁵and Salmon the father of Boaz by Rahab, and Boaz the father of Obed by Ruth, and Obed the father of Jesse, ⁶and Jesse the father of King David.

And David was the father of Solomon by the wife of Uriah, ⁷and Solomon the father of Rehoboam, and Rehoboam the father of Abijah, and Abijah the father of Asaph, ⁸and Asaph the father of Jehoshaphat, and Jehoshaphat the father of Joram, and Joram the father of Uzziah, ⁹and Uzziah the father of Jotham, and Jotham the father of Ahaz, and Ahaz the father of Hezekiah, ¹⁰and Hezekiah the father of Manasseh, and Manasseh the father of Amos, and Amos the father of Josiah, ¹¹and Josiah the father of Jechoniah and his brothers, at the time of the deportation to Babylon.

12 And after the deportation to Babylon: Jechoniah was the father of Salathiel, and Salathiel the father of Zerubbabel, ¹³and Zerubbabel the father of Abiud, and Abiud the father of Eliakim, and Eliakim the father of Azor, ¹⁴and Azor the father of Zadok, and Zadok the father of Achim, and Achim the father of Eliud, ¹⁵and Eliud the father of Eleazar, and Eleazar the father of Matthan, and Matthan the father of Jacob, ¹⁶and Jacob the father of Joseph the husband of Mary, of whom Jesus was born, who is called the Messiah.

17 So all the generations from Abraham to David are fourteen generations; and from David to the deportation to Babylon, fourteen generations; and from the deportation to Babylon to the Messiah, fourteen generations.

The Birth of Jesus the Messiah

18 Now the birth of Jesus the Messiah took place in this way. When his mother Mary had been engaged to Joseph, but before they lived together, she was found to be with child from the Holy Spirit. ¹⁹Her husband Joseph, being a righteous man and unwilling to expose her to public disgrace, planned to dismiss her quietly. ²⁰But just when he had resolved to do this, an angel of the Lord appeared to him in a dream and said, "Joseph, son of David, do not be afraid to take Mary as your wife, for the child conceived in her is from the Holy Spirit. ²¹She will bear a son, and you are to name him Jesus, for he will save his people from their sins." ²²All this took place to fulfill what had been spoken by the Lord through the prophet:

23 "Look, the virgin shall conceive and bear a son,
 and they shall name him Emmanuel,"

which means, "God is with us." ²⁴When Joseph awoke from sleep, he did as the angel of the Lord commanded him; he took her as his wife, ²⁵but had no marital relations with her until she had borne a son; and he named him Jesus.

Scripture quotations are from the *New Revised Standard Version of the Bible*, copyright 1989 by the Division of Christian Education of the National Council of the Churches of Christ in the USA. Used by permission. All rights reserved.

The Visit of the Wise Men

2 In the time of King Herod, after Jesus was born in Bethlehem of Judea, wise men from the East came to Jerusalem, ²asking, "Where is the child who has been born king of the Jews? For we observed his star at its rising, and have come to pay him homage." ³When King Herod heard this, he was frightened, and all Jerusalem with him; ⁴and calling together all the chief priests and scribes of the people, he inquired of them where the Messiah was to be born. ⁵They told him, "In Bethlehem of Judea; for so it has been written by the prophet:
⁶ 'And you, Bethlehem, in the land of Judah,
   are by no means least among the rulers of
      Judah;
   for from you shall come a ruler
      who is to shepherd my people Israel.'"

7 Then Herod secretly called for the wise men and learned from them the exact time when the star had appeared. ⁸Then he sent them to Bethlehem, saying, "Go and search diligently for the child; and when you have found him, bring me word so that I may also go and pay him homage." ⁹When they had heard the king, they set out; and there, ahead of them, went the star that they had seen at its rising, until it stopped over the place where the child was. ¹⁰When they saw that the star had stopped, they were overwhelmed with joy. ¹¹On entering the house, they saw the child with Mary his mother; and they knelt down and paid him homage. Then, opening their treasure chests, they offered him gifts of gold, frankincense, and myrrh. ¹²And having been warned in a dream not to return to Herod, they left for their own country by another road.

The Escape to Egypt

13 Now after they had left, an angel of the Lord appeared to Joseph in a dream and said, "Get up, take the child and his mother, and flee to Egypt, and remain there until I tell you; for Herod is about to search for the child, to destroy him." ¹⁴Then Joseph got up, took the child and his mother by night, and went to Egypt, ¹⁵and remained there until the death of Herod. This was to fulfill what had been spoken by the Lord through the prophet, "Out of Egypt I have called my son."

The Massacre of the Infants

16 When Herod saw that he had been tricked by the wise men, he was infuriated, and he sent and killed all the children in and around Bethlehem who were two years old or under, according to the time that he had learned from the wise men. ¹⁷Then was fulfilled what had been spoken through the prophet Jeremiah:
¹⁸ "A voice was heard in Ramah,
      wailing and loud lamentation,
   Rachel weeping for her children;
      she refused to be consoled, because they are
         no more."

The Return from Egypt

19 When Herod died, an angel of the Lord suddenly appeared in a dream to Joseph in Egypt and said, ²⁰"Get up, take the child and his mother, and go to the land of Israel, for those who were seeking the child's life are dead." ²¹Then Joseph got up, took the child and his mother, and went to the land of Israel. ²²But when he heard that Archelaus was ruling over Judea in place of his father Herod, he was afraid to go there. And after being warned in a dream, he went away to the district of Galilee. ²³There he made his home in a town called Nazareth, so that what had been spoken through the prophets might be fulfilled, "He will be called a Nazorean."

The Proclamation of John the Baptist

3 In those days John the Baptist appeared in the wilderness of Judea, proclaiming, ²"Repent, for the kingdom of heaven has come near." ³This is the one of whom the prophet Isaiah spoke when he said,
   "The voice of one crying out in the wilderness:
      'Prepare the way of the Lord, make his paths
         straight.'"

⁴Now John wore clothing of camel's hair with a leather belt around his waist, and his food was locusts and wild honey. ⁵Then the people of Jerusalem and all Judea were going out to him, and all the region along the Jordan, ⁶and they were baptized by him in the river Jordan, confessing their sins.

7 But when he saw many Pharisees and Sadducees coming for baptism, he said to them, "You brood of vipers! Who warned you to flee from the wrath to come? ⁸Bear fruit worthy of repentance. ⁹Do not presume to say to yourselves, 'We have Abraham as our ancestor'; for I tell you, God is able from these stones to raise up children to Abraham. ¹⁰Even now the ax is lying at the root of the trees; every tree therefore that does not bear good fruit is cut down and thrown into the fire.

11 "I baptize you with water for repentance, but one who is more powerful than I is coming after me; I am not worthy to carry his sandals. He will baptize you with the Holy Spirit and fire. ¹²His winnowing fork is in his hand, and he will clear his threshing floor and will gather his wheat into the granary; but the chaff he will burn with unquenchable fire."

The Baptism of Jesus

13 Then Jesus came from Galilee to John at the Jordan, to be baptized by him. ¹⁴John would have prevented him, saying, "I need to be baptized by you, and do you come to me?"
¹⁵But Jesus answered him, "Let it be so now; for it is proper for us in this way to fulfill all righteousness." Then he consented. ¹⁶And when Jesus had been baptized, just as he came up from the water, suddenly the heavens were opened to him and he saw the Spirit of God descending like a dove and alighting on him. ¹⁷And a voice from heaven said, "This is my Son, the Beloved, with whom I am well pleased."

The Temptation of Jesus

4 Then Jesus was led up by the Spirit into the wilderness to be tempted by the devil. ²He fasted forty days and forty nights, and afterwards he was famished. ³The tempter came and said to him, "If you are the Son of God, command these stones to become loaves of bread." ⁴But he answered, "It is written,

'One does not live by bread alone,
 but by every word that comes from the mouth of God.'"

5 Then the devil took him to the holy city and placed him on the pinnacle of the temple, ⁶saying to him, "If you are the Son of God, throw yourself down; for it is written,

'He will command his angels concerning you,'
 and 'On their hands they will bear you up,
 so that you will not dash your foot against a stone.'"

⁷Jesus said to him, "Again it is written, 'Do not put the Lord your God to the test.'"

8 Again, the devil took him to a very high mountain and showed him all the kingdoms of the world and their splendor; ⁹and he said to him, "All these I will give you, if you will fall down and worship me." ¹⁰Jesus said to him, "Away with you, Satan! for it is written,

'Worship the Lord your God,
 and serve only him.'"

¹¹Then the devil left him, and suddenly angels came and waited on him.

Jesus Begins His Ministry in Galilee

12 Now when Jesus heard that John had been arrested, he withdrew to Galilee. ¹³He left Nazareth and made his home in Capernaum by the sea, in the territory of Zebulun and Naphtali, ¹⁴so that what had been spoken through the prophet Isaiah might be fulfilled:
¹⁵ "Land of Zebulun, land of Naphtali,
 on the road by the sea, across the Jordan,
 Galilee of the Gentiles—
¹⁶ the people who sat in darkness
 have seen a great light,
 and for those who sat in the region and
 shadow of death
 light has dawned."

¹⁷From that time Jesus began to proclaim, "Repent, for the kingdom of heaven has come near."

Jesus Calls the First Disciples

18 As he walked by the Sea of Galilee, he saw two brothers, Simon, who is called Peter, and

Andrew his brother, casting a net into the sea—for they were fishermen. ¹⁹And he said to them, "Follow me, and I will make you fish for people." ²⁰Immediately they left their nets and followed him. ²¹As he went from there, he saw two other brothers, James son of Zebedee and his brother John, in the boat with their father Zebedee, mending their nets, and he called them. ²²Immediately they left the boat and their father, and followed him.

Jesus Ministers to Crowds of People

23 Jesus went throughout Galilee, teaching in their synagogues and proclaiming the good news of the kingdom and curing every disease and every sickness among the people. ²⁴So his fame spread throughout all Syria, and they brought to him all the sick, those who were afflicted with various diseases and pains, demoniacs, epileptics, and paralytics, and he cured them. ²⁵And great crowds followed him from Galilee, the Decapolis, Jerusalem, Judea, and from beyond the Jordan.

The Beatitudes

5 When Jesus saw the crowds, he went up the mountain; and after he sat down, his disciples came to him. ²Then he began to speak, and taught them, saying:

3 "Blessed are the poor in spirit, for theirs is the kingdom of heaven.

4 "Blessed are those who mourn, for they will be comforted.

5 "Blessed are the meek, for they will inherit the earth.

6 "Blessed are those who hunger and thirst for righteousness, for they will be filled.

7 "Blessed are the merciful, for they will receive mercy.

8 "Blessed are the pure in heart, for they will see God.

9 "Blessed are the peacemakers, for they will be called children of God.

10 "Blessed are those who are persecuted for righteousness' sake, for theirs is the kingdom of heaven.

11 "Blessed are you when people revile you and persecute you and utter all kinds of evil against you falsely on my account. ¹²Rejoice and be glad, for your reward is great in heaven, for in the same way they persecuted the prophets who were before you.

Salt and Light

13 "You are the salt of the earth; but if salt has lost its taste, how can its saltiness be restored? It is no longer good for anything, but is thrown out and trampled under foot.

14 "You are the light of the world. A city built on a hill cannot be hid. ¹⁵No one after lighting a lamp puts it under the bushel basket, but on the lampstand, and it gives light to all in the house. ¹⁶In the same way, let your light shine before others, so that they may see your good works and give glory to your Father in heaven.

The Law and the Prophets

17 "Do not think that I have come to abolish the law or the prophets; I have come not to abolish but to fulfill. ¹⁸For truly I tell you, until heaven and earth pass away, not one letter, not one stroke of a letter, will pass from the law until all is accomplished. ¹⁹Therefore, whoever breaks one of the least of these commandments, and teaches others to do the same, will be called least in the kingdom of heaven; but whoever does them and teaches them will be called great in the kingdom of heaven. ²⁰For I tell you, unless your righteousness exceeds that of the scribes and Pharisees, you will never enter the kingdom of heaven.

Concerning Anger

21 "You have heard that it was said to those of ancient times, 'You shall not murder'; and 'whoever murders shall be liable to judgment.' ²²But I say to you that if you are angry with a brother or sister, you will be liable to judgment; and if you insult a brother or sister, you will be liable to the council; and if you say, 'You fool,' you will be liable to the hell of fire. ²³So when you are offering your gift at the altar, if you remem-

ber that your brother or sister has something against you, ²⁴leave your gift there before the altar and go; first be reconciled to your brother or sister, and then come and offer your gift. ²⁵Come to terms quickly with your accuser while you are on the way to court with him, or your accuser may hand you over to the judge, and the judge to the guard, and you will be thrown into prison. ²⁶Truly I tell you, you will never get out until you have paid the last penny.

Concerning Adultery

27 "You have heard that it was said, 'You shall not commit adultery.' ²⁸But I say to you that everyone who looks at a woman with lust has already committed adultery with her in his heart. ²⁹If your right eye causes you to sin, tear it out and throw it away; it is better for you to lose one of your members than for your whole body to be thrown into hell. ³⁰And if your right hand causes you to sin, cut it off and throw it away; it is better for you to lose one of your members than for your whole body to go into hell.

Concerning Divorce

31 "It was also said, 'Whoever divorces his wife, let him give her a certificate of divorce.' ³²But I say to you that anyone who divorces his wife, except on the ground of unchastity, causes her to commit adultery; and whoever marries a divorced woman commits adultery.

Concerning Oaths

33 "Again, you have heard that it was said to those of ancient times, 'You shall not swear falsely, but carry out the vows you have made to the Lord.' ³⁴But I say to you, Do not swear at all, either by heaven, for it is the throne of God, ³⁵or by the earth, for it is his footstool, or by Jerusalem, for it is the city of the great King. ³⁶And do not swear by your head, for you cannot make one hair white or black. ³⁷Let your word be 'Yes, Yes' or 'No, No'; anything more than this comes from the evil one.

Concerning Retaliation

38 "You have heard that it was said, 'An eye for an eye and a tooth for a tooth.' ³⁹But I say to you, Do not resist an evildoer. But if anyone strikes you on the right cheek, turn the other also; ⁴⁰and if anyone wants to sue you and take your coat, give your cloak as well; ⁴¹and if anyone forces you to go one mile, go also the second mile. ⁴²Give to everyone who begs from you, and do not refuse anyone who wants to borrow from you.

Love for Enemies

43 "You have heard that it was said, 'You shall love your neighbor and hate your enemy.' ⁴⁴But I say to you, Love your enemies and pray for those who persecute you, ⁴⁵so that you may be children of your Father in heaven; for he makes his sun rise on the evil and on the good, and sends rain on the righteous and on the unrighteous. ⁴⁶For if you love those who love you, what reward do you have? Do not even the tax collectors do the same? ⁴⁷And if you greet only your brothers and sisters, what more are you doing than others? Do not even the Gentiles do the same? ⁴⁸Be perfect, therefore, as your heavenly Father is perfect.

Concerning Almsgiving

6 "Beware of practicing your piety before others in order to be seen by them; for then you have no reward from your Father in heaven.

2 "So whenever you give alms, do not sound a trumpet before you, as the hypocrites do in the synagogues and in the streets, so that they may be praised by others. Truly I tell you, they have received their reward. ³But when you give alms, do not let your left hand know what your right hand is doing, ⁴so that your alms may be done in secret; and your Father who sees in secret will reward you.

Concerning Prayer

5 "And whenever you pray, do not be like the hypocrites; for they love to stand and pray in the synagogues and at the street corners, so that they may be seen by others. Truly I tell you, they have received their reward. ⁶But whenever you pray, go into your room and shut the door and pray to your Father who is in secret; and your Father who sees in secret will reward you.

7 "When you are praying, do not heap up empty phrases as the Gentiles do; for they think that they will be heard because of their many words. ⁸Do not be like them, for your Father knows what you need before you ask him.
9 "Pray then in this way:
Our Father in heaven,
hallowed be your name.
10 Your kingdom come.
Your will be done,
on earth as it is in heaven.
11 Give us this day our daily bread.
12 And forgive us our debts,
as we also have forgiven our debtors.
13 And do not bring us to the time of trial,
but rescue us from the evil one.
¹⁴For if you forgive others their trespasses, your heavenly Father will also forgive you; ¹⁵but if you do not forgive others, neither will your Father forgive your trespasses.

Concerning Fasting

16 "And whenever you fast, do not look dismal, like the hypocrites, for they disfigure their faces so as to show others that they are fasting. Truly I tell you, they have received their reward. ¹⁷But when you fast, put oil on your head and wash your face, ¹⁸so that your fasting may be seen not by others but by your Father who is in secret; and your Father who sees in secret will reward you.

Concerning Treasures

19 "Do not store up for yourselves treasures on earth, where moth and rust consume and where thieves break in and steal; ²⁰but store up for yourselves treasures in heaven, where neither moth nor rust consumes and where thieves do not break in and steal. ²¹For where your treasure is, there your heart will be also.

The Sound Eye

22 "The eye is the lamp of the body. So, if your eye is healthy, your whole body will be full of light; ²³but if your eye is unhealthy, your whole body will be full of darkness. If then the light in you is darkness, how great is the darkness!

Serving Two Masters

24 "No one can serve two masters; for a slave will either hate the one and love the other, or be devoted to the one and despise the other. You cannot serve God and wealth.

Do Not Worry

25 "Therefore I tell you, do not worry about your life, what you will eat or what you will drink, or about your body, what you will wear. Is not life more than food, and the body more than clothing? ²⁶Look at the birds of the air; they neither sow nor reap nor gather into barns, and yet your heavenly Father feeds them. Are you not of more value than they? ²⁷And can any of you by worrying add a single hour to your span of life? ²⁸And why do you worry about clothing? Consider the lilies of the field, how they grow; they neither toil nor spin, ²⁹yet I tell you, even Solomon in all his glory was not clothed like one of these. ³⁰But if God so clothes the grass of the field, which is alive today and tomorrow is thrown into the oven, will he not much more clothe you—you of little faith? ³¹Therefore do not worry, saying, 'What will we eat?' or 'What will we drink?' or 'What will we wear?' ³²For it is the Gentiles who strive for all these things; and indeed your heavenly Father knows that you need all these things. ³³But strive first for the kingdom of God and his righteousness, and all these things will be given to you as well.

34 "So do not worry about tomorrow, for tomorrow will bring worries of its own. Today's trouble is enough for today.

Judging Others

7 "Do not judge, so that you may not be judged. ²For with the judgment you make you will be judged, and the measure you give will be the measure you get. ³Why do you see the speck in your neighbor's eye, but do not notice the log in your own eye? ⁴Or how can you say to your neighbor, 'Let me take the speck out of your eye,' while the log is in your own eye? ⁵You hypocrite, first take the log out of your own eye, and then you will see clearly to take the speck out of your neighbor's eye.

Profaning the Holy

6 "Do not give what is holy to dogs; and do not throw your pearls before swine, or they will trample them under foot and turn and maul you.

Ask, Search, Knock

7 "Ask, and it will be given you; search, and you will find; knock, and the door will be opened for you. ⁸For everyone who asks receives, and everyone who searches finds, and for everyone who knocks, the door will be opened. ⁹Is there anyone among you who, if your child asks for bread, will give a stone? ¹⁰Or if the child asks for a fish, will give a snake? ¹¹If you then, who are evil, know how to give good gifts to your children, how much more will your Father in heaven give good things to those who ask him!

The Golden Rule

12 "In everything do to others as you would have them do to you; for this is the law and the prophets.

The Narrow Gate

13 "Enter through the narrow gate; for the gate is wide and the road is easy that leads to destruction, and there are many who take it. ¹⁴For the gate is narrow and the road is hard that leads to life, and there are few who find it.

A Tree and Its Fruit

15 "Beware of false prophets, who come to you in sheep's clothing but inwardly are ravenous wolves. ¹⁶You will know them by their fruits. Are grapes gathered from thorns, or figs from thistles? ¹⁷In the same way, every good tree bears good fruit, but the bad tree bears bad fruit. ¹⁸A good tree cannot bear bad fruit, nor can a bad tree bear good fruit. ¹⁹Every tree that does not bear good fruit is cut down and thrown into the fire. ²⁰Thus you will know them by their fruits.

Concerning Self-Deception

21 "Not everyone who says to me, 'Lord, Lord,' will enter the kingdom of heaven, but only the one who does the will of my Father in heaven. ²²On that day many will say to me, 'Lord, Lord, did we not prophesy in your name, and cast out demons in your name, and do many deeds of power in your name?' ²³Then I will declare to them, 'I never knew you; go away from me, you evildoers.'

Hearers and Doers

24 "Everyone then who hears these words of mine and acts on them will be like a wise man who built his house on rock. ²⁵The rain fell, the floods came, and the winds blew and beat on that house, but it did not fall, because it had been founded on rock. ²⁶And everyone who hears these words of mine and does not act on them will be like a foolish man who built his house on sand. ²⁷The rain fell, and the floods came, and the winds blew and beat against that house, and it fell—and great was its fall!"

28 Now when Jesus had finished saying these things, the crowds were astounded at his teaching, [29]for he taught them as one having authority, and not as their scribes.

Jesus Cleanses a Leper

8 When Jesus had come down from the mountain, great crowds followed him; [2]and there was a leper who came to him and knelt before him, saying, "Lord, if you choose, you can make me clean." [3]He stretched out his hand and touched him, saying, "I do choose. Be made clean!" Immediately his leprosy was cleansed. [4]Then Jesus said to him, "See that you say nothing to anyone; but go, show yourself to the priest, and offer the gift that Moses commanded, as a testimony to them."

Jesus Heals a Centurion's Servant

5 When he entered Capernaum, a centurion came to him, appealing to him [6]and saying, "Lord, my servant is lying at home paralyzed, in terrible distress." [7]And he said to him, "I will come and cure him." [8]The centurion answered, "Lord, I am not worthy to have you come under my roof; but only speak the word, and my servant will be healed. [9]For I also am a man under authority, with soldiers under me; and I say to one, 'Go,' and he goes, and to another, 'Come,' and he comes, and to my slave, 'Do this,' and the slave does it." [10]When Jesus heard him, he was amazed and said to those who followed him, "Truly I tell you, in no one in Israel have I found such faith. [11]I tell you, many will come from east and west and will eat with Abraham and Isaac and Jacob in the kingdom of heaven, [12]while the heirs of the kingdom will be thrown into the outer darkness, where there will be weeping and gnashing of teeth." [13]And to the centurion Jesus said, "Go; let it be done for you according to your faith." And the servant was healed in that hour.

Jesus Heals Many at Peter's House

14 When Jesus entered Peter's house, he saw his mother-in-law lying in bed with a fever; [15]he touched her hand, and the fever left her, and she got up and began to serve him. [16]That evening they brought to him many who were possessed with demons; and he cast out the spirits with a word, and cured all who were sick. [17]This was to fulfill what had been spoken through the prophet Isaiah, "He took our infirmities and bore our diseases."

Would-Be Followers of Jesus

18 Now when Jesus saw great crowds around him, he gave orders to go over to the other side. [19]A scribe then approached and said, "Teacher, I will follow you wherever you go." [20]And Jesus said to him, "Foxes have holes, and birds of the air have nests; but the Son of Man has nowhere to lay his head." [21]Another of his disciples said to him, "Lord, first let me go and bury my father." [22]But Jesus said to him, "Follow me, and let the dead bury their own dead."

Jesus Stills the Storm

23 And when he got into the boat, his disciples followed him. [24]A windstorm arose on the sea, so great that the boat was being swamped by the waves; but he was asleep. [25]And they went and woke him up, saying, "Lord, save us! We are perishing!" [26]And he said to them, "Why are you afraid, you of little faith?" Then he got up and rebuked the winds and the sea; and there was a dead calm. [27]They were amazed, saying, "What sort of man is this, that even the winds and the sea obey him?"

Jesus Heals the Gadarene Demoniacs

28 When he came to the other side, to the country of the Gadarenes, two demoniacs coming out of the tombs met him. They were so fierce

that no one could pass that way. ²⁹Suddenly they shouted, "What have you to do with us, Son of God? Have you come here to torment us before the time?" ³⁰Now a large herd of swine was feeding at some distance from them. ³¹The demons begged him, "If you cast us out, send us into the herd of swine." ³²And he said to them, "Go!" So they came out and entered the swine; and suddenly, the whole herd rushed down the steep bank into the sea and perished in the water. ³³The swineherds ran off, and on going into the town, they told the whole story about what had happened to the demoniacs. ³⁴Then the whole town came out to meet Jesus; and when they saw him, they begged him to leave their neighborhood.

9

¹And after getting into a boat he crossed the sea and came to his own town.

Jesus Heals a Paralytic

2 And just then some people were carrying a paralyzed man lying on a bed. When Jesus saw their faith, he said to the paralytic, "Take heart, son; your sins are forgiven." ³Then some of the scribes said to themselves, "This man is blaspheming." ⁴But Jesus, perceiving their thoughts, said, "Why do you think evil in your hearts? ⁵For which is easier, to say, 'Your sins are forgiven,' or to say, 'Stand up and walk'? ⁶But so that you may know that the Son of Man has authority on earth to forgive sins"—he then said to the paralytic—" Stand up, take your bed and go to your home." ⁷And he stood up and went to his home. ⁸When the crowds saw it, they were filled with awe, and they glorified God, who had given such authority to human beings.

The Call of Matthew

9 As Jesus was walking along, he saw a man called Matthew sitting at the tax booth; and he said to him, "Follow me." And he got up and followed him.

10 And as he sat at dinner in the house, many tax collectors and sinners came and were sitting with him and his disciples. ¹¹When the Pharisees saw this, they said to his disciples, "Why does your teacher eat with tax collectors and sinners?"

¹²But when he heard this, he said, "Those who are well have no need of a physician, but those who are sick. ¹³Go and learn what this means, 'I desire mercy, not sacrifice.' For I have come to call not the righteous but sinners."

The Question about Fasting

14 Then the disciples of John came to him, saying, "Why do we and the Pharisees fast often, but your disciples do not fast?" ¹⁵And Jesus said to them, "The wedding guests cannot mourn as long as the bridegroom is with them, can they? The days will come when the bridegroom is taken away from them, and then they will fast. ¹⁶No one sews a piece of unshrunk cloth on an old cloak, for the patch pulls away from the cloak, and a worse tear is made. ¹⁷Neither is new wine put into old wineskins; otherwise, the skins burst, and the wine is spilled, and the skins are destroyed; but new wine is put into fresh wineskins, and so both are preserved."

A Girl Restored to Life and a Woman Healed

18 While he was saying these things to them, suddenly a leader of the synagogue came in and knelt before him, saying, "My daughter has just died; but come and lay your hand on her, and she will live." ¹⁹And Jesus got up and followed him, with his disciples. ²⁰Then suddenly a woman who had been suffering from hemorrhages for twelve years came up behind him and touched the fringe of his cloak, ²¹for she said to herself, "If I only touch his cloak, I will be made well." ²²Jesus turned, and seeing her he said, "Take heart, daughter; your faith has made you well." And instantly the woman was made well. ²³When Jesus came to the leader's house and saw the flute players and the crowd making a commotion, ²⁴he said, "Go away; for the girl is not dead but sleeping." And they laughed at him. ²⁵But when the crowd had been put outside, he went in and took her by the hand, and the girl got up. ²⁶And the report of this spread throughout that district.

Jesus Heals Two Blind Men

27 As Jesus went on from there, two blind men followed him, crying loudly, "Have mercy on us, Son of David!" ²⁸When he entered the house, the blind men came to him; and Jesus said to them, "Do you believe that I am able to do this?" They said to him, "Yes, Lord." ²⁹Then he touched their eyes and said, "According to your faith let it be done to you." ³⁰And their eyes were opened. Then Jesus sternly ordered them, "See that no one knows of this." ³¹But they went away and spread the news about him throughout that district.

Jesus Heals One Who Was Mute

32 After they had gone away, a demoniac who was mute was brought to him. ³³And when the demon had been cast out, the one who had been mute spoke; and the crowds were amazed and said, "Never has anything like this been seen in Israel." ³⁴But the Pharisees said, "By the ruler of the demons he casts out the demons."

The Harvest Is Great, the Laborers Few

35 Then Jesus went about all the cities and villages, teaching in their synagogues, and proclaiming the good news of the kingdom, and curing every disease and every sickness. ³⁶When he saw the crowds, he had compassion for them, because they were harassed and helpless, like sheep without a shepherd. ³⁷Then he said to his disciples, "The harvest is plentiful, but the laborers are few; ³⁸therefore ask the Lord of the harvest to send out laborers into his harvest."

The Twelve Apostles

10 Then Jesus summoned his twelve disciples and gave them authority over unclean spirits, to cast them out, and to cure every disease and every sickness. ²These are the names of the twelve apostles: first, Simon, also known as Peter, and his brother Andrew; James son of Zebedee, and his brother John; ³Philip and Bartholomew; Thomas and Matthew the tax collector; James son of Alphaeus, and Thaddaeus; ⁴Simon the Cananaean, and Judas Iscariot, the one who betrayed him.

The Mission of the Twelve

5 These twelve Jesus sent out with the following instructions: "Go nowhere among the Gentiles, and enter no town of the Samaritans, ⁶but go rather to the lost sheep of the house of Israel. ⁷As you go, proclaim the good news, 'The kingdom of heaven has come near.' ⁸Cure the sick, raise the dead, cleanse the lepers, cast out demons. You received without payment; give without payment. ⁹Take no gold, or silver, or copper in your belts, ¹⁰no bag for your journey, or two tunics, or sandals, or a staff; for laborers deserve their food. ¹¹Whatever town or village you enter, find out who in it is worthy, and stay there until you leave. ¹²As you enter the house, greet it. ¹³If the house is worthy, let your peace come upon it; but if it is not worthy, let your peace return to you. ¹⁴If anyone will not welcome you or listen to your words, shake off the dust from your feet as you leave that house or town. ¹⁵Truly I tell you, it will be more tolerable for the land of Sodom and Gomorrah on the day of judgment than for that town.

Coming Persecutions

16 "See, I am sending you out like sheep into the midst of wolves; so be wise as serpents and innocent as doves. ¹⁷Beware of them, for they will hand you over to councils and flog you in their synagogues; ¹⁸and you will be dragged before governors and kings because of me, as a testimony to them and the Gentiles. ¹⁹When they hand you over, do not worry about how you are to speak or what you are to say; for what you are to say will be given to you at that time; ²⁰for it is not you who speak, but the Spirit of your Father speaking through you. ²¹Brother will betray brother to death, and a father his child, and children will rise against parents and have them put to death; ²²and you will be hated by all because of my name. But the one who endures to the end

will be saved. ²³When they persecute you in one town, flee to the next; for truly I tell you, you will not have gone through all the towns of Israel before the Son of Man comes.

24 "A disciple is not above the teacher, nor a slave above the master; ²⁵it is enough for the disciple to be like the teacher, and the slave like the master. If they have called the master of the house Beelzebul, how much more will they malign those of his household!

Whom to Fear

26 "So have no fear of them; for nothing is covered up that will not be uncovered, and nothing secret that will not become known. ²⁷What I say to you in the dark, tell in the light; and what you hear whispered, proclaim from the housetops. ²⁸Do not fear those who kill the body but cannot kill the soul; rather fear him who can destroy both soul and body in hell. ²⁹Are not two sparrows sold for a penny? Yet not one of them will fall to the ground apart from your Father. ³⁰And even the hairs of your head are all counted. ³¹So do not be afraid; you are of more value than many sparrows.

32 "Everyone therefore who acknowledges me before others, I also will acknowledge before my Father in heaven; ³³but whoever denies me before others, I also will deny before my Father in heaven.

Not Peace, but a Sword

34 "Do not think that I have come to bring peace to the earth; I have not come to bring peace, but a sword.
35 For I have come to set a man against his father,
and a daughter against her mother,
and a daughter-in-law against her mother-in-law;
36 and one's foes will be members of one's own household.
³⁷Whoever loves father or mother more than
me is not worthy of me; and whoever
loves son or daughter more than me is
not worthy of me; ³⁸and whoever does
not take up the cross and follow me is
not worthy of me. ³⁹Those who find
their life will lose it, and those who
lose their life for my sake will find it.

Rewards

40 "Whoever welcomes you welcomes me, and whoever welcomes me welcomes the one who sent me. ⁴¹Whoever welcomes a prophet in the name of a prophet will receive a prophet's reward; and whoever welcomes a righteous person in the name of a righteous person will receive the reward of the righteous; ⁴²and whoever gives even a cup of cold water to one of these little ones in the name of a disciple—truly I tell you, none of these will lose their reward."

11 Now when Jesus had finished instructing his twelve disciples, he went on from there to teach and proclaim his message in their cities.

Messengers from John the Baptist

2 When John heard in prison what the Messiah was doing, he sent word by his disciples ³and said to him, "Are you the one who is to come, or are we to wait for another?" ⁴Jesus answered them, "Go and tell John what you hear and see: ⁵the blind receive their sight, the lame walk, the lepers are cleansed, the deaf hear, the dead are raised, and the poor have good news brought to them. ⁶And blessed is anyone who takes no offense at me."

Jesus Praises John the Baptist

7 As they went away, Jesus began to speak to the crowds about John: "What did you go out into the wilderness to look at? A reed shaken by the wind? ⁸What then did you go out to see? Someone dressed in soft robes? Look, those who wear soft robes are in royal palaces. ⁹What then did you go out to see? A prophet? Yes, I tell you, and more than a prophet. ¹⁰This is the one about whom it is written,
'See, I am sending my messenger ahead of you,
who will prepare your way before you.'

¹¹"Truly I tell you, among those born of women no one has arisen greater than John the Baptist; yet the least in the kingdom of heaven is greater than he. ¹²From the days of John the Baptist until now the kingdom of heaven has suffered violence, and the violent take it by force. ¹³For all the prophets and the law prophesied until John came; ¹⁴and if you are willing to accept it, he is Elijah who is to come. ¹⁵Let anyone with ears listen!

16 "But to what will I compare this generation? It is like children sitting in the marketplaces and calling to one another,

¹⁷ 'We played the flute for you, and you did not dance;
we wailed, and you did not mourn.'

¹⁸For John came neither eating nor drinking, and they say, 'He has a demon'; ¹⁹the Son of Man came eating and drinking, and they say, 'Look, a glutton and a drunkard, a friend of tax collectors and sinners!' Yet wisdom is vindicated by her deeds."

Woes to Unrepentant Cities

20 Then he began to reproach the cities in which most of his deeds of power had been done, because they did not repent. ²¹"Woe to you, Chorazin! Woe to you, Bethsaida! For if the deeds of power done in you had been done in Tyre and Sidon, they would have repented long ago in sackcloth and ashes. ²²But I tell you, on the day of judgment it will be more tolerable for Tyre and Sidon than for you. ²³And you, Capernaum,

will you be exalted to heaven?

No, you will be brought down to Hades. For if the deeds of power done in you had been done in Sodom, it would have remained until this day. ²⁴But I tell you that on the day of judgment it will be more tolerable for the land of Sodom than for you."

Jesus Thanks His Father

25 At that time Jesus said, "I thank you, Father, Lord of heaven and earth, because you have hidden these things from the wise and the intelligent and have revealed them to infants; ²⁶yes, Father, for such was your gracious will. ²⁷All things have been handed over to me by my Father; and no one knows the Son except the Father, and no one knows the Father except the Son and anyone to whom the Son chooses to reveal him.

28 "Come to me, all you that are weary and are carrying heavy burdens, and I will give you rest. ²⁹Take my yoke upon you, and learn from me; for I am gentle and humble in heart, and you will find rest for your souls. ³⁰For my yoke is easy, and my burden is light."

Plucking Grain on the Sabbath

12 At that time Jesus went through the grainfields on the sabbath; his disciples were hungry, and they began to pluck heads of grain and to eat. ²When the Pharisees saw it, they said to him, "Look, your disciples are doing what is not lawful to do on the sabbath." ³He said to them, "Have you not read what David did when he and his companions were hungry? ⁴He entered the house of God and ate the bread of the Presence, which it was not lawful for him or his companions to eat, but only for the priests. ⁵Or have you not read in the law that on the sabbath the priests in the temple break the sabbath and yet are guiltless? ⁶I tell you, something greater than the temple is here. ⁷But if you had known what this means, 'I desire mercy and not sacrifice,' you would not have condemned the guiltless. ⁸For the Son of Man is lord of the sabbath."

The Man with the Withered Hand

9 He left that place and entered their synagogue; ¹⁰a man was there with a withered hand, and they asked him, "Is it lawful to cure on the sabbath?" so that they might accuse him. ¹¹He said to them, "Suppose one of you has only one sheep and it falls into a pit on the sabbath; will you not lay hold of it and lift it out? ¹²How much more valuable is a human being than a sheep! So it is lawful to do good on the sabbath." ¹³Then he said to the man, "Stretch out your hand." He stretched it out, and it was restored, as sound as the other. ¹⁴But the Pharisees went out and conspired against him, how to destroy him.

God's Chosen Servant

15 When Jesus became aware of this, he departed. Many crowds followed him, and he cured all of them, [16]and he ordered them not to make him known. [17]This was to fulfill what had been spoken through the prophet Isaiah:
[18] "Here is my servant, whom I have chosen,
  my beloved, with whom my soul is well pleased.
  I will put my Spirit upon him,
   and he will proclaim justice to the Gentiles.
[19] He will not wrangle or cry aloud,
   nor will anyone hear his voice in the streets.
[20] He will not break a bruised reed
   or quench a smoldering wick
  until he brings justice to victory.
[21] And in his name the Gentiles will hope."

Jesus and Beelzebul

22 Then they brought to him a demoniac who was blind and mute; and he cured him, so that the one who had been mute could speak and see. [23]All the crowds were amazed and said, "Can this be the Son of David?" [24]But when the Pharisees heard it, they said, "It is only by Beelzebul, the ruler of the demons, that this fellow casts out the demons." [25]He knew what they were thinking and said to them, "Every kingdom divided against itself is laid waste, and no city or house divided against itself will stand. [26]If Satan casts out Satan, he is divided against himself; how then will his kingdom stand? [27]If I cast out demons by Beelzebul, by whom do your own exorcists cast them out? Therefore they will be your judges. [28]But if it is by the Spirit of God that I cast out demons, then the kingdom of God has come to you. [29]Or how can one enter a strong man's house and plunder his property, without first tying up the strong man? Then indeed the house can be plundered. [30]Whoever is not with me is against me, and whoever does not gather with me scatters. [31]Therefore I tell you, people will be forgiven for every sin and blasphemy, but blasphemy against the Spirit will not be forgiven. [32]Whoever speaks a word against the Son of Man will be forgiven, but whoever speaks against the Holy Spirit will not be forgiven, either in this age or in the age to come.

A Tree and Its Fruits

33 "Either make the tree good, and its fruit good; or make the tree bad, and its fruit bad; for the tree is known by its fruit. [34]You brood of vipers! How can you speak good things, when you are evil? For out of the abundance of the heart the mouth speaks. [35]The good person brings good things out of a good treasure, and the evil person brings evil things out of an evil treasure. [36]I tell you, on the day of judgment you will have to give an account for every careless word you utter; [37]for by your words you will be justified, and by your words you will be condemned."

The Sign of Jonah

38 Then some of the scribes and Pharisees said to him, "Teacher, we wish to see a sign from you." [39]But he answered them, "An evil and adulterous generation asks for a sign, but no sign will be given to it except the sign of the prophet Jonah. [40]For just as Jonah was three days and three nights in the belly of the sea monster, so for three days and three nights the Son of Man will be in the heart of the earth. [41]The people of Nineveh will rise up at the judgment with this generation and condemn it, because they repented at the proclamation of Jonah, and see, something greater than Jonah is here! [42]The queen of the South will rise up at the judgment with this generation and condemn it, because she came from the ends of the earth to listen to the wisdom of Solomon, and see, something greater than Solomon is here!

The Return of the Unclean Spirit

43 "When the unclean spirit has gone out of a person, it wanders through waterless regions looking for a resting place, but it finds none. [44]Then it says, 'I will return to my house from which I came.' When it comes, it finds it empty, swept, and put in order. [45]Then it goes and brings along seven other spirits more evil than itself, and they enter and live there; and the last state of that person is worse than the first. So will it be also with this evil generation."

The True Kindred of Jesus

46 While he was still speaking to the crowds, his mother and his brothers were standing outside, wanting to speak to him. ⁴⁷Someone told him, "Look, your mother and your brothers are standing outside, wanting to speak to you." ⁴⁸But to the one who had told him this, Jesus replied, "Who is my mother, and who are my brothers?" ⁴⁹And pointing to his disciples, he said, "Here are my mother and my brothers! ⁵⁰For whoever does the will of my Father in heaven is my brother and sister and mother."

The Parable of the Sower

13 That same day Jesus went out of the house and sat beside the sea. ²Such great crowds gathered around him that he got into a boat and sat there, while the whole crowd stood on the beach. ³And he told them many things in parables, saying: "Listen! A sower went out to sow. ⁴And as he sowed, some seeds fell on the path, and the birds came and ate them up. ⁵Other seeds fell on rocky ground, where they did not have much soil, and they sprang up quickly, since they had no depth of soil. ⁶But when the sun rose, they were scorched; and since they had no root, they withered away. ⁷Other seeds fell among thorns, and the thorns grew up and choked them. ⁸Other seeds fell on good soil and brought forth grain, some a hundredfold, some sixty, some thirty. ⁹Let anyone with ears listen!"

The Purpose of the Parables

10 Then the disciples came and asked him, "Why do you speak to them in parables?" ¹¹He answered, "To you it has been given to know the secrets of the kingdom of heaven, but to them it has not been given. ¹²For to those who have, more will be given, and they will have an abundance; but from those who have nothing, even what they have will be taken away. ¹³The reason I speak to them in parables is that 'seeing they do not perceive, and hearing they do not listen, nor do they understand.' ¹⁴With them indeed is fulfilled the prophecy of Isaiah that says:

'You will indeed listen, but never understand,
 and you will indeed look, but never perceive.
¹⁵ For this people's heart has grown dull,
 and their ears are hard of hearing,
 and they have shut their eyes;
 so that they might not look with their eyes,
 and listen with their ears,
 and understand with their heart and turn—
 and I would heal them.'

¹⁶But blessed are your eyes, for they see, and your ears, for they hear. ¹⁷Truly I tell you, many prophets and righteous people longed to see what you see, but did not see it, and to hear what you hear, but did not hear it.

The Parable of the Sower Explained

18 "Hear then the parable of the sower. ¹⁹When anyone hears the word of the kingdom and does not understand it, the evil one comes and snatches away what is sown in the heart; this is what was sown on the path. ²⁰As for what was sown on rocky ground, this is the one who hears the word and immediately receives it with joy; ²¹yet such a person has no root, but endures only for a while, and when trouble or persecution arises on account of the word, that person immediately falls away. ²²As for what was sown among thorns, this is the one who hears the word, but the cares of the world and the lure of wealth choke the word, and it yields nothing. ²³But as for what was sown on good soil, this is the one who hears the word and understands it, who indeed bears fruit and yields, in one case a hundredfold, in another sixty, and in another thirty."

The Parable of Weeds among the Wheat

24 He put before them another parable: "The kingdom of heaven may be compared to someone who sowed good seed in his field; ²⁵but while everybody was asleep, an enemy came and sowed weeds among the wheat, and then went away. ²⁶So when the plants came up and bore grain, then the weeds appeared as well. ²⁷And

the slaves of the householder came and said to him, 'Master, did you not sow good seed in your field? Where, then, did these weeds come from?' ²⁸He answered, 'An enemy has done this.' The slaves said to him, 'Then do you want us to go and gather them?' ²⁹But he replied, 'No; for in gathering the weeds you would uproot the wheat along with them. ³⁰Let both of them grow together until the harvest; and at harvest time I will tell the reapers, Collect the weeds first and bind them in bundles to be burned, but gather the wheat into my barn.'"

The Parable of the Mustard Seed

31 He put before them another parable: "The kingdom of heaven is like a mustard seed that someone took and sowed in his field; ³²it is the smallest of all the seeds, but when it has grown it is the greatest of shrubs and becomes a tree, so that the birds of the air come and make nests in its branches."

The Parable of the Yeast

33 He told them another parable: "The kingdom of heaven is like yeast that a woman took and mixed in with three measures of flour until all of it was leavened."

The Use of Parables

34 Jesus told the crowds all these things in parables; without a parable he told them nothing. ³⁵This was to fulfill what had been spoken through the prophet:

"I will open my mouth to speak in parables;
 I will proclaim what has been hidden from the foundation of the world."

Jesus Explains the Parable of the Weeds

36 Then he left the crowds and went into the house. And his disciples approached him, saying, "Explain to us the parable of the weeds of the field." ³⁷He answered, "The one who sows the good seed is the Son of Man; ³⁸the field is the world, and the good seed are the children of the kingdom; the weeds are the children of the evil one, ³⁹and the enemy who sowed them is the devil; the harvest is the end of the age, and the reapers are angels. ⁴⁰Just as the weeds are collected and burned up with fire, so will it be at the end of the age. ⁴¹The Son of Man will send his angels, and they will collect out of his kingdom all causes of sin and all evildoers, ⁴²and they will throw them into the furnace of fire, where there will be weeping and gnashing of teeth. ⁴³Then the righteous will shine like the sun in the kingdom of their Father. Let anyone with ears listen!

Three Parables

44 "The kingdom of heaven is like treasure hidden in a field, which someone found and hid; then in his joy he goes and sells all that he has and buys that field.

45 "Again, the kingdom of heaven is like a merchant in search of fine pearls; ⁴⁶on finding one pearl of great value, he went and sold all that he had and bought it.

47 "Again, the kingdom of heaven is like a net that was thrown into the sea and caught fish of every kind; ⁴⁸when it was full, they drew it ashore, sat down, and put the good into baskets but threw out the bad. ⁴⁹So it will be at the end of the age. The angels will come out and separate the evil from the righteous ⁵⁰and throw them into the furnace of fire, where there will be weeping and gnashing of teeth.

Treasures New and Old

51 "Have you understood all this?" They answered, "Yes." ⁵²And he said to them, "Therefore every scribe who has been trained for the kingdom of heaven is like the master of a household who brings out of his treasure what is new and what is old." ⁵³When Jesus had finished these parables, he left that place.

The Rejection of Jesus at Nazareth

54 He came to his hometown and began to teach the people in their synagogue, so that they were astounded and said, "Where did this man get this wisdom and these deeds of power? [55]Is not this the carpenter's son? Is not his mother called Mary? And are not his brothers James and Joseph and Simon and Judas? [56]And are not all his sisters with us? Where then did this man get all this?" [57]And they took offense at him. But Jesus said to them, "Prophets are not without honor except in their own country and in their own house." [58]And he did not do many deeds of power there, because of their unbelief.

The Death of John the Baptist

14 At that time Herod the ruler heard reports about Jesus; [2]and he said to his servants, "This is John the Baptist; he has been raised from the dead, and for this reason these powers are at work in him." [3]For Herod had arrested John, bound him, and put him in prison on account of Herodias, his brother Philip's wife, [4]because John had been telling him, "It is not lawful for you to have her." [5]Though Herod wanted to put him to death, he feared the crowd, because they regarded him as a prophet. [6]But when Herod's birthday came, the daughter of Herodias danced before the company, and she pleased Herod [7]so much that he promised on oath to grant her whatever she might ask. [8]Prompted by her mother, she said, "Give me the head of John the Baptist here on a platter." [9]The king was grieved, yet out of regard for his oaths and for the guests, he commanded it to be given; [10]he sent and had John beheaded in the prison. [11]The head was brought on a platter and given to the girl, who brought it to her mother. [12]His disciples came and took the body and buried it; then they went and told Jesus.

Feeding the Five Thousand

13 Now when Jesus heard this, he withdrew from there in a boat to a deserted place by himself. But when the crowds heard it, they followed him on foot from the towns. [14]When he went ashore, he saw a great crowd; and he had compassion for them and cured their sick. [15]When it was evening, the disciples came to him and said, "This is a deserted place, and the hour is now late; send the crowds away so that they may go into the villages and buy food for themselves." [16]Jesus said to them, "They need not go away; you give them something to eat." [17]They replied, "We have nothing here but five loaves and two fish." [18]And he said, "Bring them here to me." [19]Then he ordered the crowds to sit down on the grass. Taking the five loaves and the two fish, he looked up to heaven, and blessed and broke the loaves, and gave them to the disciples, and the disciples gave them to the crowds. [20]And all ate and were filled; and they took up what was left over of the broken pieces, twelve baskets full. [21]And those who ate were about five thousand men, besides women and children.

Jesus Walks on the Water

22 Immediately he made the disciples get into the boat and go on ahead to the other side, while he dismissed the crowds. [23]And after he had dismissed the crowds, he went up the mountain by himself to pray. When evening came, he was there alone, [24]but by this time the boat, battered by the waves, was far from the land, for the wind was against them. [25]And early in the morning he came walking toward them on the sea. [26]But when the disciples saw him walking on the sea, they were terrified, saying, "It is a ghost!" And they cried out in fear. [27]But immediately Jesus spoke to them and said, "Take heart, it is I; do not be afraid."

28 Peter answered him, "Lord, if it is you, command me to come to you on the water." [29]He said, "Come." So Peter got out of the boat, started walking on the water, and came toward Jesus. [30]But when he noticed the strong wind, he became frightened, and beginning to sink, he cried out, "Lord, save me!" [31]Jesus immediately reached out his hand and caught him, saying to him, "You of little faith, why did you doubt?" [32]When they got into the boat, the wind ceased. [33]And those in the boat worshiped him, saying, "Truly you are the Son of God."

Jesus Heals the Sick in Gennesaret

34 When they had crossed over, they came to land at Gennesaret. [35]After the people of that place recognized him, they sent word throughout the region and brought all who were sick to him, [36]and begged him that they might touch even the fringe of his cloak; and all who touched it were healed.

The Tradition of the Elders

15 Then Pharisees and scribes came to Jesus from Jerusalem and said, [2]"Why do your disciples break the tradition of the elders? For they do not wash their hands before they eat." [3]He answered them, "And why do you break the commandment of God for the sake of your tradition? [4]For God said, 'Honor your father and your mother,' and, 'Whoever speaks evil of father or mother must surely die.' [5]But you say that whoever tells father or mother, 'Whatever support you might have had from me is given to God,' then that person need not honor the father. [6]So, for the sake of your tradition, you make void the word of God. [7]You hypocrites! Isaiah prophesied rightly about you when he said:
[8] 'This people honors me with their lips,
　　but their hearts are far from me;
[9] in vain do they worship me,
　　teaching human precepts as doctrines.'"

Things That Defile

10 Then he called the crowd to him and said to them, "Listen and understand: [11]it is not what goes into the mouth that defiles a person, but it is what comes out of the mouth that defiles." [12]Then the disciples approached and said to him, "Do you know that the Pharisees took offense when they heard what you said?" [13]He answered, "Every plant that my heavenly Father has not planted will be uprooted. [14]Let them alone; they are blind guides of the blind. And if one blind person guides another, both will fall into a pit." [15]But Peter said to him, "Explain this parable to us." [16]Then he said, "Are you also still without understanding? [17]Do you not see that whatever goes into the mouth enters the stomach, and goes out into the sewer? [18]But what comes out of the mouth proceeds from the heart, and this is what defiles. [19]For out of the heart come evil intentions, murder, adultery, fornication, theft, false witness, slander. [20]These are what defile a person, but to eat with unwashed hands does not defile."

The Canaanite Woman's Faith

21 Jesus left that place and went away to the district of Tyre and Sidon. [22]Just then a Canaanite woman from that region came out and started shouting, "Have mercy on me, Lord, Son of David; my daughter is tormented by a demon." [23]But he did not answer her at all. And his disciples came and urged him, saying, "Send her away, for she keeps shouting after us." [24]He answered, "I was sent only to the lost sheep of the house of Israel." [25]But she came and knelt before him, saying, "Lord, help me." [26]He answered, "It is not fair to take the children's food and throw it to the dogs." [27]She said, "Yes, Lord, yet even the dogs eat the crumbs that fall from their masters' table." [28]Then Jesus answered her, "Woman, great is your faith! Let it be done for you as you wish." And her daughter was healed instantly.

Jesus Cures Many People

29 After Jesus had left that place, he passed along the Sea of Galilee, and he went up the mountain, where he sat down. [30]Great crowds came to him, bringing with them the lame, the maimed, the blind, the mute, and many others. They put them at his feet, and he cured them, [31]so that the crowd was amazed when they saw the mute speaking, the maimed whole, the lame walking, and the blind seeing. And they praised the God of Israel.

Feeding the Four Thousand

32 Then Jesus called his disciples to him and said, "I have compassion for the crowd, because they have been with me now for three days and have nothing to eat; and I do not want to send

them away hungry, for they might faint on the way." ³³The disciples said to him, "Where are we to get enough bread in the desert to feed so great a crowd?" ³⁴Jesus asked them, "How many loaves have you?" They said, "Seven, and a few small fish." ³⁵Then ordering the crowd to sit down on the ground, ³⁶he took the seven loaves and the fish; and after giving thanks he broke them and gave them to the disciples, and the disciples gave them to the crowds. ³⁷And all of them ate and were filled; and they took up the broken pieces left over, seven baskets full. ³⁸Those who had eaten were four thousand men, besides women and children. ³⁹After sending away the crowds, he got into the boat and went to the region of Magadan.

The Demand for a Sign

16 The Pharisees and Sadducees came, and to test Jesus they asked him to show them a sign from heaven. ²He answered them, "When it is evening, you say, 'It will be fair weather, for the sky is red.' ³And in the morning, 'It will be stormy today, for the sky is red and threatening.' You know how to interpret the appearance of the sky, but you cannot interpret the signs of the times. ⁴An evil and adulterous generation asks for a sign, but no sign will be given to it except the sign of Jonah." Then he left them and went away.

The Yeast of the Pharisees and Sadducees

5 When the disciples reached the other side, they had forgotten to bring any bread. ⁶Jesus said to them, "Watch out, and beware of the yeast of the Pharisees and Sadducees." ⁷They said to one another, "It is because we have brought no bread." ⁸And becoming aware of it, Jesus said, "You of little faith, why are you talking about having no bread? ⁹Do you still not perceive? Do you not remember the five loaves for the five thousand, and how many baskets you gathered? ¹⁰Or the seven loaves for the four thousand, and how many baskets you gathered? ¹¹How could you fail to perceive that I was not speaking about bread? Beware of the yeast of the Pharisees and Sadducees!" ¹²Then they understood that he had not told them to beware of the yeast of bread, but of the teaching of the Pharisees and Sadducees.

Peter's Declaration about Jesus

13 Now when Jesus came into the district of Caesarea Philippi, he asked his disciples, "Who do people say that the Son of Man is?" ¹⁴And they said, "Some say John the Baptist, but others Elijah, and still others Jeremiah or one of the prophets." ¹⁵He said to them, "But who do you say that I am?" ¹⁶Simon Peter answered, "You are the Messiah, the Son of the living God." ¹⁷And Jesus answered him, "Blessed are you, Simon son of Jonah! For flesh and blood has not revealed this to you, but my Father in heaven. ¹⁸And I tell you, you are Peter, and on this rock I will build my church, and the gates of Hades will not prevail against it. ¹⁹I will give you the keys of the kingdom of heaven, and whatever you bind on earth will be bound in heaven, and whatever you loose on earth will be loosed in heaven." ²⁰Then he sternly ordered the disciples not to tell anyone that he was the Messiah.

Jesus Foretells His Death and Resurrection

21 From that time on, Jesus began to show his disciples that he must go to Jerusalem and undergo great suffering at the hands of the elders and chief priests and scribes, and be killed, and on the third day be raised. ²²And Peter took him aside and began to rebuke him, saying, "God forbid it, Lord! This must never happen to you." ²³But he turned and said to Peter, "Get behind me, Satan! You are a stumbling block to me; for you are setting your mind not on divine things but on human things."

The Cross and Self-Denial

24 Then Jesus told his disciples, "If any want to become my followers, let them deny themselves and take up their cross and follow me. ²⁵For those who want to save their life will lose it, and those who lose their life for my sake will

find it. ²⁶For what will it profit them if they gain the whole world but forfeit their life? Or what will they give in return for their life?

27 "For the Son of Man is to come with his angels in the glory of his Father, and then he will repay everyone for what has been done. ²⁸Truly I tell you, there are some standing here who will not taste death before they see the Son of Man coming in his kingdom."

The Transfiguration

17 Six days later, Jesus took with him Peter and James and his brother John and led them up a high mountain, by themselves. ²And he was transfigured before them, and his face shone like the sun, and his clothes became dazzling white. ³Suddenly there appeared to them Moses and Elijah, talking with him. ⁴Then Peter said to Jesus, "Lord, it is good for us to be here; if you wish, I will make three dwellings here, one for you, one for Moses, and one for Elijah." ⁵While he was still speaking, suddenly a bright cloud overshadowed them, and from the cloud a voice said, "This is my Son, the Beloved; with him I am well pleased; listen to him!" ⁶When the disciples heard this, they fell to the ground and were overcome by fear. ⁷But Jesus came and touched them, saying, "Get up and do not be afraid." ⁸And when they looked up, they saw no one except Jesus himself alone.

9 As they were coming down the mountain, Jesus ordered them, "Tell no one about the vision until after the Son of Man has been raised from the dead." ¹⁰And the disciples asked him, "Why, then, do the scribes say that Elijah must come first?" ¹¹He replied, "Elijah is indeed coming and will restore all things; ¹²but I tell you that Elijah has already come, and they did not recognize him, but they did to him whatever they pleased. So also the Son of Man is about to suffer at their hands." ¹³Then the disciples understood that he was speaking to them about John the Baptist.

Jesus Cures a Boy with a Demon

14 When they came to the crowd, a man came to him, knelt before him, ¹⁵and said, "Lord, have mercy on my son, for he is an epileptic and he suffers terribly; he often falls into the fire and often into the water. ¹⁶And I brought him to your disciples, but they could not cure him." ¹⁷Jesus answered, "You faithless and perverse generation, how much longer must I be with you? How much longer must I put up with you? Bring him here to me." ¹⁸And Jesus rebuked the demon, and it came out of him, and the boy was cured instantly. ¹⁹Then the disciples came to Jesus privately and said, "Why could we not cast it out?" ²⁰He said to them, "Because of your little faith. For truly I tell you, if you have faith the size of a mustard seed, you will say to this mountain, 'Move from here to there,' and it will move; and nothing will be impossible for you."

Jesus Again Foretells His Death and Resurrection

22 As they were gathering in Galilee, Jesus said to them, "The Son of Man is going to be betrayed into human hands, ²³and they will kill him, and on the third day he will be raised." And they were greatly distressed.

Jesus and the Temple Tax

24 When they reached Capernaum, the collectors of the temple tax came to Peter and said, "Does your teacher not pay the temple tax?" ²⁵He said, "Yes, he does." And when he came home, Jesus spoke of it first, asking, "What do you think, Simon? From whom do kings of the earth take toll or tribute? From their children or from others?" ²⁶When Peter said, "From others," Jesus said to him, "Then the children are free. ²⁷However, so that we do not give offense to them, go to the sea and cast a hook; take the first fish that comes up; and when you open its mouth, you will find a coin; take that and give it to them for you and me."

True Greatness

18 At that time the disciples came to Jesus and asked, "Who is the greatest in the kingdom of heaven?" ²He called a child, whom he put

among them, ³and said, "Truly I tell you, unless you change and become like children, you will never enter the kingdom of heaven. ⁴Whoever becomes humble like this child is the greatest in the kingdom of heaven. ⁵Whoever welcomes one such child in my name welcomes me.

Temptations to Sin

6 "If any of you put a stumbling block before one of these little ones who believe in me, it would be better for you if a great millstone were fastened around your neck and you were drowned in the depth of the sea. ⁷Woe to the world because of stumbling blocks! Occasions for stumbling are bound to come, but woe to the one by whom the stumbling block comes!

8 "If your hand or your foot causes you to stumble, cut it off and throw it away; it is better for you to enter life maimed or lame than to have two hands or two feet and to be thrown into the eternal fire. ⁹And if your eye causes you to stumble, tear it out and throw it away; it is better for you to enter life with one eye than to have two eyes and to be thrown into the hell of fire.

The Parable of the Lost Sheep

10 "Take care that you do not despise one of these little ones; for, I tell you, in heaven their angels continually see the face of my Father in heaven. ¹²What do you think? If a shepherd has a hundred sheep, and one of them has gone astray, does he not leave the ninety-nine on the mountains and go in search of the one that went astray? ¹³And if he finds it, truly I tell you, he rejoices over it more than over the ninety-nine that never went astray. ¹⁴So it is not the will of your Father in heaven that one of these little ones should be lost.

Reproving Another Who Sins

15 "If another member of the church sins against you, go and point out the fault when the two of you are alone. If the member listens to you, you have regained that one. ¹⁶But if you are not listened to, take one or two others along with you, so that every word may be confirmed by the evidence of two or three witnesses. ¹⁷If the member refuses to listen to them, tell it to the church; and if the offender refuses to listen even to the church, let such a one be to you as a Gentile and a tax collector. ¹⁸Truly I tell you, whatever you bind on earth will be bound in heaven, and whatever you loose on earth will be loosed in heaven. ¹⁹Again, truly I tell you, if two of you agree on earth about anything you ask, it will be done for you by my Father in heaven. ²⁰For where two or three are gathered in my name, I am there among them."

Forgiveness

21 Then Peter came and said to him, "Lord, if another member of the church sins against me, how often should I forgive? As many as seven times?" ²²Jesus said to him, "Not seven times, but, I tell you, seventy-seven times.

The Parable of the Unknowing Servant

23 "For this reason the kingdom of heaven may be compared to a king who wished to settle accounts with his slaves. ²⁴When he began the reckoning, one who owed him ten thousand talents was brought to him; ²⁵and, as he could not pay, his lord ordered him to be sold, together with his wife and children and all his possessions, and payment to be made. ²⁶So the slave fell on his knees before him, saying, 'Have patience with me, and I will pay you everything.' ²⁷And out of pity for him, the lord of that slave released him and forgave him the debt. ²⁸But that same slave, as he went out, came upon one of his fellow slaves who owed him a hundred denarii; and seizing him by the throat, he said, 'Pay what you owe.' ²⁹Then his fellow slave fell down and pleaded with him, 'Have patience with me, and I will pay you.' ³⁰But he refused; then he went and threw him into prison until he would pay the debt. ³¹When his fellow slaves saw what had happened, they were greatly distressed, and they went and reported to their lord all that had taken place. ³²Then his lord summoned him and said to him, 'You wicked slave! I forgave you all that debt because you pleaded with me. ³³Should you not have had mercy on your fellow slave, as I had mercy on you?' ³⁴And in anger his lord handed

him over to be tortured until he would pay his entire debt. ³⁵So my heavenly Father will also do to every one of you, if you do not forgive your brother or sister from your heart."

Teaching about Divorce

19 When Jesus had finished saying these things, he left Galilee and went to the region of Judea beyond the Jordan. ²Large crowds followed him, and he cured them there.

3 Some Pharisees came to him, and to test him they asked, "Is it lawful for a man to divorce his wife for any cause?" ⁴He answered, "Have you not read that the one who made them at the beginning 'made them male and female,' ⁵and said, 'For this reason a man shall leave his father and mother and be joined to his wife, and the two shall become one flesh'? ⁶So they are no longer two, but one flesh. Therefore what God has joined together, let no one separate." ⁷They said to him, "Why then did Moses command us to give a certificate of dismissal and to divorce her?" ⁸He said to them, "It was because you were so hard-hearted that Moses allowed you to divorce your wives, but from the beginning it was not so. ⁹And I say to you, whoever divorces his wife, except for unchastity, and marries another commits adultery."

10 His disciples said to him, "If such is the case of a man with his wife, it is better not to marry." ¹¹But he said to them, "Not everyone can accept this teaching, but only those to whom it is given. ¹²For there are eunuchs who have been so from birth, and there are eunuchs who have been made eunuchs by others, and there are eunuchs who have made themselves eunuchs for the sake of the kingdom of heaven. Let anyone accept this who can."

Jesus Blesses Little Children

13 Then little children were being brought to him in order that he might lay his hands on them and pray. The disciples spoke sternly to those who brought them; ¹⁴but Jesus said, "Let the little children come to me, and do not stop them; for it is to such as these that the kingdom of heaven belongs." ¹⁵And he laid his hands on them and went on his way.

The Rich Young Man

16 Then someone came to him and said, "Teacher, what good deed must I do to have eternal life?" ¹⁷And he said to him, "Why do you ask me about what is good? There is only one who is good. If you wish to enter into life, keep the commandments." ¹⁸He said to him, "Which ones?" And Jesus said, "You shall not murder; You shall not commit adultery; You shall not steal; You shall not bear false witness; ¹⁹Honor your father and mother; also, You shall love your neighbor as yourself." ²⁰The young man said to him, "I have kept all these; what do I still lack?" ²¹Jesus said to him, "If you wish to be perfect, go, sell your possessions, and give the money to the poor, and you will have treasure in heaven; then come, follow me." ²²When the young man heard this word, he went away grieving, for he had many possessions.

23 Then Jesus said to his disciples, "Truly I tell you, it will be hard for a rich person to enter the kingdom of heaven. ²⁴Again I tell you, it is easier for a camel to go through the eye of a needle than for someone who is rich to enter the kingdom of God." ²⁵When the disciples heard this, they were greatly astounded and said, "Then who can be saved?" ²⁶But Jesus looked at them and said, "For mortals it is impossible, but for God all things are possible."

27 Then Peter said in reply, "Look, we have left everything and followed you. What then will we have?" ²⁸Jesus said to them, "Truly I tell you, at the renewal of all things, when the Son of Man is seated on the throne of his glory, you who have followed me will also sit on twelve thrones, judging the twelve tribes of Israel. ²⁹And everyone who has left houses or brothers or sisters or father or mother or children or fields, for my name's sake, will receive a hundredfold, and will inherit eternal life. ³⁰But many who are first will be last, and the last will be first.

The Laborers in the Vineyard

20 "For the kingdom of heaven is like a landowner who went out early in the morning to hire laborers for his vineyard. ²After agreeing with the laborers for the usual daily wage, he sent them into his vineyard. ³When he went out about nine o'clock, he saw others standing idle in the marketplace; ⁴and he said to them, 'You also go into the vineyard, and I will pay you whatever is right.' So they went. ⁵When he went out again about noon and about three o'clock, he did the same. ⁶And about five o'clock he went out and found others standing around; and he said to them, 'Why are you standing here idle all day?' ⁷They said to him, 'Because no one has hired us.' He said to them, 'You also go into the vineyard.' ⁸When evening came, the owner of the vineyard said to his manager, 'Call the laborers and give them their pay, beginning with the last and then going to the first.' ⁹When those hired about five o'clock came, each of them received the usual daily wage. ¹⁰Now when the first came, they thought they would receive more; but each of them also received the usual daily wage. ¹¹And when they received it, they grumbled against the landowner, ¹²saying, 'These last worked only one hour, and you have made them equal to us who have borne the burden of the day and the scorching heat.' ¹³But he replied to one of them, 'Friend, I am doing you no wrong; did you not agree with me for the usual daily wage? ¹⁴Take what belongs to you and go; I choose to give to this last the same as I give to you. ¹⁵Am I not allowed to do what I choose with what belongs to me? Or are you envious because I am generous?' ¹⁶So the last will be first, and the first will be last."

A Third Time Jesus Foretells His Death and Resurrection

17 While Jesus was going up to Jerusalem, he took the twelve disciples aside by themselves, and said to them on the way, ¹⁸"See, we are going up to Jerusalem, and the Son of Man will be handed over to the chief priests and scribes, and they will condemn him to death; ¹⁹then they will hand him over to the Gentiles to be mocked and flogged and crucified; and on the third day he will be raised."

The Request of the Mother of James and John

20 Then the mother of the sons of Zebedee came to him with her sons, and kneeling before him, she asked a favor of him. ²¹And he said to her, "What do you want?" She said to him, "Declare that these two sons of mine will sit, one at your right hand and one at your left, in your kingdom." ²²But Jesus answered, "You do not know what you are asking. Are you able to drink the cup that I am about to drink?" They said to him, "We are able." ²³He said to them, "You will indeed drink my cup, but to sit at my right hand and at my left, this is not mine to grant, but it is for those for whom it has been prepared by my Father."

24 When the ten heard it, they were angry with the two brothers. ²⁵But Jesus called them to him and said, "You know that the rulers of the Gentiles lord it over them, and their great ones are tyrants over them. ²⁶It will not be so among you; but whoever wishes to be great among you must be your servant, ²⁷and whoever wishes to be first among you must be your slave; ²⁸just as the Son of Man came not to be served but to serve, and to give his life a ransom for many."

Jesus Heals Two Blind Men

29 As they were leaving Jericho, a large crowd followed him. ³⁰There were two blind men sitting by the roadside. When they heard that Jesus was passing by, they shouted, "Lord, have mercy on us, Son of David!" ³¹The crowd sternly ordered them to be quiet; but they shouted even more loudly, "Have mercy on us, Lord, Son of David!" ³²Jesus stood still and called them, saying, "What do you want me to do for you?" ³³They said to him, "Lord, let our eyes be opened." ³⁴Moved with compassion, Jesus touched their eyes. Immediately they regained their sight and followed him.

Jesus' Triumphal Entry into Jerusalem

21 When they had come near Jerusalem and had reached Bethphage, at the Mount of Olives, Jesus sent two disciples, ²saying to them, "Go into the village ahead of you, and immediately you will find a donkey tied, and a colt with her; untie them and bring them to me. ³If anyone says anything to you, just say this, 'The Lord needs them.' And he will send them immediately." ⁴This took place to fulfill what had been spoken through the prophet, saying,

5 "Tell the daughter of Zion, Look, your king is coming to you,
> humble, and mounted on a donkey,
> and on a colt, the foal of a donkey."

⁶The disciples went and did as Jesus had directed them; ⁷they brought the donkey and the colt, and put their cloaks on them, and he sat on them. ⁸A very large crowd spread their cloaks on the road, and others cut branches from the trees and spread them on the road. ⁹The crowds that went ahead of him and that followed were shouting, "Hosanna to the Son of David! Blessed is the one who comes in the name of the Lord! Hosanna in the highest heaven!"

¹⁰When he entered Jerusalem, the whole city was in turmoil, asking, "Who is this?" ¹¹The crowds were saying, "This is the prophet Jesus from Nazareth in Galilee."

Jesus Cleanses the Temple

12 Then Jesus entered the temple and drove out all who were selling and buying in the temple, and he overturned the tables of the money changers and the seats of those who sold doves. ¹³He said to them, "It is written,

> 'My house shall be called a house of prayer';
> but you are making it a den of robbers."

14 The blind and the lame came to him in the temple, and he cured them. ¹⁵But when the chief priests and the scribes saw the amazing things that he did, and heard the children crying out in the temple, "Hosanna to the Son of David," they became angry ¹⁶and said to him, "Do you hear what these are saying?" Jesus said to them, "Yes; have you never read,

> 'Out of the mouths of infants and nursing babies
> you have prepared praise for yourself'?"

¹⁷He left them, went out of the city to Bethany, and spent the night there.

Jesus Curses the Fig Tree

18 In the morning, when he returned to the city, he was hungry. ¹⁹And seeing a fig tree by the side of the road, he went to it and found nothing at all on it but leaves. Then he said to it, "May no fruit ever come from you again!" And the fig tree withered at once. ²⁰When the disciples saw it, they were amazed, saying, "How did the fig tree wither at once?" ²¹Jesus answered them, "Truly I tell you, if you have faith and do not doubt, not only will you do what has been done to the fig tree, but even if you say to this mountain, 'Be lifted up and thrown into the sea,' it will be done. ²²Whatever you ask for in prayer with faith, you will receive."

The Authority of Jesus Questioned

23 When he entered the temple, the chief priests and the elders of the people came to him as he was teaching, and said, "By what authority are you doing these things, and who gave you this authority?" ²⁴Jesus said to them, "I will also ask you one question; if you tell me the answer, then I will also tell you by what authority I do these things. ²⁵Did the baptism of John come from heaven, or was it of human origin?" And they argued with one another, "If we say, 'From heaven,' he will say to us, 'Why then did you not believe him?' ²⁶But if we say, 'Of human origin,' we are afraid of the crowd; for all regard John as a prophet." ²⁷So they answered Jesus, "We do not know." And he said to them, "Neither will I tell you by what authority I am doing these things.

The Parable of the Two Sons

28 "What do you think? A man had two sons; he went to the first and said, 'Son, go and work in the vineyard today.' ²⁹He answered, 'I will

not'; but later he changed his mind and went. ³⁰The father went to the second and said the same; and he answered, 'I go, sir'; but he did not go. ³¹Which of the two did the will of his father?" They said, "The first." Jesus said to them, "Truly I tell you, the tax collectors and the prostitutes are going into the kingdom of God ahead of you. ³²For John came to you in the way of righteousness and you did not believe him, but the tax collectors and the prostitutes believed him; and even after you saw it, you did not change your minds and believe him.

The Parable of the Wicked Tenants

33 "Listen to another parable. There was a landowner who planted a vineyard, put a fence around it, dug a wine press in it, and built a watchtower. Then he leased it to tenants and went to another country. ³⁴When the harvest time had come, he sent his slaves to the tenants to collect his produce. ³⁵But the tenants seized his slaves and beat one, killed another, and stoned another. ³⁶Again he sent other slaves, more than the first; and they treated them in the same way. ³⁷Finally he sent his son to them, saying, 'They will respect my son.' ³⁸But when the tenants saw the son, they said to themselves, 'This is the heir; come, let us kill him and get his inheritance." ³⁹So they seized him, threw him out of the vineyard, and killed him. ⁴⁰Now when the owner of the vineyard comes, what will he do to those tenants?" ⁴¹They said to him, "He will put those wretches to a miserable death, and lease the vineyard to other tenants who will give him the produce at the harvest time."

42 Jesus said to them, "Have you never read in the scriptures: 'The stone that the builders rejected has become the cornerstone; this was the Lord's doing, and it is amazing in our eyes'? ⁴³Therefore I tell you, the kingdom of God will be taken away from you and given to a people that produces the fruits of the kingdom. ⁴⁴The one who falls on this stone will be broken to pieces; and it will crush anyone on whom it falls."

45 When the chief priests and the Pharisees heard his parables, they realized that he was speaking about them. ⁴⁶They wanted to arrest him, but they feared the crowds, because they regarded him as a prophet.

The Parable of the Wedding Banquet

22 Once more Jesus spoke to them in parables, saying: ²"The kingdom of heaven may be compared to a king who gave a wedding banquet for his son. ³He sent his slaves to call those who had been invited to the wedding banquet, but they would not come. ⁴Again he sent other slaves, saying, 'Tell those who have been invited: Look, I have prepared my dinner, my oxen and my fat calves have been slaughtered, and everything is ready; come to the wedding banquet.' ⁵But they made light of it and went away, one to his farm, another to his business, ⁶while the rest seized his slaves, mistreated them, and killed them. ⁷The king was enraged. He sent his troops, destroyed those murderers, and burned their city. ⁸Then he said to his slaves, 'The wedding is ready, but those invited were not worthy. ⁹Go therefore into the main streets, and invite everyone you find to the wedding banquet.' ¹⁰Those slaves went out into the streets and gathered all whom they found, both good and bad; so the wedding hall was filled with guests.

11 "But when the king came in to see the guests, he noticed a man there who was not wearing a wedding robe, ¹²and he said to him, 'Friend, how did you get in here without a wedding robe?' And he was speechless. ¹³Then the king said to the attendants, 'Bind him hand and foot, and throw him into the outer darkness, where there will be weeping and gnashing of teeth.' ¹⁴For many are called, but few are chosen."

The Question about Paying Taxes

15 Then the Pharisees went and plotted to entrap him in what he said. ¹⁶So they sent their disciples to him, along with the Herodians, saying, "Teacher, we know that you are sincere, and teach the way of God in accordance with truth, and show deference to no one; for you do not regard people with partiality. ¹⁷Tell us, then, what you think. Is it lawful to pay taxes to the emperor, or not?" ¹⁸But Jesus, aware of their malice, said, "Why are you putting me to the test, you hypocrites? ¹⁹Show me the coin used for the tax." And they brought him a denarius. ²⁰Then he

said to them, "Whose head is this, and whose title?" ²¹They answered, "The emperor's." Then he said to them, "Give therefore to the emperor the things that are the emperor's, and to God the things that are God's." ²²When they heard this, they were amazed; and they left him and went away.

The Question about the Resurrection

23 The same day some Sadducees came to him, saying there is no resurrection; and they asked him a question, saying, ²⁴"Teacher, Moses said, 'If a man dies childless, his brother shall marry the widow, and raise up children for his brother.' ²⁵Now there were seven brothers among us; the first married, and died childless, leaving the widow to his brother. ²⁶The second did the same, so also the third, down to the seventh. ²⁷Last of all, the woman herself died. ²⁸In the resurrection, then, whose wife of the seven will she be? For all of them had married her."

29 Jesus answered them, "You are wrong, because you know neither the scriptures nor the power of God. ³⁰For in the resurrection they neither marry nor are given in marriage, but are like angels in heaven. ³¹And as for the resurrection of the dead, have you not read what was said to you by God, ³²'I am the God of Abraham, the God of Isaac, and the God of Jacob'? He is God not of the dead, but of the living." ³³And when the crowd heard it, they were astounded at his teaching.

The Greatest Commandment

34 When the Pharisees heard that he had silenced the Sadducees, they gathered together, ³⁵and one of them, a lawyer, asked him a question to test him. ³⁶"Teacher, which commandment in the law is the greatest?" ³⁷He said to him, "'You shall love the Lord your God with all your heart, and with all your soul, and with all your mind.' ³⁸This is the greatest and first commandment. ³⁹And a second is like it: 'You shall love your neighbor as yourself.' ⁴⁰On these two commandments hang all the law and the prophets."

The Question about David's Son

41 Now while the Pharisees were gathered together, Jesus asked them this question: ⁴²"What do you think of the Messiah? Whose son is he?" They said to him, "The son of David." ⁴³He said to them, "How is it then that David by the Spirit calls him Lord, saying,
⁴⁴ 'The Lord said to my Lord,
   "Sit at my right hand,
      until I put your enemies under your feet"'?
⁴⁵If David thus calls him Lord, how can he be his son?" ⁴⁶No one was able to give him an answer, nor from that day did anyone dare to ask him any more questions.

Jesus Denounces Scribes and Pharisees

23 Then Jesus said to the crowds and to his disciples, ²"The scribes and the Pharisees sit on Moses' seat; ³therefore, do whatever they teach you and follow it; but do not do as they do, for they do not practice what they teach. ⁴They tie up heavy burdens, hard to bear, and lay them on the shoulders of others; but they themselves are unwilling to lift a finger to move them. ⁵They do all their deeds to be seen by others; for they make their phylacteries broad and their fringes long. ⁶They love to have the place of honor at banquets and the best seats in the synagogues, ⁷and to be greeted with respect in the marketplaces, and to have people call them rabbi. ⁸But you are not to be called rabbi, for you have one teacher, and you are all students. ⁹And call no one your father on earth, for you have one Father—the one in heaven. ¹⁰Nor are you to be called instructors, for you have one instructor, the Messiah. ¹¹The greatest among you will be your servant. ¹²All who exalt themselves will be humbled, and all who humble themselves will be exalted.

13 "But woe to you, scribes and Pharisees, hypocrites! For you lock people out of the kingdom of heaven. For you do not go in yourselves, and when others are going in, you stop them. ¹⁵Woe to you, scribes and Pharisees, hypocrites! For you cross sea and land to make a single convert, and you make the new convert twice as much a child of hell as yourselves.

16 "Woe to you, blind guides, who say, 'Whoever swears by the sanctuary is bound by nothing, but whoever swears by the gold of the sanctuary is bound by the oath.' ¹⁷You blind fools! For which is greater, the gold or the sanctuary that has made the gold sacred? ¹⁸And you say, 'Whoever swears by the altar is bound by nothing, but whoever swears by the gift that is on the altar is bound by the oath.' ¹⁹How blind you are! For which is greater, the gift or the altar that makes the gift sacred? ²⁰So whoever swears by the altar, swears by it and by everything on it; ²¹and whoever swears by the sanctuary, swears by it and by the one who dwells in it; ²²and whoever swears by heaven, swears by the throne of God and by the one who is seated upon it.

23 "Woe to you, scribes and Pharisees, hypocrites! For you tithe mint, dill, and cummin, and have neglected the weightier matters of the law: justice and mercy and faith. It is these you ought to have practiced without neglecting the others. ²⁴You blind guides! You strain out a gnat but swallow a camel!

25 "Woe to you, scribes and Pharisees, hypocrites! For you clean the outside of the cup and of the plate, but inside they are full of greed and self-indulgence. ²⁶You blind Pharisee! First clean the inside of the cup, so that the outside also may become clean.

27 "Woe to you, scribes and Pharisees, hypocrites! For you are like whitewashed tombs, which on the outside look beautiful, but inside they are full of the bones of the dead and of all kinds of filth. ²⁸So you also on the outside look righteous to others, but inside you are full of hypocrisy and lawlessness.

29 "Woe to you, scribes and Pharisees, hypocrites! For you build the tombs of the prophets and decorate the graves of the righteous, ³⁰and you say, 'If we had lived in the days of our ancestors, we would not have taken part with them in shedding the blood of the prophets.' ³¹Thus you testify against yourselves that you are descendants of those who murdered the prophets. ³²Fill up, then, the measure of your ancestors. ³³You snakes, you brood of vipers! How can you escape being sentenced to hell? ³⁴Therefore I send you prophets, sages, and scribes, some of whom you will kill and crucify, and some you will flog in your synagogues and pursue from town to town, ³⁵so that upon you may come all the righteous blood shed on earth, from the blood of righteous Abel to the blood of Zechariah son of Barachiah, whom you murdered between the sanctuary and the altar. ³⁶Truly I tell you, all this will come upon this generation.

The Lament over Jerusalem

37 "Jerusalem, Jerusalem, the city that kills the prophets and stones those who are sent to it! How often have I desired to gather your children together as a hen gathers her brood under her wings, and you were not willing! ³⁸See, your house is left to you, desolate. ³⁹For I tell you, you will not see me again until you say, 'Blessed is the one who comes in the name of the Lord.'"

The Destruction of the Temple Foretold

24 As Jesus came out of the temple and was going away, his disciples came to point out to him the buildings of the temple. ²Then he asked them, "You see all these, do you not? Truly I tell you, not one stone will be left here upon another; all will be thrown down."

Signs of the End of the Age

3 When he was sitting on the Mount of Olives, the disciples came to him privately, saying, "Tell us, when will this be, and what will be the sign of your coming and of the end of the age?" ⁴Jesus answered them, "Beware that no one leads you astray. ⁵For many will come in my name, saying, 'I am the Messiah!' and they will lead many astray. ⁶And you will hear of wars and rumors of wars; see that you are not alarmed; for this must take place, but the end is not yet. ⁷For nation will rise against nation, and kingdom against kingdom, and there will be famines and earthquakes in various places: ⁸all this is but the beginning of the birth pangs.

Persecutions Foretold

9 "Then they will hand you over to be tortured and will put you to death, and you will be hated by all nations because of my name. [10]Then many will fall away, and they will betray one another and hate one another. [11]And many false prophets will arise and lead many astray. [12]And because of the increase of lawlessness, the love of many will grow cold. [13]But the one who endures to the end will be saved. [14]And this good news of the kingdom will be proclaimed throughout the world, as a testimony to all the nations; and then the end will come.

The Desolating Sacrilege

15 "So when you see the desolating sacrilege standing in the holy place, as was spoken of by the prophet Daniel (let the reader understand), [16]then those in Judea must flee to the mountains; [17]the one on the housetop must not go down to take what is in the house; [18]the one in the field must not turn back to get a coat. [19]Woe to those who are pregnant and to those who are nursing infants in those days! [20]Pray that your flight may not be in winter or on a sabbath. [21]For at that time there will be great suffering, such as has not been from the beginning of the world until now, no, and never will be. [22]And if those days had not been cut short, no one would be saved; but for the sake of the elect those days will be cut short. [23]Then if anyone says to you, 'Look! Here is the Messiah!' or 'There he is!'—do not believe it. [24]For false messiahs and false prophets will appear and produce great signs and omens, to lead astray, if possible, even the elect. [25]Take note, I have told you beforehand. [26]So, if they say to you, 'Look! He is in the wilderness,' do not go out. If they say, 'Look! He is in the inner rooms,' do not believe it. [27]For as the lightning comes from the east and flashes as far as the west, so will be the coming of the Son of Man. [28]Wherever the corpse is, there the vultures will gather.

The Coming of the Son of Man

29 "Immediately after the suffering of those days
the sun will be darkened,
and the moon will not give its light;
the stars will fall from heaven,
and the powers of heaven will be shaken.
[30]Then the sign of the Son of Man will appear in heaven, and then all the tribes of the earth will mourn, and they will see 'the Son of Man coming on the clouds of heaven' with power and great glory. [31]And he will send out his angels with a loud trumpet call, and they will gather his elect from the four winds, from one end of heaven to the other.

The Lesson of the Fig Tree

32 "From the fig tree learn its lesson: as soon as its branch becomes tender and puts forth its leaves, you know that summer is near. [33]So also, when you see all these things, you know that he is near, at the very gates. [34]Truly I tell you, this generation will not pass away until all these things have taken place. [35]Heaven and earth will pass away, but my words will not pass away.

The Necessity for Watchfulness

36 "But about that day and hour no one knows, neither the angels of heaven, nor the Son, but only the Father. [37]For as the days of Noah were, so will be the coming of the Son of Man. [38]For as in those days before the flood they were eating and drinking, marrying and giving in marriage, until the day Noah entered the ark, [39]and they knew nothing until the flood came and swept them all away, so too will be the coming of the Son of Man. [40]Then two will be in the field; one will be taken and one will be left. [41]Two women will be grinding meal together; one will be taken and one will be left. [42]Keep awake therefore, for you do not know on what day your Lord is coming. [43]But understand this: if the owner of the house had known in what part of the night the thief was coming, he would have stayed awake and would not have let his house be broken into. [44]Therefore you also must be ready, for the Son of Man is coming at an unexpected hour.

The Faithful or the Unfaithful Slave

45 "Who then is the faithful and wise slave, whom his master has put in charge of his household, to give the other slaves their allowance of food at the proper time? ⁴⁶Blessed is that slave whom his master will find at work when he arrives. ⁴⁷Truly I tell you, he will put that one in charge of all his possessions. ⁴⁸But if that wicked slave says to himself, 'My master is delayed,' ⁴⁹and he begins to beat his fellow slaves, and eats and drinks with drunkards, ⁵⁰the master of that slave will come on a day when he does not expect him and at an hour that he does not know. ⁵¹He will cut him in pieces and put him with the hypocrites, where there will be weeping and gnashing of teeth.

The Parable of the Ten Bridesmaids

25 "Then the kingdom of heaven will be like this. Ten bridesmaids took their lamps and went to meet the bridegroom. ²Five of them were foolish, and five were wise. ³When the foolish took their lamps, they took no oil with them; ⁴but the wise took flasks of oil with their lamps. ⁵As the bridegroom was delayed, all of them became drowsy and slept. ⁶But at midnight there was a shout, 'Look! Here is the bridegroom! Come out to meet him.' ⁷Then all those bridesmaids got up and trimmed their lamps. ⁸The foolish said to the wise, 'Give us some of your oil, for our lamps are going out.' ⁹But the wise replied, 'No! there will not be enough for you and for us; you had better go to the dealers and buy some for yourselves.' ¹⁰And while they went to buy it, the bridegroom came, and those who were ready went with him into the wedding banquet; and the door was shut. ¹¹Later the other bridesmaids came also, saying, 'Lord, lord, open to us.' ¹²But he replied, 'Truly I tell you, I do not know you.' ¹³Keep awake therefore, for you know neither the day nor the hour.

The Parable of the Talents

14 "For it is as if a man, going on a journey, summoned his slaves and entrusted his property to them; ¹⁵to one he gave five talents, to another two, to another one, to each according to his ability. Then he went away. ¹⁶The one who had received the five talents went off at once and traded with them, and made five more talents. ¹⁷In the same way, the one who had the two talents made two more talents. ¹⁸But the one who had received the one talent went off and dug a hole in the ground and hid his master's money. ¹⁹After a long time the master of those slaves came and settled accounts with them. ²⁰Then the one who had received the five talents came forward, bringing five more talents, saying, 'Master, you handed over to me five talents; see, I have made five more talents.' ²¹His master said to him, 'Well done, good and trustworthy slave; you have been trustworthy in a few things, I will put you in charge of many things; enter into the joy of your master.' ²²And the one with the two talents also came forward, saying, 'Master, you handed over to me two talents; see, I have made two more talents.' ²³His master said to him, 'Well done, good and trustworthy slave; you have been trustworthy in a few things, I will put you in charge of many things; enter into the joy of your master.' ²⁴Then the one who had received the one talent also came forward, saying, 'Master, I knew that you were a harsh man, reaping where you did not sow, and gathering where you did not scatter seed; ²⁵so I was afraid, and I went and hid your talent in the ground. Here you have what is yours.' ²⁶But his master replied, 'You wicked and lazy slave! You knew, did you, that I reap where I did not sow, and gather where I did not scatter? ²⁷Then you ought to have invested my money with the bankers, and on my return I would have received what was my own with interest. ²⁸So take the talent from him, and give it to the one with the ten talents. ²⁹For to all those who have, more will be given, and they will have an abundance; but from those who have nothing, even what they have will be taken away. ³⁰As for this worthless slave, throw him into the outer darkness, where there will be weeping and gnashing of teeth.'

The Judgment of the Nations

31 "When the Son of Man comes in his glory, and all the angels with him, then he will sit on the throne of his glory. ³²All the nations will be gathered before him, and he will separate people one from another as a shepherd separates the sheep from the goats, ³³and he will put the sheep at his right hand and the goats at the left. ³⁴Then the king will say to those at his right hand, 'Come, you that are blessed by my Father, inherit the kingdom prepared for you from the foundation of the world; ³⁵for I was hungry and you gave me food, I was thirsty and you gave me something to drink, I was a stranger and you welcomed me, ³⁶I was naked and you gave me clothing, I was sick and you took care of me, I was in prison and you visited me.' ³⁷Then the righteous will answer him, 'Lord, when was it that we saw you hungry and gave you food, or thirsty and gave you something to drink? ³⁸And when was it that we saw you a stranger and welcomed you, or naked and gave you clothing? ³⁹And when was it that we saw you sick or in prison and visited you?' ⁴⁰And the king will answer them, 'Truly I tell you, just as you did it to one of the least of these who are members of my family, you did it to me.' ⁴¹Then he will say to those at his left hand, 'You that are accursed, depart from me into the eternal fire prepared for the devil and his angels; ⁴²for I was hungry and you gave me no food, I was thirsty and you gave me nothing to drink, ⁴³I was a stranger and you did not welcome me, naked and you did not give me clothing, sick and in prison and you did not visit me.' ⁴⁴Then they also will answer, 'Lord, when was it that we saw you hungry or thirsty or a stranger or naked or sick or in prison, and did not take care of you?' ⁴⁵Then he will answer them, 'Truly I tell you, just as you did not do it to one of the least of these, you did not do it to me.' ⁴⁶And these will go away into eternal punishment, but the righteous into eternal life."

The Plot to Kill Jesus

26 When Jesus had finished saying all these things, he said to his disciples, ²"You know that after two days the Passover is coming, and the Son of Man will be handed over to be crucified."

3 Then the chief priests and the elders of the people gathered in the palace of the high priest, who was called Caiaphas, ⁴and they conspired to arrest Jesus by stealth and kill him. ⁵But they said, "Not during the festival, or there may be a riot among the people."

The Anointing at Bethany

6 Now while Jesus was at Bethany in the house of Simon the leper, ⁷a woman came to him with an alabaster jar of very costly ointment, and she poured it on his head as he sat at the table. ⁸But when the disciples saw it, they were angry and said, "Why this waste? ⁹For this ointment could have been sold for a large sum, and the money given to the poor." ¹⁰But Jesus, aware of this, said to them, "Why do you trouble the woman? She has performed a good service for me. ¹¹For you always have the poor with you, but you will not always have me. ¹²By pouring this ointment on my body she has prepared me for burial. ¹³Truly I tell you, wherever this good news is proclaimed in the whole world, what she has done will be told in remembrance of her."

Judas Agrees to Betray Jesus

14 Then one of the twelve, who was called Judas Iscariot, went to the chief priests ¹⁵and said, "What will you give me if I betray him to you?" They paid him thirty pieces of silver. ¹⁶And from that moment he began to look for an opportunity to betray him.

The Passover with the Disciples

17 On the first day of Unleavened Bread the disciples came to Jesus, saying, "Where do you want us to make the preparations for you to eat the Passover?" ¹⁸He said, "Go into the city to a certain man, and say to him, 'The Teacher says, My time is near; I will keep the Passover at your house with my disciples.'" ¹⁹So the disciples did as Jesus had directed them, and they prepared the Passover meal.

20 When it was evening, he took his place with the twelve; ²¹and while they were eating, he said, "Truly I tell you, one of you will betray me."

22And they became greatly distressed and began to say to him one after another, "Surely not I, Lord?" 23He answered, "The one who has dipped his hand into the bowl with me will betray me. 24The Son of Man goes as it is written of him, but woe to that one by whom the Son of Man is betrayed! It would have been better for that one not to have been born." 25Judas, who betrayed him, said, "Surely not I, Rabbi?" He replied, "You have said so."

The Institution of the Lord's Supper

26 While they were eating, Jesus took a loaf of bread, and after blessing it he broke it, gave it to the disciples, and said, "Take, eat; this is my body." 27Then he took a cup, and after giving thanks he gave it to them, saying, "Drink from it, all of you; 28for this is my blood of the covenant, which is poured out for many for the forgiveness of sins. 29I tell you, I will never again drink of this fruit of the vine until that day when I drink it new with you in my Father's kingdom."

30 When they had sung the hymn, they went out to the Mount of Olives.

Peter's Denial Foretold

31 Then Jesus said to them, "You will all become deserters because of me this night; for it is written,
'I will strike the shepherd,
    and the sheep of the flock will be scattered.'
32But after I am raised up, I will go ahead of you to Galilee." 33Peter said to him, "Though all become deserters because of you, I will never desert you." 34Jesus said to him, "Truly I tell you, this very night, before the cock crows, you will deny me three times." 35Peter said to him, "Even though I must die with you, I will not deny you." And so said all the disciples.

Jesus Prays in Gethsemane

36 Then Jesus went with them to a place called Gethsemane; and he said to his disciples, "Sit here while I go over there and pray." 37He took with him Peter and the two sons of Zebedee, and began to be grieved and agitated. 38Then he said to them, "I am deeply grieved, even to death; remain here, and stay awake with me." 39And going a little farther, he threw himself on the ground and prayed, "My Father, if it is possible, let this cup pass from me; yet not what I want but what you want." 40Then he came to the disciples and found them sleeping; and he said to Peter, "So, could you not stay awake with me one hour? 41Stay awake and pray that you may not come into the time of trial; the spirit indeed is willing, but the flesh is weak." 42Again he went away for the second time and prayed, "My Father, if this cannot pass unless I drink it, your will be done." 43Again he came and found them sleeping, for their eyes were heavy. 44So leaving them again, he went away and prayed for the third time, saying the same words. 45Then he came to the disciples and said to them, "Are you still sleeping and taking your rest? See, the hour is at hand, and the Son of Man is betrayed into the hands of sinners. 46Get up, let us be going. See, my betrayer is at hand."

The Betrayal and Arrest of Jesus

47 While he was still speaking, Judas, one of the twelve, arrived; with him was a large crowd with swords and clubs, from the chief priests and the elders of the people. 48Now the betrayer had given them a sign, saying, "The one I will kiss is the man; arrest him." 49At once he came up to Jesus and said, "Greetings, Rabbi!" and kissed him. 50Jesus said to him, "Friend, do what you are here to do." Then they came and laid hands on Jesus and arrested him. 51Suddenly, one of those with Jesus put his hand on his sword, drew it, and struck the slave of the high priest, cutting off his ear. 52Then Jesus said to him, "Put your sword back into its place; for all who take the sword will perish by the sword. 53Do you think that I cannot appeal to my Father, and he will at once send me more than twelve legions of angels? 54But how then would the scriptures be fulfilled, which say it must happen in this way?" 55At that hour Jesus said to the crowds, "Have you come out with swords and clubs to arrest me as though I were a bandit? Day after day I sat in the temple teaching, and you did not arrest me. 56But all this has taken place, so that the scriptures of the prophets may be fulfilled." Then all the disciples deserted him and fled.

Jesus Before the High Priest

57 Those who had arrested Jesus took him to Caiaphas the high priest, in whose house the scribes and the elders had gathered. ⁵⁸But Peter was following him at a distance, as far as the courtyard of the high priest; and going inside, he sat with the guards in order to see how this would end. ⁵⁹Now the chief priests and the whole council were looking for false testimony against Jesus so that they might put him to death, ⁶⁰but they found none, though many false witnesses came forward. At last two came forward ⁶¹and said, "This fellow said, 'I am able to destroy the temple of God and to build it in three days.'" ⁶²The high priest stood up and said, "Have you no answer? What is it that they testify against you?" ⁶³But Jesus was silent. Then the high priest said to him, "I put you under oath before the living God, tell us if you are the Messiah, the Son of God." ⁶⁴Jesus said to him, "You have said so. But I tell you,

> From now on you will see the Son of Man
> seated at the right hand of Power
> and coming on the clouds of heaven."

⁶⁵Then the high priest tore his clothes and said, "He has blasphemed! Why do we still need witnesses? You have now heard his blasphemy. ⁶⁶What is your verdict?" They answered, "He deserves death." ⁶⁷Then they spat in his face and struck him; and some slapped him, ⁶⁸saying, "Prophesy to us, you Messiah! Who is it that struck you?"

Peter's Denial of Jesus

69 Now Peter was sitting outside in the courtyard. A servant-girl came to him and said, "You also were with Jesus the Galilean." ⁷⁰But he denied it before all of them, saying, "I do not know what you are talking about." ⁷¹When he went out to the porch, another servant-girl saw him, and she said to the bystanders, "This man was with Jesus of Nazareth." ⁷²Again he denied it with an oath, "I do not know the man." ⁷³After a little while the bystanders came up and said to Peter, "Certainly you are also one of them, for your accent betrays you." ⁷⁴Then he began to curse, and he swore an oath, "I do not know the man!" At that moment the cock crowed. ⁷⁵Then Peter remembered what Jesus had said: "Before the cock crows, you will deny me three times." And he went out and wept bitterly.

Jesus Brought before Pilate

27 When morning came, all the chief priests and the elders of the people conferred together against Jesus in order to bring about his death. ²They bound him, led him away, and handed him over to Pilate the governor.

The Suicide of Judas

3 When Judas, his betrayer, saw that Jesus was condemned, he repented and brought back the thirty pieces of silver to the chief priests and the elders. ⁴He said, "I have sinned by betraying innocent blood." But they said, "What is that to us? See to it yourself." ⁵Throwing down the pieces of silver in the temple, he departed; and he went and hanged himself. ⁶But the chief priests, taking the pieces of silver, said, "It is not lawful to put them into the treasury, since they are blood money." ⁷After conferring together, they used them to buy the potter's field as a place to bury foreigners. ⁸For this reason that field has been called the Field of Blood to this day. ⁹Then was fulfilled what had been spoken through the prophet Jeremiah, "And they took the thirty pieces of silver, the price of the one on whom a price had been set, on whom some of the people of Israel had set a price, ¹⁰and they gave them for the potter's field, as the Lord commanded me."

Pilate Questions Jesus

11 Now Jesus stood before the governor; and the governor asked him, "Are you the King of the Jews?" Jesus said, "You say so." ¹²But when he was accused by the chief priests and elders, he did not answer. ¹³Then Pilate said to him, "Do you not hear how many accusations they make against you?" ¹⁴But he gave him no answer, not even to a single charge, so that the governor was greatly amazed.

Barabbas or Jesus?

15 Now at the festival the governor was accustomed to release a prisoner for the crowd, anyone whom they wanted. ¹⁶At that time they had a notorious prisoner, called Jesus Barabbas. ¹⁷So after they had gathered, Pilate said to them, "Whom do you want me to release for you, Jesus Barabbas or Jesus who is called the Messiah?" ¹⁸For he realized that it was out of jealousy that they had handed him over. ¹⁹While he was sitting on the judgment seat, his wife sent word to him, "Have nothing to do with that innocent man, for today I have suffered a great deal because of a dream about him." ²⁰Now the chief priests and the elders persuaded the crowds to ask for Barabbas and to have Jesus killed. ²¹The governor again said to them, "Which of the two do you want me to release for you?" And they said, "Barabbas." ²²Pilate said to them, "Then what should I do with Jesus who is called the Messiah?" All of them said, "Let him be crucified!" ²³Then he asked, "Why, what evil has he done?" But they shouted all the more, "Let him be crucified!"

Pilate Hands Jesus over to Be Crucified

24 So when Pilate saw that he could do nothing, but rather that a riot was beginning, he took some water and washed his hands before the crowd, saying, "I am innocent of this man's blood; see to it yourselves." ²⁵Then the people as a whole answered, "His blood be on us and on our children!" ²⁶So he released Barabbas for them; and after flogging Jesus, he handed him over to be crucified.

The Soldiers Mock Jesus

27 Then the soldiers of the governor took Jesus into the governor's headquarters, and they gathered the whole cohort around him. ²⁸They stripped him and put a scarlet robe on him, ²⁹and after twisting some thorns into a crown, they put it on his head. They put a reed in his right hand and knelt before him and mocked him, saying, "Hail, King of the Jews!" ³⁰They spat on him, and took the reed and struck him on the head. ³¹After mocking him, they stripped him of the robe and put his own clothes on him. Then they led him away to crucify him.

The Crucifixion of Jesus

32 As they went out, they came upon a man from Cyrene named Simon; they compelled this man to carry his cross. ³³And when they came to a place called Golgotha (which means Place of a Skull), ³⁴they offered him wine to drink, mixed with gall; but when he tasted it, he would not drink it. ³⁵And when they had crucified him, they divided his clothes among themselves by casting lots; ³⁶then they sat down there and kept watch over him. ³⁷Over his head they put the charge against him, which read, "This is Jesus, the King of the Jews."

38 Then two bandits were crucified with him, one on his right and one on his left. ³⁹Those who passed by derided him, shaking their heads ⁴⁰and saying, "You who would destroy the temple and build it in three days, save yourself! If you are the Son of God, come down from the cross." ⁴¹In the same way the chief priests also, along with the scribes and elders, were mocking him, saying, ⁴²"He saved others; he cannot save himself. He is the King of Israel; let him come down from the cross now, and we will believe in him. ⁴³He trusts in God; let God deliver him now, if he wants to; for he said, 'I am God's Son.'" ⁴⁴The bandits who were crucified with him also taunted him in the same way.

The Death of Jesus

45 From noon on, darkness came over the whole land until three in the afternoon. ⁴⁶And about three o'clock Jesus cried with a loud voice, "Eli, Eli, lema sabachthani?" that is, "My God, my God, why have you forsaken me?" ⁴⁷When some of the bystanders heard it, they said, "This man is calling for Elijah." ⁴⁸At once one of them ran and got a sponge, filled it with sour wine, put it on a stick, and gave it to him to drink. ⁴⁹But the others said, "Wait, let us see whether Elijah will come to save him." ⁵⁰Then Jesus cried again with a loud voice and breathed his last. ⁵¹At that moment the curtain of the temple was torn in two, from top to bottom. The earth shook, and the rocks were split. ⁵²The tombs also were opened,

and many bodies of the saints who had fallen asleep were raised. ⁵³After his resurrection they came out of the tombs and entered the holy city and appeared to many. ⁵⁴Now when the centurion and those with him, who were keeping watch over Jesus, saw the earthquake and what took place, they were terrified and said, "Truly this man was God's Son!"

55 Many women were also there, looking on from a distance; they had followed Jesus from Galilee and had provided for him. ⁵⁶Among them were Mary Magdalene, and Mary the mother of James and Joseph, and the mother of the sons of Zebedee.

The Burial of Jesus

57 When it was evening, there came a rich man from Arimathea, named Joseph, who was also a disciple of Jesus. ⁵⁸He went to Pilate and asked for the body of Jesus; then Pilate ordered it to be given to him. ⁵⁹So Joseph took the body and wrapped it in a clean linen cloth ⁶⁰and laid it in his own new tomb, which he had hewn in the rock. He then rolled a great stone to the door of the tomb and went away. ⁶¹Mary Magdalene and the other Mary were there, sitting opposite the tomb.

The Guard at the Tomb

62 The next day, that is, after the day of Preparation, the chief priests and the Pharisees gathered before Pilate ⁶³and said, "Sir, we remember what that impostor said while he was still alive, 'After three days I will rise again.' ⁶⁴Therefore command the tomb to be made secure until the third day; otherwise his disciples may go and steal him away, and tell the people, 'He has been raised from the dead,' and the last deception would be worse than the first." ⁶⁵Pilate said to them, "You have a guard of soldiers; go, make it as secure as you can." ⁶⁶So they went with the guard and made the tomb secure by sealing the stone.

The Resurrection of Jesus

28 After the sabbath, as the first day of the week was dawning, Mary Magdalene and the other Mary went to see the tomb. ²And suddenly there was a great earthquake; for an angel of the Lord, descending from heaven, came and rolled back the stone and sat on it. ³His appearance was like lightning, and his clothing white as snow. ⁴For fear of him the guards shook and became like dead men. ⁵But the angel said to the women, "Do not be afraid; I know that you are looking for Jesus who was crucified. ⁶He is not here; for he has been raised, as he said. Come, see the place where he lay. ⁷Then go quickly and tell his disciples, 'He has been raised from the dead, and indeed he is going ahead of you to Galilee; there you will see him.' This is my message for you." ⁸So they left the tomb quickly with fear and great joy, and ran to tell his disciples. ⁹Suddenly Jesus met them and said, "Greetings!" And they came to him, took hold of his feet, and worshiped him. ¹⁰Then Jesus said to them, "Do not be afraid; go and tell my brothers to go to Galilee; there they will see me."

The Report of the Guard

11 While they were going, some of the guard went into the city and told the chief priests everything that had happened. ¹²After the priests had assembled with the elders, they devised a plan to give a large sum of money to the soldiers, ¹³telling them, "You must say, 'His disciples came by night and stole him away while we were asleep.' ¹⁴If this comes to the governor's ears, we will satisfy him and keep you out of trouble." ¹⁵So they took the money and did as they were directed. And this story is still told among the Jews to this day.

The Commissioning of the Disciples

16 Now the eleven disciples went to Galilee, to the mountain to which Jesus had directed them. ¹⁷When they saw him, they worshiped him; but some doubted. ¹⁸And Jesus came and said to them, "All authority in heaven and on earth has been given to me. ¹⁹Go therefore and make disciples of all nations, baptizing them in the name of the Father and of the Son and of the Holy Spirit, ²⁰and teaching them to obey everything that I have commanded you. And remember, I am with you always, to the end of the age."

A Seminar on the *Gospel of Matthew*

The faculty of the Intellectual Heritage Program at Temple University often hold seminars in which they discuss the issues of the texts we teach. Here we present a rare opportunity to students—the chance to overhear their professors talking together about the books. These are the notes from a meeting held in Fall of 1997.

Yesterday's "*Matthew* Chat" was rich and highly informative.

Much of the discussion was about the crisis of the Jews living under Roman rule, which is the historical setting of the *Gospel of Matthew*. We recalled that Jesus and the Disciples are Jewish as are the Pharisees. *Matthew* gives us an argument within Judaism. The Pharisees, despite what many readers think they know, are not non-believers, or doubters of Jesus, so much as a group of highly righteous and learned Jews battling to keep their community from forgetting its traditions under the assaults of Rome. In their strict adherence, the Gospel would tell us, they have forgotten what it is that Jesus is ready to remind them of—the deeper truths of the tradition they struggle to uphold. These confrontations (Professor Gross suggested) should remind us of Socrates and his street discussions with the traditional and pious members of his community, his gadfly role in urging his fellow citizens to think clearly.

Much was said also about the tradition of the Messiah. The Gospel records the confusion of two very different notions of salvation. The more obvious liberator is the return of the Maccabees (2nd Century B.C.E.), a warrior-leader who will throw off the yoke of Rome and restore the Davidic Kingdom of a thousand years earlier. Barrabas seems a much more likely liberator in this tradition. Even within the Jewish tradition there is a second conception of the Messiah, the priestly purifier, descended from Aaron. But this other Messiah (this *Christos*—Greek term for annointed one) changes everything. It would seem that the *Gospel of Matthew* was aimed at Jewish audiences to persuade them of the rightness of this new way of being liberated and of being Jewish.

We spent some time discussing the political situation of Judea in this Roman period. Herod (there are two in the story, a grandfather and grandson of the Herodians who were chosen to administer the rule of Rome), Caiaphas (the High Priest of the Temple, whose vestments were loaned out to him by the Romans who regulated religious observation), Pontius Pilate (the Roman Governor who was removed by the Romans for being too harsh). The Jews lived in degradation under Rome, their hopes for national sovereignty broken by centuries of defeat; the promises of ancient covenants seemingly empty; and after centuries of self-laceration (*Lamentations, Isaiah, Jeremiah,* etc.), perhaps ready to dismiss their own essential identity. Pompey, the conquering Roman general, had invaded the Holy of Holies, the inner sanctum of the Temple, and found it empty! And, of course, the Temple itself was to be destroyed in 70 C.E. by the Romans as the price for the rebelliousness of the Jews. These are terrible times when a revolution is appropriate.

We noted, also, that later political purposes seem to be included in the text. The Romans seem absolved as the source of cruelty, and the figure of the Centurion who sees Jesus as the Christ (a familiar figure in Hollywood Christ films) helps us all see how Romans really are a proper community for conversion. Matthew insists that it is those "other Jews" and not the gentiles that are really the source of the troubles for Jesus.

We observed that Jesus as presented is not the "gentle Jesus" of the Sunday School account. He is exacting and demanding and stern; he whips the money changers from the Temple, he curses the fig tree, he damns people to hell. The Wedding Feast Parable promises destruction for those who will not respond to the invitation of this new salvation. His debates with the

Pharisees are spirited and tough. He is the one figure who is fully awake (Socrates, again) in a world of sleep-walkers!

We talked about the sources of the Gospels. In Matthew almost everything is from Jewish history; in John and Paul, from Greek Mystery (the dead god revived; the ritual partaking of flesh and blood).

We discussed *Matthew* as a revolutionary text—that is, a text that changes everything. What changes?—the law is "fulfilled" (no more divorces, which were allowed in the Mosaic law—see *Matthew* 19, for Jesus' teaching on this; and there is an insistence on interior/psychological reality); religion is now universal in its impact, where previously Judaism was for the Israelites alone; and, finally, there is the promise of eternal life for the righteous. One might add the inclusion of women, at least in the direct teachings of Jesus. He is clearly a man/god who loves women and has a significant place for them (later Church teachings reverse this democratization). And another is the social class appeal, in which the poor and meek are privileged and the rich and powerful are condemned. An interesting text in this regard is *1Corinthians* 13, where all the attainments that a Greek would treasure (knowledge, wisdom, rhetorical skill, etc.) are rejected for love of one's fellows (charity).

This led us to some discussion of the difficulty of Christ's teachings. How can we be expected to turn the other cheek? To love one's enemies? Not only to resist, but indeed never to have impure thoughts? One answer is that these high ideals introduce the glory of grace—i.e., although these ideals are a far reach for us, a loving God is ready to forgive us so long as our effort is there.

Another set of demands—leaving one's family behind, giving away all earthly possessions—makes sense if we imagine that the promised end of this world is imminent. This eschatology, along with the images of Armageddon (a word taken from the name of a wide plain near Jerusalem and the only place where a battle of armies employing chariots—the ultimate weapon of the time—could take place) dominates the last portions of the *Gospel of Matthew*. We recall, too, that Jesus promises that within the lifetime of those in his audience, all this would take place. John Yeatts explained that within Christian teaching this Kingdom arrived on earth with Jesus' coming and that a second coming is promised when the world will indeed be judged finally.

It is interesting to note, too, that Christian churches have had a hard time since knowing how to come at the teachings against gathering worldly goods and the condemnations of the rich. A student of mine from Spain explained that the "eye of the needle" (through which a rich man would have to pass with all his goods in order to enter heaven) was actually an entry gate to the City of Jerusalem, and that a heavily laden camel (i.e., that of a rich man) would have to unload some of its treasure to gain entry. The teaching, then, means that some wealth would have to be "offloaded" for the rich to gain heaven. The student was taught that by the priests of his parish.

In general, there was tension in the group discussion concerning tradition and innovation—that nothing is new in the *New Testament* because everything in it has a textual and cultural source, and that everything is fundamentally new!

Some "Literature" people emphasized the beauties of the language and the need for students to become acquainted with the phrases and metaphors that have entered our language (King James) from *Matthew* and are now common terms—". . . not by bread alone"; "a millstone around your neck"; "a house divided against itself . . ."; "practice what you preach"; and hundreds of others.

Gospel of John

The Word Became Flesh

1 In the beginning was the Word, and the Word was with God, and the Word was God. ²He was in the beginning with God. ³All things came into being through him, and without him not one thing came into being. What has come into being ⁴in him was life, and the life was the light of all people. ⁵The light shines in the darkness, and the darkness did not overcome it.

6 There was a man sent from God, whose name was John. ⁷He came as a witness to testify to the light, so that all might believe through him. ⁸He himself was not the light, but he came to testify to the light. ⁹The true light, which enlightens everyone, was coming into the world.

10 He was in the world, and the world came into being through him; yet the world did not know him. ¹¹He came to what was his own, and his own people did not accept him. ¹²But to all who received him, who believed in his name, he gave power to become children of God, ¹³who were born, not of blood or of the will of the flesh or of the will of man, but of God.

14 And the Word became flesh and lived among us, and we have seen his glory, the glory as of a father's only son, full of grace and truth. ¹⁵(John testified to him and cried out, "This was he of whom I said, 'He who comes after me ranks ahead of me because he was before me.'") ¹⁶From his fullness we have all received, grace upon grace. ¹⁷The law indeed was given through Moses; grace and truth came through Jesus Christ. ¹⁸No one has ever seen God. It is God the only Son, who is close to the Father's heart, who has made him known.

The Testimony of John the Baptist

19 This is the testimony given by John when the Jews sent priests and Levites from Jerusalem to ask him, "Who are you?" ²⁰He confessed and did not deny it, but confessed, "I am not the Messiah." ²¹And they asked him, "What then? Are you Elijah?" He said, "I am not." "Are you the prophet?" He answered, "No." ²²Then they said to him, "Who are you? Let us have an answer for those who sent us. What do you say about yourself?" ²³He said,

"I am the voice of one crying out in the wilderness,
'Make straight the way of the Lord,'" as the prophet Isaiah said.

24 Now they had been sent from the Pharisees. ²⁵They asked him, "Why then are you baptizing if you are neither the Messiah, nor Elijah, nor the prophet?" ²⁶John answered them, "I baptize with water. Among you stands one whom you do not know, ²⁷the one who is coming after me; I am not worthy to untie the thong of his sandal." ²⁸This took place in Bethany across the Jordan where John was baptizing.

The Lamb of God

29 The next day he saw Jesus coming toward him and declared, "Here is the Lamb of God who takes away the sin of the world! ³⁰This is he of whom I said, 'After me comes a man who ranks ahead of me because he was before me.' ³¹I myself did not know him; but I came baptizing with water for this reason, that he might be revealed to Israel." ³²And John testified, "I saw the Spirit descending from heaven like a dove, and it re-

---

Scripture quotations are from the *New Revised Standard Version of the Bible,* copyright 1989 by the Division of Christian Education of the National Council of the Churches of Christ in the USA. Used by permission. All rights reserved.

mained on him. ³³I myself did not know him, but the one who sent me to baptize with water said to me, 'He on whom you see the Spirit descend and remain is the one who baptizes with the Holy Spirit.' ³⁴And I myself have seen and have testified that this is the Son of God."

The First Disciples of Jesus

35 The next day John again was standing with two of his disciples, ³⁶and as he watched Jesus walk by, he exclaimed, "Look, here is the Lamb of God!" ³⁷The two disciples heard him say this, and they followed Jesus. ³⁸When Jesus turned and saw them following, he said to them, "What are you looking for?" They said to him, "Rabbi" (which translated means Teacher), "where are you staying?" ³⁹He said to them, "Come and see." They came and saw where he was staying, and they remained with him that day. It was about four o'clock in the afternoon. ⁴⁰One of the two who heard John speak and followed him was Andrew, Simon Peter's brother. ⁴¹He first found his brother Simon and said to him, "We have found the Messiah" (which is translated Anointed). ⁴²He brought Simon to Jesus, who looked at him and said, "You are Simon son of John. You are to be called Cephas" (which is translated Peter).

Jesus Calls Philip and Nathanael

43 The next day Jesus decided to go to Galilee. He found Philip and said to him, "Follow me." ⁴⁴Now Philip was from Bethsaida, the city of Andrew and Peter. ⁴⁵Philip found Nathanael and said to him, "We have found him about whom Moses in the law and also the prophets wrote, Jesus son of Joseph from Nazareth." ⁴⁶Nathanael said to him, "Can anything good come out of Nazareth?" Philip said to him, "Come and see." ⁴⁷When Jesus saw Nathanael coming toward him, he said of him, "Here is truly an Israelite in whom there is no deceit!" ⁴⁸Nathanael asked him, "Where did you get to know me?" Jesus answered, "I saw you under the fig tree before Philip called you." ⁴⁹Nathanael replied, "Rabbi, you are the Son of God! You are the King of Israel!" ⁵⁰Jesus answered, "Do you believe because I told you that I saw you under the fig tree? You will see greater things than these." ⁵¹And he said to him, "Very truly, I tell you, you will see heaven opened and the angels of God ascending and descending upon the Son of Man."

The Wedding at Cana

2 On the third day there was a wedding in Cana of Galilee, and the mother of Jesus was there. ²Jesus and his disciples had also been invited to the wedding. ³When the wine gave out, the mother of Jesus said to him, "They have no wine." ⁴And Jesus said to her, "Woman, what concern is that to you and to me? My hour has not yet come." ⁵His mother said to the servants, "Do whatever he tells you." ⁶Now standing there were six stone water jars for the Jewish rites of purification, each holding twenty or thirty gallons. ⁷Jesus said to them, "Fill the jars with water." And they filled them up to the brim. ⁸He said to them, "Now draw some out, and take it to the chief steward." So they took it. ⁹When the steward tasted the water that had become wine, and did not know where it came from (though the servants who had drawn the water knew), the steward called the bridegroom ¹⁰and said to him, "Everyone serves the good wine first, and then the inferior wine after the guests have become drunk. But you have kept the good wine until now." ¹¹Jesus did this, the first of his signs, in Cana of Galilee, and revealed his glory; and his disciples believed in him.

12 After this he went down to Capernaum with his mother, his brothers, and his disciples; and they remained there a few days.

Jesus Cleanses the Temple

13 The Passover of the Jews was near, and Jesus went up to Jerusalem. ¹⁴In the temple he found people selling cattle, sheep, and doves, and the money changers seated at their tables. ¹⁵Making a whip of cords, he drove all of them out of the temple, both the sheep and the cattle. He also poured out the coins of the money changers and overturned their tables. ¹⁶He told those who were selling the doves, "Take these things out of here! Stop making my Father's house a marketplace!" ¹⁷His disciples remembered that it was written, "Zeal for your house will consume

me." ¹⁸The Jews then said to him, "What sign can you show us for doing this?" ¹⁹Jesus answered them, "Destroy this temple, and in three days I will raise it up." ²⁰The Jews then said, "This temple has been under construction for forty-six years, and will you raise it up in three days?" ²¹But he was speaking of the temple of his body. ²²After he was raised from the dead, his disciples remembered that he had said this; and they believed the scripture and the word that Jesus had spoken.

23 When he was in Jerusalem during the Passover festival, many believed in his name because they saw the signs that he was doing. ²⁴But Jesus on his part would not entrust himself to them, because he knew all people ²⁵and needed no one to testify about anyone; for he himself knew what was in everyone.

Nicodemus Visits Jesus

3 Now there was a Pharisee named Nicodemus, a leader of the Jews. ²He came to Jesus by night and said to him, "Rabbi, we know that you are a teacher who has come from God; for no one can do these signs that you do apart from the presence of God." ³Jesus answered him, "Very truly, I tell you, no one can see the kingdom of God without being born from above." ⁴Nicodemus said to him, "How can anyone be born after having grown old? Can one enter a second time into the mother's womb and be born?" ⁵Jesus answered, "Very truly, I tell you, no one can enter the kingdom of God without being born of water and Spirit. ⁶What is born of the flesh is flesh, and what is born of the Spirit is spirit. ⁷Do not be astonished that I said to you, 'You must be born from above.' ⁸The wind blows where it chooses, and you hear the sound of it, but you do not know where it comes from or where it goes. So it is with everyone who is born of the Spirit." ⁹Nicodemus said to him, "How can these things be?" ¹⁰Jesus answered him, "Are you a teacher of Israel, and yet you do not understand these things?

11 "Very truly, I tell you, we speak of what we know and testify to what we have seen; yet you do not receive our testimony. ¹²If I have told you about earthly things and you do not believe, how can you believe if I tell you about heavenly things? ¹³No one has ascended into heaven except the one who descended from heaven, the Son of Man. ¹⁴And just as Moses lifted up the serpent in the wilderness, so must the Son of Man be lifted up, ¹⁵that whoever believes in him may have eternal life.

16 "For God so loved the world that he gave his only Son, so that everyone who believes in him may not perish but may have eternal life.

17 "Indeed, God did not send the Son into the world to condemn the world, but in order that the world might be saved through him. ¹⁸Those who believe in him are not condemned; but those who do not believe are condemned already, because they have not believed in the name of the only Son of God. ¹⁹And this is the judgment, that the light has come into the world, and people loved darkness rather than light because their deeds were evil. ²⁰For all who do evil hate the light and do not come to the light, so that their deeds may not be exposed. ²¹But those who do what is true come to the light, so that it may be clearly seen that their deeds have been done in God."

Jesus and John the Baptist

22 After this Jesus and his disciples went into the Judean countryside, and he spent some time there with them and baptized. ²³John also was baptizing at Aenon near Salim because water was abundant there; and people kept coming and were being baptized ²⁴John, of course, had not yet been thrown into prison.

25 Now a discussion about purification arose between John's disciples and a Jew. ²⁶They came to John and said to him, "Rabbi, the one who was with you across the Jordan, to whom you testified, here he is baptizing, and all are going to him." ²⁷John answered, "No one can receive anything except what has been given from heaven. ²⁸You yourselves are my witnesses that I said, 'I am not the Messiah, but I have been sent ahead of him.' ²⁹He who has the bride is the bridegroom. The friend of the bridegroom, who stands and hears him, rejoices greatly at the bridegroom's voice. For this reason my joy has been fulfilled. ³⁰He must increase, but I must decrease."

The One Who Comes from Heaven

31 The one who comes from above is above all; the one who is of the earth belongs to the earth and speaks about earthly things. The one who comes from heaven is above all. [32]He testifies to what he has seen and heard, yet no one accepts his testimony. [33]Whoever has accepted his testimony has certified this, that God is true. [34]He whom God has sent speaks the words of God, for he gives the Spirit without measure. [35]The Father loves the Son and has placed all things in his hands. [36]Whoever believes in the Son has eternal life; whoever disobeys the Son will not see life, but must endure God's wrath.

1 Corinthians

The Gift of Love

13 If I speak in the tongues of mortals and of angels, but do not have love, I am a noisy gong or a clanging cymbal. ²And if I have prophetic powers, and understand all mysteries and all knowledge, and if I have all faith, so as to remove mountains, but do not have love, I am nothing. ³If I give away all my possessions, and if I hand over my body so that I may boast, but do not have love, I gain nothing.

4 Love is patient; love is kind; love is not envious or boastful or arrogant ⁵or rude. It does not insist on its own way; it is not irritable or resentful; ⁶it does not rejoice in wrongdoing, but rejoices in the truth. ⁷It bears all things, believes all things, hopes all things, endures all things.

8 Love never ends. But as for prophecies, they will come to an end; as for tongues, they will cease; as for knowledge, it will come to an end. ⁹For we know only in part, and we prophesy only in part; ¹⁰but when the complete comes, the partial will come to an end. ¹¹When I was a child, I spoke like a child, I thought like a child, I reasoned like a child; when I became an adult, I put an end to childish ways. ¹²For now we see in a mirror, dimly, but then we will see face to face. Now I know only in part; then I will know fully, even as I have been fully known. ¹³And now faith, hope, and love abide, these three; and the greatest of these is love.

Qur'an

We include the *Qur'an* in Intellectual Heritage for several reasons. Although this Holy Book is less well known to us than the Bible, it is growing in prominence in the United States. Indeed, Islam is growing faster than any other religion in our country, and especially in the Northern cities one sees evidence everywhere of the Muslim community. One should note also that close to 800 million people world-wide are Muslims and that in the West we read about Islamic movements daily, and often in ignorant and belligerent terms.

In addition, Islam was for many centuries a center of world learning and scientific excellence. When Europe was suffering through the period known as the Dark Ages (roughly from the fall of Rome in 453 until the flourishing of the Renaissance 1450), Muslim scholars preserved the texts of ancient philosophers, scientists, astronomers, mathematicians, and themselves advanced the knowledge in those fields of study (ever wonder why the names of most stars are Arabic and our numbers are called "Arabic numerals," and such terms as "chemistry," "algebra," and "zero" are borrowed from Arabic?).

The Great Mosque at Mecca is the central site for Muslims the world over. Their pilgrimage is to this place where there stands the Ka'bah, a stone house of prayer built by Abraham and Ishmael. The Ka'bah is visible in this picture at the very center of the Great Mosque. UPI/Corbis-Bettmann.

The *Qur'an* is a complex text for most of us. Unlike the Bible, it does not contain many stories. Instead, it teaches very directly what Allah (God) wants from us. Muslims recite the *Qur'an* at family gatherings, social gatherings, and in their daily prayers. Many Muslims memorize large portions of the *Qur'an*, and it is not uncommon to find followers of Islam who have committed the entire book to memory. Muslims agree that the *Qur'an* exists only in Arabic, and that "translations" are merely commentaries because no matter how true to the original, they introduce many changes that can be misleading.

This demand for absolute fidelity can be explained by understanding the origins of the *Qur'an*. In the year 610, as Muhammad meditated alone in a cave nearby the city of Mecca (located today in Saudi Arabia), he was visited by the angel Gabriel with a message from God. The angel commanded Muhammad to "recite" what the angel relayed to him. The word "Qur'an" means "the recitation." Muhammad proceeded to recite these messages to his followers over the next 22 years. They were recorded by scribes, and the slight variations have since been regularized. Muslims, therefore, can claim that their scriptures do not suffer from the major editing, selection process, and accidents of translation of the Bible. There is no question in the *Qur'an* of what parts are authoritative since it is all in the voice of God's angel.

We have selected Surah Two, "The Cow," as our main reading. This Surah (Chapter) contains the main tenets of the faith and many of the laws for living of Islam. Therefore, it is often called the "little *Qur'an*." The name of this Surah comes from a central incident it reports regarding Moses and his efforts to bring God's message to the Israelites. The reluctance of these people to hear God's message and submit themselves is the central teaching; instead, the people wish to delay and haggle over the rules. The *Qur'an* is forceful about the need to submit to God. After all, the word "Islam" means "to submit."

Most notable for Christian readers is the direct embrace of the benefits of life in this world. As Surah Two makes clear, God does not wish us to suffer but to enjoy his bounty, and that includes not only food and the glories of nature but even sexual pleasure. In addition, we are to understand that one can prosper in this world and still gain eternal salvation. Finally, the very proof of God's existence and compassion for us is in the abundance of nature which we are to enjoy. Although Islam imposes strict disciplines upon its followers, these do not include a wish to eradicate the appetites, only to have them enjoyed in moderation.

One also sees in this "little *Qur'an*" how much of Islamic teaching touches everyday matters and supplies specific rules. For example, observe the rules governing divorce and how specific and how realistic these are. So too, issues concerning cleanliness and business dealings are presented as a straightforward guide to living

Perhaps most worth our notice are the passages addressed to the condition of women. Islam has acquired in our time a poor reputation for its treatment of women. This reputation is most unfair and unenlightened. Surah Two, for example, shows just how progressive Islam was in its time. Women are permitted to own property (a legal right won only in the late 19th century in the United States); and they are specifically invested with the legal rights of men. Emerging as does this advanced view in 7th century Arabia is truly remarkable. Before Islam, women were treated as property and often as prizes in plundering raids and business dealings. Marriage dowries seem to have been more highly prized than wives and mothers. Muhammad brings God's word to change all this brutality, and women have followed Islam with great fervor from the 7th century until this day.

The collection of very short Surahs that we have included represent the earliest recitations. They treat, quite lyrically, some of the more mystical issues of existence and the mystery of our spirit. Here we can gather in a clearer sense of the beauties of the *Qur'an* and why Muslims are enraptured at this central treasure of their existence. As any Muslim will happily tell you, however, these transcendent beauties are really only available in the original Arabic and the love-filled human voice that recites.

Introduction to the *Qur'an*

Some Notes

One of the surprises for most of us in opening up the *Qur'an* is to discover that it is, among other things, a continuation of the Bible with which we are familiar. We find Surahs (chapters) discussing Joseph, Noah, Moses, Mary and so on. We find Allah to be the same one God of the Judeo-Christian tradition.

We find many of the same laws and the same general format that includes:

   a. An announcement of God and His purposes and rituals required to honor God
   b. Laws of Social Obligation (ethics)
   c. Laws regarding Dispositions of the Heart
   d. A Guide to Everyday Life (handling property disputes, rules of marriage and divorce, practices of cleanliness, etc.).

In this regard, the *Qur'an* is much like the Hebrew Bible. The *New Testament* includes the first three but has much less on (d) the fourth category because (1) it anticipates an imminent end to this world, and (2) Christianity in its early days happens within the rule of Rome and cannot articulate and enforce its own civil law.

There is another initial connection we need to observe. Arab Muslims trace their origin to Abraham of the Hebrew Bible. As *Genesis* tells us, Abraham was first the father of Ishmael (with his servant woman Hagar, identified as an Egyptian) because Sarah was unable to conceive a child. Only in her old age was Sarah blessed by the Lord with the ability to conceive Isaac. Hagar and Ishmael are sent away into the desert. And in their despair they are comforted by God with the promise that Ishmael shall be the father of a mighty people. This reference is understood to be relating to the Arabs.

A confirmation of this is the holy building known as the Ka'bah. This small stone structure is identified as a house of prayer constructed by Abraham and Ishmael. The Ka'bah sits today as the focal structure in the great mosque at Meccah, the destination of the journey all Muslims are invited to make at least once during their lifetime.

This means, surprisingly enough, that for all their present emnity, Jews and Arabs are descended from half-brothers and are therefore kin.

Some Themes

1. The *Qur'an* is a forthright Text, announcing right off that it is "not to be doubted." Part of this air of certainty results from the way the *Qur'an* is known to have been received and transmitted. Gabriel, delivering God's message directly, speaks to Muhammad. Muhammad recites the messages to scribes. And that is it. There is none of the problem that exists with the Hebrew Bible and *New Testament* about how this text came to be compiled, edited, translated, and worked to the advantage of certain political moments. The *Qur'an*, Muslims maintain, is purely the word of God.
2. The *Qur'an* advises tolerance towards other peoples and their religion. Jews, Christians, and others can be saved if they follow God's word as it is known to them.

This tolerance was not always perfectly realized in the days of Muslim conquest. On the other hand, Islam contained a large Jewish population that flourished under Muslim rule.

3. The *Qur'an* specifically rejects the Divinity of Jesus although Muslims accept Jesus as a major prophet of God. For Muslims, God is indivisible and would have no reason to seek an indirect route, like containing His majesty within a human form, to make his law and Being known.

4. The *Qur'an* sees God in nature everywhere, and some of the finest poetry directs us to the beauties and generosity of the natural world for our pleasure. Thus, the *Qur'an* is not squeamish about sexual matters and invites Muslims to recognize the blessing of sexual pleasure within the bonds of marriage. Sexual joy is one feature of the promise of heavenly bliss. In addition, the *Qur'an* permits such natural feeling as the need for retaliation against injuries. Not only does retaliation protect you from further assault, but human beings need to express their anger in a direct physical expression or risk becoming twisted with hate. All of this acceptance of nature and certain features of human nature are in stark contrast to the puritanical features of Christianity.

5. The *Qur'an* also addresses social law and issues of justice. Like the *Hebrew Bible*, the *Qur'an* presents the basis of civil law (recall that early Christianity exists within the rule of Rome). The *Qur'an* treats many issues of ethics and social process, such as how to settle economic disputes, marriage and divorce, the lending of money, and so forth. The *Qur'an* also offers a guide on such matters as diet and cleanliness.

6. Women benefit most particularly from the *Qur'an*. They are accorded legal rights, including rights to property. They are also taught modesty of dress and manner as a protection against the terrible depredations they faced before the coming of Islam at

This man reads the Qur'an in absolute devotion. The world over, Muslims center their lives upon the Qur'an and its teachings. Islam welcomes a love of this book as the guide to life and celebration of God. It is not unusual for Muslims to memorize large portions of the Qur'an and sometimes even the entire book. Dean Conger/Corbis.

the hands of a crude and lawless people. Muhammad was beloved of women and continues to be so in the Muslim world for the honor and protection accorded women by Islam.
7. There is a realism about Islam that finds its roots in the *Qur'an*. Human beings can do well in this world, live a life of abundance, so long as they do not forget God's laws and the real force of the Final Judgment. They owe the poor and oppressed protection and charity; a pious life and a successful life in this world are not mutually exclusive. We all have our measure of suffering, but the successful are not singled out for rejection and future torments.

The Story of the Qur'an

Muhammad M. Pickthall

Part I
At Makkah

Muhammad, son of 'Abd Allāh, son of 'Abd al Muṭṭalib, of the tribe of Quraysh, was born in Makkah fifty-three years before the Hijrah. As his father died before he was born, the young Muhammad was raised under the protection of his grandfather 'Abd al Muṭṭalib and, after this man's death, by his uncle Abū Ṭalib. As a young boy, he travelled with his uncle in the merchants' caravan to Syria and, some years later, made the same journey in the service of a wealthy widow named Khadījah. So faithfully did he transact her business and so excellent was the report of his behavior that she received from her old servant who had accompanied him, that she soon proposed to and then married her young agent. The marriage proved to be a very happy one, though she was fifteen years older than he was. Throughout the twenty-six years of their life together, Muhammad was devoted to her. Even after her death, when he married other women, he always mentioned her name with the greatest love and reverence. This marriage gave him rank among the Makkan notables, while his conduct earned for him the surname *al Amīn*, the "trustworthy."

The Makkans claimed descent from Abraham through Ishmael, and tradition stated that their temple (the Ka'bah) had been built by Abraham for the worship of the One God. It was still called the House of Allah, even though by the Prophet's time it housed the chief objects of the local pagan cult: several idols known as the "daughters of Allah" and regarded as intercessors. The few who were disgusted with the prevailing idolatry, which had prevailed for centuries, longed for the religion of Abraham and tried to discover its original teachings. Such seekers of the truth were known as Ḥunafā' (sing. Ḥanīf), a word that had originally meant "those who turn away" (from the existing idol-worship) but later on came to have the sense of "upright" or "by nature upright," because such persons held the way of truth to be right conduct. The Ḥunafā' did not form a community: they were the agnostics of their day, each seeking truth by the light of his own inner consciousness.

Muhammad became one of these people. It was his practice to retire for one month (Ramaḍan, the "month of heat") every year to a cave in the desert for meditation. His place of retreat was Ḥirā,' a desert hill located close to Makkah. It was there one night toward the end of his retreat that the first revelation came to him when he was forty years old. He was asleep or in a trance when he heard a voice say: "Read!" He replied: "I cannot read." The voice again said: "Read!" and he again replied: "I cannot read." A third time, the voice commanded: "Read!" He said: "What can I read?" The voice said:

"Read: In the name of your Lord who creates, creates man from a clot. Read: And your Lord is the Most Bounteous Who teaches by the pen, teaches man that which he knew not."

When he awoke, the words remained "as if inscribed upon his heart." He went out of the cave and heard the same awe-inspiring voice say: "O Muhammad! You are Allah's Messenger, and I am Gabriel." Then he raised his eyes and saw the angel, in the likeness of a man, standing in the sky above the horizon. Again the awesome voice said: "O Muhammad! You are Allah's Messenger, and I am Gabriel." Muhammad (God's

---

From *The Meaning of the Glorious Qur'an* by Muhammad Marmaduke Pickthall, edited and revised by Arafat El Ashi. Copyright © 1996 by Amana Publications. Reprinted by permission.

grace and peace be with him) stood quite still, turning his face away from the brightness of the vision. But wherever he turned his face, the angel was always standing there, confronting him. He remained thus a long while, until the angel vanished, and then returned in great distress to his wife Khadījah. She did her best to reassure him, saying that his conduct had been such that Allah would not let a harmful spirit come to him and that she hoped that he would become the prophet of his people. She took him to her cousin Waraqa ibn Nawfal, a very old man "who knew the Scriptures of Jews and Christians." This man declared his belief that the heavenly messenger who had come to Moses had now come to Muhammad and that he had been chosen to serve as the prophet of his people.

To understand why the Prophet felt extreme distress after this, it must be remembered that the Ḥunafā' sought true religion in the natural world and distrusted any communication with those spirits about which men "avid of the Unseen,"' sorcerers, soothsayers, and even poets boasted in those days. Moreover, he was a man of humble and devout intelligence, a lover of quiet and solitude. The very thought of being chosen to face mankind alone with such a message at first appalled him. His recognition of the divine nature of the call caused a change in his whole mental outlook that was enough to disturb his sensitive and honest mind and caused him to forsake his quiet and honored way of life. The early biographers tell how Khadījah "tried the spirit" that came to him and proved it to be good, and how, when the revelations continued and his conviction in them grew, he at length accepted the tremendous task and was filled with an enthusiasm of obedience that justifies his proudest title: "The Slave of Allah."

The words that were revealed to him are held sacred by all Muslims and are never confounded with those uttered when no physical change was apparent in him. The former make up the Qur'an, while the latter form the Hadith or the Sunnah of the Prophet. Since the angel on Mt. Ḥira' commanded him to "Read!" and insisted on his "reading," even though the Prophet was illiterate, the sacred book is known as al Qur'an, "The Reading,"' the Reading of the man who did not know how to read.

During the first three years of his mission, the Prophet preached only to his family and intimate friends. The people of Makkah as a whole regarded him as having become a little mad. His first convert was Khadījah, the second was his first cousin 'Alī (whom he had adopted), and the third was his servant Zayd (a former slave). His old friend Abū Bakr was among the early converts, along with some of his slaves and dependents.

At the end of the third year, the Prophet received the command to "arise and Warn." He now began to preach in public, pointing out the wretched folly of idolatry in face of the tremendous laws of day and night, of life and death, of growth and decay, all of which manifest the power of Allah and attest to His sovereignty. When he began to speak against their gods, the Quraysh became actively hostile and began to persecute his poorer disciples and to mock and insult him. The one consideration that prevented them from killing him was their fear of the Prophet's clan's right to blood-vengeance in the event of his murder. Strong in his inspiration, the Prophet continued to warn, plead, and threaten while the Quraysh did what they could to ridicule his teaching and spread dejection among his followers. The converts of the first four years were mostly humble folk who could not defend themselves. So cruel was the persecution they endured that the Prophet advised all who could possibly do so to emigrate to Abyssinia, a Christian country.

Despite the persecution and emigration, the number of Muslims grew. The Quraysh were seriously alarmed. The idol worship at the Ka'bah, the holy place to which all inhabitants of Arabia made pilgrimage and of which they were the guardian, was among their most important vested interests. During the pilgrimage season, they posted men on all the roads to warn the tribes against the madman preaching in their midst. They tried to persuade the Prophet to compromise by offering to accept his religion if he would modify it to make room for their gods as intercessors with Allah. When this failed, they said that he could be their king if he would give up attacking idolatry. When their efforts at negotiation failed, they went to his uncle Abū Ṭalib and said that they would give him the best of their young men in place of Muhammad and, moreover, give him all that he desired, if only he would let them kill Muhammad. Abū Ṭalib refused.

The exasperation of the idolaters was increased by the conversion of 'Umar, one of their stalwarts. They grew more and more embittered, till things came to such a pass that they decided to ostracize the Prophet's whole clan, regardless of whether or not they believed in his message. Their chief men drew up a document to the effect that none of them or their dependents would have any dealings, business or otherwise, with the Prophet's clan. They all signed this document and deposited it in the Ka'bah. For the next three years, the Prophet and his people were enclosed in their stronghold, which was located in one of the gorges leading to Makkah. Only at the time of pilgrimage could he go out and preach or did any of his kinsfolk dare go into the city.

Finally, some of the more sensitive members of the Quraysh grew weary of this boycott against their old friends and neighbors. They managed to have the document brought out of the Ka'bah for reconsideration. It was then discovered that all of the writing had been destroyed by white ants, except for the words *Bismika Allāhuma* ("In Your name, O God"). When the elders saw this miracle, they lifted the ban and allowed the Prophet to resume his former way of life in the city. However, as the opposition to his preaching had grown rigid, he had little success among the Makkans. In addition, his attempt to preach in the city of Ṭā'if also ended in failure. Judged by the narrow worldly standards, his mission was until then a failure.

But then he met a small group of men who listened to him and believed. They came from Yathrib, a city more than two hundred miles away, which has since become famous as al Madinah, "the City" *par excellence*. Among Yathrib's inhabitants were Jewish tribes whose learned rabbis had often spoken to the Arab pagans of a soon-to-come prophet who, along with the Jews, would destroy them as the tribes of 'Ād and Thamūd had been destroyed for their idolatry. After this group of men listened to Muhammad, they recognized him as the prophet described by the Jewish rabbis. On their return to Yathrib, they told others what they had seen and heard. As a result, when the next season of pilgrimage arrived, a deputation came from Yathrib in order to meet the Prophet. Its members swore allegiance to him in the first pact of al 'Aqabah. They returned to Yathrib with a Muslim teacher in their company, and soon "there was not a house in Yathrib wherein there was not a mention of the Messenger of Allah."

In the following year at the time of pilgrimage, seventy-three Muslims from Yathrib came to Makkah to swear allegiance to the Prophet and invite him to their city. At al 'Aqabah, they swore to defend him as they would their own wives and children. It was then that the Hijrah, or the Flight to Yathrib, was decided.

Soon those Muslims who could began to sell their property and leave Makkah unobtrusively. The Quraysh eventually learned what was going on and, although they hated having Muhammad in their midst, they were even more afraid of what he might do if he was beyond their reach. They decided that it would be better to kill him as soon as possible. When his chief protector, Abū Ṭālib, was removed by death, they saw their chance, even though they would still have to reckon with the vengeance of his clan. To avoid this, they cast lots and chose one member from every clan to participate in the attack on the Prophet. These men then pledged themselves to strike the Prophet at exactly the same time, so that his blood would be on the entire Quraysh tribe. It was at this time (asserts Ibn Khaldūn, and it is the only satisfactory explanation of what happened afterwards) that the Prophet received the first revelation ordering him to make war upon his persecutors "until persecution is no more and religion is for Allah only."

The last of the able Muslims in Makkah were Abū Bakr, 'Alī, and the Prophet. Abū Bakr, who was a wealthy man, had bought two riding camels and retained a guide in readiness for the Prophet's departure, which would take place when God ordered it.

On the appointed night, the murderers gathered in front of the Prophet's house. The Prophet gave his cloak to 'Alī and asked him to lie down on the bed so that if anyone looked in, they would think that it was the Prophet lying there. The murderers had decided to attack the Prophet whenever he came out of his house. Knowing that they would not injure 'Alī, the Prophet left the house unseen by his opponents. It is said that blindness fell upon the would-be murderers: he put dust on their heads as he passed by without them being aware of his departure. After picking up Abū Bakr at the latter's house, the two men went to a cave in the nearby mountains and stayed there until the immediate danger was past. Abū Bakr's son, daughter, and his herdsman brought them food and news after nightfall. The Makkans sent out search parties, one of which came quite near to their hiding place. Seeing that Abū Bakr was sad, the Prophet told him: "Grieve not! Allah is with us."' When the coast was clear, Abū Bakr told the guide to bring the riding camels to the cave one night so that they could begin the long ride to Yathrib.

After travelling for many days by unfrequented paths, the fugitives reached a suburb of Yathrib. The people of the city had been going there every morning for weeks in anticipation of the Prophet's arrival. They would give up their watch only when it became so hot that they had to seek shelter. It was at just such a time that the two travellers arrived. The man who spread the news was a Jew, who called out to the Muslims in derisive tones that the men for whom they were waiting had arrived at last. Such was the Hijrah, the Flight from Makkah to Yathrib, which marks the beginning of the Muslim era. The thirteen years of humiliation, persecution, apparent failure, unfulfilled prophecies were now over. The ten years of success, the fullest period that has ever crowned one man's endeavor, would now begin.

The Hijrah marks a clear division in the story of the Prophet's mission, which is evident in the Qur'an. Up until this time, he had only been a preacher. From now on, he would be the ruler of a state, admittedly at first a very small one, but one that would grow during the next ten years into the empire of Arabia. The kind of guidance that he and his people needed after the Hijrah was different from that which they had received in Makkah. Therefore, the surahs revealed during this period differ from those revealed earlier. Whereas the Makkan surahs give guidance to the individual soul and to the Prophet in his capacity as a warner, the Madinan surahs give guidance to a growing social and political community and to the Prophet as example, lawgiver, and reformer.

For classification purposes, the Makkan surahs are subdivided into four groups: very early, early, middle, and late. Though the historical data and traditions are insufficient for a strict chronological grouping, the very early surahs were, roughly speaking, revealed before the persecution began; the early surahs were revealed between the beginning of the persecution and 'Umar's conversion; the middle surahs were revealed between 'Umar's conversion and the destruction of the deed of ostracism; and the late surahs were revealed between the end of the ostracism and the Hijrah.

Part II
At al Madinah

In the first year of his reign at Yathrib, the Prophet and the Jews negotiated a solemn treaty by which the latter were given full rights of citizenship and religious liberty in exchange for their support of the new state. However, their idea of a prophet was an individual who would give them dominion over others, not one who would make those who followed the same message (i.e., Arab Muslims) their brothers and equals. When they discovered that they could not use the Prophet for their own purposes, they tried to weaken his faith in his mission and to seduce his followers. They received secret support for these efforts from some professing Muslims who thought that the presence of the Prophet in their city would weaken or even end their influence and therefore resented his presence. In the Madinah surahs, such Jews and Hypocrites are mentioned with great frequency.

Until this time, the *qiblah* (the place toward which Muslims face when praying) had been Jerusalem. The Jews, believing that this implied a pro-Judaism bias on the part of the Prophet, began to say that he needed to be instructed by them. To clear up this misunderstanding, it was revealed to the Prophet that the Muslims should turn their faces toward Makkah and the Ka'bah when praying. The whole first part of the second surah deals with this Jewish controversy.

Now that he was a ruler, the Prophet's first concern was to establish public worship and to lay down his state's constitution. He did not forget, however, that the Quraysh had sworn to oppose his religion or that he had been ordered by God to fight against his persecutors until they were completely defeated. One year after his arrival in Yathrib, he sent out small expeditions, led by himself or someone else, in order to see what was going on and to persuade other local tribes not to side with the Quraysh.

These are generally represented as warlike but, considering their weakness and the fact that there was no actual fighting (although they were prepared to fight), they can hardly have been that. It is noteworthy that these expeditions were composed only of Muslims who had originally come from Makkah. The natives of Yathrib did not participate, for the reason that (if we accept Ibn Khaldūn's theory) the command to fight had been revealed to the Prophet at Makkah after the men from Yathrib had sworn their oath of allegiance at al 'Aqabah, and in their absence. They had undertaken to protect the Prophet from attack, not to fight with him in actual campaigns. Blood was shed and booty taken—against the Prophet's express orders—in only one of those early expeditions. One purpose of those expeditions may have been to prepare the Makkan Muslims for actual warfare. For thirteen years they had been strict pacifists and it is clear from several Qur'anic passages that many, including perhaps even the Prophet, hated the idea of fighting even in self-defence and had to accept it gradually.

In the second year of the Hijrah, a caravan belonging to Makkan merchants was returning from Syria by the usual route, which happened to be located not far from Yathrib. Its leader, Abū Sufyān, learned of the Prophet's plan to capture the caravan as he approached the territory of Yathrib. At once he sent a camel-rider to Makkah. Upon his arrival, the exhausted rider shouted frantically from the valley to the Quraysh to ride as fast as they could to protect their wealth and honor. A force of one thousand warriors was soon on its way to Yathrib—apparently less concerned with saving the caravan than with punishing the raiders, since the Prophet might have taken the caravan before their departure.

Did the Prophet ever intend to raid the caravan? According to Ibn Hishām's account of the Tabūk expedition, on that one occasion the Prophet did not hide his real objective. The caravan was the pretext for the campaign of Badr, and the real objective was the Makkan army. He had received the command to fight his persecutors, had been promised victory, and was ready to fight against all odds (as was the case with the battle of Badr). The Muslims, until then not very eager for war and also ill-equipped, would have despaired if they had known at the outset that they would face a well-armed force three times their number.

The Qurayshī army advanced more than halfway to Yathrib before the Prophet set out. The two armies, in addition to the caravan, were all heading for the water located at Badr. Abū Sufyān, the caravan leader, heard from one of his scouts that the Muslims were near the water and so turned back to the coastal plain. The Muslims met the Quraysh by the water. Before the battle, the Prophet was prepared to increase the odds against him. He told the Anṣār (natives of Yathrib) that they could return to their homes unreproached, since their oath did not include participating in actual warfare. The Anṣar, however, were hurt by the very thought that they would even consider leaving the Prophet when he was in danger.

Despite the clear difference in numbers in favor of the Quraysh, Muslims emerged victorious. This victory gave the Prophet new prestige among the Arab tribes, but it also resulted in a blood feud, in addition to the religious conflict, between the Quraysh and the Prophet. The Qur'anic passages that refer to the battle of Badr warn of much greater struggles to come.

In fact, the very next year saw an army of three thousand Makkan warriors on their way to Yathrib to destroy it. The Prophet's first idea was to defend the city. This plan received the strong support of 'Abd Allah ibn 'Ubayy, leader of "the Hypocrites" (or lukewarm Muslims). However, the veterans of Badr believed that God would help them against any odds and thought they would shame themselves if they remained behind walls. The Prophet, approving of their faith and zeal, agreed and set out with one thousand men toward the enemy encampment at Mt. Uhud. 'Abd Allāh ibn 'Ubayy opposed this change in plan, for he claimed that the Prophet would really fight in such disadvantageous circumstances and did not want to take part in a demonstration of power. He therefore withdrew with his men and decreased the size of the Muslim army by one-third.

Despite the heavy odds, the battle at Mt. Uhud would have been an even greater Muslim victory than that at Badr if the band of fifty Muslim archers, whom the Prophet set to guard a pass against the enemy cavalry, had not deserted their posts upon seeing their comrades victorious, fearing that they might miss out on the resulting spoils. The Qurayshī cavalry rode through the gap, fell on the exultant Muslims, and wounded the Prophet. The cry arose that the Prophet had been killed. However, someone recognized him and shouted that he was still living, which caused the demoralized Muslims to rally. They gathered around the Prophet and began to retreat, leaving many fallen warriors on the hillside.

On the following day, the Prophet again sallied forth with what remained of his army so that the Quraysh would hear that he was in the field and perhaps be deterred from attacking the city. The stratagem succeeded, thanks to a friendly bedouin who, after meeting and talking with the Muslims, encountered the Quraysh. Upon being questioned by Abū Sufyān, he said that Muhammad was in the field, stronger than ever, and thirsting for revenge. Based on this information, Abū Sufyān decided to quickly return to Makkah.

This setback lowered the Muslims' prestige with the Arab tribes and also with the Jews of Yathrib. Tribes that had inclined towards the Muslims before now inclined towards the Quraysh. The Prophet's followers were attacked and murdered when they went abroad in little companies. Khubayb, an envoy of the Prophet, was captured by a desert tribe and sold to the Quraysh, who then tortured him to death before the people of Makkah. The Jews, despite their treaty with the Prophet, became almost open in their hostility and told the Quraysh that their pagan religion was superior to Islam. The Prophet was obliged to take punitive action against some of them. The Banī Naḍīr tribe was besieged in its strong forts, eventually subdued, and then forced to emigrate. The Hypocrites had sympathized with the Jews and encouraged them secretly.

In the fifth year of the Hijrah, the idolaters made a great effort to destroy Islam in an event called the War of the Clans or War of the Trench. The Quraysh gathered all of its clans and allied its army with that of the Ghatafān, a great desert tribe. This alliance, ten thousand warriors strong, then marched on Yathrib, by now known as al Madinah. The Prophet ordered (supposedly upon the advice of Salmān the Persian) and participated in the digging of a deep trench in front the city. The enemy army did not know what to do when faced with such a novelty; they had never seen such a defense before. As their cavalry, which formed their strength, did not know how, or was unable, to breach it, they camped in sight of it and daily showered their arrows on its defenders.

While the Muslims awaited the assault, news came that Banī Qurayẓah, a Jewish tribe of Yathrib that had till then been loyal, had gone over to the enemy. The case seemed desperate. However, the delay caused by the trench had dampened the enemy's enthusiasm, and an individual who was secretly a Muslim was able to sow distrust between the Quraysh and their Jewish allies. This caused both sides to hesitate. During their hesitation, a bitter wind from the sea reached them. It engulfed them for three days and nights and was so strong that no tent could be kept standing, no fire lit, or no water boiled. Seeing that the tribesmen were in utter misery, one night the leader of the Qurayshī army decided that the torment could be borne no longer and gave the order to retire. When the Ghatafān awoke the next morning and saw that the Quraysh had departed, they gathered their supplies and retreated.

Upon his return from the trench, the Prophet ordered war against the treacherous Banī Qurayẓah who, conscious of their guilt, had already taken to their towers of refuge. After a siege of nearly a month, they surrendered unconditionally and begged to be judged by a member of the Arab tribe to which they were affiliated. The Prophet granted their request and carried out the sentence of the judge: the execution of the men and the enslavement of the women and children.

Early in the sixth year of the Hijrah, the Prophet led a campaign against the Banī Mustaliq tribe, as it had been preparing to attack the Muslims. During the return from this campaigning, 'A'ishah, the Prophet's young wife, was left behind. A young soldier found her and brought her back to the Muslim camp. This incident gave rise to the scandal denounced in Surah 24. In addition, 'Abd Allāh ibn 'Ubayy, the "Hypocrite" chief, planned to exploit the situation. He is reported to have said: "When we return to the city the mightier will soon expel the weaker," upon witnessing a quarrel between the Muhājirīn (immigrants from Makkah) and the Anṣar (natives of Yathrib).

In the same year, the Prophet had a vision in which he saw himself entering the holy precincts of Makkah unopposed and made the intention to perform the pilgrimage. Along with a number of Muslims from Yathrib (which we shall here-after call al Madinah), he called upon those Arabs who were sympathetic to his cause, whose numbers had increased since the miraculous (as it was considered) discomfiture of the clans, to accompany him. Most of them did not respond. This did not deter him, however, and he set out for Makkah with fourteen hundred men attired as pilgrims and bearing the customary offerings. As they approached the holy valley, they were met by a friend from the city who warned the Prophet that the Quraysh had put on their leopardskins (a badge of valor), had sworn to prevent him from entering the sanctuary, and that their cavalry was on the road in front of him. After hearing this, the Prophet ordered a detour through mountain gorges. When his exhausted troops finally reached al Ḥudaytbīyah, a site located within the valley of Makkah, they set up camp and rested.

The Prophet now sought to open negotiations. He sent a messenger to the enemy camp to inform the Quraysh that he and his men wanted to enter Makkah only as pilgrims. This man was maltreated, his camel was hamstrung, and he had to return before he could deliver his message. The Quraysh then sent a man to convey their message in a very threatening and arrogant tone. Another of their messengers was too familiar and had to be reminded sternly of the respect due to the Prophet. When this second messenger returned to Makkah, he said: "I have seen Caesar and Chosroes in their pomp, but never have I seen a man so honored by his comrades as is Muhammad."

The Prophet decided to send another messenger whom the Quraysh would be forced to treat with respect. Eventually, he chose to send 'Uthmān, who had ties of kinship with the powerful 'Umayyad family. While the Muslims were awaiting his return, they received the news that he had been murdered. This turn of events caused the Prophet, who was sitting under a tree at al Ḥudaybīyah, to bind his followers to an oath that they would all stand or fall together. After a while, however, it became known that 'Uthmān had not been murdered. A group of Makkan warriors that tried to harm the Muslims in their camp was captured before any harm was done, and the men were forgiven and released after they promised the Prophet that they would renounce their previous hostility.

This incident marked the beginning of serious negotiations, for the Quraysh now sent proper envoys. The resulting agreement, known as the truce of al Ḥudabīyah, enshrined a cessation of hostilities for a period of ten years. The Prophet was to return to al Madīnah without visiting the Ka'bah with the understanding that he and his comrades would be able to perform the pilgrimage the following year. At that time, the Quraysh would evacuate Makkah for three days so that his pilgrimage could be made properly. The Prophet promised to return all members of the Quraysh who sought to join the Muslims, even though the Quraysh did not have to assume a corresponding obligation. It was also accepted by both sides that any tribe or clan that wished to participate in the treaty as allies of the Prophet or of the Quraysh could do so.

There was dismay among the Muslims when they learned of the terms. They asked one another: "Where is the victory that we were promised?" In response, Surah at Fatḥ (Victory) was revealed while the troops were returning to al Madīnah. What these men did not know was that this truce would prove to be the greatest victory achieved by the Muslims up to that time, for armed hostilities, which had been a barrier between them and the non-Muslims, had prevented both parties from meeting and talking with each other. Now that this barrier had been removed, the new religion spread more rapidly. In the two years that elapsed between the signing of the truce and the fall of Makkah, more people embraced Islam than had done so since the beginning of the Prophet's mission. The Prophet had travelled to al Ḥudaybīyah with 1400 men. Two years later, when the Makkans broke the truce, he marched against them with an army of ten thousand.

In the seventh year of the Hijrah, the Prophet led a campaign against the Jewish stronghold of Khaybar, which was located in northern Arabia and had become a focal point for his enemies. The forts of Khaybar were reduced one by one, and their Jewish inhabitants were turned into tenants of the Muslims until all Jews were expelled from Arabia during the caliphate of 'Umar. On the day when the last fort surrendered, Ja'far, son of Abū Ṭālib and the Prophet's cousin, arrived from Abyssinia with the Muslims whom the Prophet had advised to leave Makkah fifteen years earlier.

After the Muslims' victory at Khaybar, a Jewess prepared a meal of poisoned meat for the Prophet. He tasted, but did not swallow, a small piece of it and then told his comrades that it was poisoned. One Muslim, who had already swallowed some of it, did instantly. The Prophet, even though he had only tasted it, contracted the illness that eventually caused his death. When the guilty woman was brought before him, she said that she had done it to avenge the humiliation of her people. The Prophet forgave her.

During this same year, the Prophet's vision was fulfilled; he visited the holy place at Makkah unopposed. In accordance with the terms of the truce, the non-Muslims evacuated the city and watched the Muslim pilgrimage from the surrounding heights. At the end of the stipulated three days, the chiefs of the Quraysh sent word to the Prophet to remind him that they had fulfilled their part of the treaty and that it was now time for him to leave Makkah. He withdrew, and the idolaters reoccupied the city.

In the eighth year of the Hijrah, hearing that the Byzantine emperor was gathering a force in Syria to send against the Muslims, the Prophet dispatched three thousand men under the command of his freedman Zayd. The campaign was not successful, but the reckless valor of the Muslims—three thousand of them did not hesitate to take the battle field against one hundred thousand enemy troops—left an impression on the Syrians. When all of the three leaders appointed by the Prophet had been killed, the survivors obeyed Khālid ibn al Walīd, whose strategy and courage preserved the Muslim army and got it back to al Madīnah.

Also in this year, the Quraysh broke the truce by attacking a tribe allied to the Prophet and massacring its members even in the sanctuary at Makkah. After this breach, the Quraysh sent Abū Sufyān to al Madīnah to ask for the existing treaty to be renewed and prolonged before the Prophet learned what had happened to his allies. His mission ended in failure, however, for a survivor was able to reach the Prophet and inform him of the massacre.

The Prophet now summoned all of the Muslims who could bear arms and marched on Makkah. The Quraysh were overwhelmed and, after putting up a show of defense in front of the town, were routed without bloodshed. The Prophet, upon entering Makkah as a conqueror, proclaimed a general amnesty for all but a few known criminals, most of whom were eventually forgiven. In their relief and surprise, the whole population of Makkah hastened to swear allegiance to him. The Prophet then destroyed all of the idols housed in the Ka'bah, saying: "Truth has come; falsehood has vanished," and the Muslim call to prayer rang out over Makkah.

But not all tribes were so eager to embrace Islam. In that same year, an angry gathering of pagan tribes tried to regain control of the Ka'bah. The Prophet, who led twelve thousand men against them, met this new enemy at Ḥunayn. When the Muslims advanced into a deep ravine, they were ambushed and almost put to flight. With difficulty, they managed to rally to the Prophet and his bodyguard of faithful comrades who stood firm. But the victory, when it came, was complete and the booty enormous, for many of the hostile tribes had brought with them all of their possessions. The tribe of Thaqīf, which had participated in this campaign, soon saw its own city of Ṭā'if besieged and reduced to submission.

After all of this, the Prophet appointed a governor for Makkah and returned to al Madinah to the boundless joy of the Anṣār, who had feared that he might forsake them and return to his native city.

In the ninth year of the Hijrah, hearing that a new army was being assembled in Syria, the Prophet called upon the Muslims to support him in a great campaign. Many excused themselves on the grounds that the distances involved were great, that it was the hot season, that it was harvest time, and that the enemy had a great deal of prestige. Others just refused to go without offering any excuse. Both groups were denounced in the Qur'an. The campaign ended peacefully, for the Muslims advanced to Tabūk, on the borders of Syria, and discovered that the enemy had not yet gathered.

Although Makkah had been conquered and its people were now Muslims, the official order of the pilgrimage had not been changed: the pagan Arabs performed it as usual, and the Muslims performed it in the way ordained by God. Only after the pilgrims' caravan left al Madinah in the ninth year of the Hijrah, by which time Islam was dominant in northern Arabia, was the Declaration of Disavowal revealed. The Prophet sent a copy of it by messenger to Abū Bakr, leader of the pilgrimage, with the instructions that 'Alī was to read it to the multitudes at Makkah. In essence, it stated that after that year only Muslims and certain non-Muslims (those who had never broken their treaties with the Muslims or actively sided against them) would be allowed to make the pilgrimage. These treaties would be honored until their expiration date, after which these non-Muslims would be treated like all of the other non-Muslims. This proclamation marks the end of idol worship in Arabia.

The ninth year of the Hijrah, the Year of Deputations, saw delegations from all over Arabia coming to al Madinah to swear allegiance to the Prophet and to hear the Qur'an. The Prophet had become, in fact, the emperor of Arabia, but his way of life remained as simple as before.

During the last ten years of his life, the Prophet led twenty-seven campaigns, nine of which saw heavy fighting. He planned, but let other people lead, a further thirty-eight expeditions. He personally controlled each detail of the organization, judged each case, and was accessible to each suppliant. He destroyed idolatry in Arabia, raised women from the status of chattel to human beings with complete legal equality vis-à-vis men, and ended the drunkenness and immorality that had until his time disgraced the Arabs. His followers fell in love with faith, sincerity, and honest dealing. Previously ignorant tribes who had been content with their ignorance were transformed into tribes with a great thirst for knowledge. And, for the first time in history, the ideal of universal human brotherhood was a fact and a principle of common law. The Prophet's support and guide in all of this work was the Qur'an.

In the tenth year of the Hijrah, the Prophet performed the pilgrimage to Makkah for the last time. This has become known as the Farewell Pilgrimage. From Mount 'Arafat, he preached to an enormous throng of pilgrims, reminded them of the duties enjoined upon them by God, and that one day they would meet and be judged by their Lord on the basis of what they had done here on Earth. At the end of the discourse, he asked: "Have I conveyed the message?" And from that great multitude of people, who a few months or years before had all been conscienceless idolaters, the shout went up: "O Allah! Yes!" The Prophet said: "O Allah! You are a witness!"

It was during this Farewell Pilgrimage that Surah al Naṣr (Succour), which he received as an announcement of his approaching death, was revealed. Soon after his return to al Madinah he fell ill, an event that caused dismay throughout Arabia and anguish to the people of al Madinah, Makkah, and Ṭā'if. In the early dawn on his last day of earthly life, he came out of his room beside the mosque at al Madinah and joined the public prayer, which Abū Bakr had been leading since his illness. This event caused a great relief among the people, who took this as an indication that he was well again.

When later in the day the rumour spread that he had died, 'Umar declared it a crime to think that the Prophet could die and threatened to punish severely anyone who said such a thing. Abū Bakr, upon entering the mosque and seeing what 'Umar was doing, went to 'Ā'ishah's (his daughter's) chamber to see the Prophet. Ascertaining that the Prophet really was dead, he kissed the Prophet's forehead, returned to the mosque, and tried to whisper the information to 'Umar, who was still threatening the people. Finally, because 'Umar refused to listen to him, Abū Bakr called out to the people. Recognizing his voice, they left 'Umar and turned their attention to Abū Bakr who, after praising God, said: "O people! As for him who used to worship Muhammad, Muhammad is dead. But as for him who used to worship Allah, Allah is alive and does not die." He then recited the following verse:

And Muhammad is but a Messenger, messengers the like of whom have passed away before him. Will it be that, when he dies or is slain, you will turn back on your heels? He who turns back does no hurt to Allah and Allah will reward the thankful.

"And," says the narrator, an eye-witness, "it was as if the people had not known that such a verse had been revealed until Abū Bakr recited it." Another witness tells how 'Umar used to say: "As soon as I heard Abū Bakr recite that verse, my feet were cut from beneath me and I fell to the ground, for I knew that Allah's Messenger was dead. May Allah bless and keep him!"

All the surahs of the Qur'an had been recorded in writing before the Prophet's death, and many Muslims had committed the whole Qur'an to memory. But the written surahs were dispersed among the people. This soon became a problem, for within two years of the Prophet's death, many of those who had memorized the entire Qur'an were killed during a battle. It was therefore decided to collect the written portions and prepare a complete and undeniably authentic written copy of the Qur'an. This was done under the instruction of Abū Bakr, the first caliph. A master copy of the Qur'an was kept in the custody of Ḥafṣah, one of the Prophet's wives.

With the passage of time, people in different places started to differ on the Qur'an's contents. To end such disputes once and for all, Caliph 'Uthmān formed a committee composed of the Prophet's Companions and those who had memorized either all or part of the Qur'an. All existing copies were collected during the reign of 'Uthmān, and an authoritative version based on Abū Bakr's collection and the testimony of those who could recite the entire Qur'an from memory was compiled. This is the Qur'an that exists today, which is regarded as traditional and as being arranged according to the Prophet's own instructions. The caliph 'Uthmān and his helpers, all Companions of the Prophet and the most devout students of the revelation, saw that this task was completed. The Qur'an has thus been very carefully preserved.

The arrangement is not easy to understand. Revelations of various dates and on different subjects are found together; verses revealed in al Madinah are found in Makkan surahs; some Madinan surahs that were revealed quite late are found in the front of the Qur'an while the very early Makkan surahs come at the end. This arrangement is not haphazard, however, as some have hastily supposed. Closer study reveals a sequence and significance, for instance, with regard to placing the very early Makkan surahs at the end. The inspiration of the Prophet progressed from the internal to the external, whereas most people find their way through the external to the internal.

Another disconcerting peculiarity proceeds from one of the beauties of the original and is unavoidable without abolishing the division of the verses, which is of great importance for reference. In Arabic, verses are divided according to the rhythm of the language. When a certain sound marking the rhythm recurs, there is a strong pause and the verse ends naturally, although the sentence may go on to the next verse or to several subsequent verses. This is the spirit of the Arabic language. Unfortunately, attempts to reproduce such rhythm in English have the opposite effect. Here only the division is preserved, the verses being divided as in the Qur'an, and numbered.

The Qur'an

Exordium

IN THE NAME OF GOD THE COMPASSIONATE THE MERCIFUL 1:1

Praise be to God, Lord of the Universe,

The Compassionate, the Merciful,

Sovereign of the Day of Judgement!

You alone we worship, and to You alone we turn for help.

Guide us to the straight path,

The path of those whom You have favoured,

Not of those who have incurred Your wrath, 1:7

Nor of those who have gone astray.

The Cow

In the Name of God, the Compassionate, the Merciful

Alif lām mīm. This Book is not to be doubted. It is a guide for the righteous, who have faith in the unseen and are steadfast in prayer; who give in alms[1] from what We gave them; who trust what has been revealed to you[2] and to others before you, and firmly believe in the life to come. These are rightly guided by their Lord; these shall surely triumph. 2:1

As for the unbelievers, it is the same whether or not you forewarn them; they will not have faith. God has set a seal upon their hearts and ears; their sight is dimmed and grievous punishment awaits them.

There are some who declare: "We believe in God and the Last Day," yet they are no true believers. They seek to deceive God and those who believe in Him: but they deceive none save themselves, though they may not perceive it. There is a sickness in their hearts which God has aggravated: they shall be sternly punished for the lies they tell. 2:10

When they are told: "Do not commit evil in the land," they reply: "We do nothing but good." But it is they who are the evil-doers, though they may not perceive it.

And when they are told: "Believe as others believe," they reply: "Are we to believe as fools believe?" It is they who are the fools, if they but knew it!

When they meet the faithful, they declare: "We, too, are believers." But when alone with their devils they say to them: "We follow none but you: we were only mocking." God will mock them and keep them long in sin, blundering blindly along.

Such are those that barter guidance for error: they profit nothing, nor are they on the right path. They are like one who kindled a fire, but as soon as it lit up all around him God put it out and he was left in darkness: they do not see. Deaf, dumb, and blind, they will never return to the right path. 2:17

Or like those who, beneath a dark storm-cloud charged with thunder and lightning, thrust their fingers in their ears at the sound of every thunder-clap for fear of death (God thus encompasses the unbelievers). The 2:18

From *The Koran* translated by N.J. Dawood (Penguin Classics 1956, Fifth revised edition 1990). Copyright © N.J. Dawood, 1956, 1959, 1966, 1968, 1974, 1990. Reproduced by permission of Penguin Books Ltd.

1 Or "give to the cause."
2 Muḥammad.

lightning almost takes away their sight: whenever it flashes upon them they walk on, but as soon as it darkens they stand still. Indeed, if God pleased, He could take away their hearing and their sight: God has power over all things.

Men, serve your Lord, who has created you and those who have gone before you, so that you may guard yourselves against evil; who has made the earth a bed for you and the sky a dome, and has sent down water from the sky to bring forth fruits for your sustenance. Do not knowingly set up other gods beside God.

If you doubt what We have revealed to Our servant, produce one chapter comparable to it. Call upon your idols to assist you, if what you say be true. But if you fail (as you are sure to fail) then guard yourselves against the Fire whose fuel is men and stones, prepared for the unbelievers. 2:23

Proclaim good tidings to those who have faith and do good works. They shall dwell in gardens watered by running streams: whenever they are given fruit to eat they will say: "This is what we used to eat before," for they shall be given the like. Wedded to chaste spouses, they shall abide therein for ever.

God does not disdain to make a comparison with a gnat or with a larger creature. The faithful know that it is the truth from their Lord, but the unbelievers ask: "What could God mean by this comparison?"

By such comparisons God confounds many and enlightens many. But He confounds none except the evil-doers, who break His covenant after accepting it, and put asunder what He has bidden to be united, and perpetrate corruption in the land. These will surely be the losers. 2:27

How can you deny God? Did He not give you life when you were dead, and will He not cause you to die and then restore you to life? Will you not return to Him at last? He created for you all that the earth contains; then, ascending to the sky, He fashioned it into seven heavens. He has knowledge of all things. 2:28

When your Lord said to the angels: "I am placing on the earth one that shall rule as My deputy," they replied: "Will You put there one that will do evil and shed blood, when we have for so long sung Your praises and sanctified Your name?"

He said: "I know what you know not."

He taught Adam the names of all things and then set them before the angels, saying: "Tell Me the names of these, if what you say be true."

"Glory to You," they replied, "we have no knowledge except that which You have given us. You alone are all-knowing and wise." 2:32

Then said He: "Adam, tell them their names." And when Adam had named them, He said: "Did I not tell you that I know the secrets of the heavens and the earth, and all that you reveal and all that you conceal?"

And when We said to the angels: "Prostrate yourselves before Adam," they all prostrated themselves except Satan, who in his pride refused and became an unbeliever.

We said: "Adam, dwell with your wife in Paradise and eat of its fruits to your hearts' content wherever you will. But never approach this tree or you shall both become transgressors."

But Satan removed them thence and brought about their banishment. "Get you down," We said, "and be enemies to each other. The earth will for a while provide your dwelling and your sustenance."

Then Adam received commandments from his Lord, and his Lord relented towards him. He is the Forgiving One, the Merciful.

"Get you down hence, all," We said. "When My guidance is revealed to you, those that accept My guidance shall have nothing to fear or to regret; but those that deny and reject Our revelations shall be the inmates of the Fire, and there they shall abide for ever." 2:38 2:39

Children of Israel, remember the favour I have bestowed upon you. Keep your covenant, and I will be true to Mine. Dread My power. Have faith in My revelations, which confirm your Scriptures, and do not be the first to deny them. Do not sell My revelations for a paltry price; fear Me. Do not confound truth with falsehood, nor knowingly conceal the truth. Attend to your prayers, render the alms levy, and kneel down with those who kneel down. Would you enjoin righteousness on others and forget it yourselves? Yet you read the Scriptures. Have you no sense?

Fortify yourselves with patience and prayer. This may indeed be an exacting discipline, but not to the devout, who know that they will meet their Lord and that to Him they will return.

Children of Israel, remember the favour I have bestowed upon you, and that I exalted you above the nations. Guard yourselves against the day on which no soul shall stand for another: when neither intercession shall be accepted for it, nor any ransom be taken from it, nor any help be given it. *2:47*

Remember how We delivered you from Pharaoh's people, who had oppressed you cruelly, slaying your sons and sparing only your daughters. Surely that was a great trial from your Lord. We parted the sea for you and, taking you to safety, drowned Pharaoh's men before your very eyes. We communed with Moses for forty nights, but in his absence you took up the calf and thus committed evil. Yet after that We pardoned you, so that you might give thanks.

We gave Moses the Scriptures and knowledge of right and wrong, so that you might be rightly guided. Moses said to his people: "You have wronged yourselves, my people, in worshipping the calf. Turn in repentance to your Creator and slay the culprits among you. That will be best for you in your Creator's sight." And He relented towards you. He is the Forgiving One, the Merciful. *2:54*

When you said to Moses: "We will not believe in you until we see God with our own eyes," the thunderbolt struck you whilst you were looking on. Then We revived you from your stupor, so that you might give thanks. *2:55*

We caused the clouds to draw their shadow over you and sent down for you manna and quails, saying: "Eat of the good things We have given you." Indeed, they[3] did not wrong Us, but they wronged themselves.

"Enter this city," We said, "and eat where you will to your hearts' content. Make your way reverently through the gates, saying: 'We repent.' We shall forgive you your sins and bestow abundance on the righteous." But that which they were told the wrongdoers replaced with other words; and We let loose on the wrongdoers a scourge from heaven as punishment for their misdeeds.

When Moses requested water for his people We said to him: "Strike the Rock with your staff." Thereupon twelve springs gushed from the Rock, and each tribe knew their drinking-place. We said: "Eat and drink of that which God has provided and do not foul the land with evil."

"Moses," you[3] said, "we will no longer put up with this monotonous diet. Call on your Lord to give us some of the varied produce of the earth, green herbs and cucumbers, corn and lentils and onions."

"What!" he answered. "Would you exchange that which is good for what is worse? Go back to some city. There you will find all you have asked for."

Shame and misery were stamped upon them[3] and they incurred the wrath of God; because they disbelieved God's signs and slew the prophets unjustly; because they were rebels and transgressors.

Believers, Jews, Christians, and Sabaeans—whoever believes in God and the Last Day and does what is right—shall be rewarded by their Lord; they have nothing to fear or to regret.

We made a covenant with you[3] and raised the Mount above you, saying: "Receive what We have given you with earnestness and bear in mind its precepts, that you may guard yourselves against evil." Yet after that you turned away, and but for God's grace and mercy you would have surely been among the lost. *2:63* *2:64*

You have heard of those of you that broke the Sabbath. We said to them: "You shall be changed into detested apes." We made their fate an example to their own generation and to those who followed them, and a lesson to the righteous.

When Moses said to his people: "God commands you to sacrifice a cow," they replied: "Are you making game of us?"

"God forbid that I should be so foolish!" he rejoined.

"Call on your Lord," they said, "to make known to us what kind of cow she shall be."

He replied: "Your Lord says: 'Let her be neither an old cow nor a young heifer, but in between.' Do, therefore, as you are bidden."

"Call on your Lord," they said, "to make known to us what her colour shall be."

He replied: "Your Lord says: 'Let the cow be yellow, a rich yellow, pleasing to those that see it.'"

---

3   The Israelites.

"Call on your Lord," they said, "to make known to us the exact type of cow she shall be; for to us cows look all alike. If God wills we shall be rightly guided."

Moses replied: "Your Lord says: 'Let her be a healthy cow, not worn out with ploughing the earth or watering the field; a cow free from any blemish.'"

"Now you have told us all," they answered. And they slaughtered a cow, after they had nearly declined.

And when you slew a man and then fell out with one another concerning him, God made known what you concealed. We said: "Strike him with a part of it." Thus God restores the dead to life and shows you His signs, that you may grow in understanding.

Yet after that your hearts became as hard as rock or even harder; for from some rocks rivers take their course: some break asunder and water gushes from them: and others tumble down through fear of God. God is not unaware of what you do.

Do you[4] then hope that they will believe in you, when some of them have already heard the Word of God and knowingly perverted it, although they understood its meaning?

When they meet the faithful they declare: "We, too, are believers." But when alone they say to each other: "Must you preach to them what God has revealed to you? They will only dispute with you about it in your Lord's presence. Have you no sense?"

Do they not know that God has knowledge of all they hide and all that they reveal?

There are illiterate men among them who, ignorant of the Scriptures, know of nothing but wishful fancies and vague conjecture. Woe to those that write the scriptures with their own hands and then declare: "This is from God," in order to gain some paltry end. Woeful shall be their fate, because of what their hands have written, because of that which they have gained!

They declare: "The Fire will never touch us—except for a few days." Say: "Did God make you such a promise—God will not break His promise—or do you assert about Him what you have no means of knowing?"

Truly, those that commit evil and become engrossed in sin shall be the inmates of the Fire; there they shall abide for ever. But those that have faith and do good works are the heirs of Paradise; there they shall abide for ever.

When We made a covenant with the Israelites We said: "Serve none but God. Show kindness to your parents, to your kinsfolk, to the orphans, and to the destitute. Exhort men to righteousness. Attend to your prayers and render the alms levy." But you all broke your covenant except a few, and gave no heed.

And when We made a covenant with you We said: "You shall not shed your kinsmen's blood or turn them out of their dwellings." To this you consented and bore witness. Yet there you were, slaying your own kinsfolk, and turning a number of them out of their dwellings, and helping each other against them with sin and aggression. Though had they come to you as captives, you would have ransomed them. Surely their expulsion was unlawful. Can you believe in one part of the Scriptures and deny another?

Those of you that act thus shall be rewarded with disgrace in this world and with grievous punishment on the Day of Resurrection. God is never heedless of what you do.

Such are they who buy the life of this world at the price of the life to come. Their punishment shall not be lightened, nor shall they be helped.

To Moses We gave the Scriptures and after him We sent other apostles. We gave Jesus the son of Mary veritable signs and strengthened him with the Holy Spirit. Will you then scorn each apostle whose message does not suit your fancies, charging some with imposture and slaying others?

They say: "Our hearts are sealed." But God has cursed them for their unbelief. They have but little faith.

And now that a Book confirming their own has come to them from God, they deny it, although they know it to be the truth and have long prayed for help against the unbelievers. God's curse be upon the infidels! Evil is that for which they have bartered away their souls. To deny God's own revelation, grudging that He should reveal His bounty to whom He chooses from among

---

4 The believers are here addressed.

His servants! They have incurred God's most inexorable wrath. An ignominious punishment awaits the unbelievers.

When they are told: "Believe in what God has revealed," they reply: "We believe in what was revealed to *us*." But they deny what has since been revealed, although it is the truth, corroborating their own scriptures.

Say: "Why did you kill the prophets of God, if you are true believers? Moses came to you with veritable signs, but in his absence you worshipped the calf and committed evil." 2:92

When We made a covenant with you and raised the Mount above you, saying: "Take what We have given you with willing hearts and hear Our commandments," you[5] replied: "We hear but disobey." 2:93

For their unbelief they were made to drink the calf into their very hearts. Say: "Evil is that to which your faith prompts you if you are indeed believers."

Say: "If God's Abode of the Hereafter is for yourselves alone, to the exclusion of all others, then wish for death if your claim be true!"

But they will never wish for death, because of what they did; for God knows the evil-doers. Indeed, you will find they love this life more than other men: more than the pagans do. Each one of them would love to live a thousand years.

But even if their lives were indeed prolonged, that will surely not save them from Our scourge. God is watching all their actions.

Say: "Whoever is an enemy of Gabriel" (who has by God's grace revealed to you[6] the Koran as a guide and joyful tidings for the faithful, confirming previous scriptures) "whoever is an enemy of God, His angels, or His apostles, or of Gabriel or Michael, will surely find that God is the enemy of the unbelievers." 2:98

We have sent down to you clear revelations: none will deny them except the evil-doers. What! Whenever they make a covenant, must some of them cast it aside? Most of them are unbelievers.

And now that an apostle has come to them from God confirming their own Scriptures, some of those to whom the Scriptures were given cast off the Book of God behind their backs as though they know nothing and accept what the devils tell of Solomon's kingdom. Not that Solomon was an unbeliever: it is the devils who are unbelievers. They teach men witchcraft and that which was revealed to the angels Hārūt and Mārūt in Babylon. Yet they never instruct any man without saying to him beforehand: "We have been sent to tempt you; do not renounce your faith." From these two, they learn a charm by which they can create discord between husband and wife, although they can harm none with what they learn except by God's leave. They learn, indeed, what harms them and does not profit them; yet they know full well that anyone who engaged in that traffic would have no share in the life to come. Vile is that for which they have sold their souls, if they but knew it! Had they embraced the Faith and kept from evil, far better for them would God's reward have been, if they but knew it 2:102

Believers do not say *Rā'inā*, but say *Unzurnā*.[7] Take heed; woeful punishment awaits the unbelievers. 2:103

The unbelievers among the People of the Book, and the pagans, resent that any blessings should have been sent down to you from your Lord. But God chooses whom He will for His mercy. God's grace is infinite.

If We abrogate a verse or cause it to be forgotten, We will replace it by a better one or one similar. Did you not know that God has power over all things? Did you not know that it is God who has sovereignty over the heavens and the earth, and that there is none besides God to protect or help you? 2:106

Would you rather demand of your Apostle that which was once demanded of Moses? He that barters faith for unbelief has surely strayed from the right path.

Many among the People of the Book wish, through envy, to lead you back to unbelief, now that you have embraced the Faith and the truth has been made plain to 2:109

---

5 Lit., they.
6 Muḥammad.
7 These words mean "Listen to us" and "Look upon us" respectively; but in Judaeo-Arabic the sound of the first conveys the sense, "Our evil one." Jewish Arabs used the expression as a derisive pun.

them. Forgive them and bear with them until God make known His will. God has power over all things.

Attend to your prayers and render the alms levy. Whatever good you do shall be rewarded by God. God is watching all your actions. 2:110

They declare: "None shall enter Paradise but Jews and Christians." Such are their wishful fancies. Say: "Let us have your proof, if what you say be true." Indeed, those that surrender themselves to God and do good works shall be rewarded by their Lord: they shall have nothing to fear or to regret.

The Jews say the Christians are misguided, and the Christians say it is the Jews who are misguided. Yet they both read the Scriptures. And the ignorant say the same of both. God will judge their disputes on the Day of Resurrection.

Who is more wicked than the men who seek to destroy the mosques of God and forbid His name to be mentioned in them, when it behooves these men to enter them with fear in their hearts? They shall be held up to shame in this world and sternly punished in the hereafter.

To God belongs the east and the west. Whichever way you turn there is the face of God. He is omnipresent and all-knowing. 2:115

They say: "God has begotten a son." Glory be to Him! His is what the heavens and the earth contain; all things are obedient to Him. Creator of the heavens and the earth! When He decrees a thing, He need only say "Be," and it is.

The ignorant ask: "Why does God not speak to us or give us a sign?" The same demand was made by those before them: their hearts are all alike. But to those whose faith is firm We have already revealed Our signs.

We have sent you forth to proclaim the truth and to give warning. You shall not be questioned about the heirs of Hell.

You will please neither the Jews nor the Christians unless you follow their faith. Say: "God's guidance is the only guidance." And if after all the knowledge you have been given you yield to their desires, there shall be none to help or protect you from the wrath of God. Those to whom We have given the Book, and who read it as it ought to be read, truly believe in it; those that deny it will surely be the losers. 2:121

Children of Israel, remember the favour I have bestowed upon you, and that I exalted you above the nations. Guard yourselves against a day on which no soul shall stand for another: when neither ransom shall be accepted from it, nor intercession avail it, nor any help be given it. 2:122

When his Lord put Abraham to the proof by enjoining on him certain commandments and Abraham fulfilled them, He said: "I have appointed you a leader of mankind."

"And what of my descendants?" asked Abraham.

"My covenant," said He, "does not apply to the evil-doers."

We made the House[8] a resort and a sanctuary for mankind, saying: "Make the place where Abraham stood a home of worship." We enjoined Abraham and Ishmael to cleanse Our House for those who walk round it, who meditate in it, and who kneel and prostrate themselves.

"Lord," said Abraham, "make this a secure land and bestow plenty upon its people, those of them that believe in God and the Last Day."

"As for those that do not," He answered, "I shall let them live awhile, and then shall drag them to the scourge of the Fire: an evil fate."

Abraham and Ishmael built the House and dedicated it, saying: "Accept this from us, Lord. You are the One that hears all and knows all. Lord, make us submissive to You; make of our descendants a nation that will submit to You. Teach us our rites of worship and turn to us with mercy; You are forgiving and merciful. Lord, send forth to them an apostle of their own who shall declare to them Your revelations, and shall instruct them in the Book and in wisdom, and shall purify them of sin. You are the Mighty, the Wise One." 2:127

Who but a foolish man would renounce the faith of Abraham? We chose him in this world, and in the world to come he shall abide among the righteous. When his Lord said to him: "Submit," he answered: "I have submitted to the Lord of the Universe." 2:131

---

8 The Ka'bah at Mecca.

Abraham enjoined the faith on his children, and so did Jacob, saying: "My children, God has chosen for you the true faith. Do not depart this life except as men who have submitted to Him." 2:132

Were you present when death came to Jacob? He said to his children: "What will you worship when I am gone?" They replied: "We will worship your God and the God of your forefathers Abraham and Ishmael and Isaac: the One God. To Him we will surrender ourselves."

That nation have passed away. Theirs is what they did and yours what you have done. You shall not be questioned about their actions.

They say: "Accept the Jewish or the Christian faith and you shall be rightly guided." 2:135

Say: "By no means! We believe in the faith of Abraham, the upright one. He was no idolater."

Say: "We believe in God and that which is revealed to us; in what was revealed to Abraham, Ishmael, Isaac, Jacob, and the tribes; to Moses and Jesus and the other prophets by their Lord. We make no distinction among any of them, and to God we have surrendered ourselves."

If they accept your faith, they shall be rightly guided; if they reject it, they shall surely be in schism. Against them God is your all-sufficient defender. He hears all and knows all.

We take on God's own dye. And who has a better dye than God's? Him will we worship.

Say: "Would you dispute with us about God, who is our Lord and your Lord? We shall both be judged by our works. To Him alone we are devoted.

"Do you claim that Abraham, Ishmael, Isaac, Jacob, and the tribes, were all Jews or Christians?" Say: "Who knows better, you or God? Who is more wicked than the man who hides a testimony he has received from God? God is never heedless of what you do."

That nation have passed away. Theirs is what they did and yours what you have done. You shall not be questioned about their actions. 2:141

The foolish will ask: "What has made them turn away from their *qiblah*?"[9] 2:142

Say: "The East and the West are God's. He guides whom He will to the right path."

We have made you a just community, so that you may testify against mankind and that your own Apostle may testify against you. We decreed your former *qiblah* only in order that We might know the Apostle's true adherents and those who were to disown him. It was indeed a hard test, but not to those whom God has guided. He was not to make your faith fruitless. He is compassionate and merciful to men.

Many a time have We seen you[10] turn your face towards the sky. We will make you turn towards a *qiblah* that will please you. Turn your face towards the Holy Mosque; wherever you[11] be, turn your faces towards it. 2:144

Those to whom the Scriptures were given know this to be the truth from their Lord. God is never heedless of what they do. But even if you gave them every proof they would not accept your *qiblah*, nor would you accept theirs; nor would any of them accept the *qiblah* of the other. If, after all the knowledge you have been given, you yield to their desires, then you will surely become an evil-doer.

Those to whom We gave the Scriptures know Our apostle as they know their own sons. But some of them deliberately conceal the truth. This is the truth from your Lord: therefore never doubt it.

Each one has a goal towards which he turns. But wherever you be, emulate one another in good works. God will bring you all before Him. God has power over all things.

Whichever way you depart, face towards the Holy Mosque. This is surely the truth from your Lord. God is never heedless of what you do. 2:149

Whichever way you depart, face towards the Holy Mosque: and wherever you are, face towards it, so that men will have no cause to reproach you, except the evil-doers 2:150

---

9 The direction which the Muslim faces in prayer. At first the believers were ordered to turn toward Jerusalem, afterwards to Mecca.
10 Muḥammad.
11 The faithful.

among them. Have no fear of them; fear Me, so that I may perfect My favour to you and that you may be rightly guided.

Thus have We sent forth to you an apostle of your own who will recite to you Our revelations and purify you of sin, who will instruct you in the Book and in wisdom and teach you that of which you have no knowledge. Remember Me, then, and I will remember you. Give thanks to Me and never deny Me.

Believers, fortify yourselves with patience and prayer. God is with those that are patient. Do not say that those slain in the cause of God are dead. They are alive, but you are not aware of them.

We shall test your steadfastness with fear and famine, with loss of property and life and crops. Give good news to those who endure with fortitude; who in adversity say: "We belong to God, and to Him we shall return." On such men will be God's blessing and mercy; such men are rightly guided. 2:156

Ṣafā and Marwa[12] are two of God's beacons. It shall be no offence for the pilgrim or the visitor to the Sacred House to walk around them. He that does good of his own accord shall be rewarded by God. God has knowledge of all things.

Those that hide the clear proofs and the guidance We have revealed after We had proclaimed them in the Scriptures shall be cursed by God and cursed by those who invoke damnation; except those that repent and mend their ways and make known the truth. Towards them I shall relent. I am the Relenting One, the Merciful. But the infidels who die unbelievers shall incur the curse of God, the angels, and all mankind. Under it they shall remain for ever; their punishment shall not be lightened, nor shall they be reprieved. 2:162

Your God is one God. There is no god but Him. He is the Compassionate, the Merciful. 2:163

In the creation of the heavens and the earth; in the alternation of night and day; in the ships that sail the ocean with cargoes beneficial to man; in the water which God sends down from the sky and with which He revives the earth after its death, dispersing over it all manner of beasts; in the disposal of the winds, and in the clouds that are driven between sky and earth: surely in these there are signs for rational men.

Yet there are some who worship idols, bestowing on them the adoration due to God (though the love of God is stronger in the faithful). But when they face their punishment the wrongdoers will know that might is God's alone, and God is stern in retribution. When they face their punishment those who were followed will disown their followers, and the bonds which now unite them will break asunder. Those who followed them will say: "Could we but live again, we would disown them as they have now disowned us."

Thus will God show them their own works. They shall sigh with remorse, but shall never come out of the Fire.

Men, eat of what is lawful and wholesome on the earth and do not walk in Satan's footsteps, for he is your inveterate foe. He enjoins you to commit evil and indecency and to assert about God what you know not. 2:168

When they are told: "Follow what God has revealed," they reply: "We will follow what our fathers practised," even though their fathers were senseless men lacking in guidance.

The unbelievers are like beasts which, call out to them as one may, can hear nothing but a shout and a cry. Deaf, dumb, and blind, they understand nothing.

Believers, eat of the wholesome things with which We have provided you and give thanks to God, if it is Him you worship.

He has forbidden you carrion, blood, and the flesh of swine; also any flesh that is consecrated other than in the name of God. But whoever is compelled through necessity, intending neither to sin nor to transgress, shall incur no guilt. God is forgiving and merciful. 2:173

Those that suppress any part of the Scriptures which God has revealed in order to gain some paltry end shall swallow nothing but fire into their bellies. On the Day of Resurrection God will neither speak to them nor purify them. Theirs shall be a woeful punishment. 2:174

Such are those that barter guidance for error and forgiveness for punishment. How steadfastly they seek the Fire! That is be-

---

12 Two hills near Mecca, held in reverence by pagan Arabs.

cause God has revealed the Book with the truth; those that disagree about it are in extreme schism.

Righteousness does not consist in whether you face towards the East or the West. The righteous man is he who believes in God and the Last Day, in the angels and the Book and the prophets; who, though he loves it dearly, gives away his wealth to kinsfolk, to orphans, to the destitute, to the traveller in need and to beggars, and for the redemption of captives; who attends to his prayers and renders the alms levy; who is true to his promises and steadfast in trial and adversity and in times of war. Such are the true believers; such are the God-fearing.

Believers, retaliation is decreed for you in bloodshed: a free man for a free man, a slave for a slave, and a female for a female. He who is pardoned by his aggrieved brother shall be prosecuted according to usage and shall pay him a liberal fine. This is a merciful dispensation from your Lord. He that transgresses thereafter shall be sternly punished. *2:178*

Men of understanding! In retaliation you have a safeguard for your lives; perchance you will guard yourselves against evil.

It is decreed that when death approaches, those of you that leave property shall bequeath it equitably to parents and kindred. This is a duty incumbent on the righteous. He that alters a will after hearing it shall be accountable for his crime. God hears all and knows all.

He that suspects an error or an injustice on the part of a testator and brings about a settlement among the parties incurs no guilt. God is forgiving and merciful. *2:182*

Believers, fasting is decreed for you as it was decreed for those before you; perchance you will guard yourselves against evil. Fast a certain number of days, but if any one among you is ill or on a journey, let him fast a similar number of days later; and for those that cannot[13] endure it there is a ransom: the feeding of a poor man. He that does good of his own accord shall be well rewarded; but to fast is better for you, if you but knew it.

In the month of Ramaḍān the Koran was revealed, a book of guidance for mankind with proofs of guidance distinguishing right from wrong.[14] Therefore whoever of you is present in that month let him fast. But he who is ill or on a journey shall fast a similar number of days later on.

God desires your well-being, not your discomfort. He desires you to fast the whole month so that you may magnify God and render thanks to Him for giving you His guidance.

When My servants question you about Me, tell them that I am near. I answer the prayer of the suppliant when he calls to Me; therefore let them answer My call and put their trust in Me, that they may be rightly guided. *2:186*

It is now lawful for you to lie with your wives on the night of the fast; they are a comfort to you as you are to them. God knew that you were deceiving yourselves. He has relented towards you and pardoned you. Therefore you may now lie with them and seek what God has ordained for you; Eat and drink until you can tell a white thread from a black one in the light of the coming dawn. Then resume the fast till nightfall and do not approach them, but stay at your prayers in the mosques.

These are the bounds set by God: do not come near them. Thus He makes known His revelations to mankind that they may guard themselves against evil.

Do not devour one another's property by unjust means, nor bribe with it the judges in order that you may wrongfully and knowingly usurp the possessions of other men. *2:188*

They question you about the phases of the moon. Say: "They are seasons fixed for mankind and for the pilgrimage." *2:189*

Righteousness does not consist in entering your dwellings from the back.[15] The righteous man is he that fears God. Enter your dwellings by their doors and fear God, so that you may prosper.

Fight for the sake of God those that fight against you, but do not attack them first. God does not love the aggressors.

---

13 Thus Al-Jalālayn; the negative being understood. Alternatively: ". . . and for those well able to fast there is a ransom:"
14 Alternatively: ". . . with proofs of guidance and *salvation*."
15 It was the custom of pagan Arabs, on returning from pilgrimage, to enter their homes from the back.

Slay them wherever you find them. Drive them out of the places from which they drove you. Idolatry is more grievous than bloodshed. But do not fight them within the precincts of the Holy Mosque unless they attack you there; if they attack you put them to the sword. Thus shall the unbelievers be rewarded: but if they mend their ways, know that God is forgiving and merciful.

Fight against them until idolatry is no more and God's religion reigns supreme. But if they desist, fight none except the evil-doers.

A sacred month for a sacred month: sacred things too are subject to retaliation. If anyone attacks you, attack him as he attacked you. Have fear of God, and know that God is with the righteous.

Give generously for the cause of God and do not with your own hands cast yourselves into destruction. Be charitable; God loves the charitable. *2:195*

Make the pilgrimage and visit the Sacred House for His sake. If you cannot, send such offerings as you can afford and do not shave your heads until the offerings have reached their destination. But if any of you is ill or suffers from an ailment of the head, he must pay a ransom either by fasting or by almsgiving or by offering a sacrifice. *2:196*

If in peacetime anyone among you combines the visit with the pilgrimage, he must offer such gifts as he can afford; but if he lacks the means let him fast three days during the pilgrimage and seven when he has returned; that is, ten days in all. That is incumbent on him whose family are not present at the Holy Mosque. Have fear of God: know that God is stern in retribution.

Make the pilgrimage in the appointed months. He that intends to perform it in those months must abstain from sexual intercourse, obscene language, and acrimonious disputes while on pilgrimage. God is aware of whatever good you do. Provide well for yourselves: the best provision is piety. Fear Me, then, you that are endowed with understanding. *2:197*

It shall be no offence for you to seek the bounty of your Lord. When you come running from 'Arafat[16] remember God as you approach the sacred monument. Remember Him that gave you guidance when you were in error. Then go out from the place whence the pilgrims will go out and implore the forgiveness of God. God is forgiving and merciful. And when you have fulfilled your sacred duties, remember God as you remember your forefathers or with deeper reverence.

There are some who say: "Lord, give us abundance in this world." These shall have no share in the world to come. But there are others who say: "Lord, give us what is good both in this world and in the hereafter and keep us from the torment of the Fire." These shall have a share, according to what they did. Swift is God's reckoning. *2:201*

Give glory to God on the appointed days. He that departs on the second day incurs no sin, nor does he who stays on longer, if he truly fears God. Have fear of God, then, and know that you shall all be gathered before Him.

There are some whose views on this life please you: they even call on God to vouch for that which is in their hearts; whereas in fact they are the deadliest of your opponents. No sooner do they leave you than they hasten to do evil in the land, destroying crops and cattle. God does not love evil. *2:205*

When they are told: "Have fear of God," vanity carries them off to sin. Hell shall be enough for them, a dismal resting-place. *2:206*

But there are others who would give away their lives in order to find favour with God. God is compassionate to His servants.

Believers, submit all of you to God and do not walk in Satan's footsteps; he is your inveterate foe. If you lapse back after the veritable signs that have been shown to you, know that God is mighty and wise.

Are they waiting for God to come down to them in the shadow of a cloud, with all the angels? Their fate will have been settled then. To God shall all things return.

Ask the Israelites how many veritable signs We have given them. He that tampers with the boon of God after it has been bestowed on him shall find that God is stern in retribution.

For the unbelievers the life of this world is decked with all manner of temptations. They scoff at the faithful, but those that fear God shall be above them on the Day of Res-

---

16 Near Mecca.

urrection. God gives without measure to whom He will.

Mankind were once one community. Then God sent forth prophets to give them good news and to warn them, and with these He sent down the Book with the Truth, that it might judge the disputes of men. (None disputed it save those to whom it was given, and that was through envy of one another, after veritable signs had been vouchsafed them.) So God guided by His will those who believed in the truth which had been disputed. God guides whom He will to a straight path. 2:213

Did you suppose that you would go to Paradise untouched by the suffering which was endured by those before you? Affliction and adversity befell them; and so battered were they that each apostle, and those who shared his faith, cried out: "When will God's help come?" God's help is ever near.

They will ask you about almsgiving. Say: "Whatever you bestow in charity must go to parents and to kinsfolk, to the orphans and to the destitute and to the traveller in need. God is aware of whatever good you do." 2:215

Fighting is obligatory for you, much as you dislike it. But you may hate a thing although it is good for you, and love a thing although it is bad for you. God knows, but you know not.

They ask you about the sacred month. Say: "To fight in this month is a grave offence; but to debar others from the path of God, to deny Him, and to expel His worshippers from the Holy Mosque, is far more grave in His sight. Idolatry is more grievous than bloodshed."

They will not cease to fight against you until they force you to renounce your faith—if they are able. But whoever of you recants and dies an unbeliever, his works shall come to nothing in this world and in the world to come. Such men shall be the tenants of the Fire, wherein they shall abide for ever.

Those that have embraced the Faith and those that have fled their land and fought for the cause of God, may hope for God's mercy. God is forgiving and merciful.

They ask you about drinking and gambling. Say: "There is great harm in both, although they have some benefit for men; but their harm is far greater than their benefit." 2:219

They ask you what they should give in alms. Say: "What you can spare." Thus God makes plain to you His revelations so that you may reflect upon this world and the hereafter.

They question you concerning orphans. Say: "To deal justly with them is best. If you mix their affairs with yours, remember they are your brothers. God knows the unjust from the just. If God pleased, He could afflict you. God is mighty and wise."

You shall not wed pagan women, unless they embrace the Faith. A believing slave-girl is better than an idolatress, although she may please you. Nor shall you wed idolaters, unless they embrace the Faith. A believing slave is better than an idolater, although he may please you. These call you to the Fire; but God calls you, by His will, to Paradise and to forgiveness. He makes plain His revelations to mankind, so that they may take heed. 2:221

They ask you about menstruation. Say: "It is an indisposition. Keep aloof from women during their menstrual periods and do not approach them until they are clean again; when they are clean, have intercourse with them whence God enjoined you. God loves those that turn to Him in repentance and strive to keep themselves clean." 2:222

Women are your fields: go, then, into your fields whence you please. Do good works and fear God. Bear in mind that you shall meet Him. Give good tidings to the believers.

Do not make God, when you swear by Him, a means to prevent you from dealing justly, from guarding yourselves against evil, and from making peace among men. God knows all and hears all. God will not call you to account for that which is inadvertent in your oaths. But He will take you to task for that which is intended in your hearts. God is forgiving and lenient.

Those that renounce their wives on oath must wait four months. If they change their minds, God is forgiving and merciful; but if they decide to divorce them, know that God hears all and knows all.

Divorced women must wait, keeping themselves from men, three menstrual courses. It is unlawful for them, if they believe in God and the Last Day, to hide what God has created in their wombs: in which case their husbands would do well to take 2:228

them back, should they desire reconciliation.

Women shall with justice have rights similar to those exercised against them, although men have a status above women. God is mighty and wise.

Divorce[17] may be pronounced twice, and then a woman must be retained in honour or allowed to go with kindness. It is unlawful for husbands to take from them anything they have given them, unless both fear that they may not be able to keep within the bounds set by God; in which case it shall be no offence for either of them if the wife ransoms herself.

2:229

These are the bounds set by God; do not transgress them. Those that transgress the bounds of God are wrongdoers.

If a man divorces[18] his wife, he cannot remarry her until she has wedded another man and been divorced by him; in which case it shall be no offence for either of them to return to the other, if they think that they can keep within the bounds set by God.

2:230

Such are the bounds of God. He makes them plain to men of knowledge.

When you have renounced your wives and they have reached the end of their waiting period, either retain them in honour or let them go with kindness. But you shall not retain them in order to harm them or to wrong them. Whoever does this wrongs his own soul.

Do not make game of God's revelations. Remember the favour God has bestowed upon you, and the Book and the wisdom He has revealed for your instruction. Fear God and know that God has knowledge of all things.

If a man has renounced his wife and she has reached the end of her waiting period, do not prevent her from remarrying her husband if they have come to an honourable agreement. This is enjoined on every one of you who believes in God and the Last Day; it is more honourable for you and more chaste. God knows, but you know not

Mothers shall give suck to their children for two whole years if the father wishes the sucking to be completed. They must be maintained and clothed in a reasonable manner by the child's father. None should be charged with more than one can bear. A mother should not be allowed to suffer on account of her child, nor should a father on account of his child. The same duties devolve upon the father's heir. But if, after consultation, they choose by mutual consent to wean the child, they shall incur no guilt. Nor shall it be any offence for you if you prefer to have a nurse for your children, provided that you pay her what you promise, according to usage. Have fear of God and know that God is cognizant of all your actions.

2:233

Widows shall wait, keeping themselves apart from men, for four months and ten days after their husbands' death. When they have reached the end of their waiting period, it shall be no offence for you to let them do whatever they choose for themselves, provided that it is decent. God is cognizant of all your actions.

2:234

It shall be no offence for you openly to propose marriage to such women or to cherish them in your hearts. God knows that you will remember them. Do not arrange to meet them in secret, and if you do, speak to them honourably. But you shall not consummate the marriage before the end of their waiting period. Know that God has knowledge of all your thoughts. Therefore take heed and bear in mind that God is forgiving and lenient.

It shall be no offence for you to divorce your wives before the marriage is consummated or the dowry settled. Provide for them with fairness; the rich man according to his means and the poor man according to his. This is binding on righteous men. If you divorce them before the marriage is consummated, but after their dowry has been settled, give them the half of their dowry, unless they or the husband agree to waive it. But it is more proper that the husband should waive it. Do not forget to show kindness to each other. God observes your actions.

2:236

Attend regularly to your prayers, including the middle prayer, and stand up with all devotion before God. When you are exposed to danger pray on foot or while riding; and when you are restored to safety

---

17 Revocable divorce, or the renunciation of one's wife on oath.
18 By pronouncing the formula "I divorce you" for the third time.

remember God, as He has taught you what you did not know.

You shall bequeath your widows a year's maintenance without causing them to leave their homes; but if they leave of their own accord, no blame shall be attached to you for any course they may deem fit to pursue. God is mighty and wise. Reasonable provision shall also be made for divorced women. That is incumbent on righteous men. 2:241

Thus God makes known to you His revelations that you may grow in understanding. 2:242

Consider those that fled their homes in their thousands for fear of death. God said to them: "You shall perish," and then He brought them back to life. Surely God is bountiful to mankind, but most men do not give thanks.

Fight for the cause of God and bear in mind that God hears all and knows all.

Who will grant God a generous loan? He will repay him many times over. It is God who enriches and makes poor. To Him you shall return.

Have you not heard of what the leaders of the Israelites demanded of one of their prophets after the death of Moses? "Raise up for us a king," they said, "and we will fight for the cause of God."

He replied: "What if you refuse to fight, when ordered so to do?"

"Why should we refuse to fight for the cause of God," they said, "when we have been driven from our dwellings and our children?"

But when at last they were ordered to fight, they all refused, except a few of them. God knows the evil-doers.

Their prophet said to them: "God has appointed Saul to be your king." But they replied: "Should he be given the kingship, when we are more deserving of it than he? Besides, he is not rich at all." 2:247

He said: "God has chosen him to rule over you and made him grow in wisdom and in stature. God gives His sovereignty to whom He will. God is munificent and all-knowing."

Their prophet also said to them: "The advent of the Ark shall be the portent of his reign. Therein shall be tranquillity[19] from your Lord, and the relics which the House 2:248 of Moses and the House of Aaron left behind. It will be borne by the angels. That will be a sign for you, if you are true believers."

And when Saul marched out with his army, he said: "God will put you to the proof at a certain river. He that drinks from it shall cease to be my soldier, but he that does not drink from it, or contents himself with a taste of it in the hollow of his hand, shall fight by my side." 2:249

But they all drank from it, except a few of them. And when Saul had crossed the river with those who shared his faith, they said: "We have no power this day against Goliath and his warriors."

But those of them who believed that they would meet God replied: "Many a small band has, by God's grace, vanquished a mighty army. God is with those who endure with fortitude."

When they met Goliath and his warriors they cried: "Lord, fill our hearts with steadfastness. Make us firm of foot and help us against the unbelievers." 2:250

By God's will they routed them. David slew Goliath, and God bestowed on him sovereignty and wisdom and taught him what He pleased. Had God not defeated some by the might of others, the earth would have been utterly corrupted. But God is bountiful to mankind.

Such are God's revelations. We recite them to you in all truth, for you are one of Our messengers. Of these messengers We have exalted some above others. To some God spoke directly; others He raised to a lofty status. We gave Jesus the son of Mary veritable signs and strengthened him with the Holy Spirit. Had God pleased, those who succeeded them would not have fought against one another after the veritable signs had been given them. But they disagreed among themselves; some had faith and others had none. Yet had God pleased they would not have fought against one another. God does what He will.

Believers, bestow in alms a part of what We have given you before that day arrives when commerce and friendship and intercession shall be no more. Truly, it is the unbelievers who are unjust. 2:254

---

19 This is the meaning of the Arabic word *sakīnah*, which, however, may well be related to *shekbīna*, (the holy Presence) in the Old Testament.

God: there is no god but Him, the Living, the Eternal One. Neither slumber nor sleep overtakes Him. His is what the heavens and the earth contain. Who can intercede with Him except by His permission? He knows what is before and behind men. They can grasp only that part of His knowledge which He wills. His throne is as vast as the heavens and the earth, and the preservation of both does not weary Him. He is the Exalted, the Immense One. 2:255

There shall be no compulsion in religion. True guidance is now distinct from error, He that renounces idol-worship and puts his faith in God shall grasp a firm handle that will never break. God hears all and knows all.

God is the Patron of the faithful. He leads them from darkness to the light. As for the unbelievers, their patrons are false gods, who lead them from light to darkness. They are the heirs of the Fire and shall abide in it for ever.

Have you not heard of him who argued with Abraham about his Lord because God had bestowed sovereignty upon him? Abraham said: "My Lord is He who has power to give life and to cause death." 2:258

"I, too," replied the other, "have power to give life and to cause death."

"God brings up the sun from the east," said Abraham. "Bring it up yourself from the west."

The unbeliever was confounded. God does not guide the evil-doers.

Or of him, who, when passing by a ruined and desolate city, remarked: "How can God give life to this city, now that it is dead?" Thereupon God caused him to die, and after a hundred years brought him back to life. 2:259

"How long have you stayed away?" asked God.

"A day," he replied, "or part of a day."

"Know, then," said God, "that you have stayed away a hundred years. Yet look at your food and drink: they have not rotted. And look at your ass. We will make you a sign to mankind: see how We will raise the bones and clothe them with flesh."

And when it had all become manifest to him, he said: "Now I know that God has power over all things."

When Abraham said: "Show me, Lord, how You will raise the dead. He replied: "Have you no faith?" 2:260

"Yes," said Abraham, "but just to reassure my heart."

"Take four birds," said He, "draw them to you, and cut their bodies to pieces. Scatter them over the mountain-tops, then call them back. They will come swiftly to you. Know that God is mighty and wise."

Those that give their wealth for the cause of God can be compared to a grain of corn which brings forth seven ears, each bearing a hundred grains. God gives abundance to whom He will; God is munificent and all-knowing.

Those that give their wealth for the cause of God and do not follow their almsgiving with taunts and insults shall be rewarded by their Lord; they shall have nothing to fear or to regret.

A kind word with forgiveness is better than charity followed by insult, God is self-sufficient and indulgent. 2:263

Believers, do not mar your almsgiving with taunts and mischief-making, like those who spend their wealth for the sake of ostentation and believe neither in God nor in the Last Day. Such men are like a rock covered with earth: a shower falls upon it and leaves it hard and bare. They shall gain nothing from their works. God does not guide the unbelievers.

But those that give away their wealth from a desire to please God and to reassure their own souls are like a garden on a hillside: if a shower falls upon it, it yields up twice its normal produce; and if no rain falls, it is watered by the dew, God takes cognizance of all your actions.

Would any one of you, being a man well-advanced in age with helpless children to support, wish to have his garden—a garden planted with palm-trees, vines and all manner of fruits, and watered by running streams—blasted and consumed by a fiery whirlwind? 2:266

Thus God makes plain to you His revelations, so that you may give thought.

Believers, give in alms of the wealth you have lawfully earned and of that which We have brought out of the earth for you; not worthless things which you yourselves would but reluctantly accept. Know that God is self-sufficient and glorious. 2:267

Satan threatens you with poverty and orders you to commit what is indecent. But God promises you His forgiveness and His bounty. God is munificent and all-knowing.

He gives wisdom to whom He will; and he that receives the gift of wisdom is rich indeed. Yet none but men of sense bear this in mind.

Whatever alms you give and whatever vows you make are known to God. The evil-doers shall have none to help them.

To be charitable in public is good, but to give alms to the poor in private is better and will atone for some of your sins. God has knowledge of all your actions.

It is not for you to guide them. God gives guidance to whom He will. 2:272

Whatever alms you give shall rebound to your own advantage, provided that you give them for the love of God. And whatever alms you give shall be paid back to you in full: you shall not be wronged.

As for those needy men who, being wholly preoccupied with fighting for the cause of God, cannot travel the land in quest of trading ventures: the ignorant take them for men of wealth on account of their modest behaviour. But you can recognize them by their look—they never importune men for alms. Whatever alms you give are known to God.

Those that give alms by day and by night, in private and in public, shall be rewarded by their Lord. They shall have nothing to fear or to regret. 2:275

Those that live on usury shall rise up before God like men whom Satan has demented by his touch; for they claim that trading is no different from usury. But God has permitted trading and made usury unlawful. He that has received an admonition from his Lord and mended his ways may keep his previous gains; God will be his judge. Those that turn back shall be the inmates of the Fire, wherein they shall abide for ever.

God has laid his curse on usury and blessed almsgiving with increase. God bears no love for the impious and the sinful. 2:276

Those that have faith and do good works, attend to their prayers and render the alms levy, will be rewarded by their Lord and will have nothing to fear or to regret.

Believers, have fear of God and waive what is still due to you from usury, if your faith be true; or war shall be declared against you by God and His apostle. If you repent, you may retain your principal, suffering no loss and causing loss to none.

If your debtor be in straits, grant him a delay until he can discharge his debt; but if you waive the sum as alms it will be better for you, if you but knew it.

Fear the day when you shall all return to God; when every soul shall be requited according to its deserts. None shall be wronged.

Believers, when you contract a debt for a fixed period, put it in writing. Let a scribe write it down for you with fairness; no scribe should refuse to write as God has taught him. Therefore let him write; and let the debtor dictate, fearing God his Lord and not diminishing the sum he owes. If the debtor be an ignorant or feeble-minded person, or one who cannot dictate, let his guardian dictate for him in fairness. Call in two male witnesses from among you, but if two men cannot be found, then one man and two women whom you judge fit to act as witnesses; so that if either of them commit an error, the other will remind her. Witnesses must not refuse to give evidence if called upon to do so. So do not fail to put your debts in writing, be they small or big, together with the date of payment. This is more just in the sight of God; it ensures accuracy in testifying and is the best way to remove all doubt. But if the transaction in hand be a bargain concluded on the spot, it is no offence for you if you do not commit it to writing. 2:282

See that witnesses are present when you barter with one another, and let no harm be done to either scribe or witness. If you harm them you will commit a transgression. Have fear of God; God teaches you, and God has knowledge of all things.

If you are travelling the road and a scribe cannot be found, then let pledges be taken. If any one of you entrusts another with a pledge, let the trustee restore the pledge to its owner; and let him fear God, his Lord 2:283

You shall not withhold testimony. He that withholds it sinful is his heart. God has knowledge of all your actions.

To God belongs all that the heavens and the earth contain. Whether you reveal your thoughts or hide them, God will bring you to account for them. He will forgive whom He will and punish whom He pleases; God has power over all things.

The Apostle believes in what has been revealed to him by his Lord, and so do the faithful. They all believe in God and His angels, His scriptures, and His apostles: We discriminate against none of His apostles. They say: "We hear and obey. Grant us Your forgiveness, Lord; to You we shall all return. God does not charge a soul with more than it can bear. It shall be requited for whatever good and whatever evil it has done. Lord, do not be angry with us if we forget or lapse into error. Lord, do not lay on us the burden You laid on those before us. Lord, do not charge us with more than we can bear. Pardon us, forgive us our sins, and have mercy upon us. You alone are our Protector. Give us victory over the unbelievers." *2:286*

Women

In the Name of God, the Compassionate, the Merciful

Men, have fear of your Lord, who created you from a single soul. From that soul He created its mate, and through them He bestrewed the earth with countless men and women. *4:1*

Fear God, in whose name you plead with one another, and honour the mothers who bore you. God is ever watching you.

Give orphans the property which belongs to them. Do not exchange their valuables for worthless things or cheat them of their possessions; for this would surely be a great sin. If you fear that you cannot treat orphans[20] with fairness, then you may marry other women who seem good to you: two, three, or four of them. But if you fear that you cannot maintain equality among them, marry one only or any slave-girls you may own. This will make it easier for you to avoid injustice.

Give women their dowry as a free gift; but if they choose to make over to you a part of it, you may regard it as lawfully yours.

Do not give the feeble-minded the property with which God has entrusted you for their support; but maintain and clothe them with its proceeds, and give them good advice. *4:5*

Put orphans to the test until they reach a marriageable age. If you find them capable *4:6* of sound judgement, hand over to them their property, and do not deprive them of it by squandering it before they come of age.

Let not the rich guardian touch the property of his orphan ward; and let him who is poor use no more than a fair portion of it for his own advantage.

When you hand over to them their property, call in some witnesses; sufficient is God's accounting of your actions.

Men shall have a share in what their parents and kinsmen leave; and women shall have a share in what their parents and kinsmen leave: whether it be little or much, they shall be legally entitled to a share.

If relatives, orphans, or needy men are present at the division of an inheritance, give them, too, a share of it, and speak to them kind words.

Let those who are solicitous about the welfare of their young children after their own death take care not to wrong orphans. Let them fear God and speak for justice.

Those that devour the property of orphans unjustly, swallow fire into their bellies; they shall burn in a mighty conflagration. *4:10*

God has thus enjoined you concerning your children:

A male shall inherit twice as much as a female. If there be more than two girls, they shall have two-thirds of the inheritance; but if there be one only, she shall inherit the half. Parents shall inherit a sixth each, if the deceased have a child; but if he leave no child and his parents be his heirs, his mother shall have a third. If he have brothers, his mother shall have a sixth after payment of any legacy he may have bequeathed or any debt he may have owed.

You may wonder whether your parents or your children are more beneficial to you. But this is the law of God; surely God is all-knowing and wise.

You shall inherit the half of your wives' estate if they die childless. If they leave children, a quarter of their estate shall be yours after payment of any legacy they may have bequeathed or any debt they may have owed. *4:12*

Your wives shall inherit one quarter of your estate if you die childless. If you leave children, they shall inherit one-eighth, after

---

20 Orphan girls.

payment of any legacy you may have bequeathed or any debt you may have owed.

If a man or a woman leave neither children nor parents and have a brother or a sister, they shall each inherit one-sixth. If there be more, they shall equally share the third of the estate, after payment of any legacy he may have bequeathed or any debt he may have owed, without prejudice to the rights of the heirs. That is a commandment from God. God is all-knowing, and gracious.

Such are the bounds set by God. He that obeys God and His apostle shall dwell for ever in gardens watered by running streams. That is the supreme triumph. But he that defies God and His apostle and transgresses His bounds, shall be cast into a Fire wherein he will abide for ever. Shameful punishment awaits him. 4:13

If any of your women commit fornication, call in four witnesses from among yourselves against them; if they testify to their guilt confine them to their houses till death overtakes them or till God finds another way for them.

If two men among you commit indecency, punish them both. If they repent and mend their ways, let them be. God is forgiving and merciful.

God forgives those who commit evil in ignorance and then quickly turn to Him in repentance. God will pardon them. God is all-knowing and wise. But He will not forgive those who do evil and, when death comes to them, say: "Now we repent!" Nor those who die unbelievers: for them We have prepared a woeful scourge. 4:16

Believers, it is unlawful for you to inherit the women of your deceased kinsmen against their will, or to bar them from remarrying, in order that you may force them to give up a part of what you have given them, unless they be guilty of a proven indecent act. Treat them with kindness; for even if you dislike them, it may well be that you dislike a thing which God has meant for your own abundant good. 4:19

If you wish to replace a wife with another, do not take from her the dowry you have given her even if it be a talent of gold. That would be improper and grossly unjust; for how can you take it back when you have lain with each other and entered into a firm contract? 4:20

You shall not marry the women whom your fathers married: all previous such marriages excepted. That was an evil practice, indecent and abominable.

Forbidden to you are your mothers, your daughters, your sisters, your paternal and maternal aunts, the daughters of your brothers and sisters, your foster-mothers, your foster-sisters, the mothers of your wives, your step-daughters who are in your charge, born of the wives with whom you have lain (it is no offence for you to marry your step-daughters if you have not consummated your marriage with their mothers), and the wives of your own begotten sons. You are also forbidden to take in marriage two sisters at one and the same time: all previous such marriages excepted. Surely God is forgiving and merciful. Also married women, except those whom you own as slaves. Such is the decree of God. All women other than these are lawful to you, provided you seek them with your wealth in modest conduct, not in fornication. Give them their dowry for the enjoyment you have had of them as a duty; but it shall be no offence for you to make any other agreement among yourselves after you have fulfilled your duty. Surely God is all-knowing and wise. 4:24

If any one of you cannot afford to marry a free believing woman, let him marry a slave-girl who is a believer (God best knows your faith: you are born one of another). Marry them with the permission of their masters and give them their dowry in all justice, provided they are honourable and chaste and have not entertained other men. If after marriage they commit adultery, they shall suffer half the penalty inflicted upon free adulteresses. Such is the law for those of you who fear to commit sin: but if you abstain, it will be better for you. God is forgiving and merciful. 4:25

God desires to make this known to you and to guide you along the paths of those who have gone before you, and to turn to you in mercy. God is all-knowing and wise. 4:26

God wishes to forgive you, but those who follow their own appetites wish to see you far astray. God wishes to lighten your burdens, for man was created weak.

Believers, do not consume your wealth among yourselves in vanity, but rather trade with it by mutual consent.

Do not kill yourselves. God is merciful to you, but he that does that through wickedness and injustice shall be burned in fire. That is easy enough for God.

If you avoid the enormities you are forbidden, We shall pardon your misdeeds and usher you in with all honour. Do not covet the favours by which God has exalted some among you above others. Men shall be rewarded according to their deeds, and women shall be rewarded according to their deeds. Rather implore God to bestow on you His gifts. God has knowledge of all things.

To every parent and kinsman We have appointed heirs who will inherit from them. As for those with whom you have entered into agreements, let them, too, have their due. Surely God bears witness to all things.

Men have authority over women because God has made the one superior to the other, and because they spend their wealth to maintain them. Good women are obedient. They guard their unseen parts because God has guarded them. As for those from whom you fear disobedience, admonish them and send them to beds apart and beat them. Then if they obey you, take no further action against them. Surely God is high, supreme.

If you fear a breach between a man and his wife, appoint an arbiter from his people and another from hers. If they wish to be reconciled God will bring them together again. Surely God is all-knowing and wise.

Serve God and associate none with Him. Show kindness to parents and kindred, to orphans and to the destitute, to near and distant neighbours, to those that keep company with you, to the traveller in need, and to the slaves you own. God does not love arrogant and boastful men, who are themselves niggardly and enjoin others to be niggardly; who conceal the riches which God of His bounty has bestowed upon them (We have prepared a shameful punishment for the unbelievers); and who spend their wealth for the sake of ostentation, believing neither in God nor in the Last Day. He that chooses Satan for his friend, an evil friend has he.

4:34

4:36

4:37

Those That Are Sent Forth

In the Name of God, the Compassionate, the Merciful

By the gales, sent forth in swift succession; by the raging tempests and the rain-spreading winds; by your Lord's revelations, discerning good from evil and admonishing by plea and warning: that which you have been promised shall be fulfilled!

When the stars are blotted out; when the sky is rent asunder and the mountains crumble into dust; when the apostles are brought together on the appointed day—when will all this be? Upon the Day of Judgement!

Would that you knew what the Day of Judgement is! Woe on that day to the disbelievers! Did We not destroy the men of old and cause others to follow them? Thus shall We deal with the guilty.

Woe on that day to the disbelievers! Did We not create you from a humble fluid, which We kept in a safe receptacle[21] for an appointed term? All this We did; how excellent is Our work!

Woe on that day to the disbelievers! Have We not made the earth a home for the living and for the dead? Have We not placed high mountains upon it, and given you fresh water for your drink?

Woe on that day to the disbelievers! Begone to that Hell which you deny! Depart into the shadow that will rise high in three columns, giving neither shade nor shelter from the flames, and throwing up sparks as huge as towers, as bright as yellow camels!

Woe on that day to the disbelievers! On that day they shall not speak, nor shall their pleas be heeded.

Woe on that day to the disbelievers! Such is the Day of Judgement. We will assemble you all, together with past generations. If then you are cunning, try your spite against Me!

Woe on that day to the disbelievers! The righteous shall dwell amidst cool shades and fountains, and feed on such fruits as they desire. We shall say to them: "Eat and

77:1

77:24

77:41

77:42

---

21 The womb.

drink, and may every joy attend you! This is the guerdon of your labours." Thus shall the righteous be rewarded.

Woe on that day to the disbelievers! Eat and enjoy yourselves awhile. Surely you are sinners all.

Woe on that day to the disbelievers! When they are bidden to kneel down, they do not kneel.

Woe on that day to the disbelievers! In what revelation, after this, will they believe? *77:50*

The Tidings

In the Name of God, the Compassionate, the Merciful

About what are they asking? *78:1*

About the fateful tidings—the theme of their disputes.

But they shall know the Truth; before long they shall know it.

Did We not spread the earth like a bed, and raise the mountains like supporting poles?

We created you in pairs, and gave you rest in sleep. We made the night a mantle, and ordained the day for work. We built above you seven mighty heavens and placed in them a shining lamp. We sent down abundant water from the clouds, bringing forth grain and varied plants, and gardens thick with foliage.

Fixed is the Day of Judgement. On that day the Trumpet shall be sounded, and you *78:17* shall come in multitudes. The gates of heaven shall swing open, and the mountains shall pass away and become like vapour.

Hell will lie in ambush, a home for the transgressors. There they shall abide long ages; there they shall taste neither refreshment nor any drink, save scalding water and decaying filth: a fitting recompense.

They disbelieved in Our reckoning, and roundly denied Our revelations. But We counted all their doings and wrote them down. We shall say: "Taste this: you shall *78:30* have nothing but mounting torment!"

As for the righteous, they shall surely triumph. Theirs shall be gardens and vine- *78:31* yards, and high-bosomed maidens for companions: a truly overflowing cup.

There they shall hear no idle talk, nor any falsehood. Such is the recompense of your Lord—a gift that will suffice them: the Lord of the heavens and the earth and all that lies between them; the Merciful, with whom no one can speak.

On the day when the Spirit and the angels stand up in their ranks, they shall not speak; except him who shall receive the sanction of the Merciful and declare what is right.

That day is sure to come. Let him who will, seek a way back to his Lord. We have forewarned you of an imminent scourge: *78:40* the day when man will look upon his works and the unbeliever cry: "Would that I were dust!"

The Soul-Snatchers

In the Name of God, the Compassionate, the Merciful

By those who snatch away men's souls, and those who gently release them; by those *79:1* who float at will, and those who speed headlong; by those who govern the affairs of this world! On the day the Trumpet sounds its first and second blast, all hearts shall be filled with terror, and all eyes shall stare with awe.

They say: "When we are turned to hollow bones, shall we be restored to life? A fruitless transformation!" But with one blast they shall return to the earth's surface.

Have you heard the story of Moses?

His Lord called out to him in the sacred valley of Ṭuwā, saying: "Go to Pharaoh: he has transgressed all bounds; and say: 'Will you reform yourself? I will guide you to your Lord, so that you may have fear of Him.'"

He showed Pharaoh the mightiest sign, but he denied it and rebelled. He quickly went away and, summoning all his men, made to them a proclamation. "I am your supreme Lord," he said.

God smote him with the scourge of the *79:25* hereafter, and of this life. Surely in this there *79:26* is a lesson for the God-fearing.

Are you harder to create than the heaven which He has built? He raised it high and fashioned it, giving darkness to its night and brightness to its day.

After that He spread the earth, and, drawing water from its depth, brought forth its pastures. He set down the mountains, for you and for your cattle to delight in.

But when the supreme disaster strikes—the day when man will call to mind his labours—when the Fire is brought in sight of all—he that transgressed and chose this present life shall have his home in Hell; but he that feared to stand before his Lord and curbed his soul's desire shall have his home in Paradise.

They question you about the Hour of Doom. "When will it come?" they ask. But how are you to know? Only your Lord knows when it will come. Your duty is but to warn those that fear it.

On the day when they behold that hour, they will think they stayed in the grave but one evening, or one morning. 79:46

He Frowned

In the Name of God, the Compassionate, the Merciful

He[22] frowned and turned his back when the blind man came towards him. 80:1

How could you[21] tell? He might have sought to purify himself. He might have been forewarned, and might have profited from Our warning.

But to the wealthy man you were all attention: although the fault would not be yours if he remained uncleansed. Yet to him that came to you with zeal and awe, you gave no heed.

Indeed, this is an admonition; let him who will, bear it in mind. It is set down on honoured pages, purified and exalted, by the hands of devout and gracious scribes.

Perish man! How ungrateful he is! 80:17
From what did God create him? From a little germ He created him and proportioned him. He makes his path smooth for him, then causes him to die and stows him 80:18

in a grave. He will surely bring him back to life when He pleases. Yet he declines to do His bidding.

Let man reflect on the food he eats: how We pour down the rain in torrents and cleave the earth asunder; how We bring forth the corn, the grapes and the fresh vegetation; the olive and the palm, the thickets, the fruit-trees and the green pasture, for you and for your cattle to delight in.

But when the dread blast is sounded, on that day each man will forsake his brother, his mother and his father, his wife and his children: for each one of them will on that day have enough sorrow of his own.

On that day there shall be beaming faces, smiling and joyful. On that day there shall be faces veiled with darkness, covered with dust. These shall be the faces of the sinful unbelievers. 80:42

The Cessation

In the Name of God, the Compassionate, the Merciful

When the sun ceases to shine; when the stars fall down and the mountains are blown away; when camels big with young are left untended, and the wild beasts are brought together; when the seas are set alight and men's souls are reunited; when the infant girl,[23] buried alive, is asked for what crime she was slain; when the records of men's deeds are laid open, and heaven is stripped bare; when Hell burns fiercely and Paradise is brought near: then each soul shall know what it has done. 81:1

I swear by the turning planets, and by the stars that rise and set; by the night, when it descends, and the first breath of morning: this is the word of a gracious and mighty messenger, held in honour by the Lord of the Throne, obeyed in heaven, faithful to his trust. 81:15 81:21

No, your compatriot[24] is not mad. He saw him[25] on the clear horizon. He does not 81:22

---

22 Muḥammad.
23 An allusion to the pre-Islamic custom of burying unwanted newborn girls.
24 Muḥammad.
25 Gabriel.

grudge the secrets of the unseen; nor is this the utterance of an accursèd devil.

Whither then are you going?

This is but an admonition to all men: to those among you that have the will to be upright. Yet you cannot will, except by the will of God, Lord of the Universe. *81:29*

The Cataclysm

In the Name of God, the Compassionate, the Merciful

When the sky is rent asunder; when the stars scatter and the oceans roll together; when the graves are hurled about; each soul shall know what it has done and what it has failed to do. *82:1*

O man! What evil has enticed you from your gracious Lord who created you, gave you an upright form, and proportioned you? In whatever shape He willed He could have moulded you.

Yet you deny the Last Judgement. Surely there are guardians watching over you, noble recorders who know of all your actions. *82:9*

The righteous will surely dwell in bliss. But the wicked shall burn in Hell upon the Judgement-day: nor shall they ever escape from it.

Would that you knew what the Day of Judgement is! Oh, would that you knew what the Day of Judgement is! It is the day when every soul will stand alone and God will reign supreme. *82:19*

The Unjust

In the Name of God, the Compassionate, the Merciful

Woe to the unjust who, when others measure for them, exact in full, but when they measure or weigh for others, defraud them! *83:1*

Do they not think they will be raised to life upon a fateful day, the day when all mankind will stand before the Lord of the Universe?

Truly, the record of the sinners is in Sijjīn. Would that you knew what Sijjīn is! It is a sealed book.

Woe on that day to the disbelievers who deny the Last Judgement! None denies it except the evil transgressor who, when Our revelations are recited to him, cries: "Fables of the ancients!"

No! Their own deeds have cast a veil over their hearts.

No! On that day a barrier shall be set between them and their Lord. They shall burn in Hell, and shall be told: "This is the scourge that you denied!"

But the record of the righteous shall be in 'Illiyyūn. Would that you knew what 'Illiyyūn is! It is a sealed book, seen only by the favoured.

The righteous will surely dwell in bliss. Reclining upon soft couches they will gaze around them: and in their faces you shall mark the glow of joy. They shall be given a pure wine to drink, securely sealed, whose very dregs are musk (for this let all men emulously strive); a wine tempered with the waters of Tasnīm, a spring at which the favoured will refresh themselves. *83:22*

The evil-doers mock the faithful and wink at one another as they pass by them. When they meet their own folk they speak of them with jests, and when they see them, they say: "These are surely erring men!" Yet they were not sent to be their guardians.

But on that day the faithful will mock the unbelievers as they recline upon their couches and gaze around them.

Shall not the unbelievers be rewarded according to their deeds? *83:36*

The Rending

In the Name of God, the Compassionate, the Merciful

When the sky is rent apart, obeying her Lord in true submission; when the earth expands and casts out all that is within her and becomes empty, obeying her Lord in true submission; then, O man, who labour constantly to meet your Lord, shall you meet Him. *84:1*

He that is given his book in his right hand shall have a lenient reckoning, and shall go back rejoicing to his people. But he that is given his book behind his back shall call down destruction on himself and burn in the fire of Hell; for he lived without a care among his people and thought he would never return to God. Yes; but his Lord was ever watching him.

I swear by the glow of sunset; by the night, and all that it brings together; by the moon, in her full perfection: that you shall march onwards from state to state.

Why then do they not have faith, or kneel in prayer when the Koran is read to them?

The unbelievers indeed deny it; but God knows best the falsehoods they believe in.

Therefore proclaim to all a woeful doom, save those who embrace the true Faith and do good works; for theirs is an unfailing recompense.

84:16

84:25

The Constellations

In the Name of God, the Compassionate, the Merciful

By the heaven with its constellations! By the Promised Day! By the Witness, and that which is witnessed!

Cursed be the diggers of the trench, who lighted the consuming fire and sat around it to watch the faithful being put to the torture! Nor did they torture them for any reason save that they believed in God, the Mighty, the Praised One, who has sovereignty over the heavens and the earth. God is the Witness of all things.

Those that persecute believers, men or women, and never repent shall be rewarded with the scourge of Hell, the scourge of the Conflagration. But those that have faith and do good works shall be rewarded with gardens watered by running streams. That is the supreme triumph.

Stern indeed is the vengeance of your Lord. It is He who brings into being and then restores to life. Forgiving and benignant, He is the Lord of the Glorious Throne, the Executor of His own will.

Have you not heard the story of the warriors, of Pharaoh and of Thamūd? Yet the unbelievers still deny it.

God surrounds them all. Surely this is a glorious Koran, inscribed on an imperishable tablet.

85:1

85:9

85:10

85:22

---

26 The Koran.

The Nightly Visitant

In the Name of God, the Compassionate, the Merciful

By the heaven, and by the nightly visitant!

Would that you knew what the nightly visitant is!

It is the star of piercing brightness.

For every soul there is a guardian watching it. Let man reflect from what he is created. He is created from an ejaculated fluid that issues from between the loins and the ribs.

Surely He has power to bring him back to life, on the day when men's consciences are searched. Helpless shall he be, with none to succour him.

By the heaven with its recurring cycles, and by the earth, ever bursting with new growth; this[26] is a discerning utterance, no flippant jest.

They scheme and scheme: and I, too, scheme and scheme. Therefore bear with the unbelievers, and let them be awhile.

86:1

86:11

86:17

The Most High

In the Name of God, the Compassionate, the Merciful

Praise the Name of your Lord, the Most High, who has created all things and proportioned them; who has ordained their destinies and guided them; who brings forth the green pasture, then turns it to withered grass.

We shall make you recite Our revelations, so that you shall forget none of them except as God pleases. He has knowledge of all that is manifest, and all that is hidden.

We shall guide you to the smoothest path. Therefore give warning, if warning will avail. He that fears God will heed it, but the wicked sinner will flout it. He shall burn in the gigantic Fire, where he shall neither die nor live. Happy shall be the man who

87:1

87:11

purifies himself, who remembers the name of his Lord and prays.

Yet you[27] prefer this life, although the life to come is better and more lasting.

All this is written in earlier scriptures; the scriptures of Abraham and Moses. *87:19*

The Overwhelming Event

In the Name of God, the Compassionate, the Merciful

Have you heard of the Event which will overwhelm mankind?

On that day there shall be downcast faces, of men broken and worn out, burnt by a scorching fire, drinking from a seething fountain. Their only food shall be bitter thorns, which will neither sustain them nor satisfy their hunger. *88:1*

On that day there shall be radiant faces, of men well-pleased with their labours, in a lofty garden. There they shall hear no idle talk. A gushing fountain shall be there, and raised soft couches with goblets placed before them; silken cushions ranged in order and carpets richly spread. *88:16*

Do they never reflect on the camels, and how they were created? The heaven, how it was raised on high? The mountains, how they were set down? The earth, how it was levelled flat? *88:17*

Therefore give warning. Your duty is only to give warning: you are not their keeper. As for those that turn their backs and disbelieve, God will inflict on them the supreme chastisement. To Us they shall return, and We will bring them to account. *88:26*

The Dawn

In the Name of God, the Compassionate, the Merciful

By the Dawn and the Ten Nights;[28] by that which is dual, and that which is single; by the night, when it comes! *89:1*

Is there not in this a mighty oath for a man of sense?

Have you not heard how your Lord dealt with 'Ād?[29] The people of the many-columned city of Iram, whose like has never been built in the whole land? And with Thamūd,[28] who hewed out their dwellings among the rocks of the valley? And with Pharaoh, who impaled his victims upon the stake?

They had all led sinful lives, and made the land teem with wickedness. Therefore your Lord let loose on them His scourge; for from His eminence your Lord observes all.

As for man, when his Lord tests him by exalting him and bestowing favours on him, he says: "My Lord is bountiful to me." But when He tests him by grudging him His favours, he says: "My Lord despises me." *89:15*

No! But you show no kindness to the orphan, nor do you vie with each other in feeding the destitute. Greedily you lay your hands on the inheritance of the weak, and you love riches with all your hearts. *89:20*

No! But when the earth is crushed to fine dust, and your Lord comes down with the angels, in their ranks, and Hell is brought near—on that day man will remember his deeds. But what will memory avail him? *89:21*

He will say: "Would that I had been charitable in my lifetime!" But on that day none will punish as He will punish, and none will bind with chains like His.

O serene soul! Return to your Lord, joyful, and pleasing in His sight. Join My servants and enter My Paradise. *89:30*

---

27 The unbelievers of Mecca.
28 The first ten nights of the sacred month of Dhūl-Ḥajjah.
29 Tradition has it that the tribes of 'Ād and Thamūd were destroyed on account of their sins.

The City

In the Name of God, the Compassionate, the Merciful

I swear by this city (and you[30] are a resident of this city), by the begetter[31] and all whom he begot: We created man to try him with afflictions.

Does he think that none has power over him? "I have squandered vast riches!" he boasts. Does he think that none observes him?

Have We not given him two eyes, a tongue, and two lips, and shown him the two paths?[32] Yet he would not scale the Height.

Would that you knew what the Height is. It is the freeing of a bondsman; the feeding, in the day of famine, of an orphaned relation or a needy man in distress; to have faith, and to enjoin fortitude and mercy.

Those that do this shall stand on the right hand; but those that deny Our revelations shall stand on the left, with Hell-fire close above them.

The Sun

In the Name of God, the Compassionate, the Merciful

By the sun and his midday brightness; by the moon, which rises after him; by the day, which reveals his splendour; by the night, which veils him!

By the heaven and Him that built it; by the earth and Him that spread it; by the soul and Him that moulded it and inspired it with knowledge of sin and piety: blessed shall be the man who has kept it pure, and ruined he that has corrupted it!

In their presumptuous pride the people of Thamūd denied their apostle when their arch-sinner rose against him. God's apostle said: "This is God's own she-camel. Let her drink."

They disbelieved and slaughtered her. And for that crime their Lord let loose His scourge upon them and razed their city to the ground. He did not fear the consequences.

Night

In the Name of God, the Compassionate, the Merciful

By the night, when she lets fall her darkness, and by the radiant day! By Him that created the male and the female, your endeavours have varied ends!

For him that gives in charity and guards himself against evil and believes in goodness, We shall smooth the path of salvation; but for him that neither gives nor takes and disbelieves in goodness, We shall smooth the path of affliction. When he breathes his last, his riches will not avail him.

It is for Us to give guidance. Ours is the life to come, Ours the life of this world. I warn you, then, of the blazing fire, in which none shall burn save the hardened sinner, who denies the Truth and gives no heed. But the good man who purifies himself by alms-giving shall keep away from it: and so shall he that does good works for the sake of the Most High only, seeking no recompense. Such men shall be content.

Daylight

In the Name of God, the Compassionate, the Merciful

By the light of day, and by the dark of night, your Lord has not forsaken you,[33] nor does He abhor you.

The life to come holds a richer prize for you than this present life. You shall be gratified with what your Lord will give you.

---

30 Muḥammad.
31 Adam.
32 Of right and wrong.
33 Muḥammad.

Did He not find you an orphan and give you shelter? Did He not find you in error and guide you?

Did He not find you poor and enrich you?

Therefore do not wrong the orphan, nor chide away the beggar. But proclaim the goodness of your Lord.

93:11

Comfort

In the Name of God, the Compassionate, the Merciful

94:1

Have we not lifted up your heart and relieved you[32] of the burden which weighed down your back?

Have We not given you high renown?

94:8

Every hardship is followed by ease. Every hardship is followed by ease.

When your prayers are ended resume your toil, and seek your Lord with all fervour.

The Fig

In the Name of God, the Compassionate, the Merciful

95:1

By the Fig, and by the Olive!

By Mount Sinai, and by this inviolate City.[34]

We created man in a most noble image and in the end We shall reduce him to the lowest of the low: except the believers who do good works, for theirs shall be a boundless recompense.

What then after this can make you deny the Last Judgement?

Is God not the best of judges?

95:8

Clots of Blood

In the Name of God, the Compassionate, the Merciful

Recite in the name of your Lord who created—created man from clots of blood.

96:1

Recite! Your Lord is the Most Bountiful One, who by the pen taught man what he did not know.

Indeed, man transgresses in thinking himself his own master: for to your Lord all things return.

Observe the man who rebukes Our servant when he prays. Think: does he follow the right guidance or enjoin true piety?

96:13

Think: if he denies the Truth and gives no heed, does he not realize that God observes all?

No. Let him desist, or We will drag him by the forelock, his lying, sinful forelock.

Then let him call his helpmates. We will call the guards of Hell.

96:19

No, never obey him! Prostrate yourself and come nearer.

Qadr

In the Name of God, the Compassionate, the Merciful

We revealed this on the Night of Qadr.[35] Would that you knew what the Night of Qadr is like!

97:1

Better is the Night of Qadr than a thousand months.

On that night the angels and the Spirit by their Lord's leave come down with each decree.

That night is peace, till break of dawn.

97:5

---

34 Mecca.
35 Lit., glory.

The Proof

In the Name of God, the Compassionate, the Merciful

The unbelievers among the People of the Book[36] and the pagans did not desist from unbelief until the Proof was given them: an apostle from God reciting from purified pages infallible decrees.

Nor did those who were vouchsafed the Book disagree among themselves until the Proof was given them. Yet they were enjoined only to serve God and to worship none but Him, to attend to their prayers and to render the alms levy. That, surely, is the infallible faith.

The unbelievers among the People of the Book and the pagans shall burn for ever in the fire of Hell. They are the vilest of all creatures.

But of all creatures those that embrace the Faith and do good works are the noblest. Their reward, in their Lord's presence, shall be the gardens of Eden, gardens watered by running streams, where they shall dwell for ever.

God is well pleased with them, and they are well pleased with Him. Thus shall the God-fearing be rewarded.

The Earthquake

In the Name of God, the Compassionate, the Merciful

When Earth is rocked in her last convulsion; when Earth shakes off her burdens and man asks, "What may this mean?"—on that day she will proclaim her tidings, for your Lord will have inspired her.

On that day mankind will come in broken bands to be shown their labours. Whoever does an atom's weight of good shall see it, and whoever does an atom's weight of evil shall see it also.

The War Steeds

In the Name of God, the Compassionate, the Merciful

By the snorting war steeds, which strike fire with their hoofs as they gallop to the raid at dawn and with a trail of dust split apart a massed army; man is ungrateful to his Lord! To this he himself shall bear witness.

He loves riches with all his heart. But is he not aware that when the dead are thrown out from their graves and men's hidden thoughts are laid open, their Lord will on that day have full knowledge of them all?

The Disaster

In the Name of God, the Compassionate, the Merciful

The Disaster! What is the Disaster?
Would that you knew what the Disaster is!
On that day men shall become like scattered moths and the mountains like tufts of carded wool.
Then he whose scales are heavy shall dwell in bliss; but he whose scales are light, the Abyss shall be his home.
Would that you knew what this is like!
It is a scorching fire.

Worldly Gain

In the Name of God, the Compassionate, the Merciful

Your hearts are taken up with worldly gain from the cradle to the grave.
But you shall know. You shall before long come to know.
Indeed, if you knew the truth with certainty, you would see the fire of Hell: you would see it with your very eyes.

---

36 Jews and Christians.

Then, on that day, you shall be questioned about your joys. *102:8*

The Declining Day

In the Name of God, the Compassionate, the Merciful

I swear by the declining day that perdition shall be the lot of man, except for those who have faith and do good works; who exhort each other to justice and to fortitude. *103:1–103:3*

The Slanderer

In the Name of God, the Compassionate, the Merciful

Woe to every back-biting slanderer who amasses riches and sedulously hoards them, thinking his wealth will render him immortal! *104:1*

By no means! He shall be flung to the Destroying Flame.

Would that you knew what the Destroying Flame is like!

It is God's own kindled fire, which will rise up to the hearts of men. It will close upon them from every side, in towering columns. *104:9*

The Elephant

In the Name of God, the Compassionate, the Merciful

Have you not considered how God dealt with the Army of the Elephant?[37] *105:1*

Did He not confound their stratagem and send against them flocks of birds which pelted them with clay-stones, so that they became like the withered stalks of plants which cattle have devoured? *105:5*

Quraysh[38]

In the Name of God, the Compassionate, the Merciful

For the protection of Quraysh: their protection in their summer and winter journeyings. *106:1*

Therefore let them worship the Lord of this House who fed them in the days of famine and shielded them from all peril. *106:4*

Alms

In the Name of God, the Compassionate, the Merciful

Have you thought of him that denies the Last Judgement? It is he who turns away the orphan and has no urge to feed the destitute. *107:1*

Woe to those who pray but are heedless in their prayer; who make a show of piety and forbid alsmgiving. *107:7*

Abundance

In the Name of God, the Compassionate, the Merciful

We have given you[39] abundance. Pray to your Lord and sacrifice to Him. He that hates you shall remain childless. *108:1–108:3*

The Unbelievers

In the Name of God, the Compassionate, the Merciful

Say: "Unbelievers, I do not worship what you worship, nor do you worship what I worship. *109:1*

---

37 The allusion is to the expedition of Abraha, the Christian King of Ethiopia, against Mecca, said to have taken place in the year of Muḥammad's birth.
38 Muḥammad's own clan. Some commentators connect this chapter with the preceding one.
39 Muḥammad.

I shall never worship what you worship, nor will you ever worship what I worship. You have your own religion, and I have mine." *109:6*

Help

In the Name of God, the Compassionate, the Merciful

When God's help and victory come, and you see men embrace God's faith in multitudes, give glory to your Lord and seek His pardon. He is ever disposed to mercy. *110:1 – 110:3*

Al-lahab[40]

In the Name of God, the Compassionate, the Merciful

May the hands of Abu-Lahab[41] perish! May he himself perish! Nothing shall his wealth and gains avail him. He shall be burnt in a flaming fire[42] and his wife, laden with firewood, shall have a rope of fibre round her neck! *111:1 – 111:5*

Oneness

In the Name of God, the Compassionate, the Merciful

Say: "God is One, the Eternal God. He begot none, nor was He begotten. None is equal to Him." *112:1 – 112:4*

Daybreak

In the Name of God, the Compassionate, the Merciful

Say: "I seek refuge in the Lord of Daybreak from the mischief of His creation; from the mischief of the night when she spreads her darkness; from the mischief of conjuring witches; from the mischief of the envier, when he envies." *113:1 – 113:5*

Men

In the Name of God, the Compassionate, the Merciful

Say: "I seek refuge in the Lord of men, the King of men, the God of men, from the mischief of the slinking prompter who whispers in the hearts of men; from jinn and men." *114:1 – 114:6*

---

40 This *sūrah* is also known by another title: "Al-Masad" (Fibre).
41 The Prophet's uncle, and one of his staunchest opponents.
42 A pun on the meaning of Abu-Lahab, "father of flame."

Basic Features of Islam

Main Articles of Faith:

1. Allah, who is the only God ("Allah" is the same word as "Eli," a familiar Hebrew word for "God." Islam knows Allah to be the same God as that of the Hebrew Bible and the New Testament).
2. The angels (Gabriel and others).
3. The Prophets (Muhammad, Abraham, Noah, Moses, and Jesus).
4. The sacred books (The Koran and, to a lesser extent, the Hebrew Bible, New Testament, and the Psalms of David).
5. The Qadar (God's plan for the collective benefit of all humanity).
6. Resurrection of the Day of Judgment.

The Five Pillars of Faith Identify the Religious Duties of Muslims:

1. "There is no God but Allah, and Muhammad is his prophet." This is the Shahadah. Any person wishing to be accepted as a Muslim need only recite this statement of faith.
2. The obligation of five daily prayers (dawn, midday, midafternoon, sunset, and nightfall).
3. Giving to the poor (once voluntary, now an assessment).
4. Fasting during Ramadan.
5. Pilgrimage (Hijrah) to Mecca.

A sixth obligation, the Jihad (holy war), is no longer in effect. In the early days of Islam, each caliph (or "successor" to Muhammad) felt obligated to reduce the infidel "territory of war" by armed conquest in the name of Allah. Except for Spain and Israel, all those territories converted by the sword remain Muslim to this day.

The Arabic word for submission is "Islam," and this is the name of the religion; a person who submits is a "Muslim," a Believer.

English Words That Come from Arabic

Alchemy—al-kimiya'	Coffee—qahwa	Orange—naranj
Algebra—al-jabr	Cotton—qutun	Rice—ruzz
Amber—anbar	Giraffe—zurafa	Safari—safara
Amulet—hama'il	jasmine—yasmin	Saffron—za'faran
Artichoke—al-kharshuf	Lemon—limun	Sofa—suffa
Banana—banana	Magazine—makhazin	Sugar—sukkar
Cable—habl	Mask—maskhara	Syrup—sharab, shurb
Camel—jamal	Monsoon—mawsim	Troubadour—tarrab
Checkmate—shah-mat	Musk—musk	Zero—sifr

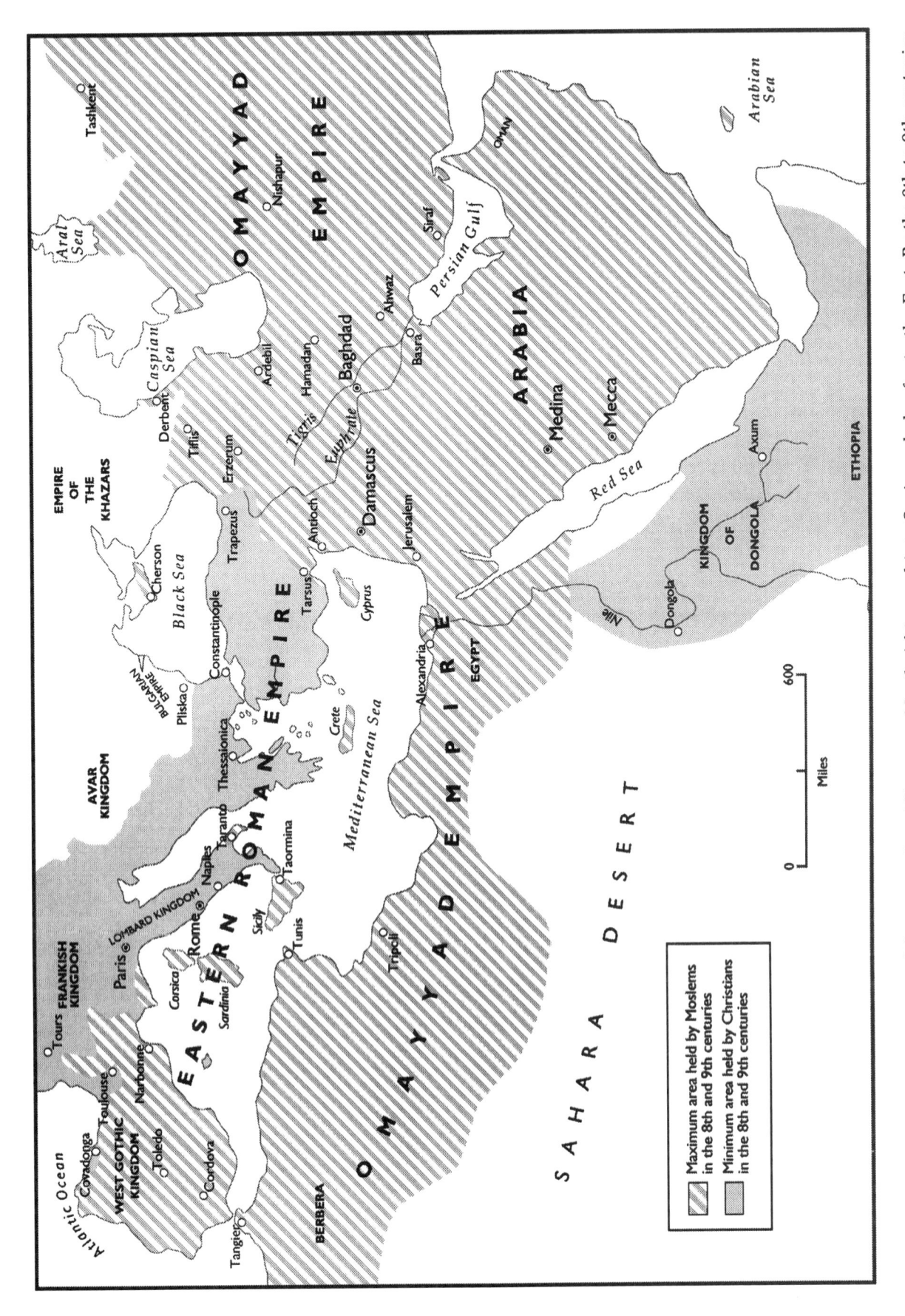

After its inception in the 7th century, Islam spread rapidly across North Africa and into Spain and also far to the East. By the 8th to 9th centuries, Islam had a decisive advantage over Christianity in political power and influence and had laid the foundation for a flourishing culture.

RELIGIOUS FOUNDATIONS

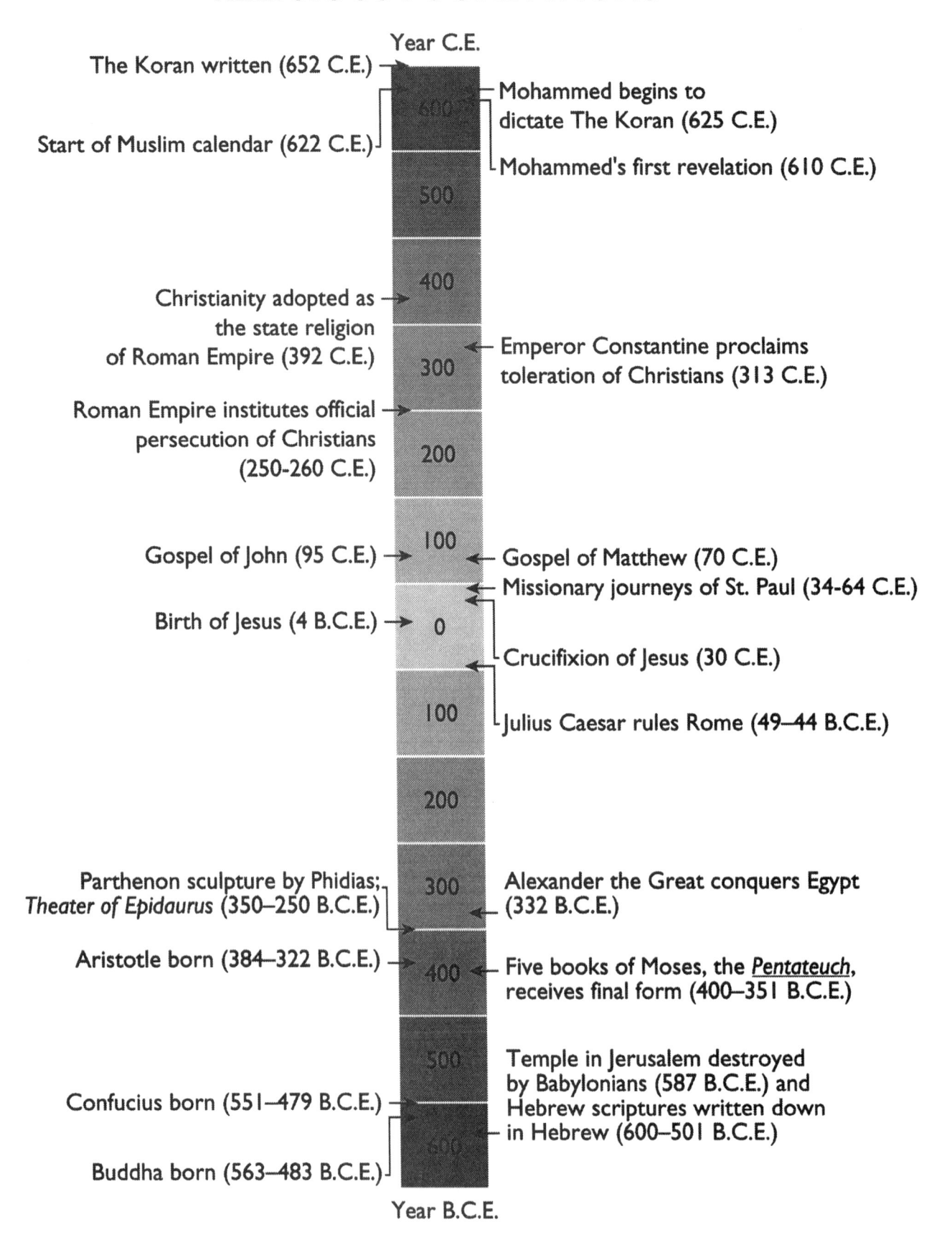

Year C.E.

- The Koran written (652 C.E.)
- Mohammed begins to dictate The Koran (625 C.E.)
- Start of Muslim calendar (622 C.E.)
- Mohammed's first revelation (610 C.E.)

— 600 —
— 500 —
— 400 —

- Christianity adopted as the state religion of Roman Empire (392 C.E.)
- Emperor Constantine proclaims toleration of Christians (313 C.E.)

— 300 —

- Roman Empire institutes official persecution of Christians (250–260 C.E.)

— 200 —

- Gospel of John (95 C.E.)
- Gospel of Matthew (70 C.E.)
- Missionary journeys of St. Paul (34–64 C.E.)

— 100 —

- Birth of Jesus (4 B.C.E.)

— 0 —

- Crucifixion of Jesus (30 C.E.)

— 100 —

- Julius Caesar rules Rome (49–44 B.C.E.)

— 200 —
— 300 —

- Parthenon sculpture by Phidias; *Theater of Epidaurus* (350–250 B.C.E.)
- Alexander the Great conquers Egypt (332 B.C.E.)

— 400 —

- Aristotle born (384–322 B.C.E.)
- Five books of Moses, the *Pentateuch*, receives final form (400–351 B.C.E.)

— 500 —

- Temple in Jerusalem destroyed by Babylonians (587 B.C.E.) and Hebrew scriptures written down in Hebrew (600–501 B.C.E.)
- Confucius born (551–479 B.C.E.)

— 600 —

- Buddha born (563–483 B.C.E.)

Year B.C.E.

Introduction to Sundiata

Sundiata: an Epic of Old Mali, is the one work in Paths of Civilization that is not part of the Western tradition. This means that not only was it not written by Europeans, but unlike the Qur'an it was unknown until very recently and has as yet had little impact on Western literature and thinking. The reason for including such a work is to help us think about some matters that are so familiar to us that we take them very much for granted. The Sundiata introduces us to animism, magic, and a view of the relation between humankind and nature that is radically different from our traditional view.

In the story, we encounter people whose spirits live sometimes in animal form. And people in the world of Sundiata generally seem to have an animal totem that helps form their identity. The hero is both a buffalo and a lion, a formidable legacy. His mother is so much buffalo that she takes this physical form at critical times. What can all this mean?

One way for us to think about it is to recognize how far we in Western culture have turned away from nature as a part of ourselves. Native Americans, for example, acquired their names from observed similarities with animals (Sundiata calls animals "our dumb brothers in the bush"). For them, it was impossible to claim ownership of a piece of land, of a stream, or a stand of trees because all those were part of nature, had spirits of their own, and were far beyond the creative powers of mere mortals. The claim of Europeans to own the landscape was at first ridiculous to them.

In the West we follow Genesis, which informs us that we are not part of nature and that, indeed, God has given us "dominion" over nature. We alone are created in God's image. Nature is there for our pleasure and sustenance. We owe it nothing at all. Sundiata reminds us of what modern science affirms, that we are made of the same stuff as the world around us, share the same fate, and even feelings and emotions with the creatures all about us. Animism may be closer to the truth of things than our thinking allows us to know.

Sundiata also challenges our commitment to literacy. The Griot who tells the tale, Djeli Mamadou Kouyate (a real person), asserts that oral culture is more true and more powerful than literate culture. A story told face-to-face by an expert story-teller schooled in the art and informed of the story to an extraordinary degree is more reliable and more effective than reading it in a "dumb book." Books are dumb because they cannot talk. We cannot ask them questions, and they cannot provide vivid inflection to their story. Also, they allow anyone to think he knows when he does not really grasp the force and deeper significance of the story. This is much harder to miss in a face-to-face telling. In the Griot's view, literacy breeds ignorance and arrogance and destroys traditional authority in knowledge. He may just be right about that.

But Sundiata has a life and form of its own apart from its difference from our cultural assumptions. It is an epic, the only one we read in Intellectual Heritage. Its hero founds an empire and brings the law to protect the people. In this regard, he is like not only epic heroes but like Pericles and Moses, too. Unlike them, Sundiata must defeat a sorcerer and himself engage in the magic arts. However, the true source of his power is his goodness and the brave way he engages his destiny.

The *Sundiata* is also a work of political science—the Griot is traditionally a counselor to kings and must advise the man of power wisely. Although the people's best interest is paramount, Sundiata does not conduct himself in a democratic style. He is a superior person, and he lets this be known by his exacting manner towards others. The Griot tells us that this is really what people want in a leader, not fellowship. At the same time, the leader depends upon alliances with others. Sundiata's exile allows him to find friends among other peoples, who become critical to his victory in the end. Women, too, play an important role in his victory. The bravery and resourcefulness of his half-sister is critical to his success. Finally, when he is victorious, Sundiata knows how to withhold his vengeance and thereby to make friends of former enemies. He is a general but also a statesman. Building an empire requires many talents.

Sundiata is one of the favorite moments for many students. It is an enjoyable story, and one with much to teach us.

Further Notes on *Sundiata*

There are many versions of the story of Sundiata and under several different names (SonJara being a variation). Many of the people influenced by the accomplishments of the real 13th century emperor favor their own version, and there are Christian, Muslim, and animist tellings of the tale. Our version has been heavily adapted for Western readers, and looks something like a novel. Without that adaptation, it is unlikely that we could read it. However, the original is nothing like this version. In truth, the *Sundiata* exists only in its oral form.

The *Sundiata* is in reality a performance piece presented by a griot. It has no written form (note the comments of the griot at the opening of the chapter entitled "History"). The griot, as our story shows, is an important member of the community. First, he serves as the historian, recalling the genealogies and stories of past personages back through the centuries. Thus, in the book *Roots*, by Alex Haley, we find that the author was able to authenticate the stories his enslaved forebears had passed down by checking the record through a griot's tale. The griot is also a counselor to kings. Knowing the events of the past, the griot is able to advise which actions were successful and which failed in similar situations. The stories he tells carry this practical sort of wisdom and other kinds as well. The griot is also an official at court and helps arrange alliances and important marriages. Griots are educated within their families, which carry this art across the centuries. The performances of the griot's tale is done to the accompaniment of musical instruments, and a performance may take place over several days. Our version, then, is only a thin slice of the story and of the griot's art.

Still, what comes through to us is powerful and enlightening. D. T. Niane, the translator of the tale, is a well known French-speaking scholar from Senegal who persuaded a griot by the name of Djeli Mamoudou Kouyate to recite his tale for him. Niane then adapted his telling so that modern "readers" could grasp something of this traditional knowledge and art. The book was originally published in French as *Soundjata, ou l'Epopee Mandingue*. So, this version of the tale has made its journey over the centuries from Mandinke, to French, to English. As Niane writes: "May this book open the eyes of more than one African and induce him to come and sit humbly beside the ancients and hear the words of the griots who teach wisdom and history."

We have published *Sundiata* without the notes Niane included, most of which are technical and scholarly. Three items, however, require comment.

Sundiata comes from a world that takes the spirit life seriously. People have totems; Sundiata, for example, is both the Buffalo and the Lion from his parentage. This means that he can draw upon the spiritual powers of both those animals. In addition, and far stranger, there is the figure of the *wraith*. A wraith is part of our spirit that goes wandering and can enter into other forms and have adventures of which we are unaware. Thus, the old woman who is the buffalo can be both a human being and the rampaging menace assaulting the village of Do. The concept does help explain where we are when we are sleeping—think about it.

The second item that needs some discussion is the end of the evil sorcerer Soumaoro. The secret of his power is discovered to involve avoiding contact with the substance ergot, of which the cock's spur is composed. Once Soumaoro is touched by this substance, he loses his magic powers and becomes vulnerable to human weapons. There are several versions of the end of Soumaoro. In one he is transformed into a stone, in another he simply disappears on the battlefield never to reappear. In our version he enters a cave and is never heard from again.

And finally, you will notice that Sundiata is known by many names—this is confusing to us. The idea was that having many names was a protection against sorcery since the enemy was unable to invoke evil magic against an opponent whose name was not precisely known.

Sundiata: An Epic of Old Mali

—D.T.N.

The Words of the Griot Mamadou Kouyaté

I am a griot. It is I, Djeli Mamoudou Kouyaté, son of Bintou Kouyaté and Djeli Kedian Kouyaté, master in the art of eloquence. Since time immemorial the Kouyatés have been in the service of the Keita princes of Mali; we are vessels of speech, we are the repositories which harbour secrets many centuries old. The art of eloquence has no secrets for us; without us the names of kings would vanish into oblivion, we are the memory of mankind; by the spoken word we bring to life the deeds and exploits of kings for younger generations.

I derive my knowledge from my father Djeli Kedian, who also got it from his father; history holds no mystery for us; we teach to the vulgar just as much as we want to teach them, for it is we who keep the keys to the twelve doors of Mali.

I know the list of all the sovereigns who succeeded to the throne of Mali. I know how the black people divided into tribes, for my father bequeathed to me all his learning; I know why such and such is called Kamara, another Keita, and yet another Sibibé or Traoré; every name has a meaning, a secret import.

I teach kings the history of their ancestors so that the lives of the ancients might serve them as an example, for the world is old, but the future springs from the past.

My word is pure and free of all untruth; it is the word of my father; it is the word of my father's father. I will give you my father's words just as I received them; royal griots do not know what lying is. When a quarrel breaks out between tribes it is we who settle the difference, for we are the depositories of oaths which the ancestors swore.

Listen to my word, you who want to know; by my mouth you will learn the history of Mali.

By my mouth you will get to know the story of the ancestor of great Mali, the story of him who, by his exploits, surpassed even Alexander the Great; he who, from the East, shed his rays upon all the countries of the West.

Listen to the story of the son of the Buffalo, the son of the Lion. I am going to tell you of Maghan Sundiata, of Mari-Djata, of Sogolon Djata, of Naré Maghan Djata; the man of many names against whom sorcery could avail nothing.

The First Kings of Mali

Listen then, sons of Mali, children of the black people, listen to my word, for I am going to tell you of Sundiata, the father of the Bright Country, of the savanna land, the ancestor of those who draw the bow, the master of a hundred vanquished kings.

I am going to talk of Sundiata, Manding Diara, Lion of Mali, Sogolon Djata, son of Sogolon, Naré Maghan Djata, son of Naré Maghan, Sogo Sogo Simbon Salaba, hero of many names.

I am going to tell you of Sundiata, he whose exploits will astonish men for a long time yet. He was great among kings, he was peerless among

---

From *Sundiata: An Epic of Old Mali* by Niane. Copyright © 1965. Reprinted by permission of Addison Wesley Longman Ltd.

men; he was beloved of God because he was the last of the great conquerors.

Right at the beginning then, Mali was a province of the Bambara kings; those who are today called Mandingo, inhabitants of Mali, are not indigenous; they come from the East. Bilali Bounama, ancestor of the Keitas, was the faithful servant of the Prophet Muhammad (may the peace of God be upon him). Bilali Bounama had seven sons of whom the eldest, Lawalo, left the Holy City and came to settle in Mali; Lawalo had Latal Kalabi for a son, Latal Kalabi had Damul Kalabi who then had Lahilatoul Kalabi.

Lahilatoul Kalabi was the first black prince to make the Pilgrimage to Mecca. On his return he was robbed by brigands in the desert; his men were scattered and some died of thirst, but God saved Lahilatoul Kalabi, for he was a righteous man. He called upon the Almighty and jinn appeared and recognized him as king. After seven years' absence Lahilatoul was able to return, by the grace of Allah the Almighty, to Mali where none expected to see him any more.

Lahilatoul Kalabi had two sons, the elder being called Kalabi Bomba and the younger Kalabi Dauman; the elder chose royal power and reigned, while the younger preferred fortune and wealth and became the ancestor of these who go from country to country seeking their fortune.

Kalabi Bomba had Mamadi Kani for a son. Mamadi Kani was a hunter king like the first kings of Mali. It was he who invented the hunter's whistle; he communicated with the jinn of the forest and bush. These spirits had no secrets from him and he was loved by Kondolon Ni Sané. His followers were so numerous that he formed them into an army which became formidable; he often gathered them together in the bush and taught them the art of hunting. It was he who revealed to hunters the medicinal leaves which heal wounds and cure diseases. Thanks to the strength of his followers, he became king of a vast country; with them Mamadi Kani conquered all the lands which stretch from the Sankarani to the Bouré. Mamadi Kani had four sons—Kani Simbon, Kamignogo Simbon, Kabala Simbon and Simbon Tagnogokelin. They were all initiated into the art of hunting and deserved the title of Simbon. It was the lineage of Bamari Tagnogokelin which held on to the power, his son was M'Bali Nènè whose son was Bello. Bello's son was called Bello Bakon and he had a son called Maghan Kon Fatta, also called Frako Maghan Keigu, Maghan the handsome.

Maghan Kon Fatta was the father of the great Sundiata and had three wives and six children— three boys and three girls. His first wife was called Sassouma Bérété, daughter of a great divine; she was the mother of King Dankaran Touman and Princess Nana Triban. The second wife, Sogolon Kedjou, was the mother of Sundiata and the two princesses Sogolon Kolonkan and Sogolon Djamarou. The third wife was one of the Kamaras and was called Namandjé; she was the mother of Manding Bory (or Manding Bakary), who was the best friend of his half-brother Sundiata . . . .

The Buffalo Woman

Maghan Kon Fatta, the father of Sundiata, was renowned for his beauty in every land; but he was also a good king loved by all the people. In his capital of Nianiba he loved to sit often at the foot of the great silk-cotton tree which dominated his palace of Canco. Maghan Kon Fatta had been reigning a long time and his eldest son Dankaran Touman was already eight years old and often came to sit on the ox-hide beside his father.

Well now, one day when the king had taken up his usual position under the silk-cotton tree surrounded by his kinsmen he saw a man dressed like a hunter coming towards him; he wore the tight-fitting trousers of the favourites of Kondolon Ni Sané, and his blouse oversewn with cowries showed that he was a master of the hunting art. All present turned towards the unknown man whose bow, polished with frequent usage, shone in the sun. The man walked up in front of the king, whom he recognized in the midst of his courtiers. He bowed and said, "I salute you, king of Mali, greetings all you of Mali. I am a hunter chasing game and come from Sangaran; a fearless doe has guided me to the walls of Nianiba. By the grace of my master the great Simbon my arrows have hit her and now she lies not far from your walls. As is fitting, oh king, I have come to bring you your portion." He took a leg from his leather sack whereupon the king's griot, Gnankouman Doua, seized upon the leg and said, "Stranger, whoever you may be you will be the king's guest because you respect custom; come and take your place on the mat beside us. The king is pleased because he loves righteous men." The king nodded his approval and all the courtiers agreed. The griot continued in a more familiar tone, "Oh you who come from the Sangaran, land of the favourites of Kondolon Ni Sané, you who have doubtless had an expert master, will you open your pouch of knowledge for us and instruct us with your conversation, for you have no doubt visited several lands."

The king, still silent, gave a nod of approval and a courtier added, "The hunters of Sangaran are the best soothsayers; if the stranger wishes we could learn a lot from him."

The hunter came and sat down near Gnankouman Doua who vacated one end of the mat to him. Then he said, "Griot of the king, I am not one of these hunters whose tongues are more dexterous than their arms; I am no spinner of adventure yarns, nor do I like playing upon the credulity of worthy folk; but, thanks to the lore which my master has imparted to me, I can boast of being a seer among seers."

He took out of his hunter's bag twelve cowries which he threw on the mat. The king and all his entourage now turned towards the stranger who was jumbling up the twelve shiny shells with his bare hand. Gnankouman Doua discreetly brought to the king's notice that the soothsayer was left-handed. The left hand is the hand of evil, but in the divining art it is said that left-handed people are the best. The hunter muttered some incomprehensible words in a low voice while he shuffled and jumbled the twelve cowries into different positions which he mused on at length. All of a sudden he looked up at the king and said, "Oh king, the world is full of mystery, all is hidden and we know nothing but what we can see. The silk-cotton tree springs from a tiny seed—that which defies the tempest weighs in its germ no more than a grain of rice. Kingdoms are like trees; some will be silk-cotton trees, others will remain dwarf palms and the powerful silk-cotton tree will cover them with its shade. Oh, who can recognize in the little child the great king to come? The great comes from the small; truth and falsehood have both suckled at the same breast. Nothing is certain, but, sire, I can see two strangers over there coming towards your city."

He fell silent and looked in the direction of the city gates for a short while. All present silently turned towards the gates. The soothsayer returned to his cowries. He shook them in his palm with a skilled hand and then threw them out.

"King of Mali, destiny marches with great strides, Mali is about to emerge from the night. Nianiba is lighting up, but what is this light that comes from the east?"

"Hunter," said Gnankouman Doua, "your words are obscure. Make your speech comprehensible to us, speak in the clear language of your savanna."

"I am coming to that now, griot. Listen to my message. Listen, sire. You have ruled over the kingdom which your ancestors bequeathed to you and you have no other ambition but to pass on this realm, intact if not increased, to your descendants; but, fine king, your successor is not yet born. I see two hunters coming to your city; they have come from afar and a woman accompanies them. Oh, that woman! She is ugly, she is hideous, she bears on her back a disfiguring hump. Her monstrous eyes seem to have been merely laid on her face, but, mystery of mysteries, this is the woman you must marry, sire, for she will be the mother of him who will make the name of Mali immortal for ever. The child will be the seventh star, the seventh conqueror of the earth. He will be more mighty than Alexander. But, oh king, for destiny to lead this woman to you a sacrifice is necessary; you must offer up a red bull, for the bull is powerful. When its blood soaks into the ground nothing more will hinder the arrival of your wife. There, I have said what I had to say, but everything is in the hands of the Almighty."

The hunter picked up his cowries and put them away in his bag.

"I am only passing through, king of Mali, and now I return to Sangaran. Farewell."

The hunter disappeared but neither the king, Naré Maghan, nor his griot, Gnankouman Doua, forgot his prophetic words; soothsayers see far ahead, their words are not always for the immediate present; man is in a hurry but time is tardy and everything has its season.

Now one day the king and his suite were again seated under the great silk-cotton tree of Nianiba, chatting as was their wont. Suddenly their gaze was drawn by some strangers who came into the city. The small entourage of the king watched in silent surprise.

Two young hunters, handsome and of fine carriage, were walking along preceded by a young maid. They turned towards the Court. The two men were carrying shining bows of silver on their shoulders. The one who seemed the elder of the two walked with the assurance of a master hunter. When the strangers were a few steps from the king they bowed and the elder spoke thus:

"We greet King Naré Maghan Kon Fatta and his entourage. We come from the land of Do, but my brother and I belong to Mali and we are of the tribe of Traoré. Hunting and adventure led us as far as the distant land of Do where King Mansa

Gnemo Diarra reigns. I am called Oulamba and my brother Oulani. The young girl is from Do and we bring her as a present to the king, for my brother and I deemed her worthy to be a king's wife."

The king and his suite tried in vain to get a look at the young girl, for she stayed kneeling, her head lowered, and had deliberately let her kerchief hang in front of her face. If the young girl succeeded in hiding her face, she did not, however, manage to cover up the hump which deformed her shoulders and back. She was ugly in a sturdy sort of way. You could see her muscular arms, and her bulging breasts pushing stoutly against the strong pagne of cotton fabric which was knotted just under her armpit. The king considered her for a moment, then the handsome Maghan turned his head away. He stared a long time at Gnankouman Doua then he lowered his head. The griot understood all the sovereign's embarrassment.

"You are the guests of the king; hunters, we wish you peace in Nianiba, for all the sons of Mali are but one. Come and sit down, slake your thirst and relate to the king by what adventure you left Do with this maiden."

The king nodded his approval. The two brothers looked at each other and, at a sign from the elder, the younger went up to the king and put down on the ground the calabash of cold water which a servant had brought him.

The hunter said: "After the great harvest my brother and I left our village to hunt. It was in this way that our pursuit of game led us as far as the approaches of the land of Do. We met two hunters, one of whom was wounded, and we learnt from them that an amazing buffalo was ravaging the countryside of Do. Every day it claimed some victims and nobody dared leave the village after sunset. The king, Do Mansa-Gnemo Diarra, had promised the finest rewards to the hunter who killed the buffalo. We decided to try our luck too and so we penetrated into the land of Do. We were advancing warily, our eyes well skinned, when we saw an old woman by the side of a river. She was weeping and lamenting, gnawed by hunger. Until then no passer-by had deigned to stop by her. She beseeched us, in the name of the Almighty, to give her something to eat. Touched by her tears I approached and took some pieces of dried meat from my hunter's bag. When she had eaten well she said, 'Hunter, may God requite you with the charity you have given me.' We were making ready to leave when she stopped me. 'I know,' she said, 'that you are going to try your luck against the Buffalo of Do, but you should know that many others before you have met their death through their foolhardiness, for arrows are useless against the buffalo; but, young hunter, your heart is generous and it is you who will be the buffalo's vanquisher. I am the buffalo you are looking for, and your generosity has vanquished me. I am the buffalo that ravages Do. I have killed a hundred and seven hunters and wounded seventy-seven; every day I kill an inhabitant of Do and the king, Gnemo Diarra, is at his wit's end which jinn to sacrifice to. Here, young man, take this distaff and this egg and go to the plain of Ourantamba where I browse among the king's crops. Before using your bow you must take aim at me three times with this distaff; then draw your bow and I shall be vulnerable to your arrow. I shall fall but shall get up and pursue you into a dry plain. Then throw the egg behind you and a great mire will come into being where I shall be unable to advance and then you will kill me. As a proof of your victory you must cut off the buffalo's tail, which is of gold, and take it to the king, from whom you will exact your due reward. As for me, I have run my course and punished the king of Do, my brother, for depriving me of my part of the inheritance.' Crazy with joy, I seized the distaff and the egg, but the old woman stopped me with a gesture and said, 'There is one condition, hunter.' 'What condition?' I replied impatiently. 'The king promises the hand of the most beautiful maiden of Do to the victor. When all the people of Do are gathered and you are told to choose her whom you want as a wife you must search in the crowd and you will find a very ugly maid—uglier than you can imagine—sitting apart on an observation platform; it is her you must choose. She is called Sogolon Kedjou, or Sogolon Kondouto, because she is a hunchback. You will choose her for she is my wraith. She will be an extraordinary woman if you manage to possess her. Promise me you will choose her, hunter.' I swore to, solemnly, between the hands of the old woman, and we continued on our way. The plain of Ourantamba was half a day's journey from there. On the way we saw hunters who were fleeing and who watched us quite dumbfounded. The buffalo was at the other end of the plain but when it saw us it charged with menacing horns. I did as the old woman had told me and killed the buffalo. I cut off its tail and we went back to the town of Do as night was falling, but we did not go before the king before midday all the inhabitants of the country were gathered in the main square. The mutilated carcass of the buffalo had been placed in the middle of the square and the delirious crowd abused it, while our names were sung in a thousand refrains. When the king appeared a deep silence settled on the crowd. 'I promised the hand of the most beautiful maiden in Do to the brave hunter who saved us from the scourge which overwhelmed us. The buffalo of Do is dead and here is the hunter who has killed it. I am a man of my word. Hunter, here are all the daughters of Do; take your pick.' And the crowd showed its approval by a great cheer. On that day all the daughters of Do wore their festive dress; gold shone in their hair and fragile wrists bent under the weight of heavy silver bracelets. Never did so much beauty come together in one place. Full of pride, my quiver on my back, I swaggered before the beautiful girls of Do who were smiling at me, with their teeth as white as the rice of Mali. But I remembered the words of the old woman. I went round the great circle many times until at last I saw Sogolon Kedjou sitting apart on a raised platform. I elbowed my way through the crowd, took Sogolon by the hand and drew her into the middle of the circle. Showing her to the king, I said, 'Oh King Gnemo Diarra, here is the one I have chosen from among the young maids of Do; it is her I would like for a wife.' The choice was so paradoxical that the king could not help laughing, and then general laughter broke out and the people split their sides with mirth. They took me for a fool, and I became a ludicrous hero. 'You've got to belong to the tribe of Traoré to do things like that,' said somebody in the crowd, and it was thus that my brother and I left Do the very same day pursued by the mockery of the Kondés."

The hunter ended his story and the noble king Naré Maghan determined to solemnize his marriage with all the customary formalities so that nobody could dispute the rights of the son to be born to him. The two hunters were considered as being relatives of Sogolon and it was to them that Gnankouman Doua bore the traditional cola nuts. By agreement with the hunters the marriage was fixed for the first Wednesday of the new moon. The twelve villages of old Mali and all the peoples allied to them were acquainted with this and on the appointed day delegations flocked from all sides to Nianiba, the town of Maghan Kon Fatta.

Sogolon had been lodged with an old aunt of the king's. Since her arrival in Nianiba she had never once gone out and everyone longed to see the woman for whom Naré Maghan was preparing such a magnificent wedding. It was known that she was not beautiful, but the curiosity of everyone was aroused, and already a thousand anecdotes were circulating, most of them put about by Sassouma Bérété, the king's first wife.

The royal drums of Nianiba announced the festivity at crack of dawn. The town awoke to the sound of tam-tams which answered each other from one district to another; from the midst of the crowds arose the voices of griots singing the praises of Naré Maghan.

At the home of the king's old aunt, the hairdresser of Nianiba was plaiting Sogolon Kedjou's hair. As she lay on her mat, her head resting on the hairdresser's legs, she wept softly, while the king's sisters came to chaff her, as was the custom.

"This is your last day of freedom; from now onwards you will be our woman."

"Say farewell to your youth," added another.

"You won't dance in the square any more and have yourself admired by the boys," added a third.

Sogolon never uttered a word and from time to time the old hairdresser said, "There, there, stop crying. It's a new life beginning, you know, more beautiful than you think. You will be a mother and you will know the joy of being a queen surrounded by your children. Come now, daughter, don't listen to the gibes of your sisters-in-law." In front of the house the poetesses who belonged to the king's sisters chanted the name of the young bride.

During this time the festivity was reaching its height in front of the king's enclosure. Each village was represented by a troupe of dancers and musicians; in the middle of the courtyard the elders were sacrificing oxen which the servants carved up, while ungainly vultures, perched on the great silk-cotton tree, watched the hecatomb with their eyes.

Sitting in front of the palace, Naré Maghan listened to the grave music of the "bolon" in the midst of his courtiers. Doua, standing amid the eminent guests, held his great spear in his hand and sang the anthem of the Mandingo kings. Everywhere in the village people were dancing and singing and members of the royal family envinced their joy, as was fitting, by distributing grain, clothes, and even gold. Even the jealous Sassouma Bérété took part in this largesse and, among other things, bestowed fine loin-cloths on the poetesses.

But night was falling and the sun had hidden behind the mountain. It was time for the marriage procession to form up in front of the house of the king's aunt. The tam-tams had fallen silent.

The old female relatives of the king had washed and perfumed Sogolon and now she was dressed completely in white with a large veil over her head.

Sogolon walked in front held by two old women. The king's relatives followed and, behind, the choir of young girls of Mali sang the bride's departure song, keeping time to the songs by clapping their hands. The villagers and guests were lined up along the stretch of ground which separated the aunt's house from the palace in order to see the procession go by. When Sogolon had reached the threshold of the king's antechamber one of his young brothers lifted her vigorously from the ground and ran off with her towards the palace while the crowd cheered.

The women danced in front of the palace of the king for a long while, then, after receiving money and presents from members of the royal family, the crowd dispersed and night darkened overhead.

"She will be an extraordinary woman if you manage to possess her." Those were the words of the old woman of Do, but the conqueror of the buffalo had not been able to conquer the young girl. It was only as an afterthought that the two hunters, Oulani and Oulamba, had the idea of giving her to the king of Mali.

That evening, then, Naré Maghan tried to perform his duty as a husband but Sogolon repulsed his advances. He persisted, but his efforts were in vain and early the next morning Doua found the king exhausted, like a man who had suffered a great defeat.

"What is the matter, my king?" asked the griot.

"I have been unable to possess her—and besides, she frightens me, this young girl. I even doubt whether she is a human being; when I drew close to her during the night her body became covered with long hairs and that scared me very much. All night long I called upon my wraith but he was unable to master Sogolon's."

All that day the king did not emerge and Doua was the only one to enter and leave the palace. All Nianiba seemed puzzled. The old women who had come early to seek the virginity pagne had been discreetly turned away. And this went on for a week.

Naré Maghan had vainly sought advice from some great sorcerers but all their tricks were powerless in overcoming the wraith of Sogolon. But one night, when everyone was asleep, Naré Maghan got up. He unhooked his hunter's bag from the wall and, sitting in the middle of the house, he spread on the ground the sand which the bag contained. The king began tracing mysterious signs in the sand; he traced, effaced and began again. Sogolon woke up. She knew that sand talks, but she was intrigued to see the king so absorbed at dead of night. Naré Maghan stopped drawing signs and with his hand under his chin he seemed to be brooding on the signs. All of a sudden he jumped up, bounded after his sword which hung above his bed, and said, "Sogolon, Sogolon, wake up. A dream has awakened me out of my sleep and the protective spirit of the Mandingo kings has appeared to me. I was mistaken in the interpretation I put upon the words of the hunter who led you to me. The jinn has revealed to me their real meaning. Sogolon, I must sacrifice you to the greatness of my house. The blood of a virgin of the tribe of Kondé must be spilt, and you are the Kondé virgin whom fate has brought under my roof. Forgive me, but I must accomplish my mission. Forgive the hand which is going to shed your blood."

"No, no—why me?—no, I don't want to die."

"It is useless," said the king. "It is not me who has decided."

He seized Sogolon by the hair with an iron grip, but so great had been her fright that she had already fainted. In this faint, she was congealed in her human body and her wraith was no longer in her, and when she woke up, she was already a wife. That very night, Sogolon conceived.

The Lion Child

A wife quickly grows accustomed to her state. Sogolon now walked freely in the king's great enclosure and people also got used to her ugliness. But the first wife of the king, Sassouma Bérété, turned out to be unbearable. She was restless, and smarted to see the ugly Sogolon proudly flaunting her pregnancy about the palace. What would become of her, Sassouma Bérété, if her son, already eight years old, was disinherited in favour of the child that Sogolon was going to bring into the world? All the king's attentions went to the mother-to-be. On returning from the wars he would bring her the best portion of the booty—fine loin-cloths and rare jewels. Soon, dark schemes took form in the mind of Sassouma Bérété; she determined to kill Sogolon. In great secrecy she had the foremost sorcerers of Mali come to her, but they all declared themselves incapable of tackling Sogolon. In fact, from twilight onwards, three owls came and perched on the roof of her house and watched over her. For the sake of peace and quiet Sassouma said to herself, "Very well then, let him be born, this child, and then we'll see."

Sogolon's time came. The king commanded the nine greatest midwives of Mali to come to Niani, and they were now constantly in attendance on the damsel of Do. The king was in the midst of his courtiers one day when someone came to announce to him that Sogolon's labours were beginning. He sent all his courtiers away and only Gnankouman Doua stayed by his side. One would have thought that this was the first time that he had become a father, he was so worried and agitated. The whole palace kept complete silence. Doua tried to distract the sovereign with his one-stringed guitar but in vain. He even had to stop this music as it jarred on the king. Suddenly the sky darkened and great clouds coming from the east hid the sun, although it was still the dry season. Thunder began to rumble and swift lightning rent the clouds; a few large drops of rain began to fall while a strong wind blew up. A flash of lightning accompanied by a dull rattle of thunder burst out of the east and lit up the whole sky as far as the west. Then the rain stopped and the sun appeared and it was at this very moment that a midwife came out of Sogolon's house, ran to the antechamber and announced to Naré Maghan that he was the father of a boy.

The king showed no reaction at all. He was as though in a daze. Then Doua, realizing the king's emotion, got up and signalled to two slaves who were already standing near the royal "tabala." The hasty beats of the royal drum announced to Mali the birth of a son; the village tam-tams took it up and thus all Mali got the good news the same day. Shouts of joy, tam-tams and "balafons" took the place of the recent silence and all the musicians of Niani made their way to the palace. His initial emotion being over, the king had got up and on leaving the antechamber he was greeted by the warm voice of Gnankouman Doua singing:

"I salute you, father; I salute you, king Naré Maghan; I salute you, Maghan Kon Fatta, Frako Maghan Keigu. The child is born whom the world awaited. Maghan, oh happy father, I salute you. The lion child, the buffalo child is born, and to announce him the Almighty has made the thunder peal, the whole sky has lit up and the earth has trembled. All hail, father, hail king Naré Maghan!"

All the griots were there and had already composed a song in praise of the royal infant. The generosity of kings makes griots eloquent, and Maghan Kon Fatta distributed on this day alone six granaries of rice among the populace. Sassouma Bérété distinguished herself by her largesses, but that deceived nobody. She was suffering in her heart but did not want to betray anything.

The name was given the eighth day after his birth. It was a great feast day and people came from all the villages of Mali while each neighbouring people brought gifts to the king. First thing in the morning a great circle had formed in front of the palace. In the middle, serving women were pounding rice which was to serve as bread, and sacrificed oxen lay at the foot of the great silk-cotton tree.

In Sogolon's house the king's aunt cut off the baby's first crop of hair while the poetesses, equipped with large fans, cooled the mother who was nonchalantly stretched out on soft cushions.

The king was in his antechamber but he came out followed by Doua. The crowd fell silent and Doua cried, "The child of Sogolon will be called Maghan after his father, and Mari Djata, a name which no Mandingo prince has ever borne. Sogolon's son will be the first of this name."

Straight away the griots shouted the name of the infant and the tam-tams sounded anew. The king's aunt, who had come out to hear the name of the child, went back into the house, and whispered the double name of Maghan and Mari Djata in the ear of the newly-born so that he would remember it.

The festivity ended with the distribution of meat to the heads of families and everyone dispersed joyfully. The near relatives one by one went to admire the newly-born.

Childhood

God has his mysteries which none can fathom. You, perhaps, will be a king. You can do nothing about it. You, on the other hand, will be unlucky, but you can do nothing about that either. Each man finds his way already marked out for him and he can change nothing of it.

Sogolon's son had a slow and difficult childhood. At the age of three he still crawled along on all-fours while children of the same age were already walking. He had nothing of the great beauty of his father Naré Maghan. He had a head so big that he seemed unable to support it; he also had large eyes which would open wide whenever anyone entered his mother's house. He was taciturn and used to spend the whole day just sitting in the middle of the house. Whenever his mother went out he would crawl on all fours to rummage about in the calabashes in search of food, for he was very greedy.

Malicious tongues began to blab. What three-year-old has not yet taken his first steps? What three-year-old is not the despair of his parents through his whims and shifts of mood? What three-year-old is not the joy of his circle through his backwardness in talking? Sogolon Djata (for it was thus that they called him, prefixing his mother's name to his), Sogolon Djata, then, was very different from others of his own age. He spoke little and his severe face never relaxed into a smile. You would have thought that he was already thinking, and what amused children of his age bored him. Often Sogolon would make some of them come to him to keep him company. These children were already walking and she hoped that Djata, seeing his companions walking, would be tempted to do likewise. But nothing came of it. Besides, Sogolon Djata would brain the poor little things with his already strong arms and none of them would come near him any more.

The king's first wife was the first to rejoice at Sogolon Djata's infirmity. Her own son, Dankaran Touman, was already eleven. He was a fine and lively boy, who spent the day running about the village with those of his own age. He had even begun his initiation in the bush. The king had had a bow made for him and he used to go behind the town to practise archery with his companions. Sassouma was quite happy and snapped her fingers at Sogolon, whose child was still crawling on the ground. Whenever the latter happened to pass by her house, she would say, "Come, my son, walk, jump, leap about. The jinn didn't promise you anything out of the ordinary, but I prefer a son who walks on his two legs to a lion that crawls on the ground." She spoke thus whenever Sogolon went by her door. The innuendo would go straight home and then she would burst into laughter, that diabolical laughter which a jealous woman knows how to use so well.

Her son's infirmity weighed heavily upon Sogolon Kedjou; she had resorted to all her talent as a sorceress to give strength to her son's legs, but the rarest herbs had been useless. The king himself lost hope.

How impatient man is! Naré Maghan became imperceptibly estranged but Gnankouman Doua never ceased reminding him of the hunter's words. Sogolon became pregnant again. The king hoped for a son, but it was a daughter called Kolonkan. She resembled her mother and had nothing of her father's beauty. The disheartened king debarred Sogolon from his house and she lived in semi-disgrace for a while. Naré Maghan married the daughter of one of his allies, the king of the Kamaras. She was called Namandjé and her beauty was legendary. A year later she brought a boy into the world. When the king consulted soothsayers on the destiny of this son he received the reply that Namandjé's child would be the right hand of some mighty king. The king gave the newly-born the name of Boukari. He was to be called Manding Boukari or Manding Bory later on.

Naré Maghan was very perplexed. Could it be that the stiff-jointed son of Sogolon was the one the hunter soothsayer had foretold?

"The Almighty has his mysteries," Gnankouman Doua would say and, taking up the hunter's words, added, "The silk-cotton tree emerges from a tiny seed."

One day Naré Maghan came along to the house of Nounfaïri, the blacksmith seer of Niani. He was an old, blind man. He received the king in the anteroom which served as his workshop. To the king's question he replied, "When the seed germinates growth is not always easy; great trees grow slowly but they plunge their roots deep into the ground."

"But has the seed really germinated?" said the king.

"Of course" replied the blind seer. "Only the growth is not as quick as you would like it; how impatient man is."

This interview and Doua's confidence gave the king some assurance. To the great displeasure of Sassouma Bérété the king restored Sogolon to favour and soon another daughter was born to her. She was given the name of Djamarou.

However, all Niani talked of nothing else but the stiff-legged son of Sogolon. He was now seven and he still crawled to get about. In spite of all the king's affection, Sogolon was in despair. Naré Maghan aged and he felt his time coming to an end. Dankaran Touman, the son of Sassouma Bérété, was now a fine youth.

One day Naré Maghan made Mari Djata come to him and he spoke to the child as one speaks to an adult. "Mari Djata, I am growing old and soon I shall be no more among you, but before death takes me off I am going to give you the present each king gives his successor. In Mali every prince has his own griot. Doua's father was my father's griot, Doua is mine and the son of Doua, Balla Fasséké here, will be your griot. Be inseparable friends from this day forward. From his mouth you will hear the history of your ancestors, you will learn the art of governing Mali according to the principles which our ancestors have bequeathed to us. I have served my term and done my duty too. I have done everything which a king of Mali ought to do. I am handing an enlarged kingdom over to you and I leave you sure allies. May your destiny be accomplished, but never forget that Niani is your capital and Mali the cradle of your ancestors."

The child, as if he had understood the whole meaning of the king's words, beckoned Balla Fasséké to approach. He made room for him on the hide he was sitting on and then said, "Balla, you will be my griot."

"Yes, son of Sogolon, if it pleases God," replied Balla Fasséké.

The king and Doua exchanged glances that radiated confidence.

The Lion's Awakening

A short while after this interview between Naré Maghan and his son the king died. Sogolon's son was no more than seven years old. The council of elders met in the king's palace. It was no use Doua's defending the king's will which reserved the throne for Mari Djata, for the council took no account of Naré Maghan's wish. With the help of Sassouma Bérété's intrigues, Dankaran Touman was proclaimed king and a regency council was formed in which the queen mother was all-powerful. A short time after, Doua died.

As men have short memories, Sogolon's son was spoken of with nothing but irony and scorn. People had seen one-eyed kings, one-armed kings, and lame kings, but a stiff-legged king had never been heard tell of. No matter how great the destiny promised for Mari Djata might be, the throne could not be given to someone who had no power in his legs; if the jinn loved him, let them begin by giving him the use of his legs. Such were the remarks that Sogolon heard every day. The queen mother, Sassouma Bérété, was the source of all this gossip.

Having become all-powerful, Sassouma Bérété persecuted Sogolon because the late Naré Maghan had preferred her. She banished Sogolon and her son to a back yard of the palace. Mari Djata's mother now occupied an old hut which had served as a lumber-room of Sassouma's.

The wicked queen mother allowed free passage to all those inquisitive people who wanted to see the child that still crawled at the age of seven. Nearly all the inhabitants of Niani filed into the palace and the poor Sogolon wept to see herself thus given over to public ridicule. Mari Djata took on a ferocious look in front of the crowd of sightseers. Sogolon found a little consolation only in the love of her eldest daughter, Kolonkan. She was four and she could walk. She seemed to understand all her mother's miseries and already she helped her with the housework. Sometimes, when Sogolon was attending to the chores, it was she who stayed beside her sister Djamarou, quite small as yet.

Sogolon Kedjou and her children lived on the queen mother's left-overs, but she kept a little garden in the open ground behind the village. It was there that she passed her brightest moments looking after her onions and gnougous. One day she happened to be short of condiments and went to the queen mother to beg a little baobab leaf.

"Look you," said the malicious Sassouma, "I have a calabash full. Help yourself, you poor woman. As for me, my son knew how to walk at seven and it was he who went and picked these baobab leaves. Take them then, since your son is unequal to mine." Then she laughed derisively with that fierce laughter which cuts through your flesh and penetrates right to the bone.

Sogolon Kedjou was dumbfounded. She had never imagined that hate could be so strong in a human being. With a lump in her throat she left Sassouma's. Outside her hut Mari Djata, sitting on his useless legs, was blandly eating out of a calabash. Unable to contain herself any longer, Sogolon burst into sobs and seizing a piece of wood, hit her son.

"Oh son of misfortune, will you never walk? Through your fault I have just suffered the greatest affront of my life! What have I done, God, for you to punish me in this way?"

Mari Djata seized the piece of wood and, looking at his mother, said, "Mother, what's the matter?"

"Shut up, nothing can ever wash me clean of this insult."

"But what then?"

"Sassouma has just humiliated me over a matter of a baobab leaf. At your age her own son could walk and used to bring his mother baobab leaves."

"Cheer up, Mother, cheer up."

"No. It's too much. I can't."

"Very well then, I am going to walk today," said Mari Djata. "Go and tell my father's smiths to make me the heaviest possible iron rod. Mother, do you want just the leaves of the baobab or would you rather I brought you the whole tree?"

"Ah, my son, to wipe out this insult I want the tree and its roots at my feet outside my hut."

Balla Fasséké, who was present, ran to the master smith, Farakourou, to order an iron rod.

Sogolon had sat down in front of her hut. She was weeping softly and holding her head between her two hands. Mari Djata went calmly back to his calabash of rice and began eating again as if nothing had happened. From time to time he looked up discreetly at his mother who was murmuring in a low voice, "I want the whole tree, in front of my hut, the whole tree."

All of a sudden a voice burst into laughter behind the hut. It was the wicked Sassouma telling one of her serving women about the scene of humiliation and she was laughing loudly so that Sogolon could hear. Sogolon fled into the hut and hid her face under the blankets so as not to have before her eyes this heedless boy, who was more preoccupied with eating than with anything else. With her bead buried in the bed-clothes Sogolon wept and her body shook violently. Her daughter, Sogolon Djamarou, had come and sat down beside her and she said, "Mother, Mother, don't cry. Why are you crying?"

Mari Djata had finished eating and, dragging himself along on his legs, he came and sat under the wall of the hut for the sun was scorching. What was he thinking about? He alone knew.

The royal forges were situated outside the walls and over a hundred smiths worked there. The bows, spears, arrows and shields of Niani's warriors came from there. When Balla Fasséké came to order the iron rod, Farakourou said to him, "The great day has arrived then?"

"Yes. Today is a day like any other, but it will see what no other day has seen."

The master of the forges, Farakourou, was the son of the old Nounfaïri, and he was a soothsayer like his father. In his workshops there was an enormous iron bar wrought by his father Nounfaïri. Everybody wondered what this bar was destined to be used for. Farakourou called six of his apprentices and told them to carry the iron bar to Sogolon's house

When the smiths put the gigantic iron bar down in front of the hut the noise was so frightening that Sogolon, who was lying down, jumped up with a start. Then Balla Fasséké, son of Gnankouman Doua, spoke.

"Here is the great day, Mari Djata. I am speaking to you, Maghan, son of Sogolon. The waters of the Niger can efface the stain from the body, but they cannot wipe out an insult. Arise, young lion, roar, and may the bush know that from henceforth it has a master."

The apprentice smiths were still there, Sogolon had come out and everyone was watching Mari Djata. He crept on all-fours and came to the iron bar. Supporting himself on his knees and one hand, with the other hand he picked up the iron bar without any effort and stood it up vertically. Now he was resting on nothing but his knees and held the bar with both his hands. A deathly silence had gripped all those present. Sogolon Djata closed his eyes, held tight, the muscles in his arms tensed. With a violent jerk he threw his weight on to it and his knees left the ground. Sogolon Kedjou was all eyes and watched her son's legs which were trembling as though from an electric shock. Djata was sweating and the sweat ran from his brow. In a great effort he straightened up and was on his feet at one go—but the great bar of iron was twisted and had taken the form of a bow!

Then Balla Fasséké sang out the "Hymn to the Bow," striking up with his powerful voice:

"Take your bow, Simbon,
Take your bow and let us go.
Take your bow, Sogolon Djata."

When Sogolon saw her son standing she stood dumb for a moment, then suddenly she sang these words of thanks to God who had given her son the use of his legs:

"Oh day, what a beautiful day,
Oh day, day of joy;
Allah Almighty, you never created a finer day.
So my son is going to walk!"

Standing in the position of a soldier at ease, Sogolon Djata, supported by his enormous rod, was sweating great beads of sweat. Balla Fasséké's song had alerted the whole palace and people came running from all over to see what had happened, and each stood bewildered before Sogolon's son. The queen mother had rushed there and when she saw Mari Djata standing up she trembled from head to foot. After recovering his breath Sogolon's son dropped the bar and the crowd stood to one side. His first steps were those of a giant. Balla Fasséké fell into step and pointing his finger at Djata, he cried:

"Room, room, make room!
The lion has walked;
Hide antelopes,
Get out of his way."

Behind Niani there was a young baobab tree and it was there that the children of the town came to pick leaves for their mothers. With all his might the son of Sogolon tore up the tree and put it on his shoulders and went back to his mother. He threw the tree in front of the hut and said, "Mother, here are some baobab leaves for you. From henceforth it will be outside your hut that the women of Niani will come to stock up."

Sogolon Djata walked. From that day forward the queen mother had no more peace of mind. But what can one do against destiny? Nothing. Man, under the influence of certain illusions, thinks he can alter the course which God has mapped out, but everything he does falls into a higher order which he barely understands. That is why Sassouma's efforts were vain against Sogolon's son, everything she did lay in the child's destiny. Scorned the day before and the object of public ridicule, now Sogolon's son was as popular as he had been despised. The multitude loves and fears strength. All Niani talked of nothing but Djata; the mothers urged their sons to become hunting companions of Djata and to share his games, as if they wanted their offspring to profit from the nascent glory of the buffalo-woman's son. The words of Doua on the name-giving day came back to men's minds and Sogolon was now surrounded with much respect; in conversation people were fond of contrasting Sogolon's modesty with the pride and malice of Soussouma Bérété. It was because the former had been an exemplary wife and mother that God had granted strength to her son's legs for, it was said, the more a wife loves and respects her husband and the more she suffers for her child, the more valorous will the child be one day. Each is the child of his mother; the child is worth no more than the mother is worth. It was not astonishing that the king Dankaran Touman was so colourless, for his mother had never shown the slightest respect to her husband and never, in the presence of the late king, did she show that humility which every wife should show before her husband. People recalled her scenes of jealousy and the spiteful remarks she circulated about her co-wife and her child. And people would conclude gravely, "Nobody knows God's mystery. The snake has no legs yet it is as swift as any other animal that has four."

Sogolon Djata's popularity grew from day to day and he was surrounded by a gang of children of the same age as himself. These were Fran Kamara, son of the king of Tabon; Kamandjan, son of the king of Sibi; and other princes whose fathers had sent them to the court of Niani. The son of Namandjé, Manding Bory, was already joining in their games. Balla Fasséké followed Sogolon Djata all the time. He was past twenty and it was he who gave the child education and instruction according to Mandingo rules of conduct. Whether in town or at the hunt, he missed no opportunity of instructing his pupil. Many young boys of Niani came to join in the games of the royal child.

He liked hunting best of all. Farakourou, master of the forges, had made Djata a fine bow, and he proved himself to be a good shot with the bow. He made frequent hunting trips with his troops, and in the evening all Niani would be in the square to be present at the entry of the young hunters. The crowd would sing the "Hymn to the Bow" which Balla Fasséké had composed, and Sogolon Djata was quite young when he received the title of Simbon, or master hunter, which is only conferred on great hunters who have proved themselves.

Every evening Sogolon Kedjou would gather Djata and his companions outside her hut. She would tell them stories about the beasts of the bush, the dumb brothers of man. Sogolon Djata learnt to distinguish between the animals; he knew why the buffalo was his mother's wraith and also why the lion was the protector of his father's family. He also listened to the history of the kings which Balla Fasséké told him; enraptured by the story of Alexander the Great, the mighty king of gold and silver, whose sun shone over quite half the world. Sogolon initiated her son into certain secrets and revealed to him the names of the medicinal plants which every hunter should know. Thus, between his mother and his griot, the child got to know all that needed to be known.

Sogolon's son was now ten. The name Sogolon Djata in the rapid Mandingo language became Sundiata or Sondjata. He was a lad full of strength; his arms had the strength of ten and his biceps inspired fear in his companions. He had already that authoritative way of speaking which belongs to those who are destined to command. His brother, Manding Bory, became his best friend, and whenever Djata was seen, Manding Bory appeared too. They were like a man and his shadow. Fran Kamara and Kamandjan were the closest friends of the young princes, while Balla Fasséké followed them all like a guardian angel.

But Sundiata's popularity was so great that the queen mother became apprehensive for her son's throne. Dankaran Touman was the most retiring of men. At the age of eighteen he was still under the influence of his mother and a handful of old schemers. It was Sassouma Bérété who really reigned in his name. The queen mother wanted to put an end to this popularity by killing Sundiata and it was thus that one night she received the nine great witches of Mali. They were all old women. The eldest, and the most dangerous too, was called Soumosso Konkomba. When the nine old hags had seated themselves in a semi-circle around her bed the queen mother said:

"You who rule supreme at night, nocturnal powers, oh you who hold the secret of life, you who can put an end to one life, can you help me?"

"The night is potent," said Soumosso Konkomba, "Oh queen, tell us what is to be done, on whom must we turn the fatal blade?"

"I want to kill Sundiata," said Sassouma. "His destiny runs counter to my son's and he must be killed while there is still time. If you succeed, I promise you the finest rewards. First of all I bestow on each of you a cow and her calf and from tomorrow go to the royal granaries and each of you will receive a hundred measures of rice and a hundred measures of hay on my authority."

"Mother of the king," rejoined Soumosso Konkomba, "life hangs by nothing but a very fine thread, but all is interwoven here below. Life has a cause, and death as well. The one comes from the other. Your hate has a cause and your action must have a cause. Mother of the king, everything holds together, our action will have no effect unless we are ourselves implicated, but Mari Djata has done us no wrong. It is, then, difficult for us to compass his death."

"But you are also concerned," replied the queen mother, "for the son of Sogolon will be a scourge to us all."

"The snake seldom bites the foot that does not walk," said one of the witches.

"Yes, but there are snakes that attack everybody. Allow Sundiata to grow up and we will all repent of it. Tomorrow go to Sogolon's vegetable patch and make a show of picking a few gnougou leaves. Mari Djata stands guard there and you will see how vicious the boy is. He won't have any respect for your age, he'll give you a good thrashing."

"That's a clever idea" said one of the old hags.

"But the cause of our discomfiture will be ourselves, for having touched something which did not belong to us."

"We could repeat the offence," said another, "and then if he beats us again we would be able to reproach him with being unkind, heartless. In that case we would be concerned, I think."

"The idea is ingenious," said Soumosso Konkomba. "Tomorrow we shall go to Sogolon's vegetable patch."

"Now there's a happy thought," concluded the queen mother, laughing for joy. "Go to the vegetable patch tomorrow and you will see that Sogolon's son is mean. Beforehand, present yourselves at the royal granaries where you will receive the grain I promised you; the cows and calves are already yours."

The old hags bowed and disappeared into the black night. The queen mother was now alone and gloated over her anticipated victory. But her daughter, Nana Triban, woke up.

"Mother, who were you talking to? I thought I heard voices."

"Sleep, my daughter, it is nothing. You didn't hear anything."

In the morning, as usual, Sundiata got his companions together in front of his mother's hut and said, "What animal are we going to hunt today?"

Kamandjan said, "I wouldn't mind if we attacked some elephants right now."

"Yes, I am of this opinion too," said Fran Kamara. "That will allow us to go far into the bush."

And the young band left after Sogolon had filled the hunting bags with eatables. Sundiata and his companions came back late to the village, but first Djata wanted to take a look at his mother's vegetable patch as was his custom. It was dusk. There he found the nine witches stealing gnougou leaves. They made a show of running away like thieves caught red-handed.

"Stop, stop, poor old women," said Sundiata, "what is the matter with you to run away like this. This garden belongs to all."

Straight away his companions and he filled the gourds of the old hags with leaves, aubergines and onions.

"Each time that you run short of condiments come to stock up here without fear."

"You disarm us," said one of the old crones, and another added, "And you confound us with your bounty."

"Listen, Djata," said Soumosso Konkomba, "we had come here to test you. We have no need of condiments but your generosity disarms us.

We were sent here by the queen mother to provoke you and draw the anger of the nocturnal powers upon you. But nothing can be done against a heart full of kindness. And to think that we have already drawn a hundred measures of rice and a hundred measures of millet—and the queen promises us each a cow and her calf in addition. Forgive us, son of Sogolon."

"I bear you no ill-will," said Djata. "Here, I am returning from the hunt with my companions and we have killed ten elephants, so I will give you an elephant each and there you have some meat!"

"Thank you, son of Sogolon."

"Thank you, child of Justice."

"Henceforth," concluded Soumosso Konkomba, "we will watch over you." And the nine witches disappeared into the night. Sundiata and his companions continued on their way to Niani and got back after dark.

"You were really frightened; those nine witches really scared you, eh?" said Sogolon Kolonkan, Djata's young sister.

"How do you know," retorted Sundiata, astonished.

"I saw them at night hatching their scheme, but I knew there was no danger for you." Kolonkan was well versed in the art of witchcraft and watched over her brother without his suspecting it.

Exile

But Sogolon was a wise mother. She knew everything that Sassouma could do to hurt her family, and so, one evening, after the children had eaten, she called them together and said to Sundiata.

"Let us leave here, my son; Manding Bory and Djamarou are vulnerable. They are not yet initiated into the secrets of night, they are not sorcerers. Despairing of ever injuring you, Sassouma will aim her blows at your brother or sister. Let us go away from here. You will return to reign when you are a man, for it is in Mali that your destiny must be fulfilled."

It was the wisest course. Manding Bory, the son of Naré Maghan's third wife, Namandjé, had no gift of sorcery. Sundiata loved him very much and since the death of Namandjé he had been welcomed by Sogolon. Sundiata had found a great friend in his half-brother. You cannot choose your relatives but you can choose your friends. Manding Bory and Sundiata were real friends and it was to save his brother that Djata accepted exile.

Balla Fasséké, Djata's griot, prepared the departure in detail. But Sassouma Bérété kept her eye on Sogolon and her family.

One morning the king, Dankaran Touman, called the council together. He announced his intention of sending an embassy to the powerful king of Sosso, Soumaoro Kanté. For such a delicate mission he had thought of Balla Fasséké, son of Doua, his father's griot. The council approved the royal decision, the embassy was formed and Balla Fasséké was at the head of it.

It was a very clever way of taking away from Sundiata the griot his father had given him. Djata was out hunting and when he came back in the evening, Sogolon Kedjou told him the news. The embassy had left that very morning. Sundiata flew into a frightful rage.

"What! take away the griot my father gave me! No, he will give me back my griot."

"Stop!" said Sogolon. "Let it go. It is Sassouma who is acting thus, but she does not know that she obeys a higher order."

"Come with me," said Sundiata to his brother Manding Bory, and the two princes went out. Djata bundled aside the guards on the house of Dankaran Touman, but he was so angry that he could not utter a word. It was Manding Bory who spoke.

"Brother Dankaran Touman, you have taken away our part of the inheritance. Every prince has had his griot, and you have taken away Balla Fasséké. He was not yours but wherever he may be, Balla will always be Djata's griot. And since you do not want to have us around you we shall leave Mali and go far away from here."

"But I will return," added the son of Sogolon, vehemently. "I will return, do you hear?"

"You know that you are going away but you do not know if you will come back," the king replied.

"I *will* return, do you hear me?" Djata went on and his tone was categorical. A shiver ran through the king's whole body. Dankaran Touman trembled in every limb. The two princes went out. The queen mother hurried in and found her son in a state of collapse.

"Mother, he is leaving but he says he will return. But why is he leaving? I intend to give him back his griot, for my part. Why is he leaving?"

"Of course, he will stay behind since you so desire it, but in that case you might as well give up your throne to him, you who tremble before the threats of a ten-year-old child. Give your seat up to him since you cannot rule. As for me, I am going to return to my parents' village for I will not be able to live under the tyranny of Sogolon's son. I will go and finish my days among my kinsfolk and I will say that I had a son who was afraid to rule."

Sassouma bewailed her lot so much that Dankaran Touman suddenly revealed himself as a man of iron. Now he desired the death of his brothers—but he let them leave, it could not be helped, but if they should ever cross his path again—! He would reign, alone, for power could not be shared!

Thus Sogolon and her children tasted exile. We poor creatures! We think we are hurting our neighbour at the time when we are working in the very direction of destiny. Our action is not us for it is commanded of us.

Sassouma Bérété thought herself victorious because Sogolon and her children had fled from Mali. Their feet ploughed up the dust of the roads. They suffered the insults which those who leave their country know of. Doors were shut against them and kings chased them from their courts. But all that was part of the great destiny of Sundiata. Seven years passed, seven winters followed one another and forgetfulness crept into the souls of men, but time marched on at an even pace. Moons succeeded moons in the same sky and rivers in their beds continued their endless course.

Seven years passed and Sundiata grew up. His body became sturdy and his misfortunes made his mind wise. He became a man. Sogolon felt the weight of her years and of the growing hump on her back, while Djata, like a young tree, was shooting up to the sky.

After leaving Niani, Sogolon and her children had sojourned at Djedeba with the king, Mansa Konkon, the great sorcerer. Djedeba was a town on the Niger two days away from Niani. The king received them with a little mistrust, but everywhere the stranger enjoys the right to hospitality, so Sogolon and her children were lodged in the very enclosure of the king and for two months Sundiata and Manding Bory joined in the games of the king's children. One night, as the children were playing at knuckle-bones outside the palace in the moonlight, the king's daughter, who was no more than twelve, said to Manding Bory, "You know that my father is a great sorcerer."

"Really?" said the artless Manding Bory.

"Why yes, you mean you did not know? Well anyway, his power lies in the game of wori; you can play wori."

"My brother now, he is a great sorcerer."

"No doubt he does not come up to my father."

"But what did you say? Your father plays at wori?"

Just then Sogolon called the children because the moon had just waned.

"Mother is calling us," said Sundiata, who was standing at one side. "Come Manding Bory. If I am not mistaken, you are fond of that daughter of Mansa Konkon's."

"Yes brother, but I would have you know that to drive a cow into the stable it is necessary to take the calf in."

"Of course, the cow will follow the kidnapper. But take care, for if the cow is in a rage so much the worse for the kidnapper."

The two brothers went in swopping proverbs. Men's wisdom is contained in proverbs and when children wield proverbs it is a sign that they have profited from adult company. That morning Sundiata and Manding Bory did not leave the royal enclosure but played with the king's children beneath the meeting tree. At the beginning of the afternoon Mansa Konkon ordered the son of Sogolon into his palace.

The king lived in a veritable maze and after several twists and turns through dark corridors a servant left Djata in a badly-lit room. He looked about him but was not afraid. Fear enters the heart of him who does not know his destiny, whereas Sundiata knew that he was striding towards a great destiny. He did not know what fear was. When his eyes were accustomed to the semi-darkness Sundiata saw the king sitting with his back to the light on a great ox-hide. He saw some splendid weapons hanging on the walls and exclaimed:

"What beautiful weapons you have, Mansa Konkon," and, seizing a sword, he began to fence on his own against an imaginary foe. The king, astonished, watched the extraordinary child.

"You had me sent for," said the latter, "and here I am." He hung the sword back up.

"Sit down," said the king. "It is a habit with me to invite my guests to play, so we are going to play, we are going to play at wori. But I make rather unusual conditions; if I win—and I shall win—I kill you."

"And if it is I who win," said Djata without being put out.

"In that case I will give you all that you ask of me. But I would have you know that I always win."

"If I win I ask for nothing more than that sword," said Sundiata, pointing to the sword he had brandished.

"All right," said the king, "you are sure of yourself, eh?" He drew up the log in which the wori holes were dug and put four pebbles in each of the holes.

"I go first," said the king, and taking the four pebbles from one hole he dealt them out, punctuating his actions with these words:

*"I don don, don don Kokodji.
Wori is the invention of a hunter.
I don don, don don Kokodji.
I am unbeatable at this game.
I am called the "exterminator king."*

And Sundiata, taking the pebbles from another hole, continued:

*"I don don, don don Kokodji.
Formerly guests were sacred.
I don don, don don Kokodji.
But the gold came only yesterday.
Whereas I came before yesterday."*

"Someone has betrayed me," roared the king Mansa Konkon, "someone has betrayed me."

"No, king, do not accuse anybody," said the child.

"What then?"

"It is nearly three moons since I have been living with you and you have never up to now suggested a game of wori. God is the guest's tongue. My words express only the truth because I am your guest."

The truth was that the queen mother of Niani had sent gold to Mansa Konkon so that he would get rid of Sundiata: "the gold came only yesterday," and Sundiata was at the king's court prior to the gold. In fact, the king's daughter had revealed the secret to Manding Bory. Then the king, in confusion, said, "You have won, but you will not have what you asked for, and I will turn you out of my town."

"Thank you for two months' hospitality, but I will return, Mansa Konkon."

Once again Sogolon and her children took to the path of exile. They went away from the river and headed west. They were going to seek hospitality from the king of Tabon in the country which is called the Fouta Djallon today. This region was at that time inhabited by the Kamara blacksmiths and the Djallonkés. Tabon was an impregnable town firmly entrenched behind mountains, and the king had been for a long time an ally of the Niani court. His son, Fran Kamara, had been one of the companions of Sundiata. After Sogolon's departure from Niani the companion princes of Sundiata had been sent back to their respective families.

But the king of Tabon was already old and did not want to fall out with whoever ruled at Niani. He welcomed Sogolon with kindness and advised her to go away as far as possible. He suggested the court of Ghana, whose king he knew. A caravan of merchants was shortly leaving for Ghana. The old king commended Sogolon and her children to the merchants and even delayed the departure for a few days to allow the mother to recover a little from her fatigues.

It was with joy that Sundiata and Manding Bory met Fran Kamara again. The latter, not without pride, showed them round the fortresses of Tabon and had them admire the huge iron gates and the king's arsenals. Fran Kamara was very glad to receive Sundiata at his home but was very grieved when the fatal day arrived, the day of departure. The night before he had given a hunting party to the princes of Mali and the youngsters had talked in the bush like men.

"When I go back to Mali," Sundiata had said, "I will pass through Tabon to pick you up and we will go to Mali together."

"Between now and then we will have grown up," Manding Bory had added.

"I will have all the army of Tabon for my own," Fran Kamara had said, "The blacksmiths and the Djallonkés are excellent warriors. I already attend the gathering of armed men which my father holds once a year."

"I will make you a great general, we will travel through many countries and emerge the strongest of all. Kings will tremble before us as a woman trembles before a man." The son of Sogolon had spoken thus.

The exiles took to the road again. Tabon was very far from Ghana, but the merchants were good to Sogolon and her children. The king had provided the mounts and the caravan headed to the north, leaving the land of Kita on the right. On the way the merchants told the princes a great deal about events of the past. Mari Djata was particularly interested in the stories bearing on the great king of the day, Soumaoro Kanté. It was to him at Sosso that Balla Fasséké had gone as envoy. Djata learnt that Saumaoro was the richest and most powerful king and even the king of Ghana paid him tribute. He was also a man of great cruelty.

The country of Ghana is a dry region where water is short. Formerly the Cissés of Ghana were the most powerful of princes. They were descended from Alexander the Great, the king of gold and silver, but ever since the Cissés had broken the ancestral taboo their power had kept on declining. At the time of Sundiata the descendants of Alexander were paying tribute to the king of Sosso. After several days of travelling the caravan arrived outside Wagadou. The merchants showed Sogolon and her children the great forest of Wagadou, where the great serpent-god used to live. The town was surrounded with enormous walls, very badly maintained. The travellers noticed that there were a lot of white traders at Wagadou and many encampments were to be seen all around the town. Tethered camels were everywhere.

Ghana was the land of the Soninke, and the people there did not speak Mandingo any more, but nevertheless there were many people who understood it, for the Soninke travel a lot. They are great traders. Their donkey caravans came heavily laden to Niani every dry season. They would set themselves up behind the town and the inhabitants would come out to barter.

The merchants made their way towards the colossal city gate. The head of the caravan spoke to the guards and one of them beckoned to Sundiata and his family to follow him, and they entered the city of the Cissés. The terraced houses did not have straw roofs in complete contrast to the towns of Mali. There were also a lot of mosques in this city, but that did not astonish Sundiata in the least, for he knew that the Cissés were very religious; at Niani there was only one mosque. The travellers noticed that the anterooms were incorporated in the houses whereas in Mali the anteroom or "bollon" was a separate building. As it was evening everybody was making his way to the mosque. The travellers could understand nothing of the prattle which the passers-by exchanged when they saw them on their way to the palace.

The palace of the king of Ghana was an imposing building. The walls were very high and you would have thought it was a dwelling-place for jinn not for men. Sogolon and her children were received by the king's brother, who understood Mandingo. The king was at prayer, so his brother made them comfortable in an enormous room and water was brought for them to quench their thirst. After the prayer the king came back into his palace and received the strangers. His brother acted as interpreter.

"The king greets the strangers."

"We greet the king of Ghana," said Sogolon.

"The strangers have entered Wagadou in peace, may peace be upon them in our city."

"So be it."

"The king gives the strangers permission to speak."

"We are from Mali," began Sogolon. "The father of my children was the king Naré Maghan, who, a few years ago sent a goodwill embassy to Ghana. My husband is dead but the council has not respected his wishes and my eldest son," (she pointed to Sundiata) "has been excluded from the throne. The son of my co-wife was preferred before him. I have known exile. The hate of my co-wife has hounded me out of every town and I have trudged along every road with my children. Today I have come to ask for asylum with the Cissés of Wagadou."

There was silence for a few moments; during Sogolon's speech the king and his brother had not taken their eyes off Sundiata for an instant. Any other child of eleven would have been disconcerted by the eyes of adults, but Sundiata kept cool and calmly looked at the rich decorations of the king's reception hall—the rich carpets, the fine scimitars hanging on the wall—and the splendid garments of the courtiers.

To the great astonishment of Sogolon and her children the king also spoke in the very same Mandingo language.

"No stranger has ever found our hospitality wanting. My court is your court and my palace is yours. Make yourself at home. Consider that in coming from Niani to Wagadou you have done no more than change rooms. The friendship which unites Mali and Ghana goes back to a very distant age, as the elders and griots know. The people of Mali are our cousins."

And, speaking to Sundiata, the king said in a familiar tone of voice, "Approach, cousin, what is your name?"

"My name is Mari-Djata and I am also called Maghan, but most commonly people call me Sundiata. As for my brother, he is called Manding Boukary, my youngest sister is called Djamarou and the other Sogolon-Kolonkan."

"There's one that will make a great king. He forgets nobody."

Seeing that Sogolon was very tired, the king said, "Brother, look after our guests. Let Sogolon and her children be royally treated and from tomorrow let the princes of Mali sit among our children."

Sogolon recovered fairly quickly from her exertions. She was treated like a queen at the court of king Soumaba Cissé. The children were clothed in the same fashion as those of Wagadou. Sundiata and Manding Bory had long smocks splendidly embroidered. They were showered with so many attentions that Manding Bory was embarrassed by them, but Sundiata found it quite natural to be treated like this. Modesty is the portion of the average man, but superior men are ignorant of humility. Sundiata even became exacting, and the more exacting he became the more the servants trembled before him. He was held in high esteem by the king, who said to his brother one day, "If he has a kingdom one day everything will obey him because he knows how to command."

However, Sogolon found no more lasting peace at Wagadou than she had found at the courts of Djedeba or Tabon; she fell ill after a year.

King Soumaba Cissé decided to send Sogolon and her people to Mema to the court of his cousin, Tounkara. Mema was the capital of a great kingdom on the Niger beyond the land of Do. The king reassured Sogolon of the welcome she would be given there. Doubtless the air which blew from the river would be able to restore Sogolon's health.

The children were sorry to leave Wagadou for they had made many friends, but their destiny lay elsewhere and they had to go away.

King Soumaba Cissé entrusted the travellers to some merchants who were going to Mema. It was a large caravan and the journey was done by camel. The children had for a long time accustomed themselves to these animals which were unknown in Mali. The king had introduced Sogolon and her children as members of his family and they were thus treated with much consideration by the merchants. Always keen to learn, Sundiata asked the caravaneers many questions. They were very well-informed people and told Sundiata a lot of things. He was told about the countries beyond Ghana; the land of the Arabs; the Hejaz, cradle of Islam, and of Djata's ancestors (for Bibali Bounama, the faithful servant of the Prophet, came from Hejaz). He learnt many things about Alexander the Great, too, but it was with terror that the merchants spoke of Soumaoro, the sorcerer-king, the plunderer who would rob the merchants of everything when he was in a bad mood.

A courier, despatched earlier from Wagadou, had heralded the arrival of Sogolon at Mema; a great escort was sent to meet the travellers and a proper reception was held before Mema. Archers and spearmen formed up in a double line and the merchants showed even more respect to their travelling companions. Surprisingly enough, the king was absent. It was his sister who had organized this great reception. The whole of Mema was at the city gate and you would have thought it was the king's homecoming. Here many people could speak Mandingo and Sogolon and her children could understand the amazement of the people, who were saying to each other, "Where do they come from? Who are they?"

The king's sister received Sogolon and her children in the palace. She spoke Maninkakan very well and talked to Sogolon as if she had known her for a long time. She lodged Sogolon in a wing of the palace. As usual, Sundiata very soon made his presence felt among the young princes of Mema and in a few days he knew every corner of the royal enclosure.

The air of Mema, the air of the river, did Sogolon's health a lot of good, but she was even more affected by the friendliness of the king's sister, who was called Massiran. Massiran disclosed to Sogolon that the king had no children and that the new companions of Sundiata were only the sons of Mema's vassal kings. The king had gone on a campaign against the mountain tribes who lived on the other side of the river. It was like this every year, because as soon as these tribes were left in peace they came down from the mountains to pillage the country.

Sundiata and Manding Bory again took up their favourite pastime, hunting, and went out with the young vassals of Mema.

At the approach of the rainy season the king's return was announced. The city of Mema gave a triumphal welcome to its king. Moussa Tounkara, richly dressed, was riding on a magnificent horse while his formidable cavalry made an impressive escort. The infantry marched in ranks carrying on their heads the booty taken from the enemy. The war drums rolled while the captives, heads lowered and hands tied behind their backs, moved forward mournfully to the accompaniment of the crowd's derisive laughter.

When the king was in his palace, Massiran, his sister, introduced Sogolon and her children and handed him the letter from the king of Ghana. Moussa Tounkara was very affable and said to Sogolon, "My cousin Soumaba recommends you and that is enough. You are at home. Stay here as long as you wish."

It was at the court of Mema that Sundiata and Manding Bory went on their first campaign. Moussa Tounkara was a great warrior and therefore he admired strength. When Sundiata was fifteen the king took him with him on campaign. Sundiata astonished the whole army with his strength and with his dash in the charge. In the course of a skirmish against the mountaineers he hurled himself on the enemy with such vehemence that the king feared for his life, but Mansa

Tounkara admired bravery too much to stop the son of Sogolon. He followed him closely to protect him and he saw with rapture how the youth sowed panic among the enemy. He had remarkable presence of mind, struck right and left and opened up for himself a glorious path. When the enemy had fled the old "sofas" said, "There's one that'll make a good king." Moussa Tounkara took the son of Sologon in his arms and said, "It is destiny that has sent you to Mema. I will make a great warrior out of you."

From that day Sundiata did not leave the king any more. He eclipsed all the young princes and was the friend of the whole army. They spoke about nothing but him in the camp. Men were even more surprised by the lucidity of his mind. In the camp he had an answer to everything and the most puzzling situations resolved themselves in his presence.

Soon it was in Mema itself that people began to talk about Sundiata. Was it not Providence which had sent this boy at a time when Mema had no heir? People already averred that Sundiata would extend his dominion from Mema to Mali. He went on all the campaigns. The enemy's incursions became rarer and rarer and the reputation of Sogolon's son spread beyond the river.

After three years the king appointed Sundiata Kan-Koro-Sigui, his Viceroy, and in the king's absence it was he who governed. Djata had now seen eighteen winters and at that time he was a tall young man with a fat neck and a powerful chest. Nobody else could bend his bow. Everyone bowed before him and he was greatly loved. Those who did not love him feared him and his voice carried authority.

The king's choice was approved of both by the army and the people; the people love all who assert themselves over them. The soothsayers of Mema revealed the extraordinary destiny of Djata. It was said that he was the successor of Alexander the Great and that he would be even greater; the soldiers already had a thousand dreams of conquest. What was impossible with such a gallant chief? Sundiata inspired confidence in the sofas by his example, for the sofa loves to see his chief share the hardship of battle.

Djata was now a man, for time had marched on since the exodus from Niani and his destiny was now to be fulfilled. Sogolon knew that the time had arrived and she had performed her task. She had nurtured the son for whom the world was waiting and she knew that now her mission was accomplished, while that of Djata was about to begin. One day she said to her son, "Do not deceive yourself. Your destiny lies not here but in Mali. The moment has come. I have finished my task and it is yours that is going to begin, my son. But you must be able to wait. Everything in its own good time."

Soumaoro Kanté, the Sorcerer King

While Sogolon's son was fighting his first campaign far from his native land, Mali had fallen under the domination of a new master, Soumaoro Kanté, king of Sosso.

When the embassy sent by Dankaran Touman arrived at Sosso, Suomaoro demanded that Mali should acknowledge itself tributary to Sosso. Balla Fasséké found delegates from several other kingdoms at Soumaoro's court. With his powerful army of smiths the king of Sosso had quickly imposed his power on everybody. After the defeat of Ghana and Diaghan no one dared oppose him any more. Soumaoro was descended from the line of smiths called Diarisso who first harnessed fire and taught men how to work iron, but for a long time Sosso had remained a little village of no significance. The powerful king of Ghana was the master of the country. Little by little the kingdom of Sosso had grown at the expense of Ghana and now the Kantés dominated their old masters. Like all masters of fire, Soumaoro Kanté was a great sorcerer. His fetishes had a terrible power and it was because of them that all kings trembled before him, for he could deal a swift death to whoever he pleased. He had fortified Sosso with a triple curtain wall and in the middle of the town loomed his palace, towering over the thatched huts of the villages. He had had an immense seven-storey tower built for himself and he lived on the seventh floor in the midst of his fetishes. This is why he was called "The Untouchable King."

Soumaoro let the rest of the Mandingo embassy return but he kept Balla Fasséké back and threatened to destroy Niani if Dankaran Touman did not make his submission. Frightened, the son of Sassouma immediately made his submission, and he even sent his sister, Nana Triban, to the king of Sosso.

One day when the king was away, Balla Fasséké managed to get right into the most secret chamber of the palace where Soumaoro safeguarded his fetishes. When he had pushed the door open he was transfixed with amazement at what he saw. The walls of the chamber were tapestried with human skins and there was one in the middle of the room on which the king sat; around an earthenware jar nine heads formed a circle; when Balla had opened the door the water had become disturbed and a monstrous snake had raised its head. Balla Fasséké, who was also well versed in sorcery, recited some formulas and everything in the room fell quiet, so he continued his inspection. He saw on a perch above the bed three owls which seemed to be asleep; on the far wall hung strangely-shaped weapons, curved swords and knives with three cutting edges. He looked at the skulls attentively and recognized the nine kings killed by Soumaoro. To the right of the door he discovered a great balafon, bigger than he had ever seen in Mali. Instinctively he pounced upon it and sat down to play. The griot always has a weakness for music, for music is the griot's soul.

He began to play. He had never heard such a melodious balafon. Though scarcely touched by the hammer, the resonant wood gave out sounds of an infinite sweetness, notes clear and as pure as gold dust; under the skilful hand of Balla the instrument had found its master. He played with all his soul and the whole room was filled with wonderment. The drowsy owls, eyes half closed, began to move their heads as though with satisfaction. Everything seemed to come to life upon the strains of this magic music. The nine skulls resumed their earthly forms and blinked at hearing the solemn "Vulture Tune"; with its head resting on the rim, the snake seemed to listen from the jar. Balla Fasséké was pleased at the effect his music had had on the strange inhabitants of this ghoulish chamber, but he quite understood that this balafon was not at all like any other. It was that of a great sorcerer. Soumaoro was the only one to play this instrument. After each victory he would come and sing his own praises. No griot had ever touched it. Not all ears were made to hear that music. Soumaoro was constantly in touch with this xylophone and no matter how far away he was, one only had to touch it for him to know that someone had got into his secret chamber.

The king was not far from the town and he rushed back to his palace and climbed up to the seventh storey. Balla Fasséké heard hurried steps in the corridor and Soumaoro bounded into the room, sword in hand.

"Who is there?" he roared. "It is you, Balla Fasséké!"

The king was foaming with anger and his eyes burnt fiercely like hot embers. Yet without losing his composure the son of Doua changed key and improvised a song in honour of the king:

There he is, Soumaoro Kanté.
All hail, you who sit on the skins of kings.
All hail, Simbon of the deadly arrow.
I salute you, you who wear clothes of human skin.

This improvised tune greatly pleased Soumaoro and he had never heard such fine words. Kings are only men, and whatever iron cannot achieve against them, words can. Kings, too, are susceptible to flattery, so Soumaoro's anger abated, his heart filled with joy as he listened attentively to this sweet music:

All hail, you who wear clothes of human skin.
I salute you, you who sit on the skins of kings.

Balla sang and his voice, which was beautiful, delighted the king of Sosso.

"How sweet it is to hear one's praises sung by someone else; Balla Fasséké, you will nevermore return to Mali for from today you are my griot."

Thus Balla Fasséké, whom king Naré Maghan had given to his son Sundiata, was stolen from the latter by Dankaran Touman; now it was the king of Sosso, Soumaoro Kanté, who, in turn, stole the precious griot from the son of Sassouma Bérété. In this way war between Sundiata and Soumaoro became inevitable.

History

We are now coming to the great moments in the life of Sundiata. The exile will end and another sun will arise. It is the sun of Sundiata. Griots know the history of kings and kingdoms and that is why they are the best counsellors of kings. Every king wants to have a singer to perpetuate his memory, for it is the griot who rescues the memories of kings from oblivion, as men have short memories.

Kings have prescribed destinies just like men, and seers who probe the future know it. They have knowledge of the future, whereas we griots are depositories of the knowledge of the past. But whoever knows the history of a country can read its future.

Other peoples use writing to record the past, but this invention has killed the faculty of memory among them. They do not feel the past any more, for writing lacks the warmth of the human voice. With them everybody thinks he knows, whereas learning should be a secret. The prophets did not write and their words have been all the more vivid as a result. What paltry learning is that which is congealed in dumb books!

I, Djeli Mamoudou Kouyaté, am the result of a long tradition. For generations we have passed on the history of kings from father to son. The narrative was passed on to me without alteration and I deliver it without alteration, for I received it free from all untruth.

Listen now to the story of Sundiata, the Na'Kamma, the man who had a mission to accomplish.

At the time when Sundiata was preparing to assert his claim over the kingdom of his fathers, Soumaoro was the king of kings, the most powerful king in all the lands of the setting sun. The fortified town of Sosso was the bulwark of fetishism against the word of Allah. For a long time Soumaoro defied the whole world. Since his accession to the throne of Sosso he had defeated nine kings whose heads served him as fetishes in his macabre chamber. Their skins served as seats and he cut his footwear from human skin. Soumaoro was not like other men, for the jinn had revealed themselves to him and his power was beyond measure. So his countless sofas were very brave since they believed their king to be invincible. But Soumaoro was an evil demon and his reign had produced nothing but bloodshed. Nothing was taboo for him. His greatest pleasure was publicly to flog venerable old men. He had defiled every family and everywhere in his vast empire there were villages populated by girls whom he had forcibly abducted from their families without marrying them.

The tree that the tempest will throw down does not see the storm building up on the horizon. Its proud head braves the winds even when it is near its end. Soumaoro had come to despise everyone. Oh! how power can pervert a man. If man had but a mithkal of divine power at his disposal the world would have been annihilated long ago. Soumaoro arrived at a point where he would stop at nothing. His chief general was his nephew the smith, Fakoli Koroma. He was the son of Soumaoro's sister, Kassia. Fakoli had a wonderful wife, Keleya, who was a great magician like her husband. She could cook better than the three hundred wives of Soumaoro put together. Soumaoro abducted Keleya and locked her up in his palace. Fakoli fell into a dreadful rage and went to his uncle and said, "Since you are not ashamed to commit incest by taking my wife, I am freed from all my ties with you from this day forward. Henceforth I shall be on the side of your enemies. I shall combine insurgent Mandingoes with my own troops and wage war against you." And he left Sosso with the smiths of the Koroma tribe.

It was like a signal. All those long-repressed hates and rancours burst out and everywhere men answered the call of Fakoli. Straight away Dankaran Touman, the king of Mali, mobilized and marched to join Fakoli. But Soumaoro, casting his nephew's threat aside, swooped down on Dankaran Touman, who gave up the struggle and fled to the land of the cola; and in those forested regions he founded the town of Kissidougou. During this period Soumaoro, in his anger, punished all the Mandingo towns which had revolted. He destroyed the town of Niani and reduced it to ashes. The inhabitants cursed the king who had fled

It is in the midst of calamity that man questions himself about his destiny. After the flight of Dankaran Touman, Soumaoro proclaimed himself king of Mali by right of conquest, but he was not recognized by the populace and resistance was organized in the bush. Soothsayers were consulted as to the fate of the country. The soothsayers were unanimous in saying that it would be the rightful heir to the throne who would save Mali. This heir was "The Man with Two Names." The elders of the court of Niani then remembered the son of Sogolon. The man with two names was no other than Maghan Sundiata.

But where could he be found? No one knew where Sogolon and her children lived. For seven years nobody had had any news of them. Now the problem was to find them. Nevertheless a search party was formed to seek him out. Among the people included must be mentioned Kountoun Manian, an old griot from the court of Naré Maghan; Mandjan Bérété, a brother of Sassouma's, who did not want to follow Dankaran Touman in flight; Singbin Mara Cissé, a divine of the court; Siriman Touré, another divine; and, finally, a woman, Magnouma. According to the clues of the soothsayers they had to search towards the riverine lands, that is, towards the east. The searchers left Mali while war raged between Sosso Soumaoro and his nephew Fakoli Koroma.

The Baobab Leaves

At Mema Sundiata learnt that Soumaoro had invaded Mali and that his own brother, Dankaran Touman, had fled. He learnt also that Fakoli was holding his own against the king of Sosso. That year the kingdom of Mema was at peace and the king's viceroy had a lot of leisure time. As always, he went out hunting, but since the news about Mali had arrived Sundiata had become very gloomy. The aged Sogolon was ill. Manding Bory was fifteen and was now a lively youth like his brother and friend Sundiata. Djata's sisters had grown up and Kolonkan was now a tall maiden of marriageable age. Now that Sogolon had grown old it was she who did the cooking and she often went to the town market with her serving women.

Well, one day when she was at the market she noticed a woman who was offering for sale nafiola and gnougou, condiments unknown to the people of Mema, who looked in astonishment at the woman who was selling them. Kolonkan approached. She recognized baobab leaves and many other vegetables which her mother used to grow in her garden at Niani.

"Baobab leaves," she muttered, "and gnougou, I know these," she said, taking some.

"How do you know them princess?" said the woman. "I have been offering them for sale here in the market of Mema for days but nobody wants any here."

"But I am from Mali. At home my mother used to have a vegetable garden and my brother would go to seek baobab leaves for us."

"What is your brother's name princess?"

"He is called Sogolon Djata, and the other one is called Manding Bory. I also have a sister called Sogolon Djamarou."

Meanwhile a man had drawn near and he spoke thus to Sogolon Kolonkan, "Princess, we are also from Mali. We are merchants and are going from town to town. I am selling colas myself. Here, I give you one. Princess, could your mother receive us today?"

"Of course, she will be happy to talk to people who come from Mali. Don't budge from here and I'll go and talk to her about it."

Kolonkan, without caring about the scandal of the viceroy's sister being seen running across the market-place, had knotted her long dress about her middle and was running at full speed towards the royal enclosure.

"N'na," she said, out of breath and addressing her mother, "I have found baobab leaves, gnougou and many other things at the market, look. Some merchants from Mali are selling them. They would like to see you."

Sogolon took the baobab leaves and gnougou in her hand and put her nose to them as though to inhale all the scent. She opened her eyes wide and looked at her daughter.

"They come from Mali, you say? Then run to the market and tell them that I am waiting for them, run, my daughter."

Sogolon remained alone. She was turning the precious condiments over and over in her hands when she heard Sundiata and Manding Bory returning from the hunt.

"Hail, mother. We have returned," said Manding Bory.

"Hail, mother," said Sundiata, "we have brought you some game."

"Come in and sit down," she said, and held out to them what she had in her hand.

"Why, it's gnougou," said Sundiata, "where did you find it? The people here grow it very little."

"Yes, some merchants from Mali are offering it for sale in the market. Kolonkan has gone to fetch them for they want to see me. We are going to have some news of Mali."

Kolonkan soon appeared followed by four men and a woman; straight away Sogolon recognized the eminent members of her husband's court. The salutations began and greetings were exchanged with all the refinement demanded by Mandingo courtesy. At last Sogolon said, "Here are my children; they have grown up far from their native country. Now let us talk of Mali."

The travellers quickly exchanged meaningful glances, then Mandjan Bérété, Sassouma's brother, began to speak in these words:

"I give thanks to God the Almighty that we are here in the presence of Sogolon and her children. I give thanks to God that our journey will not have been in vain. It is two months since we left Mali. We went from one royal town to another posing as merchants and Magnouma offered vegetables of Mali for sale. In these eastern lands people are unacquainted with these vegetables. But at Mema our plan worked out perfectly. The person who bought some gnougou was able to tell us of your fate and that person, by a crowning stroke of fortune, turned out to be Sogolon Kolonkan."

"Alas! I bring you sad tidings. That is my mission. Soumaoro Kanté, the powerful king of Sosso, has heaped death and desolation upon

Mali. The king, Dankaran Touman, has fled and Mali is without a master, but the war is not finished yet. Courageous men have taken to the bush and are waging tireless war against the enemy. Fakoli Koroma, the nephew of the king of Sosso, is fighting pitilessly against his incestuous uncle who robbed him of his wife. We have consulted the jinn and they have replied that only the son of Sogolon can deliver Mali. Mali is saved because we have found you, Sundiata."

"Maghan Sundiata, I salute you; king of Mali, the throne of your fathers awaits you. Whatever rank you may hold here, leave all these honours and come and deliver your fatherland. The brave await you, come and restore rightful authority to Mali. Weeping mothers pray only in your name, the assembled kings await you, for your name alone inspires confidence in them. Son of Sogolon, your hour has come, the words of the old Gnankouman Doua are about to come to pass, for you are the giant who will crush the giant Soumaoro."

After these words a profound silence reigned over the room of Sogolon. She, her eyes cast down, remained silent; Kolonkan and Manding Bory had their eyes fixed on Sundiata.

"Very well," he said, "it is no longer the time for words. I am going to ask the king's leave and we will return immediately. Manding Bory, take charge of the envoys from Mali. The king will return this evening and we will set out first thing tomorrow."

Sundiata got up and all the envoys stood up while Djata went out. He was already king.

The king returned to Mema at nightfall. He had gone to spend the day in one of his neighbouring residences. The viceroy was not at the king's reception and nobody knew where he was. He returned at night and before going to bed he went and saw Sogolon. She had a fever and was trembling under the blankets. With a feeble voice she wished her son good night. When Sundiata was in his chamber alone he turned to the east and spoke thus:

"Almighty God, the time for action has come. If I must succeed in the reconquest of Mali, Almighty, grant that I may bury my mother in peace here." Then he lay down,

In the morning, Sogolon Kedjou, the buffalo woman, passed away, and all the court of Mema went into mourning, for the viceroy's mother was dead. Sundiata went to see the king, who offered his condolences. He said to the king, "King, you gave me hospitality at your court when I was without shelter. Under your orders I went on my first campaign. I shall never be able to thank you for so much kindness. However, my mother is dead; but I am now a man and I must return to Mali to claim the kingdom of my fathers. Oh king, I give you back the powers you conferred upon me, and I ask leave to depart. In any case, allow me to bury my mother before I go."

These words displeased the king. Never did he think that the son of Sogolon could leave him. What was he going to seek in Mali? Did he not live happy and respected by all at Mema? Was he not already the heir to the throne of Mema? How ungrateful, thought the king, the son of another is always the son of another.

"Ungrateful creature," said the king, "since this is how it is, go away, leave my kingdom, but take your mother's remains with you; you will not bury her at Mema."

But after a pause he went on, "Very well then, since you insist on burying your mother, you will pay me the price of the earth where she will lie."

"I will pay later," replied Sundiata. "I will pay when I reach Mali."

"No, now, or you will have to take your mother's corpse with you."

Then Sundiata got up and went out. He came back after a short while and brought the king a basket full of bits of pottery, guinea fowl feathers, feathers of young partridges and wisps of straw. He said, "Very well king, here is the price of the land."

"You are mocking, Sundiata, take your basket of rubbish away. That is not the price of the land. What do you mean by it?"

Then the old Arab who was the king's adviser said, "Oh king, give this young man the land where his mother must rest. What he has brought you has a meaning. If you refuse him the land he will make war on you. These broken pots and wisps of straw indicate that he will destroy the town. It will only be recognized by the fragments of broken pots. He will make such a ruin of it that guinea-fowl and young partridges will come to take their dust baths there. Give him the land for if he reconquers his kingdom he will deal gently with you, your family, and his will be forever allied."

The king understood. He gave him the land and Sogolon received her funeral honours with all the regal obsequies.

The Return

Every man to his own land! If it is foretold that your destiny should be fulfilled in such and such a land, men can do nothing against it. Mansa Tounkara could not keep Sundiata back because the destiny of Sogolon's son was bound up with that of Mali. Neither the jealousy of a cruel stepmother, nor her wickedness, could alter for a moment the course of great destiny.

The snake, man's enemy, is not long-lived, yet the serpent that lives hidden will surely die old. Djata was strong enough now to face his enemies. At the age of eighteen he had the stateliness of the lion and the strength of the buffalo. His voice carried authority, his eyes were live coals, his arm was iron, he was the husband of power.

Moussa Tounkara, king of Mema, gave Sundiata half of his army. The most valiant came forward of their own free will to follow Sundiata in the great adventure. The cavalry of Mema, which he had fashioned himself, formed his iron squadron. Sundiata, dressed in the Muslim fashion of Mema, left the town at the head of his small but redoubtable army. The whole population sent their best wishes with him. He was surrounded by five messengers from Mali and Manding Bory rode proudly at the side of his brother. The horsemen of Mema formed behind Djata a bristling iron squadron. The troop took the direction of Wagadou, for Djata did not have enough troops to confront Soumaoro directly, and so the king of Mema advised him to go to Wagadou and take half of the men of the king, Soumaba Cissé. A swift messenger had been sent there and so the king of Wagadou came out in person to meet Sundiata and his troops. He gave Sundiata half of his cavalry and blessed the weapons. Then Manding Bory said to his brother, "Djata, do you think yourself able to face Soumaoro now?"

"No matter how small a forest may be, you can always find there sufficient fibres to tie up a man. Numbers mean nothing; it is worth that counts. With my cavalry I shall clear myself a path to Mali."

Djata gave out his orders. They would head south, skirting Soumaoro's kingdom. The first objective to be reached was Tabon, the iron-gated town in the midst of the mountains, for Sundiata had promised Fran Kamara that he would pass by Tabon before returning to Mali. He hoped to find that his childhood companion had become king. It was a forced march and during the halts the divines, Singbin Mara Cissé and Mandjan Bérété, related to Sundiata the history of Alexander the Great and several other heroes, but of all of them Sundiata preferred Alexander, the king of gold and silver, who crossed the world from west to east. He wanted to outdo his prototype both in the extent of his territory and the wealth of his treasury.

However, Soumaoro Kanté, being a great sorcerer, knew that the son of Sogolon had set out and that he was coming to lay claim to Mali. The soothsayers told him to forestall this calamity by attacking Sundiata, but good fortune makes men blind. Soumaoro was busy fighting Fakoli, the insurgent nephew who was holding out against him. Even before he had given battle the name of Sundiata was already well known throughout the kingdom. Those of the western frontier who had seen his army marching southwards spread extraordinary reports. Having just ascended the throne that year, Fran Kamara, the friend of Sundiata, had revolted in his turn against Soumaoro. In place of the policy of prudence followed by the old king of Tabon, Fran Kamara pursued a policy of war. Proud of his troops and above all spurred on by the imminent arrival of Sundiata, Fran Kamara, now called Tabon Wana (the Dread One of Tabon), had called to arms all the smiths and the mountain-dwelling Djallonkés.

Soumaoro sent a detachment under his son Sosso Balla to block Sundiata's route to Tabon. Sosso Balla was about the same age as Sundiata. He promptly deployed his troops at the entrance to the mountains to oppose Sundiata's advance to Tabon.

In the evening, after a long day's march, Sundiata arrived at the head of the great valley which led to Tabon. The valley was quite black with men, for Sosso Balla had deployed his men everywhere in the valley, and some were positioned on the heights which dominated the way through. When Djata saw the layout of Sosso Balla's men he turned to his generals laughing.

"Why are you laughing, brother, you can see that the road is blocked."

"Yes, but no mere infantrymen can halt my course towards Mali," replied Sundiata.

The troops stopped. All the war chiefs were of the opinion that they should wait until the next day to give battle because, they said, the men were tired.

"The battle will not last long," said Sundiata, "and the men will have time to rest. We must not allow Soumaoro the time to attack Tabon."

Sundiata was immovable, so the orders were given and the war drums began to beat. On his proud horse Sundiata turned to right and left in front of his troops. He entrusted the rearguard, composed of a part of the Wagadou cavalry, to his younger brother Manding Bory. Having drawn his sword, Sundiata led the charge, shouting his war cry.

The Sossos were surprised by this sudden attack for they all thought that the battle would be joined the next day. The lightning that flashes across the sky is slower, the thunderbolts less frightening and floodwaters less surprising than Sundiata swooping down on Sosso Balla and his smiths. In a trice, Sundiata was in the middle of the Sossos like a lion in the sheepfold. The Sossos, trampled under the hooves of his fiery charger, cried out. When he turned to the right the smiths of Soumaoro fell in their tens, and when he turned to the left his sword made heads fall as when someone shakes a tree of ripe fruit. The horsemen of Mema wrought a frightful slaughter and their long lances pierced flesh like a knife sunk into a paw-paw. Charging ever forwards, Sundiata looked for Sosso Balla; he caught sight of him and like a lion bounded towards the son of Soumaoro, his sword held aloft. His arm came sweeping down but at that moment a Sosso warrior came between Djata and Sosso Balla and was sliced like a calabash. Sosso Balla did not wait and disappeared from amidst his smiths. Seeing their chief in flight, the Sossos gave way and fell into a terrible rout. Before the sun disappeared behind the mountains there were only Djata and his men left in the valley. Manding Bory, who was keeping an eye on the men perched on the heights, seeing that his brother had got the upper hand, dispatched some horsemen across the mountains to dislodge the Sossos. The Sossos were pursued until nightfall and several of them were taken prisoner.

Tabon Wana arrived too late, for the victory had already fallen to the son of Sogolon. The meeting of the two armies occasioned an all-night celebration in the very valley where the Sossos had been defeated. Tabon Wana Fran Kamara had a lot of food brought to the army of Sundiata and dancing went on all night, then at break of day the victors entered impregnable Tabon to the cheering of women standing on the ramparts.

The news of the battle of Tabon spread like wildfire in the plains of Mali. It was known that Soumaoro was not present at the battle, but the mere fact that his troops had retreated before Sundiata sufficed to give hope to all the peoples of Mali. Soumaoro realized that from now on he would have to reckon with this young man. He got to know of the prophecies of Mali, yet he was still too confident. When Sosso Balla returned with the remnant he had managed to save at Tabon, he said to his father, "Father, he is worse than a lion; nothing can withstand him."

"Be quiet, you ill-starred son," Soumaoro had said, "what, you tremble before a lad of your own age!" Nonetheless, these words of Balla made a deep impression on Soumaoro and he decided to march on Tabon with the largest of his forces.

The son of Sogolon had already decided on his plan of campaign—to beat Soumaoro, destroy Sosso and return triumphantly to Niani. He now had five army corps at his disposal, namely, the cavalry and infantry of Mema, those of Wagadou and the three tribes forming the army of Tabon Wana Fran Kamara. He must assume the offensive as soon as possible.

Soumaoro marched out to meet Sundiata. The meeting took place at Neguéboria in the Bouré country. As usual, the son of Sogolon wanted to join battle straight away. Soumaoro thought to draw Sundiata into the plain, but Sundiata did not allow him the time to do it. Compelled to give battle, the king of Sosso drew up his men across the narrow valley of Neguéboria, the wings of his army occupying the slopes. Sundiata adopted a very original form of deployment. He formed a tight square with all his cavalry in the front line. The archers of Wagadou and Tabon were stationed at the back. Soumaoro was on one of the hills dominating the valley and he could be distinguished by his height and his helmet bristling with horns. Under an overpowering sun the trumpets sounded, on both sides the drums and bolons echoed and courage entered the hearts of the Sofas. Sundiata charged at the gallop and the valley soon disappeared in a cloud of red dust kicked up by thousands of feet and hooves. Without giving an inch, the smiths of Soumaoro stopped the wave.

As though detached from the battle, Soumaoro Kanté watched from the top of his hill. Sundiata and the king of Tabon were laying about them with mighty blows. Sundiata could be distinguished by his white turban and Soumaoro could see the breach he was opening up in the middle of his troops. The centre was about to cave in under the crushing pressure of Djata.

Soumaoro made a sign and from the hills came smiths swooping down into the bottom of the valley to encircle Sundiata. Then, without the slightest order from Sundiata, who was in the thick of the struggle, his square stretched and elongated itself into a great rectangle. Everything had been foreseen. The change was so quick that Soumaoro's men, halted in their mad career, could not use their weapons. In Djata's rear the archers of Wagadou and those of Tabon, on one knee, shot arrows into the sky, which fell thickly, like a rain of iron, on the ranks of Soumaoro. Like a stretching piece of elastic, Djata's line ascended to attack the hills. Djata caught sight of Sosso Balla and bore down on him, but the latter slipped away and the warriors of the buffalo woman's son raised a huzza of triumph. Soumaoro rushed up and his presence in the centre revived the courage of the Sossos. Sundiata caught sight of him and tried to cut a passage through to him. He struck to the right and struck to the left and trampled underfoot. The murderous hooves of his "Daffeké" dug into the chests of the Sossos. Soumaoro was now within spear range and Sundiata reared up his horse and hurled his weapon. It whistled away and bounced off Soumaoro's chest as off a rock and fell to the ground. Sogolon's son bent his bow but with a motion of the hand Soumaoro caught the arrow in flight and showed it to Sundiata as if to say "Look, I am invulnerable."

Furious, Sundiata snatched up his spear and with his head bent charged at Soumaoro, but as he raised his arm to strike his enemy he noticed that Soumaoro had disappeared. Manding Bory riding at his side pointed to the hill and said, "Look, brother."

Sundiata saw Soumaoro on the hill, sitting on his black-coated horse. How could he have done it, he who was only two paces from Sundiata? By what power had he spirited himself away on to the hill? The son of Sogolon stopped fighting to watch the king of Sosso. The sun was already very low and Soumaoro's smiths gave way but Sundiata did not give the order to pursue the enemy. Suddenly, Soumaoro disappeared!

How can I vanquish a man capable of disappearing and reappearing where and when he likes? How can I affect a man invulnerable to iron? Such were the questions which Sogolon's son asked himself. He had been told many things about Sosso-Soumaoro but he had given little credence to so much gossip. Didn't people say that Soumaoro could assume sixty-nine different shapes to escape his enemies? According to some, he could transform himself into a fly in the middle of the battle and come and torment his opponent; he could melt into the wind when his enemies encircled him too closely—and many other things.

The battle of Neguéboria showed Djata, if he needed to be shown, that to beat the king of Sosso other weapons were necessary.

The evening of Neguéboria, Sundiata was master of the field, but he was in a gloomy mood. He went away from the field of battle with its agonized cries of the wounded, and Manding Bory and Tabon Wana watched him go. He headed for the hill where he had seen Soumaoro after his miraculous disappearance from the midst of his troops. From the top of the hill he watched the compact mass of Soumaoro's smiths withdrawing in a cloud of dust.

"How was he able to escape me? Why did neither my spear nor my arrow wound him?" he wondered. "What is the jinn that protects Soumaoro? What is the mystery of his power?"

He dismounted from his horse and picked up a piece of the earth which Soumaoro's horse had trampled on. Complete darkness had already fallen, the village of Neguéboria was not far away and the Djallonkés came out in a crowd to greet Sundiata and his men. The fires were already lit in the camp and the soldiers were beginning to prepare a meal, but what was their joy when they saw a long procession of girls from Neguéboria carrying on their heads enormous gourds of rice. All the sofas took up the girls' song in chorus. The chief of the village and its notables followed behind. Djata came down from the hill and received the Djallonké chief of Neguéboria, who was a vassal of Tabon Wana. For the sofas the day had been a victory because Soumaoro had fled, so the drums of war became drums of joy and Djata let his men celebrate what they called a victory. He stayed in his tent. In the life of every man there comes a moment when doubt settles in and the man questions himself on his own destiny, but on this evening it was not yet doubt which assailed Djata, for he was thinking rather of what powers he could employ to injure Sosso-Soumaoro. He did not sleep that night. At daybreak they struck camp. Peasants on their line of march told Sundiata that Soumaoro and his men were making a forced march without stopping so only in the evening did Sundiata halt the army to take a little food and rest. This was near the village of Kankigné. The men set up camp in the middle of the plain whilst guards were stationed on the heights. As usual, the men grouped themselves by tribes and busied themselves cooking their food. The tent of Sundiata stood in the middle of the camp surrounded by makeshift huts hastily built by the Mema horsemen.

But all of a sudden the sound of warning horns was heard. The men hardly had time to snatch their weapons before the camp was surrounded by enemies looming out of the darkness. The men of Mema were used to these surprise attacks on their camp and therefore unsaddled their horses. As the camp did not constitute a single unit, each kin group had to defend itself individually. Having escaped encirclement, Djata and the horsemen of Mema went to the help of Tabon Wana who seemed to be overwhelmed by numbers. In the pitch dark, no one knows how the men acquitted themselves. All that can be said is that the son of Sogolon broke the vice that was squeezing the breath out of Tabon Wana. The archers of Wagadou had quickly pulled themselves together and fired into the air torches and flaming arrows which fell among the enemy. Suddenly there was a panic. The burning brands crashed on to the bare backs of Soumaoro's sofas, cries of pain filled the sky and the Sossos began a headlong retreat while the cavalry cut them to pieces. The overwhelmed Sossos took to flight, again leaving many captives in the hands of Sundiata's men. Leaving to Tabon Wana the task of regrouping the men, Sundiata pursued the enemy with his cavalry to beyond the village of Kankigné. When he returned the struggle was over. The Sossos' night attack had caused more fright than real damage. On the ground near Tabon Wana's tent were found several split skulls. The king of Tabon never hit a man twice! The battle of Kankigné was not a great victory but it demoralized the Sossos. However, there had been great fear in Djata's ranks and that is why the griots sing:

"Kankigné Tabe bara djougonya."

The Names of the Heroes

The surprise attack at Kankigné had turned out badly for Soumaoro and succeeded only in increasing the wrath of Sundiata, who decimated the whole of the Sosso rearguard.

Soumaoro got back to Sosso to recover his strength while on all sides villages opened their gates to Sundiata. In all these villages Sundiata recruited soldiers. In the same way as light precedes the sun, so the glory of Sundiata, overleaping the mountains, shed itself on all the Niger plain.

All the rebellious kings of the savanna country had gathered at Sibi under the command of Kamandjan, the very same childhood friend of Sundiata and now himself the king of Sibi. Kamandjan and Tabon Wana were cousins, the former being the king of the Dalikimbon group of Kamaras, the latter being king of the iron-working Kamaras who were called Sinikimbon. Thus the Niani trio were going to meet again. Fakoli, the nephew of Soumaoro, had gone right to the south to recruit troops. He was bent on having his revenge on his uncle and recovering his wife, Keleya, she who was called "the woman of the three hundred and thirty-three gourds of rice."

Sundiata had now entered the region of the plains, the land of the powerful Niger. The trees that he saw were those of Mali, everything indicated that old Mali was near.

All the allies had arranged to meet up in the great plain of Sibi, and all the children of the savanna were there about their kings. There they were, the valorous sons of Mali, awaiting what destiny had promised them. Pennants of all colours fluttered above the sofas divided up by tribes.

With whom should I begin; with whom end?

I shall begin with Siara Kouman Konaté. Siara Kouman Konaté, the cousin of Sundiata was there. He was the ancestor of those who live in the land of Toron. His spear-armed troops formed a thick hedge around him.

I will also mention Faony Kondé, Faony Diarra, the king of the land of Do whence came Sogolon. Thus the uncle had come to meet his nephew. Faony, king of Do and Kri, was surrounded by sofas armed with deadly arrows. They formed a solid wall around his standard.

You also will I cite, Mansa Traoré, king of the Traoré tribe; Mansa Traoré, the double-sighted king, was at Sibi. Mansa Traoré could see what was going on behind him just as other men can see in front of them. His sofas, formidable archers with quivers on their shoulders, thronged around him.

As for you, Kamandjan, I cannot forget you among those whom I extol, for you are the father of the Dalikimbon Kamaras. The Kamaras, armed with long spears, raised their menacing pikes around Kamandjan.

In short, all the sons of Mali were there, all those who say "N'Ko," all who speak the clear language of Mali were represented at Sibi.

When the son of the buffalo woman and his army appeared, the trumpets, drums and tam-tams blended with the voices of the griots. The son of Sogolon was surrounded by his swift horsemen and his horse pranced along. All eyes were fixed on the child of Mali, who shone with glory and splendour. When he was within call, Kamandjan made a gesture and the drums, tam-tams and voices fell silent. Leaving the ranks, the king of Sibi went towards Sundiata and cried, "Maghan Sundiata, son of Sogolon, son of Naré Maghan, assembled Mali awaits you. Hail to you, I am Kamandjan, king of Sibi."

Raising his hand, Maghan Sundiata spoke thus: "I salute you all, sons of Mali, and I salute you, Kamandjan. I have come back, and as long as I breathe Mali will never be in thrall—rather death than slavery. We will live free because our ancestors lived free. I am going to avenge the indignity that Mali has undergone."

A shout of joy issuing from thousands of throats filled the whole heaven. The drums and tam-tams rumbled while the griots struck up Balla Fasséké's "Hymn to the Bow." It was thus that Sundiata met the sons of Mali gathered at Sibi.

Nana Triban and Balla Fasséké

Sundiata and his mighty army stopped at Sibi for a few days. The road into Mali lay open, but Soumaoro was not yet vanquished. The king of Sosso had mustered a powerful army and his sofas were numbered by the thousand. He had raised contingents in all the lands over which he held sway and got ready to pounce again on Mali.

With scrupulous care, Sundiata had made his preparations at Sibi. Now he had sufficient sofas to meet Soumaoro in the open field, but it was not a question of having a lot of troops. In order to defeat Soumaoro it was necessary first of all to destroy his magical power. At Sibi, Sundiata decided to consult the soothsayers, of whom the most famous in Mali were there.

On their advice Djata had to sacrifice a hundred white bulls, a hundred white rams and a hundred white cocks. It was in the middle of this slaughter that it was announced to Sundiata that his sister Nana Triban and Balla Fasséké, having been able to escape from Sosso, had now arrived. Then Sundiata said to Tabon Wana, "If my sister and Balla have been able to escape from Sosso, Soumaoro has lost the battle."

Leaving the site of the sacrifices, Sundiata returned to Sibi and met his sister and his griot.

"Hail, my brother," said Nana Triban.
"Greetings, sister."
"Hail Sundiata," said Balla Fasséké.
"Greetings, my griot."

After numerous salutations, Sundiata asked the fugitives to relate how they had been able to elude the vigilance of a king such as Soumaoro. But Triban was weeping for joy. Since the time of their childhood she had shown much sympathy towards the crippled child that Sundiata had been. Never had she shared the hate of her mother, Sassouma Bérété.

"You know, Djata," she said, weeping, "for my part I did not want you to leave the country. It was my mother who did all that. Now Niani is destroyed, its inhabitants scattered, and there are many whom Soumaoro has carried off into captivity in Sosso."

She cried worse than ever. Djata was sympathetic to all this, but he was in a hurry to know something about Sosso. Balla Fasséké understood and said, "Triban, wipe away your tears and tell your story, speak to your brother. You know that he has never thought ill of you, and besides, all that was in his destiny."

Nana Triban wiped her tears away and spoke.

"When you left Mali, my brother sent me by force to Sosso to be the wife of Soumaoro, whom he greatly feared. I wept a great deal at the beginning but when I saw that perhaps all was not lost I resigned myself for the time being. I was nice to Soumaoro and was the chosen one among his numerous wives. I had my chamber in the great tower where he himself lived. I knew how to flatter him and make him jealous. Soon I became his confidante and I pretended to hate you, to share the hate which my mother bore you. It was said that you would come back one day, but I swore to him that you would never have the presumption to claim a kingdom you had never possessed, and that you had left never to see Mali again. However, I was in constant touch with Balla Fasséké, each of us wanting to pierce the mystery of Soumaoro's magic power. One night I took the bull by the horns and said to Soumaoro: 'Tell me, oh you whom kings mention with trembling, tell me Soumaoro, are you a man like others or are you the same as the jinn who protects humans? No one can bear the glare of your eyes, your arm has the strength of ten arms. Tell me, king of kings, tell me what jinn protects you so that I can worship him also.' These words filled him with pride and he himself boasted to me of the might of his Tana. That very night he took me into his magic chamber and told me all.

"Then I redoubled my zeal to show myself faithful to his cause, I seemed more overwhelmed than him. It was even he who went to the extent of telling me to take courage, that nothing was yet lost. During all this time, in complicity with Balla Fasséké, I was preparing for the inevitable flight. Nobody watched over me any more in the royal enclosure, of which I knew the smallest twists and turns. And one night when Soumaoro was away, I left that fearsome tower. Balla Fasséké was waiting for me at the gate to which I had the key. It was thus, brother, that we left Sosso."

Balla Fasséké took up the story.

"We hastened to you. The news of the victory of Tabon made me realize that the lion had burst his chains. Oh son of Sogolon, I am the word and you are the deed, now your destiny begins."

Sundiata was very happy to recover his sister and his griot. He now had the singer who would perpetuate his memory by his words. There would not be any heroes if deeds were condemned to man's forgetfulness, for we ply our trade to excite the admiration of the living, and to evoke the veneration of those who are to come.

Djata was informed that Soumaoro was advancing along the river and was trying to block his route to Mali. The preparations were complete, but before leaving Sibi, Sundiata arranged a great military review in the camp so that Balla Fasséké, by his words, should strengthen the hearts of his sofas. In the middle of a great circle formed by the sofas, Balla Fasséké extolled the heroes of Mali. To the king of Tabon he said: "You whose iron arm can split ten skulls at a time, you, Tabon Wana, king of the Sinikimbon and the Djallonké, can you show me what you are capable of before the great battle is joined?"

The griots words made Fran Kamara leap up. Sword in hand and mounted on his swift steed he came and stood before Sundiata and said, "Maghan Sundiata, I renew my oath to you in the sight of all the Mandingoes gathered together. I pledge myself to conquer or to die by your side. Mali will be free or the smiths of Tabon will be dead."

The tribes of Tabon shouted their approval, brandishing their weapons, and Fran Kamara, stirred by the shouts of the sofas, spurred his charger and charged forward. The warriors opened their ranks and he bore down on a great mahogany tree. With one stroke of his sword he split the giant tree just as one splits a paw-paw. The flabbergasted army shouted, "Wassa Wassa ... Ayé ..."

Then, coming back to Sundiata, his sword held aloft, the king of Tabon said, "Thus on the Niger plain will the smiths of Tabon cleave those of Sosso in twain." And the hero came and fell in beside Sundiata.

Turning towards Kamandjan, the king of Sibi and cousin of the king of Tabon, Balla Fasséké said, "Where are you, Kamandjan, where is Fama Djan? Where is the king of the Dalikimbon Kamaras. Kamandjan of Sibi, I salute you. But what will I have to relate of you to future generations?"

Before Balla had finished speaking, the king of Sibi, shouting his war-cry, started his fiery charger off at full gallop. The sofas, stupefied, watched the extraordinary horseman head for the mountain that dominates Sibi. . . . Suddenly a tremendous din filled the sky, the earth trembled under the feet of the sofas and a cloud of red dust covered the mountain. Was this the end of the world? . . . But slowly the dust cleared and the sofas saw Kamandjan coming back holding a fragment of a sword. The mountain of Sibi, pierced through and through, disclosed a wide tunnel!

Admiration was at its highest pitch. The army stood speechless and the king of Sibi, without saying a word, came and fell in beside Sundiata.

Balla Fasséké mentioned all the chiefs by name and they all performed great feats; then the army, confident in its leadership, left Sibi.

Krina

Sundiata went and pitched camp at Dayala in the valley of the Niger. Now it was he who was blocking Soumaoro's road to the south. Up till that time, Sundiata and Soumaoro had fought each other without a declaration of war. One does not wage war without saying why it is being waged. Those fighting should make a declaration of their grievances to begin with. Just as a sorcerer ought not to attack someone without taking him to task for some evil deed, so a king should not wage war without saying why he is taking up arms.

Soumaoro advanced as far as Krina, near the village of Dayala on the Niger and decided to assert his rights before joining battle. Soumaoro knew that Sundiata also was a sorcerer, so, instead of sending an embassy, he committed his words to one of his owls. The night bird came and perched on the roof of Djata's tent and spoke. The son of Sogolon in his turn sent his owl to Soumaoro. Here is the dialogue of the sorcerer kings:

"Stop, young man. Henceforth I am the king of Mali. If you want peace, return to where you came from," said Soumaoro.

"I am coming back, Soumaoro, to recapture my kingdom. If you want peace you will make amends to my allies and return to Sosso where you are the king."

"I am king of Mali by force of arms. My rights have been established by conquest."

"Then I will take Mali from you by force of arms and chase you from my kingdom."

"Know, then, that I am the wild yam of the rocks; nothing will make me leave Mali."

"Know, also that I have in my camp seven master smiths who will shatter the rocks. Then, yam, I will eat you."

"I am the poisonous mushroom that makes the fearless vomit."

"As for me, I am the ravenous cock, the poison does not matter to me."

"Behave yourself, little boy, or you will burn your foot, for I am the red-hot cinder."

"But me, I am the rain that extinguishes the cinder; I am the boisterous torrent that will carry you off."

"I am the mighty silk-cotton tree that looks from on high on the tops of other trees."

"And I, I am the strangling creeper that climbs to the top of the forest giant."

"Enough of this argument. You shall not have Mali."

"Know that there is not room for two kings on the same skin, Soumaoro; you will let me have your place."

"Very well, since you want war I will wage war against you, but I would have you know that I have killed nine kings whose heads adorn my room. What a pity, indeed, that your head should take its place beside those of your fellow madcaps."

"Prepare yourself, Soumaoro, for it will be long before the calamity that is going to crash down upon you and yours comes to an end."

Thus Sundiata and Soumaoro spoke together. After the war of mouths, swords had to decide the issue. Sogolon's son was in his tent when someone came to announce to him the arrival of Fakoli, Soumaoro's insurgent nephew. All the men stood to arms and the war chiefs drew up their men. When everything was in order in the camp, Djata and the Mandingo leaders received Fakoli followed by his warriors. Fakoli halted before Sundiata and spoke thus:

"I salute you, Sundiata. I am Fakoli Koroma, king of the tribe of Koroma smiths. Soumaoro is the brother of my mother Kassia. I have taken up arms against my uncle because he has outraged me. Without fearing incest he has pushed his effrontery to the lengths of robbing me of my wife Keleya. As for you, you are coming to reconquer the kingdom of your fathers, you are fighting Soumaoro. We have the same goal and therefore I come to place myself under your orders. I bring you my strong-armed smiths, I bring you sofas who do not know what fear is. Sundiata, I and my men are yours."

Balla, Sundiata's griot, said, "Fakoli, come and sit among your brothers whom Soumaoro's injustice has smitten, the judge folds you to his bosom. You could not do better than entrust your cause to the son of Sogolon."

Sundiata made a sign indicating that the griot had spoken well, but he added, "I defend the weak, I defend the innocent, Fakoli. You have suffered an injustice so I will render you justice, but I have my lieutenants about me and I would like to know their opinions."

All the war chiefs agreed. Fakoli's cause became Sundiata's cause. Justice had to be granted to the man who came to implore justice. Thus Sundiata accepted Fakoli Da-Ba, Large-Mouthed Fakoli, among his war chiefs.

Sundiata wanted to have done with Soumaoro before the rainy season, so he struck camp and marched on Krina where Soumaoro was encamped. The latter realized that the decisive battle had come. Sundiata deployed his men on the little hill that dominates the plain. The great battle was for the next day.

In the evening, to raise the men's spirits, Djata gave a great feast, for he was anxious that his men should wake up happy in the morning. Several oxen were slaughtered and that evening Balla Fasséké, in front of the whole army, called to mind the history of old Mali. He praised Sundiata, seated amidst his lieutenants, in this manner:

"Now I address myself to you, Maghan Sundiata, I speak to you king of Mali, to whom dethroned monarchs flock. The time foretold to you by the jinn is now coming. Sundiata, kingdoms and empires are in the likeness of man; like him they are born, they grow and disappear. Each sovereign embodies one moment of that life. Formerly, the kings of Ghana extended their kingdom over all the lands inhabited by the black man, but the circle has closed and the Cissés of Wagadou are nothing more than petty princes in a desolate land. Today, another kingdom looms up, powerful, the kingdom of Sosso. Humbled kings have borne their tribute to Sosso, Soumaoro's arrogance knows no more bounds and his cruelty is equal to his ambition. But will Soumaoro dominate the world? Are we, the griots of Mali, condemned to pass on to future generations the humiliations which the king of Sosso cares to inflict on our country? No, you may be glad, children of the 'Bright Country,' for the kingship of Sosso is but the growth of yesterday, whereas that of Mali dates from the time of Bilali. Each kingdom has its childhood, but Soumaoro wants to force the pace, and so Sosso will collapse under him like a horse worn out beneath its rider.

"You, Maghan, you are Mali. It has had a long and difficult childhood like you. Sixteen kings have preceded you on the throne of Niani, sixteen kings have reigned with varying fortunes, but from being village chiefs the Keitas have become tribal chiefs and then kings. Sixteen generations have consolidated their power. You are the outgrowth of Mali just as the silk-cotton tree is the growth of the earth, born of deep and mighty roots. To face the tempest the tree must have long roots and gnarled branches. Maghan Sundiata, has not the tree grown?

"I would have you know, son of Sogolon, that there is not room for two kings around the same calabash of rice. When a new cock comes to the poultry run the old cock picks a quarrel with him and the docile hens wait to see if the new arrival asserts himself or yields. You have come to Mali. Very well, then, assert yourself. Strength makes a law of its own self and power allows no division.

"But listen to what your ancestors did, so that you will know what you have to do.

"Bilali, the second of the name, conquered old Mali. Latal Kalabi conquered the country between the Niger and the Sankarani. By going to Mecca, Lahibatoul Kalabi, of illustrious memory, brought divine blessing upon Mali. Mamadi Kani made warriors out of hunters and bestowed armed strength upon Mali. His son Bamari Tagnokelin, the vindictive king, terrorized Mali with this army, but Maghan Kon Fatta, also called Naré Maghan, to whom you owe your being, made peace prevail and happy mothers yielded Mali a populous youth.

"You are the son of Naré Maghan, but you are also the son of your mother Sogolon, the buffalo-woman, before whom powerless sorcerers shrank in fear. You have the strength and majesty of the lion, you have the might of the buffalo.

"I have told you what future generations will learn about your ancestors, but what will we be able to relate to our sons so that your memory will stay alive, what will we have to teach our sons about you? What unprecedented exploits, what unheard-of feats? By what distinguished actions will our sons be brought to regret not having lived in the time of Sundiata?

"Griots are men of the spoken word, and by the spoken word we give life to the gestures of kings. But words are nothing but words; power lies in deeds. Be a man of action; do not answer me any more with your mouth, but tomorrow, on the plain of Krina, show me what you would have me recount to coming generations. Tomorrow allow me to sing the 'Song of the Vultures' over the bodies of the thousands of Sossos whom your sword will have laid low before evening."

It was on the eve of Krina. In this way Balla Fasséké reminded Sundiata of the history of Mali so that, in the morning, he would show himself worthy of his ancestors,

At break of day, Fakoli came and woke up Sundiata to tell him that Soumaoro had begun to move his sofas out of Krina. The son of Sogolon appeared dressed like a hunter king. He wore tight-fitting, ochre-coloured trousers. He gave the order to draw up the sofas across the plain, and while his chiefs bustled about, Manding Bory and Nana Triban came into Djata's tent.

"Brother," said Manding Bory, "have you got the bow ready?"

"Yes," replied Sundiata. "Look."

He unhooked his bow from the wall, along with the deadly arrow. It was not an iron arrow at all, but was made of wood and pointed with the spur of a white cock. The cock's spur was the Tana of Soumaoro, the secret which Nana Triban had managed to draw out of the king of Sosso.

"Brother," said Nana Triban, "Soumaoro now knows that I have fled from Sosso. Try to get near him for he will avoid you the whole battle long."

These words of Nana Triban left Djata worried, but Balla Fasséké, who had just come into the tent, said to Sundiata that the soothsayer had seen the end of Soumaoro in a dream.

The sun had risen on the other side of the river and already lit the whole plain. Sundiata's troops deployed from the edge of the river across the plain, but Soumaoro's army was so big that other sofas remaining in Krina had ascended the ramparts to see the battle. Soumaoro was already distinguishable in the distance by his tall headdress, and the wings of his enormous army brushed the river on one side and the hills on the other. As at Neguéboria, Sundiata did not deploy all his forces. The bowmen of Wagadou and the Djallonkés stood at the rear ready to spill out on the left towards the hills as the battle spread. Fakoli Koroma and Kamandjan were in the front line with Sundiata and his cavalry.

With his powerful voice Sundiata cried "An gnewa." The order was repeated from tribe to tribe and the army started off. Soumaoro stood on the right with his cavalry.

Djata and his cavalry charged with great dash but they were stopped by the horsemen of Diaghan and a struggle to the death began. Tabon Wana and the archers of Wagadou stretched out their lines towards the hills and the battle spread over the entire plain, while an unrelenting sun climbed in the sky. The horses of Mema were extremely agile, and they reared forward with their fore hooves raised and swooped down on the horsemen of Diaghan, who rolled on the ground trampled under the horses' hooves. Presently the men of Diaghan gave ground and fell back towards the rear. The enemy centre was broken.

It was then that Manding Bory galloped up to announce to Sundiata that Soumaoro, having thrown in all his reserve, had swept down on Fakoli and his smiths. Obviously Soumaoro was bent on punishing his nephew. Already overwhelmed by the numbers, Fakoli's men were beginning to give ground. The battle was not yet won.

His eyes red with anger, Sundiata pulled his cavalry over to the left in the direction of the hills where Fakoli was valiantly enduring his uncle's blows. But wherever the son of the buffalo passed, death rejoiced. Sundiata's presence restored the balance momentarily, but Soumaoro's sofas were too numerous all the same. Sogolon's son looked for Soumaoro and caught sight of him in the middle of the fray. Sundiata struck out right and left and the Sossos scrambled out of his way. The king of Sosso, who did not want Sundiata to get near him, retreated far behind his men, but Sundiata followed him with his eyes. He stopped and bent his bow. The arrow flew and grazed Soumaoro on the shoulder. The cock's spur no more than scratched him, but the effect was immediate and Soumaoro felt his powers leave him. His eyes met Sundiata's. Now trembling like a man in the grip of a fever, the vanquished Soumaoro looked up towards the sun. A great black bird flew over above the fray and he understood. It was a bird of misfortune.

"The bird of Krina," he muttered.

The king of Sosso let out a great cry and, turning his horse's head, he took to flight. The Sossos saw the king and fled in their turn. It was a rout. Death hovered over the great plain and blood poured out of a thousand wounds. Who can tell how many Sossos perished at Krina? The rout was complete and Sundiata then dashed off in pursuit of Soumaoro. The sun was at the middle of its course. Fakoli had caught up with Sundiata and they both rode in pursuit of the fugitives. Soumaoro had a good start. Leaving the plain, the king of Soso had dashed across the open bush followed by his son Balla and a few Sosso chiefs. When night fell Sundiata and Fakoli stopped at a hamlet. There they took a little food and rest. None of the inhabitants had seen Soumaoro. Sundiata and Fakoli started off in pursuit again as soon as they were joined by some horsemen of Mema. They galloped all night and at daybreak Djata learnt from some peasants that some horsemen had passed that way when it was still dark. The king of Sosso shunned all centres of population for he knew that the inhabitants, seeing him on the run, would no longer hesitate to lay hands on him in order to get into favour with the new master. Soumaoro was followed by none but his son Balla. After having changed his mount at daybreak, the king of Sosso was still galloping to the north.

With difficulty Sundiata found the trail of the fugitives. Fakoli was as resolute as Djata and he knew this country better. It was difficult to tell which of these two men harboured the greatest hatred towards Soumaoro. The one was avenging his humiliated country while the other was prompted by the love of a wife. At noon the horses of Sundiata and Fakoli were out of breath and the pursuers halted at Bankoumana. They took a little food and Djata learnt that Soumaoro was heading for Koulikoro. He had only given himself enough time to change horses. Sundiata and Fakoli set off again straight away. Fakoli said, "I know a short cut to Koulikoro, but it is a difficult track and our horses will be tired!"

"Come on," said Djata.

They tackled a difficult path scooped out by the rain in a gully. Cutting across country they now crossed the bush until, pointing a finger in front of him, Fakoli said, "Look at the hills over there which herald Koulikoro. We have made up some time."

"Good," replied Djata simply.

However, the horses were fatigued, they went more slowly and painfully lifted their hooves from the ground. As there was no village in sight, Djata and Fakoli dismounted to let their mounts get their wind back. Fakoli, who had a small bag of millet in his saddle, fed them. The two men rested under a tree. Fakoli even said that Soumaoro, who had taken an easy but lengthy route, would not arrive at Koulikoro until nightfall. He was speaking like a man who had ridden over the whole country.

They continued on their way and soon climbed the hills. Arrived at the top, they saw two horsemen at the bottom of the valley going towards the mountain.

"There they are," cried Djata.

Evening was coming on and the sun's rays were already kissing the summit of Koulikoro mountain. When Soumaoro and his son saw the two riders behind them, they broke off and began to climb the mountain. The kin of Sosso and his son Balla seemed to have fresher horses. Djata and Fakoli redoubled their efforts.

The fugitives were within spear range when Djata shouted to them, "Stop, stop."

Like Djata, Fakoli wanted to take Soumaoro alive. Keleya's husband sheered off and outflanked Soumaoro on the right, making his horse jump. He was going to lay hands on his uncle but the latter escaped him by a sudden turn. Through his impetus Fakoli bumped into Balla and they both rolled on the ground. Fakoli got up and seized his cousin while Sundiata, throwing his spear with all his might, brought Soumaoro's horse tumbling down. The old king got up and the foot race began. Soumaoro was a sturdy old man and he climbed the mountain with great agility. Djata did not want either to wound him or kill him. He wanted to take him alive

The sun had just disappeared completely. For a second time the king of Sosso escaped from Djata. Having reached the summit of Koulikoro, Soumaoro hurried down the slope followed by Djata. To the right he saw the gaping cave of Koulikoro and without hesitation he entered the black cavern. Sundiata stopped in front of the cave. At this moment arrived Fakoli who had just tied the hands of Sosso Balla, his cousin.

"There," said Sundiata, "he has gone into the cave."

"But it is connected to the river," said Fakoli.

The noise of horses' hooves was heard and it turned out to be a detachment of Mema horsemen. Straight away the son of Sogolon sent some of them towards the river and had all the mountain guarded. The darkness was complete. Sundiata went into the village of Koulikoro and waited there for the rest of his army.

The victory of Krina was dazzling. The remains of Soumaoro's army went to shut themselves up in Sosso. But the empire of Sosso was done for. From everywhere around kings sent their submission to Sundiata. The king of Guidimakhan sent a richly furnished embassy to Djata and at the same time gave his daughter in marriage to the victor. Embassies flocked to Koulikoro, but when Djata had been joined by all the army he marched on Sosso. Soumaoro's city, Sosso, the impregnable city, the city of smiths skilled in wielding the spear.

In the absence of the king and his son, Noumounkeba, a tribal chief, directed the defence of the city. He had quickly amassed all that he could find in the way of provisions from the surrounding countryside.

Sosso was a magnificent city. In the open plain her triple rampart with awe-inspiring towers reached into the sky. The city comprised a hundred and eighty-eight fortresses and the palace of Soumaoro loomed above the whole city like a gigantic tower. Sosso had but one gate; colossal and made of iron, the work of the sons of fire. Noumounkeba hoped to tie Sundiata down outside of Sosso, for he had enough provisions to hold out for a year.

The sun was beginning to set when Sogolon-Djata appeared before Sosso the Magnificent. From the top of a hill, Djata and his general staff gazed upon the fearsome city of the sorcerer king. The army encamped in the plain opposite the great gate of the city and fires were lit in the camp. Djata resolved to take Sosso in the course of a morning. He fed his men a double ration and the tam-tams beat all night to stir up the victors of Krina.

At daybreak the towers of the ramparts were black with sofas. Others were positioned on the ramparts themselves. They were the archers. The Mandingoes were masters in the art of storming a town. In the front line Sundiata placed the sofas of Mali, while those who held the ladders were in the second line protected by the shields of the spearmen. The main body of the army was to attack the city gate. When all was ready, Djata gave the order to attack. The drums resounded, the horns blared and like a tide the Mandingo front line moved off, giving mighty shouts. With their shields raised above their heads the Mandingoes advanced up to the foot of the wall, then the Sossos began to rain large stones down on the assailants. From the rear, the bowmen of Wagadou shot arrows at the ramparts. The attack spread and the town was assaulted at all points. Sundiata had a murderous reserve; they were the bowmen whom the king of the Bobos had sent shortly before Krina. The archers of Bobo are the best in the world. On one knee the archers fired flaming arrows over the ramparts. Within the walls the thatched huts took fire and the smoke swirled up. The ladders stood against the curtain wall and the first Mandingo sofas were already at the top. Seized by panic through seeing the town on fire, the Sossos hesitated a moment. The huge tower surmounting the gate surrendered, for Fakoli's smiths had made themselves masters of it. They got into the city where the screams of women and children brought the Sossos' panic to a head. They opened the gates to the main body of the army.

Then began the massacre. Women and children in the midst of fleeing Sossos implored mercy of the victors. Djata and his cavalry were now in front of the awesome tower palace of Soumaoro. Noumounkeba, conscious that he was lost, came out to fight. With his sword held aloft he bore down on Djata, but the latter dodged him and, catching hold of the Sosso's braced arm, forced him to his knees whilst the sword dropped to the ground. He did not kill him but delivered him into the hands of Manding Bory.

Soumaoro's palace was now at Sundiata's mercy. While everywhere the Sossos were begging for quarter, Sundiata, preceded by Balla Fasséké, entered Soumaoro's tower. The griot knew every nook and cranny of the palace from his captivity and he led Sundiata to Soumaoro's magic chamber.

When Balla Fasséké opened the door to the room it was found to have changed its appearance since Soumaoro had been touched by the fatal arrow. The inmates of the chamber had lost their power. The snake in the pitcher was in the throes of death, the owls from the perch were flapping pitifully about on the ground. Everything was dying in the sorcerer's abode. It was all up with the power of Soumaoro. Sundiata had all Soumaoro's fetishes taken down and before the palace were gathered together all Soumaoro's wives, all princesses taken from their families by force. The prisoners, their hands tied behind their backs, were already herded together. Just as he had wished, Sundiata had taken Sosso in the course of a morning. When everything was outside of the town and all that there was to take had been taken out, Sundiata gave the order to complete its destruction. The last houses were set fire to and prisoners were employed in the razing of the walls. Thus, as Djata intended, Sosso was destroyed to its very foundations.

Yes, Sosso was razed to the ground. It has disappeared, the proud city of Soumaoro. A ghastly wilderness extends over the places where kings came and humbled themselves before the sorcerer king. All traces of the houses have vanished and of Soumaoro's seven-storey palace there remains nothing more. A field of desolation, Sosso is now a spot where guinea fowl and young partridges come to take their dust baths.

Many years have rolled by and many times the moon has traversed the heaven since these places lost their inhabitants. The bourein, the tree of desolation, spreads out its thorny undergrowth and insolently grows in Soumaoro's capital. Sosso the Proud is nothing but a memory in the mouths of griots. The hyenas come to wail there at night, the hare and the hind come and feed on the site of the palace of Soumaoro, the king who wore robes of human skin.

Sosso vanished from the earth and it was Sundiata, the son of the buffalo, who gave these places over to solitude. After the destruction of Soumaoro's capital the world knew no other master but Sundiata.

The Empire

While Sosso succumbed to the mattocks of its own sons, Sundiata marched on Diaghan. The king of Diaghan had been Soumaoro's most formidable ally and after Krina he still remained faithful to Soumaoro's cause. He had shut himself up in his city, which was proud of its cavalry, but like a hurricane Sundiata beat upon Diaghan, the city of divines. Like Sosso, Diaghan was taken in one morning. Sundiata had the heads of all the young men shaved and made sofas of them.

Sundiata had divided his army into three bodies; the first, under the command of Fakoli Koroma, waged war in Bambougou; the second, under the command of Fran Kamara, fought in the mountains of the Fouta; Sundiata and the main body of the army marched on the great city of Kita.

Kita Mansa was a powerful king and was under the protection of the jinn of the great mountain which dominates the town of Kita, Kita Kourou. In the middle of the mountain was a little pool of magic water. Whoever got as far as this pool and drank its waters became powerful, but the jinn of the pool were very evil and only the king of Kita had access to the mysterious pool.

Sundiata camped to the east of Kita and demanded submission of the king. Vainglorious in the protection of the mountain jinn, Kita Mansa answered Djata with arrogance. Sogolon's son had in his army some infallible soothsayers. On their advice, Sundiata invoked the jinn of Kita Kourou and sacrificed to them a hundred white oxen, a hundred white rams and a hundred white cocks. All the cocks died on their backs, facing upwards; the jinn had replied favourably. Then Sundiata did not hesitate any longer and first thing in the morning he gave the signal to attack. The assaulting sofas sang the "Hymn to the Bow." Balla Fesséké, dressed as a great griot, rode at Djata's side. At the first assault the east gate surrendered, but there was no massacre at all. Men, women and children all were spared, but Kita Mansa had been killed outside his palace. Sundiata accorded him royal obsequies. Sundiata did not take one prisoner at Kita and the inhabitants, who were Kamaras, became his allies.

First thing next morning Sundiata determined to go into the mountain to sacrifice to the jinn and thank them for his victory over Kita. The whole army followed him. The mountain of Kita is as steep as a wall and Sundiata resolved to go all round it to receive the submission of the numerous villages lying at the foot of Kita Kourou. At Boudofou, a Kamara village, there was a great celebration between Kamandjan's tribes and the inhabitants. There was dancing and eating around the sacred stone of Boudofou. Today the Kamaras still sacrifice at this stone, but only those Kamaras who have known how to respect the Dio of their ancestors. In the evening the army camped at Kourou-Koto on the slope of the mountain opposite. Kita Djata was well received by the king Mansa Kourou and several tribes fraternized there.

At break of day Sundiata, followed by Balla Fasséké and a few members of the royal tribe of Mali went to the foot of a large rock. He sacrificed a hundred cocks to the jinn of the mountain, then, accompanied by Balla Fasséké alone, Sundiata went off in search of the pool. He found it in the midst of the mountain. He knelt down at the water's edge and said,

"Oh jinn of the water, Master of the Moghoya-Dji, master of the magic water, I sacrificed to you a hundred bulls, I sacrificed to you a hundred rains, and I sacrificed to you a hundred cocks. You gave me the victory but I have not destroyed Kita. I, the successor to Kita Mansa, come to drink the magic water, the moghoya dji."

He scooped up some water in his two hands and drank. He found the water good and drank three times of it, then he washed his face.

When Djata rejoined his men his eyes had an unbearable brilliance. He radiated like a star. The moghoya dji had transfigured him.

From Kourou-Koto Sundiata returned to Kita, the trip round the mountain having lasted two days. At Kita he found delegations from the kingdoms conquered by Fakoli and Tabon Wana. The king of Mali stayed at Kita for some time and often went hunting with his brother Manding Bory and Sibi Kamandjan. The people of Kita never hunted the mountain game for fear of the jinn. As for Sundiata, he hunted on the mountain for he had become the chosen one of the jinn. A Simbon from his early years, he was well enough versed in the art of Sané ni Kondolon. He and his companions used to bathe in one of the mountain springs and the people of Kita still distinguish this spring and surround it with great veneration.

Leaving Kita, Sundiata and his large army headed for Do, the country of his mother Sogolon. At Do Sundiata was received as the uncle receives the nephew. Djata and Balla Fasséké betook themselves to the famous plain of Ourantamba and a member of the Traoré tribe accompanied them. The inhabitants of Do had raised a great mound on the spot where the buffalo had expired. Sundiata sacrificed a white cock on the mound. When the cock had died on its back a big whirlwind swirled up and blew towards the west.

"Look," said Balla Fasséké, "the whirlwind is going towards Mali."

"Yes, it is time to go back there."

From Do, Sundiata sent a richly furnished embassy to Mema loaded with costly gifts. Thus he paid off his contracted debt and the embassy made it known to the king that the Cissé-Tounkaras and the Keitas would be allies for ever.

It was from Do, also, that Sundiata ordered all his generals to meet him at Ka-ba on the Niger in the land of the king of Sibi. Fakoli had completed his conquests and the king of Tabon had subjugated the mountaineers of the Fouta. The arms of Sundiata had subdued all the countries of the savanna. From Ghana in the north to Mali in the south and from Mema in the east to the Fouta in the west, all the lands had recognized Sundiata's authority.

Djata's army followed the Niger valley to make its way to Ka-ba.

Kouroukan Fougan or The Division of the World

Leaving Do, the land of ten thousand guns, Sundiata wended his way to Ka-ba, keeping to the river valley. All his armies converged on Ka-ba and Fakoli and Tabon Wana entered it laden with booty. Sibi Kamandjan had gone ahead of Sundiata to prepare the great assembly which was to gather at Ka-ba, a town situated on the territory belonging to the country of Sibi.

Ka-ba was a small town founded by Niagalin M'Bali Faly, a hunter of Sibi, and by Sounoumba Traore, a fisherman. Ka-ba belonged to the king of Sibi and nowadays you can also find Keitas at Ka-ba, but the Keitas did not come there until after Sundiata's time. Ka-ba stands on the left bank of the Niger and it is through Ka-ba that the road to old Mali passes.

To the north of the town stretches a spacious clearing and it is there that the great assembly was to foregather. King Kamandjan had the whole clearing cleaned up and a great dais was got ready. Even before Djata's arrival the delegations from all the conquered peoples had made their way to Ka-ba. Huts were hastily built to house all these people. When all the armies had reunited, camps had to be set up in the big plain lying between the river and the town. On the appointed day the troops were drawn up on the vast square that had been prepared. As at Sibi, each people was gathered round its king's pennant. Sundiata had put on robes such as are worn by a great Muslim king. Balla Fasséké, the high master of ceremonies, set the allies around Djata's great throne. Everything was in position. The sofas, forming a vast semicircle bristling with spears, stood motionless. The delegations of the various peoples had been planted at the foot of the dais. A complete silence reigned. On Sundiata's right, Balla Fasséké, holding his mighty spear, addressed the throng in this manner:

"Peace reigns today in the whole country; may it always be thus...."

"Amen," replied the crowd, then the herald continued:

"I speak to you, assembled peoples. To those of Mali I convey Maghan Sundiata's greeting; greetings to those of Do, greetings to those of Ghana, to those from Mema greetings, and to those of Fakoli's tribe. Greetings to the Bobo warriors and, finally, greetings to those of Sibi and Ka-ba. To all the peoples assembled, Djata gives greetings.

"May I be humbly forgiven if I have made any omission. I am nervous before so many people gathered together.

"Peoples, here we are, after years of hard trials, gathered around our saviour, the restorer of peace and order. From the east to the west, from the north to the south, everywhere his victorious arms have established peace. I convey to you the greetings of Soumaoro's vanquisher, Maghan Sundiata, king of Mali.

"But in order to respect tradition, I must first of all address myself to the host of us all, Kamandjan, king of Sibi; Djata greets you and gives you the floor."

Kamandjan, who was sitting close by Sundiata, stood up and stepped down from the dais. He mounted his horse and brandished his sword, crying "I salute you all, warriors of Mali, of Do, of Tabon, of Mema, of Wagadou, of Bobo, of Fakoli . . .; warriors, peace has returned to our homes, may God long preserve it."

"Amen," replied the warriors and the crowd. The king of Sibi continued.

"In the world man suffers for a season, but never eternally. Here we are at the end of our trials. We are at peace. May God be praised. But we owe this peace to one man who, by his courage and his valiance, was able to lead our troops to victory.

"Which one of us, alone, would have dared face Soumaoro? Ay, we were all cowards. How many times did we pay him tribute? The insolent rogue thought that everything was permitted him. What family was not dishonoured by Soumaoro? He took our daughters and wives from us and we were more craven than women. He carried his insolence to the point of stealing the wife of his nephew Fakoli! We were prostrated and humiliated in front of our children. But it was in the midst of so many calamities that our destiny suddenly changed. A new sun arose in the east. After the battle of Tabon we felt ourselves to be men, we realized that Soumaoro was a human being and not an incarnation of the devil, for he was no longer invincible. A man came to us. He had heard our groans and came to our aid, like a father when he sees his son in tears. Here is that man. Maghan Sundiata, the man with two names foretold by the soothsayers.

"It is to you that I now address myself, son of Sogolon, you, the nephew of the valorous warriors of Do. Henceforth it is from you that I derive my kingdom for I acknowledge you my sovereign. My tribe and I place ourselves in your hands. I salute you, supreme chief, I salute you, Fama of Famas. I salute you, Mansa!"

The huzza that greeted these words was so loud that you could hear the echo repeat the tremendous clamour twelve times over. With a strong hand Kamandjan stuck his spear in the ground in front of the dais and said, "Sundiata, here is my spear, it is yours."

Then he climbed up to sit in his place. Thereafter, one by one, the twelve kings of the bright savanna country got up and proclaimed Sundiata "Mansa" in their turn. Twelve royal spears were stuck in the ground in front of the dais. Sundiata had become emperor. The old tabala of Niani announced to the world that the lands of the savanna had provided themselves with one single king. When the imperial tabala had stopped reverberating, Balla Fasséké, the grand master of ceremonies, took the floor again following the crowd's ovation.

"Sundiata, Maghan Sundiata, king of Mali, in the name of the twelve kings of the 'Bright Country,' I salute you as 'Mansa.'" The crowd shouted "Wassa, Wassa. . . . Ayé."

It was amid such joy that Balla Fasséké composed the great hymn "Niama" which the griots still sing:

Niama, Niama, Niama,
You, you serve as a shelter for all,
All come to seek refuge under you.
And as for you, Niama,
Nothing serves you for shelter,
God alone protects you.

The festival began. The musicians of all the countries were there. Each people in turn came forward to the dais under Sundiata's impassive gaze. Then the war dances began. The sofas of all the countries had lined themselves up in six ranks amid a great clatter of bows and spears knocking together. The war chiefs were on horseback. The warriors faced the enormous dais and at a signal from Balla Fasséké, the musicians, massed on the right of the dais, struck up. The heavy war drums thundered, the bolons gave off muted notes while the griot's voice gave the throng the pitch for the "Hymn to the Bow." The spearmen, advancing like hyenas in the night, held their spears above their heads; the archers of Wagadou and Tabon, walking with a noiseless tread, seemed to be lying in ambush behind bushes. They rose suddenly to their feet and let fly their arrows at imaginary enemies. In front of the great dais the Kéké-Tigui, or war chiefs, made their horses perform dance steps under the eyes of the Mansa. The horses whinnied and reared, then, overmastered by the spurs, knelt, got up and cut little capers, or else scraped the ground with their hooves.

The rapturous people shouted the "Hymn to the Bow" and clapped their hands. The sweating bodies of the warriors glistened in the sun while the exhausting rhythm of the tam-tams wrenched from them shrill cries. But presently they made way for the cavalry, beloved by Djata. The horsemen of Mema threw their swords in the air and caught them in flight, uttering mighty shouts. A smile of contentment took shape on Sundiata's lips, for he was happy to see his cavalry manoeuvre with so much skill.

In the afternoon the festivity took on a new aspect. It began with the procession of prisoners and booty. Their hands tied behind their backs and in triple file, the Sosso prisoners made their entry into the giant circle. All their heads had been shaved. Inside the circle they turned and passed by the foot of the dais. Their eyes lowered, the poor prisoners walked in silence, abuse heaped upon them by the frenzied crowd. Behind came the kings who had remained faithful to Soumaoro and who had not intended to make their submission. They also had their heads shorn, but they were on horseback so that everyone could see them. At last, right at the back, came Sosso Balla, who had been placed in the midst of his father's fetishes. The fetishes had been loaded onto donkeys. The crowd gave loud cries of horror on seeing the inmates of Soumaoro's grisly chamber. People pointed with terror at the snake's pitcher, the magic balafon, and the king of Sosso's owls. Soumaoro's son Balla, his hands bound, was on a horse but did not dare look up at this throne, which formerly used to tremble with fear at mere talk of his father. In the crowd could be heard:

"Each in his turn, Sosso Balla; lift up your head a bit, impudent little creature!" Or else: "Did you have any idea that one day you would be a slave, you vile fellow!"

"Look at your useless fetishes. Call on them then, son of a sorcerer!"

When Sosso Balla was in front of the dais, Djata made a gesture. He had just remembered the mysterious disappearance of Soumaoro inside the mountain. He became morose, but his griot Balla Fasséké noticed it and so he spoke thus:

"The son will pay for the father, Soumaoro can thank God that he is already dead."

When the procession had finished Balla Fasséké silenced everyone. The sofas got into line and the tam-tams stopped.

Sundiata got up and a graveyard silence settled on the whole place. The Mansa moved forward to the edge of the dais. Then Sundiata spoke as Mansa. Only Balla Fasséké could hear him, for a Mansa does not speak like a town-crier.

"I greet all the peoples gathered here." And Djata mentioned them all. Pulling the spear of Kamandjan, king of Sibi, out of the ground, he said:

"I give you back your kingdom, king of Sibi, for you have deserved it by your bravery; I have known you since childhood and your speech is as frank as your heart is straightforward.

"Today I ratify for ever the alliance between the Kamaras of Sibi and the Keitas of Mali. May these two people be brothers henceforth. In future, the land of the Keitas shall be the land of the Kamaras, and the property of the Kimaras shall be henceforth the property of the Keitas.

"May there nevermore be falsehood between a Kamara and a Keita, and may the Kamaras feel at home in the whole extent of my empire."

He returned the spear to Kamandjan and the king of Sibi prostrated himself before Djata, as is done when honoured by a Fama.

Sundiata took Tabon Wana's spear and said, "Fran Kamara, my friend, I return your kingdom to you. May the Djallonkés and Mandingoes be forever allies. You received me in your own domain, so may the Djallonkés be received as friends throughout Mali. I leave you the lands you have conquered, and henceforth your children and your children's children will grow up at the court of Niani where they will be treated like the princes of Mali."

One by one all the kings received their kingdoms from the very hands of Sundiata, and each one bowed before him as one bows before a Mansa.

Sundiata pronounced all the prohibitions which still obtain in relations between the tribes. To each he assigned its land, he established the rights of each people and ratified their friendships. The Kondés of the land of Do became henceforth the uncles of the imperial family of Keita, for the latter, in memory of the fruitful marriage between Naré Maghan and Sogolon, had to take a wife in Do. The Tounkaras and the Cissés became "banter-brothers" of the Keitas. While the Cissés, Bérétés and Tourés were proclaimed great divines of the empire. No kin group was forgotten at Kouroukan Fougan; each had its share in the division. To Fakoli Koroma, Sundiata gave the kingdom of Sosso, the majority of whose inhabitants were enslaved. Fakoli's tribe, the Koromas, which others call Doumbouya or Sissoko, had the monopoly of the forge, that is, of iron working. Fakoli also received from Sundiata part of the lands situated between the Bafing and Bagbé rivers. Wagadou and Mema kept their kings who continued to bear the title of Mansa, but these two kingdoms acknowledged the suzerainty of the supreme Mansa. The Konaté of Toron became the cadets of the Keitas so that on reaching maturity a Konaté could call himself Keita.

When Sogolon's son had finished distributing lands and power he turned to Balla Fasséké, his griot, and said: "As for you, Balla Fasséké, my griot, I make you grand master of ceremonies. Henceforth the Keitas will choose their griot from your tribe, from among the Kouyatés. I give the Kouyatés the right to make jokes about all the tribes, and in particular about the royal tribe of Keita."

Thus spoke the son of Sogolon at Kouroukan Fougan. Since that time his respected word has become law, the rule of conduct for all the peoples, who were represented at Ka-ba.

So, Sundiata had divided the world at Kouroukan Fougan. He kept for his tribe the blessed country of Kita, but the Kamaras inhabiting the region remained masters of the soil.

If you go to Ka-ba, go and see the glade of Kouroukan Fougan and you will see a linké tree planted there, perpetuating the memory of the great gathering which witnessed the division of the world.

Niani

After this great assembly Sundiata stayed a few more days at Ka-ba. For the people these were days of festivity. For them Djata caused hundreds of oxen, taken from Soumaoro's immense exchequer, to be slaughtered every day. In the main square of Ka-ba the girls of the town came and laid big calabashes of rice and meat at the foot of the observation platforms. Anybody could come and eat his fill and go away. Soon Ka-ba was full of people who had come from all directions attracted by the opulence. A year of war had emptied all the granaries so each came to take his share of the king of Sosso's reserves. It is even said that certain people had set up their household gods on that very spot during Djata's stay at Ka-ba. These were the summer months so these people slept on the observation platforms during the night and on awakening found calabashes of rice at their feet. That was the time when people sang the "Hymn to Abundance" in Sundiata's honour:

He has come
And happiness has come
Sundiata is here
And happiness is here.

But it was time to return to his native Mali. Sundiata assembled his army in the plain and each people provided a contingent to accompany the Mansa to Niani. At Ka-ba all the peoples separated in friendship and in joy at their newfound peace.

Sundiata and his men had to cross the Niger in order to enter old Mali. One might have thought that all the dug-out canoes in the world had arranged to meet at the port of Ka-ba. It was the dry season and there was not much water in the river. The fishing tribe of Somono, to whom Djata had given the monopoly of the water, were bent on expressing their thanks to the son of Sogolon. They put all their dug-outs side by side across the Niger so that Sundiata's sofas could cross without wetting their feet.

When the whole army was on the other side of the river, Sundiata ordered great sacrifices. A hundred oxen and a hundred rams were sacrificed. It was thus that Sundiata thanked God on returning to Mali.

The villages of Mali gave Maghan Sundiata an unprecedented welcome. At normal times a traveller on foot can cover the distance from Ka-ba to Niani with only two halts, but Sogolon's son with his army took three days. The road to Mali from the river was flanked by a double human hedge. Flocking from every corner of Mali, all the inhabitants were resolved to see their saviour from close up. The women of Mali tried to create a sensation and they did not fail. At the entrance to each village they had carpeted the road with their multi-coloured pagnes so that Sundiata's horse would not so much as dirty its feet on entering their village. At the village exits the children, holding leafy branches in their hands, greeted Djata with cries of "Wassa, Wassa, Ayé."

Sundiata was leading the van. He had donned his costume of a hunter king—a plain smock, skin-tight trousers and his bow slung across his back. At his side Balla Fasséké was still wearing his festive garments gleaming with gold. Between Djata's general staff and the army Sosso Balla had been placed, amid his father's fetishes. But his hands were no longer tied. As at Ka-ba, abuse was everywhere heaped upon him and the prisoner did not dare look up at the hostile crowd. Some people, always ready to feel sympathy, were saying among themselves:

"How few things good fortune prizes!"

"Yes, the day you are fortunate is also the day when you are the most unfortunate, for in good fortune you cannot imagine what suffering is."

The troops were marching along singing the "Hymn to the Bow," which the crowd took up. New songs flew from mouth to mouth. Young women offered the soldiers cool water and cola nuts. And so the triumphal march across Mali ended outside Niani, Sundiata's city.

It was a ruined town which was beginning to be rebuilt by its inhabitants. A part of the ramparts had been destroyed and the charred walls still bore the marks of the fire. From the top of the hill Djata looked on Niani, which looked like a dead city. He saw the plain of Sounkarani, and he also saw the site of the young baobab tree. "The survivors of the catastrophe were standing in rows on the Mali road. The children were waving branches, a few young women were singing, but the adults were mute.

"Rejoice," said Balla Fasséké to Sundiata, "for your part you will have the bliss of rebuilding Niani, the city of your fathers, but nevermore will anyone rebuild Sosso out of its ruins. Men will lose recollection of the very site of Soumaoro's city."

With Sundiata peace and happiness entered Niani. Lovingly Sogolon's son had his native city rebuilt. He restored in the ancient style his father's old enclosure where he had grown up. People came from all the villages of Mali to settle in Niani. The walls had to be destroyed to enlarge the town, and new quarters were built for each kin group in the enormous army.

Sundiata had left his brother Manding Bory at Bagadou-Djeliba on the river. He was Sundiata's Kankoro Sigui, that is to say, viceroy. Manding Bory had looked after all the conquered countries. When reconstruction of the capital was finished he went to wage war in the south in order to frighten the forest peoples. He received an embassy from the country of Sangaran where a few Kondé clans had settled, and although these latter had not been represented at Kouroukan Fougan, Sundiata granted his alliance and they were placed on the same footing as the Kondés of the land of Do.

After a year Sundiata held a new assembly at Niani, but this one was the assembly of dignitaries and kings of the empire. The kings and notables of all the tribes came to Niani. The kings spoke of their administration and the dignitaries talked of their kings. Fakoli, the nephew of Soumaoro, having proved himself too independent, had to flee to evade the Mansa's anger. His lands were confiscated and the taxes of Sosso were payed directly into the granaries of Niani. In this way, every year, Sundiata gathered about him all the kings and notables so justice prevailed everywhere, for the kings were afraid of being denounced at Niani.

Djata's justice spared nobody. He followed the very word of God. He protected the weak against the strong and people would make journeys lasting several days to come and demand justice of him. Under his sun the upright man was rewarded and the wicked one punished.

In their new-found peace the villages knew prosperity again, for with Sundiata happiness had come into everyone's home. Vast fields of millet, rice, cotton, indigo and fonio surrounded the villages. Whoever worked always had something to live on. Each year long caravans carried the taxes in kind to Niani. You could go from village to village without fearing brigands. A thief would have his right hand chopped off and if he stole again he would be put to the sword.

New villages and new towns sprang up in Mali and elsewhere. "Dyulas," or traders, became numerous and during the reign of Sundiata the world knew happiness.

There are some kings who are powerful through their military strength. Everybody trembles before them, but when they die nothing but ill is spoken of them. Others do neither good nor ill and when they die they are forgotten. Others are feared because they have power, but they know how to use it and they are loved because they love justice. Sundiata belonged to this group. He was feared, but loved as well. He was the father of Mali and gave the world peace. After him the world has not seen a greater conqueror, for he was the seventh and last conqueror. He had made the capital of an empire out of his father's village, and Niani became the navel of the earth. In the most distant lands, Niani was talked of and foreigners said, "Travellers from Mali can tell lies with impunity," for Mali was a remote country for many peoples.

The griots, fine talkers that they were, used to boast of Niani and Mali saying: "If you want salt, go to Niani, for Niani is the camping place of the Sahel caravans. If you want gold, go to Niani, for Bouré, Bambougou and Wagadou work for Niani. If you want fine cloth, go to Niani, for the Mecca road passes by Niani. If you want fish, go to Niani, for it is there that the fishermen of Maouti and Djenné come to sell their catches. If you want meat, go to Niani, the country of the great hunters, and the land of the ox and the sheep. If you want to see an army, go to Niani, for it is there that the united forces of Mali are to be found. If you want to see a great king, go to Niani, for it is there that the son of Sogolon lives, the man with two names."

This is what the masters of the spoken word used to sing.

I must mention Kita among the great cities of the empire, the city of holy water which became the second capital of the Keitas. I shall mention vanished Tabon, the iron-gated city. I shall not forget Do, nor Kri, the motherland of Sogolon, the buffalo woman. I shall also cite Koukouba, Batamba and Kambasiga, towns of the sofas. I shall mention the town of Diaghan, Mema, the town of hospitality, and Wagadou where the descendants of Alexander the Great used to reign. How many heaped-up ruins, how many vanished cities! How many wildernesses peopled by the spirits of great kings! The silk-cotton trees and baobabs that you see in Mali are the only traces of extinct cities.

Eternal Mali

How many piled-up ruins, how much buried splendour! But all the deeds I have spoken of took place long ago and they all had Mali as their background. Kings have succeeded kings, but Mali has always remained the same.

Mali keeps its secrets jealously. There are things which the uninitiated will never know, for the griots, their depositaries, will never betray them. Maghan Sundiata, the last conqueror on earth, lies not far from Niani-Niani at Balandougou, the weir town.

After him many kings and many Mansas reigned over Mali and other towns sprang up and disappeared. Hajji Mansa Moussa, of illustrious memory, beloved of God, built houses at Mecca for pilgrims coming from Mali, but the towns which he founded have all disappeared, Karanina, Bouroun-Kouna—nothing more remains of these towns. Other kings carried Mali far beyond Djata's frontiers, for example Mansa

Samanka and Fadima Moussa, but none of them came near Djata.

Maghan Sundiata was unique. In his own time no one equalled him and after him no one had the ambition to surpass him. He left his mark on Mali for all time and his taboos still guide men in their conduct.

Mali is eternal. To convince yourself of what I have said go to Mali. At Tigan you will find the forest dear to Sundiata. There you will see Fakoli Koroma's plastron. Go to Kirikoroni near Niassola and you will see a tree which commemorates Sundiata's passing through these parts. Go to Bankoumana on the Niger and you will see Soumaoro's balafon, the balafon which is called Balguintiri. Go to Ka-ba and you will see the clearing of Kouroukan Fougan, where the great assembly took place which gave Sundiata's empire its constitution. Go to Krina near Ka-ba and you will see the bird that foretold the end to Soumaoro. At Keyla, near Ka-ba, you will find the royal drums belonging to Djolofin Mansa, king of Senegal, whom Djata defeated. But never try, wretch, to pierce the mystery which Mali hides from you. Do not go and disturb the spirits in their eternal rest. Do not ever go into the dead cities to question the past, for the spirits never forgive. Do not seek to know what is not to be known.

Men of today, how small you are beside your ancestors, and small in mind too, for you have trouble in grasping the meaning of my words. Sundiata rests near Niani-Niani, but his spirit lives on and today the Keitas still come and bow before the stone under which lies the father of Mali.

To acquire my knowledge I have journeyed all round Mali. At Kita I saw the mountain where the lake of holy water sleeps; at Segou, I learnt the history of the kings of Do and Kri; at Fadama, in Hamana, I heard the Kondé griots relate how the Keitas, Kondés and Kamaras conquered Wouroula. At Keyla, the village of the great masters, I learnt the origins of Mali and the art of speaking. Everywhere I was able to see and understand what my masters were teaching me, but between their hands I took an oath to teach only what is to be taught and to conceal what is to be kept concealed.

Creation Stories from around the World

The Creation Stories

—adapted by S.Z.

The earliest known creation myth is from the third millennium B.C.E. from Sumer. It says that first there was the goddess Nammu, the primeval sea. She gave birth to An, the sky god, and Ki, the earth god. Earth and sky were both solid elements, and they were joined together to produce Enlil, the god of air, who separated them. Enlil lit his realm by begetting Nanna, the moon god, who fathered Utu, the sun god. Enlil then impregnated Ki, who gave birth to Enki, the god of water and wisdom. Enki ordered the universe, but was unable to create man. This was done by the goddess Nintu who molded him out of clay.

There are several parallels between this myth and the Babylonian creation story in the *Enuma Elish*, which extend to Genesis, chapters one and two. The most obvious borrowing is the creation of man formed out of clay. In the *Enuma Elish*, the Babylonian warrior god Marduk slays Tiamat, who according to tradition is, like Nammu, the sea, represented as a dragon goddess. Marduk creates the heaven and earth from the two halves of Tiamat's body, and goes on to arrange the stars and planets. Marduk forms man out of the blood and bones of Kingu, a servant of the goddess Tiamat. This sequence of creation closely parallels the account in Genesis, chapter one.

Many scholars have pointed out the distinct parallels between the creation in the *Enuma Elish* and in chapter one of Genesis. A close reading of both shows that the Hebrew sacred writing has to be placed in the context of other Near Eastern sacred literatures, and that the Hebrews did not create their culture in a vacuum. They were, in fact, influenced by their neighbors. A close reading of the story of Marduk compared with Psalm 74:12–17 will also demonstrate this point, since it is structurally similar to the Marduk myth and portrays Yahweh as a warrior god: "You divided the sea by your might; you broke the heads of the dragon in the waters." This psalm, combined with a textual analysis of a God who divides the waters in Genesis chapter one, demonstrates the complexity of the Hebrew scriptures, particularly in regard to its development of monotheism.

There are many important traditions that include distinctive creation myths. There follow condensed retellings of a Sumarian and a Babylonian story, the Greek poet Hesiod's account of Greek creation stories, two Native American tales, and several African tales. Comparing and contrasting these with the creation story of Genesis should prove enlightening.

Atrahasis

A Babylonian Flood Myth

At the beginning, the gods—sky-god (Anu), Earth deity (Enlil), and god of the deep waters (Enki)—were alone in the universe. The Great Ones put many lesser gods to work digging canals to irrigate food crops, but after 40 years' hard labor they rebelled—so the Great Ones decided to create the human race to provide workers. They proceeded to slaughter a lesser god, mix his flesh and blood with clay, and feed it to 14 birth goddesses, who then bore the original 14 humans: seven males and seven females.

As the human race multiplied and spread over the Earth, they made so much noise that the Earth-god Enlil could not sleep. He sent a plague to kill some, but the wise king Atrahasis appealed to Enlil, and the plague ceased. But again the humans multiplied and made so much noise that Enlil could not sleep, so he sent a drought to Earth. Again, Atrahasis prayed until Enki intervened and, behind Enlil's back, sent rain through the storm god Adad. Once again the human race multiplied and became noisy; Enlil sent a second drought; but Enki again saved mankind—denying his fellow gods by sending fish in a whirlwind for humans to eat.

Finally, the major gods had a meeting and decided that never again should a god save mankind, but Enki refused to join in and laughed at the other gods' decision. Enlil then decided to take matters into his own hands and wipe out this troublesome mankind once and for all with a terrible flood.

Atrahasis foresaw the disaster in a dream and asked "his lord" Enki to show him its meaning. Enki instructed him to destroy his reed house, build a boat with the reeds and "spurn property and save life." The boat was to be roofed, waterproofed with pitch, and loaded with clean animals, fat animals from the farm and also birds and wild creatures.

After loading the animals, Atrahasis invited his people to a banquet, but sent his family to board the boat. He was heartbroken and ill as he anticipated the fate of the majority. Soon the storm god Adad thundered, and Atrahasis boarded his ship, sealed the door with pitch and cast off as the flood came and destroyed everything living. As the earth became dark, the mother goddess, Mami, repented agreeing to the destruction and denounced Enlil for killing her offspring. It stormed for seven days and nights, while some of the gods wept.

When the flood subsided, Atrahasis made an offering and the gods smelled the smoke and gathered round. Nintu, the birth goddess, berated the others for trying to destroy humanity and vowed she would remember the disaster always.

Tiamat and Marduk

A Babylon Creation Myth

Neither earth nor sky existed—nothing but a watery chaos in which the fresh waters of the sea, Apsu (imagined as male), mingled with the salt waters of the sea, Tiamat (imagined as female). At first there were no gods—but then Apsu engendered two gods, who were born of Tiamat. Generations of gods followed, all inhabiting a formless void. The shaping of the world still lay in the future.

Yet as soon as they came into being the gods introduced a new principle into the world—movement. Apsu and Tiamat represented rest, inertia; unimaginably old, they wanted only to be left in peace. The gods, on the contrary, were active, restless. When they came together to dance, it was too much for Apsu. He complained to Tiamat that such behavior was depriving him of rest by day, sleep at night—and announced his intention of smashing all the gods to bits.

Tiamat, as a mother, could not assent in the destruction of her offspring. But Apsu continued to plot their destruction, until the gods came to hear of it. Their reaction was panic—until Ea found a solution: by means of a magical spell he put Apsu to sleep. Then he stripped him of his crown and royal robe, killed him, and established his own abode above him. So the waters underground were mastered while Ea set up his temple at Eridu, on the waters of a lagoon.

Marduk was born at Eridu as Ea's son. A magnificent creature from birth onwards, supernaturally wise and strong, he is the real hero of the myth. His adventures began when his grandfather Anu created storm winds for him to play with. Now some of the gods were kept awake. The gods, kindred spirits to Apsu, succeeded where Apsu had failed: they persuaded Tiamat to take action herself against the main body of the gods, associates of Anu and Ea and Marduk—who after all were collectively responsible for depriving her of her consort Apsu.

Tiamat prepared for war and spawned troops to fight that war: monstrous serpents with sharp fangs, their bodies filled with poison. She even endowed these gruesome beings with a fearful, quasi-divine aura, so that anyone who looked on them would die of terror. And she added reinforcements: vipers, dragons, huge lions, mad dogs, mighty storm-demons, bisons, flying creatures, scorpion-men—all of them lethally equipped and thirsting for battle. To lead this host Tiamat appointed her second husband, the god Kingu—and to ensure his success she entrusted him with that supreme vehicle of power, the register of destinies.

When the news reached the gods, they were once more aghast. First Ea, that embodiment of wisdom, then Anu, that embodiment of authority, shrank back in terror at the sight of Tiamat. Finally the gods appealed to young Marduk. He agreed to tackle Tiamat, but on one condition: that the authority of all the gods should be given to him alone—in short, that he should be made king over the gods. This was granted. Marduk was given all the rights that went with kingship: power to promote and demote gods as he saw fit, authority to wage war, power to kill or spare prisoners of war.

Equipped with the royal insignia and armed with bow and arrows, a mace, and a net, Marduk filled himself with blazing fire and mounted his storm-chariot. Like a thunderstorm, preceded by lightnings, followed by storm-winds, he faced Tiamat and her allies. Kingu and his army were at once overcome with terror; only Tiamat held her ground. Marduk tackled her in single combat. As she opened her mouth to swallow him he drove his "evil wind" into her, jamming her mouth wide open and distending her belly An arrow shot into her gullet cut through her insides and tore her heart asunder.

Tiamat dead, her followers were captured, disarmed and made prisoner, and Kingu was deprived of the register of destinies. Now the young god was free to deploy his powers constructively. Standing on Tiamat's carcass he split her into two parts like a "shell-fish." Out of one half he made the sky and secured it: to prevent Tiamat's water from escaping he set bars in place and posted guards. In the newly created sky, at a spot immediately opposite the dwelling that his father had built over Apsu, he built an exact replica, his own heavenly dwelling. Next he made constellations and organized the calendar. The moon and the sun were instructed on how to conduct themselves. Finally Marduk made the earth, using the fluids in Tiamat's body to supply the rivers of Mesopotamia.

A retelling of the *Enuma Elish* from Babylon

From *The Theogony of Hesiod*

First the Void came into being, next broad-bosomed Earth, the solid and eternal home of all, and Eros [Desire], the most beautiful of the immortal gods, who in every man and every god softens the sinews and overpowers the prudent purpose of the mind. Out of Void came Darkness and black Night, and out of Night came Light and Day, her children conceived after union in love with Darkness. Earth first produced starry Sky [Uranus], equal in size with herself, to cover her on all sides. Next she produced the tall mountains, the pleasant haunts of the gods, and also gave birth to the barren waters, sea with its raging surges—all this without the passion of love. Thereafter she lay with Sky and gave birth to Ocean with its deep current, Coeus and Crius and Hyperion and Iapetus; Thea and Rhea and Themis [Law] and Mnemosyne [Memory]; also golden-crowned Phoebe and lovely Tethys. After these came cunning Cronus, the youngest and boldest of her children, who grew to hate the father who had begotten him.

Earth also gave birth to the violent Cyclopes who made and gave to Zeus the thunder and the lightning-bolt. A single eye stood in the middle of their foreheads, and their strength and power and skill were in their hands. There were also born to Earth and Sky three more children, big, strong, and horrible, Cottus and Briareus and Gyes. This unruly brood had a hundred monstrous hands sprouting from their shoulders, and fifty heads on top of their shoulders growing from their sturdy bodies. They had monstrous strength to match their huge size....

Of all the children born of Earth and Uranus these were the boldest, and their father hated them from the beginning. As each of them was about to be born, Sky would not let them reach the light of day; instead he hid them all away in the bowels of Mother Earth. Sky took pleasure in doing this evil. In spite of her enormous size, Earth felt the strain within her and groaned. Finally she thought of a cunning stratagem. She instantly produced a new metal, gray steel, and made a huge sickle. Then she laid the matter before her children; the anguish in her heart made her speak boldly: "My children, you have a savage father; if you will listen to me, we may be able to take vengeance for his evil outrage." But all the children were gripped with fear, and not one of them spoke a word. Then great Cronus, the cunning trickster, took courage and answered: "Mother, I am willing to carry through your plan. I have no respect for our infamous father, since he was the one who started the violence."

Enormous Earth was very pleased. She hid him in ambush and put in his hands the sickle with jagged teeth, and instructed him fully in her plot. Huge Uranus came, drawing night behind him and desiring to make love; he lay on top of earth, stretched all over her. Then from his ambush his son reached out with his left hand and with his right took the huge sickle with its long jagged teeth and quickly sheared the genitals from his own father and threw them away, backward over his shoulder. But that was not the end of them. The drops of blood that spurted from them were all taken in by Mother Earth, and in the course of the revolving years she gave birth to the powerful Erinyes [Spirits of Vengeance] and the huge Giants with shining armor and long spears. As for the organs themselves, for a long time they drifted round the sea just as they were when Cronus cut them off with the steel edge and threw them from the land into the waves of the ocean; then white foam issued from the divine flesh, and in the foam a girl began to grow. At Cyprus, the land surrounded by sea, she stepped out, a goddess, tender and beautiful, and round her slender feet the green grass shot up. She is called Aphrodite by gods and men. Eros [Desire] and beautiful Passion were her attendants both at her birth and at her first going to join the family of the gods. There she presides over the whispers and smiles and tricks which girls employ, and the sweet delight and tenderness of love.

Napi

A Native American Creation Story

According to one version of a Plains Indian creation story first written down in the 19th Century, in olden times the Sun was a great fiery chief who lived in his lodge in the sky. His principal servant was Napi, an immense being who did the Sun's bidding, so he wouldn't be distracted from keeping the Earth warm.

Napi was usually occupied with the Sun's many tasks, but one day he found himself with some free time and sat down to smoke his pipe near a spring. As he sat, he noticed some damp clay next to him, so he picked up some lumps and started to form them into shapes. He made a great many little sculptures out of the clay, then let them all dry in the sun. As they hardened, Napi smoked and studied them.

Finally, he picked one up, blew his breath on it, and said, "Go you now, my son. Be a Bighorn Sheep and live out on the plains." And the sheep galloped off.

Then Napi blew on the others, giving life to the Bear, the Antelope, the Beaver, the Badger, and many more. To each animal he gave a name and then sent them to where they were supposed to live.

One strange little clay shape was left, one with two legs, instead of four, and Napi smoked and looked at it for a long time. After a while, he blew the breath of life into it, and said, "Go you now, my son. Be a man. Live with the wolves, and hunt meat on the plains."

Napi thought he had done well, and that all the creatures would be happy. But a few days later, when he went to the spring again to smoke his pipe, all the animals came to complain. First, the Buffalo said "Grandfather, I cannot live in the mountains where you sent me. The hills are too steep, the rocks break my hooves, and there is no grass. I cannot live there."

The Bighorn Sheep complained that he could not live on the plains. "Grandfather," he said, "my hooves grow too fast there and curl up. There is no moss, no hills to climb, and my legs get weak." And the Antelope had similar complaints about living in the mountains with the Buffalo.

"Alright," said Napi, "I have thought how to fix this, and here is what we will do. My sons, I will give you each a home suited to you. You, Bighorn Sheep, go up to the mountains, and take the Goat and live there, too. Bear, my son, you go and live among the forested hills; Cougar, you go there also. Buffalo, my son, go and take Antelope and live in the plains and eat the grass there. Badger and Prairie Dog, go also to the plains and dig burrows in the earth, where you will find food. And Wolf, you will share the meat of the plains with Man."

So all the animals listened to Napi and went where he told them to live, and they have lived there and been content ever since. All except Man, who is never satisfied anywhere and always wants everything.

"The Old-One and the Earth, Sun, and People"

A Pacific Northwest Native American Myth

The Thompson Indians

A long time ago, before the world was formed, there lived a number of people together. They were the Stars, Moon, Sun, and Earth. The latter was a woman, and her husband was the Sun. The Earth-woman always found fault with her husband, and was disagreeable with him, saying he was nasty, ugly, and too hot. They had several children. At last the Sun felt annoyed at her grumbling, and deserted her. The Moon and the Stars, who were relatives of the Sun, also left her, and moved over to where the Sun had taken up his abode. When the Earth-woman saw that her husband and his friends had all deserted her, she became very sorrowful, and wept much. Now Old-One appeared, and transformed Sun, Moon, and Stars into those we see in the sky at the present day, and placed them all so that they should look on the Earth-woman, and she could look at them. He said, "Henceforth, you shall not desert people, nor hide yourselves, but shall remain where you can always be seen at night or by day. Henceforth you will look down on the Earth." Then he transformed the woman into the present earth. Her hair became the trees and grass; her flesh, the clay; her bones, the rocks; and her blood, the springs of water. Old-One said, "Henceforth you will be the earth, and people will live on you, and trample on your belly. You will be as their mother, for from you, bodies will spring, and to you they will go back. People will live as in your bosom, and sleep on your lap. They will derive nourishment from you, for you are fat; and they will utilize all parts of your body. You will no more weep when you see your children.... [And the Old-One said to the people] When you die, you will return to your mother's body. You will be covered with her flesh as a blanket, under which your bones will rest in peace."

African Tales

The Creation of Land

A Yoruba Myths of Creation

At the beginning everything was water. Then Oludumare the supreme god sent Obatala down from heaven to create the dry land. Obatala descended on a chain and he carried with him: a snail shell filled with earth, some pieces of crow, and a cock. When he arrived he placed the crow on the water, spread the earth over it and placed the cock on top. The cock immediately started to scratch and thus the land spread far and wide.

When the land had been created, the other Orisha [a lesser deity] descended from heaven in order to live on the land with Obatala.

The Creation of Man

A Yoruba Myths of Creation

Obatala made man out of earth. After shaping men and women he gave them to Oludumare to blow in the breath of life.

One day Obatala drank palm wine. Then he started to make hunchbacks and cripples, albinos and blind men.

From that day onward hunchbacks and albinos and all deformed persons are sacred to Obatala. But his worshippers are forbidden to drink palm wine.

Obatala is still the one who gives shape to the new babe in the mother's womb.

Mulungu and the Beasts

A Myth of the Yak Peoples from Northern Mozambique

In the beginning man was not, only Mulungu and his people, the beasts. They lived happily on earth.

One day a chameleon found a human pair in his fish trap. He had never seen such creatures before and he was surprised. The chameleon reported his discovery to Mulungu. Mulungu said, "Let us wait and see what the creatures will do."

The men started making fires. They set fire to the bush so that the beasts fled into the forest. Then the men set traps and killed Mulungu's people. At last Mulungu was compelled to leave the earth. Since he could not climb a tree he called for a spider.

The spider spun a thread up to the sky and down again. When he returned he said, "I have gone on high nicely, now you Mulungu go on high." And Mulungu ascended to the sky on the spider's thread to escape the wickedness of men.

Withdrawal of God

A Ngome Myth from Zaire

Akongo was not always as he is now. In the beginning the creator lived among men; but men were quarrelsome. One day they had a big quarrel and Akongo left them to themselves. He went and hid in the forest and nobody has seen him since. People today can't tell what he is like.

The Humanist Revival

The Humanist Revival is another way to refer to the Renaissance. "Renaissance" means "rebirth," and it is precisely the rebirth of ancient learning to which the term refers. Europe had passed through what some call the "Dark Ages." After the fall of Rome, Europe indeed was at a low ebb. Its economy lay in ruins, and the wonderful network of communication and trade built by the Romans had been destroyed. Europeans retreated to a world of village life and faced bands of marauding warriors who partook of an economy of plunder rather than production.

Under such grim circumstances learning and the productive arts were abandoned and all that was left between the people and pure savagery was the Christian Church. While the Islamic world flourished and became the center of learning, science, art and trade, Europe languished in its misery. The crusades, an ill-conceived assault upon Islam by Christian warriors hoping to reclaim the Holy Land, at least showed some signs of returning energy but hardly of the right kind as European nations squandered what little resource they had on their failed crusade.

In the latter stages of this bleak period Europe produced some remarkable cultural achievements. The Medieval period saw the construction of great Cathedrals that remain monuments to a total community devotion to God. Feudal manors supported a tightly knit social structure based upon a code of homage and responsibility from vassal to lord. Cities began to emerge, and with them new crafts and the guild corporations that protected and advanced these crafts. Literature, music, and the arts began to revive, first in the form of religious devotions.

The stirrings of renewal belong to the Italians in particular. Although there was no such nation as Italy, the several principalities of Italians—notably the city states of Florence, of Genoa, of Venice—became centers of trade, production, and banking. With economic success came the remarkable flourishing of the arts and the reclamation of ancient literary skill and philosophy. It is fitting to call this humanism, for at the center of the rebirth was the vigorous claim that human beings are at the center of importance. As merchants, and artists, and designers of new technologies, and politicians began to take command, it was obvious that man was the measure, if not of all things, of a great many of them.

We study Galileo, Machiavelli, and Shakespeare. It makes some sense to take the two Italians out of order, simply because it is easier to see the revolution that Galileo brings about in science than it is with Machiavelli and political science.

Galileo (1564–1642) designs his telescope and immediately publishes a shocking record of what he sees. The entire picture of the universe that had prevailed for thousands of years is overthrown in an instant. The "celestial bodies," far from being perfect, are revealed to be as irregular and imperfect as the earth. The earth is simply another ball in space—still a difficult thought for us. And worse yet, the earth is not at the center of it all, a bad blow to our self-esteem. And how did Galileo conclude all this? Not by going to the library and reading books, not by referring to the Bible, not by conversing with the authorities in the Church, and not even by referring to the appearances of things. His answer to the Cardinals who challenged him was to ask them to have a look for themselves. Direct experience and the careful collection of data was now to replace the authority of time-honored sources and institutions. Galileo had taken a walk outside of the cave and returned to tell what he saw. His reception was pretty much what Plato had predicted.

Niccolo Machiavelli (1469–1527) had brought about a similar shift in understanding in politics. Where Plato, for example, had tried to understand politics by constructing a perfect city (the "kallipolis"), Machiavelli asked instead what men had done in the past and what had worked and what had failed. Like Galileo, Machiavelli looked at things as they are instead of as they are supposed to be. And the answers his researches brought back were also irregular and highly disturbing. Although Machiavelli was attempting to figure out what to do to rescue his beloved city of Florence from additional indignities and plundering by foreign invaders, he wrote a book that continues to intrigue and haunt us, a book about political power and how it works that is as new as today's newspaper.

William Shakespeare (1564–1616) shares this humanist revolution with our Italians. Shakespeare also has a sharp eye for things as they are, and his characters, rather than representing types or fantastical personages, seem to be as real (or more real) than any of us. Shakespeare's plots, too, are well informed by real concerns and events that unfold according to real world plausibility. Compared to his Greek predecessors, Shakespeare explores his characters in far greater psychological depth. His language is ripe with conversational vigor and careful shading; he accords each speech to the individual character and the emotions that character is experiencing. Again, we see a highly expressive sense of realism, and a world that at the center follows the passage ways inscribed by human beings.

This rebirth of confidence and human arts and powers is one of the truly remarkable events in our history. Hundreds of years later, we remain the beneficiaries of these bold innovators who have taken their journey upward to the light.

Notes on Galileo

If you read the introduction by Stillman Drake with some care, you will recognize that Galileo isn't only making some discoveries about the heavens, but he is also introducing a new way of thinking about nature. The ancients, of course, had no way to observe the heavens in any kind of close detail. Instead, they tried their best to imagine what was there, guided by mathematics (and geometry)—i.e, activities of pure thoughts—and their ability to employ metaphor to establish relationships.

In such a fashion, they were able to conclude that the moon was a pure object, a sphere without irregularity. What, after all, is more perfect than a sphere? It has no beginning and no end (like God), and it has a central point from which all edges are equally distant. It represents mathematical perfection. Like all objects in the heavens, indeed, the moon is a celestial object representing the perfection of divinity. Only the earth, this sink of sin, has imperfection in it and therefore death (things come and go). The objects in the heavens are situated on crystal spheres, which rotate in their own fashion. To the ears of the morally and intellectually pure, there is a celestial music in their movement ("the music of the spheres"). Now, this is very pleasant thinking, and especially pleasant because it aligns the physical

Galileo invites a gentleman to observe the heavens "with the aid of a spyglass which I devised." Authority on astronomical subjects is no longer in ancient books but in the direct observations available to anyone willing to look. Corbis-Bettmann.

with the moral, Aristotle with the Church. There is surely great pleasure in constructing a world of "should be."

Galileo constructs a world of "actually is." The moon is made of the same perishable stuff as the earth, and is even more irregular than the surface of our planet. This science of the irregular goes even further when it maintains the heliocentric premise. While all our sense impressions tell us that the earth, our vantage point, is at the center of everything, the new science places the earth among several other objects that orbit the sun. This displacement is very troubling.

Galileo, like Machiavelli before him, creates a science of facts and not "imaginary republics." When the cardinals disputed his findings, Galileo could invite them to look for themselves through the "spyglass" he had made. The facts were there for all to see. The new science chases away the realm of metaphor, some say only to replace it with details that invite an even greater sort of wonder and new kinds of stories. However it is, after Galileo, nothing is the same.

Introduction to *The Starry Messenger*

Stillman Drake

I

A century ago Giacomo Leopardi, in an essay on fame, remarked that continual progress in science obscures the achievements of men who have devoted their lives to it. He took Galileo as an example. "Who reads the works of Galileo any more?' he asked. "Certainly they were quite remarkable in their time, yet any average physicist of our age is far superior to Galileo in his science."*

We may let Galileo retort in his own words. Writing in praise of William Gilbert, his great predecessor in the study of magnetism, he said: "I do not doubt that in the course of time this new science will be improved by further observations, and still more by true and conclusive proofs. But this need not diminish the glory of the first observer. My regard for the inventor of the harp is not made less by knowing that his instrument was very crudely constructed and still more crudely played. Rather, I admire him more than I do the hundreds of craftsmen who in ensuing centuries have brought this art to the highest perfection. . . . To apply oneself to great inventions, starting from the smallest beginnings, is no task for ordinary minds; to divine that wonderful arts lie hid behind trivial and childish things is a conception for superhuman talents."**

If modern physicists care nothing for the works of Galileo, that is a matter of taste and not merely one of progress. Modern poets still read Homer, and modern philosophers Plato, not only because those works are excellently written but also because they throw light upon the origins of poetry and philosophy—matters of special interest to poets and philosophers, and not without a certain value and attraction to the rest of us. Similarly the works of Galileo are well written, and throw light upon the origins of modern science; hence, even if few physicists are interested in them today, it does not necessarily follow that no one else ought to be.

Leopardi was an Italian man of letters, and it was natural that he should choose an Italian scientist to illustrate his idea. Unfortunately his reasoning implies that Galileo's books were intended to be read only, or at least primarily, by physicists. This is as if one were to suppose that Homer wrote only for poets, or Plato primarily for philosophers. But the fact is that Galileo scarcely ever got around to writing for physicists at all. Nearly without exception he wrote and published for the benefit of his countrymen in every walk of life who happened to share his insatiable curiosity about the universe and his ardent wish to discover the laws of nature. Indeed, there were no physicists in his day except philosophers, and these soon became his principal opponents. During most of his life Galileo ignored his professorial colleagues abroad by refusing to write in Latin. The readers he especially cultivated at home lived outside the universities, as we shall presently learn from his own words.

From *Discoveries and Opinions of Galileo* by Galileo Galilei. Copyright © 1957 by Stillman Drake. Used by permission of Doubleday, a division of Random House, Inc.

* Quoted from Enrico Persico, *Galileo e la fisica* (Milan, 1942). Cf. Leopardi, *Parini's Discourse on Glory*, ch. 11.

** *Dialogue Concerning the Two Chief World Systems* (Berkeley, 1953) pp. 406–7. (Cited hereafter as *Dialogue*.)

And they were delighted by his barbed attacks against pedantry as well as by the colloquial fashion in which he presented his own discoveries and opinions.

For the sake of argument we may grant that if in Leopardi's time the physicists had little reason to read the works of Galileo, they have still less reason now. But what about the rest of us? Science now dominates every phase of our culture to a degree that can hardly be exaggerated. It follows that we ought to have an interest in every truly significant phase of this phenomenon which so profoundly affects our lives and thoughts. To the most recent developments in science we are indeed almost obliged to pay some attention, but these are not necessarily its most significant aspects in a cultural sense. So far as scientific facts are concerned, no layman can hope to acquire more than the most superficial smattering; it is a commonplace that today even the best-informed man is not fully in touch with the latest developments in more than a few specialized fields. Facts, however, constitute only a part of what science has to teach us, and they make up neither the most interesting nor the most significant part in relation to the age in which we live. The truly influential and pervasive aspects of modern science are not its facts at all, but rather its method of inquiry and its criterion of truth.

Now those are precisely the things whose introduction created modern science. They were, moreover, first made clear in the writings of Galileo, and perhaps even today there is no other source from which they may be obtained more easily, more clearly, or more entertainingly by the nonscientific reader. It was to the man of general interests that Galileo originally addressed his works, and his remarkable success in explaining his method and revealing his criterion of truth is attested by the prompt and vigorous opposition which he inspired, led by professors who regarded the new method as injurious to philosophy and by priests who believed the new criterion of truth to be inimical to religion. All later attempts to explain scientific method and define scientific truth, however much more logical and thorough, have been considerably less effective.

We may be inclined to take it for granted that we fully understand the implications of scientific method; that we can easily tell whether or not any given statement may properly be called scientific. But the things we take for granted are not always those which we best understand. Thoughtful men of our time are often disturbed to hear the term "scientific" carelessly applied. Some say that it is a term not truly comprehended by anyone unless he has personally confronted laboratory problems or conscientiously designed experiments of his own. No doubt the best way to find out all that is implied by the word "scientific" is to become a scientist, but that is a course not open to everyone. A quite reasonable alternative is to read the writings of a man who was obliged to work out for himself, step by step, all the required procedures. Such a man was Galileo. If we wish to capture the true and living spirit of scientific inquiry without seeking this in the laboratory ourselves, then we cannot do better than to read his works.

II

The true originators of new lines of thought speak perforce not to specialists but to all who will listen. Hence it is not to Galileo, who wrote for laymen, so much as to Newton, who wrote for physicists, that Leopardi's explanation of neglect might truly apply. By 1687, when Newton published his monumental *Mathematical Principles of Natural Philosophy*, the educated layman for whom Galileo had written was left far behind. Newton's work had to be interpreted to the public by popularizers, and ever since his time we have depended upon such intermediaries for news of scientific advances and explanations of their significance to us. But Galileo was his own popularizer. He had to be, for he wanted both the methods and the rudiments of the new sciences he was founding to be understood by everyone who could read. Because his literary talents were considerable he was able to present his discoveries attractively and his opinions persuasively. The purely scientific material in his books was enlivened for the reader by the devastating sarcasm with which he was accustomed to puncture his pompous opponents. This sort of thing went out of fashion in physical science as rapidly as the old criteria of truth gave way to those which Galileo himself introduced. Thus Galileo's polemics in science rendered polemics in science obsolete. But at the same time they make his work eminently readable, and moreover they contribute substantially to our understanding of the origin and essential nature of modern scientific thought by giving us a glimpse of what preceded it.

Less than fifty years elapsed between Galileo's last book and Newton's first, but the changes that had taken place during that interval were enormous. The focus of intellectual interest had moved; the thin edge of the wedge which now separates the scientist from the public had been driven. Since we shall not have occasion to explore the changes that took place after Galileo's time, we may suggest them here by contrasting the two men themselves. Each spent a period as professor in a prominent university and then entered a sort of government service. But there all resemblance ends. Galileo's work had gone counter to every accepted tradition of his age; Newton's fitted intimately into the spirit of his time. Newton shrank from controversy and declined even to answer ignorant critics; Galileo was nothing if not combative, and used his most obstinate opponents as foils for his own purposes. Newton cared little for society, particularly that of women. Galileo thrived on companionship, and his mistress bore him three children. Newton tended to be abstemious, while Galileo delighted in wine—which he called "light held together by moisture"—and even when under close arrest he insisted on having a well-stocked cellar. Whenever he could find time he diverted himself by gardening, and he loved to observe the growth of plants; Newton, though he took an occasional turn in his garden, could not abide the sight of a weed there. Galileo took pleasure in conversing with artisans and applying his science to their practical problems; Newton preferred the precisely designed experiment and the deductive application of scientific laws. While Newton spent much of his life in alchemical pursuits and theological speculations, Galileo (almost alone in his age) ridiculed the alchemists, and ventured into theology only when it encroached upon his science. Galileo was personally skilled in art, talented in music, and devoted to literature; to Newton these appear to have remained passive enjoyments. In Galileo it is hard to say whether the qualities of the man of the Renaissance were dominant, or those of our own scientific age. Of Newton this question cannot even be asked.

III

The spirit of modern science, the conditions of its origin, and the reasons for its eventual triumph shine through the vestiges of older thought in the works of Galileo. But that is not all. The very issues for which Galileo fought are by no means settled, though for a long time they appeared to be. Now, after a period of quiescence, they have once again come vividly to life.

Science has afforded man an unprecedented mastery over nature. But to those who do not regard the conquest of nature as a proper end in itself, science has never appeared as an unmixed blessing. In the beginning, men who viewed it with distrust were very numerous and influential, and wherever they held power scientific thought was quickly subordinated to their authority. Gradually their number and influence diminished as the value to mankind of free scientific inquiry became apparent, and the effectiveness with which they could enforce their authority weakened. A final attempt to subordinate science to religion was made a century ago when the doctrine of organic evolution was propounded, and that attempt merely added to the prestige of science. As a result we became accustomed to seeing the protests of the antiscientific treated with impatience if not contempt.

But within the last decade events have created a new alarm concerning the unchecked progress of scientific knowledge. This time it is not the church but the state which feels morally obliged to impose external limitations upon the freedom of scientific inquiry and the communication of knowledge and opinion. This time the universities are impelled by public opinion and governmental policies to reconsider the scope of academic freedom, rather than by philosophical opinion and theological policies. But it is not the issues which are new, nor even the forms in which they confront us; only the center around which antiscientific forces rally has been changed. The issues are very similar to those which were fought out in the time of Galileo; the stakes are not much higher now than they were then, and the balance of power between the two sides is about the same as before.

Whether or not the fears of those who would now save us from science are any better grounded than were those of the men who opposed its unrestrained advance at the very beginning remains to be seen. Meanwhile it is instructive to reconsider the first battle that was waged in this long war of ideas—a battle which began with skirmishes between Galileo and his adversaries, and ended with their official but brief victory and his punishment. We shall be concerned only with those first skirmishes and the uneasy armistice that preceded the pitched battle; his ultimate defeat has been much discussed in other books, where these early but significant thrusts and parries of opinion have been relatively neglected.

Even in those early stages the forces that came into play were many and varied. It is of course impossible to do justice here to many of the factors that historically were involved, or even to avoid misrepresenting them to some extent by necessarily arbitrary selection and emphasis. Nevertheless a brief sketch of the background of the age will be attempted in the hope of making clearer the impact of Galileo's discoveries and opinions upon his contemporaries.

IV

European life in the Middle Ages displays even to the casual student a unifying web of religious beliefs and aspirations. Despite the myriad political sovereignties, despite the limited contact between men of different lands, despite the barriers of caste and a host of other conditions of daily life which tended to divide and separate men, all shared a common faith that dominated the intellectual spirit of the time. Scholarship was possible only through patronage except in rare and unusual cases, and it therefore tended to center upon the interests of the church that in return provided its chief support. The study and interpretation of texts occupied a high place among scholarly pursuits, and next after purely religious texts those of a philosophical nature received the most attention. Hence it appears that few practical problems of a physical nature were presented to scholars for consideration and solution, or indeed came to their attention in any way. Philosophical problems of physics were the subject of much discussion, but the method employed was that of logical argument as applied to the opinions of ancient writers, rather than direct observation and investigation. Not the laws of nature, but the divine will which underlay them, was considered the proper object of inquiry.

The pursuit of learning during the Middle Ages brought students into association around teachers of great reputation in many European cities. These associations, which at first were informal congregations of mature men in quest of specific instruction, gradually evolved into formal universities with recognized civil jurisdictions and having the power to confer degrees and to accredit teachers. As repositories of accumulated knowledge and as establishments responsible for the continuance of authoritative instruction, the universities necessarily became conservative institutions in every sense of the term. Although not controlled by the church, they were predominantly peopled by churchmen and every teacher was imbued with church doctrines. Because scholars came to them from every land and migrated continually from one university to another, all instruction was given in Latin. Thus the universities had great influence in preserving the religious emphasis of scholarly researches, in resisting the intrusion of unorthodox doctrines, and in maintaining a separation of language between scholars and men in other walks of life.

With the opening of the Renaissance, rifts appeared in the unity of medieval intellectual life. Preoccupation with religious matters began to give way before the wonders of reported explorations and discoveries. Intellectual interests and the desire for knowledge commenced to spread beyond the circles of professional scholarship into those of the nobility and the rising merchant class. Texts of works from classical antiquity and from oriental lands became available in much greater number and variety. While these were distracting some of the scholars from their traditional hair-splitting disputes, men of culture generally became curious about the origins of familiar things and the nature of alien ones. Even before any open split occurred within the church itself, a diversion of intellectual interest from God and his word into man and his works had taken place in the ranks of scholars. This humanist movement was originally neither hostile to, nor irreconcilable with, Christian theology; it was at first simply the opening of a new outlet for intellectual energy. Yet with its advent the monopoly of theology and philosophy upon the minds of men, so to speak, was broken. Humanism captured the imagination of a large proportion of the liveliest geniuses of the time, and though its intention was not to weaken religious institutions, its effect was to undermine their power.

V

Italy was pre-eminently the land of the Renaissance and the home of the humanist movement in its greatest vitality. Of the many ways in which this manifested itself, two are of primary interest here—the cultivation of the colloquial language and the spontaneous appearance of informal academies. Both these phenomena are inextricably linked with the origin of modern science and do much to explain its astonishingly rapid progress and its characteristic points of emphasis.

The origin of Italian literature and emergence of the Tuscan dialect as the literary language considerably antedates the Renaissance; in this the works of Dante, Petrarch and Boccaccio had been decisive. During the early Renaissance there was in fact a definite return to Latin, largely as a result of excessive admiration for and imitation of classical works. The scholarly language was also preferred for translations of newly discovered Greek texts. But before long the previous literary movement was resumed, and great pride came to be taken in the power and expressiveness of the native tongue. During the sixteenth century a large number of classic works were translated into Italian. The center of this movement was Florence, and a guiding spirit in it was the *Accademia degli Umidi*—the "Academy of Moistures." The founders of this organization were literary men who at first met merely to enjoy the pleasure of mutual discussion; as it grew in size and influence the society gained the patronage of the Grand Duke and was transformed into the Florentine Academy. In the cultivation of their mother tongue the academicians not only translated many classics but composed popular books of philosophy and science, and proposed the compilation of a complete dictionary of spoken Italian. This latter project was eventually carried out by an offshoot of the Florentine Academy which called itself the *Accademia della Crusca*—the "Academy of Chaff."

These fanciful names, and others adopted by many of the academies founded during this period everywhere in Italy, bespeak the half-serious, half-deprecatory attitude of men who pursued their studies outside the universities and who concentrated their attention upon subjects not recognized in orthodox and conservative curricula. Anything related to man was considered by them a legitimate object of research—his artistic as well as his philosophical, his literary as well as his political history. Music, architecture, sculpture, and painting found new vigor in activities independent of the requirements of the church, while their origins and history were eagerly traced among ruins and relics of the past and in allusions by classical authors. Often enough the men who undertook these tasks had been trained in the universities, but were not associated with them in any other way. Applying their education in the directions and fashions that best suited their own tastes, they in turn formed associations in order to communicate their ideas and spread their interests, yet without quite daring to represent themselves seriously as organizations of learned men in competition with or in opposition to the universities. The modest and sometimes even abject names which they therefore applied to their academies tend to hide the enormous importance of those institutions in the development of new fields of scholarship and the transmission of new knowledge to the public.

VI

We must next consider, though briefly, the state of astronomy prior to the time of Galileo. Although it was a good deal more scientific in its approach than was physics, still it bore little resemblance to the astronomy with which we are familiar today. Heavenly bodies were not regarded as physical objects made of ordinary matter. They were supposed instead to consist of some superior kind of substance free from all change. Their motions were investigated geometrically, but there was no thought of reducing their behavior to mechanical laws. Ancient Greek astronomers had adopted perfectly circular motion of all heavenly bodies as axiomatic. Philosophers supported this idea by asserting that only perfectly circular motion was appropriate to these perfect and unchanging bodies. Yet observation had revealed many difficulties in allowing simple circular motion around the earth to all the planets, among which the sun and moon were included at that time. Various devices had been invented to "save the appearances." In the Ptolemaic system* there were two. First, the centers of planetary orbits were placed at some distance from the center of the earth, and such orbits were called *eccentric*. Second, most planets were given small circular orbits around centers which

---

* This system took its name from Claudius Ptolemy, who brought it to completion about 150 A.D. It had been set forth by Hipparchus about three centuries earlier. Although the Ptolemaic system was defended by the followers of Aristotle, in reality it was the much older astronomy of Eudoxus (ca. 408–355 B.C.) to which Aristotle's statements were originally intended to apply.

moved in large circles around the earth, and these smaller circles were called *epicycles*. The latter were of special value in accounting for the fact that planets appear from time to time to slow down, stop, and temporarily reverse their motion among the fixed stars.*

With the passage of time and the accumulation of more accurate observations, a great number of eccentrics and epicycles had to be introduced in order to account for various irregularities. As a result, astronomical computations had become very complex. Even worse, in the eyes of mathematicians, was the increasing departure of the entire astronomical system from that symmetry and elegance which they and the philosophers expected of it. Early in the sixteenth century the Polish astronomer Copernicus, impelled by distaste for this inelegance, suggested placing the sun at or near the center of the heavens and giving the earth an orbit equivalent to that which had previously been assigned to the sun. This reduced the complexity of the calculations relatively little, but it had the very great advantage of introducing greater order and symmetry into man's conception of the heavens. At the same time it had the objectionable feature of removing the earth from its unique and distinguished situation at the center of the universe—a result which could not fail to antagonize the philosophers and above all the theologians, who taught that the heavenly bodies were created especially for the use and service of man, and that man was the subject of God's principal care and concern. The Copernican system had the further disadvantage of requiring vast and rapid motions of the earth, which seemed to contradict all common sense and everyday experience. Fully aware of the controversy this would create, Copernicus long refrained from publishing his ideas, though they circulated among other scholars in manuscript form and in a brief published description by one of his pupils. Eventually he was persuaded to publish them in full in the great book *De revolutionibus orbium coelestium*, the first copy of which was placed in his hands while he by on his deathbed in 1543. Unknown to Copernicus a preface had been anonymously added to his book by an officious clergyman, advising readers that the ideas in it were to be construed not literally but merely as hypotheses useful in simplifying the work of astronomers.

The storm of controversy which might have been expected did not take place at once. Most writers on astronomy continued to accept the arguments Ptolemy had set forth against any motion of the earth and against its being situated anywhere except at the center of the universe. A few adhered to the new system but made little effort to popularize it.

In 1572 a supernova and in 1577 an exceptionally conspicuous comet appeared and were carefully observed by the Danish astronomer, Tycho Brahe, who determined that both these phenomena were located in the celestial regions; that is, beyond the moon. The motion of the comet destroyed for him the possibility of solid crystalline spheres in the heavens such as were generally assumed to carry the stars and planets in their courses, for the comet would necessarily have penetrated them. These and other considerations induced him to forsake the Ptolemaic system, though he did not accept that of Copernicus. Instead he proposed a third alternative in which the earth remained fixed at the center of the universe while the moon and sun went around it, the planets revolving about the sun as it went around the earth.

This system offered a convenient escape for those who were aware of the untenability of the Ptolemaic view but could not accept a motion of the earth. It seems absurd to us, because we think of the planetary motions in terms of the laws of mechanics, but from a strictly geometrical point of view such as was taken by astronomers of that period the Tychonic system was equivalent to its rivals. Some well-informed astronomers connected with the Catholic Church, particularly among the Jesuits, supported Tycho, while those associated with the universities generally adhered to Ptolemy in deference to the philosophers who had linked his views with those of Aristotle. Hence the system of Copernicus was not widely discussed, and the great controversy over its merits was to await the time when it first came to the attention of large numbers of people with evidence in support of it that had not been known to its author.

---

* This happens, for example, when the earth in its annual course about the sun overtakes and passes (so to speak) one of the slower-moving outer planets.

VII

The old and distinguished Florentine family from which Galileo[*] was descended had originally been called Bonajuti. His great-great-grandfather had changed the family name to Galilei in honor of a brother, a noted physician of the fifteenth century whose given name was Galileo. Vincenzio Galilei, the father of the great scientist, was by trade a cloth merchant. He had moved the family from Florence to Pisa in the hope of improving its fortunes, and it was there that Galileo was born on February 15, 1564, about the same time as Shakespeare. Vincenzio was an accomplished musician, composer, and music theorist who wrote several books on these subjects that reveal some traits later characteristic of his son—a good knowledge of mathematics, distrust and even contempt of reliance upon authority, and a pugnacious temper. From him Galileo received instruction not only in music but probably in drawing, a field in which his skill is said to have been noteworthy and his judgment to have been such as to have enjoyed the respect of several noted artists. His love for music endured all his life, and he found solace in his years of adversity by playing on the lute.

Galileo's unusual abilities soon became sufficiently evident to justify his enrollment at the University of Pisa despite the family's meager funds. His father wished him to study medicine, but at that time university instruction in this subject consisted largely in lecturing from the texts of Galen and Aristotle and inculcating respect for those authors. This Galileo found very tiresome. He frequently disputed the doctrines thus handed down, and acquired a reputation among his professors as obstinate and argumentative. Meanwhile his own interest turned to mathematics, in which his first instruction is said to have come from outside the university at the hands of a teacher attached to the Tuscan court, Ostilio Ricci by name. Ricci was a practical rather than an academic mathematician, and it is probably significant that Galileo's introduction to mathematics came from such a source, as his ultimate great contributions to physics consisted in the application of mathematical concepts to observed phenomena—something that has never had much appeal to pure mathematicians.

At the age of twenty-five, with assistance from Guidobaldo dal Monte, a nobleman of great scientific talent, Galileo secured the chair of mathematics at the University of Pisa. It was a miserably paid post, but one that enabled him to pursue his real interests. During his professorship at Pisa he is said to have proved the incorrectness of Aristotle's ideas about the speeds of falling bodies by dropping unequal weights from the Leaning Tower. Such demonstrations, however conclusive they would be for us, had little effect upon the professors of philosophy, who felt an antipathy in any case toward this former pupil of theirs who had so often set himself up against the authority of the ancients. Either because of this mutual dislike or because of political pressure used against Galileo by an illegitimate son of the Grand Duke whom he had offended, the appointment at Pisa did not last long. In the summer of 1592, being then twenty-eight years old, Galileo left his native Tuscany for the Republic of Venice, having obtained the long-vacant chair of mathematics at the University of Padua.

VIII

Galileo remained at Padua for eighteen years. There he accomplished most of the work in mechanics which lies at the basis of modern physics, though he did not publish this until long afterward. It appears that he taught only conventional courses in mathematics and astronomy, but that he went somewhat beyond these in the private instruction which he gave to many students in order to supplement his salary. Several of these private pupils became lifelong friends who were able later to give him valuable support. At Padua he lived for several years with a Venetian woman named Marina Gamba, who bore him two daughters (in 1600 and 1601) and a son (in 1606). The years he spent at Padua were later recalled by Galileo as the happiest of his life. Yet while there he seems never to have abandoned the idea of returning to Tuscany, and when he succeeded in doing so he never revisited Padua or Venice despite many promises that he would.

Around the year 1597 Galileo devised a mathematical instrument which he called the "geomet-

---

[*] With the exception of rulers, Galileo is the last of the great Italians to enjoy the distinction of being known almost universally by his given name.

ric and military compass."* This was not unlike the proportional compass already in use elsewhere in Europe, though Galileo's model was an improvement in several respects and bore a number of additional scales of his own invention. The instrument enabled its user to solve a wide variety of problems, and in this period before the invention of logarithms it was invaluable to engineers and military men. There was sufficient demand for it to justify Galileo in employing a craftsman to produce his compasses in quantity for sale. A dispute originating over this invention first precipitated Galileo into the realm of polemic writing—a field in which he must have enjoyed himself a good deal, as he never again left it. This first literary feud arose as follows.

As early as 1601 Galileo had applied to the reigning family at Florence, the Medici, for appointment as tutor in mathematics to the heir apparent, Cosimo. This action was part of his quiet campaign to remain in the minds of the Tuscan rulers in the hope of returning there in a position of distinction. When Cosimo was old enough to benefit from such instruction, which was not until the summer vacation of 1605, Galileo was invited to give him private lessons. The course included instruction in the use of his compass. When Galileo returned to Padua he prepared his first book, published at his own house in 1606. It was in effect a handbook of instructions for buyers of the compass, and he dedicated it to the young prince. He wrote it in the Tuscan dialect partly to gratify his noble pupil and partly in order to assure its usefulness to practical men. For the use of scholars, especially those outside Italy, a Latin work on the same subject was promptly published by a student at Padua named Baldassar Capra. To Galileo's irritation a large part of Capra's production was merely a translation (or rather a Latin paraphrase) of Galileo's book; moreover, Capra practically accused Galileo of having stolen the invention from him. This combination of plagiarism and effrontery was too much for Galileo, who brought charges against the author before the university officials and had the book suppressed and Capra severely censured. But since not all copies were recovered, and Galileo feared that Capra's insolent charges might have damaged his reputation both in Italy and abroad, he published in 1607 a *Defense against the Calumnies and Impostures of Baldassar Capra*. In this very entertaining book Galileo first displayed those polemic talents which were soon to be brought to bear in much more serious subjects upon far more formidable opponents.

IX

The year 1609 was a turning point in the history of astronomy and in Galileo's own career. In that year the great German astronomer Johannes Kepler, with whom Galileo had been in correspondence intermittently for many years, published a momentous book called *Astronomia Nova*—the New Astronomy. This book contained the key to the true description of the planetary motions and foreshadowed their explanation decades later by Sir Isaac Newton. Kepler had been an assistant to Tycho, upon whose death in 1601 he acquired the Danish astronomer's incomparably accurate observations of the orbit of Mars. After many years of painstaking analysis applied to these data, Kepler had finally succeeded in discovering the source of confusion and error which had existed in all previous theories of the planets. His discovery was that the shape of a planetary orbit is not circular, but elliptical, and that the sun is not at the center but at one focus of the ellipse. This discovery cleared the path to the elimination of the eccentric circles and epicycles which had beset all previous astronomy.

The importance of Kepler's work was not immediately recognized, even by Galileo; in fact it was not fully appreciated until the time of Newton, who showed that Kepler's findings could be mathematically deduced from the law of universal gravitation. The *Astronomia Nova* was an enormous volume in which the crucial proof was buried amid a long description of Kepler's researches, including all the wrong leads and blind alleys which he took an unaccountable interest in relating. Moreover, Kepler's Latin was not always clear even to his contemporaries, and relatively few really studied his work. Even among those who did, there were not many men open-minded enough to consider seriously the possibility of noncircular orbits in the heavens. Hence, although Kepler's greatest contribution to astronomy belongs to the year 1609, it remained almost unknown until much later.

---

* This instrument, later called the "sector," served among other purpose that of today's proportional compass or proportional divider.

In the same year that Kepler in Germany was publishing his great but unappreciated contribution to theoretical astronomy, Galileo in Italy was preparing a contribution to observational astronomy which was destined to have a very different fate. In June or July of 1609 word reached him that a curious optical device had been invented in Holland, by means of which distant objects could be made to appear closer. The details were unknown to Galileo but he promptly set to work to figure them out for himself if he could. His own account of the events which followed will be found in the first and last of the works here translated. Whether or not he was the first to apply the telescope to celestial objects (a matter of perennial debate among historians of science), Galileo was certainly the first to publish the results of that momentous event.

The book describing Galileo's observations appeared in March 1610. Unlike Kepler's massive tome it was scarcely more than a pamphlet. There was no doubt in Galileo's mind of the authenticity and importance of the discoveries he announced, and since he wished to have them reach astronomers and philosophers all over Europe as quickly as possible he addressed his book to them and wrote it in Latin. He called it the *Sidereus Nuncius*, which was generally taken to mean "the messenger of the stars," not only by Galileo's contemporaries but by translators in succeeding generations.[*] Several booklets appeared in reply with titles referring to this "messenger," and there were allusions to this idea in many poems and literary works. Galileo did not correct these authors, but he may not have meant the title to be so interpreted. Several years later a Jesuit critic assailed him for having represented himself as the ambassador of heaven; in the margin of his copy of this attack Galileo noted that the word nuncius means "message" as well as "messenger," and asserted that he had intended only the humbler meaning. On the basis of this and other evidence, modern scholars have suggested that the word in question has always been mistranslated in this title. But it is now too late to change that, and perhaps even if the established tradition is incorrect it ought to be preserved. Se *non è vero, è ben trovato*; from a literary standpoint there can hardly be a question which word is preferable. And if "starry" is not quite synonymous with "sidereal," it may be excused as rather more intelligible.

---

[*] A previous English translation was published in 1880 by Edward Stafford Carlos. Other published translations include one into French by the Abbé Alexandre Tinelis, *Le Mesager Céleste* (Paris, 1681) and two into Italian; *Annunzio Siderio* (Florence, 1948, tr. Maria Timpanaro Cardini) and *Nunzio Siderio* (Milan, 1953, tr. Luisa Lanzillotta, in vol. 34 of *La Letteratura Italiana*.)

The Starry Messenger

Galileo Galilei

Revealing great, unusual, and remarkable spectacles, opening these to the consideration of every man, and especially of philosophers and astronomers;
AS OBSERVED By GALILEO GALILEI
Gentleman of Florence
Professor of Mathematics in the
University of Padua,
WITH THE AID OF A
SPYGLASS
lately invented by him,
In the surface of the Moon, in innumerable
Fixed Stars, in Nebulae, and above all
in FOUR PLANETS
swift revolving about Jupiter at
differing distances and periods,
and known to no one before the
Author recently perceived them
and decided that they should
be named
THE MEDICEAN STARS

Venice
1610

To the Most Serene Cosimo II De' Medici Fourth Grand Duke of Tuscany

Surely a distinguished public service has been rendered by those who have protected from envy the noble achievements of men who have excelled in virtue, and have thus preserved from oblivion and neglect those names which deserve immortality. In this way images sculptured in marble or cast in bronze have been handed down to posterity; to this we owe our statues, both pedestrian and equestrian; thus have we those columns and pyramids whose expense (as the poet says) reaches to the stars; finally, thus cities have been built to bear the names of men deemed worthy by posterity of commendation to all the ages. For the nature of the human mind is such that unless it is stimulated by images of things acting upon it from without, all remembrance of them passes easily away.

Looking to things even more stable and enduring, others have entrusted the immortal fame of illustrious men not to marble and metal but to the custody of the Muses and to imperishable literary monuments. But why dwell upon these things as though human wit were satisfied with earthly regions and had not dared advance beyond? For, seeking further, and well understanding that all human monuments ultimately perish through the violence of the elements or by old age, ingenuity has in fact found still more incorruptible monuments over which voracious time and envious age have been unable to assert any rights. Thus turning to the sky, man's wit has inscribed on the familiar and everlasting orbs of most bright stars the names of those whose eminent and godlike deeds have caused them to be accounted worthy of eternity in the company of the stars. And so the fame of Jupiter, of Mars, of Mercury, Hercules, and other heroes by whose names the stars are called, will not fade before the extinction of the stars themselves.

Yet this invention of human ingenuity, noble and admirable as it is, has for many centuries been out of style. Primeval heroes are in possession of those bright abodes, and hold them in their own right. In vain did the piety of Augustus attempt to elect Julius Caesar into their number, for when he tried to give the name of "Julian" to a star which appeared in his time (one of those bodies which the Greeks call "comets" and which the Romans likewise named for their hairy appearance), it vanished in a brief time and mocked his too ambitious wish. But we are able, most serene Prince, to read Your Highness in the heavens far more accurately and auspiciously. For scarce have the immortal graces of your spirit begun to shine on earth when in the heavens bright stars appear as tongues to tell and celebrate your exceeding virtues to all time. Behold, then, four stars reserved to bear your famous name; bodies which belong not to the inconspicuous multitude of fixed stars, but to the bright ranks of the planets. Variously moving about most noble Jupiter as children of his own, they complete their orbits with marvelous velocity—at the same time executing with one harmonious accord mighty revolutions every dozen years about the center of the universe; that is, the sun.*

Indeed, the Maker of the stars himself has seemed by clear indications to direct that I assign to these new planets Your Highness's famous name in preference to all others. For just as these stars, like children worthy of their sire, never leave the side of Jupiter by any appreciable distance, so (as indeed who does not know?) clemency, kindness of heart, gentleness of manner, splendor of royal blood, nobility in public affairs, and excellency of authority and rule have all fixed their abode and habitation in Your Highness. And who, I ask once more, does not know that all these virtues emanate from the benign star of Jupiter, next after God as the source of all things good? Jupiter; Jupiter, I say, at the instant of Your Highness's birth, having already emerged from the turbid mists of the horizon and occupied the midst of the heavens, illuminating the eastern sky from his own royal house, looked out from that exalted throne upon your auspicious birth and poured forth all his splendor and majesty in order that your tender body and your mind (already adorned by God with the most noble ornaments) might imbibe with their first breath that universal influence and power.

But why should I employ mere plausible arguments, when I may prove my conclusion absolutely? It pleased Almighty God that I should instruct Your Highness in mathematics, which I did four years ago at that time of year when it is

---

* This is the first published intimation by Galileo that he accepted the Copernican system. Tycho had made Jupiter revolve about the sun, but considered the earth to be the center of the universe. It was not until 1613, however, that Galileo unequivocally supported Copernicus in print.

customary to rest from the most exacting studies. And since clearly it was mine by divine will to serve Your Highness and thus to receive from near at hand the rays of your surpassing clemency and beneficence, what wonder is it that my heart is so inflamed as to think both day and night of little else than how I, who am indeed your subject not only by choice but by birth and lineage, may become known to you as most grateful and most anxious for your glory? And so, most serene Cosimo, having discovered under your patronage these stars unknown to every astronomer before me, I have with good right decided to designate them by the august name of your family. And if I am first to have investigated them, who can justly blame me if I likewise name them, calling them the Medicean Stars, in the hope that this name will bring as much honor to them as the names of other heroes have bestowed on other stars? For, to say nothing of Your Highness's most serene ancestors, whose everlasting glory is testified by the monuments of all history, your virtue alone, most worthy Sire, can confer upon these stars an immortal name. No one can doubt that you will fulfill those expectations, high though they are, which you have aroused by the auspicious beginning of your reign, and will not only meet but far surpass them. Thus when you have conquered your equals you may still vie with yourself, and you and your greatness will become greater every day.

Accept then, most clement Prince, this gentle glory reserved by the stars for you. May you long enjoy those blessings which are sent to you not so much from the stars as from God, their Maker and their Governor.

Your Highness's most devoted servant,
GALILEO GALILEI

PADUA, March 12, 1610

Astronomical Message

Which contains and explains recent observations made with the aid of a new spyglass* concerning the surface of the moon, the Milky Way, nebulous stars, and innumerable fixed stars, as well as four planets never before seen, and now named THE MEDICEAN STARS

Great indeed are the things which in this brief treatise I propose for observation and consideration by all students of nature. I say great because of the excellence of the subject itself, the entirely unexpected and novel character of these things, and finally because of the instrument by means of which they have been revealed to our senses.

Surely it is a great thing to increase the numerous host of fixed stars previously visible to the unaided vision, adding countless more which have never before been seen, exposing these plainly to the eye in numbers ten times exceeding the old and familiar stars.

It is a very beautiful thing, and most gratifying to the sight, to behold the body of the moon, distant from us almost sixty earthly radii,** as if it were no farther away than two such measures—so that its diameter appears almost thirty times larger, its surface nearly nine hundred times, and its volume twenty-seven thousand times as large as when viewed with the naked eye. In this way one may learn with all the certainty of sense evidence that the moon is not robed in a smooth and polished surface but is in fact rough and uneven, covered everywhere, just like the earth's surface, with huge prominences, deep valleys, and chasms.

Again, it seems to me a matter of no small importance to have ended the dispute about the Milky Way by making its nature manifest to the very senses as well as to the intellect. Similarly it will be a pleasant and elegant thing to demonstrate that the nature of those stars which astronomers have previously called "nebulous" is far different from what has been believed hitherto. But what surpasses all wonders by far, and what particularly moves us to seek the attention of all astronomers and philosophers, is the discovery of four wandering stars not known or observed by any man before us. Like Venus and Mercury, which have their own periods about the sun, these have theirs about a certain star that is conspicuous among those already known, which they sometimes precede and sometimes follow, without ever departing from it beyond certain limits. All these facts were discovered and observed by me not many days ago with the aid of a spyglass which I devised, after first being illuminated by divine grace. Perhaps other things, still more remarkable, will in time be discovered by me or by other observers with the aid of such an instrument, the form and construction of which I shall first briefly explain, as well as the occasion of its having been devised. Afterwards I shall relate the story of the observations I have made.

About ten months ago a report reached my ears that a certain Fleming*** had constructed a spyglass by means of which visible objects, though very distant from the eye of the observer, were distinctly seen as if nearby. Of this truly remarkable effect several experiences were related, to which some persons gave credence while others denied them. A few days later the report was confirmed to me in a letter from a noble Frenchman at Paris, Jacques Badovere,**** which caused me to apply myself wholeheartedly to inquire into the means by which I might arrive at the invention of a similar instrument. This I did shortly afterwards, my basis being the theory of refraction. First I prepared a tube of

---

* The word "telescope" was not coined until 1611. A detailed account of its origin is given by Edward Rosen in *The Naming of the Telescope* (New York, 1947). In the present translation the modern term has been introduced for the sake of dignity and ease of reading, but only after the passage in which Galileo describes the circumstances which led him to construct the instrument (pp. 28–29).

** The original text reads "diameters" here and in another place. That this error was Galileo's and not the printer's has been convincingly shown by Edward Rosen (*Isis*, 1952, pp. 344 ff.). The slip was a curious one, as astronomers of all schools had long agreed that the maximum distance of the moon was approximately sixty terrestrial radii. Still more curious is the fact that neither Kepler nor any other correspondent appears to have called Galileo's attention to this error; not even a friend who ventured to criticize the calculations in this very passage.

*** Credit for the original invention is generally assigned to Hans Lipperhey, a lens grinder in Holland who chanced upon this property of combined lenses and applied for a patent on it in 1608.

**** Badovere studied in Italy toward the close of the sixteenth century and is said to have been a pupil of Galileo's about 1598. When he wrote concerning the new instrument in 1609 he was in the French diplomatic service at Paris, where he died in 1620.

lead, at the ends of which I fitted two glass lenses, both plane on one side while on the other side one was spherically convex and the other concave. Then placing my eye near the concave lens I perceived objects satisfactorily large and near, for they appeared three times closer and nine times larger than when seen with the naked eye alone. Next I constructed another one, more accurate, which represented objects as enlarged more than sixty times. Finally, sparing neither labor nor expense, I succeeded in constructing for myself so excellent an instrument that objects seen by means of it appeared nearly one thousand times larger and over thirty times closer than when regarded with our natural vision.

It would be superfluous to enumerate the number and importance of the advantages of such an instrument at sea as well as on land. But forsaking terrestrial observations, I turned to celestial ones, and first I saw the moon from as near at hand as if it were scarcely two terrestrial radii away. After that I observed often with wondering delight both the planets and the fixed stars, and since I saw these latter to be very crowded, I began to seek (and eventually found) a method by which I might measure their distances apart.

Here it is appropriate to convey certain cautions to all who intend to undertake observations of this sort, for in the first place it is necessary to prepare quite a perfect telescope, which will show all objects bright, distinct, and free from any haziness, while magnifying them at least four hundred times and thus showing them twenty times closer. Unless the instrument is of this kind it will be vain to attempt to observe all the things which I have seen in the heavens, and which will presently be set forth. Now in order to determine without much trouble the magnifying power of an instrument, trace on paper the contour of two circles or two squares of which one is four hundred times as large as the other, as it will be when the diameter of one is twenty times that of the other. Then, with both these figures attached to the same wall, observe them simultaneously, from a distance, looking at the smaller one through the telescope and at the larger one with the other eye unaided. This may be done without inconvenience while holding both eyes open at the same time; the two figures will appear to be of the same size if the instrument magnifies objects in the desired proportion.

Such an instrument having been prepared, we seek a method of measuring distances apart. This we shall accomplish by the following contrivance.

Let ABCD be the tube and E be the eye of the observer. Then if there were no lenses in the tube, the rays would reach the object FG along the straight lines ECF and EDG. But when the lenses have been inserted, the rays go along the refracted lines ECH and EDI; thus they are brought closer together, and those which were previously directed freely to the object FG now include only the portion of it HI. The ratio of the distance EH to the line HI then being found, one may by means of a table of sines determine the size of the angle formed at the eye by the object HI, which we shall find to be but a few minutes of arc. Now, if to the lens CD we fit thin plates, some pierced with larger and some with smaller apertures, putting now one plate and now another over the lens as required, we may form at pleasure different angles subtending more or fewer minutes of arc, and by this means we may easily measure the intervals between stars which are but a few minutes apart, with no greater error than one or two minutes. And for the present let it suffice that we have touched lightly on these matters and scarcely more than mentioned them, as on some other occasion we shall explain the entire theory of this instrument.

Now let us review the observations made during the past two months, once more inviting the attention of all who are eager for true philosophy to the first steps of such important contemplations. Let us speak first of that surface of the moon which faces us. For greater clarity I distinguish two parts of this surface, a lighter and a darker; the lighter part seems to surround and to pervade the whole hemisphere, while the darker part discolors the moon's surface like a kind of cloud, and makes it appear covered with spots. Now those spots which are fairly dark and rather large are plain to everyone and have been seen throughout the ages; these I shall call the "large" or "ancient" spots, distinguishing them from others that are smaller in size but so numerous as to occur all over the lunar surface, and especially the lighter part. The latter spots had never been seen by anyone before me. From observations of these spots repeated many times I have been led to the opinion and conviction that the surface of the moon is not smooth, uniform, and precisely spherical as a great number of philosophers believe it (and the other heavenly bodies) to be, but is uneven, rough, and full of cavities and prominences, being not unlike the face of the earth, relieved by chains of mountains and deep valleys. The things I have seen by which I was enabled to draw this conclusion are as follows.

On the fourth or fifth day after new moon, when the moon is seen with brilliant horns, the boundary which divides the dark part from the light does not extend uniformly in an oval line as would happen on a perfectly spherical solid, but traces out an uneven, rough, and very wavy line as shown in the figure below. Indeed, many luminous excrescences extend beyond the boundary into the darker portion, while on the other hand some dark patches invade the illuminated part. Moreover a great quantity of small blackish spots, entirely separated from the dark region, are scattered almost all over the area illuminated by the sun with the exception only of that part which is occupied by the large and ancient spots. Let us note, however, that the said small spots always agree in having their blackened parts directed toward the sun, while on the side opposite the sun they are crowned with bright contours, like shining summits. There is a similar sight on earth about sunrise, when we behold the valleys not yet flooded with light though the mountains surrounding them are already ablaze with glowing splendor on the side opposite the sun. And just as the shadows in the hollows on earth diminish in size as the sun rises higher, so these spots on the moon lose their blackness as the illuminated region grows larger and larger.

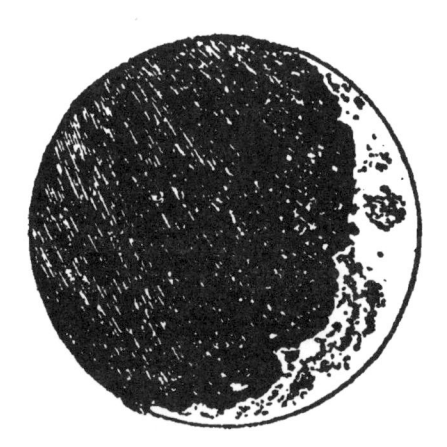

Again, not only are the boundaries of shadow and light in the moon seen to be uneven and wavy, but still more astonishingly many bright points appear within the darkened portion of the moon, completely divided and separated from the illuminated part and at a considerable distance from it. After a time these gradually increase in size and brightness, and an hour or two later they become joined with the rest of the lighted part which has now increased in size. Meanwhile more and more peaks shoot up as if sprouting now here, now there, lighting up within the shadowed portion; these become larger, and finally they too are united with that same luminous surface which extends ever further. An illustration of this is to be seen in the figure above. And on the earth, before the rising of the sun, are not the highest peaks of the mountains illuminated by the sun's rays while the plains remain in shadow? Does not the light go on spreading while the larger central parts of those mountains are becoming illuminated? And when the sun has finally risen, does not the illumination of plains and hills finally become one? But on the moon the variety of elevations and depressions appears to surpass in every way the roughness of the terrestrial surface, as we shall demonstrate further on.

At present I cannot pass over in silence something worthy of consideration which I observed when the moon was approaching first quarter, as shown in the previous figure. Into the luminous part there extended a great dark gulf in the neighborhood of the lower cusp. When I had observed it for a long time and had seen it completely dark, a bright peak began to emerge, a little below its center, after about two hours. Gradually growing, this presented itself in a triangular shape, remaining completely detached and separated from the lighted surface. Around it three other small points soon began to shine, and finally, when the moon was about to set, this triangular shape (which had meanwhile become more widely extended) joined with the rest of the illuminated region and suddenly burst into the gulf of shadow like a vast promontory of light, surrounded still by the three bright peaks already mentioned. Beyond the ends of the cusps, both above and below, certain bright points emerged which were quite detached from the remaining lighted part, as may be seen depicted in the same figure. There were also a great number of dark spots in both the horns, especially in the lower one; those nearest the boundary of light and shadow appeared larger and darker, while those more distant from the boundary were not so dark and distinct. But in all cases, as we have mentioned earlier, the blackish portion of each spot is turned toward the source of the sun's radiance, while a bright rim surrounds the spot on the side away from the sun in the direction of the shadowy region of the moon. This part of the moon's surface, where it is spotted as the tail of a peacock is sprinkled with azure eyes, resembles those glass vases which have been plunged while still hot into cold water and have thus acquired a crackled and wavy surface, from which they receive their common name of "ice-cups."

As to the large lunar spots, these are not seen to be broken in the above manner and full of cavities and prominences; rather, they are even and uniform, and brighter patches crop up only here and there. Hence if anyone wished to revive the old Pythagorean* opinion that the moon is like another earth, its brighter part might very fitly represent the surface of the land and its darker region that of the water. I have never doubted that if our globe were seen from afar when flooded with sunlight, the land regions would appear brighter and the watery regions darker.** The large spots in the moon are also seen to be less elevated than the brighter tract, for whether the moon is waxing or waning there are always seen, here and there along its boundary of light and shadow, certain ridges of brighter hue around the large spots (and we have attended to this in preparing the diagrams); the edges of these spots are not only lower, but also more uniform, being uninterrupted by peaks or ruggedness.

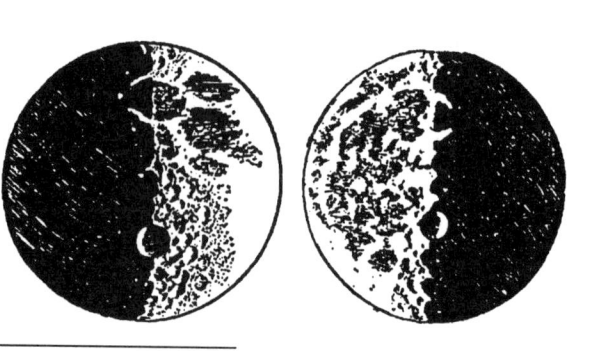

Near the large spots the brighter part stands out particularly in such a way that before first quarter and toward last quarter, in the vicinity of a certain spot in the upper (or northern) region of the moon, some vast prominences arise both above and below as shown in the figures reproduced below. Before last quarter this same spot is seen to be walled about with certain blacker contours which, like the loftiest mountaintops, appear darker on the side away from the sun and brighter on that which faces the sun. (This is the opposite of what happens in the cavities, for there the part away from the sun appears brilliant, while that which is turned toward the sun is dark and in shadow.) After a time, when the lighted portion of the moon's surface has diminished in size and when all (or nearly all) the said spot is covered with shadow, the brighter ridges of the mountains gradually emerge from the shade. This double aspect of the spot is illustrated in the ensuing figures.

There is another thing which I must not omit, for I beheld it not without a certain wonder; this is that almost in the center of the moon there is a cavity larger than all the rest and perfectly round in shape. I have observed it near both first and last quarters, and have tried to represent it as correctly as possible in the second of the above figures.

As to light and shade, it offers the same appearance as would a region like Bohemia*** if that

---

* Pythagoras was a mathematician and philosopher of the sixth century B.C., a semilegendary figure whose followers were credited at Galileo's time with having anticipated the Copernican system. This tradition was based upon misunderstanding. The Pythagoreans made the earth revolve about a "central fire" whose light and heat were reflected to the earth by the sun.
** Leonardo da Vinci had previously suggested that the dark and light regions of the moon were bodies of land and water, though Galileo probably did not know this. Da Vinci, however, had mistakenly supposed that the water would appear brighter than the land.
*** This casual comparison between a part of the moon and a specific region on earth was later the basis of much trouble for Galileo; see the letter of Piero Dini, p. 158. Even in antiquity the idea that the moon (or any other heavenly body) was of the same nature as the earth had been dangerous to hold. The Athenians banished the philosopher Anaxagoras for teaching such notions, and charged Socrates with blasphemy for repeating them.

were enclosed on all sides by very lofty mountains arranged exactly in a circle. Indeed, this area on the moon is surrounded by such enormous peaks that the bounding edge adjacent to the dark portion of the moon is seen to be bathed in sunlight before the boundary of light and shadow reaches halfway across the same space. As in other spots, its shaded portion faces the sun while its lighted part is toward the dark side of the moon; and for a third time I draw attention to this as a very cogent proof of the ruggedness and unevenness that pervades all the bright region of the moon. Of these spots, moreover, those are always darkest which touch the boundary line between light and shadow, while those farther off appear both smaller and less dark, so that when the moon ultimately becomes full (at opposition* to the sun), the shade of the cavities is distinguished from the light of the places in relief by a subdued and very tenuous separation.

The things we have reviewed are to be seen in the brighter region of the moon. In the large spots, no such contrast of depressions and prominences is perceived as that which we are compelled to recognize in the brighter parts by the changes of aspect that occur under varying illumination by the sun's rays throughout the multiplicity of positions from which the latter reach the moon. In the large spots there exist some holes rather darker than the rest, as we have shown in the illustrations. Yet these present always the same appearance, and their darkness is neither intensified nor diminished, although with some minute difference they appear sometimes a little more shaded and sometimes a little lighter according as the rays of the sun fall on them more or less obliquely. Moreover, they join with the neighboring regions of the spots in a gentle linkage, the boundaries mixing and mingling. It is quite different with the spots which occupy the brighter surface of the moon; these, like precipitous crags having rough and jagged peaks, stand out starkly in sharp contrasts of light and shade. And inside the large spots there are observed certain other zones that are brighter, some of them very bright indeed. Still, both these and the darker parts present always the same appearance; there is no change either of shape or of light and shadow; hence one may affirm beyond any doubt that they owe their appearance to some real dissimilarity of parts.

They cannot be attributed merely to irregularity of shape, wherein shadows move in consequence of varied illuminations from the sun, as indeed is the case with the other, smaller, spots which occupy the brighter part of the moon and which change, grow, shrink, or disappear from one day to the next, as owing their origin only to shadows of prominences.

But here I foresee that many persons will be assailed by uncertainty and drawn into a grave difficulty, feeling constrained to doubt a conclusion already explained and confirmed by many phenomena. If that part of the lunar surface which reflects sunlight more brightly is full of chasms (that is, of countless prominences and hollows), why is it that the western edge of the waxing moon, the eastern edge of the waning moon and the entire periphery of the full moon are not seen to be uneven, rough, and wavy? On the contrary they look as precisely round as if they were drawn with a compass; and yet the whole periphery consists of that brighter lunar substance which we have declared to be filled with heights and chasms. In fact not a single one of the great spots extends to the extreme periphery of the moon, but all are grouped together at a distance from the edge.

Now let me explain the twofold reason for this troublesome fact, and in turn give a double solution to the difficulty. In the first place, if the protuberances and cavities in the lunar body existed only along the extreme edge of the circular periphery bounding the visible hemisphere, the moon might (indeed, would necessarily) look to us almost like a toothed wheel, terminated by a warty or wavy edge. Imagine, however, that there is not a single series of prominences arranged only along the very circumference, but a great many ranges of mountains together with their valleys and canyons disposed in ranks near the edge of the moon, and not only in the hemisphere visible to us but everywhere near the boundary line of the two hemispheres. Then an eye viewing them from afar will not be able to detect the separation of prominences by cavities, because the intervals between the mountains located in a given circle or a given chain will be hidden by the interposition of other heights situated in yet other ranges. This will be especially true if the eye of the observer is placed in the same straight line with the summits of these ele-

---

* Opposition of the sun and moon occurs when they are in line with the earth between them (full moon, or lunar eclipse); conjunction, when they are in line on the same side of the earth (new moon, or eclipse of the sun).

vations. Thus on earth the summits of several mountains close together appear to be situated in one plane if the spectator is a long way off and is placed at an equal elevation. Similarly in a rough sea the tops of the waves seem to lie in one plane, though between one high crest and another there are many gulfs and chasms of such depth as not only to hide the hulls but even the bulwarks, masts, and rigging of stately ships. Now since there are many chains of mountains and chasms on the moon in addition to those around its periphery, and since the eye, regarding these from a great distance, lies nearly in the plane of their summits, no one need wonder that they appear as arranged in a regular and unbroken line.

To the above explanation another may be added; namely, that there exists around the body of the moon, just as around the earth, a globe of some substance denser than the rest of the aether.* This may serve to receive and reflect the sun's radiations without being sufficiently opaque to prevent our seeing through it, especially when it is not illuminated. Such a globe, lighted by the sun's rays, makes the body of the moon appear larger than it really is, and if it were thicker it would be able to prevent our seeing the actual body of the moon. And it actually is thicker near the circumference of the moon; I do not mean in an absolute sense, but relative, to the rays of our vision, which cut it obliquely there. Thus it may obstruct our vision, especially when it is lighted, and cloak the lunar periphery that is exposed to the sun. This may be more clearly understood from the figure below, in which the body of the moon, ABC, is surrounded by the vaporous globe DEG.

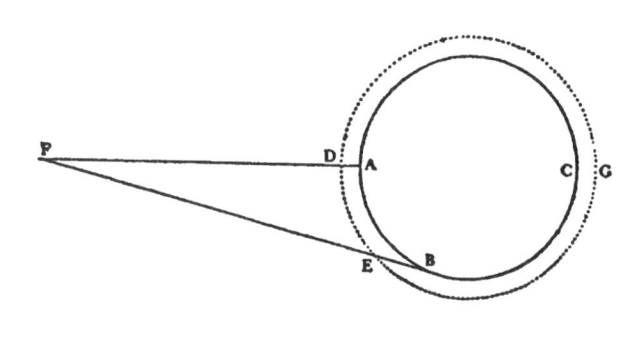

The eyesight from F reaches the moon in the central region, at A for example, through a lesser thickness of the vapors DA, while toward the extreme edges a deeper stratum of vapors, EB, limits and shuts out our sight. One indication of this is that the illuminated portion of the moon appears to be larger in circumference than the rest of the orb, which lies in shadow. And perhaps this same cause will appeal to some as reasonably explaining why the larger spots on the moon are nowhere seen to reach the very edge, probable though it is that some should occur there. Possibly they are invisible by being hidden under a thicker and more luminous mass of vapors.

That the lighter surface of the moon is everywhere dotted with protuberances and gaps has, I think, been made sufficiently clear from the appearances already explained. It remains for me to speak of their dimensions, and to show that the earth's irregularities are far less than those of the moon. I mean that they are absolutely less, and not merely in relation to the sizes of the respective globes. This is plainly demonstrated as follows.

I had often observed, in various situations of the moon with respect to the sun, that some summits within the shadowy portion appeared lighted, though lying some distance from the boundary of the light. By comparing this separation to the whole diameter of the moon, I found that it sometimes exceeded one-twentieth of the diameter. Accordingly, let CAF be a great circle of the lunar body, E its center, and CF a diameter, which is to the diameter of the earth as two is to seven.

Since according to very precise observations the diameter of the earth is seven thousand miles, CF will be two thousand, CE one thousand, and one-twentieth of CF will be one hundred miles. Now let CF be the diameter of the great circle which divides the light part of the moon from the dark part (for because of the very great distance of the sun from the moon, this does not differ appreciably from a great circle), and let A be distant from C by one-twentieth of this. Draw the radius EA, which, when produced, cuts the tangent line GCD (representing the illuminating ray) in the point D. Then the arc CA, or rather the straight line CD, will consist of one hundred units whereof CE contains one thousand, and the

---

* The aether, or "ever-moving," was the special substance of which the sky and all the heavenly bodies were supposed to be made, a substance essentially different from all the earthly "elements." In later years Galileo abandoned his suggestion here that the moon has a vaporous atmosphere.

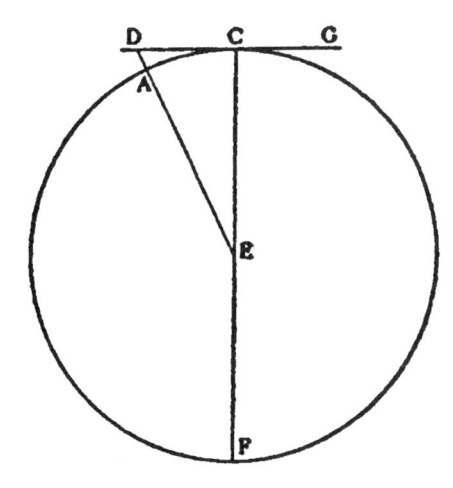

sum of the squares of DC and CE will be 1,010,000. This is equal to the square of DE; hence ED will exceed 1,004, and AD will be more than four of those units of which CE contains one thousand. Therefore the altitude AD on the moon, which represents a summit reaching up to the solar ray GCD and standing at the distance CD from C, exceeds four miles. But on the earth we have no mountains which reach to a perpendicular height of even one mile.* Hence it is quite clear that the prominences on the moon are loftier than those on the earth.

Here I wish to assign the cause of another lunar phenomenon well worthy of notice. I observed this not just recently, but many years ago, and pointed it out to some of my friends and pupils, explaining it to them and giving its true cause. Yet since it is rendered more evident and easier to observe with the aid of the telescope, I think it not unsuitable for introduction in this place, especially as it shows more clearly the connection between the moon and the earth.

When the moon is not far from the sun, just before or after new moon, its globe offers itself to view not only on the side where it is adorned with shining horns, but a certain faint light is also seen to mark out the periphery of the dark part which faces away from the sun, separating this from the darker background of the aether. Now if we examine the matter more closely, we shall see that not only does the extreme limb of the shaded side glow with this uncertain light, but the entire face of the moon (including the side which does not receive the glare of the sun) is whitened by a not inconsiderable gleam. At first glance only a thin luminous circumference appears, contrasting with the darker sky coterminous with it; the rest of the surface appears darker from its contact with the shining horns which distract our vision. But if we place ourselves so as to interpose a roof or chimney or some other object at a considerable distance from the eye, the shining horns may be hidden while the rest of the lunar globe remains exposed to view. It is then found that this region of the moon, though deprived of sunlight, also shines not a little. The effect is heightened if the gloom of night has already deepened through departure of the sun, for in a darker field a given light appears brighter.

Moreover, it is found that this secondary light of the moon (so to speak) is greater according as the moon is closer to the sun. It diminishes more and more as the moon recedes from that body until, after the first quarter and before the last, it is seen very weakly and uncertainly even when observed in the darkest sky. But when the moon is within sixty degrees of the sun it shines remarkably, even in twilight; so brightly indeed that with the aid of a good telescope one may distinguish the large spots. This remarkable gleam has afforded no small perplexity to philosophers, and in order to assign a cause for it some have offered one idea and some another. Some would say it is an inherent and natural light of the moon's own; others, that it is imparted by Venus; others yet, by all the stars together; and still other derive it from the sun, whose rays they would have permeate the thick solidity of the moon. But statements of this sort are refuted and their falsity evinced with little difficulty. For if this kind of light were the moon's own, or were contributed by the stars, the moon would retain it and would display it particularly during eclipses, when it is left in an unusually dark sky. This is contradicted by experience, for the brightness which is seen on the moon during eclipses is much fainter and is ruddy, almost copper-colored, while this is brighter and whitish. Moreover the other light is variable and movable, for it covers the face of the moon in such a way that the place near the edge of the earth's shadow is always seen to be brighter than the rest of the moon; this undoubtedly results from contact of the tangent solar rays

---

* Galileo's estimate of four miles for the height of some lunar mountains was a very good one. His remark about the maximum height of mountains on the earth was, however, quite mistaken. An English propagandist for his views, John Wilkins took pains to correct this error in his anonymous *Discovery of a New World . . . in the Moon* (London, 1638), Prop. ix.

with some denser zone which girds the moon about.* By this contact a sort of twilight is diffused over the neighboring regions of the moon, just as on earth a sort of crepuscular light is spread both morning and evening; but with this I shall deal more fully in my book on the system of the world.**

To assert that the moon's secondary light is imparted by Venus is so childish as to deserve no reply. Who is so ignorant as not to understand that from new moon to a separation of sixty degrees between moon and sun, no part of the moon which is averted from the sun can possibly be seen from Venus? And it is likewise unthinkable that this light should depend upon the sun's rays penetrating the thick solid mass of the moon, for then this light would never dwindle, inasmuch as one hemisphere of the moon is always illuminated except during lunar eclipses. And the light does diminish as the moon approaches first quarter, becoming completely obscured after that is passed.

Now since the secondary light does not inherently belong to the moon, and is not received from any star or from the sun, and since in the whole universe there is no other body left but the earth, what must we conclude? What is to be proposed? Surely we must assert that the lunar body (or any other dark and sunless orb) is illuminated by the earth. Yet what is there so remarkable about this? The earth, in fair and grateful exchange, pays back to the moon an illumination similar to that which it receives from her throughout nearly all the darkest gloom of night.

Let us explain this matter more fully. At conjunction the moon occupies a position between the sun and the earth; it is then illuminated by the sun's rays on the side which is turned away from the earth. The other hemisphere, which faces the earth, is covered with darkness; hence the moon does not illuminate the surface of the earth at all. Next, departing gradually from the sun, the moon comes to be lighted partly upon the side it turns toward us, and its whitish horns, still very thin, illuminate the earth with a faint light. The sun's illumination of the moon increasing now as the moon approaches first quarter, a reflection of that light to the earth also increases.

Soon the splendor on the moon extends into a semicircle, and our nights grow brighter; at length the entire visible face of the moon is irradiated by the sun's resplendent rays, and at full moon the whole surface of the earth shines in a flood of moonlight. Now the moon, waning, sends us her beams more weakly, and the earth is less strongly lighted; at length the moon returns to conjunction with the sun, and black night covers the earth.

In this monthly period, then, the moonlight gives us alternations of brighter and fainter illumination; and the benefit is repaid by the earth in equal measure. For while the moon is between us and the sun (at new moon), there lies before it the entire surface of that hemisphere of the earth which is exposed to the sun and illuminated by vivid rays. The moon receives the light which this reflects, and thus the nearer hemisphere of the moon—that is, the one deprived of sunlight—appears by virtue of this illumination to be not a little luminous. When the moon is ninety degrees away from the sun it sees but half the earth illuminate (the western half), for the other (the eastern half) is enveloped in night. Hence the moon itself is illuminated less brightly from the earth, and as a result its secondary light appears fainter to us. When the moon is in opposition to the sun, it faces a hemisphere of the earth that is steeped in the gloom of night, and if this position occurs in the plane of the ecliptic the moon will receive no light at all, being deprived of both the solar and the terrestrial rays. In its various other positions with respect to the earth and sun, the moon receives more or less light according as it faces a greater or smaller portion of the illuminated hemisphere of the earth. And between these two globes a relation is maintained such that whenever the earth is most brightly lighted by the moon, the moon is least lighted by the earth, and vice versa.

Let these few remarks suffice us here concerning this matter, which will be more fully treated in our *System of the world*. In that book, by a multitude of arguments and experiences, the solar reflection from the earth will be shown to be quite real—against those who argue that the earth must be excluded from the dancing whirl of stars for the specific reason that it is devoid of

---

* Kepler had correctly accounted for the existence of this light and its ruddy color. It is caused by refraction of sunlight in the earth's atmosphere, and does not require a lunar atmosphere as supposed by Galileo.

** The book thus promised was destined not to appear for more than two decades. Events which will presently be recounted prevented its publication for many years, and then it had to be modified to present the arguments for both the Ptolemaic and Copernican systems instead of just the latter as Galileo here planned. Even then it was suppressed, and the author was condemned to life imprisonment.

motion and of light. We shall prove the earth to be a wandering body surpassing the moon in splendor, and not the sink of all dull refuse of the universe; this we shall support by an infinitude of arguments drawn from nature.

Thus far we have spoken of our observations concerning the body of the moon. Let us now set forth briefly what has thus far been observed regarding the fixed stars. And first of all, the following fact deserves consideration: The stars, whether fixed or wandering,* appear not to be enlarged by the telescope in the same proportion as that in which it magnifies other objects, and even the moon itself. In the stars this enlargement seems to be so much less that a telescope which is sufficiently powerful to magnify other objects a hundredfold is scarcely able to enlarge the stars four or five times. The reason for this is as follows.

When stars are viewed by means of unaided natural vision, they present themselves to us not as of their simple (and, so to speak, their physical) size, but as irradiated by a certain fulgor and as fringed with sparkling rays, especially when the night is far advanced. From this they appear larger than they would if stripped of those adventitious hairs of light, for the angle at the eye is determined not by the primary body of the star but by the brightness which extends so widely about it. This appears quite clearly from the fact that when stars first emerge from twilight to sunset they look very small, even if they are of the first magnitude; Venus itself, when visible in broad daylight, is so small as scarcely to appear equal to a star of the sixth magnitude. Things fall out differently with other objects, and even with the moon itself; these, whether seen in daylight or the deepest night, appear always of the same bulk. Therefore the stars are seen crowned among shadows, while daylight is able to remove their headgear; and not daylight alone but any thin cloud that interposes itself between a star and the eye of the observer. The same effect is produced by black veils or colored glasses, through the interposition of which obstacles the stars are abandoned by their surrounding brilliance. A telescope similarly accomplishes the same result. It removes from the stars their adventitious and accidental rays, and then it enlarges their simple globes (if indeed the stars are naturally globular) so that they seem to be magnified in a lesser ratio than other objects. In fact a star of the fifth or sixth magnitude when seen through a telescope presents itself as one of the first magnitude.

Deserving of notice also is the difference between the appearances of the planets and of the fixed stars.** The planets show their globes perfectly round and definitely bounded, looking like little moons, spherical and flooded all over with light; the fixed stars are never seen to be bounded by a circular periphery, but have rather the aspect of blazes whose rays vibrate about them and scintillate a great deal. Viewed with a telescope they appear of a shape similar to that which they present to the naked eye, but sufficiently enlarged so that a star of the fifth or sixth magnitude seems to equal the Dog Star, largest of all the stars. Now, in addition to stars of the sixth magnitude, a host of other stars are perceived through the telescope which escape the naked eye; these are so numerous as almost to surpass belief. One may, in fact, see more of them than all the stars included among the first six magnitudes. The largest of these, which we may call stars of the seventh magnitude, or the first magnitude of invisible stars, appear through the telescope as larger and brighter than stars of the second magnitude when the latter are viewed with the naked eye. In order to give one or two proofs of their almost inconceivable number, I have adjoined pictures of two constellations. With these as samples, you may judge of all the others.

In the first I had intended to depict the entire constellation of Orion, but I was overwhelmed by the vast quantity of stars and by limitations of time, so I have deferred this to another occasion. There are more than five hundred new stars distributed among the old ones within limits of one or two degrees of arc. Hence to the three stars in the Belt of Orion and the six in the Sword which were previously known, I have added eighty adjacent stars discovered recently, preserving the intervals between them as exactly as I could. To distinguish the known or ancient stars, I have

---

* That is, planets. Among these bodies Galileo counted his newly discovered satellites of Jupiter. The term "satellites" was introduced somewhat later by Kepler.

** Fixed stars are so distant that their light reaches the earth as from dimensionless points. Hence their images are not enlarged by even the best telescopes, which serve only to gather more of their light and in that way increase their visibility. Galileo was never entirely clear about this distinction. Nevertheless, by applying his knowledge of the effects described here, he greatly reduced the prevailing overestimation of visual dimensions of stars and planets.

depicted them larger and have outlined them doubly; the other (invisible) stars I have drawn smaller and without the extra line. I have also preserved differences of magnitude as well as possible.

The Belt and Sword of Orion

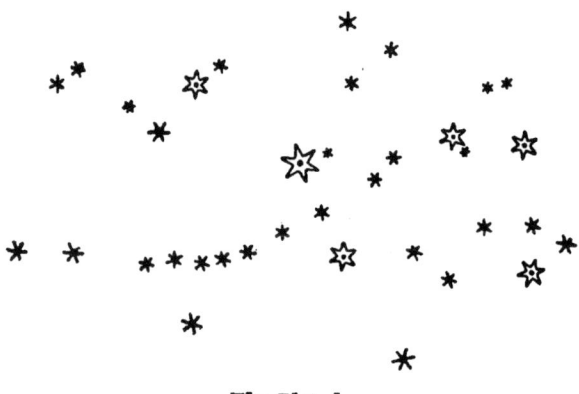

The Pleiades

In the second example I have depicted the six stars of Taurus known as the Pleiades (I say six, inasmuch as the seventh is hardly ever visible) which lie within very narrow limits in the sky. Near them are more than forty others, invisible, no one of which is much more than half a degree away from the original six. I have shown thirty-six of these in the diagram; as in the case of Orion I have preserved their intervals and magnitudes, as well as the distinction between old stars and new.

Third, I have observed the nature and the material of the Milky Way. With the aid of the telescope this has been scrutinized so directly and with such ocular certainty that all the disputes which have vexed philosophers through so many ages have been resolved, and we are at last freed from wordy debates about it. The galaxy is, in fact, nothing but a congeries of innumerable stars grouped together in clusters. Upon whatever part of it the telescope is directed, a vast crowd of stars is immediately presented to view. Many of them are rather large and quite bright, while the number of smaller ones is quite beyond calculation.

But it is not only in the Milky Way that whitish clouds are seen; several patches of similar aspect shine with faint light here and there throughout the aether, and if the telescope is turned upon any of these it confronts us with a tight mass of stars. And what is even more remarkable, the stars which have been called "nebulous" by every astronomer up to this time turn out to be groups of very small stars arranged in a wonderful manner. Although each star separately escapes our sight on account of its smallness or the immense distance from us, the mingling of their rays gives rise to that gleam which was formerly believed to be some denser part of the aether that was capable of reflecting rays from stars or from the sun. I have observed some of these constellations and have decided to depict two of them.

In the first you have the nebula called the Head of Orion, in which I have counted twenty-one stars. The second contains the nebula called Praesepe,* which is not a single star but a mass of more than forty starlets. Of these I have shown thirty-six, in addition to the Aselli, arranged in the order shown.

We have now briefly recounted the observations made thus far with regard to the moon, the fixed stars, and the Milky Way. There remains the matter which in my opinion deserves to be considered the most important of all—the disclosure of four PLANETS never seen from the creation of the world up to our own time, together

---

* Praesepe, "the Manger," is a small whitish cluster of stars lying between the two Aselli (ass-colts) which are imagined as feeding from it. It lies in the constellation Cancer.

Nebula of Orion   *Nebula of Praesepe*

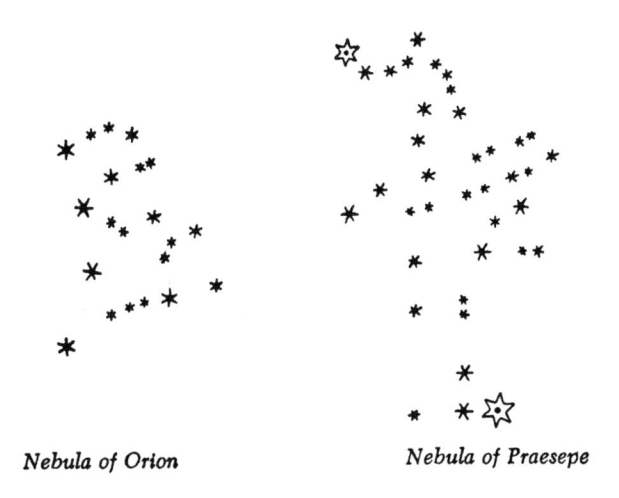

with the occasion of my having discovered and studied them, their arrangements, and the observations made of their movements and alterations during the past two months. I invite all astronomers to apply themselves to examine them and determine their periodic times, something which has so far been quite impossible to complete, owing to the shortness of the time. Once more, however, warning is given that it will be necessary to have a very accurate telescope such as we have described at the beginning of this discourse.

On the seventh day of January in this present year 1610, at the first hour of night, when I was viewing the heavenly bodies with a telescope, Jupiter presented itself to me; and because I had prepared a very excellent instrument for myself, I perceived (as I had not before, on account of the weakness of my previous instrument) that beside the planet there were three starlets, small indeed, but very bright. Though I believed them to be among the host of fixed stars, they aroused my curiosity somewhat by appearing to lie in an exact straight line parallel to the ecliptic, and by their being more splendid than others of their size. Their arrangement with respect to Jupiter and each other was the following:

East   *   *   O   *   West

that is, there were two stars on the eastern side and one to the west. The most easterly star and the western one appeared larger than the other. I paid no attention to the distances between them and Jupiter, for at the outset I thought them to be fixed stars, as I have said.* But returning to the same investigation on January eighth—led by what I do not know—I found a very different arrangement. The three starlets were now all to the west of Jupiter, closer together, and at equal intervals from one another as shown in the following sketch:

East   O   *   *   *   West

At this time, though I did not yet turn my attention to the way the stars had come together, I began to concern myself with the question how Jupiter could be east of all these stars when on the previous day it had been west of two of them. I commenced to wonder whether Jupiter was not moving eastward at that time, contrary to the computations of the astronomers, and had got in front of them by that motion.** Hence it was with great interest that I awaited the next night. But I was disappointed in my hopes, for the sky was then covered with clouds everywhere.

On the tenth of January, however, the stars appeared in this position with respect to Jupiter:

East   *   *   O   West

that is, there were but two of them, both easterly, the third (as I supposed) being hidden behind Jupiter. As at first, they were in the same straight line with Jupiter and were arranged precisely in the line of the zodiac. Noticing this, and knowing that there was no way in which such alterations could be attributed to Jupiter's motion, yet being certain that these were still the same stars I had observed (in fact no other was to be found along the line of the zodiac for a long way on either side of Jupiter), my perplexity was now transformed into amazement. I was sure that the apparent

---

* The reader should remember that the telescope was nightly revealing to Galileo hundreds of fixed stars never previously observed. His unusual gifts for astronomical observation are illustrated by his having noticed and remembered these three merely by reason of their alignment, and recalling them so well that when by chance he happened to see them the following night he was certain that they had changed their positions. No such plausible and candid account of the discovery was given by the rival astronomer Simon Mayr, who four years later claimed priority. See pp. 233 ff. and note 4, pp. 233–34.

** See note 4, p. 12. Jupiter was at this time in "retrograde" motion; that is, the earth's motion made the planet appear to be moving westward among the fixed stars.

changes belonged not to Jupiter but to the observed stars, and I resolved to pursue this investigation with greater care and attention.

And thus, on the eleventh of January, I saw the following disposition:

East   ✳ ✱   ○   *West*

There were two stars, both to the east, the central one being three times as far from Jupiter as from the one farther east. The latter star was nearly double the size of the former, whereas on the night before they had appeared approximately equal.

I had now decided beyond all question that there existed in the heavens three stars wandering about Jupiter as do Venus and Mercury about the sun, and this became plainer than daylight from observations on similar occasions which followed. Nor were there just three such stars; four wanderers complete their revolutions about Jupiter, and of their alterations as observed more precisely later on we shall give a description here. Also I measured the distances between them by means of the telescope, using the method explained before. Moreover I recorded the times of the observations, especially when more than one was made during the same night—for the revolutions of these planets are so speedily completed that it is usually possible to take even their hourly variations.

Thus on the twelfth of January at the first hour of night I saw the stars arranged in this way:

East   ✳ ✱○✳   *West*

The most easterly star was larger than the western one, though both were easily visible and quite bright. Each was about two minutes of arc distant from Jupiter. The third star was invisible at first, but commenced to appear after two hours; it almost touched Jupiter on the east, and was quite small. All were on the same straight line directed along the ecliptic.

On the thirteenth of January four stars were seen by me for the first time, in this situation relative to Jupiter:

East   ✳   ○✱✳✳   *West*

Three were westerly and one was to the east; they formed a straight line except that the middle western star departed slightly toward the north. The eastern star was two minutes of arc away from Jupiter, and the intervals of the rest from one another and from Jupiter were about one minute. All the stars appeared to be of the same magnitude, and though small were very bright, much brighter than fixed stars of the same size.*

On the twenty-sixth of February, midway in the first hour of night, there were only two stars:

East   ✳   ○   ✳   *West*

One was to the east, ten minutes from Jupiter; the other to the west, six minutes away. The eastern one was somewhat smaller than the western. But at the fifth hour three stars were seen:

East   ✳   ○ ✳   ✳   *West*

In addition to the two already noticed, a third was discovered to the west near Jupiter; it had at first been hidden behind Jupiter and was now one minute away. The eastern one appeared farther away than before, being eleven minutes from Jupiter.

This night for the first time I wanted to observe the progress of Jupiter and its accompanying planets along the line of the zodiac in relation to some fixed star, and such a star was seen to the east eleven minutes distant from the easterly starlet and a little removed toward the south, in the following manner:

East   ✳   ○✳   ✳   *West*
★

On the twenty-seventh of February, four minutes after the first hour, the stars appeared in this configuration:

---

* Galileo's day-by-day journal of observations continued in unbroken sequence until ten days before publication of the book, which he remained in Venice to supervise. The observations omitted here contained nothing of a novel character.

```
East    *        *○ *✳︎         West
         ★
```

The most easterly was ten minutes from Jupiter; the next, thirty seconds; the next to the west was two minutes thirty seconds from Jupiter, and the most westerly was one minute from that. Those nearest Jupiter appeared very small, while the end ones were plainly visible, especially the westernmost. They marked out an exactly straight line along the course of the ecliptic. The progress of these planets toward the east is seen quite clearly by reference to the fixed star mentioned, since Jupiter and its accompanying planets were closer to it, as may be seen in the figure above. At the fifth hour, the eastern star closer to Jupiter was one minute away.

At the first hour on February twenty-eighth, two stars only were seen; one easterly, distant nine minutes from Jupiter, and one to the west, two minutes away. They were easily visible and on the same straight line. The fixed star, perpendicular to this line, now fell under the eastern planet as in this figure:

```
East      *           ○  *           West
           ★
```

At the fifth hour a third star, two minutes east of Jupiter, was seen in this position:

```
East      *        * ○ *            West
```

On the first of March, forty minutes after sunset, four stars all to the east were seen, of which the nearest to Jupiter was two minutes away, the next was one minute from this, the third two seconds from that and brighter than any of the others; from this in turn the most easterly was four minutes distant, and it was smaller than the rest. They marked out almost a straight line, but the third one counting from Jupiter was a little to the north. The fixed star formed an equilateral triangle with Jupiter and the most easterly star, as in this figure:

```
East       *   *** ○                West
              ★
```

On March second, half an hour after sunset, there were three planets, two to the east and one to the west, in this configuration:

```
East         **       ○   *          West
                    ★
```

The most easterly was seven minutes from Jupiter and thirty seconds from its neighbor; the western one was two minutes away from Jupiter. The end stars were very bright and were larger than that in the middle, which appeared very small. The most easterly star appeared a little elevated toward the north from the straight line through the other planets and Jupiter. The fixed star previously mentioned was eight minutes from the western planet along the line drawn from it perpendicularly to the straight line through all the planets, as shown above.

I have reported these relations of Jupiter and its companions with the fixed star so that anyone may comprehend that the progress of those planets, both in longitude and latitude, agrees exactly with the movements derived from planetary tables.

Such are the observations concerning the four Medicean planets recently first discovered by me, and although from these data their periods have not yet been reconstructed in numerical form, it is legitimate at least to put in evidence some facts worthy of note. Above all, since they sometimes follow and sometimes precede Jupiter by the same intervals, and they remain within very limited distances either to east or west of Jupiter, accompanying that planet in both its retrograde and direct movements in a constant manner, no one can doubt that they complete their revolutions about Jupiter and at the same time effect all together a twelve-year period about the center of the universe. That they also revolve in unequal circles is manifestly deduced from the fact that at the greatest elongation* from Jupiter it is never possible to see two of these planets in conjunction, whereas in the vicinity of Jupiter they are found united two, three, and sometimes all four together. It is also observed that the revolutions are swifter in those planets which describe smaller circles about Jupiter, since the stars closest to Jupiter are usually seen to the east when on the previous day they appeared to the west, and vice versa, while the planet which traces the largest orbit appears upon accurate observation of its returns to have a semimonthly period.

Here we have a fine and elegant argument for quieting the doubts of those who, while accepting with tranquil mind the revolutions of the planets about the sun in the Copernican system, are mightily disturbed to have the moon alone revolve about the earth and accompany it in an annual rotation about the sun. Some have believed that this structure of the universe should be rejected as impossible. But now we have not just one planet rotating about another while both run through a great orbit around the sun; our own eyes show us four stars which wander around Jupiter as does the moon around the earth, while all together trace out a grand revolution about the sun in the space of twelve years.

And finally we should not omit the reason for which the Medicean stars appear sometimes to be twice as large as at other times, though their orbits about Jupiter are very restricted. We certainly cannot seek the cause in terrestrial vapors, as Jupiter and its neighboring fixed stars are not seen to change size in the least while this increase and diminution are taking place. It is quite unthinkable that the cause of variation should be their change of distance from the earth at perigee and apogee, since a small circular rotation could by no means produce this effect, and an oval motion (which in this case would have to be nearly straight) seems unthinkable and quite inconsistent with the appearances.** But I shall gladly explain what occurs to me on this matter, offering it freely to the judgment and criticism of thoughtful men. It is known that the interposition of terrestrial vapors makes the sun and moon appear large, while the fixed stars and planets are made to appear smaller. Thus the two great luminaries are seen larger when close to the horizon, while the stars appear smaller and for the most part hardly visible. Hence the stars appear very feeble by day and in twilight, though the moon does not, as we have said. Now from what has been said above, and even more from what we shall say at greater length in our *System*, it follows that not only the earth but also the moon is surrounded by an envelope of vapors, and we may apply precisely the same judgment to the rest of the planets. Hence it does not appear entirely impossible to assume that around Jupiter also there exists an envelope denser than the rest of the aether, about which the Medicean planets revolve as does the moon about the elemental sphere. Through the interposition of this envelope they appear larger when they are in perigee by the removal, or at least the attenuation, of this envelope.

Time prevents my proceeding further, but the gentle reader may expect more soon.

Finis

---

* By this is meant the greatest angular separation from Jupiter attained by any of the satellites.
** The marked variation in brightness of the satellites which Galileo observed may be attributed mainly to markings upon their surfaces, though this was not determined until two centuries later. The mention here of a possible oval shape of the orbits is the closest Galileo ever came to accepting Kepler's great discovery of the previous year (cf. p. 17). Even here, however, he was probably not thinking of Kepler's work but of an idea proposed by earlier astronomers for the moon and the planet Venus.

Galileo and Ancient Science

—S.Z.

The ancients had no effective way to observe and measure the heavens directly. Still, they had a hunger to understand the nature of the world and worlds about them. Limited in observation, some turned to structures and structures of the mind with which they were familiar. They reasoned, since the cosmos was created by the gods and the gods were creatures attaining perfection, that the cosmos itself must be shaped after perfect geometrical or mathematical models.

A Pythagorean, believing in the mystical powers of numbers, might conclude that the earth was shaped as a dodecahedron (a 12-sided, 3-dimensional object—think of a soccer ball!). The thinking was that the number twelve was very special. Think of the way in which twelve contains so many factors (12 X 1; 6 X 2; 4 X 3—thus, the numbers 1, 2,3,4,6 are all accounted for). If we add that each side of the dodecahedron is a pentagon (5), you can see why thinkers who believed in the power of numbers might conclude that the earth was shaped in this way.

Another form of argument established that the heavens were shaped as a set of nested crystalline spheres. Again, if the gods work on the pattern of perfection, they might well choose the sphere as a geometrical model fully to their liking. The sphere is the only object that has a center point from which radii in all directions are equal; another way of seeing this is to say that a sphere is "perfectly round."

Why crystal? Well, since the heavenly bodies set on those spheres (the moon, the sun, the planets, and the fixed stars) are all visible, it must be the case that the spheres, on the surface of each of which these objects are embedded, must be transparent. Crystal, again, suggests perfection (since it is all imaginary, why not have the best).

Another thought was to associate the heavenly realms with perfection and especially immortality. These celestial fires may indeed be divinities, gods that can never change and surely never die because they are pure and perfect. We do know, however, that here on the earth everything comes and goes. One might think this occurs because everything we know is imperfect and therefore flawed and unstable. The Church would maintain that the ancient Greeks had intuited what scripture explains—that is, this world is a world of sin and death. The conclusion was that the heavens were perfect, but this world, sitting at the center of it all, was a sink of decay towards which all broken and imperfect things flow from the inner orbit of the moon on down to the earth.

All this makes a kind of sense, but not what we have come to call science. It is a dream of things rather than a close factual account. Galileo demands that knowledge of the heavens be founded upon observation and calculation. Now, this is science! However, before we boast too triumphantly about the silliness of the ancients, we need to recall that Einstein, like Newton, based his description of the heavens not on observation but on pure mathematics. Pythagoras may have been on to something!

Another issue that arises concerning Copernicus and Galileo is their new claim that the earth is not the center of the universe and that indeed it moves. This was not a new thought. Ptolemy, a Hellenic Egyptian and surely the most knowledgeable astronomer of his time, entertained the possibility that the earth moved around the sun. However, he rejected this idea because it seemed just too silly. And if you thought about it, you too would see just how silly this is (even though it happens to be true).

Suppose the earth did orbit the sun (which it does) and rotate on its axis in order to produce the effect of day and night (which it also does). First, imagine you are standing at the equator. If the earth rotates completely every 24 hours and (as we know) the circumference of the earth is approximately 25,000 miles, that would mean that you would be traveling at more than 1,000 miles per hour. Hold onto your hat! Now, you might object that we are not standing at the equator, so I will split the difference and round off and tell you now that you are traveling at 500 mph. You would think you would notice if you were speeding along at that rate. And think, too, what it would mean for a baseball lofted skyward. Since the earth is turning towards the East at 500 mph (if it is turning, which it is), any baseball pop-up would land far behind you to the West (which it surely does not do).

But it gets worse. If the earth orbits the sun (which it does), it would be traveling the circumference of a circle (again we will round off) the radius of which is about 93 million miles (the distance from the earth to the sun) and would be completing this journey each year (that's what a year is, the journey from one point and back to that starting point). Geometry from 10th grade will tell you the sobering answers (2 X 3.14 X 93 million—a journey of 584 million miles a year). Now, if we make that journey in 365 days, you begin to see the appalling speeds at which the earth would have to be traveling (and it does). Again, you would think you would notice traveling close to 67,000 mph!—a truly ridiculous fact (which happens also to be true).

Ptolemy, despite having a difficult name, was no dope. He knew that he could not account for these speeds, nor could he explain what would be pushing the earth to make it move. Not only that, he reasoned (and like all great scientists, he was an excellent reasoner) that a journey across the heavens would cause the view of the stars to shift in relation to one another (that circle, after all, is 186 million miles across, so observations of the heavens at one point and again six months later would stretch across this vast distance). The shift (the parallax effect) did not occur. So, Ptolemy was certain that the earth could not be moving and that the heavens instead wheeled around the earth (which is just what appearances say happens).

A final point: when Galileo asserted his theory that the earth revolved around the sun, he could not answer these objections that stumped Ptolemy 1500 years earlier. A friend of his, a Churchmen friendly to Galileo's new science, begged Galileo to keep quiet about his idea precisely because, as he pointed out, Galileo was unable to prove it. Galileo, however, knew he was right. So much so, that when the Church later forced him to reject his theory in public, Galileo, rising from his humiliation, was heard to mutter defiantly: "Still, it does move!"

The Prince—Notes on Connections

Why include Machiavelli's *The Prince* in *Paths to Civilization?*

It must be that Machiavelli's book is concerned with more than simply instructing the prince in how to realize his personal ambitions.

Clearly, many books in our intellectual heritage share an important concern. Pericles affords us an example of a statesman at work, employing rhetoric to rally his fellow citizens for ultimate sacrifices. He also presents an argument on how best to order the community to realize its best desires.

Plato, in *The Republic* presents us examples and discussion of the liberator who will free his fellow citizens from their confusions. In *The Republic* he speaks more directly (through Socrates) about the best kind of government and the sort of education that produces the best kind of leader.

Exodus presents us another example of a community in formation and the kind of leader best able to carry out this difficult task. The comparison of Aaron and Moses makes clear that the author(s) of *Exodus* endorse a strong leader and not a follower of the people's wishes. Moses is not only a prophet but also a political liberator of his people.

Jesus is a liberator but of a different kind. He leads no political state, however, and provides in himself no clear example of how to do this. His "state" is not of this world. What belongs to Caesar, belongs to Caesar.

Muhammad, however, clearly does. He, like Moses, is not only a prophet ("The Slave of Allah") but also a political liberator who leads his people in battle and later forms the civil order, a theocratic state (like that of Moses). Allah tells him, in Surah Two, that he must do these hard things even though he doesn't feel equipped, as a holy man, to carry them out. Allah shows him the way.

Sundiata is, of course, another example of a political leader whose efforts are to establish an empire on the basis of justice and military strength. If you read closely, you

This famous portrait of Machiavelli seems almost like a cartoon. Machiavelli looks shrewd and fox-like, with penetrating eyes, and a sly grin. Other portraits look different, but this one has served as an emblem for *The Prince* for obvious reasons. Corbis-Bettmann.

notice that the *Sundiata* presents discussions on whether fear or love is the best approach for a leader, whether the leader should be like other people or set himself apart, how punishment (or withholding punishment) is the best policy when dealing with former enemies, and so on. The griot, as counselor to kings, is also a political scientist of the sort that Machiavelli would have appreciated.

So, it should be clear that the issues we encounter in *The Prince* are not new ones in the course overall. And also, we should read Machiavelli not as a guide to the ambition of a prince but to the question of how best to form and maintain a vigorous and just political arrangement.

The best way to see this is to read the last chapter of *The Prince* intensely. There we discover the urgency for saving Italy (and Florence most particularly) from the assaults of its neighbors. Machiavelli also reviews several of the people we read and read about in *Paths to Civilization* in his book, so he is aware that he is in this tradition. Like the others, his topic is how to organize society so it works best.

The model for Machiavelli's prince was Cesare Borgia, also known as Duke Valentino, and son of Pope Alexander VI. Machiavelli describes him as "greathearted and ambitious" and admired his *virtu* (capability). Cesare Borgia was struck down by illness before he could achieve his goal of consolidating power in Italy. Leonard de Selva/Corbis.

The Prince

*Nicolo Machiavelli
translated by David Wootton*

Chapter One: How many types of principality are there? And how are they acquired?

All states, all forms of government that have had and continue to have authority over men, have been and are either republics or principalities. And principalities are either hereditary, when their rulers' ancestors have long been their rulers, or they are new. And if they are new, they are either entirely new, as was Milan for Francesco Sforza,[1] or they are like limbs added on to the hereditary state of the ruler who acquires them, as the kingdom of Naples has been added on to the kingdom of Spain.[2] Those dominions that are acquired by a ruler are either used to living under the rule of one man, or accustomed to being free; and they are either acquired with soldiers belonging to others, or with one's own; either through fortune or through strength [*virtù*].

Chapter Two: On hereditary principalities.

I will leave behind me the discussion of republics, for I have discussed them at length elsewhere. I will concern myself only with principalities. The different types of principality I have mentioned will be the threads from which I will weave my account. I will debate how these different types of principality should be governed and defended.

I maintain, then, it is much easier to hold on to hereditary states, which are accustomed to being governed by the family that now rules them, than it is to hold on to new acquisitions. All one has to do is preserve the structures established by one's forebears, and play for time if things go badly. For, indeed, an hereditary ruler, if he is of no more than normal resourcefulness, will never lose his state unless some extraordinary and overwhelming force appears that can take it away from him; and even then, the occupier has only to have a minor setback, and the original ruler will get back to power.

Let us take a contemporary Italian example: The Duke of Ferrara was able to resist the assaults of the Venetians in '84, and of Pope Julius in 1510, only because his family was long established as rulers of that state. For a ruler who inherits power has few reasons and less cause to give offense; as a consequence he is more popular; and, as long as he does not have exceptional vices that make him hateful, it is to be expected he will naturally have the goodwill of his people. Because the state has belonged to his family from one generation to another, memories of how they came to power, and motives to overthrow them, have worn away. For every change in government creates grievances that those who wish to bring about further change can exploit.

Chapter Three: On mixed principalities.

New principalities are the ones that present problems. And first of all, if the whole of the

---

The Prince, by Niccolo Machiavelli, translated by David Wootton. Copyright © 1995 by Hackett Publishing Company. Reprinted by permission of Hackett Publishing Company. All rights reserved.

principality is not new, but rather a new part has been added on to the old, creating a whole one may term "mixed," instability derives first of all from a natural difficulty that is to be found in all new principalities. The problem is that people willingly change their ruler, believing the change will be for the better; and this belief leads them to take up arms against him. But they are mistaken, and they soon find out in practice they have only made things worse. The reason for this, too, is natural and typical: You always have to give offense to those over whom you acquire power when you become a new ruler, both by imposing troops upon them, and by countless other injuries that follow as necessary consequences of the acquisition of power. Thus, you make enemies of all those to whom you have given offense in acquiring power, and in addition you cannot keep the goodwill of those who have put you in power, for you cannot satisfy their aspirations as they thought you would. At the same time you cannot use heavy-handed methods against them, for you are obliged to them. Even if you have an overwhelmingly powerful army, you will have needed the support of the locals to take control of the province. This is why Louis XII of France lost Milan as quickly as he gained it.[3] All that was needed to take it from him the first time were Ludovico's own troops. For those who had opened the gates to him, finding themselves mistaken in their expectations and disappointed in their hopes of future benefit, could not put up with the burdensome rule of a new sovereign.

Of course it is true that, after a ruler has regained power in rebel territories, he is much more likely to hang on to it. For the rebellion gives him an excuse, and he is able to take firmer measures to secure his position, punishing delinquents, checking up on suspects, and taking precautions where needed. So, if the first time the King of France lost Milan all that was needed to throw him out was Duke Ludovico growling on his borders, to throw him out a second time it took the whole world united against him, and the destruction or expulsion from Italy of his armies.[4] We have seen why this was so.

Nevertheless, he lost Milan both times. We have discussed why he was almost bound to lose it the first time; now we must discuss why he managed to lose it the second. What remedies should he have adopted? What can someone in the King of France's position do to hold on to an acquisition more effectively than he did?

Let me start by saying these territories that are newly added on to a state that is already securely in the possession of a ruler are either in the same geographical region as his existing possessions and speak the same language, or they are not. When they are, it is quite straightforward to hold on to them, especially if they are not used to governing themselves. In order to get a secure hold on them one need merely eliminate the surviving members of the family of their previous rulers. In other respects one should keep things as they were, respecting established traditions. If the old territories and the new have similar customs, the new subjects will live quietly. Thus, Burgundy, Brittany, Gascony, and Normandy have for long quietly submitted to France. Although they do not all speak exactly the same language, nevertheless their customs are similar, and they can easily put up with each other. He who acquires neighboring territories in this way, intending to hold on to them, needs to see to two things: First, he must ensure their previous ruler has no heirs; and second, he must not alter their old laws or impose new taxes. If he follows these principles they will quickly become inseparable from his hereditary domains.

But when you acquire territories in a region that has a different language, different customs, and different institutions, then you really have problems, and you need to have great good fortune and great resourcefulness if you are going to hold on to them. One of the best policies, and one of the most effective, is for the new ruler to go and live in his new territories. This will make his grasp on them more secure and more lasting. This is what the Sultan of Turkey has done in Greece.[5] All the other measures he has taken to hold on to that territory would have been worthless if he had not settled there. For if you are on the spot, you can identify difficulties as they arise, and can quickly take appropriate action. If you are at a distance, you only learn of them when they have become serious, and when it is too late to put matters right. Moreover, if you are there in person, the territory will not be plundered by your officials. The subjects can appeal against their exactions to you, their ruler. As a consequence they have more reason to love you, if they behave themselves, and, if they do not, more reason to fear you. Anyone who wants to attack the territory from without will have to think twice, so that, if you live there, you will be unlucky indeed to lose it.

The second excellent policy is to send colonies to settle in one or two places; they will serve to tie your new subjects down. For it is necessary either to do this, or to garrison your new territory with a substantial army. Colonies do not cost much to run. You will have to lay out little or nothing to establish and maintain them. You will only offend those from whom you seize fields and houses to give to your settlers, and they will be only a tiny minority within the territory. Those whom you offend will be scattered and become poor, so they will be unable to do you any harm. All the rest will remain uninjured, and so ought to remain quiet; at the same time they will be afraid to make a false move, for they will have before them the fate of their neighbors as an example of what may happen to them. I conclude such colonies are economical, reliable, and do not give excessive grounds for resistance; those who suffer by their establishment are in no position to resist, being poor and scattered, as I have said. There is a general rule to be noted here: People should either be caressed or crushed. If you do them minor damage they will get their revenge; but if you cripple them there is nothing they can do. If you need to injure someone, do it in such a way that you do not have to fear their vengeance.

But if, instead of establishing colonies, you rely on an occupying army, it costs a good deal more, for your army will eat up all your revenues from your new territory. As a result, your acquisition will be a loss, not a gain. Moreover, your army will make more enemies than colonies would, for the whole territory will suffer from it, the burden moving from one place to another as the troops are billeted first here, then there. Everybody suffers as a result, and everyone becomes your enemy. And these are enemies who can hurt you, for they remain, even if beaten, in their own homes. In every respect, then, an occupying army is a liability, while colonies are an asset.

In addition, anyone who finds himself with territory in a region with different customs from those of his hereditary possessions should make himself the leader and protector of neighboring powers who are weaker than he is, and should set out to weaken his powerful neighbors. He should also take care no outsider as powerful as himself has any occasion to intervene. Outside powers will always be urged to intervene by those in the region who are discontented, either because their ambitions are unsatisfied, or because they are afraid of the dominant powers. So, long ago, the Aetolians invited the Romans into Greece;[6] and, indeed, in every other region the Romans occupied they were invited by local people. It is in the nature of things that, as soon as a foreign power enters into a region, all the local states that are weak rally to it, for they are driven by the envy they have felt for the state that has exercised predominance over them. As a result, the invader does not have to make any effort at all to win over these lesser states, because they all immediately ally themselves to the territory he has acquired there. He only has to take care they do not become too strong and exercise too much influence. He can easily, with his own troops and his new allies' support, strike down the powerful states, and make himself the arbiter of all the affairs of the region. Anyone who does not see how to play this role successfully will quickly lose what he has gained, and, while he holds it, will have innumerable difficulties and vexations.

The Romans, in the regions they seized, obeyed these principles admirably. They settled colonies; were friendly towards the weaker rulers, without building up their strength; broke the powerful; and did not allow foreign powers to build up support. Let me take just the region of Greece as an example.[7] The Romans favored the Acheans and the Aetolians; they crushed the Kingdom of Macedon; they expelled Antiochus[8] from the region. Despite the credit the Acheans and the Aetolians had earned with them, they never allowed them to build up any independent power; nor did the blandishments of Philip[9] ever persuade them to treat him as a friend before they had destroyed his power; nor did Antiochus's strength intimidate them into permitting him to retain any territory in that region.

The Romans did in such matters what all wise rulers ought to do. It is necessary not only to pay attention to immediate crises, but to foresee those that will come, and to make every effort to prevent them. For if you see them coming well in advance, then you can easily take the appropriate action to remedy them, but if you wait until they are right on top of you, then the prescription will no longer take effect, because the disease is too far advanced. In this matter it is as doctors say of consumption: In the beginning the disease is easy to cure, difficult to diagnose; but, after a while, if it has not been diagnosed and treated early, it becomes easy to diagnose and hard to cure. So, too, in politics, for if you foresee problems while they are far off (which only a prudent man is able to do) they can easily be dealt with; but when, because you have failed to see them coming, you allow them to grow to the point that anyone can recognize them, then it is too late to do anything.

The Romans always looked ahead and took action to remedy problems before they developed. They never postponed action in order to avoid a war, for they understood you cannot escape wars, and when you put them off only your opponents benefit. Thus, they wanted to have a war with Philip and Antiochus in Greece, so as not to have one with them in Italy. At the time they could have avoided having a war at all, but this they did not want. They never approved the saying that nowadays is repeated *ad nauseam* by the wise: "Take advantage of the passage of time." Rather they relied on their strength [*virtù*] and prudence, for in time anything can happen, and the passage of time brings good mixed with evil, and evil mixed with good.

But let us return to the kings of France, and let us see whether they followed any of the principles I have outlined. I will discuss Louis, not Charles, for, since Louis held territory in Italy for a longer time, we can have a better understanding of the policies he was following.[10] We will see he did the opposite of what one ought to do in order to hold on to territory in a region unlike one's hereditary lands.

King Louis was brought into Italy by the ambition of the Venetians, who hoped to gain half of the territory of Lombardy as a result of his invasion. I do not want to criticize the king's decision to ally with the Venetians. Since he wanted to get a foothold in Italy, and since he had no friends in that region (rather the opposite, for all the gateways to Italy were closed against him as a result of the actions of King Charles), he was obliged to take what allies he could get. His decision would have been a good one, if he had done everything else right. Now when the king had conquered Lombardy, he at once recovered the reputation Charles had lost for him. Genoa gave itself up and the Florentines became his friends. Everybody came forward to meet him as he advanced and sought his friendship: the Marquis of Mantua, the Duke of Ferrara, Bentivoglio, the Countess of Forlì, the rulers of Faenza, Pesaro, Rimini, Camerino, Piombino, the citizens of Lucca, Pisa, and Siena. Then the Venetians were able to see the risk they had chosen to run; in order to acquire a couple of fortresses in Lombardy, they had made the King of France master of two-thirds of Italy.

Now consider how easy it would have been for the king to preserve his authority in Italy if he had followed the principles I have laid out, and if he had protected and defended all his new friends. They were numerous, weak, and fearful, some afraid of the Church, some of the Venetians, and so had no choice but to remain loyal to him; and with their help he could easily have overwhelmed the surviving great powers. But he had no sooner got to Milan than he did the opposite, coming to the assistance of Pope Alexander so he could occupy the Romagna.[11] He did not realize that by this decision he weakened himself, alienating his friends and those who had flung themselves into his arms; and at the same time strengthened the Church, adding to its already extensive spiritual authority an increased temporal power. And having made one error he was forced to make another, for, in order to put a stop to Alexander's ambitions, and to prevent his gaining control of Tuscany, he was obliged to march into Italy once more. Nor was he satisfied with having strengthened the Church and thrown away his alliances, but in addition, because he wanted the Kingdom of Naples, he agreed to divide it with the King of Spain.[12] Where he had been all-powerful in Italy, he now shared his power with another, giving ambitious rulers in the region and those who were discontented with him someone to whom they could turn. Where he could have left in the Kingdom of Naples a king who was on his payroll, he threw him out, and replaced him with someone who might aspire to kick out the French.

It is perfectly natural and normal to want to acquire new territory; and whenever men do what will succeed towards this end, they will be praised, or at least not condemned. But when they are not in a position to make gains, and try nevertheless, then they are making a mistake, and deserve condemnation. If the King of France had the military capacity to attack Naples, he should have done so; if he did not have it, he should not have proposed to partition the territory. The division of Lombardy between France and Venice was justified because it gave the French a foothold in Italy; the division of Naples was blameworthy, for it was not justifiable on the same grounds.

Thus, Louis had made the following five mistakes: He wasted his alliance with the lesser states; he increased the strength of one of the more powerful Italian states; he invited an extremely powerful foreign state to intervene in Italy; he did not go and live in Italy; he did not establish settlements there. Even these mistakes might have had no evil consequences while he lived, had he not made a sixth, attacking the Venetians. Had he not strengthened the Church and brought the Spanish into Italy, then it would have been reasonable and appropriate to attack them; but having done what he had done, he should never have given his consent to a policy aimed at their destruction. For as long as they remained powerful, the others would never have been prepared to undertake an attack upon Lombardy. For the Venetians would not have consented to Lombardy's falling into the hands of others, and not themselves; while the others would not have wanted to take Lombardy from the King of France only to give it to the Venetians, and would not have had the courage to try to take it away from both of them.

And if someone were to reply that King Louis allowed Alexander to take the Romagna, and the King of Spain to have the Kingdom of Naples, in order to avoid a war, I would answer as I did above: One should never allow a problem to develop in order to avoid a war, for you end up not avoiding the war, but deferring it to a time that will be less favorable. And if others were to appeal to the promise the king had given to the pope, to help him seize the Romagna in return for the pope's giving him a divorce and making the Bishop of Rouen a cardinal, I would reply with what I will say later on the subject of whether and to what extent rulers should keep their word.

Thus, King Louis lost Lombardy because he did not follow any of the policies others have adopted when they have established predominance within a region and have wanted to hold on to it. There is nothing remarkable about what happened: It is entirely natural and predictable. I spoke about these matters with the Cardinal of Rouen in Nantes, when Valentino (as Cesare Borgia, son of Pope Alexander, was commonly called) was taking possession of the Romagna. The cardinal said to me that the Italians did not understand war; so I told him that the French did not understand politics, for if they did, they would not allow the church to acquire so much power. And in practice we have seen that the strength of the papacy and of the King of Spain within Italy has been brought about by the King of France, and they in turn have been the cause of his own ruin. From this one can draw a general conclusion that will never (or hardly ever) be proved wrong: He who is the cause of someone else's becoming powerful is the agent of his own destruction; for he makes his protegé powerful either through his own skill or through his own strength, and either of these must provoke his protegé's mistrust once he has become powerful.

Chapter Four: Why the kingdom of Darius, which Alexander occupied, did not rebel against his successors after Alexander's death.

When you think of the difficulties associated with trying to hold on to a newly acquired state, you might well be puzzled: Since Alexander the Great had conquered Asia in the space of a few years, and then died when he had scarcely had time to take possession of it, at that point you would expect the whole state to rebel.[13] Nevertheless, Alexander's successors maintained possession of it and had no difficulty in keeping hold of it, beyond the conflicts that sprung up between themselves as a result of their own ambitions. My explanation is that the principalities recorded in history have been governed in two different ways: either by a single individual, and everyone else has been his servant, and they have helped to govern his kingdom as ministers, appointed by his grace and benevolence; or by a monarch together with barons, who, not by concession of the ruler, but by virtue of their noble lineage, hold that rank. Such barons have their own territories and their own subjects: subjects who recognize them as their lords and feel a natural affection for them. In those states that are governed by a single individual and his servants, the sovereign has more authority in his own hands; for in all his territories there is no one recognized as having a right to rule except him alone; and if his subjects obey anyone else, they do so because he is the ruler's minister and representative, and they do not feel any particular loyalty to these subordinate authorities.

In our own day the obvious examples of these two types of ruler are the Sultan of Turkey and the King of France. All the kingdom of Turkey is ruled by a single monarch, and everyone else is his servant. He divides his kingdom into sanjaks,[14] sending administrators, whom he replaces and transfers as he thinks best, to rule them. But the King of France is placed among a multitude of long-established nobles, whose rights are recognized by their subjects and who are loved by them. They have their own inherited privileges, and the king cannot take them away without endangering himself. If you compare these two states, you will realize it would be difficult to seize the sultan's kingdom, but, once you had got control of it, it would be very easy to hold on to it.

It would be difficult to occupy the lands of the sultan for two reasons: The local authorities of that kingdom will not invite you to invade, nor can you hope those around the ruler will rebel, making your task easier. And this for the reasons I have explained. For, since they are all his slaves, and indebted to him, it is harder to corrupt them; and even if you can corrupt them, they are not going to be much use to you, for they cannot command the obedience of the people, as I have explained. Consequently, anyone attacking the sultan must expect to find the Turks united in his defense and must rely more on his own strength than on the disorder of his opponents. But once he has defeated them and has destroyed their forces on the field of battle so completely they cannot muster an army, then he has no one to worry about except the sultan's close relatives. Once he has got rid of them, then there is no one left for him to fear, for there is no one else with influence over the people. Just as the invader, before his victory, had no reason to hope for support, so, after his victory, he has no reason to fear opposition.

The opposite is true in kingdoms governed like that of France. For it is easy to invade them, once one has gained the support of some local noble. For in such kingdoms one can always find malcontents who hope to benefit from innovation. These, as we have seen, can ease your entrance into the state and help you win victory. But then, when you try to hold on to power, you will find the nobility, both those who have been your allies and those you have defeated, present you with an infinity of problems. It simply is not sufficient to kill the ruler and his close relatives, for the rest of the nobility will survive to provide leadership for new insurrections. You cannot win their loyalty or wipe them out, so you will always be in danger of losing your kingdom should anything go wrong.

Now if you ask yourself what sort of state it was Darius ruled, you will see it was similar to that of the sultan. So it was necessary for Alexander, first to take on his forces and seize control of the territory. Once he was victorious, and Darius was dead, Alexander had a firm grip on his new lands, for the reasons I have given. And his successors, if they had stayed united, could have enjoyed them at their leisure; nor was there any resistance to them in that kingdom, apart from their own conflicts with one another. But states that are organized after the French model cannot be held onto, once seized, with such ease. This is why there were frequent rebellions in Spain, France,[15] and Greece against the Romans. For there were many rulers in those territories, and as long as people remembered them, the Romans were always unsure of their grip. Once the memory of these rulers had faded completely away, thanks to the long duration of Roman rule, they became secure in their possession. Even after that, each faction among the Romans, when they fought among themselves, could call on the support of a section of those provinces, depending on the influence they had built up within them. The subjects of these territories, because their former rulers had no heirs, had no loyalties except to Roman leaders. Once you have considered all these matters, you will not be at all surprised at the ease with which Alexander held on to Asia or at the difficulties other conquerors (one might take Pyrrhus as one example among many) have had in keeping control of their acquisitions. The crucial factor in these differing outcomes is not the strength [virtù] or weakness of the conqueror but the contrasting character of the societies that have been conquered.

Chapter Five: How you should govern cities or kingdoms that, before you acquired them, lived under their own laws.

When the states one acquires by conquest are accustomed to living under their own laws and in freedom, there are three policies one can follow in order to hold on to them: The first is to lay them waste; the second is to go and live there in person; the third is to let them continue to live under their own laws, make them pay you, and create there an administrative and political elite who will remain loyal to you. For since the elite are the creation of the head of state, its members know they cannot survive without both his friendship and his power, and they know it is in their interest to do everything to sustain it. It is easier to rule a city that is used to being self-governing by employing its own citizens than by other means, assuming you do not wish to destroy it.

Examples are provided by the Spartans and the Romans. The Spartans took Athens and Thebes, establishing oligarchies there. However, they lost them again.[16] The Romans, in order to hold on to Capua, Carthage, and Numantia razed them and never lost them.[17] They sought to govern Greece according to more or less the same policies as those used by Sparta, letting the Greek cities rule themselves and enforce their own laws, but the policy failed, so in the end they were obliged to demolish many cities in that territory in order to hold on to them. The simple truth is there is no reliable way of holding on to a city and the territory around it, short of demolishing the city itself. He who becomes the ruler of a city that is used to living under its own laws and does not knock it down, must expect to be knocked down by it. Whenever it rebels, it will find strength in the language of liberty and will seek to restore its ancient constitution. Neither the passage of time nor good treatment will make its citizens forget their previous liberty. No matter what one does, and what precautions one takes, if one does not scatter and drive away the original inhabitants, one will not destroy the memory of liberty or the attraction of the old institutions. As soon as there is a crisis, they will seek to restore them. This is what happened in Pisa after it had been enslaved by the Florentines for a hundred years.[18]

But when cities or provinces are used to being ruled by a monarch, and one has wiped out his relatives and descendants, then matters are very different. They are used to being obedient. Their old ruler is gone, and they cannot agree among themselves as to who should replace him. They do not know how to rule themselves. The result is that they are slower to take up arms, and it is easier for a new ruler to win them over and establish himself securely in power. But in former republics there is more vitality, more hatred, more desire for revenge. The memory of their former freedom gives them no rest, no peace. So the best thing to do is to demolish them or to go and live there oneself.

Chapter Six: About new kingdoms acquired with one's own armies and one's own skill [virtù].

No one should be surprised if, in talking about completely new kingdoms (that is, states that are governed by someone who was not a ruler before, and were themselves not previously principalities), I point to the greatest of men as examples to follow. For men almost always walk along the beaten path, and what they do is almost always an imitation of what others have done before. But you cannot walk exactly in the footsteps of those who have gone before, nor is it easy to match the skill [virtù] of those you have chosen to imitate. Consequently, a prudent man will always try to follow in the footsteps of great men and imitate those who have been truly outstanding, so that, if he is not quite as skillful [virtù] as they, at least some of their ability may rub off on him. One should be like an experienced archer, who, trying to hit someone at a distance and knowing the range [virtù] of his bow, aims at a point above his target, not so his arrow will strike the point he is aiming at, but so, by aiming high, he can reach his objective.

I maintain that, in completely new kingdoms, the new ruler has more or less difficulty in keeping hold of power depending on whether he is more or less skillful [virtuoso]. Now you only find yourself in this situation, a private individual only becomes a ruler, if you are either lucky, or skillful [virtù]. Both luck and skill enable you to overcome difficulties. Nevertheless, he who relies least on luck has the best prospect of success. One advantage is common to any completely new sovereign: Because he has no other territories, he has no choice but to come in person and live in his new kingdom. Let us look at those who through their own skill [virtù], and not merely through chance, have become rulers. In my view, the greatest have been Moses, Cyrus, Romulus, Theseus, and others like them.[19]

Obviously, we should not discuss Moses' skill, for he was a mere agent, following the instructions given him by God. So he should be admired, not for his own skill, but for that grace that made him worthy to talk with God. But let us discuss Cyrus and the others who have acquired existing kingdoms or founded new ones. You will find them all admirable. And if you look at the actions and strategies of each one of them, you will find they do not significantly differ from those of Moses, who could not have had a better teacher. If you look at their deeds and their lives, you will find they were dependent on chance only for their first opportunity. They seized their chance to make of it what they wanted. Without that first opportunity their strength [virtù] of purpose would never have been revealed. Without their strength [virtù] of purpose, the opportunity they were offered would not have amounted to anything.

Thus, it was necessary for Moses to find the people of Israel in Egypt, enslaved and oppressed by the Egyptians, so they, in order to escape from slavery, would be prepared to follow him. It was essential for Romulus to have no future in Alba, it was appropriate he should have been exposed at birth, otherwise he would not have formed the ambition of becoming King of Rome and succeeded in founding that nation. It was necessary that Cyrus should find the Persians hostile to the rule of the Medes, and the Medes weak and effeminate from too much peace. Theseus could not have demonstrated his strength of purpose [*virtù*] if he had not found the Athenians scattered. These opportunities made these men lucky; but it was their remarkable political skill [*virtù*] that enabled them to recognize these opportunities for what they were. Thanks to them their nations were ennobled and blessed with good fortune.

Those who become rulers through strength of purpose [*vie virtuose*], as they did, acquire their kingdoms with difficulty, but they hold on to them with ease. And much of the difficulty they have in getting to power derives from the new institutions and customs they are obliged to establish in order to found their governments and make them secure. One ought to pause and consider the fact that there is nothing harder to undertake, nothing more likely of failure, nothing more risky to pull off, than to set oneself up as a leader who plans to found a new system of government. For the founder makes enemies of all those who are doing well under the old system, and has only lukewarm support from those who hope to do well under the new one. The weakness of their support springs partly from their fear of their adversaries, who have the law on their side, partly from their own want of faith. For men do not truly believe in new things until they have had practical experience of them. So it is that, whenever those who are enemies of the new order have a chance to attack it, they do so ferociously, while the others defend it halfheartedly. So the new ruler is in danger, along with his supporters.

It is necessary, however, if we are going to make sense of his situation, to find out if our innovator stands on his own feet, or depends on others to prop him up. That is, we need to know if he is obliged to try to obtain his objectives by pleading, or whether he can resort to force. In the first case, he is bound to come to a bad end, and won't achieve anything. But when he can stand on his own feet, and can resort to force, then he can usually overcome the dangers he faces. Thus it is that all armed prophets are victorious, and disarmed ones are crushed. For there is another problem: People are by nature inconstant. It is easy to persuade them of something, but it is difficult to stop them from changing their minds. So you have to be prepared for the moment when they no longer believe: Then you have to force them to believe. Moses, Cyrus, Theseus, and Romulus would not have been able to make their peoples obey their new structures of authority for long if they had been unarmed. This is what happened, in our own day, to Friar Girolamo Savonarola.[20] He and his new constitution were destroyed as soon as the multitude began to stop believing in him. He had no way of stiffening the resolution of those who had been believers or of forcing disbelievers to obey.

Thus the founders of new states have immense difficulties to overcome, and dangers beset their path, dangers they must overcome by skill and strength of purpose [*virtù*]. But, once they have overcome them, and they have begun to be idolized, having got rid of those who were jealous of their superior qualities, they are established, they are powerful, secure, honored, happy.

We have looked at some noble examples, and to them I want to add one less remarkable. Nevertheless, it has some points of similarity to them, and I want it to stand for all the other lesser examples I could have chosen. My example is Hiero of Syracuse.[21] He was a private individual who became ruler of Syracuse. He, too, did not depend on luck once he had been given his opportunity. The people of Syracuse were oppressed and elected him as their military commander; so he deserved to be made their ruler. He was so remarkable [*di tanta virtù*], even before he became a ruler, history records "that he had everything one would look for in a king, except a kingdom." He disbanded the old militia and instituted a new one. Dropped his old friends and chose new ones. Since both his friends and his soldiers were his creatures, he had laid the foundations for constructing any political system he chose. He, too, had difficulties enough to overcome in acquiring power, and few in holding on to it.

Chapter Seven: About new principalities that are acquired with the forces of others and with good luck.

Those who, having started as private individuals, become rulers merely out of good luck, acquire power with little trouble but have a hard time holding on to it. They have no problems on the road to power, because they leap over all the obstacles; but dangers crowd around them once they are in power. I am talking about people who are given a state, either in return for money, or out of the goodwill of him who hands it over to them. This happened to many individuals in Greece, in the cities of Ionia and the Hellespont, who were made rulers by Darius, who wanted them to hold their cities for his own greater safety and glory.[22] So, too, with those who, having been private citizens, were made emperors of Rome because they had corrupted the soldiers.[23] Such rulers are entirely dependent on the goodwill and good fortune of whoever has given them power. Good will and good fortune are totally unreliable and capricious. Such rulers do not know how to hold on to their position and cannot do so. They do not know how, because they have always been private citizens, and only a brilliant and immensely skillful [di grande virtù] man is likely to know how to command without having had training and experience. They cannot because they have no troops of their own on whose loyalty and commitment they can count.

Moreover, states that spring up overnight, like all other things in nature that are born and grow in a hurry, cannot have their roots deep in the soil, so they shrivel up in the first drought, blow over in the first storm. Unless, as I have said, those who are suddenly made into rulers are of such extraordinary capacity [virtù] they can work out on the spot how to hold on to the gift fortune has unexpectedly handed them; and those preparations the others made before they became rulers, they must find a way of making after the event.

I want to add to the one and the other of these two ways of becoming a ruler, by skill [virtù] or by luck, two examples drawn from the events that have occurred in our own lifetimes: the examples of Francesco Sforza and Cesare Borgia. Francesco, by using the right methods and consummate skill [virtù], started out as a private citizen and ended up as Duke of Milan. And what he had acquired with painstaking effort, he held on to without trouble.[24] On the other hand Cesare Borgia, who was called Duke Valentino by the common people, acquired his state thanks to the good fortune of his father, and when that came to an end he lost it.[25] This despite the fact he used every technique and did all the things a prudent and skillful [virtuoso] man ought to do, to entrench himself in those territories that the arms and fortune of others had acquired for him.

For, as I said above, he who does not prepare the foundations first can (in principle), if he is immensely skillful [virtù], make up for it later, although the architect will find catching up a painful process, and there is a real danger the building will collapse. So, if we look at all the things Borgia did, we will see he had laid solid foundations for future power. I do not think it irrelevant to discuss his policies, because I cannot think of any better example I could offer a new ruler than that of his actions. And if his strategy did not lead to success, this was not his fault; his failure was due to extraordinary and exceptional hostility on the part of fortune.

Pope Alexander VI, in setting out to make his son the duke into a ruler, was faced with considerable immediate and long-term difficulties. In the first place, he could find no way of making him the lord of any territory, except territory that belonged to the church. And he knew if he took land from the church to give to Cesare, he would have to overcome the opposition of the Duke of Milan, and also of the Venetians, for both Faenza and Rimini were already under Venetian protection. Secondly, he saw the armed forces of Italy, and particularly those he could hope to employ, were under the control of individuals who had reason to fear any increase in papal power. Consequently, he could not regard them as reliable. He could not trust the Orsini, the Colonna, or their associates, but there was no one else to whom he could turn.[26] So it was necessary to break out of this framework, and to bring disorder to the territories of his opponents, so he could safely seize a part of them. This proved easy, for he found the Venetians, for reasons of their own, had decided to invite the French to invade Italy. He not only did not oppose this, but he facilitated it by dissolving the previous marriage of King Louis. So the king marched into Italy, with the help of the Venetians and the consent of Alexander. No sooner was he in Milan than the pope had borrowed forces from him for the attack on the Romagna, which was ceded to him out of fear of the King of France.

So, once Cesare had been made Duke of the Romagna, and the Colonnesi had been beaten, wanting to hang on to his new territories and make further conquests, he was faced with two obstacles. In the first place, his military forces did not appear reliable. In the second, the King of France might oppose him. He had made use of the troops of the Orsini, but they were likely to abandon him, and not only prevent him from making further acquisitions, but take from him what he had already acquired. And the same was true of the king. He had an indication of how far he could trust the Orsini when, after Faenza had been taken by storm, he attacked Bologna, for he discovered they had no appetite for that battle.[27] And as for the king, he discovered his attitude when, having seized the Duchy of Urbino, he attacked Tuscany, for Louis made him abandon that enterprise.[28] So the duke decided he must no longer depend on the troops and the good fortune of others.

The first thing he did was to weaken the factions of the Orsini and the Colonna in Rome. All the nobles who were allied to these families he won over to himself, making them members of his court, and giving them substantial pensions. He favored them with civil and military appointments appropriate to their standing. Thus, in the course of a few months, their attachment to their factions was dissolved, and they became committed to the duke. Next, he looked for a chance to crush the Orsini, having already defeated the forces of the Colonna family. He soon had his chance and he made the most of it. For the Orsini, having realized late in the day that the growing strength of the duke and the pope would be their ruin, called a meeting at Magione, near Perugia. From that meeting sprang the rebellion of Urbino and the uprisings in the Romagna that almost destroyed the duke; but he overcame all resistance with the help of the French.[29] And, having got back his authority and realizing he could trust neither the French nor other external forces, he decided that, in order to prevent their allying against him, he must deceive them. He so successfully concealed his intentions that the Orsini, represented by Signor Paolo, made peace with him. The duke took every opportunity to ingratiate himself with Paolo, giving him money, clothes, and horses. So the leaders of the Orsini were brought, unsuspecting, to Sinigallia, where they were at his mercy.[30] Having got rid of the leaders and won the allegiance of their followers, the duke could feel he had laid decent foundations for his future power. He had control of all the Romagna and the Duchy of Urbino, and it looked as though he had won over the Romagna and acquired the support of its population, who were beginning to enjoy a new prosperity.

Now, since it is worth paying attention to this question, and since it would be sensible to imitate Cesare's actions, I want to amplify what I have just said. Once the duke had subdued the Romagna, he found it had been under the control of weak nobles, who had rather exploited than governed their subjects and had rather been the source of conflict than of order, with the result the whole province was full of robbers, bandits, and every other type of criminal. So he decided it was necessary, if he was going to make the province peaceful and obedient to his commands, to give it good government. He put Mr. Remiro d'Orco, a man both cruel and efficient, in charge, and gave him absolute power. D'Orco in short order established peace and unity, and acquired immense authority. At that point, the duke decided such unchecked power was no longer necessary, for he feared people might come to hate it. So he established a civil court in the center of the province, placing an excellent judge in charge of it, and requiring every city to appoint a lawyer to represent it before the court. Since he knew the harsh measures of the past had given rise to some enmity towards him, in order to purge the ill-will of the people and win them completely over to him, he wanted to make clear that, if there had been any cruelty, he was not responsible for it, and that his hard-hearted minister should be blamed. He saw his opportunity and exploited it. One morning, in the town square of Cesena, he had Remiro d'Orco's corpse laid out in two pieces, with a chopping board and a bloody knife beside it.[31] This ferocious sight made the people of the Romagna simultaneously happy and dumbfounded.

But let us get back to where we were. I was saying the duke found himself rather powerful and had taken precautions against immediate dangers, for he had built up a military force that he had planned himself and had in large part destroyed neighboring forces that could be a threat to him. So what remained, if he wanted to make further acquisitions, was the problem of the King of France; for he knew the king had, late in the day, realized his policy towards Borgia had been misconceived and would not allow him to make further conquests. So Borgia began to look for new alliances and to prevaricate with the French when they dispatched a force towards the Kingdom of Naples to attack the Spanish who were laying siege to Gaeta.[32] His intention was to protect himself against them, which he would soon have succeeded in doing, if Alexander had gone on living.

These were the policies he pursued with regard to his immediate concerns. But there were future problems he also had to consider. In the first place, he had to worry that a new pope would be hostile to him and would try to take from him what Alexander had given him. He had four ways of trying to deal with this threat. In the first place, he set out to eliminate all the relatives of those rulers whose lands he had seized, to make it difficult for the pope to restore their previous rulers. Second, he sought to acquire the allegiance of the nobility of Rome, as I have explained, so he could use them to restrict the pope's freedom of action. Third, to make as many as possible of the members of the College of Cardinals his allies. Fourth, to acquire so much power, before the pope died, that he would be able on his own to resist a first attack. Of these four policies he had successfully carried out three by the time Alexander died; the fourth he had almost accomplished. Of the rulers he had dispossessed, he murdered as many as he could get his hands on, and only a very few survived. The Roman nobility were his supporters, and he had built up a very large faction in the College of Cardinals. As far as new acquisitions were concerned, he had plans for conquering Tuscany; he already held Perugia and Piombino; and he had taken Pisa under his protection. And, as soon as he would no longer have to worry about the King of France (which was already the case, for the French had already lost the Kingdom of Naples to the Spanish, with the result that both France and Spain were now obliged to try to buy his friendship), he would be free to seize Pisa. After which, Lucca and Siena would quickly give in, partly because they hated the Florentines, and partly because they would have been terrified. The Florentines could have done nothing.

If he had succeeded in all this (and he was on the point of succeeding in the very year Alexander died) he would have acquired so much strength and so much authority he would have become his own master. He would no longer have depended on events outside his control and on the policies of others, but would have been able to rely on his own power and strength [*virtù*]. But Alexander died only five years after Cesare Borgia had unsheathed his sword.[33] He found himself with only his control over the Romagna firmly established, with everything else up in the air, caught between two powerful hostile armies, and dangerously ill. But the duke was so pugnacious and so strong [*virtù*], he so well understood what determines whether one wins or loses, and he had laid such sound foundations within such a short time, that, if he had not had these enemy armies breathing down his neck, or if he had been in good health, he could have overcome every difficulty.

I am justified in claiming he had laid sound foundations, for the Romagna remained loyal to him in his absence for more than a month; in Rome, although he was half dead, he was quite safe, and although the Ballioni, the Vitelli, and the Orsini congregated in Rome, they could not muster a following to attack him; and, if he was not in a position to choose who should be pope, he could at least veto anyone he did not trust. So, if he had been well when Alexander died he would have been able to deal with his problems without difficulty. He told me himself, on the day Julius II was elected,[34] that he had asked himself what he would do if his father died and had been confident he could handle the situation, but that it had never occurred to him that when his father died he himself would be at death's door.

So, now I have surveyed all the actions of the duke, I still cannot find anything to criticize. It seems to me I have been right to present him as an example to be imitated by all those who come to power through good luck and thanks to someone else's military might. For, since he was greathearted and ambitious, he had no choice as to what to do; and he only failed to achieve his goals because Alexander died too soon, and he himself fell ill. So anyone who decides that the policy to follow when one has newly acquired power is to destroy one's enemies, to secure some allies, to win wars, whether by force or by fraud, to make oneself both loved and feared by one's subjects, to make one's soldiers loyal and respectful, to wipe out those who can or would want to hurt one, to innovate, replacing old institutions with new practices, to be both harsh and generous, magnanimous and openhanded, to disband disloyal troops and form new armies, to build alliances with other powers, so kings and princes either have to win your favor or else think twice before going against your wishes—anyone who thinks in these terms cannot hope to find, in the recent past, a better model to imitate than Cesare Borgia.

His only mistake was to allow Julius to be elected pope, for there he made a bad choice. The choice was his to make, for as I have said, if he could not choose who should be pope, he could veto anyone he did not like, and he should never have agreed to any cardinal's being elected with whom he had been in conflict in the past, or who, once he had been elected, would have been likely to be afraid of him. For men attack either out of fear or out of hatred. Those who had scores to settle with him included San Piero ad Vincula, Colonna, San Giorgio, Ascanio; all the others, if elected pope, would have had good reason to fear him, with the exception of Rouen and of the Spanish cardinals. The Spanish were his relatives and allies; Rouen was powerful, having the support of the King of France. So the duke's first objective should have been to ensure a Spaniard was elected pope; failing that, he should have agreed to the election of Rouen and vetoed that of San Piero ad Vincula. If he imagined recent gestures of goodwill make the powerful forget old injuries, he was much mistaken. So the duke made a mistake during the election of the pope, and this mistake was, in the end, the cause of his destruction.

Chapter Eight: Of those who come to power through wicked actions.

But since there are two other ways a private citizen can become a ruler, two ways that do not simply involve the acquisition of power either through fortune or strength [*virtù*], I feel I cannot omit discussion of them, although one of them can be more fully treated elsewhere, where I discuss republics. These are, first, when one acquires power through some wicked or nefarious action, and second when a private citizen becomes ruler of his own country because he has the support of his fellow citizens. Here I will talk about the first of these two routes to power, and will use two examples, one ancient, one modern, to show how it is done. These will be sufficient, I trust, to provide a model for anyone who has no alternative options. I do not intend to discuss in detail the rights and wrongs of such a policy.

Agathocles of Sicily became King of Syracuse, although he was not merely a private citizen, but of humble and poverty-stricken origins.[35] He was the son of a potter, and from start to finish lived a wicked life; nevertheless, his wicked behavior testified to so much strength [*virtù*] of mind and of body that, when he joined the army, he was promoted through the ranks to the supreme command. Having risen so high, he decided to become the sole ruler and to hold on to power, which he had originally been granted by the consent of his fellow citizens, by violence and without being dependent on anyone else. Having entered into a conspiracy with a Carthaginian called Hamilcar, who was commander of a hostile army serving in Sicily, one morning he called together the people and the senate of Syracuse, as if he wanted to discuss matters of government policy, and, at a prearranged signal, had his soldiers kill all the senators and the richest citizens. With them out of the way, he made himself ruler of the city and held power without any resistance. Although the Carthaginians twice defeated his armies and even advanced to the walls of the city, he was not only able to defend his city, but, leaving part of his army behind to withstand the siege, he was able to attack the Carthaginians in Africa with the remainder of his forces. Within a short time he had forced them to lift the siege and was threatening to conquer Carthage. In the end they were obliged to come to terms with him, leaving Sicily to Agathocles in return for security in Africa.

If you consider Agathocles' bold achievements [*azioni e virtù*], you will not find much that can be attributed to luck; for, as I have said, he did not come to power because he had help from above, but because he worked his way up from below, climbing from rank to rank by undergoing infinite dangers and discomforts until in the end he obtained a monopoly of power, and then holding on to his position by bold and risky tactics.

One ought not, of course, to call it *virtù* [virtue or manliness] to massacre one's fellow citizens, to betray one's friends, to break one's word, to be without mercy and without religion. By such means one can acquire power but not glory. If one considers the manly qualities [*virtù*] Agathocles demonstrated in braving and facing down danger, and the strength of character he showed in surviving and overcoming adversity, then there seems to be no reason why he should be judged less admirable than any of the finest generals. But on the other hand, his inhuman cruelty and brutality, and his innumerable wicked actions, mean it would be wrong to praise him as one of the finest of men. It is clear, at any rate, that one can attribute neither to luck nor to virtue [*virtù*] his accomplishments, which owed nothing to either.

In our own day, when Alexander VI was pope, Oliverotto of Fermo, whose father had died a few years before, was raised by his maternal uncle, Giovanni Fogliani.[36] As soon as he was old enough he joined the forces of Paolo Vitelli, so that, with a good military training, he could pursue a career in the army.[37] When Paolo died, he signed up with his brother, Vitellozzo. In a very short time, because he was bright and had both a strong body and a lively spirit, he became Vitellozzo's second-in-command. Soon he thought it to be beneath his dignity to serve under another, and so he conspired to occupy Fermo, relying on the help of some citizens of that city who preferred to see their fatherland enslaved than free, and on the support of Vitellozzo. He wrote to his uncle, saying that, since he had been away from home for many years, he wanted to come to visit him and to see his city, and so, in a manner of speaking, reacquaint himself with his inheritance. He said he had only gone to war in order to acquire honor. So his fellow citizens would be able to see he had not been wasting his time, he wanted to arrive in state, accompanied by a hundred men on horseback, some of them his friends, and others his servants. He asked his uncle to ensure that the inhabitants of Fermo received him with respect: This would not only enhance his own reputation, but that of his uncle, who had raised him.

Giovanni did everything he could for his nephew. He ensured he was greeted by the people of Fermo with every honor, and he put him up in his own house. After a few days had gone by, and he had had time to make the arrangements necessary for the carrying out of his wicked plans, he held a lavish banquet at his uncle's, to which he invited his uncle and the most powerful citizens of Fermo. After the food had been eaten, and the guests had been entertained in all the ways that are customary upon such occasions, Oliverotto deliberately began discussing serious questions, talking about the greatness of Pope Alexander and his son Cesare, and about their undertakings. When his uncle Giovanni and the others picked up the subject, he sprang to his feet, saying such matters should be discussed in a more private place. He withdrew into another room, where Giovanni and all the other leading citizens followed. No sooner had they sat down than soldiers emerged from their hiding places and killed Giovanni along with all the rest. Once the killing was over, Oliverotto got on his horse and took possession of the city, laying siege to the government building. Those in authority were so terrified they agreed to obey him and to establish a new regime of which he was the head. With all those who had something to lose and would have been able to resist him dead, he was able to entrench himself by establishing new civilian and military institutions. Within a year of coming to power, he was not only securely in control of Fermo, but had become a threat to all the cities round about. It would soon have been as difficult to get rid of him as to get rid of Agathocles, had he not allowed himself to be taken in by Cesare Borgia, when, as I have already explained, he got rid of the Orsini and the Vitelli at Sinigallia. Oliverotto was seized at the same time, and, a year after he had killed his uncle, he was strangled along with Vitellozzo from whom he had learned how to be bold [*virtù*] and how to be wicked.

Perhaps you are wondering how Agathocles and others like him, despite their habitual faithlessness and cruelty, have been able to live safely in their homelands year after year, and to defend themselves against their enemies abroad. Why did their fellow subjects not conspire against them? After all, mere cruelty has not been enough to enable many other rulers to hang on to power even in time of peace, let alone during the turmoil of war. I think here we have to distinguish between cruelty well used and cruelty abused. Well-used cruelty (if one can speak well of evil) one may call those atrocities that are committed at a stroke, in order to secure one's power, and are then not repeated, rather every effort is made to ensure one's subjects benefit in the long run. An abuse of cruelty one may call those policies that, even if in the beginning they involve little bloodshed, lead to more rather than less as time goes by. Those who use cruelty well may indeed find both God and their subjects are prepared to let bygones be bygones, as was the case with Agathocles. Those who abuse it cannot hope to retain power indefinitely.

So the conclusion is: If you take control of a state, you should make a list of all the crimes you have to commit and do them all at once. That way you will not have to commit new atrocities every day, and you will be able, by not repeating your evil deeds, to reassure your subjects and to win their support by treating them well. He who acts otherwise, either out of squeamishness or out of bad judgment, has to hold a bloody knife in his hand all the time. He can never rely on his subjects, for they can never trust him, for he is always making new attacks upon them. Do all the harm you must at one and the same time, that way the full extent of it will not be noticed, and it will give least offense. One should do good, on the other hand, little by little, so people can fully appreciate it.

A ruler should, above all, behave towards his subjects in such a way that, whatever happens, whether for good or ill, he has no need to change his policies. For if you fall on evil times and are obliged to change course, you will not have time to benefit from the harm you do, and the good you do will do you no good, because people will think you have been forced to do it, and they will not be in the slightest bit grateful to you.

Chapter Nine: Of the citizen-ruler.

But, coming to the alternative possibility, when a private citizen becomes the ruler of his homeland, not through wickedness or some act of atrocity, but through the support of his fellow citizens, so that we may call him a citizen-ruler (remember we are discussing power acquired neither by pure strength *[virtù]* nor mere luck—in this case one needs a lucky cunning), I would point out there are two ways to such power: the support of the populace or the favor of the elite. For in every city one finds these two opposed classes. They are at odds because the populace do not want to be ordered about or oppressed by the elite; and the elite want to order about and oppress the populace. The conflict between these two irreconcilable ambitions has in each city one of three possible consequences: rule by one man, liberty, or anarchy.

Rule by one man can be brought about either by the populace or the elite, depending on whether one or the other of these factions hopes to benefit from it. For if the elite fear they will be unable to control the populace, they begin to build up the reputation of one of their own, and they make him sole ruler in order to be able, under his protection, to achieve their objectives. The populace on the other hand, if they fear they are going to be crushed by the elite, build up the reputation of one of their number and make him sole ruler, in order that his authority may be employed in their defense. He who comes to power with the help of the elite has more difficulty in holding on to power than he who comes to power with the help of the populace, for in the former case he is surrounded by many who think of themselves as his equals, and whom he consequently cannot order about or manipulate as he might wish. He who comes to power with the support of the populace, on the other hand, has it all to himself. There is no one, or hardly anyone, around him who is not prepared to obey. In addition, one cannot honorably give the elite what they want, and one cannot do it without harming others; but this is not true with the populace, for the objectives of the populace are less immoral than those of the elite, for the latter want to oppress, and the former not to be oppressed. Thirdly, if the masses are opposed to you, you can never be secure, for there are too many of them; but the elite, since there are few of them, can be neutralized.

The worst a ruler who is opposed by the populace has to fear is that they will give him no support; but from the elite he has to fear not only lack of support, but worse, that they will attack him. For the elite have more foresight and more cunning; they act in time to protect themselves, and seek to ingratiate themselves with rivals for power. Finally, the ruler cannot get rid of the populace but must live with them; he can, however, get by perfectly well without the members of the elite, being able to make and unmake them each day, and being in a position to give them status or take it away, as he chooses.

In order to clarify the issues, let me point out there are two principal points of view from which one should consider the elite. Either they behave in a way that ties their fortunes to yours, or they do not. Those who tie themselves to you and are not rapacious, you should honor and love; those who do not tie themselves to you are to be divided into two categories. If they retain their independence through pusillanimity and because they are lacking in courage, then you should employ them, especially if they have good judgment, for you can be sure they will help you achieve success so long as things are going well for you, and you can also be confident you have nothing to fear from them if things go badly. But if they retain their independence from you out of calculation and ambition, then you can tell they are more interested in their own welfare than yours. A ruler must protect himself against such people and fear them as much as if they were publicly declared enemies, for you can be sure that, in adversity, they will help to overthrow you.

Anyone who becomes a ruler with the support of the populace ought to ensure he keeps their support; which will not be difficult, for all they ask is not to be oppressed. But anyone who becomes a ruler with the support of the elite and against the wishes of the populace must above all else seek to win the populace over to his side, which will be easy to do if he protects their interests. And since people, when they are well-treated by someone whom they expected to treat them badly, feel all the more obliged to their benefactor, he will find that the populace will quickly become better inclined towards him than if he had come to power with their support. There are numerous ways the ruler can win the support of the populace. They vary so much depending on the circumstances they cannot be reduced to a formula, and, consequently, I will not go into them here. I will simply conclude by saying a ruler needs to have the support of the populace, for otherwise he has nothing to fall back on in times of adversity.

Nabis, ruler of the Spartans, survived an attack by the confederate forces of all Greece, together with an almost invincible Roman army, and successfully defended both his homeland and his own hold on power. All he needed to do, when faced with danger, was neutralize a few; but if he had had the populace opposed to him, this would have been insufficient.[38] Do not think you can rebut my argument by citing the well-worn proverb, "Relying on the people is like building on the sand." This is quite true when a private citizen depends upon them and gives the impression he expects the populace to free him if he is seized by his enemies or by the magistrates. In such a case one can easily find oneself disappointed, as happened to the Gracchi in Rome and to Mr. Giorgio Scali in Florence.[39] But if you are a ruler and you put your trust in the populace, if you can give commands and are capable of bold action, if you are not nonplused by adversity, if you take other necessary precautions, and if through your own courage and your policies you keep up the morale of the populace, then you will never be let down by them, and you will discover you have built on a sound foundation.

The type of one-man rule we are discussing tends to be at risk at the moment of transition from constitutional to dictatorial government. Such rulers either give commands in their own name, or act through the officers of state. In the second case, their situation is more dangerous and less secure. For they are entirely dependent on the cooperation of those citizens who have been appointed to the offices of state, who can, particularly at times of crisis, easily deprive them of their power, either by directly opposing them or by simply failing to carry out their instructions. It is too late for the ruler once a crisis is upon him to seize dictatorial authority, for the citizens and the subjects, who are used to obeying the constituted authorities, will not, in such circumstances, obey him, and he will always have, in difficult circumstances, a shortage of people on whom he can rely. For such a ruler cannot expect things to continue as they were when there were no difficulties, when all the citizens are conscious of what the government can do for them. Then everyone flocked round, everyone promised support, everyone was willing to die for him, when there was no prospect of having to do so. But when times are tough, when the government is dependent on its citizens, then there will be few who are prepared to stand by it. One does not learn the danger of such an erosion of support from experience, as the first experience proves fatal. So a wise ruler will seek to ensure that his citizens always, no matter what the circumstances, have an interest in preserving both him and his authority. If he can do this, they will always be faithful to him.

Chapter Twelve: How many types of army are there, and what opinion should one have of mercenary soldiers?

So far I have discussed one by one the various types of one-man rule I listed at the beginning, and I have to some extent described the policies that make each type succeed or fail. I have shown the various techniques employed by numerous individuals who have sought to acquire and to hold on to power. Now my task is to outline the various strategies for offense and defense that are common to all these principalities. I said above it was necessary for a ruler to lay good foundations; otherwise, he is likely to be destroyed. The principal foundations on which the power of all governments is based (whether they be new, long-established, or mixed) are good laws and good armies. And, since there cannot be good laws where there are not good armies, and since where there are good armies, there must be good laws, I will omit any discussion of laws, and will talk about armies.

Let me begin by saying, then, that a ruler defends his state with armies that are made up of his own subjects, or of mercenaries, or of auxiliary forces, or of some combination of these three types. Mercenaries and auxiliaries are both useless and dangerous. Anyone who relies on mercenary troops to keep himself in power will never be safe or secure, for they are factious, ambitious, ill-disciplined, treacherous. They show off to your allies and run away from your enemies. They do not fear God and do not keep faith with mankind. A mercenary army puts off defeat for only so long as it postpones going into battle. In peacetime they pillage you, in wartime they let the enemy do it. This is why: They have no motive or principle for joining up beyond the desire to collect their pay. And what you pay them is not enough to make them want to die for you. They are delighted to be your soldiers when you are not at war; when you are at war, they walk away when they do not run. It should not be difficult to convince you of this, because the sole cause of the present ruin of Italy has been the fact that for many years now the Italians have been willing to rely on mercenaries. It is true that occasionally a ruler seems to benefit from their use, and they boast of their own prowess, but as soon as they face foreign troops their true worth becomes apparent. This is why Charles, King of France, was able to conquer Italy with a piece of chalk; and the person who said we were being punished for our sins spoke the truth.[40] But our sins were not the ones of which he was thinking, but those I have been discussing. Because these were the sins of our rulers, our rulers as well as the common people had to pay the price for them.

I want now to make crystal clear the worthlessness of mercenary armies. Mercenary commanders are either excellent or not. If they are excellent, you cannot trust them, for they will always be looking for ways of increasing their own power, either by turning on you, their employer, or by turning on others whom you want them to leave alone. On the other hand, if they are not first rate [virtuoso], then they will be the ruin of you in the normal course of events. And if you want to reply the same problems will arise whoever makes up the army, whether they are mercenaries or not, I will argue it depends on whether they take their orders from a sovereign or from a republic. A sovereign ought to go to war himself, and be his own general. A republic has to send one of its citizens. If it chooses someone who turns out not to be a successful soldier, it must replace him; if it chooses someone who is successful, it must tie his hands with laws, to ensure he keeps within the limits assigned to him. Experience shows individual sovereigns and republics that arm the masses are capable of making vast conquests; but mercenary troops are always a liability. Moreover, it is harder for a treacherous citizen to suborn an army consisting of his own fellow subjects than one made up of foreigners.

Rome and Sparta were armed and free for many centuries. The Swiss are armed to the teeth and do not have to take orders from anyone. In ancient history, we can take the Carthaginians as an example of the consequences of relying on mercenaries. They were in danger of being oppressed by their mercenary soldiers when the first war with Rome was over,[41] despite the fact they employed their own citizens as commanders. Philip of Macedon was made general of the Theban armies after the death of Epaminondas; and, after he had won the war, he enslaved the Thebans.[42] In modern times, Milan, after Duke Filippo died, employed Francesco Sforza to fight the Venetians. Once he had defeated the enemy at Caravaggio, he joined forces with them to attack the Milanese, his employers.[43] Sforza his father, who was employed by Queen Giovanna of Naples, abandoned her without warning and without defenses.[44] As a consequence, she was obliged to throw herself into the embrace of the King of Aragon in order to hold on to her kingdom. If the Venetians and the Florentines have in the past succeeded in acquiring new territory with mercenary armies, and if their commanders have not seized the conquests for themselves, but have held onto them for their employers, this, I would argue, is because the Florentines have had more than their share of luck. For of the first-rate [virtuosi] commanders, whom they would have had reason to fear, some have not been victorious, some have not been in sole command, and some have turned their ambitions elsewhere. It was John Hawkwood who did not win: We cannot know if he would have proved reliable had he been victorious, but no one can deny that if he had won Florence would have been his for the taking.[45] Sforza always had to share command with the Braccheschi, and neither could act for fear of the other. Francesco turned his ambitions to Lombardy; Braccio[46] turned his against the church and the Kingdom of Naples.

But let us look at what happened only a short time ago. The Florentines made Paolo Vitelli their commander.[47] He was a very astute man, and, despite being of modest origin, he had acquired a tremendous reputation. If he had succeeded in taking Pisa, no one can deny the Florentines would have needed his goodwill, for, if he had transferred his support to their enemies, they would have been without defenses; and if they had managed to keep his support, they would have had no choice but to do as he told them.

Consider next the conquests made by the Venetians. You will see they ran no risks and won magnificent victories as long as they relied on their own troops, which was until they tried to conquer territory on the mainland. When they armed both the nobility and the populace they had a magnificent fighting force [operorono virtuosissimamente], but when they began to fight on the mainland they abandoned this sound policy [questa virtù], and began to copy the other Italian states. When they began their conquests on the mainland, because they had little territory there, and because their own reputation was fearsome, they had little to fear from their mercenary commanders. But as their conquests extended, as they did under Carmagnola, they began to discover their mistake.[48] They recognized he was a first-rate [virtuosissimo] general, and that they had, under his command, defeated the Duke of Milan, but they realized he had lost his taste for war, and concluded they could no longer win with him, because he no longer wanted victory; but they could not dismiss him, or the land they had acquired would go with him. So, in order to neutralize him, they had to kill him. Since then they have employed as commanders of their forces Bartolemeo of Bergamo, Roberto of San Severino, the Count of Pitigliano, and others like them. With such commanders they had reason to fear defeat, not the consequences of victory. And indeed they were defeated at Vailà, where, in one day, they lost all they had acquired with so much effort in eight hundred years.[49] For with mercenary troops one acquires new territory slowly, feebly, after many attempts; but one loses so much so quickly that it seems an act of God.

And, since these examples have been drawn from recent Italian experience, and since Italy has been entirely dependent on mercenary forces for many years, I want to trace the present state of affairs back to its source, so that, having seen the origin and development of the problem, it will be easier to see how to correct it. You need to understand, then, that in modern times, as soon as the authority of the Holy Roman Empire began to be rejected in Italy, and the pope began to acquire greater authority in temporal affairs, Italy began to be divided into a number of different states. Many of the larger cities went to war against the nobility of the surrounding countryside, who had been oppressing them, and who were, at first, supported by the emperor. The Church, on the other hand, favored the cities in order to build up its temporal authority. In many other cities individual citizens established princedoms. So Italy came to be more or less divided up between those who owed allegiance to the papacy and a number of independent republican city states. Since neither the priests nor the citizens of the republics were accustomed to fighting wars, they began to employ foreigners in their armies.

The first to win a reputation for these mercenary troops was Alberigo of Conio in the Romagna.[50] Among those who were trained by him were Braccio and Sforza, who were, at the height of their powers, the arbiters of Italian affairs. After them came all the others who have commanded mercenary forces down to the present time. The outcome of all their prowess [virtù] has been that Italy has, in quick succession, been overrun by Charles, plundered by Louis, raped by Ferdinand, and humiliated by the Swiss.

The first objective these mercenary commanders have pursued has been to destroy the reputation of the infantry in order to build up that of their own forces. They did this because they have had no resources of their own, but have been dependent on their contracts. A few infantry would have done little for their reputation, while they could not afford to feed a large number. So they specialized in cavalry, for they could feed a reasonably large number, and with them win respect. It came to the point that in an army of twenty thousand soldiers there would not even be two thousand infantry. In addition, they have done everything they could to free themselves and their troops from trouble and from danger. During skirmishes between opposing forces they did not kill each other: Indeed, they not only took prisoners, but released them without demanding a ransom. They were in no hurry to assault fortifications under cover of darkness, while the defending troops were far from eager to mount sorties against their assailants. When they made camp they did not protect themselves with trenches or palisades. They passed the winters in barracks. And all these practices were permitted by their standing orders and were invented, as I said, so they could avoid effort and risk: so much so that they have reduced Italy to a despicable slavery.

Chapter Thirteen: About auxiliary troops, native troops, and composite armies.

Auxiliaries are the other sort of useless troops. You rely on auxiliaries when you appeal to another ruler to come with his own armies to assist or defend you. This is what Pope Julius did in recent times, when, having discovered the incompetence of his mercenary troops during the siege of Ferrara, he decided to rely on auxiliaries, and reached an agreement with King Ferdinand of Spain that he would come to his assistance with his men and arms.[51] Auxiliary troops can be useful and good when fighting on their own behalf, but they are almost always a liability for anyone relying on their assistance. For if they lose, it is you who are defeated; if they win, you are their prisoner. There are plenty of examples of this in ancient history, but I do not want to stray from the contemporary case of Pope Julius II; he can have had no idea what he was doing when, in the hope of acquiring Ferrara, he placed himself entirely into the hands of a foreigner. But he was lucky: The outcome was neither defeat nor imprisonment, so he did not have to pay the price for his foolish decision. His auxiliaries were routed at Ravenna,[52] but then the Swiss came along and drove out the victors, so that, contrary to everyone's expectation, including his own, he did not end up either a prisoner of his enemies, who had fled, or of his auxiliaries, for it was not they who had been victorious. Another example: The Florentines, having no troops of their own, brought ten thousand French soldiers to take Pisa.[53] This decision placed them in more danger than at any other time during their troubles. Again, the Emperor of Constantinople, in order to attack his neighbors, brought ten thousand Turks into Greece. They, when the war was over, had no intention of leaving: This was the beginning of Greece's enslavement to the infidels.[54]

He, then, who has no desire to be the victor should use these troops, for they are much more dangerous than mercenaries. If your auxiliaries win you are ruined, for they are united in their obedience to someone else. If your mercenaries win it takes them more time and more favorable circumstances to turn against you, for they are not united among themselves, and it is you who recruited and paid them. If you appoint an outsider to command them, it takes him time to establish sufficient authority to be able to attack you. In short, where mercenaries are concerned the main risk is cowardice; with auxiliaries it is valor [virtù].

A wise ruler, therefore, will always avoid using mercenary and auxiliary troops, and will rely on his own forces. He would rather lose with his own troops than win with someone else's, for he will not regard it a true victory if it is won with troops that do not belong to him. I never hesitate to cite Cesare Borgia as a model to be imitated. This duke entered the Romagna with an auxiliary army, for his troops were all Frenchmen, and he used it to take Imola and Forlì.[55] But since he did not feel such troops were reliable, he then switched over to mercenaries, believing that using them involved fewer risks, and so he hired the Orsini and the Vitelli. But in practice he found them unreliable, treacherous, and dangerous, and so he got rid of them and formed his own army. And it is easy to see the differences among these three types of army, for you only have to consider how the duke's reputation changed, depending on whether he was relying on the French alone, on the Orsini and the Vitelli, or on his own troops and his own resources. With each change of policy it increased, but he was only taken seriously when everyone could see he was in complete command of his own forces.

I wanted to stick to examples that are both recent and Italian, but I cannot resist mentioning Hiero of Syracuse, since I have already discussed him above. He, when he was made commander-in-chief by the Syracusans, as I have described, quickly realized their mercenary army was worthless, for it was made up of condottieri like our own Italian armies. He decided he could not risk either keeping them on, or letting them go, so he had them massacred. Thereafter, he went to war with troops of his own, not with other people's soldiers. I also want to remind you of an Old Testament story that is relevant. When David proposed to Saul that he should go and fight with Goliath, the Philistine champion, Saul, in order to give him confidence, dressed him in his own armor. David, having tried it on, rejected it, saying he could not give a good account of himself if he relied on Saul's weapons. He wanted to confront the enemy armed with his sling and his knife.[56]

In short, someone else's armor either falls off, or it weighs you down, or it trips you up. Charles VII, father of King Louis XI, having through good luck and valor [virtù] driven the English out of France,[57] recognized that it was essential to have one's own weapons and, so, issued instructions for the establishment of a standing army of cavalry and infantry. Later, his son King Louis abolished the infantry[58] and began to recruit Swiss troops. It was this mistake, imitated by his successors, that was, as we can see from recent events, the cause of the dangers faced by that kingdom.[59] For he built up the reputation of the Swiss while undermining his own military capacity, for he destroyed his own infantry and made his own cavalry dependent on the support of foreign troops, for they, having become accustomed to fighting alongside the Swiss, no longer think they can win without them. The result is the French dare not fight against the Swiss, and without the Swiss they are ineffective against anyone else. So the French armies have been mixed, partly mercenary and partly native. Such a mixed army is much preferable to one made up only of auxiliaries or only of mercenaries, but it is much inferior to one made up entirely of one's own troops. The French example is sufficient to make the point, for the Kingdom of France would be able to overcome any enemy if the foundations laid by Charles VII had been built upon, or even if his instructions had merely been kept in force. But men are foolish, and they embark on something that is attractive in its outward appearance, without recognizing the evil consequences that will follow from it: a point I have already made when talking about consumption.

A ruler who cannot foresee evil consequences before they have time to develop is not truly wise; but few have such wisdom. And if one studies the first destruction of the Roman Empire one discovers it came about as a result of the first recruitment of Gothic soldiers,[60] for from that moment the armies of the Roman Empire began to grow feeble. And all the strength [virtù] that ebbed from the Romans accrued to the Goths. I conclude, therefore, that no ruler is secure unless he has his own troops. Without them he is entirely dependent on fortune, having no strength [virtù] with which to defend himself in adversity. Wise men have always believed and said that, "Nothing is so fragile as a reputation for strength that does not correspond to one's real capacities." Now one's own troops can be made up out of one's subjects, or one's citizens, or one's dependents: All others are either mercenaries or auxiliaries. And the correct way of organizing one's own troops is easy to find out by looking over the instructions given by the four rulers whose conduct I have approved, or by finding out how Philip, the father of Alexander the Great, and how many other republics and sovereigns levied and trained troops: I have complete confidence in their methods.

Chapter Fourteen: What a ruler should do as regards the militia.

A ruler, then, should have no other concern, no other thought, should pay attention to nothing aside from war, military institutions, and the training of his soldiers. For this is the only field in which a ruler has to excel. It is of such importance [virtù] that military prowess not only keeps those who have been born rulers in power, but also often enables men who have been born private citizens to come to power. On the other hand, one sees that when rulers think more about luxuries than about weapons, they fall from power. The prime reason for losing power is neglect of military matters; while being an expert soldier opens the way to the acquisition of power.

Francesco Sforza, because he had troops, became Duke of Milan,[61] having begun life as a private citizen. His descendants, who had no taste for the sweat and dust of a soldier's life, started out as dukes and ended up as private citizens. For, among the other deleterious consequences of not having one's own troops, one comes to be regarded with contempt. There are several types of disgrace a ruler should avoid, as I will explain below. This is one of them. For there is no comparison between a ruler who has his own troops and one who has not. It is not to be expected that someone who is armed should cheerfully obey someone who is defenseless, or that someone who has no weapon should be safe when his employees are armed. For the armed man has contempt for the man without weapons; the defenseless man does not trust someone who can overpower him. The two cannot get on together. So, too, a ruler who does not know how to organize a militia, beyond the other dangers he faces, which I have already described, must recognize that he will not be respected by his troops, and that he cannot trust them.

So a ruler must think only of military matters, and in time of peace he should be even more occupied with them than in time of war. There are two ways he can prepare for war: by thinking and by doing. As far as actions are concerned, he should not only keep his troops in good order and see they are well-trained; he should be always out hunting, thereby accustoming his body to fatigue. He should take the opportunity to study the lie of the land, climbing the mountains, descending into the valleys, crossing the plains, fording rivers, and wading through marshes. He should spare no effort to become acquainted with his own land, and this for two reasons. First, the knowledge will stand him in good stead if he has to defend his state against invasion; second, his knowledge and experience on his own terrain will make it easy for him to understand any other landscape with which he has to become acquainted from scratch. The hills, the valleys, the plains, the rivers, the marshes of, for example, Tuscany have a good deal in common with those of the other regions of Italy. A knowledge of the terrain in one region will make it easy for him to learn about the others. A ruler who lacks this sort of skill does not satisfy the first requirement in a military commander, for it is knowledge of the terrain that enables you to locate the enemy and to get the edge over him when deciding where to camp, in what order to march, how to draw up the troops on the field of battle, and where to build fortifications.

Philopoemon,[62] ruler of the Achaeans, is much praised by the historians,[63] but in particular he is admired because during peacetime he thought about nothing but warfare. When he was out riding in the countryside with his friends, he would often halt and ask: "If the enemy were up on those hills, and we were down here with our army, who would have the better position? How should we advance, following the rule book, to attack him? If we wanted to retreat, how would we set about it? If they were retreating, how would we pursue them?" And so he would invite them to discuss, as they rode along, all the possible eventualities an army may have to face. He listened to their views, he explained his own and backed them up with arguments. Thanks to this continual theorizing he ensured that, if he was at the head of an army, he would be perfectly prepared for anything that might happen.

Such theorizing is not enough. Every ruler should read history books, and in them he should study the actions of admirable men. He should see how they conducted themselves when at war, study why they won some battles and lost others, so he will know what to imitate and what to avoid. Above all he should set himself to imitate the actions of some admirable historical character, as great men have always imitated their glorious predecessors, constantly bearing in mind their actions and their ways of behaving. So, it is said, Alexander the Great took Achilles as his model; Caesar took Alexander; Scipio took Cyrus. If you read the life of Cyrus that was written by Xenophon and then study the life of Scipio you will realize to what extent those qualities that are admired in Scipio derive from Cyrus: His chastity, his affability, his kindness, his generosity, all are modelled upon Cyrus as Xenophon portrays him. A wise ruler will follow these examples. He will never relax during peacetime, but will always be working to take advantage of the opportunities peace presents, so he will be fully prepared when adversity comes. When his luck changes, he must be ready to fight back.

Chapter Fifteen: About those factors that cause men, and especially rulers, to be praised or censured.

Our next task is to consider the policies and principles a ruler ought to follow in dealing with his subjects or with his friends. Since I know many people have written on this subject, I am concerned it may be thought presumptuous for me to write on it as well, especially since what I have to say, as regards this question in particular, will differ greatly from the recommendations of others.[64] But my hope is to write a book that will be useful, at least to those who read it intelligently, and so I thought it sensible to go straight to a discussion of how things are in real life and not waste time with a discussion of an imaginary world. For many authors have constructed imaginary republics and principalities that have never existed in practice and never could; for the gap between how people actually behave and how they ought to behave is so great that anyone who ignores everyday reality in order to live up to an ideal will soon discover he has been taught how to destroy himself, not how to preserve himself. For anyone who wants to act the part of a good man in all circumstances will bring about his own ruin, for those he has to deal with will not all be good. So it is necessary for a ruler, if he wants to hold on to power, to learn how not to be good, and to know when it is and when it is not necessary to use this knowledge.

Let us leave to one side, then, all discussion of imaginary rulers and talk about practical realities. I maintain that all men, when people talk about them, and especially rulers, because they hold positions of authority, are described in terms of qualities that are inextricably linked to censure or to praise. So one man is described as generous, another as a miser [*misero*] (to use the Tuscan term; for "avaricious," in our language, is used of someone who has a rapacious desire to acquire wealth, while we call someone a "miser" when he is unduly reluctant to spend the money he has); one is called open-handed, another tight-fisted; one man is cruel, another gentle; one untrustworthy, another reliable; one effeminate and cowardly, another bold and violent; one sympathetic, another self-important; one promiscuous, another monogamous; one straightforward, another duplicitous; one tough, another easy-going; one serious, another cheerful; one religious, another atheistical; and so on. Now I know everyone will agree that if a ruler could have all the good qualities I have listed and none of the bad ones, then this would be an excellent state of affairs. But one cannot have all the good qualities, nor always act in a praiseworthy fashion, for we do not live in an ideal world. You have to be astute enough to avoid being thought to have those evil qualities that would make it impossible for you to retain power; as for those that are compatible with holding on to power, you should avoid them if you can; but if you cannot, then you should not worry too much if people say you have them. Above all, do not be upset if you are supposed to have those vices a ruler needs if he is going to stay securely in power, for, if you think about it, you will realize there are some ways of behaving that are supposed to be virtuous [*che parrà virtù*], but would lead to your downfall, and others that are supposed to be wicked, but will lead to your welfare and peace of mind.

Chapter Sixteen: On generosity and parsimony.

Let me begin, then, with the qualities I mentioned first. I argue it would be good to be thought generous; nevertheless, if you act in the way that will get you a reputation for generosity, you will do yourself damage. For generosity used skillfully [*virtuosamente*] and practiced as it ought to be, is hidden from sight, and being truly generous will not protect you from acquiring a reputation for parsimony. So, if you want to have a reputation for generosity, you must throw yourself into lavish and ostentatious expenditure. Consequently, a ruler who pursues a reputation for generosity will always end up wasting all his resources; and he will be obliged in the end, if he wants to preserve his reputation, to impose crushing taxes upon the people, to pursue every possible source of income, and to be preoccupied with maximizing his revenues. This will begin to make him hateful to his subjects, and will ensure no one thinks well of him, for no one admires poverty. The result is his supposed generosity will have caused him to offend the vast majority and to have won favor with few. Anything that goes wrong will destabilize him, and the slightest danger will imperil him. Recognizing the problem, and trying to economize, he will quickly find he has acquired a reputation as a miser.

So we see a ruler cannot seek to benefit from a reputation as generous [*questa virtù del liberale*] without harming himself. Recognizing this, he ought, if he is wise, not to mind being called miserly. For, as time goes by, he will be thought of as growing ever more generous, for people will recognize that as a result of his parsimony he is able to live on his income, maintain an adequate army, and undertake new initiatives without imposing new taxes. The result is he will be thought to be generous towards all those whose income he does not tax, which is almost everybody, and stingy towards those who miss out on handouts, who are only a few. In modern times nobody has succeeded on a large scale except those who have been thought miserly; the others came to nothing. Pope Julius II took advantage of a reputation for generosity in order to win election, but once elected he made no effort to keep his reputation, for he wanted to go to war. The present King of France[65] has fought many wars without having to impose additional taxes on his people, because his occasional additional expenditures are offset by his long-term parsimony. The present King of Spain[66] could not have aspired to, or achieved, so many conquests if he had had a reputation for generosity.

So a ruler should not care about being thought miserly, for it means he will be able to avoid robbing his subjects; he will be able to defend himself; he will not become poor and despicable, and he will not be forced to become rapacious. This is one of those vices that make successful government possible. And if you say: But Caesar rose to power thanks to his generosity, and many others have made their way to the highest positions of authority because they have both been and have been thought to be generous. I reply, either you are already a ruler, or you are on your way to becoming one. If you are already a ruler, generosity is a mistake; if you are trying to become one then you do, indeed, need to be thought of as generous. Caesar was one of those competing to become the ruler of Rome; but if, having acquired power, he had lived longer and had not learned to reduce his expenditures, he would have destroyed his own position. You may be tempted to reply: Many established rulers who have been thought to be immensely generous have been successful in war. But my answer is: Rulers either spend their own wealth and that of their subjects, or that of other people. Those who spend their own and their subjects' wealth should be abstemious; those who spend the wealth of others should seize every opportunity to be generous. Rulers who march with their armies, living off plunder, pillage, and confiscations are spending other people's money, and it is essential they should seem generous, for otherwise their soldiers will not follow them. With goods that belong neither to you nor to your subjects, you can afford to be generous, as Cyrus, Caesar, and Alexander were. Squandering other people's money does not do your reputation any harm, quite the reverse. The problem is with squandering your own. There is nothing so self-defeating as generosity, for the more generous you are, the less you are able to be generous. Generosity leads to poverty and disgrace, or, if you try to escape that, to rapacity and hostility. Among all the things a ruler should try to avoid, he must avoid above all being hated and despised. Generosity leads to your being both. So it is wiser to accept a reputation as miserly, which people despise but do not hate, than to aspire to a reputation as generous, and as a consequence, be obliged to face criticism for rapacity, which people both despise and hate.

Chapter Seventeen: About cruelty and compassion; and about whether it is better to be loved than feared, or the reverse.

Going further down our list of qualities, I recognize every ruler should want to be thought of as compassionate and not cruel. Nevertheless, I have to warn you to be careful about being compassionate. Cesare Borgia was thought of as cruel; but this supposed cruelty of his restored order to the Romagna, united it, rendered it peaceful and law-abiding. If you think about it, you will realize he was, in fact, much more compassionate than the people of Florence, who, in order to avoid being thought cruel, allowed Pistoia to tear itself apart.[67] So a ruler ought not to mind the disgrace of being called cruel, if he keeps his subjects peaceful and law-abiding, for it is more compassionate to impose harsh punishments on a few than, out of excessive compassion, to allow disorder to spread, which leads to murders or looting. The whole community suffers if there are riots, while to maintain order the ruler only has to execute one or two individuals. Of all rulers, he who is new to power cannot escape a reputation for cruelty, for he is surrounded by dangers. Virgil has Dido say:

Harsh necessity, and the fact my kingdom is new, oblige me to do these things,
And to mass my armies on the frontiers.[68]

Nevertheless, you should be careful how you assess the situation and should think twice before you act. Do not be afraid of your own shadow. Employ policies that are moderated by prudence and sympathy. Avoid excessive self-confidence, which leads to carelessness, and avoid excessive timidity, which will make you insupportable.

This leads us to a question that is in dispute: Is it better to be loved than feared, or vice versa?[69] My reply is one ought to be both loved and feared; but, since it is difficult to accomplish both at the same time, I maintain it is much safer to be feared than loved, if you have to do without one of the two. For of men one can, in general, say this: They are ungrateful, fickle, deceptive and deceiving, avoiders of danger, eager to gain. As long as you serve their interests, they are devoted to you. They promise you their blood, their possessions, their lives, and their children, as I said before, so long as you seem to have no need of them. But as soon as you need help, they turn against you. Any ruler who relies simply on their promises and makes no other preparations, will be destroyed. For you will find that those whose support you buy, who do not rally to you because they admire your strength of character and nobility of soul, these are people you pay for, but they are never yours, and in the end you cannot get the benefit of your investment. Men are less nervous of offending someone who makes himself lovable, than someone who makes himself frightening. For love attaches men by ties of obligation, which, since men are wicked, they break whenever their interests are at stake. But fear restrains men because they are afraid of punishment, and this fear never leaves them. Still, a ruler should make himself feared in such a way that, if he does not inspire love, at least he does not provoke hatred. For it is perfectly possible to be feared and not hated. You will only be hated if you seize the property or the women of your subjects and citizens. Whenever you have to kill someone, make sure you have a suitable excuse and an obvious reason; but, above all else, keep your hands off other people's property; for men are quicker to forget the death of their father than the loss of their inheritance. Moreover, there are always reasons why you might want to seize people's property; and he who begins to live by plundering others will always find an excuse for seizing other people's possessions; but there are fewer reasons for killing people, and one killing need not lead to another.

When a ruler is at the head of his army and has a vast number of soldiers under his command, then it is absolutely essential to be prepared to be thought cruel; for it is impossible to keep an army united and ready for action without acquiring a reputation for cruelty. Among the extraordinary accomplishments of Hannibal, we may note one in particular: He commanded a vast army, made up of men of many different nations, who were fighting far from home, yet they never mutinied and they never fell out with one another, either when things were going badly, or when things were going well.[70] The only possible explanation for this is that he was known to be harsh and cruel. This, together with his numerous virtues [virtù], meant his soldiers always regarded him with admiration and fear. Without cruelty, his other virtues [virtù] would not have done the job. Those who write about Hannibal without thinking things through both admire the loyalty of his troops and criticize the cruelty that was its principal cause. If you doubt my claim that his other virtues [virtù] would have been insufficient, take the case of Scipio.[71] He was not only unique in his own day, but history does not record anyone his equal. But his army rebelled against him in Spain.[72] The sole cause of this was his excessive leniency, which meant his soldiers had more freedom than is compatible with good military discipline. Fabius Maximus criticized him for this in the senate and accused him of corrupting the Roman armies. When Locri was destroyed by one of his commanders,[73] he did not avenge the deaths of the inhabitants, and he did not punish his officer's insubordination. He was too easygoing. This was so apparent that one of his supporters in the senate was obliged to excuse him by saying he was no different from many other men, who were better at doing their own jobs than at making other people do theirs. In course of time, had he remained in command without learning from his mistakes, this aspect of Scipio's character would have destroyed his glorious reputation. But, because his authority was subordinate to that of the senate, not only were the consequences of this defect mitigated, but it even enhanced his reputation.

I conclude, then, that, as far as being feared and loved is concerned, since men decide for themselves whom they love, and rulers decide whom they fear, a wise ruler should rely on the emotion he can control, not on the one he cannot. But he must take care to avoid being hated, as I have said.

Chapter Eighteen: How far rulers are to keep their word.

Everybody recognizes how praiseworthy it is for a ruler to keep his word and to live a life of integrity, without relying on craftiness. Nevertheless, we see that in practice, in these days, those rulers who have not thought it important to keep their word have achieved great things, and have known how to employ cunning to confuse and disorientate other men. In the end, they have been able to overcome those who have placed store in integrity.

You should therefore know there are two ways to fight: one while respecting the rules, the other with no holds barred. Men alone fight in the first fashion, and animals fight in the second.[74] But because you cannot always win if you respect the rules, you must be prepared to break them. A ruler, in particular, needs to know how to be both an animal and a man. The classical writers, without saying it explicitly, taught rulers to behave like this. They described how Achilles, and many other rulers in ancient times, were given to Chiron the centaur to be raised, so he could bring them up as he thought best. What they intended to convey, with this story of rulers' being educated by someone who was half beast and half man, was that it is necessary for a ruler to know when to act like an animal and when like a man; and if he relies on just one or the other mode of behavior he cannot hope to survive.

Since a ruler, then, needs to know how to make good use of beastly qualities, he should take as his models among the animals both the fox and the lion, for the lion does not know how to avoid traps, and the fox is easily overpowered by wolves.[75] So you must be a fox when it comes to suspecting a trap, and a lion when it comes to making the wolves turn tail. Those who simply act like a lion all the time do not understand their business. So you see a wise ruler cannot, and should not, keep his word when doing so is to his disadvantage, and when the reasons that led him to promise to do so no longer apply. Of course, if all men were good, this advice would be bad; but since men are wicked and will not keep faith with you, you need not keep faith with them. Nor is a ruler ever short of legitimate reasons to justify breaking his word. I could give an infinite number of contemporary examples to support my argument and to show how treaties and promises have been rendered null and void by the dishonesty of rulers; and he who has known best how to act the fox has come out of it the best. But it is essential to know how to conceal how crafty one is, to know how to be a clever counterfeit and hypocrite. You will find people are so simple-minded and so preoccupied with their immediate concerns, that if you set out to deceive them, you will always find plenty of them who will let themselves be deceived.

Among the numerous recent cases one could mention, there is one of particular interest. Alexander VI had only one purpose, only one thought, which was to take people in, and he always found people who were willing victims. There never has been anyone who was more convincing when he swore an oath, nor has there been anybody who has ever formulated more eloquent oaths and has at the same time been quicker to break them. Nevertheless, he was able to find gulls one after another, whenever he wanted them, for he was a master of this particular skill.

So a ruler need not have all the positive qualities I listed earlier, but he must seem to have them. Indeed, I would go so far as to say that if you have them and never make any exceptions, then you will suffer for it; while if you merely appear to have them, they will benefit you. So you should seem to be compassionate, trustworthy, sympathetic, honest, religious, and, indeed, be all these things; but at the same time you should be constantly prepared, so that, if these become liabilities, you are trained and ready to become their opposites. You need to understand this: A ruler, and particularly a ruler who is new to power, cannot conform to all those rules that men who are thought good are expected to respect, for he is often obliged, in order to hold on to power, to break his word, to be uncharitable, inhumane, and irreligious. So he must be mentally prepared to act as circumstances and changes in fortune require. As I have said, he should do what is right if he can; but he must be prepared to do wrong if necessary.

A ruler must, therefore, take great care that he never carelessly says anything that is not imbued with the five qualities I listed above. He must seem, to those who listen to him and watch him, entirely pious, truthful, reliable, sympathetic, and religious. There is no quality that it is more important he should seem to have than this last one. In general, men judge more by sight than by touch. Everyone sees what is happening, but not everyone feels the consequences. Everyone sees what you seem to be; few have direct experience of who you really are. Those few will not dare speak out in the face of public opinion when that opinion is reinforced by the authority of the state. In the behavior of all men, and particularly of rulers, against whom there is no recourse at law, people judge by the outcome. So if a ruler wins wars and holds on to power, the means he has employed will always be judged honorable, and everyone will praise them. The common man accepts external appearances and judges by the outcome; and when it comes down to it only the masses count; for the elite are powerless if the masses have someone to provide them with leadership. One contemporary ruler,[76] whom it would be unwise to name, is always preaching peace and good faith, and he has not a shred of respect for either; if he had respected either one or the other, he would have lost either his state or his reputation several times by now.

Chapter Nineteen: How one should avoid hatred and contempt.

Because I have spoken of the more important of the qualities I mentioned earlier, I want now to discuss the rest of them briefly under this general heading, that a ruler must take care (I have already referred to this in passing) to avoid those things that will make him an object of hatred or contempt. As long as he avoids these he will have done what is required of him, and he will find having a reputation for any of the other vices will do him no harm at all. You become hateful, above all, as I have said, if you prey on the possessions and the women of your subjects. You should leave both alone. The vast majority of men, so long as their goods and their honor are not taken from them, will live contentedly, so you will only have to contend with the small minority who are ambitious, and there are lots of straightforward ways of keeping them under control. You become contemptible if you are thought to be erratic, capricious, effeminate, pusillanimous, irresolute. You should avoid acquiring such a reputation as a pilot steers clear of the rocks. Make every effort to ensure your actions suggest greatness and endurance, strength of character and of purpose. When it comes to the private business of your subjects, you should aim to ensure you never have to change your decisions once they have been taken, and that you acquire a reputation that will discourage people from even considering tricking or deceiving you.

A ruler who is thought of in these terms has the sort of reputation he needs; and it is difficult to conspire against someone who is respected in this way, difficult to attack him, because people realize he is on top of his job and has the loyalty of his employees. For rulers ought to be afraid of two things: Within the state, they should fear their subjects; abroad, they should fear other rulers. Against foreign powers, a good army and reliable allies are the only defense; and, if you have a good army, you will always find your allies reliable. And you will find it easy to maintain order at home if you are secure from external threats, provided, that is, conspiracies against you have not undermined your authority. Even if foreign powers do attack, if you have followed my advice and lived according to the principles I have outlined, then, as long as you keep a grip on yourself, you will be able to resist any attack, just as I said Nabis of Sparta was able to. But where your subjects are concerned, when you are not being attacked by foreign powers, you have to be wary of secret conspiracies.[77] The best protection against these is to ensure you are not hated or despised, and the people are satisfied with your rule. It is essential to accomplish this, as I have already explained at length.

Indeed, one of the most effective defenses a ruler has against conspiracies is to make sure he is not generally hated. For conspirators always believe the assassination of the ruler will be approved by the people. If they believe the people will be angered, then they cannot screw up the courage to embark on such an enterprise, for conspirators have to overcome endless difficulties to achieve success. Experience shows the vast majority of conspiracies fail. For a conspirator cannot act alone, and he can only find associates among those whom he believes are discontented. As soon as you tell someone who is discontented what you are planning, you give him the means to satisfy his ambitions, because it is obvious he can expect to be richly rewarded if he betrays you. If he betrays you, his reward is certain; if he keeps faith with you, he faces danger, with little prospect of reward. So, you see, he needs either to be an exceptionally loyal friend or to be a completely intransigent enemy of the ruler, if he is to keep faith with you. So we can sum up as follows: The conspirators face nothing but fear, mutual distrust, and the prospect of punishment, so they lose heart; while the ruler is supported by the authority of his office and by the laws, and protected both by his supporters and by the forces of government. So, if you add to this inbuilt advantage the goodwill of the populace, then it is impossible to find anyone who is so foolhardy as to conspire against you. For in most situations a conspirator has to fear capture before he does the deed; but if the ruler has the goodwill of the people, he has to fear it afterwards as well, for the people will turn on him when the deed is done, and he will have nowhere to hide.

I could give an infinite number of examples to illustrate this, but I will confine myself to one only, a conspiracy that took place during the lifetime of our parents. Mr. Annibale Bentivoglio, grandfather of the present Mr. Annibale, was at the time ruler of Bologna. The Canneschi conspired against him and assassinated him.[78] His only surviving relative was Mr. Giovanni, who was still in the cradle. But as soon as he was killed the people rose up and killed all the Canneschi. This happened because the family of Bentivoglio had, in those days, the goodwill of the people. Their loyalty was such that, there being no surviving member of the family in Bologna who could, now Annibale was dead, take over the government, and they having heard that in Florence there was a member of the family, someone who so far had been nothing more than the son of a blacksmith, the citizens of Bologna came to Florence to fetch him and made him the ruler of their city. He ruled it until Mr. Giovanni was old enough to take office.

I conclude, then, that a ruler need not worry much about conspiracies as long as the people wish him well; but if the people are hostile to him and hate him, then he should fear everything and everyone. States that are well-governed and rulers who are wise make every effort to ensure the elite are not driven to despair, and to satisfy the masses and keep them content; for this is one of the most important tasks a ruler must set himself.

Among the states that are well-ordered and well-ruled at the present time is France. There you will find innumerable good institutions that ensure the freedom of action and security of the king. First among them is the *parlement* and its authority.[79] For whoever set up the government of that country understood the powerful are ambitious and insolent, and judged it necessary they should be bridled so they could be controlled, but on the other hand he recognized the hatred most people have for the powerful, whom they have reason to fear, and the consequent need to reassure and protect the great. So he did not want this to be the responsibility of the king, in order to avoid his alienating the powerful by favoring the people or alienating the people by favoring the powerful, and he established an independent tribunal, whose task it is, without incurring blame for the king, to crush the powerful and defend the weak. This arrangement is as intelligent and prudent as could be, and makes a substantial contribution to the security of the king and the stability of the kingdom. This institution enables us to recognize a significant general principle: Rulers should delegate responsibility for unpopular actions, while taking personal responsibility for those that will win favor. And once again I conclude a ruler should treat the powerful with respect, but at all costs he should avoid being hated by the people.

Many perhaps will think, if they consider the lives and deaths of some of the Roman emperors, that these provide examples contrary to the opinion I have expressed. For it would seem some of them lived exemplary lives and demonstrated great strength [*virtù*] of character, yet they fell from power, or rather they were killed by their retainers, who had conspired against them. Since I want to reply to this objection, I will discuss the characters of some of the emperors, explaining the reasons why they were destroyed, and show they do not tell against my argument. This will primarily involve pointing out factors that would seem significant to anyone who read the history of those times. I will confine myself to discussing all those emperors who came after Marcus Aurelius, up to and including Maximilian:[80] that is, Marcus, his son Commodus, Pertinax, Julian, Severus, his son Antoninus Caracalla, Macrinus, Heliogabulus, Alexander, and Maximilian.

The first thing to be remarked is that, where in most states one only has to contend with the ambition of the great and the effrontery of the populace, the emperors of Rome had to face a third problem: They had to put up with the cruelty and greed of their soldiers. This was so difficult to do that it caused the downfall of many of the emperors, for it was almost impossible to satisfy both the soldiers and the populace. The people loved peace and quiet and, for this reason, liked their rulers to be unassuming; but the soldiers wanted the emperor to be a man of war and liked him to be arrogant, cruel, and rapacious. They wanted him to direct his aggression against the populace, so they could double their income and give free rein to their greed and cruelty. The result was those emperors who did not have a sufficiently intimidating reputation to keep both populace and soldiers in check (either because they did not think such a reputation desirable, or because they were incapable of acquiring it) were always destroyed. Most of them, especially those who acquired power without inheriting it, recognizing the difficulty of pleasing both soldiers and people, concentrated on pleasing the soldiers, thinking it could do little harm to alienate the populace. They had no choice, for, since rulers are bound to be hated by someone, their first concern must be to ensure they are not hated by any significant group; and, if they cannot achieve this, then they must make every possible effort to avoid the hatred of those groups that are most powerful. And so those emperors who had not inherited power and, thus, were in need of particularly strong support, attached themselves to the soldiers rather than to the people; a policy that proved successful or not, depending on whether the particular ruler in question knew how to establish his reputation with the army. For these reasons, then, Marcus, Pertinax, and Alexander, all of whom were unassuming, lovers of justice, haters of cruelty, sympathetic and kind, all came, apart from Marcus, to a tragic end. Marcus alone lived honorably and died peaceably, for he inherited power, and did not have to repay a debt to either the soldiers or the populace. Moreover, since he had many virtues [*virtù*] that made him widely respected, he was able, during his own lifetime, to keep both groups in their place, and he was never hated or despised. But Pertinax was made emperor against the wishes of the soldiers, who, being accustomed to an unbridled life under Commodus, were unable to tolerate the disciplined way of life Pertinax wanted to impose on them. So he made himself hated, and to this hatred was added contempt, for he was an old man, and so his rule had scarcely begun before he fell from power.

Here we should note one can become hated for the good things one does, as much as for the bad. That is why, as I said above, a ruler who wants to hold on to power is often obliged not to be good, for when some powerful group—whether the populace, the soldiers, or the elite—whose support you feel it is essential to have if you are to survive, is corrupt, then you have to adapt to its tastes in order to satisfy it, in which case doing good will do you harm. But let us turn to Alexander. He was so good that among the other things for which he is praised is the fact that during the fourteen years he retained power, nobody was ever executed at his orders without due trial. Nevertheless, he was thought effeminate, and blamed for being under the influence of his mother, and so he came to be despised, the army conspired against him and killed him.

By contrast, let us consider the qualities of Commodus, of Severus, Antoninus Caracalla, and Maximinus. They were, you will find, in the highest degree bloodthirsty and rapacious. In order to satisfy the soldiery, they did not fail to commit every possible type of crime against the populace; and all of them, with the exception of Severus, came to a bad end. For Severus was such a strong ruler *[in Sever fu tanta virtù]* that, with the support of the army, even though the populace were oppressed by him, he could always rule successfully; for his strength *[virtù]* inspired awe in the minds of both soldiers and people: The people were always to a considerable degree stupefied and astonished by him, while the soldiers were admiring and satisfied. Because his deeds were commendable in a new ruler, I want to pause to point out how well he understood how to play the part both of the fox and of the lion: These are the two styles of action I have maintained a ruler must know how to imitate. Severus, because he knew what a coward Julian the new emperor was, persuaded the army he had under his command in Slavonia that it was a good idea to march on Rome to revenge the death of Pertinax, who had been killed by his praetorian guard. With this excuse, and without displaying any ambition to seize the throne, he set out for Rome; and his army was in Italy before anyone knew it had left its station. When he reached Rome, the senate, out of fear, elected him emperor and had Julian put to death. Severus, having begun like this, faced two problems if he wanted to gain effective control of the whole empire: In Asia there was Niger, commander of the Asiatic armies, who had had himself proclaimed emperor; in the West there was Albinus, who also aspired to power. Because he thought it would be dangerous to take on both of them at once, he decided to attack Niger and deceive Albinus. So he wrote to Albinus saying now that he had been elected emperor by the senate, he wanted to share his authority with him. He offered him the title of Caesar and had the senate appoint him co-ruler. Albinus accepted these proposals at face value. But as soon as Severus had defeated and killed Niger and pacified the eastern empire, he returned to Rome and attacked Albinus in the senate, complaining that he, far from being grateful for the generosity he had been shown, had wickedly sought to assassinate him. Severus claimed to have no choice but to go and punish this ingrate. So he attacked him in France and deprived him of his offices and of his life.

Anyone who examines Severus's actions with care will find he was both a ferocious lion and a cunning fox. He will find he was feared and respected by all, and he was not hated by the armies. So it is no surprise Severus, who had not inherited power, was able to hold on to a vast empire, for his immense reputation was a constant defense against the hatred the populace might otherwise have felt for his exactions. Antoninus his son was also a man whose remarkable abilities inspired awe in the populace and gratitude in the soldiers. For he was a man of war, able to make light of the most arduous task and contemptuous of delicate food and all other luxuries. This made all his soldiers love him. Nevertheless, his ferocity and cruelty were without parallel. He did not only kill vast numbers of individuals, but, on one occasion, a large part of the population of Rome, and, on another, the whole of Alexandria. So he came to be loathed by everyone, and even his close associates began to fear him, with the result he was killed by a centurion while he was surrounded by his own troops. One should note rulers have no protection against an assassination like this, carried out by a truly determined individual, for anyone who is prepared to die can attack them. But, nevertheless, rulers should not worry unduly about such assassins because they are extremely rare. You should try merely to avoid giving grave injury to anyone you employ who comes close to you in the course of business. Antoninus had done just this, for he had outrageously put to death a brother of the centurion who killed him, and had repeatedly threatened the centurion's own life; yet he employed him as a bodyguard. This was foolhardy, and the disastrous outcome could have been predicted.

Now we come to Commodus, who had no difficulty in holding on to power, because he had inherited it, being the son of Marcus. All he had to do was follow in his father's footsteps, and he would have been satisfactory to both soldiers and populace. But, because he was by nature cruel and brutal, he began to ingratiate himself with the soldiers and to encourage them to be undisciplined, so he would be able to give his own rapacity free rein against the people. On the other hand, he did not maintain his own dignity. Often, when he went to the amphitheater, he came down and fought with the gladiators, and he did other things that were despicable and incompatible with imperial majesty. So he became contemptible in the eyes of his soldiers. He was hated by the people and despised by the soldiers, so there was soon a conspiracy against him and he was killed.

There remains for us to discuss the character of Maximinus. He was a most warlike individual. The armies had been irritated by the feebleness of Alexander, whom I have already discussed, and so, with him out of the way, they elected Maximinus emperor. But he did not hold on to power for long, for there were two things that made him hateful and contemptible. In the first place, he was of the lowest social status, having once been a shepherd in Thrace (a fact known to everyone, and one that made them all regard him with disdain); in the second, when he was elected emperor he had delayed going to Rome and taking possession of the throne, but had acquired a reputation for terrible cruelty because his representatives, in Rome and throughout the empire, had acted with great ferocity. So everybody was worked up with disdain for his humble origins and agitated with hatred arising from their fear of his ferocity. First Africa rebelled, and then the senate and the whole population of Rome; soon all Italy was conspiring against him. His own army turned against him. They were laying siege to Aquileia, but were finding it hard to take the city, to which was added their distaste for his cruelty. Seeing so many united against him, they lost their fear of him and killed him.

I do not want to discuss Heliogabulus, Macrinus, and Julian, for they were entirely contemptible and fell from power quickly. We can now come to the end of this discussion. I would have you note the rulers of our own day do not face in such an acute form the problem of having to adopt policies that involve breaking the law in order to satisfy their soldiers' appetites; for, although you cannot afford entirely to ignore contemporary soldiers, you can handle them easily. Modern rulers do not face standing armies with long experience of ruling and administering provinces, such as the Roman armies had. But if in those days it was more important to give satisfaction to the soldiers than to the populace, that was because the soldiers were more to be feared than the populace. Now all rulers, with the exception of the sultans of Turkey and of Egypt, need to be more concerned to satisfy the populace than the soldiers, for the populace are the greater threat. I make an exception of the ruler of Turkey, for at all times he is surrounded by twelve thousand infantry and fifteen thousand cavalry, on whom depends the security and strength of his government. It is essential for him, more than anything else, to retain their loyalty. Similarly, the Sultan of Egypt is entirely at the mercy of his soldiers, so that he, too, must keep their loyalty, no matter what the consequences for the populace may be. And one should note the Sultan of Egypt is in a different position from all other rulers; for he is comparable to the Christian pope, who also cannot be described as either a hereditary or a new ruler. For the sons of the old ruler do not inherit his office and remain in power, but the new ruler is elected by a group who have the authority to appoint him. Since this arrangement has long been in existence, you cannot call the sultan a new ruler, for he faces none of the difficulties faced by those who are new to power. Even though he himself is new to power, the principle of succession is long-established, and ensures his authority is acknowledged as unquestioningly as would be the case if he were an hereditary ruler.

Let us return to our subject. I believe everyone should agree in the light of this discussion that hatred and contempt caused the fall of the emperors we have been considering, and will also understand how it comes about that, with one group of them following one line of policy and the other its opposite, in both groups one ruler was successful and the rest were killed. For it was pointless and dangerous for Pertinax and Alexander, who were new rulers, to try to imitate Marcus, who had inherited power; similarly it was a bad mistake for Caracalla, Commodus, and Maximinus to imitate Severus, for they lacked the strength [*virtù*] that would have been necessary for anyone following in his footsteps. Thus, a new ruler, who has not inherited power, should not follow the example of Marcus, but need not follow that of Severus. He ought to imitate in Severus those features that are essential for him to establish himself securely in power, and in Marcus those features that are effective and win glory for someone who is seeking to preserve a government that has already entrenched itself.

Chapter Twenty-Five: How much fortune can achieve in human affairs, and how it is to be resisted.

I am not unaware of the fact that many have held and still hold the view that the affairs of this world are so completely governed by fortune and by God that human prudence is incapable of correcting them, with the consequence that there is no way in which what is wrong can be put right. So one may conclude that there is no point in trying too hard; one should simply let chance have its way. This view has come to be more widely accepted in our own day because of the extraordinary variation in circumstances that has been seen and is still seen every day. Nobody could predict such events. Sometimes, thinking this matter over, I have been inclined to adopt a version of this view myself. Nevertheless, since our free will must not be eliminated, I think it may be true that fortune determines one half of our actions, but that, even so, she leaves us to control the other half, or thereabouts. And I compare her to one of those torrential rivers that, when they get angry, break their banks, knock down trees and buildings, strip the soil from one place and deposit it somewhere else. Everyone flees before them, everyone gives way in face of their onrush, nobody can resist them at any point. But although they are so powerful, this does not mean men, when the waters recede, cannot make repairs and build banks and barriers so that, if the waters rise again, either they will be safely kept within the sluices or at least their onrush will not be so unregulated and destructive. The same thing happens with fortune: She demonstrates her power where precautions have not been taken to resist her *[dove non è ordinata virtù a resisterle]*; she directs her attacks where she knows banks and barriers have not been built to hold her. If you think about Italy, which is the location of all these changes in circumstance, and the origin of the forces making for change, you will realize she is a landscape without banks and without any barriers. If proper precautions had been taken *[s'ella fussi reparata da conveniente virtù]*, as they were in Germany, Spain, and France, either the flood would not have had the consequences it had, or the banks would not even have been overwhelmed. And what I have said is enough, I believe, to answer the general question of how far one can resist fortune.

But, turning rather to individuals, note we see rulers who flourish one day and are destroyed the next without our being able to see any respect in which they have changed their nature or their attributes. I think the cause of this is, in the first place, the one we have already discussed at length: A ruler who depends entirely on his good fortune will be destroyed when his luck changes. I also think a ruler will flourish if he adjusts his policies as the character of the times changes; and similarly, a ruler will fail if he follows policies that do not correspond to the needs of the times. For we see men, in those activities that carry them towards the goal they all share, which is the acquisition of glory and riches, proceed differently. One acts with caution, while another is headstrong; one is violent, while another relies on skill; one is patient, while another is the opposite: And any one of them, despite the differences in their methods, may achieve his objective. One also sees that of two cautious men, one will succeed, and the other not; and similarly we see that two men can be equally successful though quite different in their behavior, one of them being cautious and the other headstrong. This happens solely because of the character of the times, which either suits or is at odds with their way of proceeding. This is the cause of what I have described: that two men, behaving differently, achieve the same result, and of two other men, who behave in the same way, one will attain his objective and the other will not. This is also the cause of the fact that the sort of behavior that is successful changes from one time to another. Take someone who acts cautiously and patiently. If the times and circumstances develop in such a way that his behavior is appropriate, he will flourish; but if the times and circumstances change, he will be destroyed for he will continue to behave in the same way. One cannot find a man so prudent he knows how to adapt himself to changing circumstances, for he will either be unable to deviate from that style of behavior to which his character inclines him, or, alternatively, having always been successful by adopting one particular style, he will be unable to persuade himself that it is time to change. And so, the cautious man, when it is time to be headstrong, does not know how to act and is destroyed. But, if one knew how to change one's character as times and circumstances change, one's luck would never change.

Pope Julius II always acted impetuously; the style of action was so appropriate to the times and circumstances in which he found himself that the outcome was always successful. Consider his first attack on Bologna, when Mr. Giovanni Bentivoglio was still alive.[81] The Venetians were not happy about it; nor was the King of Spain; he had discussed such an action with the French, who had reached no decision. Nevertheless, because he was ferocious and impetuous, he placed himself personally at the head of his troops. This gesture made the Spanish and the Venetians hesitate and do nothing: the Venetians out of fear, and the Spanish because they wanted to recover the territories they had lost from the Kingdom of Naples. On the other hand, he dragged the King of France along behind him. For the king saw it was too late to turn back, and he wanted an alliance with him in order to weaken the Venetians, so he concluded he could not deny him the support of French troops without giving him obvious grounds for resentment. So Julius, by acting impetuously, achieved something no other pope, no matter how skillful and prudent, had been able to achieve. For, if he had delayed his departure from Rome until everything had been arranged and the necessary alliances had been cemented, as any other pope would have done, he would never have succeeded. The King of France would have found a thousand excuses, and his other allies would have pointed out a thousand dangers. I want to leave aside his other actions, for they were all similar, and they were all successful. He did not live long enough to experience failure. But, if the times had changed so that it was necessary to proceed with caution, he would have been destroyed. He would never have been able to change the style of behavior to which his character inclined him.

I conclude, then, that since fortune changes, and men stubbornly continue to behave in the same way, men flourish when their behavior suits the times and fail when they are out of step. I do think, however, that it is better to be headstrong than cautious, for fortune is a lady. It is necessary, if you want to master her, to beat and strike her. And one sees she more often submits to those who act boldly than to those who proceed in a calculating fashion. Moreover, since she is a lady, she smiles on the young, for they are less cautious, more ruthless, and overcome her with their boldness.

Chapter Twenty-Six: Exhortation to seize Italy and free her from the barbarians.

Having considered all the matters we have discussed, I ask myself whether, in Italy now, we are living through times suitable for the triumph of a new ruler, and if there is an opportunity for a prudent and bold [*virtuoso*] man to take control of events and win honor for himself while benefiting everyone who lives here. It seems to me so many factors come together at the moment to help out a new ruler that I am not sure if there has ever been a more propitious time for such a man. If, as I said, Moses could only demonstrate his greatness [*virtù*] because the people of Israel were slaves in Egypt; if we would never have known what a great man Cyrus was if the Persians had not been oppressed by the Medes; if the remarkable qualities of Theseus only became apparent because the Athenians were scattered abroad; so now, the opportunity is there for some bold Italian to demonstrate his greatness [*virtù*]. For see the conditions to which Italy has been reduced: She is more enslaved than the Jews, more oppressed than the Persians, more defenseless than the Athenians. She has no leader, no organization. She is beaten, robbed, wounded, put to flight: She has experienced every sort of injury. Although so far there has been the occasional hint of exceptional qualities in someone, so that one might think he had been ordained by God to redeem Italy, yet later events have shown, as his career progressed, that he was rejected by fortune. So Italy has remained at death's door, waiting for someone who could bind her wounds and put an end to the sack of Lombardy, to the extortion of Tuscany and of the Kingdom of Naples, someone who could heal her sores which long ago became infected. One can see how she prays to God that he will send her someone who will redeem her from this ill treatment and from the insults of the barbarians. One can see every Italian is ready, everyone is eager to rally to the colors, if only someone will raise them high.

At the moment, there is nowhere Italy can turn in her search for someone to redeem her with more chance of success than to your own illustrious family, which is fortunate and resourceful [*virtù*], is favored by God and by the church (indeed the church is now at its command). The undertaking is straightforward, if you keep in mind the lives and the deeds of the leaders I have mentioned. Of course those men were exceptional and marvelous; but, nevertheless, they were only men, and none of them had as good an opportunity as you have at the moment. For their undertakings were not more just than this one, or easier, nor was God more their ally than he is yours. This is truly just: "A war is just if there is no alternative, and the resort to arms is legitimate if they represent your only hope."[82] These circumstances are ideal; and when circumstances are ideal there can be no great difficulty in achieving success, provided your family copies the policies of those I have recommended as your models. Beyond that, we have already seen extraordinary and unparalleled events. God has already shown his hand: The sea has been divided; a cloud has escorted you on your journey; water has flowed out of the rock; manna has fallen from on high. Everything has conspired to make you great. The rest you must do for yourselves. God does not want to have to do the whole thing, for he likes to leave us our free will so we can lay claim to part of the glory by earning it.

There is no need to be surprised that none of the Italian rulers I have discussed has been able to accomplish what I believe your family can achieve, or to be disheartened if during all the wars that have been fought, all the political upheavals that have taken place, it has seemed as if the Italians have completely lost their capacity to fight and win *[la virtù militare]*. This is simply because the traditional way of doing things in Italy is mistaken, and no one has appeared who has known how to bring about change. Nothing does more to establish the reputation of someone who comes new to power than do the new laws and the new institutions he establishes. These, when they are well thought out and noble in spirit, make a ruler revered and admired. In Italy we have the raw materials: You can do anything you wish with them. Here we have people capable of anything *[virtù grande]*, all they need are leaders who know what to do. When it comes to fighting one-on-one the Italians prove themselves to be stronger, quicker, cleverer. But when it comes to the clash of armies, the Italians are hopeless. The cause lies in the inadequacy of the leaders. Those who know what to do are not obeyed, and everyone thinks he knows what to do. So far there has been no one who has known how to establish an authority, based on fortune and ability *[virtù]*, such that the others will obey him. This is the reason why, through the whole of the last twenty years, during all the wars that have taken place in that time, not a single army consisting solely of Italians has done well. Twenty years ago the Italians were defeated at Taro; since then at Alexandria, Capua, Genoa, Vailà, Bologna, Mestre.

So, if your illustrious family wants to follow in the footsteps of those excellent men who liberated the nations to which they belonged, you must, before you do anything else, do the one thing that is the precondition for success in any enterprise: Acquire your own troops. You cannot hope to have more faithful, more reliable, or more skillful soldiers. And if each soldier will be good, the army as a whole will be better still, once they see their ruler place himself at their head and discover he treats them with respect and sympathy. It is necessary, though, to get such an army ready, if we are to be able to defend Italy from the foreigners with Italian strength and skill *[con la virtù italica]*.

It is true that the Swiss and Spanish infantries are thought to be intimidating; nevertheless, they both have their defects, so a third force could not only stand up to them, but could be confident of beating them. For the Spanish cannot withstand a cavalry charge; and the Swiss have reason to be afraid of infantry, should they come up against any as determined to win as they are. Thus, we have seen that the Spanish cannot withstand an attack by the French cavalry, and we will see in practice that the Swiss can be destroyed by the Spanish infantry. It is true that we have yet to see the Spanish properly defeat the Swiss, but we have seen an indication of what will happen at the Battle of Ravenna,[83] when the Spanish infantry clashed against the German battalions, for the Germans rely on the same formation as the Swiss. There the Spanish, thanks to their agility and with the help of their bucklers, were able to get underneath the pikes of the Germans and were able to attack them in safety, without the Germans' having any defense. If the cavalry had not driven them off, they would have wiped them out. So, since we know the weakness of each of these infantries, we ought to be able to train a new force that will be able to withstand cavalry and will not be afraid of infantry. To accomplish this we need specially designed weapons and new battle formations. This is the sort of new undertaking that establishes the reputation and importance of a new ruler.

So you should not let this opportunity slip by. Italy, so long enslaved, awaits her redeemer. There are no words to describe with what devotion he would be received in all those regions that have suffered from foreign invasions which have flooded across the land. No words can describe the appetite for revenge, the resolute determination, the spirit of self-sacrifice, the tears of emotion that would greet him. What gates would be closed to him? What community would refuse to obey him? Who would dare be jealous of his success? What Italian would refuse to pledge him allegiance? Everyone is sick of being pushed around by the barbarians. Your family must commit itself to this enterprise. Do it with the confidence and hope with which people embark on a just cause so that, marching behind your banner, the whole nation is ennobled. Under your patronage, may we prove Petrarch right:

Virtue [virtù] will take up arms against savagery,
And the battle will be short.
For the courage of old is not yet dead
In Italian hearts.[84]

Notes

1. Sforza acquired Milan in 1450. See below, chapter twelve.
2. Ferdinand the Catholic (1452–1516) acquired Naples in 1504. See below, chapters three and twenty-one.
3. Louis XII (1462–1515) became King of France in 1498 and invaded Italy in 1499. He gained Milan in February 1500 and lost it in April.
4. Louis regained Milan after the battle of Novara (April 1500), and lost it again after the Battle of Ravenna (April 1512). Ludovico Sforza (1451–1510), younger son of Francesco Sforza, ruled Milan from 1494 to 1500.
5. Constantinople became capital of the Turkish empire in 1453.
6. 211 B.C. See Livy, bk. 26, ch. 24.
7. The events to which Machiavelli refers occurred in 192 B.C. to 189 B.C. See Livy, bk. 37.
8. Antiochus III, King of Syria.
9. Philip V of Macedon.
10. Charles VIII (1470–98) ruled France from 1492 and invaded Italy in 1494. He was crowned King of Naples in 1494, but was forced out of Italy in 1495. Louis invaded Italy in 1499. His forces were decisively defeated at the Second Battle of Novara, 1512.
11. See below, chapter seven.
12. Louis agreed to divide the Kingdom of Naples with Ferdinand the Catholic in 1500, but lost the whole state to him in 1504.
13. Alexander conquered Asia between 334 and 327 B.C., and died in 323 B.C.
14. An administrative region.
15. Machiavelli uses "France" to refer both to modern France and the ancient province of Gaul. Because one of his beliefs is that the French have not changed, I have kept his terminology as a reminder of his conviction that there is a real continuity between the ancient world and the present.
16. The Spartan-sponsored oligarchies controlled Athens from 404 to 403 B.C. and Thebes from 382 to 379 B.C.
17. Capua in 211 B.C., Carthage in 146 B.C., Numantia in 133 B.C.
18. Pisa was controlled by Florence from 1406 to 1494, and recaptured in 1509.
19. Cyrus overcame the Medes around 550 B.C. and founded the Persian Empire. Romulus is the mythical founder of Rome, and Theseus the slayer of the Minotaur and founder of Athens (1234 B.C.): Machiavelli took them to be genuine historical persons.
20. Girolamo Savonarola (b. 1452) was a Dominican friar and prophetic preacher. He dominated Florentine politics from the expulsion of the Medici in 1494 until 1498, when he was executed as a heretic.
21. Hiero II became King of Syracuse in 269 B.C. Machiavelli's sources are Polybius, bk. 7, ch. 8, and Justin, bk. 23, ch. 4.
22. Machiavelli is referring to Greek-speaking cities in Asia and the Hellespont in the sixth century B.C.
23. See below, chapter nineteen.
24. See below, chapter twelve.
25. Cesare Borgia (1475–1507) was the natural son of Rodrigo Borgia (1431–1503), who became Pope Alexander VI in 1492. He began the conquest of the Romagna in 1499.
26. On the Orsini and the Colonna.
27. In the spring of 1501.
28. In the summer of 1502.
29. October 1502.

30. They were captured on 31 December 1502. Some were killed at once; others a few weeks later.
31. 26 December 1502.
32. 1503.
33. 18 August 1503.
34. 28 October 1503. Giuliano della Rovere (1443–1513) had been appointed Cardinal of San Piero ad Vincula in 1471, when his uncle became Pope Sixtus IV. For Machiavelli's assessment of his papacy, see below, chapter twenty-five.
35. Agathocles (361–289 B.C.) seized control of Syracuse in 317 B.C. Machiavelli's source is Justin, bk. 22.
36. Oliverotto Euffreducci (b. ca. 1475) seized Fermo in 1501. Borgia had him killed at Senigallia in December 1502.
37. The Florentines made Vitelli commander of their forces in 1498 and executed him in 1499. See below, chapter twelve.
38. Nabis (ca. 240–192 B.C.) became ruler of Sparta in 207 B.C. Livy (bk. 34) puts the number assassinated at eighty.
39. The Gracchi brothers (Tiberius Sempronius [163–133 B.C.] and Gaius Sempronius [153–121 B.C.) were advocates of agrarian reform who both died in riots. Scali was a populist leader in Florence during the Ciompi rising of 1378 but was executed for an attack on the authorities in 1382.
40. The chalk was used by Charles's quartermasters to mark the soldiers' billets. Savonarola attributed Charles's victory to sins such as fornication and usury.
41. In 346 B.C.
42. In 338 B.C.
43. In 1448.
44. In 1420.
45. Hawkwood (ca. 1320–94) began to be employed by Florence in 1380.
46. Andrea Fortebraccio (1368–1424).
47. In 1498.
48. Francesco Bussone, Count of Carmagnola (b. ca. 1390), hired by the Venetians in 1425, executed in 1432.
49. The Battle of Vailà, generally known as Agnadello, 4 May 1509.
50. Really the first Italian: He had been preceded, for example, by Hawkwood. He was victor at Marino (1379) and died in 1409.
51. In 1510.
52. 11 April 1512.
53. In 1500.
54. The war lasted from 1341 to 1347; Constantinople did not finally fall to the Turks until 1453.
55. In the winter of 1499–1500.
56. I Kings 17.
57. In 1453.
58. In 1474.
59. Machiavelli is thinking of the defeats of 1512, which had virtually forced the French out of Italy.
60. In 376.
61. In 1450.
62. 253–184 B.C.
63. Livy, bk. 25, ch. 28. Machiavelli would also have known the accounts in Plutarch and Polybius.
64. Machiavelli is thinking in particular of Cicero, *De officiis*, and Seneca, *De clementia*.
65. Louis XII.
66. Ferdinand the Catholic.
67. In 1501.
68. Virgil, *Aeneid*, I, 563–4.
69. Cicero, *De officiis*, bk. 2, ch. 7, § 23–24.
70. Hannibal (247–ca. 183 B.C.) campaigned in Italy from 218 to 203 B.C. Machiavelli's source is Polybius, bk. 11, ch. 19.
71. Scipio (ca. 236–183 B.C.) defeated Hannibal at Zama in North Africa (202 B.C.).
72. In 206 B.C. Livy, bk. 28, chs. 24–29.
73. In 205 B.C.
74. Cicero, *De officiis*, bk. 1, ch. 11, § 34.
75. The fox and the lion are from Cicero, *De officiis*, bk. 1, ch. 13, § 41.
76. Ferdinand the Catholic.
77. Influential in Machiavelli's discussion of conspiracies is Aristotle, *Politics*, bk. 8.
78. In 1445.
79. The *parlement* was the highest court of appeal. Its members belonged to a distinct social caste, the *noblesse de robe*.
80. In other words, the period from 161 to 238. Machiavelli follows Herodian closely, probably relying on Poliziano's Latin translation.
81. In 1506.
82. Livy, bk. 9, ch. 1.
83. 11 April 1512.
84. Petrarch, *Italia mia (Ai Signori d'Italia)*, ll. 93–6.

Notes on Machiavelli's *The Prince*

—M.L.

Chapter 6

Theseus. Legendary king of Athens, who came to embody Athenian civic virtues. He was credited with creating a unified Athenian city/state out of the various surrounding towns. Machiavelli treats him as an historical figure.

Cyrus. (d. 530 B.C.E.) Persian king who began a great series of conquests in 550 B.C.E., and founded the Persian Empire.

Romulus. The mythical founder of Rome, along with his brother Remus. According to legend the two brothers were raised by a she-wolf, and grew to be great warriors and leaders.

Girolamo Savonarola. (1452–1498) A Dominican friar and reformer who became a key figure in the politics of Florence during the years 1494–98. He was a popular religious leader who preached fiery sermons against worldly corruption and greed, including that of the Medicis, the family who governed Florence. When the Medicis were driven out of Florence in 1494, Savonarola became the virtual ruler of the city, and oversaw the establishment of a republican government based on strict moral laws. When he began to preach against the Papacy, however, Pope Alexander VI excommunicated him and threatened to punish Florence as well. The people of Florence turned against Savonarola; he was arrested, tortured, and executed as a heretic.

Hieron II. (c. 271–216 B.C.E.) Tyrant and later king of Syracuse. He was elected general, and then seized power in a military coup. As King he sided with the Carthaginians against Rome, but was defeated and forced into a subordinate position. He later switched sides, and became an ally of Rome during the Punic Wars.

Chapter 7

Darius. (d. 486 B.C.E.) A Persian noble who seized control of the Persian Empire through a bloody coup, and then ruthlessly put down a series of revolts. He invaded the Aegean Isles, beginning the Persian Wars, but his army was defeated by the Athenians at the battle of Marathon in 490.

Francesco Sforza. (1401–1466) One of the greatest of the mercenary captains, or *condottieri*, of fifteenth-century Italy. He usually fought for the ruling family of Milan, although he switched sides several times in his career. In 1450 he took advantage of the death of the Milanese ruler and seized power, becoming Duke of Milan. Sforza won fame as a clever military leader, but he was also important for his patronage of the arts in Milan.

Mercenaries. In Renaissance Italy, warfare on land was dominated by mercenary captains, known as *condottieri*, who led companies of armed soldiers and contracted their services to the various princes and governments. The *condottieri* were usually nobles, who could afford their own horses, armor, and weapons. Although there were exceptions, most *condottieri* were not known for their loyalty (often switching sides if offered better pay) or their desire to die for their employers.

Cesare Borgia. (1475–1507) The illegitimate son of Pope Alexander VI, Cesare was made a cardinal at the age of eighteen, but quickly showed that he had little interest in a career in the Church. Instead he shared in his father's hopes to increase his family's power and wealth. In 1499 he set out to conquer the Romagna, a territory technically controlled by the Papacy, in the hopes of carving out a principality for himself. A man of great cunning and ruthlessness, he nearly succeeded in his plans. In 1503, however, Pope Alexander died, before Cesare could establish himself as the legitimate ruler of the Romagna. Without the support of the Papacy, Cesare was forced to flee the territory. In 1506 he took shelter with the King of France, and was killed in battle the following year.

Remiro d'Orco (de Lorqua). (d. 1502) A Spanish soldier who served as one of Cesare Borgia's captains, and later governor of the Romagna. As governor he established order in the territory, but his laws were arbitrary and harsh. After he had outlived his usefulness, Borgia had him assassinated.

Pope Alexander VI (Rodrigo Borgia). (1431–1503) Originally born in Spain, Borgia worked hard to make his family one of the most powerful in Italy. He became deeply involved in the struggles among the Italian princes and noble families, and used his position as Pope to increase his family's wealth. When Charles VIII of France invaded Italy in 1494, Alexander organized a military alliance of Italian, Spanish, and German forces, and forced Charles to withdraw. The following year, however, Alexander switched sides, and allied with France against Spain in the hope of gaining tactical advantages against his enemies. Alexander placed his hopes for his family on his illegitimate son Cesare, and often used Church funds to finance his son's military ventures. Alexander became the symbol of the corruption of the Catholic Church in the Renaissance.

Chapter 8

Agathocles. (361–289 B.C.E.) Tyrannical king of Syracuse. He was exiled several times, but in 319 he became absolute ruler of Syracuse, and made an unsuccessful attempt to conquer Carthage. Known for his brutal rule, he was assassinated before he could establish a dynasty.

Oliverotto Euffreducci da Fermo. (c. 1475–1502) A *condottieri* who captured the city/state of Fermo in 1501. Along with Paolo Vitelli, he was killed by Cesare Borgia in 1502.

Paolo Vitelli. (d. 1502) The Vitelli family were originally merchants from Rome, but became famous *condottieri*. Paolo was made commander of a Florentine army in 1498, but fell prey to a plot by Cesare Borgia and was killed in 1502.

Chapter 9

Nabis. (d. 192 B.C.E.) Nabis seized the throne of Sparta in 207 B.C.E., and exiled or killed his rivals. He made many enemies, and was assassinated in 192.

The Gracchi. Tiberius Gracchus (163–133 B.C.E.) and his brother Gaius Gracchus (153–121 B.C.E.) were Roman aristocrats who sought to reform Roman law and help veteran soldiers and the urban poor. Both provoked resentment among the Roman elite, who feared their popularity, and both were killed as a result.

Giorgio Scali. In 1378, there was a popular uprising in Florence, known as the "Ciompi" revolt (*Ciompi* means cloth workers, who were protesting against unemployment and working conditions in the city). Scali was one of the leaders of the revolt; he was captured by the authorities and executed.

Chapter 18

Maximilian I. Maximilian reigned as Holy Roman Emperor from 1493 to 1519, and was known for his political deviousness. Most modern scholars, however, agree that the "certain prince" Machiavelli refers to is Ferdinand of Aragon, who ruled as King of Spain from 1479 to 1516. Ferdinand and his wife Isabella were known as the "Catholic Kings" because they were the first to unify Spain as a Christian state; in 1492, they expelled all Jews from Spain and conquered Granada, the last Moslem kingdom in Spain. Ferdinand spent his career trying to increase Spanish power and wealth, including the seizure of the Italian territory of Naples in 1504.

Chapter 19

Parlement. The French *Parlement* was not the same as the Parliament of England. Rather than a representative body, the *Parlement* was more of a supreme court, controlled by the French monarch. Medieval French kings used the *Parlement* to impose a uniform, royal law on the various regions of France. France did have an institution similar to the English Parliament, called the Estates-General, but it had much less power than its English counterpart. In 1789, the *Parlement* and the Estates General came into conflict with the French King, which helped trigger the French Revolution.

Septimius Severus. (r. 193–211) An African general who took advantage of civil war in Rome to seize power and found a brief dynasty of Roman emperors, from 193 to 235. Although Severus managed to stabilize the empire, his successors were less able rulers, who lost control of the army. When the last of the Severi was assassinated by one of his own soldiers, the empire disintegrated into another, even worse civil war.

Chapter 26

The Barbarians. In 1494 Charles VIII, King of France, invaded Italy. Ferdinand, King of Spain, did not want France to gain control of Italy, and so sent his own army in to counter the French. This begins the Italian Wars, a period which lasted until 1559. The various Italian princes, who never trusted each other, split their allegiances between France and Spain, thus dooming Italy to foreign rule. Machiavelli, as well as many other Italian writers, deplored the inability of the Italian princes to unite their efforts and expel the foreign invaders (or "barbarians"). In 1559 Spain won a decisive battle, and France withdrew its claims on Italy; the Italians were not consulted.

Who Was William Shakespeare?

—G.B.J.

Birth: 1564 (same year as Galileo) in Stratford-on-Avon, England, a prosperous market town. A market town was one in which a major market was held at frequent intervals for the sale of all kinds of goods produced in the surrounding area. In Shakespeare's time, Stratford would have been about a day's journey from London.

Family: Shakespeare's father was a glovemaker and trader in agricultural goods: in other words, a craftsman and minor merchant. He became a member of the town council and held offices in the town's government. Shakespeare's wife came from a property-owning family in a small town near Stratford.

Social class: English social classes of the sixteenth century were different from ours. There was no "middle class." As you can see below, Shakespeare's family was about at the middle of the social system in money and status. Major divisions were between:

- NOBILITY, who came from families with titles and high positions;
- GENTRY, who owned and managed landed estates but did not otherwise work;
- MERCHANTS, who conducted large businesses;
- SMALL FARMERS (Shakespeare's wife's family was in this social group);
- CRAFTSMEN, who were expert workers in one particular form of manufacture (Shakespeare's father was in this social group);
- SMALL FARMERS, who rented land from the nobility and gentry;
- SERVANTS;
- VAGRANTS, people roaming around with no means of support.

Schooling: Children of councilmen were entitled to free tuition at the Stratford Grammar School, so Shakespeare almost certainly attended it. It was a private school (like all at that time) that included levels equivalent to our elementary and high school. He would have learned Latin, the rules of prose

Shakespeare was an actor and a theater manager as well as a playwright. This manly portrait shows him unadorned and full of force and thought. The immense forehead, direct gaze, and sensual mouth announces the richness of his humanity. Corbis-Bettmann.

and poetic composition, English history, Greek and Roman history and mythology. Shakespeare did not go to college.

Marriage and children: At 18, Shakespeare married Anne Hathaway, 26. They had three children: two daughters and a son. The son died while still a child.

Career: At some time in his early twenties, Shakespeare went to London and became a member of an acting company. Acting companies were groups of actors who stayed together over time. The company was run by a manager or group of managers (sometimes a group of the actors). Each company was under the sponsorship of a member of the nobility.

Shakespeare soon began writing plays for his company. He continued in this double activity (actor and writer) until about 1612, when he retired to Stratford (aged 48). In his approximately 24-year career, he wrote 36 plays and collaborated on at least two more. His dramas comprise tragedies, comedies, plays about English history, and "romances": romantic tragicomedies. He also wrote two long narrative poems, one other longish poem of unclear meaning, and 154 sonnets.

Unlike the stereotypical poet starving in a garret, Shakespeare was financially successful. He invested in a share of his acting company that entitled him to a proportion of its profits; he was also paid as an actor and as a playwright (plays were bought outright by the company: no royalties). At the age of 33, he purchased the second largest house in his home town. Apparently he commuted; we don't know how often.

Othello: This play was probably written in 1604, a little past the middle of Shakespeare's career (he was 40). It was performed at the royal court during the Christmas season of that year, when command performances of entertainments for the king and courtiers were customary. That means it had probably already been a success.

Death: Shakespeare died in Stratford on April 23, 1616, aged 52. Both his daughters died childless; there are no Shakespeare descendants.

Some Background on Shakespeare's Theater

—G.B.J.

Shakespeare's theater, like others of its time in London, was built of wood in the shape (roughly) of a doughnut. The hole—the part with a floor but no ceiling—was standing room. Standees looked up at the stage (about 6 feet above the ground), which was covered by a roof (part of the top side of the doughnut). The rest of the doughnut was made up of covered seating, three stories high and divided into sections. There was no curtain to the stage. A balcony ran the length of the rear wall of the stage (Desdemona's father appears here in I.1). Very little scenery was used, and few props.

As on the Greek stage, all actors were male. Female roles were played by youths whose voices had not yet changed.

As costumes, actors wore appropriate contemporary clothing. They did not use masks or special shoes like Greek actors.

The scene shows Othello and his tormentor, Iago. This particular picture is from the film of Verdi's Opera *Otello*, one of the most successful adaptations to opera form of Shakespeare's works. Ira Nowinski/© Corbis.

Unlike Greek theater, the plays performed in public theaters in Shakespeare's time had no religious or ceremonial function. They were popular commercial entertainment. The audience ranged in social class from the nobility to servants and apprentices (low-paid trainees in the various crafts). The price of admission for standees was a penny, which was about a week's wages for an apprentice. Performances were held throughout the year, weather permitting.

The Tragedy of Othello, Moor of Venice

William Shakespeare

Dramatis Personae

OTHELLO, the Moor, general of the Venetian forces
DESDEMONA, his wife
IAGO, ensign to Othello
EMILIA, his wife, lady-in-waiting to Desdemona
CASSIO, lieutenant to Othello
THE DUKE OF VENICE
BRABANTIO, Venetian Senator, father of Desdemona
GRATIANO, nobleman of Venice, brother of Brabantio
LODOVICO, nobleman of Venice, kinsman of Brabantio
RODERIGO, rejected suitor of Desdemona
BIANCA, mistress of Cassio
MONTANO, a Cypriot official
A Clown in service to Othello
Senators, Sailors, Messengers, Officers, Gentlemen, Musicians, and Attendants

Scene: Venice And Cyprus

Act I. Scene I.

Venice. A street.

Enter Roderigo and Iago.

RODERIGO. Tush, never tell me! I take it much unkindly
    That thou, Iago, who hast had my purse[1]
    As if the strings were thine, shouldst know of this.
IAGO. 'Sblood,[2] but you will not hear me.
    If ever I did dream of such a matter,
    Abhor me.
RODERIGO. Thou told'st me thou didst hold him in thy hate.   5
IAGO. Despise me, if I do not. Three great ones[3] of the city,
    In personal suit to make me his lieutenant,[4]
    Off-capp'd[5] to him; and, by the faith of man,
    I know my price, I am worth no worse a place.   10
    But he, as loving his own pride and purposes,

---

1 **purse**—the conventional Elizabethan purse would have been a pouch with a drawstring, shaped much like a marble bag. Its shape and metaphorical implications allowed it to be a frequent erotic image, *scrotum*, perfect double entendre for this setting.
2 **'Sblood**—God's blood. Common Elizabethan profanity. Indicative of Iago's crude social role.
3 **Three great ones**—Three very important people (of Venice)
4 **lieutenant**—a military officer of higher rank than we are accustomed to consider for the term. This is the figure who would stand in the commanding place of the general if the general were unavailable.
5 **off-capp'd**—doffed their hats, a mark of respect and reverence

Evades them, with a bumbast circumstance
Horribly stuff'd with epithets of war,
And, in conclusion,
Nonsuits[6] my mediators; for, "Certes," says he,
"I have already chose my officer."
And what was he? 15
Forsooth,[7] a great arithmetician,
One Michael Cassio, a Florentine
(A fellow almost damn'd in a fair wife)
That never set a squadron in the field,
Nor the division of a battle knows 20
More than a spinster; unless the bookish theoric,
Wherein the tongued consuls can propose
As masterly as he. Mere prattle without practice
Is all his soldiership. But he, sir, had the election;
And I, of whom his eyes had seen the proof 25
At Rhodes, at Cyprus, and on other grounds
Christian and heathen, must be belee'd and calm'd[8]
By debitor and creditor. This counter-caster,
He, in good time, must his lieutenant be,
And I—God bless the mark!—his Moorship's ancient.[9] 30
RODERIGO. By heaven, I rather would have been his hangman.
IAGO. Why, there's no remedy. 'Tis the curse of service,
Preferment goes by letter and affection,
And not by old gradation, where each second
Stood heir to the first. Now, sir, be judge yourself 35
Whether I in any just term am affined[10]
To love the Moor.
RODERIGO. I would not follow him then.
IAGO. O, sir, content you.
I follow him to serve my turn upon him:
We cannot all be masters, nor all masters 40
Cannot be truly follow'd. You shall mark
Many a duteous and knee-crooking knave,
That doting on his own obsequious bondage
Wears out his time, much like his master's ass,
For nought but provender, and when he's old, cashier'd. 45
Whip me such honest knaves. Others there are
Who, trimm'd in forms and visages of duty,
Keep yet their hearts attending on themselves,
And throwing but shows of service on their lords
Do well thrive by them; and when they have lined their coats[11] 50
Do themselves homage. These fellows have some soul,
And such a one do I profess myself.
For, sir,
It is as sure as you are Roderigo,
Were I the Moor, I would not be Iago.
In following him, I follow but myself; 55
Heaven is my judge, not I for love and duty,
But seeming so, for my peculiar[12] end.
For when my outward action doth demonstrate
The native act and figure of my heart
In complement extern, 'tis not long after 60
But I will wear my heart upon my sleeve

---

6   **Nonsuits**—rebuffs, rejects; **certes**—certainly, without doubt
7   **Forsooth**—In truth, to tell the truth; **arithmetician**—theoretician (in this case, Cassio has only theoretical knowledge of military strategy)
8   **belee'd and calm'd**—nautical terms meaning stalled or frustrated
9   **ancient**—an anglicization of the French *ensign*, in this meaning the officer who holds the flag in battle maneuvers, a post of critical value on the battlefield, requiring fixed commitment and bravery, but not necessarily one requiring political or diplomatic acumen.
10 **affined**—affianced, promised, obligated; **Moor**—the term is used in reference to Othello, and in Elizabethan times refers generally to anyone from Africa, regardless of nationality, and quite probably regardless of color.
11 **lined their coats**—defrauded, cheated [their employers]
12 **peculiar**—particular

For daws[13] to peck at: I am not what I am.
RODERIGO. What a full fortune does the thick-lips owe,
If he can carry't thus!
IAGO.   Call up her father,
Rouse him, make after him, poison his delight, 65
Proclaim him in the streets, incense her kinsmen,
And, though he in a fertile climate dwell,
Plague him with flies. Though that his joy be joy,
Yet throw such changes of vexation on't
As it may lose some color. 70
RODERIGO. Here is her father's house; I'll call aloud.
IAGO. Do, with like timorous accent and dire yell
As when, by night and negligence, the fire
Is spied in populous cities.
RODERIGO. What, ho, Brabantio! Signior Brabantio, ho! 75
IAGO. Awake! What, ho, Brabantio! Thieves! Thieves! Thieves!
Look to your house, your daughter, and your bags!
Thieves! Thieves!

Brabantio appears above, at a window.

BRABANTIO. What is the reason of this terrible summons?
What is the matter there? 80
RODERIGO. Signior, is all your family within?
IAGO. Are your doors lock'd?
BRABANTIO.   Why? Wherefore ask you this?
IAGO. 'Zounds,[14] sir, you're robb'd! For shame, put on your gown;
Your heart is burst, you have lost half your soul;
Even now, now, very now, an old black ram 85
Is tupping[15] your white ewe. Arise, arise!
Awake the snorting citizens with the bell,
Or else the devil will make a grandsire of you.
Arise, I say!
BRABANTIO. What, have you lost your wits?
RODERIGO. Most reverend signior, do you know my voice? 90
BRABANTIO. Not I. What are you?
RODERIGO. My name is Roderigo.
BRABANTIO.   The worser welcome.
I have charged thee not to haunt about my doors.
In honest plainness thou hast heard me say
My daughter is not for thee; and now, in madness, 95
Being full of supper and distempering draughts,
Upon malicious bravery, dost thou come
To start my quiet.
RODERIGO. Sir, sir, sir—
BRABANTIO.   But thou must needs be sure
My spirit and my place have in them power 100
To make this bitter to thee.
RODERIGO.   Patience, good sir.
BRABANTIO. What tell'st thou me of robbing? This is Venice;
My house is not a grange.[16]
RODERIGO.   Most grave Brabantio,
In simple and pure soul I come to you.
IAGO. 'Zounds, sir, you are one of those that will not serve God, if the devil bid 105
you. Because we come to do you service and you think we are ruffians, you'll have your daughter covered with a Barbary[17] horse; you'll have your nephews[18] neigh to you; you'll have coursers for cousins, and gennets for germans.[19]
BRABANTIO. What profane wretch art thou? 110
IAGO. I am one, sir, that comes to tell you your daughter and the Moor are now making the beast with two backs.[20]
BRABANTIO. Thou are a villain.

---

13 **daws**—jackdaws, slighter smaller scavenger birds, similar to crows
14 **'Zounds**—God's wounds, another of the very common Elizabethan profanities
15 **tupping**—sexual intercourse
16 **grange**—isolated farmhouse or outbuilding
17 **Barbary**—Arabian, Barbary Coast (Tunisia), or Moorish
18 **nephews**—i.e. grandsons
19 **coursers for cousins, and gennets for germans**—horses for relations, Spanish horses for blood relatives
20 **making the beast with two backs**—an old and standard sexual image

IAGO. You are—a senator.
BRABANTIO. This thou shalt answer; I know thee, Roderigo. 115
RODERIGO. Sir, I will answer anything.
But, I beseech you,
If't be your pleasure and most wise consent,
As partly I find it is, that your fair daughter,
At this odd-even and dull watch o' the night,
Transported with no worse nor better guard 120
But with a knave of common hire, a gondolier,
To the gross clasps of a lascivious Moor—
If this be known to you, and your allowance,
We then have done you bold and saucy wrongs;
But if you know not this, my manners tell me 125
We have your wrong rebuke. Do not believe
That, from the sense of all civility,
I thus would play and trifle with your reverence.
Your daughter, if you have not given her leave,
I say again, hath made a gross revolt, 130
Tying her duty, beauty, wit, and fortunes
In an extravagant[21] and wheeling stranger
Of here and everywhere. Straight satisfy yourself:
If she be in her chamber or your house,
Let loose on me the justice of the state 135
For thus deluding you.
BRABANTIO. Strike on the tinder, ho!
Give me a taper! Call up all my people!
This accident is not unlike my dream;
Belief of it oppresses me already.
Light, I say, light! [Exit above.] 140
IAGO. Farewell, for I must leave you.
It seems not meet, nor wholesome to my place,
To be produced—as, if I stay, I shall—
Against the Moor; for I do know, the state,
However this may gall him with some check, 145
Cannot with safety cast him, for he's embark'd
With such loud reason to the Cyprus wars,
Which even now stands in act, that, for their souls,
Another of his fathom they have none
To lead their business; in which regard, 150
Though I do hate him as I do hell pains,
Yet for necessity of present life,
I must show out a flag and sign of love,
Which is indeed but sign. That you shall surely find him,
Lead to the Sagittary[22] the raised search, 155
And there will I be with him. So farewell. [Exit.]

Enter, below, Brabantio, in his nightgown, and Servants with torches.

BRABANTIO. It is too true an evil: gone she is,
And what's to come of my despised time
Is nought but bitterness. Now, Roderigo,
Where didst thou see her? O unhappy girl! 160
With the Moor, say'st thou? Who would be a father!
How didst thou know 'twas she? O, she deceives me
Past thought! What said she to you? Get more tapers.
Raise all my kindred. Are they married, think you?
RODERIGO. Truly, I think they are. 165
BRABANTIO. O heaven! How got she out?
O treason of the blood!
Fathers, from hence trust not your daughters' minds
By what you see them act. Is there not charms
By which the property of youth and maidhood
May be abused? Have you not read, Roderigo, 170
Of some such thing?
RODERIGO. Yes, sir, I have indeed.

---

21 **extravagant**—vagrant (Othello is not Venetian, and thus may be considered a wandering soldier of fortune)
22 **Sagittary**—a particular inn (real or imaginary) near the setting of the action in Venice

BRABANTIO. Call up my brother. O, would you had had her!
  Some one way, some another. Do you know
  Where we may apprehend her and the Moor?
RODERIGO. I think I can discover him, if you please   175
  To get good guard and go along with me.
BRABANTIO. Pray you, lead on. At every house I'll call;
  I may command at most. Get weapons, ho!
  And raise some special officers of night.
  On, good Roderigo, I'll deserve your pains.[23]   [*Exeunt.*] 180

Scene II.

Another street.

Enter Othello, Iago, and Attendants with torches.

IAGO. Though in the trade of war I have slain men,
  Yet do I hold it very stuff[24] o' the conscience
  To do no contrived murther. I lack iniquity
  Sometimes to do me service. Nine or ten times
  I had thought to have yerk'd[25] him here under the ribs.   5
OTHELLO. 'Tis better as it is.
IAGO.   Nay, but he prated[26]
  And spoke such scurvy and provoking terms
  Against your honor
  That, with the little godliness I have,
  I did full hard forbear him. But I pray you, sir,
  Are you fast married? Be assured of this,   10
  That the magnifico is much beloved,[27]
  And hath in his effect a voice potential
  As double as the Duke's. He will divorce you,
  Or put upon you what restraint and grievance
  The law, with all his might to enforce it on,   15
  Will give him cable.
OTHELLO.   Let him do his spite.
  My services, which I have done the signiory,[28]
  Shall out-tongue his complaints. 'Tis yet to know—
  Which, when I know that boasting is an honor,
  I shall promulgate—I fetch my life and being   20
  From men of royal siege,[29] and my demerits
  May speak unbonneted to as proud a fortune
  As this that I have reach'd. For know, Iago,
  But that I love the gentle Desdemona,
  I would not my unhoused free condition   25
  Put into circumscription and confine
  For the sea's worth. But, look! What lights come yond?
IAGO. Those are the raised father and his friends.
  You were best go in.
OTHELLO.   Not I; I must be found.
  My parts, my title, and my perfect soul   30
  Shall manifest me rightly. Is it they?
IAGO. By Janus, I think no.

Enter Cassio and certain Officers with torches.

OTHELLO. The servants of the Duke? And my lieutenant?
  The goodness of the night upon you, friends!
  What is the news?
CASSIO. The Duke does greet you, general,   35
  And he requires your haste-post-haste appearance,

---

23 **pains**—efforts
24 **stuff**—substance
25 **yerk'd**—stabbed
26 **prated**—idle chatter
27 **the magnifico is much beloved**—the Senator [Brabantio] is highly respected
28 **My services, which I have done the signiory,/Shall out-tongue his complaints**—the deeds I have done for the Duke [and rulers of Venice], shall overcome [Brabantio's] complaints
29 **from men of royal siege**—Othello is of royal rank

Even on the instant.
OTHELLO. What is the matter, think you?
CASSIO. Something from Cyprus, as I may divine;
It is a business of some heat. The galleys
Have sent a dozen sequent[30] messengers 40
This very night at one another's heels;
And many of the consuls, raised and met,
Are at the Duke's already. You have been hotly call'd for,
When, being not at your lodging to be found,
The Senate hath sent about three several quests 45
To search you out.
OTHELLO. 'Tis well I am found by you.
I will but spend a word here in the house
And go with you.
Exit.
CASSIO. Ancient, what makes he here?
IAGO. Faith, he tonight hath boarded a land carack;[31]
If it prove lawful prize, he's made forever. 50
CASSIO. I do not understand.
IAGO. He's married.
CASSIO. To who?

Re-enter Othello.

IAGO. Marry,[32] to—Come, captain, will you go?
OTHELLO. Have with you.
CASSIO. Here comes another troop to seek for you.
IAGO. It is Brabantio. General, be advised,
He comes to bad intent.

Enter Brabantio, Roderigo, and Officers with torches and weapons.

OTHELLO. Holla! Stand there! 55
RODERIGO. Signior, it is the Moor.
BRABANTIO. Down with him, thief!
They draw on both sides.
IAGO. You, Roderigo! Come, sir, I am for you.
OTHELLO. Keep up your bright swords, for the dew will rust them.
Good signior, you shall more command with years
Than with your weapons. 60
BRABANTIO. O thou foul thief, where hast thou stow'd my daughter?
Damn'd as thou art, thou hast enchanted her,
For I'll refer me to all things of sense,
If she in chains of magic were not bound,
Whether a maid so tender, fair, and happy, 65
So opposite to marriage that she shunn'd
The wealthy, curled darlings of our nation,
Would ever have, to incur a general mock,
Run from her guardage to the sooty bosom
Of such a thing as thou—to fear, not to delight. 70
Judge me the world, if 'tis not gross in sense
That thou hast practiced on her with foul charms,
Abused her delicate youth with drugs or minerals
That weaken motion.[33] I'll have't disputed on;
'Tis probable, and palpable to thinking. 75
I therefore apprehend and do attach thee[34]
For an abuser of the world, a practicer
Of arts inhibited and out of warrant.[35]
Lay hold upon him. If he do resist,
Subdue him at his peril.
OTHELLO. Hold your hands, 80
Both you of my inclining and the rest.
Were it my cue to fight, I should have known it
Without a prompter. Where will you that I go
To answer this your charge?
BRABANTIO. To prison, till fit time
Of law and course of direct session 85
Call thee to answer.

---

30 **sequent**—successive
31 **carack**—treasure ship, large trading ship
32 **Marry**—by Mary (another profane epithet)
33 **motion**—[not emotion but] reason
34 **I therefore apprehend and do attach thee**—I arrest you
35 **arts inhibited and out of warrant**—prohibited practices, i.e. black magic

OTHELLO. What if I do obey?
  How may the Duke be therewith satisfied,
  Whose messengers are here about my side,
  Upon some present business of the state
  To bring me to him?
FIRST OFFICER. 'Tis true, most worthy signior; 90
  The Duke's in council, and your noble self,
  I am sure, is sent for.
BRABANTIO. How? The Duke in council?
  In this time of the night? Bring him away;
  Mine's not an idle cause. The Duke himself,
  Or any of my brothers of the state, 95
  Cannot but feel this wrong as 'twere their own;
  For if such actions may have passage free,
  Bond slaves and pagans shall our statesmen be. [*Exeunt.*]

Scene III.

A council chamber. The Duke and Senators sitting at a table; Officers attending.

DUKE. There is no composition in these news
  That gives them credit.
FIRST SENATOR. Indeed they are disproportion'd;
  My letters say a hundred and seven galleys.
DUKE. And mine, a hundred and forty.
SECOND SENATOR. And mine, two hundred.
  But though they jump not on a just account— 5
  As in these cases, where the aim reports,
  'Tis oft with difference—yet do they all confirm
  A Turkish fleet, and bearing up to Cyprus.
DUKE. Nay, it is possible enough to judgement.
  I do not so secure me in the error, 10
  But the main article I do approve
  In fearful sense.
SAILOR. [*Within.*] What, ho! What, ho! What, ho!
FIRST OFFICER. A messenger from the galleys.

Enter Sailor.

DUKE. Now, what's the business?
SAILOR. The Turkish preparation makes for Rhodes,
  So was I bid report here to the state 15
  By Signior Angelo.
DUKE. How say you by this change?
FIRST SENATOR. This cannot be,
  By no assay of reason; 'tis a pageant[36]
  To keep us in false gaze. When we consider
  The importancy of Cyprus to the Turk, 20
  And let ourselves again but understand
  That as it more concerns the Turk than Rhodes,
  So may he with more facile question bear it,
  For that it stands not in such warlike brace,
  But altogether lacks the abilities 25
  That Rhodes is dress'd in. If we make thought of this,
  We must not think the Turk is so unskillful
  To leave that latest which concerns him first,
  Neglecting an attempt of ease and gain,
  To wake and wage a danger profitless. 30
DUKE. Nay, in all confidence, he's not for Rhodes.
FIRST OFFICER. Here is more news.

Enter a Messenger.

MESSENGER. The Ottomites,[37] reverend and gracious,
  Steering with due course toward the isle of Rhodes,
  Have there injointed them with an after fleet. 35
FIRST SENATOR. Ay, so I thought. How many, as you guess?
MESSENGER. Of thirty sail; and now they do re-stem
  Their backward course, bearing with frank appearance

---

36 **'tis a pageant to keep us in false gaze**—a feint (an action causing us to look in the wrong direction)
37 **Ottomites**—Turks of the Ottoman Empire

Their purposes toward Cyprus. Signior
    Montano,
  Your trusty and most valiant servitor, 40
  With his free duty[38] recommends you
    thus,
  And prays you to believe him.
DUKE. 'Tis certain then for Cyprus.
  Marcus Luccicos, is not he in town?
FIRST SENATOR. He's now in Florence. 45
DUKE. Write from us to him,
    post-post-haste dispatch.
FIRST SENATOR. Here comes Brabantio and
    the valiant Moor.

Enter Brabantio, Othello, Iago, Roderigo, and Officers.

DUKE. Valiant Othello, we must straight
    employ you
  Against the general enemy Ottoman.
  [*To Brabantio.*] I did not see you;
    welcome, gentle signior; 50
  We lack'd your counsel and your help
    tonight.
BRABANTIO. So did I yours. Good your
    Grace, pardon me:
  Neither my place nor aught I heard of
    business
  Hath raised me from my bed, nor doth
    the general care
  Take hold on me; for my particular grief 55
  Is of so flood-gate and o'erbearing
    nature
  That it engluts and swallows other
    sorrows,
  And it is still itself.
DUKE.   Why, what's the matter?
BRABANTIO. My daughter! O, my daughter!
ALL.   Dead?
BRABANTIO.   Ay, to me.
  She is abused, stol'n from me and
    corrupted 60
  By spells and medicines bought of
    mountebanks;[39]
  For nature so preposterously to err,
  Being not deficient, blind, or lame of
    sense,
  Sans witchcraft could not.
DUKE. Whoe'er he be that in this foul
    proceeding 65
  Hath thus beguiled your daughter of
    herself
  And you of her, the bloody book of law
  You shall yourself read in the bitter
    letter
  After your own sense, yea, though our
    proper[40] son
  Stood in your action.
BRABANTIO.   Humbly I thank your Grace. 70
  Here is the man, this Moor, whom now,
    it seems,
  Your special mandate for the state
    affairs
  Hath hither brought.
ALL.   We are very sorry for't.
DUKE. [*To Othello.*] What in your own part
    can you say to this?
BRABANTIO. Nothing, but this is so. 75
OTHELLO. Most potent, grave, and
    reverend signiors,
  My very noble and approved good
    masters,
  That I have ta'en[41] away this old man's
    daughter,
  It is most true; true, I have married her;
  The very head and front of my
    offending 80
  Hath this extent, no more. Rude am I in
    my speech,
  And little blest with the soft phrase of
    peace;
  For since these arms of mine had seven
    years' pith,[42]
  Till now some nine moons wasted, they
    have used
  Their dearest action in the tented field, 85
  And little of this great world can I
    speak,
  More than pertains to feats of broil and
    battle;
  And therefore little shall I grace my
    cause
  In speaking for myself. Yet, by your
    gracious patience,
  I will a round unvarnish'd tale deliver[43] 90

---

38 **free duty**—utmost respect
39 **mountebanks**—charlatans, deceivers
40 **proper**—own; **Stood in your action**—were the accused in your suit
41 **ta'en**—taken
42 **For since these arms of mine had seven years' pith**—Since my arms had the strength of seven years (since I was seven years old)
43 **a round unvarnish'd tale deliver**—a whole, honest (not deceitful) story tell

Of my whole course of love: what drugs, what charms,
What conjuration, and what mighty magic—
For such proceeding I am charged withal—
I won his daughter.
BRABANTIO.   A maiden never bold,
Of spirit so still and quiet that her motion   95
Blush'd at herself; and she—in spite of nature,
Of years, of country, credit, everything—
To fall in love with what she fear'd to look on!
It is judgement maim'd and most imperfect,
That will confess perfection so could err   100
Against all rules of nature, and must be driven
To find out practices of cunning hell
Why this should be. I therefore vouch again
That with some mixtures powerful o'er the blood,
Or with some dram conjured to this effect,   105
He wrought upon her.
DUKE.   To vouch[44] this is no proof,
Without more certain and more overt test
Than these thin habits[45] and poor likelihoods
Of modern[46] seeming do prefer against him.
FIRST SENATOR. But, Othello, speak.   110
Did you by indirect and forced courses
Subdue and poison this young maid's affections?
Or came it by request, and such fair question
As soul to soul affordeth?
OTHELLO.   I do beseech you,
Send for the lady to the Sagittary,   115
And let her speak of me before her father.
If you do find me foul in her report,
The trust, the office I do hold of you,
Not only take away, but let your sentence
Even fall upon my life.
DUKE.   Fetch Desdemona hither.   120
OTHELLO. Ancient, conduct them; you best know the place.

[*Exeunt Iago and Attendants.*]

And till she come, as truly as to heaven
I do confess the vices of my blood,
So justly to your grave ears I'll present
How I did thrive in this fair lady's love   125
And she in mine.
DUKE. Say it, Othello.
OTHELLO. Her father loved me, oft invited me,
Still question'd me the story of my life
From year to year, the battles, sieges, fortunes,
That I have pass'd.   130
I ran it through, even from my boyish days
To the very moment that he bade me tell it:
Wherein I spake of most disastrous chances,
Of moving accidents by flood and field,
Of hair-breadth 'scapes i' the imminent deadly breach,   135
Of being taken by the insolent foe
And sold to slavery, of my redemption thence
And portance[47] in my travels' history;
Wherein of antres[48] vast and deserts idle,
Rough quarries, rocks, and hills whose heads touch heaven,   140
It was my hint to speak—such was the process—
And of the Cannibals that each other eat,
The Anthropophagi,[49] and men whose heads
Do grow beneath their shoulders. This to hear
Would Desdemona seriously incline;   145
But still the house affairs would draw her thence,[50]

---

44 **vouch**—attest, charge
45 **habits**—clothes
46 **modern**—trivial
47 **portance**—manner of behaving
48 **anters(sp)**—caves
49 **Anthropophagi**—man-eaters
50 **the house affairs would draw her thence**—Desdemona was the mistress of Brabantio's house, and various

Which ever as she could with haste dispatch,
She'ld come again, and with a greedy ear
Devour up my discourse; which I observing,
Took once a pliant hour, and found good means   150
To draw from her a prayer of earnest heart
That I would all my pilgrimage dilate,[51]
Whereof by parcels she had something heard,
But not intentively. I did consent,
And often did beguile her of her tears   155
When I did speak of some distressful stroke
That my youth suffer'd. My story being done,
She gave me for my pains a world of sighs;
She swore, in faith, 'twas strange, 'twas passing strange;
'Twas pitiful, 'twas wondrous pitiful.   160
She wish'd she had not heard it, yet she wish'd
That heaven had made her such a man; she thank'd me,
And bade me, if I had a friend that loved her,
I should but teach him how to tell my story,
And that would woo her. Upon this hint I spake: 165
She loved me for the dangers I had pass'd,
And I loved her that she did pity them.
This only is the witchcraft I have used.
Here comes the lady; let her witness it.

Enter Desdemona, Iago, and Attendants.

DUKE. I think this tale would win my daughter too.   170
Good Brabantio,
Take up this mangled matter at the best:
Men do their broken weapons rather use
Than their bare hands.

BRABANTIO.   I pray you, hear her speak.
If she confess that she was half the wooer,
Destruction on my head, if my bad blame   175
Light on the man! Come hither, gentle mistress.
Do you perceive in all this noble company
Where most you owe obedience?

DESDEMONA.   My noble father,
I do perceive here a divided duty.
To you I am bound for life and education;   180
My life and education both do learn me
How to respect you; you are the lord of duty,
I am hitherto your daughter. But here's my husband,
And so much duty as my mother show'd
To you, preferring you before her father,   185
So much I challenge that I may profess
Due to the Moor, my lord.

BRABANTIO.   God be with you! I have done.
Please it your Grace, on to the state affairs;
I had rather to adopt a child than get it.
Come hither, Moor.   190
I here do give thee that with all my heart
Which, but thou hast already, with all my heart
I would keep from thee. For your sake, jewel,
I am glad at soul I have no other child;
For thy escape would teach me tyranny,   195
To hang clogs on them. I have done, my lord.

DUKE. Let me speak like yourself, and lay a sentence[52]
Which, as a grise[53] or step, may help these lovers
Into your favor.
When remedies are past, the griefs are ended
By seeing the worst, which late on hopes depended.[54]   200

---

matters of domestic management required her supervision
51 **dilate**—relate in full
52 **lay a sentence**—provide a maxim
53 **grise**—step
54 **which late on hopes depended**—which until recently hoped for [better] results

To mourn a mischief that is past and gone
Is the next[55] way to draw new mischief on.
What cannot be preserved when Fortune takes,
Patience her injury a mockery makes.
The robb'd that smiles steals something from the thief; 205
He robs himself that spends a bootless grief.
BRABANTIO. So let the Turk of Cyprus us beguile;
We lose it not so long as we can smile.
He bears the sentence well, that nothing bears
But the free comfort which from thence he hears; 210
But he bears both the sentence and the sorrow
That, to pay grief, must of poor patience borrow.
These sentences, to sugar or to gall,
Being strong on both sides, are equivocal.
But words are words; I never yet did hear 215
That the bruised heart was pierced[56] through the ear.
I humbly beseech you, proceed to the affairs of state.
DUKE. The Turk with a most mighty preparation makes for Cyprus.
Othello, the fortitude[57] of the place is best known to you; and though we 220
have there a substitute[58] of most allowed sufficiency,[59] yet opinion, a
sovereign mistress of effects, throws a more safer voice on you.[60] You must
therefore be content to slubber[61] the gloss of your new fortunes with this
more stubborn and boisterous[62] expedition. 225
OTHELLO. The tyrant custom, most grave senators,
Hath made the flinty and steel couch of war
My thrice-driven[63] bed of down. I do agnize
A natural and prompt alacrity
I find in hardness and do undertake 230
These present wars against the Ottomites.
Most humbly therefore bending to your state,
I crave fit disposition for my wife,
Due reference of place and exhibition,
With such accommodation and besort 235
As levels with her breeding.
DUKE. If you please,
Be't at her father's.
BRABANTIO. I'll not have it so.
OTHELLO. Nor I.
DESDEMONA. Nor I. I would not there reside
To put my father in impatient thoughts
By being in his eye. Most gracious Duke,
To my unfolding lend your prosperous ear, 240
And let me find a charter in your voice
To assist my simpleness.
DUKE. What would you, Desdemona?
DESDEMONA. That I did love the Moor to live with him,
My downright violence and storm of fortunes
May trumpet to the world. My heart's subdued 245
Even to the very quality of my lord.
I saw Othello's visage in his mind,
And to his honors and his valiant parts
Did I my soul and fortunes consecrate.
So that, dear lords, if I be left behind, 250

---

55 **next**—closest, surest
56 **pierced**—(some editors emend it to pieced, i.e., "healed." But *pierced* makes good sense: Brabantio is saying in effect that his heart cannot be further hurt [pierced] by the indignity of the useless, conventional advice the Duke offers him. *Pierced* can also mean, however, "lanced" in the medical sense, and would then mean "treated")
57 **fortitude**—fortification
58 **substitute**—viceroy (one who represents the Viennese Council)
59 **most allowed sufficiency**—generally acknowledged capability
60 **opinion ... you**—the general opinion, which finally controls affairs, is that you would be the best man in this situation
61 **slubber**—besmear
62 **stubborn and boisterous**—rough and violent
63 **thrice-driven**—softest (from the process of generating quality goose down); **agnize**—know in myself

  A moth of peace, and he go to the war,
  The rites for which[64] I love him are bereft me,
  And I a heavy interim shall support
  By his dear absence. Let me go with him.
OTHELLO. Let her have your voices. 255
  Vouch with me, heaven, I therefore beg it not
  To please the palate of my appetite,
  Nor to comply with heat—the young affects
  In me defunct—and proper satisfaction;
  But to be free and bounteous to her mind.[65] 260
  And heaven defend your good souls, that you think
  I will your serious and great business scant
  For she is with me. No, when light-wing'd toys
  Of feather'd Cupid seel with wanton dullness
  My speculative and officed instruments, 265
  That my disports corrupt and taint my business,
  Let housewives make a skillet of my helm,
  And all indign and base adversities
  Make head against my estimation![66]
DUKE. Be it as you shall privately determine, 270
  Either for her stay or going. The affair cries haste,
  And speed must answer't: you must hence tonight.
DESDEMONA. Tonight, my lord?
DUKE.   This night.
OTHELLO.   With all my heart.
DUKE. At nine i' the morning here we'll meet again.
  Othello, leave some officer behind, 275
  And he shall our commission bring to you,
  With such things else of quality and respect
  As doth import you.
OTHELLO. So please your Grace, my ancient;
  A man he is of honesty and trust.
  To his conveyance I assign my wife, 280
  With what else needful your good Grace shall think
  To be sent after me.
DUKE.   Let it be so.
  Good night to everyone. [*To Brabantio.*] And, noble signior,
  If virtue no delighted beauty lack,
  Your son-in-law is far more fair than black. 285
FIRST SENATOR. Adieu, brave Moor, use Desdemona well.
BRABANTIO. Look to her, Moor, if thou hast eyes to see;
  She has deceived her father, and may thee.
    [*Exeunt Duke, Senators, and Officers.*]
OTHELLO. My life upon her faith! Honest Iago,
  My Desdemona must I leave to thee. 290
  I prithee, let thy wife attend on her,
  And bring them after in the best advantage.
  Come, Desdemona, I have but an hour
  Of love, of worldly matters and direction,
  To spend with thee. We must obey the time. 295
    [*Exeunt Othello and Desdemona.*]
RODERIGO. Iago!
IAGO. What say'st thou, noble heart?
RODERIGO. What will I do, thinkest thou?
IAGO. Why, go to bed and sleep.
RODERIGO. I will incontinently drown myself. 300
IAGO. If thou dost, I shall never love thee after.
  Why, thou silly gentleman!
RODERIGO. It is silliness to live when to live is torment, and then have we a prescription to die when death is our physician. 305
IAGO. O villainous! I have looked upon the world for four times seven years,[67] and since I could distinguish betwixt a benefit and an injury, I never found man that knew how to love himself. Ere I would say I would drown myself for

---

64 **rites for which . . .**—the rites and rituals of marriage, i.e. bed, sex, mutual support, living together
65 **beg it not to please . . . bountous to her mind**—that Othello is beyond the lusty sexual heat of youth, but wants to satisfy the aims and wishes of Desdemona
66 **No, when light-wing toys . . . Make head against my estimation!**—When such frivolous temptations distract him from his military duties he has lost his commitment.
67 **four times seven years**—Iago is 28 years old

the love of a guinea hen, I would
change my humanity with a baboon. 310
RODERIGO. What should I do? I confess it
is my shame to be so fond, but it is not
in my virtue to amend it.
IAGO. Virtue? a fig! 'Tis in ourselves that
we are thus or thus.
Our bodies are gardens, to the which
our wills are gardeners; so that if we 315
will plant nettles or sow lettuce, set
hyssop and weed up thyme, supply it
with one gender of herbs or distract it
with many, either to have it sterile with
idleness or manured with industry,
why, the power and corrigible
authority of this lies in our wills. If the
balance of our lives had not one scale of 320
reason to poise another of sensuality,
the blood and baseness of our natures
would conduct us to most preposterous
conclusions.
But we have reason to cool our raging
motions, our carnal stings, our
unbitted[68] lusts; whereof I take this,
that you call love, to be a sect or scion. 325
RODERIGO. It cannot be.
IAGO. It is merely a lust of the blood and a
permission of the will. Come, be a man!
Drown thyself? Drown cats and blind
puppies. I have professed me thy
friend, and I confess me knit to thy 330
deserving with cables of perdurable
toughness; I could never better stead[69]
thee than now. Put money in thy purse;
follow thou the wars; defeat thy favor[70]
with an usurped[71] beard. I say, put
money in thy purse. It cannot be that
Desdemona should long continue her
love to the Moor—put money in thy
purse—nor he his to her. It was a 335
violent commencement, and thou shalt
see an answerable sequestration[72]—put
but money in thy purse. These Moors
are changeable in their wills—fill thy
purse with money. The food that to him
now is as luscious as locusts,[73] shall be
to him shortly as acerb as the
coloquintida.[74] She must change for 340
youth; when she is sated with his body,
she will find the error of her choice. She
must have change, she must; therefore
put money in thy purse. If thou wilt
needs damn thyself, do it a more
delicate way than drowning. Make all
the money thou canst. If sanctimony
and a frail vow betwixt an erring
barbarian and a supersubtle Venetian 345
be not too hard for my wits and all the
tribe of hell, thou shalt enjoy
her—therefore make money. A pox of
drowning thyself! It is clean out of the
way. Seek thou rather to be hanged in
compassing thy joy than to be drowned
and go without her. 350
RODERIGO. Wilt thou be fast to my hopes,
if I depend on the issue?
IAGO. Thou art sure of me—go, make
money. I have told thee often, and I
retell thee again and again, I hate the
Moor. My cause is hearted;[75] thine hath
no less reason. Let us be conjunctive[76]
in 355
our revenge against him. If thou canst
cuckold him, thou dost thyself a
pleasure, me a sport. There are many
events in the womb of time which will
be delivered. Traverse, go, provide thy
money. We will have more of this
tomorrow. Adieu.
RODERIGO. Where shall we meet i' the
morning? 360
IAGO. At my lodging.
RODERIGO. I'll be with thee betimes.
IAGO. Go to, farewell. Do you hear,
Roderigo?
RODERIGO. What say you?
IAGO. No more of drowning, do you hear? 365
RODERIGO. I am changed; I'll go sell all my
land. [*Exit.*]
IAGO. Thus do I ever make my fool my
purse;

---

68 **unbitted**—unbidden, involuntary
69 **stead**—serve
70 **defeat thy favor**—disguise your face
71 **usurped**—assumed (false)
72 **answerable sequestration**—similar continuation
73 **locusts**—(a sweet fruit)
74 **coloquintida**—(a purgative derived from a bitter apple)
75 **hearted**—deep-seated
76 **conjunctive**—joined (partners)

For I mine own gain'd knowledge[77] should profane
If I would time expend with such a snipe
But for my sport and profit. I hate the Moor, 370
And it is thought abroad that 'twixt my sheets
He has done my office.[78]
 I know not if't be true,
But I for mere suspicion in that kind
Will do as if for surety. He holds me well,
The better shall my purpose work on him. 375
Cassio's a proper man. Let me see now—
To get his place, and to plume up my will
In double knavery—How, how?—Let's see—
After some time, to abuse Othello's ear
That he is too familiar with his wife. 380
He hath a person and a smooth dispose
To be suspected—framed to make women false.
The Moor is of a free and open nature,
That thinks men honest that but seem to be so,
And will as tenderly be led by the nose 385
As asses are.
I have't. It is engender'd. Hell and night
Must bring this monstrous birth to the world's light. [*Exit.*]

Act II. Scene I.

A seaport in Cyprus. An open place near the quay.

FIRST GENTLEMAN *situated above as a lookout*

Enter Montano and two Gentlemen.

MONTANO. What from the cape can you discern at sea?
FIRST GENTLEMAN. Nothing at all. It is a high-wrought flood;
 I cannot, 'twixt the heaven and the main,[79]
 Descry a sail.
MONTANO. Methinks the wind hath spoke aloud at land; 5
 A fuller blast ne'er shook our battlements.
 If it hath ruffian'd so upon the sea,
 What ribs of oak, when mountains melt on them,
 Can hold the mortise?[80] What shall we hear of this?
SECOND GENTLEMAN. A segregation[81] of the Turkish fleet. 10
 For do but stand upon the foaming shore,
 The chidden billow seems to pelt the clouds;
 The wind-shaked surge, with high and monstrous mane,[82]
 Seems to cast water on the burning bear,
 And quench the guards of the ever-fixed pole.[83] 15
 I never did like molestation view
 On the enchafed flood.
MONTANO.   If that the Turkish fleet
 Be not enshelter'd and embay'd,[84] they are drown'd;
 It is impossible to bear it out.[85]

Enter a third Gentleman.

THIRD GENTLEMAN. News, lads! Our wars are done. 20
 The desperate tempest hath so bang'd the Turks,
 That their designment halts. A noble ship of Venice
 Hath seen a grievous wreck and sufferance
 On most part of their fleet.

---

77 **gain'd knowledge**—practical worldly wisdom
78 **'twixt my sheets/He has done my office**—in my bed he has cuckolded me
79 **'twixt the heaven and the main**—between the sky and sea [horizon]
80 **What ribs of oak ... can hold the mortise**—What [wooden] ship's hulls can hold their caulking
81 **segregation**—separation
82 **mane**—"ocean" and "power"
83 **Seems ... pole**—(the constellation Ursa Minor contains two stars which are the **guards,** or companions, of the **pole,** or North Star)
84 **enshelter'd and embay'd**—found shelter from the storm in a bay
85 **to bear it out**—to last out the storm

MONTANO. How? Is this true?
THIRD GENTLEMAN. The ship is here put in,
    A Veronesa.[86] Michael Cassio,
    Lieutenant to the warlike Moor, Othello,
    Is come on shore; the Moor himself at sea,
    And is in full commission here for Cyprus.
MONTANO. I am glad on't; 'tis a worthy governor.
THIRD GENTLEMAN. But this same Cassio, though he speak of comfort
    Touching the Turkish loss, yet he looks sadly
    And prays the Moor be safe; for they were parted
    With foul and violent tempest.
MONTANO.   Pray heavens he be,
    For I have served him, and the man commands
    Like a full soldier. Let's to the seaside, ho!
    As well to see the vessel that's come in
    As to throw out our eyes for brave Othello,
    Even till we make the main and the aerial blue
    An indistinct regard.[87]
THIRD GENTLEMAN. Come, let's do so,
    For every minute is expectancy
    Of more arrivance.

Enter Cassio.

CASSIO. Thanks, you the valiant of this warlike isle,
    That so approve[88] the Moor! O, let the heavens
    Give him defense against the elements,
    For I have lost him on a dangerous sea.
MONTANO. Is he well shipp'd?
CASSIO. His bark[89] is stoutly timber'd, and his pilot
    Of very expert and approved allowance;[90]
    Therefore my hopes, not surfeited to death,[91]
    Stand in bold cure.[92]
    [*A cry within.*] "A sail, a sail, a sail!"

Enter a fourth Gentleman.

                What noise?
FOURTH GENTLEMAN. The town is empty; on the brow o' the sea
    Stand ranks of people, and they cry, "A sail!"
CASSIO. My hopes do shape him for the governor.
                [*Guns heard.*]
SECOND GENTLEMAN. They do discharge their shot of courtesy—
    Our friends at least.
CASSIO.   I pray you, sir, go forth,
    And give us truth who 'tis that is arrived.
SECOND GENTLEMAN. I shall.
                                Exit.
MONTANO. But, good lieutenant, is your general wived?
CASSIO. Most fortunately: he hath achieved a maid
    That paragons description and wild fame,
    One that excels the quirks of blazoning pens,
    And in the essential vesture of creation
    Does tire the ingener.[93]

Re-enter second Gentleman.

                How now! who has put in?
SECOND GENTLEMAN. 'Tis one Iago, ancient to the general.
CASSIO. He has had most favorable and happy speed:
    Tempests themselves, high seas, and howling winds,
    The gutter'd rocks, and congregated sands,

---

86 **Veronesa**—[Not certain. Possibly this means a ship furnished by Verona for Venetian service; but it is also possible that this derives from an Italian word for a particular kind of ship.]
87 **make the main . . . an indistinct regard**—the sea and sky become indistinguishable
88 **approve**—honor
89 **bark**—a kind of ship
90 **expert and approved allowance**—well trained and sea-tested
91 **not surfeited to death**—not so great as to be in danger
92 **Sand in bold cure**—are likely to be restored
93 **Does tire the ingener**—(something like "taxes the skills of the poet")

Traitors ensteep'd to clog the guiltless keel, 70
As having sense of beauty, do omit
Their mortal natures, letting go safely by
The divine Desdemona.
MONTANO. What is she?
CASSIO. She that I spake of, our great captain's captain,
Left in the conduct of the bold Iago, 75
Whose footing here anticipates our thoughts
A se'nnight's speed. Great Jove, Othello guard,
And swell his sail with thine own powerful breath,
That he may bless this bay with his tall ship,
Make love's quick pants in Desdemona's arms, 80
Give renew'd fire to our extincted spirits,
And bring all Cyprus comfort.

Enter Desdemona, Emilia, Iago, Roderigo, and Attendants.

O, behold,
The riches of the ship is come on shore!
Ye men of Cyprus, let her have your knees.
[*Kneeling.*]
Hail to thee, lady! And the grace of heaven,
Before, behind thee, and on every hand, 85
Enwheel[94] thee round!
DESDEMONA. I thank you, valiant Cassio.
What tidings can you tell me of my lord?
CASSIO. He is not yet arrived, nor know I aught
But that he's well and will be shortly here.
DESDEMONA. O, but I fear—How lost you company? 90
CASSIO. The great contention of the sea and skies
Parted our fellowship—
[*A cry within.*] "A sail, a sail!"
[*Guns heard.*] But, Hark! A sail.

SECOND GENTLEMAN. They give their greeting to the citadel;
This likewise is a friend.
CASSIO. See for the news. 95
[*Exit Gentleman.*]
Good ancient, you are welcome. [*To Emilia.*] Welcome, mistress.
Let it not gall your patience, good Iago,
That I extend my manners; 'tis my breeding
That gives me this bold show of courtesy. [*Kisses her.*]
IAGO. Sir, would she give you so much of her lips 100
As of her tongue she oft bestows on me,
You'ld have enough.
DESDEMONA. Alas, she has no speech.
IAGO. In faith, too much;
I find it still when I have list to sleep.
Marry, before your ladyship I grant, 105
She puts her tongue a little in her heart
And chides with thinking.
EMILIA. You have little cause to say so.
IAGO. Come on, come on. You are pictures out of doors,
Bells in your parlors, wildcats in your kitchens,
Saints in your injuries, devils being offended, 110
Players in your housewifery, and housewives in your beds.[95]
DESDEMONA. O, fie upon thee, slanderer!
IAGO. Nay, it is true, or else I am a Turk:
You rise to play, and go to bed to work.
EMILIA. You shall not write my praise.
IAGO. No, let me not. 115
DESDEMONA. What wouldst thou write of me, if thou shouldst praise me?
IAGO. O gentle lady, do not put me to't,
For I am nothing if not critical.
DESDEMONA. Come on, assay—There's one gone to the harbor?
IAGO. Ay, madam.
DESDEMONA. [*Aside.*] I am not merry, but I do beguile 120
The thing I am by seeming otherwise.
Come, how wouldst thou praise me?
IAGO. I am about it, but indeed my invention

---

94 **Enwheel**—surrounded
95 **You are pictures .N.. in your beds**—You [women] are Models of virtues in public, music in your parlors, wildcats in your kitchens, never the causes in the injuries to others you do, devils in reaction to your being offended, deceivers in your practice of economies, and "economical" of your favors in your beds.

Comes from my pate as birdlime does from frieze;
It plucks out brains and all. But my Muse labors, 125
And thus she is deliver'd.
If she be fair and wise, fairness and wit,
The one's for use, the other useth it.
DESDEMONA. Well praised! How if she be black and witty?
IAGO. If she be black, and thereto have a wit, 130
She'll find a white that shall her blackness fit.
DESDEMONA. Worse and worse.
EMILIA. How if fair and foolish?
IAGO. She never yet was foolish that was fair,
For even her folly help'd her to an heir. 135
DESDEMONA. These are old fond paradoxes to make fools laugh i' the alehouse. What miserable praise hast thou for her that's foul and foolish?
IAGO. There's none so foul and foolish thereunto,
But does foul pranks which fair and wise ones do. 140
DESDEMONA. O heavy ignorance! Thou praisest the worst best. But what praise couldst thou bestow on a deserving woman indeed, one that in the authority of her merit did justly put on the vouch of very malice itself? 145
IAGO. She that was ever fair and never proud,
Had tongue at will and yet was never loud,
Never lack'd gold and yet went never gay,
Fled from her wish and yet said, "Now I may";
She that, being anger'd, her revenge being nigh, 150
Bade her wrong stay and her displeasure fly;
She that in wisdom never was so frail
To change the cod's head for the salmon's tail;[96]
She that could think and ne'er disclose her mind,
See suitors following and not look behind; 155
She was a wight, if ever such wight were—
DESDEMONA. To do what?
IAGO. To suckle fools and chronicle small beer.[97]
DESDEMONA. O most lame and impotent conclusion! Do not learn of him, Emilia, though he be thy husband. How say you, Cassio? Is he not a most profane 160 and liberal counselor?
CASSIO. He speaks home, madam.[98] You may relish him more in the soldier than in the scholar. [Takes Desdemona's hand.]
IAGO. [Aside.] He takes her by the palm; ay, well said, whisper! With as little 165 a web as this will I ensnare as great a fly as Cassio. Ay, smile upon her, do; I will gyve thee in thine own courtship. You say true; 'tis so, indeed. If such tricks as these strip you out of your lieutenantry, it had been better you had not kissed your three fingers so oft, which now again you are most apt to 170 play the sir in. Very good. Well kissed! An excellent courtesy! 'tis so, indeed. Yet again your fingers to your lips? Would they were clyster-pipes[99] for your sake! [Trumpet within.]
The Moor! I know his trumpet. 175
CASSIO. 'Tis truly so.
DESDEMONA. Let's meet him and receive him.
CASSIO. Lo, where he comes!

Enter Othello and Attendants.

OTHELLO. O my fair warrior!
DESDEMONA.   My dear Othello! 180
OTHELLO. It gives me wonder great as my content
To see you here before me. O my soul's joy!
If after every tempest come such calms,
May the winds blow till they have waken'd death!
And let the laboring bark climb hills of seas 185
Olympus-high, and duck again as low

---

96 **To change the cod's head for the salmon's tail**—To exchange something of value for something valueless
97 **chronicle small beer**—maintain household accounts (the very lowest of activities in Iago's opinion)
98 **He speaks home, madam**—digs deeply with his speech
99 **clyster-pipes**—enema tubes

As hell's from heaven! If it were now to die,
'Twere now to be most happy; for I fear
My soul hath her content so absolute
That not another comfort like to this   190
Succeeds in unknown fate.
DESDEMONA.   The heavens forbid
But that our loves and comforts should increase,
Even as our days do grow!
OTHELLO.   Amen to that, sweet powers!
I cannot speak enough of this content;
It stops me here [*touches his heart*]; it is too much of joy.   195
And this, and this, the greatest discords be   [*Kisses her.*]
That e'er our hearts shall make!
IAGO.   [*Aside.*] O, you are well tuned now!
But I'll set down the pegs that make this music,
As honest as I am.
OTHELLO.   Come, let us to the castle.
News, friends: our wars are done, the Turks are drown'd.   200
How does my old acquaintance of this isle?
Honey, you shall be well desired in Cyprus;
I have found great love amongst them. O my sweet,
I prattle out of fashion, and I dote
In mine own comforts. I prithee, good Iago,   205
Go to the bay and disembark my coffers.
Bring thou the master to the citadel;
He is a good one, and his worthiness
Does challenge much respect. Come, Desdemona,
Once more well met at Cyprus.   210
          [*Exeunt all but Iago and Roderigo.*]
IAGO. [*To an Attendant.*] Do thou meet me presently at the harbor.
[*To Roderigo.*] Come hither. If thou be'st valiant—as they say base men being in love have then a nobility in their natures more than is native to them—list me. The lieutenant tonight watches on the court of guard. First,   215
I must tell thee this: Desdemona is directly in love with him.
RODERIGO. With him? Why, 'tis not possible.
IAGO. Lay thy finger thus [*puts his finger to his lips*], and let thy soul be instructed. Mark me with what violence she first loved the Moor, but for bragging and   220
telling her fantastical lies. And will she love him still for prating? Let not thy discreet heart think it. Her eye must be fed; and what delight shall she have to look on the devil? When the blood is made dull with the act of sport, there should be, again to inflame it and to give satiety a fresh appetite, loveliness in favor, sympathy in years, manners,   225
and beauties—all which the Moor is defective in. Now, for want of these required conveniences, her delicate tenderness will find itself abused, begin to heave the gorge,[100] disrelish and abhor the Moor; very nature will instruct her in it and compel her to some second choice. Now sir, this granted—as it is a most pregnant and unforced position—   230
who stands so eminently in the degree of this fortune as Cassio does? A knave very voluble; no further conscionable than in putting on the mere form of civil and humane seeming, for the better compass of his salt[101] and most hidden loose affection? Why, none, why, none—a slipper and subtle knave,   235
a finder out of occasions, that has an eye can stamp and counterfeit advantages, though true advantage never present itself—a devilish knave! Besides, the knave is handsome, young, and hath all those requisites in him that folly and green minds look after—a pestilent complete knave, and the woman hath found him already.   240
RODERIGO. I cannot believe that in her; she's full of most blest condition.
IAGO. Blest fig's-end! The wine she drinks is made of grapes. If she had been blest, she would never have loved the Moor.   245

---

100 **heave the gorge**—vomit
101 **salt**—lecherous

Blest pudding! Didst thou not see her paddle with the palm of his hand?[102] Didst not mark that?

RODERIGO. Yes, that I did; but that was but courtesy.

IAGO. Lechery, by this hand; an index and obscure prologue to the history of lust and foul thoughts. They met so near with their lips that their breaths embraced together. Villainous thoughts, Roderigo! When these mutualities so marshal the way, hard at hand comes the master and main exercise, the incorporate conclusion. Pish! But, sir, be you ruled by me. I have brought you from Venice. Watch you tonight; for the command, I'll lay't upon you. Cassio knows you not. I'll not be far from you. Do you find some occasion to anger Cassio, either by speaking too loud, or tainting his discipline, or from what other course you please, which the time shall more favorably minister.

RODERIGO. Well.

IAGO. Sir, he is rash and very sudden in choler, and haply may strike at you. Provoke him, that he may; for even out of that will I cause these of Cyprus to mutiny, whose qualification shall come into no true taste again but by the displanting of Cassio. So shall you have a shorter journey to your desires by the means I shall then have to prefer them, and the impediment most profitably removed, without the which there were no expectation of our prosperity.

RODERIGO. I will do this, if I can bring it to any opportunity.

IAGO. I warrant thee. Meet me by and by at the citadel. I must fetch his necessaries ashore. Farewell.

RODERIGO. Adieu. [*Exit.*]

IAGO. That Cassio loves her, I do well believe it;
That she loves him, 'tis apt and of great credit.
The Moor, howbeit that I endure him not,
Is of a constant, loving, noble nature,
And I dare think he'll prove to Desdemona
A most dear husband. Now, I do love her too,
Not out of absolute lust, though peradventure
I stand accountant for as great a sin,
But partly led to diet my revenge,
For that I do suspect the lusty Moor
Hath leap'd into my seat; the thought whereof
Doth like a poisonous mineral gnaw my inwards,
And nothing can or shall content my soul
Till I am even'd with him, wife for wife.[103]
Or failing so, yet that I put the Moor
At least into a jealousy so strong
That judgement cannot cure. Which thing to do,
If this poor trash of Venice, whom I trace
For his quick hunting, stand the putting on,
I'll have our Michael Cassio on the hip,
Abuse him to the Moor in the rank garb
(For I fear Cassio[104] with my nightcap too),
Make the Moor thank me, love me, and reward me
For making him egregiously an ass
And practicing upon his peace and quiet
Even to madness. 'Tis here, but yet confused:
Knavery's plain face is never seen till used. [*Exit.*]

Scene II.

A street.

Enter a Herald with a proclamation; people following.

HERALD. It is Othello's pleasure, our noble and valiant general, that upon certain tidings now arrived, importing the

---

102 **paddle with the palm of his hand**—an affectionate, teasing and lecherous "invitation"
103 **even'd ... wife for wife**—(Iago suspects Othello of having cuckolded him with Emilia, and now he sees an opportunity for revenge)
104 **I fear Cassio**—Iago suspects Cassio of cuckolding him, too.

mere perdition of the Turkish fleet, every man put himself into triumph; some to dance, some to make bonfires, each man to what sport and revels his addiction leads him; for besides these beneficial news, it is the celebration of his nuptial. So much was his pleasure should be proclaimed. All offices are open, and there is full liberty of feasting from this present hour of five till the bell have told eleven. Heaven bless the isle of Cyprus and our noble general Othello! [*Exeunt.*] 10

Scene III.

A hall in the castle.

Enter Othello, Desdemona, Cassio, and Attendants.

OTHELLO. Good Michael, look you to the guard tonight.
  Let's teach ourselves that honorable stop,
  Not to outsport discretion.
CASSIO. Iago hath direction what to do;
  But notwithstanding with my personal eye
  Will I look to't.
OTHELLO.   Iago is most honest.[105]
  Michael, good night. Tomorrow with your earliest
  Let me have speech with you.
  [*To Desdemona.*] Come, my dear love, 10
  The purchase made, the fruits are to ensue;
  That profit's yet to come 'tween me and you.
  Good night.
    [*Exeunt Othello, Desdemona, and Attendants.*]

Enter Iago.

CASSIO. Welcome, Iago; we must to the watch.
IAGO. Not this hour, lieutenant; 'tis not yet ten o' the clock. Our general cast 15
us thus early for the love of his Desdemona; who let us not therefore blame. He hath not yet made wanton the night with her, and she is sport for Jove.
CASSIO. She's a most exquisite lady.
IAGO. And, I'll warrant her, full of game. 20
CASSIO. Indeed she's a most fresh and delicate creature.
IAGO. What an eye she has! Methinks it sounds a parley to provocation.
CASSIO. An inviting eye; and yet methinks right modest.
IAGO. And when she speaks, is it not an alarum to love? 25
CASSIO. She is indeed perfection.
IAGO. Well, happiness to their sheets! Come, lieutenant, I have a stope[106] of wine, and here without are a brace of Cyprus gallants that would fain have a measure to the health of black Othello. 30
CASSIO. Not tonight, good Iago. I have very poor and unhappy brains for drinking. I could well wish courtesy would invent some other custom of entertainment.
IAGO. O, they are our friends! But one cup; I'll drink for you.
CASSIO. I have drunk but one cup tonight, and that was craftily qualified[107] too, and behold what innovation it makes here. I am unfortunate in the infirmity, and dare not task my weakness with any more. 35
IAGO. What, man! 'Tis a night of revels, the gallants desire it. 40
CASSIO. Where are they?
IAGO. Here at the door; I pray you, call them in.
CASSIO. I'll do't, but it dislikes me. [*Exit.*]
IAGO. If I can fasten but one cup upon him, With that which he hath drunk tonight already, 45
  He'll be as full of quarrel and offense
  As my young mistress' dog. Now my sick fool Roderigo,
  Whom love hath turn'd almost the wrong side out,
  To Desdemona hath tonight caroused

---

105 **honest**—reliable
106 **stope**—2 qt. tankard [spelling: stoup]
107 **qualified**—diluted

Potations pottle-deep;[108] and he's to watch. 50
Three lads of Cyprus, noble swelling spirits,
That hold their honors in a wary distance,
The very elements of this warlike isle,
Have I tonight fluster'd with flowing cups,
And they watch too. Now, 'mongst this flock of drunkards, 55
Am I to put our Cassio in some action
That may offend the isle. But here they come.
If consequence do but approve my dream,
My boat sails freely, both with wind and stream.

Re-enter Cassio; with him Montano and Gentlemen; Servants following with wine.

CASSIO. 'Fore God, they have given me a rouse[109] already. 60
MONTANO. Good faith, a little one; not past a pint, as I am a soldier.
IAGO. Some wine, ho!

[*Sings.*] "And let me the canakin clink, clink;
   And let me the canakin clink. 65
   A soldier's a man;
   O, man's life's but a span;
   Why then let a soldier drink."

Some wine, boys!
CASSIO. 'Fore God, an excellent song. 70
IAGO. I learned it in England, where indeed they are most potent in potting. Your Dane, your German, and your swag-bellied Hollander—Drink, ho!—are nothing to your English.
CASSIO. Is your Englishman so expert in his drinking?
IAGO. Why, he drinks you with facility your Dane dead drunk; he sweats not to overthrow your Almain; he gives your Hollander a vomit ere the next pottle can be filled. 75
CASSIO. To the health of our general!
MONTANO. I am for it, lieutenant, and I'll do you justice.
IAGO. O sweet England! 80
[*Sings.*] "King Stephen was and-a worthy peer,
   His breeches cost him but a crown;
   He held them sixpence all too dear,
   With that he call'd the tailor lown.[110]

   "He was a wight[111] of high renown, 85
   And thou art but of low degree.
   'Tis pride that pulls the country down;
   Then take thine auld cloak about thee."

Some wine, ho!
CASSIO. Why, this is a more exquisite song than the other. 90
IAGO. Will you hear't again?
CASSIO. No, for I hold him to be unworthy of his place that does those things. Well, God's above all, and there be souls must be saved, and there be souls must not be saved.
IAGO. It's true, good lieutenant. 95
CASSIO. For mine own part—no offense to the general, nor any man of quality—I hope to be saved.
IAGO. And so do I too, lieutenant.
CASSIO. Ay, but, by your leave, not before me; the lieutenant is to be saved before the ancient. Let's have no more of this; let's to our affairs. God forgive us our sins! Gentlemen, let's look to our business. Do not think, gentlemen, I am drunk: this is my ancient, this is my right hand, and this is my left. I am not drunk now; I can stand well enough, and I speak well enough. 100
ALL. Excellent well. 105
CASSIO. Why, very well then; you must not think then that I am drunk. [*Exit.*]
MONTANO. To the platform, masters; come, let's set the watch.

---

108 **potations pottle-deep**—drinks to the bottom of the tankard
109 **rouse**—drink
110 **lown**—lout
111 **wight**—man

IAGO. You see this fellow that is gone before;
   He is a soldier fit to stand by Caesar 110
   And give direction. And do but see his vice;
   'Tis to his virtue a just equinox,[112]
   The one as long as the other. 'Tis pity of him.
   I fear the trust Othello puts him in
   On some odd time of his infirmity 115
   Will shake this island.
MONTANO.   But is he often thus?
IAGO. 'Tis evermore the prologue to his sleep.
   He'll watch the horologe a double set,[113]
   If drink rock not his cradle. 120
MONTANO.   It were well
   The general were put in mind of it.
   Perhaps he sees it not, or his good nature
   Prizes the virtue that appears in Cassio
   And looks not on his evils. Is not this true? 125

Enter Roderigo.

IAGO. [*Aside to him.*] How now, Roderigo!
   I pray you, after the lieutenant; go.
              [*Exit Roderigo.*]
MONTANO. And 'tis great pity that the noble Moor
   Should hazard such a place as his own second
   With one of an ingraft infirmity. 130
   It were an honest action to say
   So to the Moor.
IAGO.   Not I, for this fair island.
   I do love Cassio well, and would do much
   To cure him of this evil—But, hark! What noise? 135
        A cry within, "Help, help!"]

Re-enter Cassio, driving in Roderigo.

CASSIO. 'Zounds! You rogue! You rascal!
MONTANO. What's the matter, lieutenant?
CASSIO. A knave teach me my duty! But
   I'll beat the knave into a twiggen bottle.[114] 140
RODERIGO. Beat me!
CASSIO. Dost thou prate, rogue?
              [*Strikes Roderigo.*]
MONTANO. Nay, good lieutenant; I pray you, sir, hold your hand.
CASSIO. Let me go, sir, or I'll knock you o'er the mazzard.
MONTANO. Come, come, you're drunk. 145
CASSIO. Drunk?   [*They fight.*]
IAGO. [*Aside to Roderigo.*] Away, I say; go out and cry a mutiny.
              [*Exit Roderigo.*]
   Nay, good lieutenant! God's will, gentlemen!
   Help, ho!—Lieutenant—sir— Montano—sir— 150
   Help, masters!—Here's a goodly watch indeed!
              [*A bell rings.*]
   Who's that that rings the bell?—Diablo, ho!
   The town will rise. God's will, lieutenant, hold!
   You will be shamed forever.

Re-enter Othello and Attendants.

OTHELLO.   What is the matter here? 155
MONTANO. 'Zounds, I bleed still; I am hurt to the death.   [*Faints.*]
OTHELLO. Hold, for your lives!
IAGO. Hold, ho! Lieutenant—sir— Montano—gentlemen—
   Have you forgot all place of sense and duty?
   Hold! the general speaks to you! Hold, hold, for shame! 160
OTHELLO. Why, how now, ho! from whence ariseth this?
   Are we turn'd Turks, and to ourselves do that
   Which heaven hath forbid the Ottomites?
   For Christian shame, put by this barbarous brawl.
   He that stirs next to carve for his own rage 165
   Holds his soul light; he dies upon his motion.
   Silence that dreadful bell; it frights the isle

---

112 **just equinox**—equal balance [of dark and light]
113 **watch the horologe ... set**—stay awake twice around the clock
114 **twiggen bottle**—wicker covered bottle

From her propriety. What is the matter, masters?
Honest Iago, that look'st dead with grieving,
Speak: who began this? On thy love, I charge thee. 170
IAGO. I do not know. Friends all but now, even now,
In quarter, and in terms like bride and groom
Devesting them for bed; and then, but now
(As if some planet had unwitted men),
Swords out, and tilting one at other's breast, 175
In opposition bloody. I cannot speak
Any beginning to this peevish odds;
And would in action glorious I had lost
Those legs that brought me to a part of it!
OTHELLO. How comes it, Michael, you are thus forgot? 180
CASSIO. I pray you, pardon me; I cannot speak.
OTHELLO. Worthy Montano, you were wont be civil;
The gravity and stillness of your youth
The world hath noted, and your name is great
In mouths of wisest censure.[115] What's the matter, 185
That you unlace your reputation thus,
And spend your rich opinion[116] for the name
Of a night-brawler? Give me answer to it.
MONTANO. Worthy Othello, I am hurt to danger.
Your officer, Iago, can inform you— 190
While I spare speech, which something now offends me[117]—
Of all that I do know. Nor know I aught
By me that's said or done amiss this night,
Unless self-charity be sometimes a vice,
And to defend ourselves it be a sin 195
When violence assails us.
OTHELLO. Now, by heaven,
My blood begins my safer guides to rule,
And passion, having my best judgement collied,[118]
Assays to lead the way. If I once stir, 200
Or do but lift this arm, the best of you
Shall sink in my rebuke. Give me to know
How this foul rout began, who set it on,
And he that is approved[119] in this offense,
Though he had twinn'd with me, both at a birth, 205
Shall lose me. What! in a town of war,
Yet wild, the people's hearts brimful of fear,
To manage private and domestic quarrel,
In night, and on the court and guard of safety!
'Tis monstrous. Iago, who began't? 210
MONTANO. If partially affined, or leagued in office,
Thou dost deliver more or less than truth,
Thou art no soldier.
IAGO. Touch me not so near:
I had rather have this tongue cut from my mouth 215
Than it should do offense to Michael Cassio;
Yet, I persuade myself, to speak the truth
Shall nothing wrong him. Thus it is, general.
Montano and myself being in speech,
There comes a fellow crying out for help, 220
And Cassio following him with determined sword,
To execute upon him. Sir, this gentleman
Steps in to Cassio and entreats his pause.
Myself the crying fellow did pursue,
Lest by his clamor—as it so fell out— 225
The town might fall in fright. He, swift of foot,

---

115 **censure**—judgment
116 **opinion**—reputation
117 **which something now offends me**—while I am suffering such pain
118 **collied**—darkened, obscured
119 **approved**—proved

Outran my purpose; and I return'd the rather
For that I heard the clink and fall of swords,
And Cassio high in oath,[120] which till tonight
I ne'er might say before. When I came back— 230
For this was brief—I found them close together,
At blow and thrust, even as again they were
When you yourself did part them.
More of this matter cannot I report.
But men are men; the best sometimes forget. 235
Though Cassio did some little wrong to him,
As men in rage strike those that wish them best,
Yet surely Cassio, I believe, received
From him that fled some strange indignity,
Which patience could not pass. 240
OTHELLO.   I know, Iago,
Thy honesty and love doth mince this matter,
Making it light to Cassio. Cassio, I love thee,
But never more be officer of mine.

Re-enter Desdemona, attended.

Look, if my gentle love be not raised up! 245
I'll make thee an example.
DESDEMONA.   What's the matter?
OTHELLO. All's well now, sweeting; come away to bed.
Sir, for your hurts, myself will be your surgeon.
Lead him off. [*Exit Montano, attended.*] 250
Iago, look with care about the town,
And silence those whom this vile brawl distracted.
Come, Desdemona, 'tis the soldiers' life.
To have their balmy slumbers waked with strife.
       [*Exeunt all but Iago and Cassio.*]
IAGO. What, are you hurt, lieutenant? 255
CASSIO. Ay, past all surgery.
IAGO. Marry, heaven forbid!

CASSIO. Reputation, reputation, reputation! O, I have lost my reputation! I have lost the immortal part of myself, and what remains is bestial. My reputation, Iago, my reputation! 260
IAGO. As I am an honest man, I thought you had received some bodily wound; there is more sense in that than in reputation. Reputation is an idle and most false imposition; oft got without merit and lost without deserving. You have lost no reputation at all, unless you repute yourself such a loser. What, man! there are ways to recover the general again. You are but now cast in his mood, a punishment more in policy than in malice; even so as one would beat his offenseless dog to affright an imperious lion. Sue to him again, and he's yours. 265
CASSIO. I will rather sue to be despised than to deceive so good a commander with so slight, so drunken, and so indiscreet an officer. Drunk? and speak parrot? and squabble? swagger? swear? and discourse fustian[121] with one's own shadow? O thou invisible spirit of wine, if thou hast no name to be known by, let us call thee devil! 270

275
IAGO. What was he that you followed with your sword? What had he done to you?
CASSIO. I know not.
IAGO. Is't possible?
CASSIO. I remember a mass of things, but nothing distinctly; a quarrel, but nothing wherefore. O God, that men should put an enemy in their mouths to steal away their brains! that we should, with joy, pleasance, revel, and applause, transform ourselves into beasts! 280
IAGO. Why, but you are now well enough. How came you thus recovered? 285
CASSIO. It hath pleased the devil drunkenness to give place to the devil wrath: one unperfectness shows me another, to make me frankly despise myself.
IAGO. Come, you are too severe a moraler. As the time, the place, and the 290

---

120 **high in oath**—in a drunken rage
121 **discourse fustian**—speak nonsense ("fustian" was a coarse cotton cloth used for stuffing)

condition of this country stands, I could heartily wish this had not befallen; but since it is as it is, mend it for your own good.

CASSIO. I will ask him for my place again; he shall tell me I am a drunkard! Had I as many mouths as Hydra,[122] such an answer would stop them all. To be now a sensible man, by and by a fool, and presently a beast! O strange! Every inordinate cup is unblest, and the ingredient is a devil.

IAGO. Come, come, good wine is a good familiar creature, if it be well used. Exclaim no more against it. And, good lieutenant, I think you think I love you.

CASSIO. I have well approved it, sir. I drunk!

IAGO. You or any man living may be drunk at some time, man. I'll tell you what you shall do. Our general's wife is now the general. I may say so in this respect, for that he hath devoted and given up himself to the contemplation, mark, and denotement of her parts and graces. Confess yourself freely to her; importune her help to put you in your place again. She is of so free, so kind, so apt, so blessed a disposition, she holds it a vice in her goodness not to do more than she is requested. This broken joint between you and her husband entreat her to splinter; and, my fortunes against any lay[123] worth naming, this crack of your love shall grow stronger than it was before.

CASSIO. You advise me well.

IAGO. I protest, in the sincerity of love and honest kindness.

CASSIO. I think it freely; and betimes in the morning I will beseech the virtuous Desdemona to undertake for me. I am desperate of my fortunes if they check me here.

IAGO. You are in the right. Good night, lieutenant, I must to the watch.

CASSIO. Good night, honest Iago. [*Exit.*]

IAGO. And what's he then that says I play the villain? When this advice is free I give and honest, Probal to thinking, and indeed the course To win the Moor again? For 'tis most easy The inclining Desdemona to subdue In any honest suit. She's framed as fruitful As the free elements. And then for her To win the Moor, were't to renounce his baptism, All seals and symbols of redeemed sin, His soul is so enfetter'd to her love, That she may make, unmake, do what she list, Even as her appetite shall play the god With his weak function. How am I then a villain To counsel Cassio to this parallel course, Directly to his good? Divinity of hell! When devils will the blackest sins put on, They do suggest at first with heavenly shows, As I do now. For whiles this honest fool Plies Desdemona to repair his fortune, And she for him pleads strongly to the Moor, I'll pour this pestilence into his ear, That she repeals him[124] for her body's lust; And by how much she strives to do him good, She shall undo her credit with the Moor. So will I turn her virtue into pitch, And out of her own goodness make the net That shall enmesh them all.

Enter Roderigo.

How now, Roderigo!

RODERIGO. I do follow here in the chase, not like a hound that hunts, but one that fills up the cry.[125] My money is almost spent; I have been tonight exceedingly well cudgeled; and I think the issue will be, I shall have so much

---

122 **Hydra**—mythical water serpent with nine heads
123 **lay**—wager
124 **she repeals him**—Desdemona seeks to have Cassio's punishment repealed
125 **cry**—one of the baying dogs in the pack

experience for my pains; and so, with no money at all and a little more wit, return again to Venice.
IAGO. How poor are they that have not patience!
What wound did ever heal but by degrees?
Thou know'st we work by wit and not by witchcraft,
And wit depends on dilatory time. 360
Does't not go well? Cassio hath beaten thee,
And thou by that small hurt hast cashier'd Cassio.
Though other things grow fair against the sun,
Yet fruits that blossom first will first be ripe.
Content thyself awhile. By the mass, 'tis morning; 365
Pleasure and action make the hours seem short.
Retire thee; go where thou art billeted.
Away, I say. Thou shalt know more hereafter.
Nay, get thee gone. [Exit Roderigo.]
Two things are to be done: 370
My wife must move for Cassio to her mistress—
I'll set her on;
Myself the while to draw the Moor apart,
And bring him jump when he may Cassio find
Soliciting his wife. Ay, that's the way; 375
Dull not device by coldness and delay. [Exit.]

Act III. Scene I.

Before the castle.

Enter Cassio and some Musicians.

CASSIO. Masters, play here, I will content your pains;[126] Something that's brief; and bid "Good morrow, general."

Music.

Enter Clown.[127]

CLOWN. Why, masters, have your instruments been in Naples,[128] that they speak i' the nose thus? 5
FIRST MUSICIAN. How, sir, how?
CLOWN. Are these, I pray you, wind instruments?
FIRST MUSICIAN. Ay, marry, are they, sir.
CLOWN. O, thereby hangs a tail.[129] 10
FIRST MUSICIAN. Whereby hangs a tale, sir?
CLOWN. Marry, sir, by many a wind instrument that I know. But, masters, here's money for you; and the general so likes your music, that he desires you, for love's sake, to make no more noise with it. 15
FIRST MUSICIAN. Well, sir, we will not.
CLOWN. If you have any music that may not be heard, to't again; but, as they say, to hear music the general does not greatly care.
FIRST MUSICIAN. We have none such, sir. 20
CLOWN. Then put up your pipes in your bag, for I'll away.
Go, vanish into air, away! [Exeunt Musicians.]
CASSIO. Dost thou hear, my honest friend?
CLOWN. No, I hear not your honest friend; I hear you.
CASSIO. Prithee, keep up thy quillets.[130] There's a poor piece of gold for thee. If 25 the gentlewoman that attends the general's wife be stirring, tell her there's one Cassio entreats her a little favor of speech. Wilt thou do this?
CLOWN. She is stirring, sir. If she will stir hither, I shall seem to notify unto her. 30
CASSIO. Do, good my friend. [Exit Clown.]

Enter Iago.

In happy time, Iago.
IAGO. You have not been abed, then?
CASSIO. Why, no; the day had broke

---

126 **content your pains**—reward your efforts
127 **Clown**—fool
128 **Naples**—[this refers either to the nasal sound of Neapolitan dialect, or to syphilis, which breaks down nasal passages]
129 **hangs a tail**—a scatological joke having to do with "wind" and the anatomical placement of a tail
130 **quillets**—puns

Before we parted. I have made bold, Iago, 35
To send in to your wife. My suit to her
Is that she will to virtuous Desdemona
Procure me some access.
IAGO.   I'll send her to you presently;
And I'll devise a mean to draw the Moor 40
Out of the way, that your converse and business
May be more free.
CASSIO. I humbly thank you for't. [*Exit Iago.*] I never knew A Florentine more kind and honest.

Enter Emilia.

EMILIA. Good morrow, good lieutenant. I am sorry 45
For your displeasure,[131] but all will sure be well.
The general and his wife are talking of it,
And she speaks for you stoutly. The Moor replies
That he you hurt is of great fame in Cyprus
And great affinity and that in wholesome wisdom 50
He might not but refuse you; but he protests he loves you
And needs no other suitor but his likings
To take the safest occasion by the front
To bring you in again.
CASSIO.   Yet, I beseech you, 55
If you think fit, or that it may be done,
Give me advantage of some brief discourse
With Desdemona alone.
EMILIA.   Pray you, come in.
I will bestow you where you shall have time 60
To speak your bosom freely.
CASSIO.   I am much bound to you.
    [*Exeunt.*]

Scene II.

A room in the castle.

Enter Othello, Iago, and Gentlemen.

OTHELLO. These letters give, Iago, to the pilot,
And by him do my duties to the Senate.
That done, I will be walking on the works;
Repair there to me.
IAGO.   Well, my good lord, I'll do't. 5
OTHELLO. This fortification, gentlemen, shall we see't?
GENTLEMEN. We'll wait upon your lordship.   [*Exeunt.*]

Scene III.

The garden of the castle.

Enter Desdemona, Cassio, and Emilia.

DESDEMONA. Be thou assured, good Cassio, I will do
All my abilities in thy behalf.
EMILIA. Good madam, do. I warrant it grieves my husband
As if the cause were his.
DESDEMONA. O, that's an honest fellow. Do not doubt, Cassio, 5
But I will have my lord and you again
As friendly as you were.
CASSIO.   Bounteous madam,
Whatever shall become of Michael Cassio,
He's never anything but your true servant. 10
DESDEMONA. I know't: I thank you. You do love my lord:
You have known him long; and be you well assured
He shall in strangeness[132] stand no farther off
Than in a politic distance.
CASSIO.   Ay, but, lady, 15
That policy may either last so long,
Or feed upon such nice and waterish diet,
Or breed itself so out of circumstances,
That I being absent and my place supplied,

---

131 **displeasure**—discomfort
132 **strangeness**—distance, estrangement

My general will forget my love and
    service. 20
DESDEMONA. Do not doubt that. Before
    Emilia here
I give thee warrant of thy place, assure
    thee,
If I do vow a friendship, I'll perform
    it
To the last article. My lord shall never
    rest;
I'll watch him tame[133] and talk him out
    of patience; 25
His bed shall seem a school, his board a
    shrift;[134]
I'll intermingle everything he does
With Cassio's suit. Therefore be merry,
    Cassio,
For thy solicitor shall rather die
Than give thy cause away.[135] 30

Enter Othello and Iago, at a distance.

EMILIA. Madam, here comes my lord.
CASSIO. Madam, I'll take my leave.
DESDEMONA. Nay, stay and hear me speak.
CASSIO. Madam, not now. I am very ill at
    ease,
Unfit for mine own purposes. 35
DESDEMONA. Well, do your discretion.
        [*Exit Cassio.*]
IAGO. Ha! I like not that.
OTHELLO. What dost thou say?
IAGO. Nothing, my lord; or if—I know not
    what.
OTHELLO. Was not that Cassio parted
    from my wife? 40
IAGO. Cassio, my lord! No, sure, I cannot
    think it,
That he would steal away so guilty-like,
Seeing you coming.
OTHELLO.   I do believe 'twas he.
DESDEMONA. How now, my lord! 45
I have been talking with a suitor here,
A man that languishes in your
    displeasure.
OTHELLO. Who is't you mean?
DESDEMONA. Why, your lieutenant,
    Cassio. Good my lord,
If I have any grace or power to move
    you, 50
His present reconciliation take;
For if he be not one that truly loves you,
That errs in ignorance and not in
    cunning,
I have no judgement in an honest face.
I prithee, call him back. 55
OTHELLO.   Went he hence now?
DESDEMONA. Ay, sooth; so humbled
That he hath left part of his grief with
    me
To suffer with him. Good love, call him
    back.
OTHELLO. Not now, sweet Desdemona;
    some other time. 60
DESDEMONA. But shall't be shortly?
OTHELLO.   The sooner, sweet, for you.
DESDEMONA. Shall't be tonight at supper?
OTHELLO.   No, not tonight.
DESDEMONA. Tomorrow dinner then? 65
OTHELLO.   I shall not dine at home;
I meet the captains at the citadel.
DESDEMONA. Why then tomorrow night,
    or Tuesday morn,
On Tuesday noon, or night, on
    Wednesday morn.
I prithee, name the time, but let it not 70
Exceed three days. In faith, he's
    penitent;
And yet his trespass, in our common
    reason—
Save that, they say, the wars must
    make example
Out of their best—is not almost a fault
To incur a private check. When shall he
    come? 75
Tell me, Othello. I wonder in my soul,
What you would ask me, that I should
    deny,
Or stand so mammering on. What?
    Michael Cassio,
That came awooing with you, and so
    many a time
When I have spoke of you dispraisingly 80
Hath ta'en your part—to have so much
    to do
To bring him in! Trust me, I could do
    much—
OTHELLO. Prithee, no more. Let him come
    when he will;
I will deny thee nothing.

---

133 **watch him tame**—(animals were trained to tameness by keeping them awake [NOTE: the same technique which is utilized in "brain washing"])
134 **his board a shrift**—his eating table seem a confessional
135 **give thy cause away**—fail to pursue your case

DESDEMONA. Why, this is not a boon;[136] 'Tis as I should entreat you wear your gloves,
Or feed on nourishing dishes, or keep you warm,
Or sue to you to do a peculiar profit
To your own person. Nay, when I have a suit
Wherein I mean to touch your love indeed,
It shall be full of poise and difficult weight,
And fearful to be granted.
OTHELLO. I will deny thee nothing,
Whereon, I do beseech thee, grant me this,
To leave me but a little to myself.
DESDEMONA. Shall I deny you? No. Farewell, my lord.
OTHELLO. Farewell, my Desdemona; I'll come to thee straight.
DESDEMONA. Emilia, come. Be as your fancies teach you;
Whate'er you be, I am obedient.
            [Exeunt Desdemona and Emilia.]
OTHELLO. Excellent wretch! Perdition catch my soul,
But I do love thee! and when I love thee not,
Chaos is come again.
IAGO. My noble lord—
OTHELLO. What dost thou say, Iago?
IAGO. Did Michael Cassio, when you woo'd my lady,
Know of your love?
OTHELLO. He did, from first to last. Why dost thou ask?
IAGO. But for a satisfaction of my thought; No further harm.
OTHELLO. Why of thy thought, Iago?
IAGO. I did not think he had been acquainted with her.
OTHELLO. O, yes, and went between us very oft.
IAGO. Indeed!
OTHELLO. Indeed? ay, indeed. Discern'st thou aught in that?
Is he not honest?
IAGO. Honest, my lord?
OTHELLO. Honest? Ay, honest.
IAGO. My lord, for aught I know.
OTHELLO. What dost thou think?
IAGO. Think, my lord?
OTHELLO. Think, my lord? By heaven, he echoes me,
As if there were some monster in his thought
Too hideous to be shown. Thou dost mean something.
I heard thee say even now, thou like'st not that,
When Cassio left my wife. What didst not like?
And when I told thee he was of my counsel
In my whole course of wooing, thou criedst, "Indeed!"
And didst contract and purse thy brow together,
As if thou then hadst shut up in thy brain
Some horrible conceit.[137] If thou dost love me,
Show me thy thought.
IAGO. My lord, you know I love you.
OTHELLO. I think thou dost;
And for I know thou'rt full of love and honesty
And weigh'st thy words before thou givest them breath,
Therefore these stops of thine fright me the more;
For such things in a false disloyal knave
Are tricks of custom; but in a man that's just
They're close dilations,[138] working from the heart,
That passion cannot rule.
IAGO. For Michael Cassio,
I dare be sworn I think that he is honest.
OTHELLO. I think so too.
IAGO. Men should be what they seem;
Or those that be not, would they might seem none!
OTHELLO. Certain, men should be what they seem.
IAGO. Why then I think Cassio's an honest man.
OTHELLO. Nay, yet there's more in this.
I prithee, speak to me as to thy thinkings,
As thou dost ruminate, and give thy worst of thoughts

---

136 **boon**—favor
137 **conceit**—thought, image
138 **close dilations**—expressions of hidden thoughts

The worst of words.
IAGO.   Good my lord, pardon me;
　Though I am bound to every act of
　　duty,
　I am not bound to that all slaves are
　　free to.
　Utter my thoughts? Why, say they are
　　vile and false;   155
　As where's that palace whereinto foul
　　things
　Sometimes intrude not? Who has a
　　breast so pure,
　But some uncleanly apprehensions
　Keep leets and law-days,[139] and in
　　session sit
　With meditations lawful?   160
OTHELLO. Thou dost conspire against thy
　　friend, Iago,
　If thou but think'st him wrong'd and
　　makest his ear
　A stranger to thy thoughts.
IAGO.   I do beseech you—
　Though I perchance am vicious in my
　　guess,   165
　As, I confess, it is my nature's plague
　To spy into abuses, and oft my jealousy
　Shapes faults that are not—that your
　　wisdom yet,
　From one that so imperfectly conceits,
　Would take no notice, nor build
　　yourself a trouble   170
　Out of his scattering and unsure
　　observance.
　It were not for your quiet nor your
　　good,
　Nor for my manhood, honesty, or
　　wisdom,
　To let you know my thoughts.
OTHELLO.   What dost thou mean?   175
IAGO. Good name in man and woman,
　　dear my lord,
　Is the immediate jewel of their souls.
　Who steals my purse steals trash; 'tis
　　something, nothing;
　'Twas mine, 'tis his, and has been slave
　　to thousands;
　But he that filches from me my good
　　name   180
　Robs me of that which not enriches him
　And makes me poor indeed.

OTHELLO. By heaven, I'll know thy
　　thoughts.
IAGO. You cannot, if my heart were in
　　your hand;
　Nor shall not, whilst 'tis in my custody.   185
OTHELLO. Ha!
IAGO.   O, beware, my lord, of jealousy!
　It is the green-eyed monster, which
　　doth mock
　The meat it feeds on. That cuckold lives
　　in bliss
　Who, certain of his fate, loves not his
　　wronger;   190
　But O, what damned minutes tells[140] he
　　o'er
　Who dotes, yet doubts, suspects, yet
　　strongly loves!
OTHELLO. O misery!
IAGO. Poor and content is rich, and rich
　　enough;
　But riches fineless[141] is as poor as
　　winter   195
　To him that ever fears he shall be poor.
　Good heaven, the souls of all my tribe
　　defend
　From jealousy!
OTHELLO.   Why, why is this?
　Think'st thou I'ld make a life of
　　jealousy,   200
　To follow still the changes of the moon
　With fresh suspicions? No! To be once
　　in doubt
　Is once to be resolved. Exchange me for
　　a goat
　When I shall turn the business of my
　　soul
　To such exsufflicate and blown[142]
　　surmises,   205
　Matching thy inference. 'Tis not to
　　make me jealous
　To say my wife is fair, feeds well, loves
　　company,
　Is free of speech, sings, plays, and
　　dances well;
　Where virtue is, these are more
　　virtuous.
　Nor from mine own weak merits will I
　　draw   210
　The smallest fear or doubt of her revolt;

---

139 **leets and law days**—meetings of local courts
140 **tells**—counts
141 **fineless**—infinite
142 **exsufflicate and blown**—inflated and flyblown

For she had eyes and chose me. No, Iago,
I'll see before I doubt; when I doubt, prove;
And on the proof, there is no more but this—
Away at once with love or jealousy! 215
IAGO. I am glad of it, for now I shall have reason
To show the love and duty that I bear you
With franker spirit. Therefore, as I am bound,
Receive it from me. I speak not yet of proof.
Look to your wife; observe her well with Cassio; 220
Wear your eye thus, not jealous nor secure.
I would not have your free and noble nature
Out of self-bounty[143] be abused. Look to't.
I know our country disposition well;
In Venice they do let heaven see the pranks 225
They dare not show their husbands; their best conscience
Is not to leave't undone, but keep't unknown.[144]
OTHELLO. Dost thou say so?
IAGO. She did deceive her father, marrying you;
And when she seem'd to shake and fear your looks, 230
She loved them most.
OTHELLO. And so she did.
IAGO. Why, go to then.
She that so young could give out such a seeming,
To seel her father's eyes up close as oak— 235
He thought 'twas witchcraft—but I am much to blame;
I humbly do beseech you of your pardon
For too much loving you.
OTHELLO. I am bound to thee forever.
IAGO. I see this hath a little dash'd your spirits. 240
OTHELLO. Not a jot, not a jot.
IAGO. I'faith, I fear it has.
I hope you will consider what is spoke
Comes from my love. But I do see you're moved;
I am to pray you not to strain my speech 245
To grosser issues nor to larger reach
Than to suspicion.
OTHELLO. I will not.
IAGO. Should you do so, my lord,
My speech should fall into such vile success 250
Which my thoughts aim not at. Cassio's my worthy friend—
My lord, I see you're moved.
OTHELLO. No, not much moved.
I do not think but Desdemona's honest.
IAGO. Long live she so! and long live you to think so! 255
OTHELLO. And yet, how nature erring from itself—
IAGO. Ay, there's the point, as—to be bold with you—
Not to affect many proposed matches
Of her own clime, complexion, and degree,
Whereto we see in all things nature tends— 260
Foh, one may smell in such a will most rank,
Foul disproportion, thoughts unnatural.
But pardon me. I do not in position
Distinctly speak of her; though I may fear,
Her will, recoiling to her better judgement, 265
May fall to match you with her country forms,
And happily repent.
OTHELLO. Farewell, farewell.
If more thou dost perceive, let me know more;
Set on thy wife to observe. Leave me, Iago. 270
IAGO. [*Going.*] My lord, I take my leave.
OTHELLO. Why did I marry? This honest creature doubtless
Sees and knows more, much more, than he unfolds.
IAGO. [*Returning.*] My lord, I would I might entreat your honor

---

143 **self-bounty**—innate kindness (assuming others as honorable as himself)
144 **They dare not show ... unknown**—(They are publicly discreet, their morality does not forbid infidelity, but does forbid its being discovered)

To scan this thing no further; leave it to time. 275
Though it be fit that Cassio have his place,
For sure he fills it up with great ability,
Yet, if you please to hold him off awhile,
You shall by that perceive him and his means.
Note if your lady strain his entertainment[145] 280
With any strong or vehement importunity;
Much will be seen in that. In the meantime,
Let me be thought too busy in my fears—
As worthy cause I have to fear I am—
And hold her free, I do beseech your honor. 285
OTHELLO. Fear not my government.
IAGO. I once more take my leave. [Exit.]
OTHELLO. This fellow's of exceeding honesty,
And knows all qualities, with a learned spirit,
Of human dealings. If I do prove her haggard,[146] 290
Though that her jesses[147] were my dear heartstrings,
I'd whistle her off and let her down the wind[148]
To prey at fortune. Haply, for I am black
And have not those soft parts of conversation
That chamberers[149] have, or for I am declined 295
Into the vale of years—yet that's not much—
She's gone. I am abused, and my relief
Must be to loathe her. O curse of marriage,
That we can call these delicate creatures ours,
And not their appetites! I had rather be a toad, 300
And live upon the vapor of a dungeon,
Than keep a corner in the thing I love
For others' uses. Yet, 'tis the plague of great ones:
Prerogatived are they less than the base;[150]
'Tis destiny unshunnable, like death. 305
Even then this forked[151] plague is fated to us
When we do quicken.[152] Desdemona comes:

Re-enter Desdemona and Emilia.

If she be false, O, then heaven mocks itself!
I'll not believe't.
DESDEMONA. How now, my dear Othello! 310
Your dinner, and the generous islanders
By you invited, do attend your presence.
OTHELLO. I am to blame.
DESDEMONA. Why do you speak so faintly?
Are you not well? 315
OTHELLO. I have a pain upon my forehead here.
DESDEMONA. Faith, that's with watching; 'twill away again.
Let me but bind it hard, within this hour
It will be well.
OTHELLO. Your napkin is too little; 320

He puts the handkerchief from him, and she drops it.

Let it alone. Come, I'll go in with you.
DESDEMONA. I am very sorry that you are not well.
[*Exeunt Othello and Desdemona.*]
EMILIA. I am glad I have found this napkin;
This was her first remembrance from the Moor. 325
My wayward husband hath a hundred times
Woo'd me to steal it; but she so loves the token,

---

145 **strain his entertainment**—press for the reconsideration [of Cassio's punishment]
146 **haggard**—a partly trained hawk that has gone wild again
147 **jesses**—leather straps which hold the hawk's legs to the trainer's wrist
148 **I 'd whistle her off ... downwind**—I would release her (like an untamable hawk) and let her fly free
149 **chamberers**—courtiers
150 **Prerogatived are they less than the base**—Having fewer choices than the common man
151 **forked**—(a reference to the horns which are the sign of cuckoldry)
152 **do quicken**—when we are born

    For he conjured[153] her she should ever
        keep it,
    That she reserves it evermore about her
    To kiss and talk to. I'll have the work
        ta'en out,[154]   330
    And give't Iago. What he will do with it
    Heaven knows, not I;
    I nothing but to please his fantasy.

Re-enter Iago.

IAGO. How now, what do you here alone?
EMILIA. Do not you chide; I have a thing
    for you.   335
IAGO. A thing for me? It is a common
    thing[155]—
EMILIA. Ha!
IAGO. To have a foolish wife.
EMILIA. O, is that all? What will you give
    me now
    For that same handkerchief?   340
IAGO.   What handkerchief?
EMILIA. What handkerchief?
    Why, that the Moor first gave to
        Desdemona,
    That which so often you did bid me
        steal.
IAGO. Hast stol'n it from her?   345
EMILIA. No, faith; she let it drop by
    negligence,
    And, to the advantage, I being here
        took't up.
    Look, here it is.
IAGO.   A good wench; give it me.
EMILIA. What will you do with't, that you
    have been so earnest   350
    To have me filch it?
IAGO. [*Snatching it.*] Why, what is that to
    you?
EMILIA. If't be not for some purpose of
    import,
    Give't me again. Poor lady, she'll run
        mad
    When she shall lack it.   355
IAGO. Be not acknown on't;[156] I have use
    for it.
    Go, leave me.   [*Exit Emilia.*]

    I will in Cassio's lodging lose this
        napkin,
    And let him find it. Trifles light as air
    Are to the jealous confirmations strong   360
    As proofs of holy writ; this may do
        something.
    The Moor already changes with my
        poison:
    Dangerous conceits are in their natures
        poisons,
    Which at the first are scarce found to
        distaste,
    But with a little act upon the blood   365
    Burn like the mines of sulphur. I did
        say so.
    Look, where he comes!

Re-enter Othello.

            Not poppy, nor mandragora,[157]
    Nor all the drowsy syrups of the world,
    Shall ever medicine thee to that sweet
        sleep   370
    Which thou owedst[158] yesterday.
OTHELLO.   Ha, ha,
    false to me?
IAGO. Why, how now, general! No more of
    that.
OTHELLO. Avaunt! be gone! Thou hast set
    me on the rack.
    I swear 'tis better to be much abused   375
    Than but to know't a little.
IAGO.   How now, my lord?
OTHELLO. What sense had I of her stol'n
    hours of lust?
    I saw't not, thought it not, it harm'd not
        me;
    I slept the next night well, was free and
        merry;   380
    I found not Cassio's kisses on her lips.
    He that is robb'd, not wanting what is
        stol'n,
    Let him not know't and he's not robb'd
        at all.
IAGO. I am sorry to hear this.
OTHELLO. I had been happy if the general
    camp,   385

---

153 **conjured**—demanded with an oath
154 **the work ta'en out**—the embroidery copied
155 **It is a common thing**—[the "thing" is a sexual favor or sexual part, but here Iago implies that Emilia is available easily for many]
156 **Be not acknown on't**—Forget you ever saw it
157 **Not poppy, nor mandragora**—neither opium nor mandrake [another narcotic]
158 **owedst**—owned

Pioners[159] and all, had tasted her sweet
   body,
So I had nothing known. O, now forever
Farewell the tranquil mind! Farewell
   content!
Farewell the plumed troop and the big
   wars
That make ambition virtue! O, farewell,   390
Farewell the neighing steed and the
   shrill trump,
The spirit-stirring drum, the
   ear-piercing fife,
The royal banner, and all quality,
Pride, pomp, and circumstance of
   glorious war!
And O you mortal engines, whose rude
   throats   395
The immortal Jove's dread clamors
   counterfeit,
Farewell! Othello's occupation's gone!
IAGO. Is't possible, my lord?
OTHELLO. Villain, be sure thou prove my
   love a whore;
   Be sure of it. Give me the ocular proof;   400
   Or, by the worth of man's eternal soul,
   Thou hadst been better have been born
      a dog
   Than answer my waked wrath!
IAGO.   Is't come to this?
OTHELLO. Make me to see't; or at the least
   so prove it,   405
   That the probation bear no hinge nor
      loop
   To hang a doubt on; or woe upon thy
      life!
IAGO. My noble lord—
OTHELLO. If thou dost slander her and
   torture me,
   Never pray more; abandon all remorse;   410
   On horror's head horrors accumulate;
   Do deeds to make heaven weep, all
      earth amazed;
   For nothing canst thou to damnation
      add
   Greater than that.
IAGO.   O grace! O heaven defend me!   415
   Are you a man? have you a soul or
      sense?
   God be wi' you; take mine office. O
      wretched fool,
   That livest to make thine honesty a vice!
   O monstrous world! Take note, take
      note, O world,
   To be direct and honest is not safe.   420
   I thank you for this profit, and from
      hence
   I'll love no friend sith[160] love breeds
      such offense.
OTHELLO. Nay, stay; thou shouldst be
   honest.
IAGO. I should be wise; for honesty's a
   fool,
   And loses that it works for.   425
OTHELLO.   By the world,
   I think my wife be honest, and think
      she is not;
   I think that thou art just, and think
      thou art not.
   I'll have some proof. Her name, that
      was as fresh
   As Dian's visage, is now begrimed and
      black   430
   As mine own face. If there be cords or
      knives,
   Poison or fire, or suffocating streams,
   I'll not endure it. Would I were
      satisfied!
IAGO. I see, sir, you are eaten up with
   passion;
   I do repent me that I put it to you.   435
   You would be satisfied?
OTHELLO.   Would? Nay, I will.
IAGO. And may. But, how? how satisfied,
   my lord?
   Would you, the supervisor, grossly
      gape on?
   Behold her topp'd?   440
OTHELLO.   Death and damnation! O!
IAGO. It were a tedious difficulty, I think,
   To bring them to that prospect. Damn
      them then,
   If ever mortal eyes do see them
      bolster[161]
   More than their own! What then? how
      then?   445
   What shall I say? Where's satisfaction?
   It is impossible you should see this
   Were they as prime as goats, as hot as
      monkeys,
   As salt as wolves in pride, and fools as
      gross

---

159 **Pioners**—the lowest members of the army—trench diggers
160 **sith**—since
161 **bolster**—go to bed

As ignorance made drunk. But yet, I say, 450
If imputation and strong circumstances,
Which lead directly to the door of truth,
Will give you satisfaction, you may have't.
OTHELLO. Give me a living reason she's disloyal.
IAGO. I do not like the office; 455
But sith I am enter'd in this cause so far,
Prick'd to't by foolish honesty and love,
I will go on. I lay with Cassio lately
And, being troubled with a raging tooth,
I could not sleep. 460
There are a kind of men so loose of soul,
That in their sleeps will mutter their affairs;
One of this kind is Cassio.
In sleep I heard him say, "Sweet Desdemona,
Let us be wary, let us hide our loves"; 465
And then, sir, would he gripe and wring my hand,
Cry, "O sweet creature!" and then kiss me hard,
As if he pluck'd up kisses by the roots,
That grew upon my lips; then laid his leg
Over my thigh, and sigh'd and kiss'd; and then 470
Cried, "Cursed fate that gave thee to the Moor!"
OTHELLO. O monstrous! monstrous!
IAGO. Nay, this was but his dream.
OTHELLO. But this denoted a foregone conclusion.
'Tis a shrewd doubt, though it be but a dream. 475
IAGO. And this may help to thicken other proofs
That do demonstrate thinly.
OTHELLO. I'll tear her all to pieces.
IAGO. Nay, but be wise; yet we see nothing done;
She may be honest yet. Tell me but this; 480
Have you not sometimes seen a handkerchief
Spotted with strawberries in your wife's hand?
OTHELLO. I gave her such a one; 'twas my first gift.
IAGO. I know not that; but such a handkerchief—
I am sure it was your wife's—did I today 485
See Cassio wipe his beard with.
OTHELLO. If it be that—
IAGO. If it be that, or any that was hers,
It speaks against her with the other proofs.
OTHELLO. O, that the slave had forty thousand lives! 490
One is too poor, too weak for my revenge.
Now do I see 'tis true. Look here, Iago,
All my fond love thus do I blow to heaven.
'Tis gone.
Arise, black vengeance, from thy hollow hell! 495
Yield up, O love, thy crown and hearted throne
To tyrannous hate! Swell, bosom, with thy fraught,[162]
For 'tis of aspics'[163] tongues!
IAGO. Yet be content.
OTHELLO. O, blood, blood, blood! 500
IAGO. Patience, I say; your mind perhaps may change.
OTHELLO. Never, Iago. Like to the Pontic Sea,[164]
Whose icy current and compulsive course
Ne'er feels retiring ebb, but keeps due on
To the Propontic and the Hellespont, 505
Even so my bloody thoughts, with violent pace,
Shall ne'er look back, ne'er ebb to humble love,
Till that a capable and wide revenge
Swallow them up. Now, by yond marble heaven,
In the due reverence of a sacred vow
    [*Kneels.*] 510
I here engage my words.
IAGO. Do not rise yet. [*Kneels.*]
Witness, you ever-burning lights above,
You elements that clip us round about,

---

162 **fraught**—burden
163 **aspics'**—asps' (a poisonous snake)
164 **Pontic Sea**—Black Sea (famous for its strong and constant current flowing through the Bosporous to the Mediterranean)

Witness that here Iago doth give up 515
The execution of his wit, hands, heart,
To wrong'd Othello's service! Let him command,
And to obey shall be in me remorse,[165]
What bloody business ever. [*They rise.*]
OTHELLO. I greet thy love, 520
Not with vain thanks, but with acceptance bounteous,
And will upon the instant put thee to't:
Within these three days let me hear thee say
That Cassio's not alive.
IAGO. My friend is dead, 'tis done at your request; 525
But let her live.
OTHELLO. Damn her, lewd minx! O, damn her!
Come, go with me apart; I will withdraw,
To furnish me with some swift means of death
For the fair devil. Now art thou my lieutenant. 530
IAGO. I am your own forever. [*Exeunt.*]

Scene IV.

Before the castle.

Enter Desdemona, Emilia, and Clown.

DESDEMONA. Do you know, sirrah,[166] where Lieutenant Cassio lies?
CLOWN. I dare not say he lies anywhere.
DESDEMONA. Why, man?
CLOWN. He's a soldier; and for one to say a soldier lies, is stabbing. 5
DESDEMONA. Go to! Where lodges he?
CLOWN. To tell you where he lodges, is to tell you where I lie.
DESDEMONA. Can anything be made of this?
CLOWN. I know not where he lodges, and for me to devise a lodging, and say he 10
lies here or he lies there, were to lie in mine own throat.[167]
DESDEMONA. Can you inquire him out and be edified[168] by report?
CLOWN. I will catechize the world for him; that is, make questions and by them answer. 15
DESDEMONA. Seek him, bid him come hither. Tell him I have moved my lord on his behalf and hope all will be well.
CLOWN. To do this is within the compass of man's wit, and therefore I will attempt the doing it. [*Exit.*]
DESDEMONA. Where should I lose that handkerchief, Emilia? 20
EMILIA. I know not, madam.
DESDEMONA. Believe me, I had rather have lost my purse
Full of crusadoes;[169] and, but my noble Moor
Is true of mind and made of no such baseness
As jealous creatures are, it were enough 25
To put him to ill thinking.
EMILIA. Is he not jealous?
DESDEMONA. Who, he? I think the sun where he was born
Drew all such humors[170] from him.
EMILIA. Look, where he comes. 30
DESDEMONA. I will not leave him now till Cassio
Be call'd to him.

Enter Othello.

How is't with you, my lord?
OTHELLO. Well, my good lady. [*Aside.*] O, hardness to dissemble!
How do you, Desdemona? 35
DESDEMONA. Well, my good lord.
OTHELLO. Give me your hand. This hand is moist, my lady.
DESDEMONA. It yet has felt no age nor known no sorrow.

---

165 **remorse**—obligation
166 **sirrah**—a diminutive form of "sir," and often used in the context of the banter between characters and jesters. The scene can be expected to be filled with puns and bawdy. **lies**—lodges, with its obvious punning of truthfulness.
167 **to lie in my own throat**—to lie absolutely
168 **edified**—be provided with more information (Desdemona is using deliberately heightened language in jest with the jester and his play on words)
169 **crusadoes**—Portuguese gold coins
170 **humors**—characteristics

OTHELLO. This argues[171] fruitfulness and liberal[172] heart;
   Hot, hot, and moist.[173] This hand of yours requires 40
   A sequester[174] from liberty, fasting, and prayer,
   Much castigation, exercise devout,
   For here's a young and sweating devil here
   That commonly rebels. 'Tis a good hand,
   A frank one. 45
DESDEMONA. You may, indeed, say so;
   For 'twas that hand that gave away my heart.
OTHELLO. A liberal hand. The hearts of old gave hands;
   But our new heraldry[175] is hands, not hearts.[176]
DESDEMONA. I cannot speak of this. Come now, your promise. 50
OTHELLO. What promise, chuck?[177]
DESDEMONA. I have sent to bid Cassio come speak with you.
OTHELLO. I have a salt and sorry rheum[178] offends me;
   Lend me thy handkerchief.
DESDEMONA. Here, my lord. 55
OTHELLO. That which I gave you.
DESDEMONA. I have it not about me.
OTHELLO. Not?
DESDEMONA. No, faith, my lord.
OTHELLO. That's a fault. That handkerchief 60
   Did an Egyptian to my mother give;
   She was a charmer, and could almost read
   The thoughts of people. She told her, while she kept it,
   'Twould make her amiable and subdue my father
   Entirely to her love, but if she lost it 65
   Or made a gift of it, my father's eye
   Should hold her loathed and his spirits should hunt
   After new fancies. She dying gave it me,
   And bid me, when my fate would have me wive,
   To give it her. I did so, and take heed on't; 70
   Make it a darling like your precious eye;
   To lose't or give't away were such perdition
   As nothing else could match.
DESDEMONA.   Is't possible?
OTHELLO. 'Tis true; there's magic in the web of it. 75
   A sibyl,[179] that had number'd in the world
   The sun to course two hundred compasses,
   In her prophetic fury[180] sew'd the work;
   The worms were hallow'd that did breed the silk,
   And it was dyed in mummy[181] which the skillful 80
   Conserved of maiden's hearts.
DESDEMONA.   Indeed! is't true?
OTHELLO. Most veritable; therefore look to't well.
DESDEMONA. Then would to God that I had never seen't!
OTHELLO. Ha! wherefore? 85
DESDEMONA. Why do you speak so startingly and rash?
OTHELLO. Is't lost? is't gone? speak, is it out o' the way?
DESDEMONA. Heaven bless us!
OTHELLO. Say you?
DESDEMONA. It is not lost; but what an if it were? 90
OTHELLO. How?
DESDEMONA. I say, it is not lost.

---

171 **argues**—suggests
172 **liberal**—free, open (but this also suggests "licentious" and in the remainder of this scene Othello's words have double meaning, appearing polite or even praising, but simultaneously damning and suggesting Desdemona's unfaithfulness.)
173 **moist**—(a moist hand was thought to indicate a lustful nature)
174 **sequester**—separation
175 **heraldry**—heraldic symbolism, symbolism representing one's principles of behavior
176 **hands not heart**—(suggesting action over emotion)
177 **chuck**—a very familiar and casual intimate epithet, but also one showing little respect, as might be offered a "casual woman"
178 **salt and sorry rheum**—a heavy and running head cold
179 **sibyl**—women of mythical antiquity reputed to possess powers of prophecy
180 **in her prophetic fury sew'd the work**—seized by the spirit world and able prophesy
181 **mummy**—liquid drained from embalmed bodies

OTHELLO. Fetch't, let me see it.
DESDEMONA. Why, so I can, sir, but I will not now.
   This is a trick to put me from my suit. 95
   Pray you, let Cassio be received again.
OTHELLO. Fetch me the handkerchief, my mind misgives.
DESDEMONA. Come, come,
   You'll never meet a more sufficient man.
OTHELLO. The handkerchief! 100
DESDEMONA.   I pray, talk me of Cassio.
OTHELLO. The handkerchief!
DESDEMONA.   A man that all his time
   Hath founded his good fortunes on your love,
   Shared dangers with you— 105
OTHELLO. The handkerchief!
DESDEMONA. In sooth, you are to blame.
OTHELLO. Away! [Exit.]
EMILIA. Is not this man jealous?
DESDEMONA. I ne'er saw this before. 110
   Sure there's some wonder in this handkerchief;
   I am most unhappy in the loss of it.
EMILIA. 'Tis not a year or two shows us a man.[182]
   They are all but stomachs and we all but food;
   They eat us hungerly, and when they are full 115
   They belch us. Look you! Cassio and my husband.

Enter Cassio and Iago.

IAGO. There is no other way; 'tis she must do't.
   And, lo, the happiness! Go and importune her.
DESDEMONA. How now, good Cassio! What's the news with you?
CASSIO. Madam, my former suit: I do beseech you 120
   That by your virtuous means I may again
   Exist and be a member of his love
   Whom I with all the office of my heart
   Entirely honor. I would not be delay'd.
   If my offense be of such mortal kind 125
   That nor my service past nor present sorrows
   Nor purposed merit in futurity
   Can ransom me into his love again,
   But to know so must be my benefit;
   So shall I clothe me in a forced content 130
   And shut myself up in some other course
   To Fortune's alms.
DESDEMONA.   Alas, thrice-gentle Cassio!
   My advocation is not now in tune;[183]
   My lord is not my lord, nor should I know him 135
   Were he in favor as in humor alter'd.
   So help me every spirit sanctified,
   As I have spoken for you all my best
   And stood within the blank[184] of his displeasure
   For my free speech! You must awhile be patient. 140
   What I can do I will; and more I will
   Than for myself I dare. Let that suffice you.
IAGO. Is my lord angry?
EMILIA.   He went hence but now,
   And certainly in strange unquietness. 145
IAGO. Can he be angry? I have seen the cannon,
   When it hath blown his ranks into the air
   And, like the devil, from his very arm
   Puff'd his own brother. And can he be angry?
   Something of moment then. I will go meet him. 150
   There's matter in't indeed if he be angry.
DESDEMONA. I prithee, do so. [Exit Iago.]
   Something sure of state,
   Either from Venice or some unhatch'd practice
   Made demonstrable here in Cyprus to him, 155
   Hath puddled his clear spirit; and in such cases
   Men's natures wrangle with inferior things,
   Though great ones are their object. 'Tis even so;
   For let our finger ache, and it indues[185]

---

182 **'Tis not a year or two shows us a man**—Within a year or two we understand a man
183 **My advocation is not now in tune**—My support of your case is not currently welcomed
184 **blank**—bull's eye of a target
185 **indues**—leads [sp. endues?]

Our other healthful members even to
  that sense 160
Of pain. Nay, we must think men are
  not gods,
Nor of them look for such observancy
As fits the bridal. Beshrew me much,
  Emilia,
I was, unhandsome warrior as I am,
Arraigning his unkindness with my
  soul; 165
But now I find I had suborn'd the
  witness,
And he's indicted falsely.
EMILIA. Pray heaven it be state matters, as
  you think,
And no conception nor no jealous toy
Concerning you. 170
DESDEMONA. Alas the day, I never gave
  him cause!
EMILIA. But jealous souls will not be
  answer'd so;
They are not ever jealous for the cause,
But jealous for they are jealous. 'Tis a
  monster
Begot upon itself, born on itself. 175
DESDEMONA. Heaven keep that monster
  from Othello's mind!
EMILIA. Lady, amen.
DESDEMONA. I will go seek him. Cassio,
  walk hereabout.
If I do find him fit, I'll move your suit,
And seek to effect it to my uttermost. 180
CASSIO. I humbly thank your ladyship.
  [Exeunt Desdemona and Emilia.]

Enter Bianca.

BIANCA. Save you, friend Cassio!
CASSIO.   What make you from home?
  How is it with you, my most fair
    Bianca?
  I'faith, sweet love, I was coming to
    your house. 185
BIANCA. And I was going to your lodging,
  Cassio.
  What, keep a week away? seven days
    and nights?
  Eight score eight hours? and lovers'
    absent hours,
  More tedious than the dial eight score
    times?
  O weary reckoning! 190
CASSIO.   Pardon me, Bianca.
  I have this while[186] with leaden
    thoughts been press'd;
  But I shall in a more continuate time
  Strike off this score of absence. Sweet
    Bianca,
    [Gives her Desdemona's handkerchief.]
  Take me this work out. 195
BIANCA.   O Cassio, whence came this?
  This is some token from a newer friend.
  To the felt absence now I feel a cause.
  Is't come to this? Well, well.
CASSIO.   Go to, woman! 200
  Throw your vile guesses in the devil's
    teeth,
  From whence you have them. You are
    jealous now
  That this is from some mistress, some
    remembrance.
  No, by my faith, Bianca.
BIANCA.   Why, whose is it? 205
CASSIO. I know not, sweet. I found it in
  my chamber.
  I like the work well. Ere it be
    demanded—
  As like enough it will—I'ld have it
    copied.
  Take it, and do't; and leave me for this
    time.
BIANCA. Leave you! wherefore? 210
CASSIO. I do attend[187] here on the general;
  And think it no addition, nor my wish,
  To have him see me woman'd.
BIANCA.   Why, I pray you?
CASSIO. Not that I love you not. 215
BIANCA.   But that you do not love me.
  I pray you, bring me on the way a little,
  And say if I shall see you soon at night.
CASSIO. 'Tis but a little way that I can
  bring you,
  For I attend here, but I'll see you soon. 220
BIANCA. 'Tis very good; I must be
  circumstanced.[188]   [Exeunt.]

Act IV. Scene I.

Cyprus. Before the castle.

---

186 **this while**—during this time
187 **attend**—wait
188 **circumstanced**—satisfied, resigned to the conditions

Enter Othello and Iago.

IAGO. Will you think so?
OTHELLO. Think so, Iago?
IAGO. What,
   To kiss in private?
OTHELLO. An unauthorized kiss.
IAGO. Or to be naked with her friend in bed
   An hour or more, not meaning any harm?
OTHELLO. Naked in bed, Iago, and not mean harm!
   It is hypocrisy against the devil.
   They that mean virtuously and yet do so,
   The devil their virtue tempts and they tempt heaven.
IAGO. So they do nothing, 'tis a venial slip.
   But if I give my wife a handkerchief—
OTHELLO. What then?
IAGO. Why, then, 'tis hers, my lord, and being hers,
   She may, I think, bestow't on any man.
OTHELLO. She is protectress of her honor too.
   May she give that?
IAGO. Her honor is an essence that's not seen;
   They have it very oft that have it not.
   But for the handkerchief—
OTHELLO. By heaven, I would most gladly have forgot it.
   Thou said'st—O, it comes o'er my memory,
   As doth the raven o'er the infected house,
   Boding to all—he had my handkerchief.
IAGO. Ay, what of that?
OTHELLO. That's not so good now.
IAGO. What,
   If I had said I had seen him do you wrong?
   Or heard him say—as knaves be such abroad,
   Who having, by their own importunate suit,
   Or voluntary dotage of some mistress,
   Convinced or supplied them, cannot choose
   But they must blab—
OTHELLO. Hath he said anything?
IAGO. He hath, my lord; but be you well assured,
   No more than he'll unswear.
OTHELLO. What hath he said?
IAGO. Faith, that he did—I know not what he did.
OTHELLO. What? what?
IAGO. Lie—
OTHELLO. With her?
IAGO. With her, on her, what you will.
OTHELLO. Lie with her! lie on her! We say lie on her, when they belie her. Lie with her! 'Zounds, that's fulsome![189] Handkerchief—confessions—handkerchief! To confess and be hanged for his labor—first, to be hanged, and then to confess. I tremble at it. Nature would not invest herself in such shadowing passion without some instruction. It is not words that shakes me thus. Pish! Noses, ears, and lips. Is't possible? Confess? Handkerchief? O devil!
   [Falls in a trance.]
IAGO. Work on,
   My medicine, work! Thus credulous fools are caught,
   And many worthy and chaste dames even thus,
   All guiltless, meet reproach. What, ho! My lord!
   My lord, I say! Othello!

Enter Cassio.

   How now, Cassio!
CASSIO. What's the matter?
IAGO. My lord is fall'n into an epilepsy.
   This is his second fit; he had one yesterday.
CASSIO. Rub him about the temples.
IAGO. No, forbear;
   The lethargy must have his quiet course.
   If not, he foams at mouth, and by and by
   Breaks out to savage madness. Look, he stirs.
   Do you withdraw yourself a little while,
   He will recover straight. When he is gone,
   I would on great occasion speak with you.
   [Exit Cassio.]

---

189 **fulsome**—foul, repulsive

How is it, general? Have you not hurt
   your head?
OTHELLO. Dost thou mock me? 70
IAGO.   I mock you? No, by heaven.
   Would you would bear your fortune
      like a man!
OTHELLO. A horned man's[190] a monster
   and a beast.
IAGO. There's many a beast then in a
   populous city,
   And many a civil monster.
OTHELLO. Did he confess it? 75
IAGO.   Good sir, be a man;
   Think every bearded fellow that's but
      yoked
   May draw with you.[191] There's millions
      now alive
   That nightly lie in those unproper[192]
      beds
   Which they dare swear peculiar.[193]
      Your case is better. 80
   O, 'tis the spite of hell, the fiend's
      arch-mock,
   To lip a wanton in a secure couch,
   And to suppose her chaste! No, let me
      know,
   And knowing what I am, I know what
      she shall be.
OTHELLO. O, thou art wise; 'tis certain. 85
IAGO.   Stand you awhile apart,
   Confine yourself but in a patient list.
   Whilst you were here o'erwhelmed
      with your grief—
   A passion most unsuiting such a man—
   Cassio came hither. I shifted him away, 90
   And laid good 'scuse upon your ecstasy;
   Bade him anon return and here speak
      with me
   The which he promised. Do but
      encave[194] yourself
   And mark the fleers, the gibes, and
      notable scorns,
   That dwell in every region of his face; 95
   For I will make him tell the tale anew,
   Where, how, how oft, how long ago,
      and when
   He hath and is again to cope your wife.
   I say, but mark his gesture. Marry,
      patience,
   Or I shall say you are all in all in spleen, 100
   And nothing of a man.[195]
OTHELLO.   Dost thou hear, Iago?
   I will be found most cunning in my
      patience;
   But (dost thou hear?) most bloody.
IAGO.   That's not amiss; 105
   But yet keep time in all. Will you
      withdraw?

                            [*Othello retires.*]

   Now will I question Cassio of Bianca,
   A housewife[196] that by selling her
      desires
   Buys herself bread and clothes. It is a
      creature
   That dotes on Cassio, as 'tis the
      strumpet's plague 110
   To beguile many and be beguiled by
      one.
   He, when he hears of her, cannot refrain
   From the excess of laughter. Here he
      comes.

Re-enter Cassio.

   As he shall smile, Othello shall go mad;
   And his unbookish[197] jealousy must
      construe 115
   Poor Cassio's smiles, gestures, and
      light behavior
   Quite in the wrong. How do you now,
      lieutenant?
CASSIO. The worser that you give me the
   addition[198]
   Whose want even kills me.
IAGO. Ply Desdemona well, and you are
   sure on't. 120
   Now, if this suit lay in Bianca's power,
   How quickly should you speed!

---

190 **a horned man**—a cuckolded man
191 **every bearded fellow. . . you**—Do you think every cuckolded man shares your attitude
192 **unproper**—not exclusively the husband's
193 **peculiar**—uniquely for their own use
194 **encave**—hide yourself from view
195 **all in spleen, and nothing of a man**—entirely consumed in passion [anger] and in no way capable of taking manly action
196 **housewife**—here with the special meaning of prostitute
197 **unbookish**—ignorant, uninformed
198 **addition**—title

CASSIO. Alas, poor caitiff![199]
OTHELLO. Look, how he laughs already!
IAGO. I never knew a woman love man so.
CASSIO. Alas, poor rogue! I think, i'faith, she loves me.
OTHELLO. Now he denies it faintly and laughs it out.
IAGO. Do you hear, Cassio?
OTHELLO. Now he importunes him To tell it o'er. Go to; well said, well said.
IAGO. She gives it out that you shall marry her.
Do you intend it?
CASSIO. Ha, ha, ha!
OTHELLO. Do you triumph, Roman?[200] Do you triumph?
CASSIO. I marry her! What? A customer![201] I prithee, bear some charity to my wit; do not think it so unwholesome. Ha, ha, ha!
OTHELLO. So, so, so, so. They laugh that win.
IAGO. Faith, the cry goes that you shall marry her.
CASSIO. Prithee, say true.
IAGO. I am a very villain else.
OTHELLO. Have you scored[202] me? Well.
CASSIO. This is the monkey's own giving out. She is persuaded I will marry her, out of her own love and flattery, not out of my promise.
OTHELLO. Iago beckons me; now he begins the story.
CASSIO. She was here even now; she haunts me in every place. I was the other day talking on the sea bank with certain Venetians, and thither comes the bauble, and, by this hand, she falls me thus about my neck—
OTHELLO. Crying, "O dear Cassio!" as it were; his gesture imports it.
CASSIO. So hangs and lolls and weeps upon me; so hales and pulls me. Ha, ha, ha!
OTHELLO. Now he tells how she plucked him to my chamber. O, I see that nose of yours, but not that dog I shall throw it to.
CASSIO. Well, I must leave her company.
IAGO. Before me![203] look where she comes.
CASSIO. 'Tis such another fitchew![204] marry, a perfumed one.

Enter Bianca.

What do you mean by this haunting of me?
BIANCA. Let the devil and his dam haunt you! What did you mean by that same handkerchief you gave me even now? I was a fine fool to take it. I must take out the work? A likely piece of work that you should find it in your chamber and not know who left it there! This is some minx's token, and I must take out the work? There, give it your hobbyhorse.[205] Wheresoever you had it, I'll take out no work on't.
CASSIO. How now, my sweet Bianca! how now! how now!
OTHELLO. By heaven, that should be my handkerchief!
BIANCA. An you'll come to supper tonight, you may; an you will not, come when you are next prepared for.[206] [*Exit.*]
IAGO. After her, after her.
CASSIO. Faith, I must; she'll rail i' the street else.
IAGO. Will you sup there?
CASSIO. Faith, I intend so.
IAGO. Well, I may chance to see you, for I would very fain speak with you.
CASSIO. Prithee, come; will you?
IAGO. Go to; say no more. [*Exit Cassio.*]
OTHELLO. [*Advancing.*] How shall I murther him, Iago?
IAGO. Did you perceive how he laughed at his vice?
OTHELLO. O Iago!
IAGO. And did you see the handkerchief?
OTHELLO. Was that mine?

---

199 **caitiff**—wretch
200 **Roman**—exultant fellow
201 **customer**—one who sells, a merchant (here a prostitute)
202 **scored**—marked, defaced
203 **Before me!**—an exclamation of surprise, "Well, look here"
204 **fitchew**—a strong smelling creature
205 **hobbyhorse**—prostitute
206 **when you are next prepared for**—when you are next expected—i.e., never

IAGO. Yours, by this hand. And to see how he prizes the foolish woman your wife! She gave it him, and he hath given it his whore.
OTHELLO. I would have him nine years akilling. A fine woman! a fair woman! a sweet woman! 190
IAGO. Nay, you must forget that.
OTHELLO. Ay, let her rot, and perish, and be damned tonight, for she shall not live. No, my heart is turned to stone; I strike it, and it hurts my hand. O, the world hath not a sweeter creature. She might lie by an emperor's side, and command him tasks. 195
IAGO. Nay, that's not your way.
OTHELLO. Hang her! I do but say what she is. So delicate with her needle, an admirable musician. O, she will sing the savageness out of a bear. Of so high and plenteous wit and invention—
IAGO. She's the worse for all this. 200
OTHELLO. O, a thousand, a thousand times. And then, of so gentle a condition!
IAGO. Ay, too gentle.
OTHELLO. Nay, that's certain. But yet the pity of it, Iago! O Iago, the pity of it, Iago! 205
IAGO. If you are so fond over her iniquity, give her patent to offend, for, if it touch not you, it comes near nobody.
OTHELLO. I will chop her into messes.[207] Cuckold me!
IAGO. O, 'tis foul in her.
OTHELLO. With mine officer! 210
IAGO. That's fouler.
OTHELLO. Get me some poison, Iago, this night. I'll not expostulate with her, lest her body and beauty unprovide my mind[208] again. This night, Iago.
IAGO. Do it not with poison, strangle her in her bed, even the bed she hath contaminated. 215
OTHELLO. Good, good, the justice of it pleases, very good.
IAGO. And for Cassio, let me be his undertaker. You shall hear more by midnight.
OTHELLO. Excellent good. [*A trumpet within.*] What trumpet is that same? 220

IAGO. Something from Venice, sure. 'Tis Lodovico
   Come from the Duke. And, see your wife is with him.

Enter Lodovico, Desdemona, and Attendants.

LODOVICO. God save the worthy general!
OTHELLO.   With all my heart, sir. 225
LODOVICO. The Duke and Senators of Venice greet you.
                    [*Gives him a letter.*]
OTHELLO. I kiss the instrument of their pleasures.
              [*Opens the letter, and reads.*]
DESDEMONA. And what's the news, good cousin Lodovico?
IAGO. I am very glad to see you, signior; Welcome to Cyprus. 230
LODOVICO. I thank you. How does Lieutenant Cassio?
IAGO. Lives, sir.
DESDEMONA. Cousin, there's fall'n between him and my lord
   An unkind breech; but you shall make all well.
OTHELLO. Are you sure of that? 235
DESDEMONA. My lord?
OTHELLO. [*Reads.*] "This fail you not to do, as you will—"
LODOVICO. He did not call; he's busy in the paper.
   Is there division 'twixt my lord and Cassio?
DESDEMONA. A most unhappy one. I would do much 240
   To atone them, for the love I bear to Cassio.
OTHELLO. Fire and brimstone!
DESDEMONA. My lord?
OTHELLO. Are you wise?
DESDEMONA. What, is he angry? 245
LODOVICO.   May be the letter moved him;
   For, as I think, they do command him home,
   Deputing Cassio in his government.
DESDEMONA. By my troth, I am glad on't.
OTHELLO.   Indeed! 250
DESDEMONA.   My lord?
OTHELLO. I am glad to see you mad.
DESDEMONA.   Why, sweet Othello?
   OTHELLO. Devil!   [*Strikes her.*]

---

207 **messes**—bits
208 **unprovide my mind**—dissuade me from my conviction

DESDEMONA. I have not deserved this. 255
LODOVICO. My lord, this would not be believed in Venice,
  Though I should swear I saw't. 'Tis very much.
  Make her amends; she weeps.
OTHELLO.   O devil, devil!
  If that the earth could teem with woman's tears, 260
  Each drop she falls would prove a crocodile.
  Out of my sight!
DESDEMONA. [Going.] I will not stay to offend you.
LODOVICO. Truly, an obedient lady.
  I do beseech your lordship, call her back. 265
OTHELLO. Mistress!
DESDEMONA. My lord?
OTHELLO. What would you with her, sir?
LODOVICO.   Who, I, my lord?
OTHELLO. Ay, you did wish that I would make her turn. 270
  Sir, she can turn and turn, and yet go on,
  And turn again; and she can weep, sir, weep;
  And she's obedient, as you say, obedient,
  Very obedient. Proceed you in your tears.
  Concerning this, sir—O well-painted passion!— 275
  I am commanded home. Get you away;
  I'll send for you anon. Sir, I obey the mandate,
  And will return to Venice. Hence, avaunt!
                                             [Exit.]
DESDEMONA. Cassio shall have my place. And, sir, tonight,
  I do entreat that we may sup together. 280
OTHELLO. You are welcome, sir, to
  Cyprus. Goats and monkeys!
                                             [Exit.]
LODOVICO. Is this the noble Moor whom our full Senate
  Call all in all sufficient? This the nature
  Whom passion could not shake? whose solid virtue
  The shot of accident nor dart of chance 285
  Could neither graze nor pierce?
IAGO.   He is much changed.
LODOVICO. Are his wits safe? Is he not light of brain?
IAGO. He's that he is. I may not breathe my censure
  What he might be: if what he might he is not, 290
  I would to heaven he were!
LODOVICO.   What, strike his wife!
IAGO. Faith, that was not so well; yet would I knew
  That stroke would prove the worst!
LODOVICO.   Is it his use? 295
  Or did the letters work upon his blood,
  And new create this fault?
IAGO.   Alas, alas!
  It is not honesty in me to speak
  What I have seen and known. You shall observe him, 300
  And his own courses will denote him so
  That I may save my speech. Do but go after,
  And mark how he continues.
LODOVICO. I am sorry that I am deceived in him.
                                             [Exeunt.]

Scene II.

A room in the castle.

Enter Othello and Emilia.

OTHELLO. You have seen nothing, then? 5
EMILIA. Nor ever heard, nor ever did suspect.
OTHELLO. Yes, you have seen Cassio and she together.
EMILIA. But then I saw no harm, and then I heard
  Each syllable that breath made up between them.
OTHELLO. What, did they never whisper? 10
EMILIA.   Never, my lord.
OTHELLO. Nor send you out o' the way?
EMILIA. Never.
OTHELLO. To fetch her fan, her gloves, her mask, nor nothing?
EMILIA. Never, my lord. 15
OTHELLO. That's strange.
EMILIA. I durst, my lord, to wager she is honest,
  Lay down my soul at stake. If you think other,

Remove your thought; it doth abuse your bosom.
If any wretch have put this in your head, 20
Let heaven requite it with the serpent's curse!
For if she be not honest, chaste, and true,
There's no man happy; the purest of their wives
Is foul as slander.
OTHELLO. Bid her come hither; go.
    [*Exit Emilia.*] 25
She says enough; yet she's a simple bawd[209]
That cannot say as much. This is a subtle whore,
A closet lock and key of villainous secrets.
And yet she'll kneel and pray; I have seen her do't.

Enter Desdemona with Emilia.

DESDEMONA. My lord, what is your will? 30
OTHELLO. Pray, chuck, come hither.
DESDEMONA. What is your pleasure?
OTHELLO. Let me see your eyes;
    Look in my face.
DESDEMONA. What horrible fancy's this? 35
OTHELLO. [*To Emilia.*] Some of your function,[210] mistress,
Leave procreants[211] alone and shut the door;
Cough, or cry "hem," if anybody come.
Your mystery,[212] your mystery; nay, dispatch.   [*Exit Emilia.*]
DESDEMONA. Upon my knees, what doth your speech import? 40
I understand a fury in your words,
But not the words.
OTHELLO. Why, what art thou?
DESDEMONA. Your wife, my lord, your true and loyal wife.
OTHELLO. Come, swear it, damn thyself; 45
Lest, being like one of heaven, the devils themselves
Should fear to seize thee. Therefore be double-damn'd;
Swear thou art honest.
DESDEMONA. Heaven doth truly know it.
OTHELLO. Heaven truly knows that thou art false as hell. 50
DESDEMONA. To whom, my lord? with whom? how am I false?
OTHELLO. O Desdemona! Away! away! away!
DESDEMONA. Alas the heavy day! Why do you weep?
Am I the motive of these tears, my lord?
If haply you my father do suspect 55
An instrument of this your calling back,
Lay not your blame on me. If you have lost him,
Why, I have lost him too.
OTHELLO. Had it pleased heaven
To try me with affliction, had they rain'd 60
All kinds of sores and shames on my bare head,
Steep'd me in poverty to the very lips,
Given to captivity me and my utmost hopes,
I should have found in some place of my soul
A drop of patience; but, alas, to make me 65
A fixed figure for the time of scorn
To point his slow unmoving finger at!
Yet could I bear that too, well, very well;
But there, where I have garner'd up my heart,
Where either I must live or bear no life; 70
The fountain from the which my current runs,
Or else dries up; to be discarded thence!
Or keep it as a cistern for foul toads
To knot and gender in![213] Turn thy complexion there,
Patience, thou young and rose-lipp'd cherubin, 75
Ay, there, look grim as hell![214]
DESDEMONA. I hope my noble lord esteems me honest.

---

209 **bawd**—procuress, Madame of a brothel
210 **some of your function**—go do some of your work (as a madame)
211 **procreants**—sexual partners
212 **mystery**—trade
213 **to knot and gender in**—to twist and procreate
214 **Turn thy complexion ... as hell!**—"Even Patience would grow pale, turn its complexion, at Desdemona's sins, except that Othello looks on"

OTHELLO. O, ay, as summer flies are in the shambles,[215]
  That quicken even with blowing. O thou weed,
  Who art so lovely fair and smell'st so sweet
  That the sense aches at thee, would thou hadst ne'er been born!
DESDEMONA. Alas, what ignorant sin have I committed?
OTHELLO. Was this fair paper, this most goodly book,
  Made to write "whore" upon? What committed?
  Committed? O thou public commoner![216]
  I should make very forges of my cheeks,
  That would to cinders burn up modesty,
  Did I but speak thy deeds. What committed!
  Heaven stops the nose at it, and the moon winks;[217]
  The bawdy wind, that kisses all it meets,
  Is hush'd within the hollow mine of earth,
  And will not hear it. What committed?
  Impudent strumpet!
DESDEMONA.   By heaven, you do me wrong.
OTHELLO. Are not you a strumpet?
DESDEMONA.   No, as I am a Christian.
  If to preserve this vessel for my lord
  From any other foul unlawful touch
  Be not to be a strumpet, I am none.
OTHELLO. What, not a whore?
DESDEMONA.   No, as I shall be saved.
OTHELLO. Is't possible?
DESDEMONA. O, heaven forgive us!
OTHELLO.   I cry you mercy[218] then;
  I took you for that cunning whore of Venice
  That married with Othello. [*Raises his voice.*] You, mistress,
  That have the office opposite to Saint Peter,
  And keep the gate of hell!

Re-enter Emilia.

  You, you, ay, you!
  We have done our course; there's money for your pains.
  I pray you, turn the key, and keep our counsel.   [*Exit.*]
EMILIA. Alas, what does this gentleman conceive?
  How do you, madam? How do you, my good lady?
DESDEMONA. Faith, half asleep.
EMILIA. Good madam, what's the matter with my lord?
DESDEMONA. With who?
EMILIA. Why, with my lord, madam.
DESDEMONA. Who is thy lord?
EMILIA.   He that is yours, sweet lady.
DESDEMONA. I have none. Do not talk to me, Emilia;
  I cannot weep, nor answer have I none
  But what should go by water.[219]
     Prithee, tonight
  Lay on my bed my wedding sheets. Remember,
  And call thy husband hither.
EMILIA.   Here's a change indeed! [*Exit.*]
DESDEMONA. 'Tis meet I should be used so, very meet.
  How have I been behaved, that he might stick
  The small'st opinion on my least misuse?

Re-enter Emilia with Iago.

IAGO. What is your pleasure, madam? How is't with you?
DESDEMONA. I cannot tell. Those that do teach young babes
  Do it with gentle means and easy tasks.
  He might have chid me so, for in good faith,
  I am a child to chiding.
IAGO.   What's the matter, lady?
EMILIA. Alas, Iago, my lord hath so bewhored her,
  Thrown such despite and heavy terms upon her,
  As true hearts cannot bear.
DESDEMONA. Am I that name, Iago?

---

215 **shambles**—slaughterhouse
216 **commoner**—prostitute
217 **moon winks**—the moon closes its eyes (the moon was the symbol of modesty)
218 **cry you mercy**—ask your pardon
219 **go by water**—cry with tears

IAGO. What name, fair lady? 140
DESDEMONA. Such as she says my lord did say I was.
EMILIA. He call'd her whore; a beggar in his drink
Could not have laid such terms upon his callet.[220]
IAGO. Why did he so?
DESDEMONA. I do not know; I am sure I am none such. 145
IAGO. Do not weep, do not weep. Alas the day!
EMILIA. Hath she forsook so many noble matches,
Her father and her country and her friends,
To be call'd whore? Would it not make one weep?
DESDEMONA. It is my wretched fortune. 150
IAGO. Beshrew him for't!
How comes this trick upon him?
DESDEMONA. Nay, heaven doth know.
EMILIA. I will be hang'd, if some eternal villain,
Some busy and insinuating rogue, 155
Some cogging,[221] cozening slave, to get some office,
Have not devised this slander; I'll be hang'd else.
IAGO. Fie, there is no such man; it is impossible.
DESDEMONA. If any such there be, heaven pardon him!
EMILIA. A halter pardon him! And hell gnaw his bones! 160
Why should he call her whore? Who keeps her company?
What place? What time? What form? What likelihood?
The Moor's abused by some most villainous knave,
Some base notorious knave, some scurvy fellow.
O heaven, that such companions[222] thou'ldst unfold,[223] 165
And put in every honest hand a whip
To lash the rascals naked through the world
Even from the east to the west!
IAGO. Speak within door.
EMILIA. O, fie upon them! Some such squire he was 170
That turn'd your wit the seamy side without,
And made you to suspect me with the Moor.
IAGO. You are a fool; go to.
DESDEMONA. O good Iago,
What shall I do to win my lord again? 175
Good friend, go to him, for by this light of heaven,
I know not how I lost him. Here I kneel:
If e'er my will did trespass 'gainst his love
Either in discourse of thought or actual deed,
Or that mine eyes, mine ears, or any sense, 180
Delighted them in any other form,
Or that I do not yet, and ever did,
And ever will, though he do shake me off
To beggarly divorcement, love him dearly,
Comfort forswear me! Unkindness may do much, 185
And his unkindness may defeat my life,
But never taint my love. I cannot say "whore."
It doth abhor me now I speak the word;
To do the act that might the addition earn
Not the world's mass of vanity could make me. 190
IAGO. I pray you, be content; 'tis but his humor:
The business of the state does him offense,
And he does chide with you.
DESDEMONA. If 'twere no other—
IAGO. 'Tis but so, I warrant.
[Trumpets within.] 195
Hark, how these instruments summon to supper!
The messengers of Venice stay the meat.
Go in, and weep not; all things shall be well.
[Exeunt Desdemona and Emilia.]

Enter Roderigo.

---

220 **callet**—slut
221 **cogging**—cheating
222 **companions**—rogues
223 **unfold**—disclose

How now, Roderigo!
RODERIGO. I do not find that thou dealest justly with me. 200
IAGO. What in the contrary?
RODERIGO. Every day thou daffest me[224] with some device, Iago; and rather, as it seems to me now, keepest from me all conveniency than[225] suppliest me with the least advantage of hope. I will indeed no longer endure it; nor am I yet persuaded to put up in peace what 205 already I have foolishly suffered.
IAGO. Will you hear me, Roderigo?
RODERIGO. Faith, I have heard too much, for your words and performances are no kin together.
IAGO. You charge me most unjustly. 210
RODERIGO. With nought but truth. I have wasted myself[226] out of my means. The jewels you have had from me to deliver to Desdemona would half have corrupted a votarist.[227] You have told me she hath received them and returned me expectations and comforts of sudden respect and acquaintance; but I find none. 215
IAGO. Well, go to, very well.
RODERIGO. Very well! go to! I cannot go to, man; nor 'tis not very well. By this hand, I say 'tis very scurvy,[228] and begin to find myself fopped[229] in it.
IAGO. Very well. 220
RODERIGO. I tell you 'tis not very well. I will make myself known to Desdemona. If she will return me my jewels, I will give over my suit and repent my unlawful solicitation; if not, assure yourself I will seek satisfaction of you.
IAGO. You have said now. 225
RODERIGO. Ay, and said nothing but what I protest intendment of doing.
IAGO. Why, now I see there's mettle in thee; and even from this instant do build on thee a better opinion than ever before. Give me thy hand, Roderigo. Thou hast taken against me a most just 230 exception; but yet, I protest, have dealt most directly in thy affair.

RODERIGO. It hath not appeared.
IAGO. I grant indeed it hath not appeared, and your suspicion is not without wit and judgement. But, Roderigo, if thou hast that in thee indeed, which I have 235 greater reason to believe now than ever, I mean purpose, courage, and valor, this night show it; if thou the next night following enjoy not Desdemona, take me from this world with treachery and devise engines for my life.
RODERIGO. Well, what is it? Is it within reason and compass? 240
IAGO. Sir, there is especial commission come from Venice to depute Cassio in Othello's place.
RODERIGO. Is that true? Why then Othello and Desdemona return again to Venice.
IAGO. O, no; he goes into Mauritania, and takes away with him the fair 245 Desdemona, unless his abode be lingered here by some accident; wherein none can be so determinate as the removing of Cassio.
RODERIGO. How do you mean, removing of him?
IAGO. Why, by making him uncapable of Othello's place; knocking out his brains. 250
RODERIGO. And that you would have me to do?
IAGO. Ay, if you dare do yourself a profit and a right. He sups tonight with a harlotry, and thither will I go to him. He knows not yet of his honorable fortune. If you will watch his going 255 thence, which I will fashion to fall out between twelve and one, you may take him at your pleasure; I will be near to second your attempt, and he shall fall between us. Come, stand not amazed at it, but go along with me; I will show you such a necessity in his death that you shall think yourself bound to 260 put it on him. It is now high supper-time, and the night grows to waste. About it.
RODERIGO. I will hear further reason for this.

---

224 **daffest me**—puts me off
225 **conveniency than**—that is needed (or important) [rather than . . .
226 **wasted myself . . .**—I have thrown away my fortune
227 **votarist**—nun
228 **scurvy**—foul, corrupted
229 **fopped**—duped

IAGO. And you shall be satisfied. [*Exeunt.*]

Scene III.

Another room in the castle.

Enter Othello, Lodovico, Desdemona, Emilia, and Attendants.

LODOVICO. I do beseech you, sir, trouble yourself no further. 5
OTHELLO. O, pardon me; 'twill do me good to walk.
LODOVICO. Madam, good night; I humbly thank your ladyship.
DESDEMONA. Your honor is most welcome.
OTHELLO. Will you walk, sir?
  O!—Desdemona— 10
DESDEMONA. My lord?
OTHELLO. Get you to bed on the instant; I will be returned forthwith. Dismiss your attendant there; look it be done.
DESDEMONA. I will, my lord.
  [*Exeunt Othello, Lodovico, and Attendants.*]
EMILIA. How goes it now? He looks gentler than he did. 15
DESDEMONA. He says he will return incontinent.[230]
  He hath commanded me to go to bed,
  And bade me to dismiss you.
EMILIA. Dismiss me? 20
DESDEMONA. It was his bidding; therefore, good Emilia,
  Give me my nightly wearing, and adieu.
  We must not now displease him.
EMILIA. I would you had never seen him!
DESDEMONA. So would not I. My love doth so approve him, 25
  That even his stubbornness, his checks, his frowns—
  Prithee, unpin me—have grace and favor in them.
EMILIA. I have laid those sheets you bade me on the bed.
DESDEMONA. All's one. Good faith, how foolish are our minds!
  If I do die before thee, prithee shroud me 30
  In one of those same sheets.
EMILIA. Come, come, you talk.
DESDEMONA. My mother had a maid call'd Barbary;
  She was in love, and he she loved proved mad
  And did forsake her. She had a song of "willow"; 35
  An old thing 'twas, but it express'd her fortune,
  And she died singing it. That song tonight
  Will not go from my mind; I have much to do
  But to go hang my head all at one side
  And sing it like poor Barbary. Prithee, dispatch. 40
EMILIA. Shall I go fetch your nightgown?
DESDEMONA. No, unpin me here.
  This Lodovico is a proper man.
EMILIA. A very handsome man.
DESDEMONA. He speaks well. 45
EMILIA. I know a lady in Venice would have walked barefoot to Palestine for a touch of his nether lip.
DESDEMONA. [*Sings.*]

  "The poor soul sat sighing by a sycamore tree,
    Sing all a green willow;
  Her hand on her bosom, her head on her knee, 50
    Sing willow, willow, willow.
  The fresh streams ran by her, and murmur'd her moans,
    Sing willow, willow, willow;
  Her salt tears fell from her, and soften'd the stones-"

Lay by these— [*Gives Emilia her clothes.*] 55

[*Sings.*] "Sing willow, willow, willow—"
Prithee, hie thee; he'll come anon—
[*Sings.*] "Sing all a green willow must be my garland.
  Let nobody blame him; his scorn I approve—"

Nay, that's not next. Hark, who is't that knocks? 60
EMILIA. It's the wind.
DESDEMONA. [*Sings.*]

---

230 **incontinent**—at once

"I call'd my love false love; but what said he then?
  Sing willow, willow, willow.
 If I court moe women, you'll couch with moe men—"

So get thee gone; good night. Mine eyes do itch; 65
Doth that bode weeping?
EMILIA. 'Tis neither here nor there.
DESDEMONA. I have heard it said so. O, these men, these men!
 Dost thou in conscience think—tell me, Emilia—
 That there be women do abuse their husbands 70
 In such gross kind?
EMILIA. There be some such, no question.
DESDEMONA. Wouldst thou do such a deed for all the world?
EMILIA. Why, would not you?
DESDEMONA. No, by this heavenly light! 75
EMILIA. Nor I neither by this heavenly light; I might do't as well i' the dark.
DESDEMONA. Wouldst thou do such a deed for all the world?
EMILIA. The world's a huge thing; it is a great price
 For a small vice. 80
DESDEMONA. In troth, I think thou wouldst not.
EMILIA. In troth, I think I should, and undo't when I had done. Marry, I would not do such a thing for a joint-ring,[231] nor for measures of lawn,[232] nor for gowns, petticoats, nor caps, nor any petty exhibition; but, for the whole world—why, who would not make her 85
 husband a cuckold to make him a monarch? I should
 venture purgatory for't.
DESDEMONA. Beshrew me, if I would do such a wrong
 For the whole world.
EMILIA. Why, the wrong is but a wrong i' the world; and having the world for 90
 your labor, 'tis a wrong in your own world, and you might quickly make it right.

DESDEMONA. I do not think there is any such woman.
EMILIA. Yes, a dozen, and as many to the vantage as would store the world they played for. 95
 But I do think it is their husbands' faults
 If wives do fall; say that they slack their duties
 And pour our treasures into foreign laps,
 Or else break out in peevish jealousies,
 Throwing restraint upon us, or say they strike us, 100
 Or scant our former having in despite,[233]
 Why, we have galls, and though we have some grace,
 Yet have we some revenge. Let husbands know
 Their wives have sense like them; they see and smell
 And have their palates both for sweet and sour, 105
 As husbands have. What is it that they do
 When they change us for others? Is it sport?
 I think it is. And doth affection breed it?
 I think it doth. Is't frailty that thus errs?
 It is so too. And have not we affections, 110
 Desires for sport, and frailty, as men have?
 Then let them use us well; else let them know,
 The ills we do, their ills instruct us so.
DESDEMONA. Good night, good night. Heaven me such uses[234] send,
 Not to pick bad from bad, but by bad mend! 115
[Exeunt.]

Act V. Scene I.

Cyprus. A street.

Enter Iago and Roderigo:

---

[231] **joint-ring**—a ring with interlocking halves
[232] **lawn**—fine linen
[233] **scant our former having in despite**—reduce our previous allowance in retribution
[234] **uses**—practices

IAGO. Here, stand behind this bulk; straight will he come.
  Wear thy good rapier[235] bare, and put it home.
  Quick, quick; fear nothing; I'll be at thy elbow.
  It makes us, or it mars us; think on that,
  And fix most firm thy resolution. 5
RODERIGO. Be near at hand; I may miscarry in't.
IAGO. Here, at thy hand, be bold, and take thy stand.
       [Retires.]
RODERIGO. I have no great devotion to the deed;
  And yet he hath given me satisfying reasons.
  'Tis but a man gone. Forth, my sword; he dies. 10
IAGO. I have rubb'd this young quat[236] almost to the sense,[237]
  And he grows angry. Now, whether he kill Cassio,
  Or Cassio him, or each do kill the other,
  Every way makes my gain. Live Roderigo,
  He calls me to a restitution large 15
  Of gold and jewels that I bobb'd[238] from him,
  As gifts to Desdemona;
  It must not be. If Cassio do remain,
  He hath a daily beauty in his life
  That makes me ugly; and besides, the Moor 20
  May unfold me to him; there stand I in much peril.
  No, he must die. Be't so. I hear him coming.

Enter Cassio.

RODERIGO. I know his gait; 'tis he. Villain, thou diest!
       [*Makes a pass at Cassio.*]
CASSIO. That thrust had been mine enemy indeed,
  But that my coat[239] is better than thou know'st; 25
  I will make proof of thine.
       [*Draws, and wounds Roderigo.*]
RODERIGO.   O, I am slain!

Iago from behind wounds Cassio in the leg, and exit.

CASSIO. I am maim'd forever. Help, ho! Murther! Murther!
       [*Falls.*]

Enter Othello.

OTHELLO. The voice of Cassio; Iago keeps his word. 30
RODERIGO. O, villain that I am!
OTHELLO.   It is even so.
CASSIO. O, help, ho! Light! A surgeon!
OTHELLO. 'Tis he. O brave Iago, honest and just,
  That hast such noble sense of thy friend's wrong! 35
  Thou teachest me. Minion,[240] your dear lies dead,
  And your unblest fate hies.[241] Strumpet, I come!
  Forth of my heart those charms, thine eyes, are blotted;
  Thy bed lust-stain'd shall with lust's blood be spotted.
       [*Exit.*]

Enter Lodovico and Gratiano.

CASSIO. What, ho! No watch? No passage? Murther! Murther! 40
GRATIANO. 'Tis some mischance; the cry is very direful.
CASSIO. O, help!
LODOVICO. Hark!
RODERIGO. O wretched villain!
LODOVICO. Two or three groan; it is a heavy night. 45
  These may be counterfeits;[242] let's think't unsafe

---

235 **rapier**—a commonly carried light sword
236 **quat**—pimple
237 **almost to the sense**—almost raw
238 **bobb'd**—swindled
239 **coat**—a chainmail shirt or bullet proof vest
240 **Minion**—hussy (i.e. Desdemona)
241 **unblest fate hies**—condemned (unsanctified) fate calls (or comes swiftly)
242 **counterfeits**—fakes (a trap)

To come in to the cry without more help.
RODERIGO. Nobody come? Then shall I bleed to death.
LODOVICO. Hark!

Re-enter Iago, with a light.

GRATIANO. Here's one comes in his shirt, with light and weapons. 50
IAGO. Who's there? Whose noise is this that cries on murther?
LODOVICO. We do not know.
IAGO. Did not you hear a cry?
CASSIO. Here, here! for heaven's sake, help me! 55
IAGO. What's the matter?
GRATIANO. This is Othello's ancient, as I take it.
LODOVICO. The same indeed; a very valiant fellow.
IAGO. What are you here that cry so grievously?
CASSIO. Iago? O, I am spoil'd, undone by villains! 60
Give me some help.
IAGO. O me, lieutenant! What villains have done this?
CASSIO. I think that one of them is hereabout,
And cannot make away.
IAGO. O treacherous villains! 65
[*To Lodovico and Gratiano.*] What are you there?
Come in and give some help.
RODERIGO. O, help me here!
CASSIO. That's one of them.
IAGO. O murtherous slave! O villain! 70
[*Stabs Roderigo.*]
RODERIGO. O damn'd Iago! O inhuman dog!
IAGO. Kill men i' the dark! Where be these bloody thieves?
How silent is this town! Ho! Murther! Murther!
What may you be? Are you of good or evil?
LODOVICO. As you shall prove us, praise us. 75
IAGO. Signior Lodovico?
LODOVICO. He, sir.
IAGO. I cry you mercy. Here's Cassio hurt by villains.
GRATIANO. Cassio?
IAGO. How is't, brother? 80
CASSIO. My leg is cut in two.
IAGO. Marry, heaven forbid!
Light, gentlemen; I'll bind it with my shirt.

Enter Bianca.

BIANCA. What is the matter, ho? Who is't that cried?
IAGO. Who is't that cried? 85
BIANCA. O my dear Cassio, my sweet Cassio! O Cassio, Cassio, Cassio!
IAGO. O notable strumpet! Cassio, may you suspect
Who they should be that have thus mangled you?
CASSIO. No. 90
GRATIANO. I am sorry to find you thus; I have been to seek you.
IAGO. Lend me a garter. So. O, for a chair,
To bear him easily hence!
BIANCA. Alas, he faints! O Cassio, Cassio, Cassio!
IAGO. Gentlemen all, I do suspect this trash 95
To be a party in this injury.
Patience awhile, good Cassio. Come, come;
Lend me a light. Know we this face or no?
Alas, my friend and my dear countryman
Roderigo? No—yes, sure. O heaven! Roderigo. 100
GRATIANO. What, of Venice?
IAGO. Even he, sir. Did you know him?
GRATIANO. Know him! ay.
IAGO. Signior Gratiano? I cry you gentle pardon;
These bloody accidents must excuse my manners, 105
That so neglected you.
GRATIANO. I am glad to see you.
IAGO. How do you, Cassio? O, a chair, a chair!
GRATIANO. Roderigo!
IAGO. He, he, 'tis he. [*A chair brought in.*]
O, that's well said: the chair. 110
Some good man bear him carefully from hence;
I'll fetch the general's surgeon. [*To Bianca.*] For you, mistress,
Save you your labor. He that lies slain here, Cassio, 115
Was my dear friend; what malice was between you?
CASSIO. None in the world; nor do I know the man.

IAGO. [*To Bianca.*] What, look you pale? O, bear him out o' the air.
[*Cassio and Roderigo are borne off.*]
Stay you, good gentlemen. Look you pale, mistress? 120
Do you perceive the gastness of her eye?
Nay, if you stare, we shall hear more anon.
Behold her well; I pray you, look upon her.
Do you see, gentlemen? Nay, guiltiness will speak,
Though tongues were out of use. 125

Enter Emilia.

EMILIA. 'Las, what's the matter? What's the matter, husband?
IAGO. Cassio hath here been set on in the dark
By Roderigo, and fellows that are 'scaped;
He's almost slain, and Roderigo dead.
EMILIA. Alas, good gentleman! alas, good Cassio! 130
IAGO. This is the fruit of whoring. Prithee, Emilia,
Go know of Cassio where he supp'd tonight.
What, do you shake at that?
BIANCA. He supp'd at my house; but I therefore shake not.
IAGO. O, did he so? I charge you, go with me. 135
EMILIA. Fie, fie upon thee, strumpet!
BIANCA. I am no strumpet, but of life as honest
As you that thus abuse me.
EMILIA. As I! foh! fie upon thee!
IAGO. Kind gentlemen, let's go see poor Cassio dress'd.[243] 140
Come, mistress, you must tell's another tale.
Emilia, run you to the citadel,
And tell my lord and lady what hath happ'd!
Will you go on? [*Aside.*] This is the night
That either makes me or fordoes me quite. 145

[*Exeunt.*]

Scene II.

A bedchamber in the castle. Desdemona in bed asleep; a light burning.

Enter Othello.

OTHELLO. It is the cause, it is the cause, my soul.
Let me not name it to you, you chaste stars!
It is the cause. Yet I'll not shed her blood,
Nor scar that whiter skin of hers than snow
And smooth as monumental alabaster. 5
Yet she must die, else she'll betray more men.
Put out the light, and then put out the light.
If I quench thee, thou flaming minister,
I can again thy former light restore,
Should I repent me; but once put out thy light, 10
Thou cunning'st pattern of excelling nature,
I know not where is that Promethean heat[244]
That can thy light relume.[245] When I have pluck'd the rose,
I cannot give it vital growth again,
It must needs wither; I'll smell it on the tree. [*Kisses her.*] 15
O, balmy breath, that dost almost persuade
Justice to break her sword! One more, one more;
Be thus when thou art dead, and I will kill thee,
And love thee after. One more, and this the last;
So sweet was ne'er so fatal. I must weep, 20

---

243 **dress'd**—his wounds tended to
244 **Promethean heat**—[Prometheus is reputed to have brought fire to mankind, and that fire is refered to both literally as the fires by which we cook and find nightime light, and figuratively as a metaphor for life. Hence, Othello can have this figurative debate about the difference between extinguishing the candle and extinguishing Desdemona's life.]
245 **relume**—light again, or bring back to life

But they are cruel tears; this sorrow's heavenly,
It strikes where it doth love. She wakes.
DESDEMONA. Who's there? Othello?
OTHELLO. Ay, Desdemona.
DESDEMONA. Will you come to bed, my lord? 25
OTHELLO. Have you pray'd tonight, Desdemona?
DESDEMONA. Ay, my lord.
OTHELLO. If you bethink yourself of any crime
Unreconciled as yet to heaven and grace,
Solicit for it straight. 30
DESDEMONA. Alas, my lord, what may you mean by that?
OTHELLO. Well, do it, and be brief; I will walk by.
I would not kill thy unprepared spirit.
No, heaven forfend! I would not kill thy soul.
DESDEMONA. Talk you of killing? 35
OTHELLO. Ay, I do.
DESDEMONA. Then heaven have mercy on me!
OTHELLO. Amen, with all my heart!
DESDEMONA. If you say so, I hope you will not kill me.
OTHELLO. Hum! 40
DESDEMONA. And yet I fear you, for you are fatal then
When your eyes roll so. Why I should fear I know not,
Since guiltiness I know not; but yet I feel I fear.
OTHELLO. Think on thy sins.
DESDEMONA. They are loves I bear to you. 45
OTHELLO. Ay, and for that thou diest.
DESDEMONA. That death's unnatural that kills for loving.
Alas, why gnaw you so your nether lip?
Some bloody passion shakes your very frame.
These are portents; but yet I hope, I hope, 50
They do not point on me.
OTHELLO. Peace, and be still!
DESDEMONA. I will so. What's the matter?
OTHELLO. That handkerchief which I so loved and gave thee
Thou gavest to Cassio. 55
DESDEMONA. No, by my life and soul!
Send for the man, and ask him.
OTHELLO. Sweet soul, take heed,
Take heed of perjury; thou are on thy deathbed.
DESDEMONA. Ay, but not yet to die. 60
OTHELLO. Yes, presently:
Therefore confess thee freely of thy sin,
For to deny each article with oath
Cannot remove nor choke the strong conception
That I do groan withal. Thou art to die. 65
DESDEMONA. Then Lord have mercy on me!
OTHELLO. I say, amen.
DESDEMONA. And have you mercy too! I never did
Offend you in my life; never loved Cassio
But with such general warranty of heaven 70
As I might love. I never gave him token.
OTHELLO. By heaven, I saw my handkerchief in 's hand.
O perjured woman! Thou dost stone my heart,
And makest me call what I intend to do
A murther, which I thought a sacrifice. 75
I saw the handkerchief.
DESDEMONA. He found it then;
I never gave it him. Send for him hither;
Let him confess a truth.
OTHELLO. He hath confess'd. 80
DESDEMONA. What, my lord?
OTHELLO. That he hath used thee.
DESDEMONA. How? unlawfully?
OTHELLO. Ay.
DESDEMONA. He will not say so. 85
OTHELLO. No, his mouth is stopp'd;[246]
Honest Iago hath ta'en order for't.
DESDEMONA. O, my fear interprets! What, is he dead?
OTHELLO. Had all his hairs been lives, my great revenge
Had stomach for them all. 90
DESDEMONA. Alas, he is betray'd, and I undone!
OTHELLO. Out, strumpet! Weep'st thou for him to my face?
DESDEMONA. O, banish me, my lord, but kill me not!
OTHELLO. Down, strumpet!
DESDEMONA. Kill me tomorrow; let me live tonight! 95

---

246 **his mouth is stopp'd**—here, "he is dead."

OTHELLO. Nay, if you strive—
DESDEMONA. But half an hour!
OTHELLO. Being done, there is no pause.
DESDEMONA. But while I say one prayer!
OTHELLO. It is too late. [*He stifles her.*] 100
EMILIA. [*Within.*] My lord, my lord! What, ho! my lord, my lord!
OTHELLO. What noise is this? Not dead? not yet quite dead?
I that am cruel am yet merciful;
I would not have thee linger in thy pain.
So, so. 105
EMILIA. [*Within.*] What, ho! my lord, my lord!
OTHELLO. Who's there?
EMILIA. [*Within.*] O, good my lord, I would speak a word with you!
OTHELLO. Yes, 'tis Emilia. By and by.
She's dead. 110
'Tis like she comes to speak of Cassio's death.
The noise was here. Ha! no more moving?
Still as the grave. Shall she come in? were't good?
I think she stirs again. No. What's best to do?
If she come in, she'll sure speak to my wife. 115
My wife! My wife! What wife? I have no wife.
O, insupportable! O heavy hour!
Methinks it should be now a huge eclipse
Of sun and moon, and that the affrighted globe
Should yawn[247] at alteration. 120
EMILIA. [*Within.*] I do beseech you
That I may speak with you, O, good my lord!
OTHELLO. I had forgot thee. O, come in, Emilia.
Soft, by and by. Let me the curtains draw.
Where art thou?
[*Unlocks the door.*] 125

Enter Emilia.

What's the matter with thee now?

EMILIA. O, my good lord, yonder's foul murthers done!
OTHELLO. What, now?
EMILIA. But now, my lord.
OTHELLO. It is the very error[248] of the moon; 130
She comes more nearer earth than she was wont
And makes men mad.
EMILIA. Cassio, my lord, hath kill'd a young Venetian
Call'd Roderigo.
OTHELLO. Roderigo kill'd? 135
And Cassio kill'd?
EMILIA. No, Cassio is not kill'd.
OTHELLO. Not Cassio kill'd! Then murther's out of tune,
And sweet revenge grows harsh.
DESDEMONA. O, falsely, falsely murther'd! 140
EMILIA. Alas, what cry is that?
OTHELLO. That? what?
EMILIA. Out, and alas! That was my lady's voice.
Help! help, ho! help! O lady, speak again!
Sweet Desdemona! O sweet mistress, speak! 145
DESDEMONA. A guiltless death I die.
EMILIA. O, who hath done this deed?
DESDEMONA. Nobody; I myself. Farewell;
Commend me to my kind lord. O, farewell! [*Dies.*]
OTHELLO. Why, how should she be murther'd? 150
EMILIA. Alas, who knows?
OTHELLO. You heard her say herself, it was not I.
EMILIA. She said so; I must needs report the truth.
OTHELLO. She's like a liar gone to burning hell;
'Twas I that kill'd her. 155
EMILIA. O, the more angel she,
And you the blacker devil!
OTHELLO. She turn'd to folly, and she was a whore.
EMILIA. Thou dost belie her, and thou art a devil.
OTHELLO. She was false as water. 160
EMILIA. Thou art rash as fire, to say

---

247 **yawn**—gape open, as in an earthquake
248 **error**—wandering out of its regular course. Such aberrations of the heavens were seen by the Elizabethans as portents of grim activities on Earth.

That she was false. O, she was heavenly true!
OTHELLO. Cassio did top[249] her; ask thy husband else.
O, I were damn'd beneath all depth in hell,
But that I did proceed upon just grounds
To this extremity. Thy husband knew it all.
EMILIA. My husband?
OTHELLO. Thy husband.
EMILIA. That she was false to wedlock?
OTHELLO. Ay, with Cassio. Nay, had she been true,
If heaven would make me such another world
Of one entire and perfect chrysolite,
I'd not have sold her for it.
EMILIA. My husband?
OTHELLO. Ay, 'twas he that told me first.
An honest man he is, and hates the slime
That sticks on filthy deeds.
EMILIA. My husband?
OTHELLO. What needs this iteration, woman? I say thy husband.
EMILIA. O mistress, villainy hath made mocks with love!
My husband say that she was false!
OTHELLO. He, woman;
I say thy husband. Dost understand the word?
My friend, thy husband, honest, honest Iago.
EMILIA. If he say so, may his pernicious soul
Rot half a grain a day! He lies to the heart.
She was too fond of her most filthy bargain.
OTHELLO. Ha!
EMILIA. Do thy worst;
This deed of thine is no more worthy heaven
Than thou wast worthy her.
OTHELLO. Peace, you were best.
EMILIA. Thou hast not half that power to do me harm
As I have to be hurt. O gull![250] O dolt![251]
As ignorant as dirt! Thou hast done a deed—
I care not for thy sword; I'll make thee known,
Though I lost twenty lives. Help! help, ho! help!
The Moor hath kill'd my mistress! Murther, murther!

Enter Montano, Gratiano, Iago, and others.

MONTANO. What is the matter? How now, general?
EMILIA. O, are you come, Iago? You have done well,
That men must lay their murthers on your neck.
GRATIANO. What is the matter?
EMILIA. Disprove this villain, if thou be'st a man.
He says thou told'st him that his wife was false;
I know thou didst not, thou'rt not such a villain.
Speak, for my heart is full.
IAGO. I told him what I thought, and told no more
Than what he found himself was apt and true.
EMILIA. But did you ever tell him she was false?
IAGO. I did.
EMILIA. You told a lie, an odious, damned lie;
Upon my soul, a lie, a wicked lie!
She false with Cassio? Did you say with Cassio?
IAGO. With Cassio, mistress. Go to, charm your tongue.[252]
EMILIA. I will not charm my tongue; I am bound to speak.
My mistress here lies murther'd in her bed—
ALL. O heavens forfend!
EMILIA. And your reports have set the murther on.
OTHELLO. Nay, stare not, masters; it is true indeed.
GRATIANO. 'Tis a strange truth.
MONTANO. O monstrous act!

---

249 **top**—have sexual intercourse
250 **gull**—gullible one
251 **dolt**—fool
252 **charm your tongue**—say no more

EMILIA. Villainy, villainy, villainy!
　I think upon't, I think, I smell't, O villainy!
　I thought so then. I'll kill myself for grief.
　O villainy, villainy! 225
IAGO. What, are you mad? I charge you, get you home.
EMILIA. Good gentlemen, let me have leave to speak;
　'Tis proper I obey him, but not now.
　Perchance, Iago, I will ne'er go home.
OTHELLO. O! O! O! [*Falls on the bed.*] 230
EMILIA. Nay, lay thee down and roar;
　For thou hast kill'd the sweetest innocent
　That e'er did lift up eye.
OTHELLO. [*Rises.*] O, she was foul!
　I scarce did know you, uncle; there lies your niece, 235
　Whose breath indeed these hands have newly stopp'd.
　I know this act shows horrible and grim.
GRATIANO. Poor Desdemona! I am glad thy father's dead.
　Thy match was mortal to him, and pure grief
　Shore[253] his old thread in twain; did he live now, 240
　This sight would make him do a desperate turn,
　Yea, curse his better angel from his side,
　And fall to reprobation.
OTHELLO. 'Tis pitiful, but yet Iago knows
　That she with Cassio hath the act of shame 245
　A thousand times committed. Cassio confess'd it,
　And she did gratify his amorous works
　With that recognizance and pledge of love
　Which I first gave her. I saw it in his hand,
　It was a handkerchief, an antique token 250
　My father gave my mother.
EMILIA. O heaven! O heavenly powers!
IAGO. 'Zounds! Hold your peace.
EMILIA. 'Twill out, 'twill. I hold my peace, sir?
　No, I will speak as liberal as the north;[254] 255
　Let heaven and men and devils, let them all,
　All, all, cry shame against me, yet I'll speak.
IAGO. Be wise, and get you home.
EMILIA. I will not.
　　　　[*Iago offers to stab Emilia.*]
GRATIANO. Fie! 260
　Your sword upon a woman?
EMILIA. O thou dull Moor! That handkerchief thou speak'st of
　I found by fortune[255] and did give my husband,
　For often with a solemn earnestness,
　More than indeed belong'd to such a trifle, 265
　He begg'd of me to steal it.
IAGO. Villainous whore!
EMILIA. She give it Cassio? No, alas, I found it,
　And I did give't my husband.
IAGO. Filth, thou liest! 270
EMILIA. By heaven, I do not, I do not, gentlemen.
　O murtherous coxcomb! What should such a fool
　Do with so good a wife?
OTHELLO. Are there not stones in heaven
　But what serve for thunder? Precious villain! 275
　　　[*He runs at Iago, but Montano disarms him. Iago stabs Emilia.*]
GRATIANO. The woman falls; sure, he hath kill'd his wife.
EMILIA. Ay, ay! O, lay me by my mistress' side. [*Exit Iago.*]
GRATIANO. He's gone, but his wife's kill'd.
MONTANO. 'Tis a notorious villain. Take you this weapon,
　Which I have here recover'd from the Moor. 280
　Come, guard the door without; let him not pass,
　But kill him rather. I'll after that same villain,
　For 'tis a damned slave.
　　　　[*Exeunt all but Othello and Emilia.*]
OTHELLO. I am not valiant neither,
　But every puny whipster[256] gets my sword. 285

---

253 **shore**—sheared (as with a scissors)
254 **liberal as the north**—freely (and bitingly) as the north wind
255 **fortune**—by accident (good luck)
256 **whipster**—puny boy

But why should honor outlive honesty?
Let it go all.
EMILIA.   What did thy song bode, lady?
Hark, canst thou hear me? I will play the swan,
And die in music. [*Sings.*] "Willow, willow, willow." 290
Moor, she was chaste; she loved thee, cruel Moor;
So come my soul to bliss, as I speak true;
So speaking as I think, I die, I die.   [*Dies.*]
OTHELLO. I have another weapon in this chamber;
It is a sword of Spain, the ice-brook's temper— 295
O, here it is. Uncle, I must come forth.
GRATIANO. [*Within.*] If thou attempt it, it will cost thee dear.
Thou hast no weapon, and perforce must suffer.
OTHELLO. Look in upon me then, and speak with me,
Or, naked as I am, I will assault thee. 300

Re-enter Gratiano.

GRATIANO. What is the matter?
OTHELLO.   Behold, I have a weapon;
A better never did itself sustain
Upon a soldier's thigh. I have seen the day
That with this little arm and this good sword 305
I have made my way through more impediments
Than twenty times your stop. But, O vain boast!
Who can control his fate? 'Tis not so now.
Be not afraid, though you do see me weapon'd;
Here is my journey's end, here is my butt[257] 310
And very sea-mark of my utmost sail.[258]
Do you go back dismay'd? 'Tis a lost fear.
Man but a rush against Othello's breast,
And he retires. Where should Othello go?
Now, how dost thou look now? O ill-starr'd wench! 315
Pale as thy smock! When we shall meet at compt,[259]
This look of thine will hurl my soul from heaven,
And fiends will snatch at it. Cold, cold, my girl?
Even like thy chastity. O cursed, cursed slave!
Whip me, ye devils, 320
From the possession of this heavenly sight!
Blow me about in winds! Roast me in sulphur!
Wash me in steep-down gulfs of liquid fire!
O Desdemona! Desdemona! dead!
O! O! O! 325

Enter Lodovico, Montano, Cassio carried in a chair, and Officers with Iago, prisoner.

LODOVICO. Where is this rash and most unfortunate man?
OTHELLO. That's he that was Othello. Here I am.
LODOVICO. Where is that viper? Bring the villain forth.
OTHELLO. I look down towards his feet;[260] but that's a fable.
If that thou be'st a devil, I cannot kill thee.   [*Wounds Iago.*] 330
LODOVICO. Wrench his sword from him.
IAGO.   I bleed, sir, but not kill'd.
OTHELLO. I am not sorry neither. I'ld have thee live,
For, in my sense, 'tis happiness to die. 335
LODOVICO. O thou Othello, that wert once so good,
Fall'n in the practice of a damned slave,
What shall be said to thee?
OTHELLO.   Why, anything;
An honorable murtherer, if you will, 340
For nought did I in hate, but all in honor.
LODOVICO. This wretch hath part confess'd his villainy.
Did you and he consent in Cassio's death?

---

257 **butt**—target, stopping place
258 **seamark of my utmost sail**—marker of my farthest journey
259 **compt**—Judgment Day
260 **I look down towards his feet**—(to look for the cloven feet of the Devil)

OTHELLO. Ay.
CASSIO. Dear general, I never gave you cause. 345
OTHELLO. I do believe it, and I ask your pardon.
Will you, I pray, demand that demi-devil
Why he hath thus ensnared my soul and body?
IAGO. Demand me nothing; what you know, you know.
From this time forth I never will speak word. 350
LODOVICO. What, not to pray?
GRATIANO. Torments will ope your lips.
OTHELLO. Well, thou dost best.
LODOVICO. Sir, you shall understand what hath befall'n,
Which, as I think, you know not. Here is a letter 355
Found in the pocket of the slain Roderigo,
And here another. The one of them imports
The death of Cassio to be undertook By Roderigo.
OTHELLO. O villain! 360
CASSIO. Most heathenish and most gross!
LODOVICO. Now here's another discontented paper,
Found in his pocket too; and this, it seems,
Roderigo meant to have sent this damned villain;
But that, belike, Iago in the interim 365
Came in and satisfied him.
OTHELLO. O the pernicious caitiff!
How came you, Cassio, by that handkerchief
That was my wife's?
CASSIO. I found it in my chamber; 370
And he himself confess'd but even now
That there he dropp'd it for a special purpose
Which wrought to his desire.
OTHELLO. O fool! fool! fool!
CASSIO. There is besides in Roderigo's letter, 375
How he upbraids Iago, that he made him
Brave[261] me upon the watch, whereon it came
That I was cast. And even but now he spake
After long seeming dead, Iago hurt him, Iago set him on. 380
LODOVICO. You must forsake this room, and go with us.
Your power and your command is taken off,
And Cassio rules in Cyprus. For this slave,
If there be any cunning cruelty
That can torment him much and hold him long, 385
It shall be his. You shall close prisoner rest,
Till that the nature of your fault be known
To the Venetian state. Come, bring away.
OTHELLO. Soft you; a word or two before you go.
I have done the state some service, and they know't. 390
No more of that. I pray you, in your letters,
When you shall these unlucky deeds relate,
Speak of me as I am; nothing extenuate,
Nor set down aught in malice. Then must you speak
Of one that loved not wisely but too well; 400
Of one not easily jealous, but, being wrought,
Perplex'd in the extreme; of one whose hand,
Like the base Judean,[262] threw a pearl away
Richer than all his tribe; of one whose subdued eyes,
Albeit unused to the melting mood, 405
Drop tears as fast as the Arabian trees
Their medicinal gum. Set you down this;
And say besides, that in Aleppo once,
Where a malignant and a turban'd Turk
Beat a Venetian and traduced the state, 410
I took by the throat the circumcised dog
And smote him, thus. [Stabs himself.]

---

261 **brave**—challenge
262 **base Judean**—unbeliever, infidel

LODOVICO. O bloody period![263]
GRATIANO.   All that's spoke is marr'd.
OTHELLO. I kiss'd thee ere I kill'd thee. No
    way but this,   415
  Killing myself, to die upon a kiss.
                    [*Falls on the bed, and dies.*]
CASSIO. This did I fear, but thought he
    had no weapon;
  For he was great of heart.
LODOVICO.   [*To Iago.*] O Spartan dog,
  More fell[264] than anguish, hunger, or
    the sea!   420
  Look on the tragic loading of this bed;
  This is thy work. The object poisons
    sight;
Let it be hid. Gratiano, keep the house,
And seize upon the fortunes of the
    Moor,
For they succeed on you. To you, Lord
    Governor,   425
Remains the censure of this hellish
    villain,
The time, the place, the torture. O,
    enforce it!
Myself will straight aboard, and to the
    state
This heavy act with heavy heart relate.
                                        [*Exeunt.*]

THE END

---

263 **period**—end
264 **fell**—cruel

Notes on *Othello*

1. Othello, a mercenary, has been hired by the City State of Venice to lead its military against the Turks (Muslims). Othello is a Moor (from Mauretania in Northwest Africa) and a Christian (which is unusual for a Moor).
2. He marries Desdemona, the daughter of a Venetian Senator. Desdemona is much younger than Othello, she is good-looking (which Othello is not), and of course she is white. These differences can be exploited by the demonic trouble-maker Iago, who makes their relationship come to seem "unnatural."
3. One of the points of tension in the play is whether Desdemona is to be trusted. Is she simply seeking novelty and adventure in choosing Othello as a husband, or does she truly see his "visage in his mind" as she claims. Part of the tension comes from the fact that Desdemona does deceive her father (don't all daughters??), is indeed adventurous (she rejects the "curl'd darlings" of Venice who seek her love), is extremely artful (note her composure and lawyer-like intelligence in addressing the Senators), and agressive (it is Desdemona who urges on Othello to "woo her").

    How are we to think of Desdemona? Is she honest? or artful? Can one be both??? (Act IV helps us answer this question.)
4. Iago should remind us of Machiavelli's discussions of trickery and power maneuvering. Shakespeare surely has Machiavelli in mind and is probably offering his own commenatry on "Machiavellianism" in this play. An interesting question is whether Iago is a fair representative of what Machiavelli is proposing (Iago, after all, is not a prince, nor does he have the welfare of Venice in mind at any time). Still, Iago may represent the problem of the allure of deceit in its own right. Can Machiavelli's prince sustain the balance between a noble purpose and his evil arts? Iago surely has a problem even remembering what he wants to accomplish once he begins to enjoy the evil results his trickery produces.
5. *Othello* recalls several Christian themes (especially in ACT V). It does seem that Othello, like Adam, has been offered a world of blessings but is unable to appreciate this gift and so destroys it and himself. Othello does refer to a passage from *Matthew* in his agonies at the end. Iago, serpent-like, is able to turn him away from the truth.
6. One of the questions for us is why Othello gives in so easily to the suspicions aroused by Iago. Of course there is the self-doubt aroused by his "differences," but there seems to be more to it. Is there something about how men view women? something about the sexual allure itself? (Act III, iii is rich with suggestion on this theme.)
7. Everywhere one looks in *Othello*, there is a pondering about appearances and realities. Is Venice civilized, or is civility a thin membrane covering a ripe beastliness? Cassio, the most cultivated of men (look at his poetic utterances in Act II) can be transformed into a wildman after a drink or two. Of course, his trafficking with Bianca tells us that he isn't all that much better when he is sober.

    What are we to believe about ourselves? Are we angels or demons? And what would we do if an angel came among us—how would we understand her, and ourselves?
8. Lots of people would like to make *Othello* a play about race relations. While some speeches in the play seem to lead in that direction, it may not be an issue of great thematic importance in the play. Race is a ripe issue for use. However, in 1604 it would not have been an important issue for Shakespeare's audience. The racial content is already given in Shakespeare's source and is useful to motivate Othello's worries. For modern readers, of course, all this is different. Should we import our

concerns into a play written in very different circumstances? Readers and directors do this all the time.

9. An interesting question is how Shakespeare's play relates to the two other examples of Renaissance thinking. Galileo replaces the metaphorical and abstract thinking of ancient astronomers with hard data gathered by his spyglass; Machiavelli rejects Plato's theorizing and replaces it with the data of actual history (how do things really work in organizing power in the state); what then can we say about Shakespeare? (It is interesting to compare his play with the Greek plays we read earlier, and then look for what is similar to what Galileo and Machiavelli have done.)

HUMANIST FOUNDATIONS

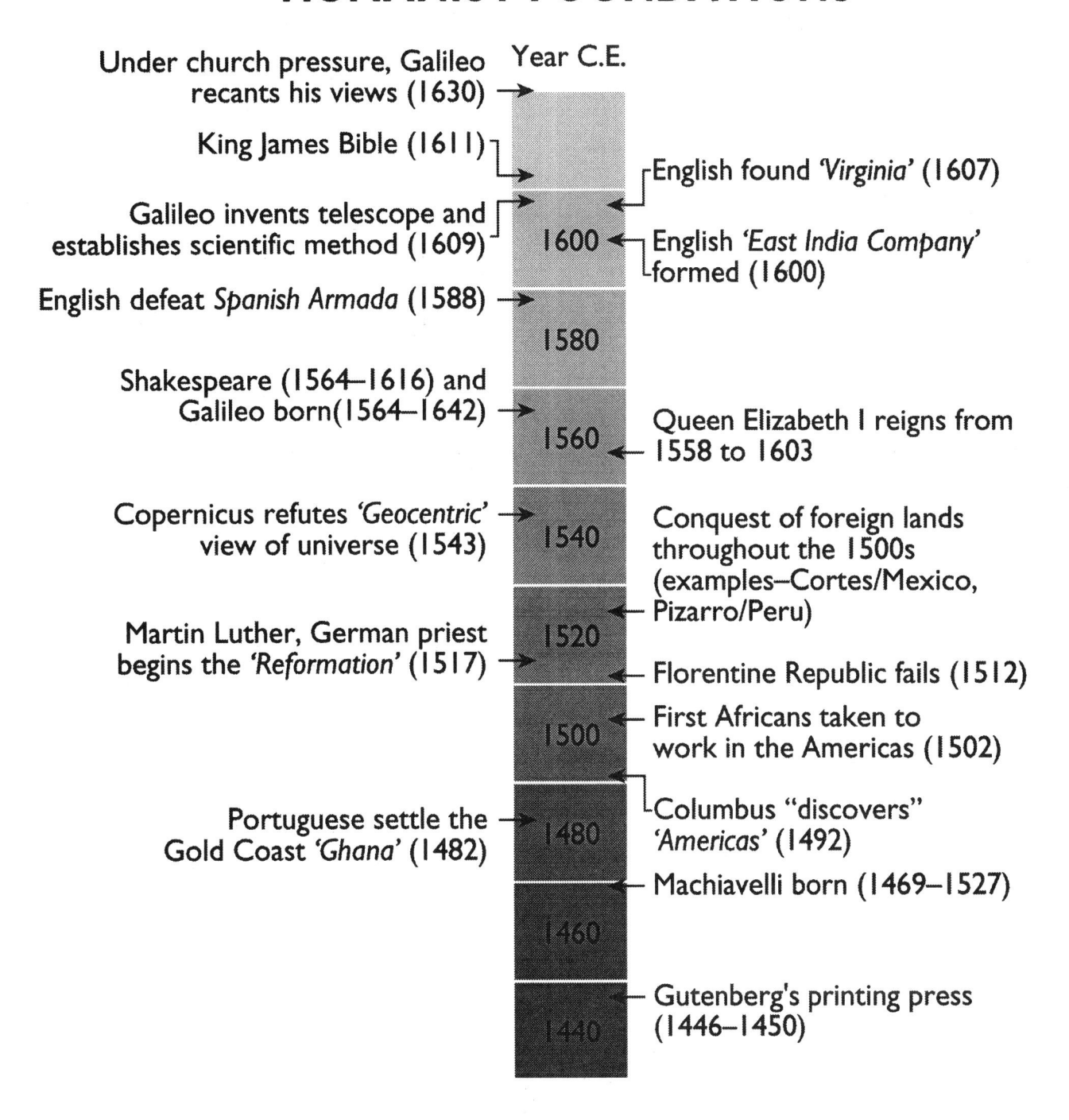

Year C.E.

Under church pressure, Galileo recants his views (1630) →

King James Bible (1611) ⤵

English found 'Virginia' (1607)

Galileo invents telescope and establishes scientific method (1609) →

1600 ← English 'East India Company' formed (1600)

English defeat *Spanish Armada* (1588) →

1580

Shakespeare (1564–1616) and Galileo born (1564–1642) →

1560 ← Queen Elizabeth I reigns from 1558 to 1603

Copernicus refutes 'Geocentric' view of universe (1543) →

1540 ← Conquest of foreign lands throughout the 1500s (examples—Cortes/Mexico, Pizarro/Peru)

Martin Luther, German priest begins the 'Reformation' (1517) →

1520 ← Florentine Republic fails (1512)

1500 ← First Africans taken to work in the Americas (1502)

Portuguese settle the Gold Coast 'Ghana' (1482) →

1480 ⤶ Columbus "discovers" 'Americas' (1492)

← Machiavelli born (1469–1527)

1460

← Gutenberg's printing press (1446–1450)

1440